When Giants Walked the Earth

Also by Mick Wall

AS AUTHOR

W.A.R.: The Unauthorized Biography of William Axl Rose
Guns N' Roses: The Most Dangerous Band in the World
Pearl Jam
Run to the Hills: The Authorized Biography of Iron Maiden
Paranoid: Black Days with Sabbath & Other Horror Stories
John Peel: A Tribute
Bono: In the Name of Love

AS COAUTHOR

Mr. Big: Ozzy, Sharon and My Life as the Godfather of Rock
with Don Arden

XS All Areas: The Status Quo Autobiography
with Francis Rossi and Rick Parfitt

When Giants Walked the Earth

A BIOGRAPHY OF

LED-ZEPPELIN

MICK WALL

 St. Martin's Griffin ❦ New York

For Linda, Evie, Mollie and Michael – always.

The Library of Congress has cataloged the hardcover edition as follows:

Wall, Mick.
    When giants walked the earth : a biography of Led Zeppelin / Mick
Wall.—1st U.S. ed.
        p. cm.
    Includes bibliographical references and index.
    ISBN 978-0-312-59000-0
        1. Led Zeppelin (Musical group)   2. Rock musicians—England—
Biography. I. Title.
    ML421.L4W35 2009
    782.42166092'2—dc22
    [B]
                                                            2009023454

ISBN 978-0-312-59039-0 (trade paperback)

First published in Great Britain by Orion Books,
an imprint of the Orion Publishing Group Ltd

First St. Martin's Griffin Edition: November 2010

10   9   8

AUTHOR'S NOTE

While I have been fortunate over the years to have enjoyed the company of various ex-members and/or former employees of Led Zeppelin, it should be born in mind at all times that this is an unauthorised biography, written objectively and with no undue pressure from any outside influence to do anything other than tell the story as I honestly see it.

It should also be clearly understood that the italicised 'flashback' passages of the text are not the actual words of Jimmy Page, Robert Plant, John Bonham, John Paul Jones and Peter Grant, nor are they actual quotes. Whilst they are all based on thorough biographical research, the facts of which can be found in the Notes & Sources section at the end of this book, the words themselves are the product of my imagination.

CONTENTS

Acknowledgements   vii

Prologue – Heaven   1

PART ONE: Ascension!   3

1. The Dawn of Now   5
2. Daze of My Youth   29
3. Light and Shade   54
4. Going To California   77
5. High in the Sky   102
6. Cannons!   126
7. Cracking the Whip   153
8. A Bustle in Your Hedgerow   178

PART TWO: The Curse of King Midas   205

9. So Mote It Be   207
10. All That Glitters   235
11. We Are Your Overlords   268
12. The Golden Gods   300
13. The Devil in His Hole   330
14. Caesar's Chariot   359
15. The Outhouse   386
16. To Be A Rock . . .   418

Epilogue – Gone, Gone, Gone . . .   451

Notes and Sources   469

Index   477

ACKNOWLEDGEMENTS

Personally, I have always disliked lengthy author acknowledgements and have consequently always tried to keep them to an absolute minimum in my own books. However, there is simply no way around the fact that this book simply could not – indeed, would not – have been written without the invaluable aid of the following people, all of whom I owe the utmost thanks.

First and foremost, to my wife Linda, who kept the walls from collapsing in on us throughout the long months and years of this endeavour. She may not have written a word of it but there is no doubt she worked harder to make this book come to life than anyone, including me. Also my agent Robert Kirby of United Agents, a gentleman and a friend, I hope, forever; and Malcolm Edwards at Orion, whose patience and understanding, coupled to a surprisingly thorough knowledge of Led Zeppelin, went far beyond the call of any normal publisher; two real-life giants of the publishing world.

Heartfelt thanks must also go to two people whose researches on my behalf again went way beyond the call of duty, and whose generosity was immense: Dave Lewis of the estimable *Tight But Loose* (see also www.tblweb.com) who not only provided music, books, access to some of his interviews (in particular, his superb Peter Grant interviews) but wonderful insight via our numerous phone conversations; and, equally, David Dickson, who provided a similarly invaluable service, including bootlegs, videos, helping arrange interviews and countless hours on the phone, sharing his own years of insight into both Zeppelin and the serious side of the occult.

I would also like to acknowledge the crucial part Jon Hotten played in helping me during the very early, very nervous days of the book's existence. He helped me overcome several sleepless nights and failures of nerve at a time when there really was no-one else to turn to. And to my editor, Ian Preece, for performing a similarly selfless task at journey's end.

Then there are those people whose input was less specific but who, again, were there for me (and the book) in all sorts of often unexpected ways, often just in the nick of time. They are: Diana and Colin Cartwright, Damian McGee, Bob Prior, Ross Halfin, Kevin Shirley, Clare Wallis, Peter Makowksi, Chris Ingham, Scott Rowley, Trevor White, Nicky Horne, Simon Porter, Maureen Rice, Sian Llewellyn, Geoff Barton, Dr Chloe Procter, Julie Bennett, Timothy d'Arch Smith, Becky Underwood, Robert Logue, Mark Blake, Ingrid Connell, Chris Welch, Lyn and Tom Cracknell, Penny and Paul Finburg, the staff at the Four Pillars Hotel in Oxford, Nigel of Oxford Cottages and – for great inspiration, would that they knew it – to the writers Paul Kimmage and David Peace.

To those people who contributed to the nuts and bolts of the book, sometimes unwittingly, or in ways so oblique it only made sense to me a long while – sometimes years – later, but again without whom things would surely have turned out differently: Burt Jansch, Ronnie Wood, Paul Rodgers, Bill Ward, Bev Bevan, Mac Poole, Jim Simpson, Tony Iommi, Geezer Butler, Ozzy Osbourne, Terry Manning, Freddie and Wendy Bannister, Jake Holmes, David Juniper, Donovan, Aynsley Dunbar, Don Arden, Jason Bonham, B.P. Fallon, and Richard Cole.

And finally, of course, to Jimmy Page, Robert Plant, John Paul Jones, John Bonham and Peter Grant, who always deserved better. Do what thou wilt.

PROLOGUE

Heaven

It could happen anywhere but it always happened best in America. Land of milk and honey, world of infinite possibility. Home of rock'n'fuckin'roll. It could happen anywhere but it never quite happened for you like it did there, those nights when you could actually feel the sparks fly, actually see the light shooting out at them, pulsing like the neon ooze of Sunset Boulevard after dark. It could happen anywhere but it never quite happened for you or them like it did in America.

From New York to LA, baby ... the Garden ... the Riot House ... somewhere under the table at the back of the Rainbow ... weed and wine and coke and pussy ... smack, baby, smack ... if god or the devil made something better they must have kept it for themselves.

Looking out at them from the stage, thousands of them, heads nodding, breasts exposed, hands aloft, a great dark mass of writhing, yearning, grasping humanity, all waiting for your signal, for the ritual to reach its dizzy peak, to spill over and engulf them, to choke and make them gasp for more. Ascension! Into the light! Learning to fly on your hands and knees ...

'That was the whole idea,' you would tell the author years later, 'to create something hypnotic, hypnotic, hypnotic ...' Dragging the violin bow across the guitar strings, making them ache and howl with the pain that burned way down inside. Then raising your arm and pointing the bow ... up there ... down there ... straight at them ... lashing it like a whip as the sound of the guitar bounced off their shining upturned faces like a well-aimed stone skimming across the surface of a pond. Hurting them with it, stabbing them, caressing, drawing them in then blowing them apart – a devil taking breath, in out, in out. Giving them a taste of what it was like, what it was really all about.

Did the others know what was going on? What you were really doing? It was possible. Standing so close to the flames though, how would they be able to tell? All they really knew was the heat and the light and the smell of it. But if they had been able to stand far enough away, they'd have been able to look into the shadows and then they might have seen. Seen the shadows within the shadows, the greys that lay entangled with the blacks, the spectral figures without face or form that looked back out at them . . .

You would drag the bow against the guitar strings, hurling your curses, and they loved you for it, fucking loved you, your right arm raised, the wand, your body bent towards them like a hook, your whole being at one with the column of light emanating from the stage, spiralling up and out and all around, a grand swirl of deep, dark colours that turned into a tower of steps, which you bade them all to take, one by one, just you, the piper, to follow. Up, up, up . . . the stairway . . . to . . .

PART ONE

Ascension!

'To worship me take wine and strange drugs whereof
I will tell my prophet, & be drunk thereof!
They shall not harm thee at all!'

—Aleister Crowley, *The Book of the Law*

1

The Dawn of Now

You are Jimmy Page. It is the summer of 1968 and you are one of the best-known guitarists in London – and one of its least famous. Even the past two years in the Yardbirds haven't brought you the recognition you know you deserve. People talk about the Yardbirds as though Jeff Beck is still the guitarist, not you, despite everything you've done for them; giving up the easy-money session gigs that bought you your house by the river; gifting them one last ride on the merry-go-round with ahead-of-the-game hits like 'Happening Ten Years Time Ago', even as Mickie Most sucked the life out of them making them do codswallop like 'Ha Ha Said The Clown'; sticking with them as their profile has slowly faded from view, along with their own self-worth. They still mean something in America, just about, but back home they are dead meat. And what's the point in traipsing around America, them and the other half-dozen acts on the same poxy package bill, earning less in a week than you used to get for a day's worth of sessions, when no-one even knows your name, knows how important you are now to the whole set-up?

Jeff Beck? Jeff is an old mate, but who had recommended him for the job in the first place? Done him a favour when he was on his uppers? You – Jimmy Page. The one who turned down the Yardbirds after Clapton had walked out, not because you were afraid, like Eric, that their craving for pop stardom would ruin your image as a 'blues purist' – you were never one of those, your love of folk, rock'n'roll, jazz, classical, Indian, Irish, anything and everything, meant you always felt sorry for those poor unfortunates that could only ever like one form of music – but because you'd secretly shuddered at the prospect of trawling the country's pubs and clubs, bouncing around in the back of a shitty bloody transit van like you'd done before with Neil Christian and the Crusaders, ending up so ill you couldn't get out of bed for three days. Not even *making any bread out of it. Stuff that for a game of soldiers.*

And so you'd recommended your old mate Jeff, who was just sat around doing nothing. Then stood back and watched as the Yardbirds with Beck had taken off like a rocket . . . 'For Your Love', 'Heart Full of Soul', 'Shapes of Things', hit after hit . . . Next thing you were in the Yardbirds too. It was never supposed to last, and you never made any promises, but you had to admit it was all right. Even when you were just supposed to be helping them out till they found a proper replacement for Samwell-Smith, twanging the bass as a bit of a laugh, the buzz was good. When they suggested moving Chris over onto bass and having you and Jeff both on guitar, you couldn't believe it! You did wonder how long Jeff would be able to hack it, but while it lasted it was actually really good. Not just the playing – you and Jeff had always played well together – but the vibe, the scene. It felt like an omen when you found yourself booked with them to appear in the Antonioni film, Blow Up. *All you had to do was make like you were playing a club, steaming it, a great laugh. Though Jeff moaned when the old director asked him to smash his guitar. Six times he had to go through it, pretending to be Pete Townshend, before the old Italian was happy. God, did he moan! You just couldn't stop smiling though.*

Then he left. Jeff Beck, the great guitar hero who had no discipline whatsoever, brilliant one night, less so the next; the so-called cool cat who couldn't write an original tune to save his life and had sold out to Mickie Most and his off-the-peg hits. Jeff is a mate and you don't like to bad-mouth him, but even Jeff knows 'Hi Ho Silver Lining' was a load of old rubbish; everyone knows it was a load of old rubbish. Yet there it was as soon as he left the Yardbirds, courtesy of Mickie, in the charts and in the discotheques; on the radio and being danced to by all the leggy birds in their miniskirts on Top of the Pops.

Well, good for Jeff Beck, but what about you, Jimmy Page? What are you gonna do now Jeff has his own thing going and the Yardbirds have finally gone kaput? You don't know. Or rather, you do, but only on an instinctual level. You don't have the proof yet but the answer, you're fairly sure, is to take the Yardbirds and build on it, take their rinky-dink rock'n'roll and so-called experimentation – their gimmicks – and turn them into something much more deliberate; something that will make you gasp, not just sigh, something that will actually compete with Hendrix and Cream and the Stones and the bloody Beatles. Really show the world who's who and what's what.

But you are also wary of letting go of the bit of fame you've finally found, however meagre. Most people may think Jeff Beck is still the guitar player in the Yardbirds but at least they've heard of the Yardbirds. Who's heard of Jimmy Page, outside of the know-all producers and record company bigwigs, the studio broom-pushers and pretty receptionists? Outside of all the guitarists you've replaced on sessions over the years – the guy in Them, the guy in Herman's Hermits, the countless others whose faces you no longer remember and who would never acknowledge what you'd done for them anyway, never thank you . . .

At least you know where you stand. Self-confident, well off, used to being on your own, you have always been someone who knew exactly where you stood, even as a kid playing on sessions for old timers like Val Doonican. You had always walked tall, always known your own worth even as others discounted it, sending you on your way to the next session – sometimes as many as three a day, six days a week, never knowing what you were going to be asked to play next, picking up good money and taking none of the risks – and none of the glory, either, when it worked.

Now it is your turn to shine. You are twenty-four, a hardened session pro who knows all about working in the studio, taking your cue from famous knob-twiddlers like Shel Talmy and Mickie Most, playing along with other session pros like Big Jim Sullivan and Bobby Graham, sharing a fag during tea breaks, taking it all in, crossing paths again and again over the years like lucky black cats. Now you want to do something for yourself. You've always wanted it. Now it's time. Something big, like Eric with Cream – only better. Like Jeff with Rod Stewart and Ronnie Wood – only better. Like George Harrison and Brian Jones with their sitars, even though you had one first – only much, much better, you wait and bloody see.

First, though, you need to put the pieces together, find the corners of the jigsaw. The years working behind the scenes – in the dark, a hired gun, doing as you were told, looking and listening and taking it all in, sharing a fag and laughing up your sleeve – have taught you about more than just the playing. You now know where to place the mikes. 'Distance makes depth,' as the old lags liked to say. You now know how to operate the desk, what makes bad groups good and good groups better. You now know it's about more than just being able to play, otherwise you'd have been a star long ago. You have also learnt something about the business. You know the value of a name and of having the right record company behind you, the right guys in suits. And for that you know you will need help. You've got a head start though. The Yardbirds still have a name – just – and you aren't about to let go of it. Not yet. You have to be sure first; have to be precise; your timing, as a pro, will have to be perfect, you know that.

The problem is time is running out. Only twenty-four but already the music is moving on without you. You wouldn't have said it out loud but you know it's true. Cream is already coming to its end and you feel like you haven't even started. Hendrix is now everybody's guitar god but you haven't shown them what you can do yet, given the opportunity, away from the sessions and the smoky studios and the bands crumbling from within, lost somewhere out there on the American road, just counting the days till something better comes along. Time is running out and though you'd never say it out loud you are starting to worry you have missed the bloody boat; that if you're not careful you will have to go back to doing sessions. 'Becoming one of those sorts of people I hate,' as you tell your friends.

The last Yardbirds tour comes to an end in Montgomery, Alabama, the gig at the Speedway Fairgrounds coming the day after Bobby Kennedy is shot in Los Angeles. You all watch it on TV back at the hotel and you all go 'wow' and shake your heads and light more cigarettes. But it means nothing to you compared to the thought of the group breaking up. By the middle of June you are at home again in your groovy riverside abode in Pangbourne – a converted Victorian boathouse thirty miles up the Thames from London with one of those basement boat moorings, not that you have a boat – wondering what on earth you are going to do now.

Fortunately, you have an ace up your sleeve; someone who knows what you can do, who you are, what you could become, and who shares your determination to make something of it, to finally let the cat out of the bag: Peter Grant. 'G'. The hulking, oversensitive giant who co-manages the Yardbirds with Mickie and who has kept you safe throughout your travels, especially on that bloody awful last American tour, when Keith Relf was going off the rails, getting drunk on stage every night and only Chris Dreja still seemed interested in keeping the whole thing together. G, who'd sat in the car with you, stuck in traffic in Shaftesbury Avenue, just days after getting back from America, both of you knowing it's over, talking about what you are going to do now. G, who sits and listens as you, in your quiet, well-mannered voice finally says what it is you've secretly been thinking all this time, finally says out it loud: that you think you can take the group and do better, add new members, write new music, do better.

The stumbling block, you both know, will be Mickie, who is only really interested in singles. Art for art's sake, hit singles for fuck's sake. That's Mickie's motto. But singles aren't where it's at anymore. The Yardbirds should be more of an albums' band now, it's obvious. You haven't said so to Mickie because you know he would only scoff, just as he had when Jeff complained he wanted to make albums too, but you say it now to Peter, who sits and listens, looking straight ahead through the windscreen at the traffic. The key, you say, feeling courageous, would be letting you have a free hand to do it the way you know it should be done. The way you hear it in your head sometimes when no-one else is listening. Not just leading the group but writing the music and lyrics, producing the records yourself, doing everything yourself except managing. That's where Peter would come in – if he's interested. G, who has worked for years in the shadows of other, more powerful music businessmen, waiting his turn in the dark, just like you. G, who sits there at the steering wheel, staring at the traffic straight ahead, and simply nods his head. 'All right then,' he says. 'Let's do it.'

There is one last Yardbirds show, a low-key contract-filler in the Student Union hall at Luton College on 7 July – almost two years to the day since the last big single in Britain, 'Over Under Sideways Down' – and then it really is all over. Only Chris has said he's willing to stick with it and give it another go with you but even he is now having second thoughts. Oh, he hasn't said anything yet to you or Peter, but you both know. So what? You're gonna need 100 per cent commitment if the new music you want to make is to sound the way you want it to. Chris is no great shakes on the bass anyway. Better he go now then, even if it does leave you on your own. Well, you're used to that. As an only child, you've never been afraid of being on your own. So when, barely a month after that last show in Luton, Chris finally owns up to the fact he isn't into it anymore, would rather go off and try for a new career as a photographer – 'He thinks he's the new fucking David Bailey,' laughs G – you are secretly relieved.

Now it's down to just the two of you, Jimmy and G. And of course, the name, for what it's still worth: the Yardbirds. Or maybe the New Yardbirds – G's suggestion. That way, at least, it won't be like starting again from scratch, he says. Not entirely, anyway. And you can still get paying gigs. Keep the wolf from the door until you can come up with something better. That's the plan anyway, this long, rainy summer of 1968 . . .

*

'I knew exactly what I wanted to do,' says Jimmy Page nearly forty
years later, sitting in his basement kitchen at the Tower House, the
nineteenth-century Gothic pile in London's Holland Park, designed by
the architect and Freemason William Burges. It's a sunny late summer's
afternoon in 2005 and we are having a cup of tea, looking back at the
early days of the band for yet another magazine profile. Over the past
twenty years this has become almost an annual ritual for us, the interest
in Zeppelin having magnified over the years to the point where they
are now more popular than they ever were in their lifetime. Of course,
the days of Jack Daniel's and cocaine, of groupies and smack – the days
of dragon suits and black swans – are long gone. Jimmy Page doesn't
drink, doesn't take drugs; doesn't even smoke cigarettes anymore. But
that doesn't mean he's forgotten what it was like, what it was all about.
Or that he is in the slightest bit repentant. Indeed, his only real regret,
he says, is that it had to end. 'It was hedonistic times, you know?' He
shrugs. 'But the thing is the playing was always there. On maybe just
a very rare occasion did it suffer – a rare occasion relative to the volume
of tours. But we wanted to be on that edge, it fed into the music.'

Of course it did. That was what it was all about for a rock monster
like Led Zeppelin, feeding on planets and shitting stars. Drugs were
their fuel, sex a form of self-expression, music merely the map to the
treasure. Think of the Stones, crammed into Keith's sweaty windowless
basement at Villa Nellcote in France in 1972, waiting for him to come
to after another three-day mindbender; waiting for him to get enough
coke and smack up his nose and in his arm before he is ready to lay
down the bones of what will become the greatest Stones album ever
made, whatever Mick and his posh new foreign bird thinks. Think of
John and George, acid buddies suddenly, united for once against strait-
laced Paul and clueless Ringo; high priests labouring devoutly to take
the Beatles beyond the yeah-yeah-yeah of their lovable mop-top past
and into the infinitely more knowing, vastly more expanded consciousness of *Revolver* and eventually *Sgt. Pepper*, the album that transformed the world from black and white into colour. Think of Dylan
smoking his weed, swallowing his pills, wearing sunglasses at midnight
and vibrating in his chair by the window as he sits up all night at the
Chelsea Hotel in New York writing 'Sad Eyed Lady Of The Lowlands'
for . . . her. Or Hendrix tripping on godhead in some beer-sticky London
dive full of fag smoke and jealous white males, as The Who and Cream

and everyone else who tried to follow him bathed in his comet trail and foolishly tried to hold onto the sparks. Of course the drugs fed into the music of Led Zeppelin. That's what the drugs were for. That's what Led Zeppelin was for. That's what it was all about, right Jimmy? Back then in the Seventies, that bridge-burning, hyper-individualistic era that began in 1968 and burst into a cultural forest-fire that would keep on spreading all the way up to around 1982; after birth control but before AIDS, when suddenly everything seemed possible and nothing was verboten. The flipside of the idealistic, consensual Sixties, the Seventies was the era when doing your own thing and letting it all hang out ceased to be mere slogans and became a birthright. When doing what thou wilt really had become the whole of the law.

How is someone like Jimmy Page supposed to put all that into words now, though, without everyone pulling a face, or worse still laughing it off? Almost impossible to do back then, it is frankly out of the question now. Even for Robert Plant, who always has an answer for everything, he thinks. Clearly, though, those early days of Zeppelin are just as vivid to Jimmy Page now, in his still smouldering old age, as they were forty years ago, in his death-defying, universe-baiting prime. In his mid-sixties now, you could forgive him for being vague on the details. But he's not; he's very precise, in fact. As he has been about everything important he's done in his career. 'I knew what I'd been working on in the framework of the Yardbirds,' he says, drinking his tea, 'and I knew that I wanted to take that further on – and you can hear all of that on the first [Zeppelin] album.'

Yes, you can. Not in the material, per se – there was little that was original about that – but in the idea; the methodology; the determination to take over the entire conversation. Recently, though, I'd read that he'd originally had something lighter, more acoustic in mind, then had a change of heart after he saw drummer John Bonham play. An idea encouraged perhaps by his solo appearance in Zeppelin's earliest days on the Julie Felix TV show, picking elegantly at 'White Summer', the acoustic guitar interlude based on legendary folk enigma Davy Graham's instrumental raga on the Irish melody 'She Moved Through The Fair' which was Page's showcase even back in Yardbirds days and that had one enthralled reviewer comparing him to flamenco guitarist Manitas de Plata.

'That's bullshit,' he told me, contemptuous of the notion that

Zeppelin might ever have been anything other than what they were. 'I had a whole sort of repertoire in my mind of songs that I wanted to put into this new format, like "Babe I'm Gonna Leave You", for example. But it wasn't just the sensitivity of doing an acoustic number, cos it was all gonna grow.' Zeppelin would not be anything so simple as all-acoustic or all-electric. Zeppelin would not be nailed down. 'I was seeing all this sort of dynamic. Because my tastes were all-encompassing, musically, it wasn't down to one particular thing. It wasn't just the blues, it wasn't just rock'n'roll. It wasn't just folk music or classical music. It went all the way through the whole thing.' Later, when I checked, I discovered he'd said much the same thing to writer Mick Houghton as far back as 1976. 'I knew exactly the style I was after and the sort of musicians I wanted to play with,' he'd declared then. 'I guess it proves that the group was really meant to be, the way it all came together.' Then again in 1990, when he told Mat Snow in *Q*: 'We knew what we were doing: treading down paths that had not been trodden before.'

So Jimmy Page had the whole thing worked out right from the start, did he? Musically, perhaps he did. Or, as he says now, what he wanted 'the framework' to be. However, the manner in which he really put the group together was much more haphazard; much more risky. Luck played a huge part. In fact, at first it appeared Lady Luck was working against him when he realised he couldn't get any of the people he really wanted in the band interested. Or if they were interested, that something else stood in the way. For example, hindsight tells us that vocalist/guitarist Terry Reid, one of the first people Page approached, was a fool to turn down the chance to join Led Zeppelin. But they weren't called Led Zeppelin then – they were still just the New Yardbirds, a new name that made the band sound very old. Reid was young, a gunslinger in his own right with, ironically, a solo deal with Mickie Most on the table. What did he want to join the *New* Yardbirds for?

Still only nineteen and hotly tipped by the music press as the 'Pop Star Most Likely To', Reid had been a star-in-the-making since he was sixteen, when Peter Jay of the Jaywalkers made him his new frontman. Then came Hendrix and Cream and just like everyone else, Terry had wanted to get in on the act too. By February 1968, his pal Graham Nash – who had just left the Hollies to do his own thing in America with two groovy new cats he'd met named David Crosby and Stephen Stills – had talked Mickie Most into signing him. When Jimmy Page came along with his offer to join the New Yardbirds, Reid was already hard at work on the songs that would end up on his *Superlungs* album – the naff nickname dreamed up for him by Most. How could he turn his back on all that just to try and help refloat a leaky boat like the Yardbirds?

Page, who'd remembered Reid from a show the Yardbirds had done at the Albert Hall two years before when Terry and the Jaywalkers had been on the bill, was devastated. Especially when Peter Grant told him the reason Terry wouldn't join was because he'd just been signed as a solo artist by Mickie, who he still shared an Oxford Street office with. Despite his growing trust in G, Jimmy felt cuckolded. 'You know their two desks faced each other, right?' he still notes sourly all these years later.

'Meanwhile,' said Reid, 'I was doing a gig. I think it was in Buxton with the Band of Joy. I'd seen them before, and I knew Robert Plant and John Bonham. And this time, as I watched them, I thought: "That's it!" I could hear the whole thing in my head. So the next day I phoned up Jimmy. He said, "What does this singer look like?" I said, "What do you mean, what does he look like? He looks like a Greek god, but what does that matter? I'm talking about how he sings. And his drummer is phenomenal. Check it out!"'

It was the same for drummer Aynsley Dunbar, a veteran of John Mayall's Bluesbreakers and the earliest incarnation of the Jeff Beck Group. As Dunbar says now, 'I was offered the chance to join the New Yardbirds. They were already talking about going to America – that was the lure, as I'd never been. There's no doubt in my mind that if I'd done so I'd have ended up in Led Zeppelin. But the Yardbirds was already sort of old news by then, and I had my own band, Retaliation, that had just signed a record deal. I liked the idea of playing with Jimmy because he was like me, very into improvisation, something which Beck couldn't manage at all – everything he did was always rehearsed right down to the last note. But joining the Yardbirds at that moment would have seemed like a step backwards, not forwards.'

It wasn't even the first time Jimmy Page had tried to put together his own group. As far back as the summer of 1966, he had tentatively imagined an outfit of his own with either Small Faces frontman Steve

Marriott on vocals and second guitar, or possibly Spencer Davis Group
protégé Steve Winwood on vocals and keyboards, along with what
Page now calls a 'super hooligan' rhythm section comprising The Who's
Keith Moon on drums and John Entwhistle on bass. That had been in
May 1966, when he had overseen the session at London's IBC studios
that would produce 'Beck's Bolero' – Jeff Beck's guitar-enflamed
version of Ravel's 'Bolero' originally intended to be his first solo single
and that Page has consistently insisted over the years that he arranged,
played on and produced – 'Jeff was playing and I was sort of in the
control booth. And even though he said he wrote it, I wrote it. Bollocks.
I'm playing all the electric and 12-string but it was supposed to be a
solo record for him. The slide bits are his and I'm just basically
playing' – and which Beck just as stubbornly flatly denies. 'No, Jimmy
didn't write that song. We sat down in his front room once, a little,
tiny, pokey room, and he was sitting on the arm of a chair and he
started playing that Ravel rhythm. And he had a 12-string and it
sounded so full, really fat and heavy. And I just played the melody and
I went home and worked out the up tempo section.'

   In the end, it hardly mattered. Mickie Most would only release it as
the B-side of 'Hi Ho Silver Lining'. Still, the guitarists continued to
argue over who did what. The only thing they did later agree on is that
the 'Beck's Bolero' line-up could have been the 'original' Led Zeppelin.
Also present on the session that night were two players Page knew
from the sessions' world: a young pianist named Nicky Hopkins and
bassist John Paul Jones. Hopkins was twenty-two, an old head on young
shoulders who had started out as a schoolboy in Lord Sutch's Savages,
then played with Cyril Davies' All Stars, as had Jimmy, which is how
they'd first met, before a serious stomach ailment landed Nicky in
hospital for eighteen months. Now he was a full-time session guy.
Good money, no travelling, easy on the tummy. Later that year the
Kinks would immortalise him on the track 'Session Man'. He was
quiet, talented and shy, hardly ever said a word to anyone, just played
his part and fucked off like a good boy afterwards. Jonesy wasn't much
of a talker, either. He was all right, though, a good player, sure of
himself. Also in his early twenties but an even older veteran of the
session scene, it wasn't the first time he and Pagey had worked together
either and it wouldn't be the last. Within weeks, in fact, he would be
brought in at Jimmy's insistence to arrange the strings on the Yardbirds

track, 'Little Games' (and later to play bass on the 'Ten Little Indians' single).

The biggest presence at the 'Bolero' session, though, was that of Keith Moon, who'd arrived at the studios in Langham Place wearing shades and a Cossack hat – 'Incognito, dear boy' – in case anybody saw and recognised him. A get-up which, unsurprisingly, had the reverse effect of making everyone stare at him intently. Moony was pissed off at The Who, fed up with Daltrey's constant fighting and Townshend's black moods. John Entwhistle, who'd also promised to turn up then backed out at the last minute, felt the same, Keith said, both boys looking for a way out of the grind of being the background to the Pete and Rog show. Sensing an opportunity, Page laughingly suggested they all team up together: Keith and Jimmy and John and Jeff. (No mention of Jonesy or Nicky, at this stage.) Moony got all excited and even accidentally suggested a name for the new line-up when he joked that it would go down like a lead zeppelin, meaning balloon. (Entwhistle would later swear blind it was he that had suggested the name but it was Moon that Page would later ask for his blessing to use the name.) Smoking cigarettes and speeding out of his head, everyone had laughed at Keith. But Jimmy had liked the idea – even the name – and tucked it away in his back pocket, like he had done a lot of good ideas over the past four years working in studios with frustrated musos.

Half-Yardbirds, half-Who; pushed in the right direction by boss man Page. All they would need was a good singer. Moony had said Entwhistle could sing but Jimmy was thinking more of Stevie Winwood. Then Traffic started taking off big time and so he thought of Steve Marriott instead. Page had been to quite a few Small Faces gigs and already knew Marriott well, knew he was up for anything. In fact, the more he thought about it, the more he liked the idea: Jimmy, Jeff, Moony and Entwhistle, with Steve Marriott upfront ... What a supergroup that would be! Or as he later told the writer, Steve Rosen, 'It would have been the first of all those sort of bands, like Cream sort of thing. But it didn't happen ...'

Not surprisingly, the success of the session had given Beck similar ideas, like two mates out for the night spotting and fancying the same bird. Keith Moon, he said, 'had the most vicious drum sound and the wildest personality. At that point, he wasn't turning up for Who sessions, so I thought that with a little wheeling and dealing, I could sneak him away.' To what, though? The Jeff Beck Group was still, at that stage, more wishful thinking than reality, and there was his old pal Pagey, in the control booth, overseeing everything, letting Jeff think it was all his idea. Not that Beck didn't cotton on to all that. As he said, 'That was probably the first Led Zeppelin band – not with that name, but that kind of thing.' Moony, he said, 'was the only hooligan who could play properly. I thought, "This is it!" You could feel the excitement, not knowing what you were going to play, but just whoosh! It was great and there were all these things going on, but nothing really happened afterwards, because Moony couldn't leave The Who.'

This fact alone wasn't enough to deter Jimmy Page, though, and despite joining the Yardbirds just weeks later – ostensibly as a temporary replacement for bassist Paul Samwell-Smith – he still put feelers out to see if Marriott might be interested in leaving the Small Faces to join forces with him in some new unspecified group project. 'He was approached,' Jimmy would later reveal, 'and seemed to be full of glee about it. A message came from the business side of Marriott, though, which said, "How would you like to play guitar with broken fingers?"'

As the 'business side of Marriott' was Don Arden, the self-proclaimed 'Al Capone of pop' and then the most notoriously gangster-like figure in the British music business, such a threat was to be taken seriously. When I asked Arden about this myself, before he succumbed to Alzheimer's disease in 2007, he merely chuckled. 'Later on I'd hang fucking Robert Stigwood over a balcony for daring to try and take Stevie Marriott away from me. You think I'd let some little schlemiel from the Yardbirds have him?' After that, said Page, 'the idea sort of fell apart. We just said, "Let's forget about the whole thing, quick." Instead of being more positive about it and looking for another singer, we just let it slip by. Then The Who began a tour, the Yardbirds began a tour and that was it.'

The idea was gone but not quite forgotten. Not by Jimmy Page anyway. So much so that when Peter Grant had asked him straight out, as they sat in the car in June 1968, what he was going to do after that final Yardbirds show, he had his answer ready. He was going to find a new singer, Page had said in his quiet but determined voice, find a new rhythm section too if needs be, and lead the band himself. Then he waited to see if G was still listening ...

*

You are Peter Grant. It is the summer of 1968, you are thirty-three and sick and tired of earning money for other fucking people. In the days when you'd worked for Don Arden, it hadn't mattered. Don could be a right cunt to work for, always on your case, giving you a hard time, always taking the piss, but at least you'd been paid regular and in cash. No fucking tax or stamp or any of that old codswallop with Don. And you'd learned a lot too. Running around on the road with nutters like Gene and Richard, Chuck and the Everly boys, you'd learned more working for Don than anything you'd done since your two years' National Service. A lot of lads hated doing Service. You'd hear 'em crying themselves to sleep at night, crying for their mummies, silly little poofs. You'd enjoyed it. Being in the army was the first time you'd experienced the feeling of what it was like to belong to a big extended family, and you'd liked it. Liked the discipline, giving and taking orders, everyone knowing where they stood even if it was in a pile of shit. Men being men, doing what they were fucking told. Enjoyed it enough to win promotion to Corporal in the RAOC – that's the Royal Army Ordinance Corps to you, sonny. Given charge of the dining hall, through which you'd got involved with the NAAFI, putting on shows, organising the tea and the sticky buns, sorting out the entertainment for the troops. 'A very cushy number,' you'd smile and say whenever you looked back.

Years later, you'd be driving through the Midlands one day in your brand new Rolls Royce convertible, being chauffeured by Richard Cole as you sat in the back telling it how it was to Atlantic Records' chief whip Phil Carson, when, realising suddenly how close you were to an important piece of your past, you decided to take a little detour and show the chaps around your old army barracks. Ordering Cole to swing right through the army camp gates, driving bold as brass past the daft bastard on duty who saluted you, you'd told Cole to park the Rolls next to the little line of huts you and the rest of the lads used to sleep in. You should have bloody well seen the look on their faces as you showed them round. So much better than the 'dreadful' holiday camp you'd later worked in, you told them. How, after you'd finished there you'd worked briefly at that Jersey hotel as 'entertainments manager', another crap job that didn't last . . .

What you didn't mention was how, as a kid, you'd dreamed of being a film star. Six foot six by the time you were old enough for the army, already well on your way to putting on the weight you would later be remembered for – not skinny, no, but bloody tall and not bad looking actually, you cheeky cunt. But it was all a dream. Instead, after the holiday camp and the hotel you'd found yourself working back in London as a doorman – a polite word for 'bouncer' – at the 2Is Coffee Bar in Old Compton Street. How even though the 2Is would later become famous as the sordid little dive where Tommy Steele started off – Tommy, Wally Whyton, Cliff Richard, Adam Faith, Wee Willie Harris and all those other cunts – it didn't bring you any closer to making any dreams come true. Later, though, you realised the 2Is had been useful in other ways. Where you first met faces like Andrew Loog Oldham, the smart-arse kid who later worked for the Beatles and Stones, who'd started out sweeping the floor at the 2Is for pin money. Then there was Lionel Bart, funny little shit who used to paint murals on the basement wall there and would later strike it lucky in the West End with Oliver, then fuck it all up by selling his copyright for a quick bit of cash, missing out on millions when it later got tuned into the film. What a fucking caper! But a lesson you were quick to learn – always get – and bloody well keep – a slice of the pie. And of course Michael Hayes, who would later change his name to Mickie Most but was working as the waiter at the 2Is when you first met. Mickie, who you would one day go into partnership with: him as the brains, you as the brawn, looking after the acts out on the road while Mickie took care of them in the studio, producing hit after hit.

'Mickie poured the coffee while I sold the tickets at the top of the stairs,' you'd tell 'em when they came to ask you about it years later. That had been 1957. The pay: eighteen shillings a night (90p) and a hot meal. Not all that but better than a poke in the eye with a sharp stick. You became known as 'a character'; the guy the girls had to charm to squeeze their way down to the small 25 x 16-foot basement; Mickie the clown at the counter who would leap out from behind it sometimes and also sing a few numbers. You the henchman who would grab their daft boyfriends and throw 'em out onto the street first sign of trouble.

Then one day you finally got your own chance to show what you could do – though not as a singer. The 2Is was owned by two Aussie wrestlers, Paul Lincoln and Ray Hunter. It was Paul who looked you up and down and suggested you might like to earn 'a few extra bob' by teaming up to 'fight' him in a few bouts. Willing to try anything, you turned up for your first wrestling match billed as His Highness Count Bruno Alassio of Milan, don't you dare fucking laugh. Paul went on as Doctor Death. And guess what? The punters loved it! Lapped it right up they did. This was the old days, before they'd cottoned on to the fact it was all a fix, so shut it. It went over so well, in fact, that Paul arranged a few more bouts between Dr Death and the Count. Sometimes you'd be billed as Count Bruno, sometimes Count Massimo. One time you put on a Lone Ranger mask and called yourself The Masked Marauder, offering to take on all-comers, while Paul, the plant, jumped up and down in the audience waving his fucking arms. 'Me! Pick me!' You'd fucking pick him one of these days all right ...

Don Arden – who gave Peter Grant his break in the biz when he hired him in the early Sixties as his 'driver', an all-purpose job title that involved 'hand-holding' some of Arden's most notorious clients, including Gene Vincent, a crippled American ex-pat alcoholic fond of brandishing knives and guns, and Little Richard, a religious-guilt freak who always carried a bible with descriptions of his orgiastic exploits scribbled in the margins – shakes his head with disgust. 'Peter Grant was never a fucking wrestler. He couldn't punch his way out of a paper bag!' I remind Don that being a wrestler is not the same as being a boxer and that Grant wouldn't have needed to punch his way out of anything. An ability to growl and look threatening – well within his range – and a nicely stage-managed forearm smash – also well within his scope – would surely have sufficed. 'All I'm saying is he traded on that reputation: the hard guy; the heavy. Well, let me tell you, Peter Grant was nothing but a big fat bully. He was so fucking fat he could barely stand up. That's why he always used to take the car everywhere. He couldn't walk more than ten feet without getting out of breath. His legs were gone.'

Even allowing for Arden's famously dark sense of humour, there's clearly some truth in what he says. As Mickie Most later told writer Chris Welch, he and Grant 'used to put up the wrestling rings for Dale Martin Promotions. Sometimes if a wrestler didn't show up for the first bout, Peter used to do a bit ... that was the basis of Peter's wrestling career.' He added: 'When Peter butted someone with his stomach, that was just using a wrestling technique. Nobody ever got hurt. If they did get hurt it was an accident. It wasn't meant to happen. There was no physical damage because it was all showbiz.'

That said, there was far more to Peter Grant than mere bulk. Shrewd enough to know a reputation as a former ring-pro only added to the air of intimidation he liked to wield over those he was determined would come off worse in their dealings with him, he was also sensitive enough to be repelled by a 1971 *Daily Mirror* article that purported to 'expose' his past life in 'the grapple game'. Wrestling was something he'd done 'for about eighteen months when I needed the money,' he said, not something he was proud of. But by then his reputation was firmly established, and not just amongst British tabloid journalists. Three years into his reign as Led Zeppelin manager he was routinely referred to in the press as the 'brute', the 'giant'; the old-school music biz hustler who looked 'like a bodyguard in a Turkish harem' as one paper unkindly but not inaccurately described him. Jibes that hurt all the more for carrying the ring of truth. For like a lot of exceptionally large men, Peter Grant was highly sensitive, particularly about his size and misleading general demeanour. While he no longer saw a potential leading man in the movies when he looked in the mirror, he didn't see an ogre, either. In fact, by the time he was in his late thirties and overseeing the affairs of the most financially successful act in the music business, he liked to see himself as a man of wealth and taste, a cultured figure who could just as easily sit and have tea with the upper crust as he could dish the dirt with the shysters of Tin Pan Alley.

According to the former promoter Freddy Bannister, who worked with Grant at the beginning and end of his career with Zeppelin, 'Peter has this reputation now as this almost gangster-like figure, and yes, he was fairly awful and intimidating in his latter days of managing Led Zeppelin. But in the early days he could be quite the gentleman, quietly spoken and very well-mannered. He was interested in antiques, and we both had a passion for vintage cars. I would often bump into him at car auctions and we would have a very jolly time together. Of course, you were always aware of this other side to him, too. When it came to negotiating deals for Zeppelin, he could be very forthright indeed. But not like later on when he really did become very nasty. But that was the drugs, too, of course.'

It also has to be borne in mind that Peter Grant came from the era before accountants and lawyers took over the music business. What his former mentor Don Arden, the ultimate poacher-turned-gamekeeper, calls 'the wild west days of the music biz'. Or in the words of someone Grant befriended later in life, Dire Straits' manager, Ed Bicknell: 'In Peter's day, you put the money in the Hammond organ and made a dash for the border.' As Mickie Most once said, '[Peter] was a dreamer and he hustled.' He was also intelligent and could spout you facts and figures from a contract at random. If that didn't work, he would take a leaf from Don Arden's book and back you up against a wall and threaten you. Unlike Don, however, who had spent his war years faking illness in an army barracks many hundreds of miles from the frontline, Peter wouldn't pull a gun on you – not in the early days anyway. But he wasn't in the least bit fazed when he saw one, and certainly not in America, where you would see them all the time. What made his manner more frightening was his unexpectedly soft voice, surprisingly high, even when shouting at you; and the beautiful, long-lashed cow eyes that would narrow into unreadable slits when angered. Word had already gone out across America long before the arrival there of Led Zeppelin: Peter Grant didn't argue. He merely told you how it was. And if that didn't work, he showed you – personally.

He also, practically unheard of then, regarded his artists as friends, members of his extended family, particularly Jimmy Page, who he treated as almost a second son. 'I always had the most respect and admiration for Jimmy,' Grant said. 'I felt that I was closer to Jimmy than any of the other members of the Yardbirds. I had immense faith in his talent and ability. I just wanted him to do whatever he felt was best for him at the time.' A man who had grown up without a large family circle for support thus went out of his way to create his own, now he was a father – manager – himself. As such, he had no precedent. In later years, people liked to compare him to Col. Tom Parker, Elvis Presley's manager. But the Colonel would – and did – sell Elvis's name to the highest bidder, both before and especially after his death. G would rather have cut off his own arm than sell his artist down the river of commercial shit the Colonel routinely sent Elvis blithely skittering down. Similarly, Brian Epstein had been intensely supportive of the Beatles, but he was a novice, weak on the small print, who would eventually throw in the towel in the most dramatic fashion possible, leaving his artists high and dry and at the mercy of much larger, more vicious predators. By comparison, Peter Grant had been around the block so many times before Zeppelin came his way he felt like he owned it. So much so, unlike the ruinous penny-ha'penny record deal Epstein negotiated for the Beatles – then failed to renegotiate after their career had lifted off into the stratosphere – Grant was able to land his act the biggest deal in music biz history. In fact, Grant had more in common with the man who eventually replaced Epstein, the pugnacious Allen Klein, who, when asked by *Playboy* magazine if he would lie or steal for his clients had replied respectively, 'Oh, sure,' and 'Probably.' Peter Grant was looking for love from his artists; to give and receive.

Even Don Arden, who was so fiercely protective of his artists he would physically go to war on their behalf – breaking bones, smashing furniture, brandishing shotguns – only did it to protect his own interests, primarily money. G was different. He was after the lolly too. But it wasn't his prime motivator. He wanted respect, he wanted loyalty, he wanted family. Most of all, he craved ultimate control of that family. Hence the surprisingly small but loyal staff Led Zeppelin would employ throughout their career, on the road and off, always the same trusted officers and infantrymen. The minute you proved yourself untrustworthy or disloyal, you were expelled – forever. It was a zero-tolerance approach that extended to record company execs, promoters, agents, merchandisers, journalists, anyone who had anything to do with the band. You were either for Peter Grant and Led Zeppelin or you were against them. And if you were against them, Peter Grant was against you – big time.

As John Paul Jones would later recall, '[Peter] trusted us to get the music together, and then just kept everybody else away, making sure we had the space to do whatever we wanted without interference from anybody – press, record company, promoters. He only had us [as clients] and reckoned that if we were going to do good, then he would do good. He always believed that we would be hugely successful and people became afraid not to go along with his terms in case they missed out. But all that stuff about renegotiating contracts through intimidation is rubbish. He wasn't hanging people out of windows and all that crap.'

Well, no. Not out of windows, perhaps. But intimidation, threats, ultra-violence, all would be used regularly by Grant at various points throughout Zeppelin's career. 'If somebody had to be trod on,' he would say, 'they got trod on. Too true!' That wasn't all there was to his style of management, nor was it even the biggest part of it. But, yes, it was always there, bubbling like a sea monster just beneath the blackest, most oily part of the surface; one that would certainly bare its teeth with ever more scary frequency as the years rolled by and the band became more and more successful and, ironically, less in need of such ferociously over the top tactics.

Back in 1968, though, Grant had found himself at a crossroads. The imminent dissolution of the Yardbirds was hardly a surprise. The group had been at each other's throats since he and Most had taken them off previous manager Simon Napier-Bell's hands two years before. What really bugged Peter, though, was the thought of going back to square one with some other group. That is, some other group controlled by Mickie. Sooner or later that, too, would come to an end and what then? It was all right for guys like Don Arden and Mickie Most with their big houses and flash cars; they had seen enough of the back end in their careers to view the whole thing as simply another business deal that had gone down before moving straight onto the next one. Peter Grant was tired of roaming around on the road to no discernible purpose, other than paying the rent. He was married, with a small son, Warren, and a baby daughter on the way and he wanted his stake in the dream to come true too. Like Jimmy, it was time for him to strike out on his own. No Mickie or Don this time, no lurking in the background this time; no more second banana. It was time for Peter – G – to show what he could do too.

When sitting in the car, passing time, Page had said he wanted to do his own thing, dreaming of the future, Grant had been pleased and surprised but not entirely sure what that would entail. All through that final Yardbirds show in Luton he had thought about it, watching Jimmy from the wings, wondering. And the more he thought about it, the more sure he became that it could – would – work. However, he was taken aback when Jimmy had mentioned Terry Reid – Terry, who Peter knew had just signed to Mickie, who he still shared an office with, their desks facing each other. Peter knew there was no chance with Terry now that Mickie had gotten his claws into him but he didn't want to discourage Jimmy. So he went along with it, knowing they'd have to look elsewhere. Sure enough, Jimmy was disappointed. If Peter knew there was no chance why hadn't he said something, tried to stop Jimmy? When Terry himself suggested someone else, it was almost too good to be true. Peter breathed a quiet sigh of relief and made himself busy trying to track the kid down . . .

*

Terry said they called him 'the Wild Man of the Black Country'. You didn't know if that sounded promising or not, but you wrote down the bloke's name and gave it to G. It was an easy one to remember anyway – Robert Plant. Made you think of flower power sort of thing, which might have been good a couple of years ago. Things had changed since then, though. The main thing was, could the bloke sing? And did he look the part? Terry seemed to think so and Terry would know, wouldn't he? So you asked G to look into it and that's when you found out that Tony Secunda, The Move's manager, was also sniffing around; had already had the bloke down to London for an audition. G suggested they move fast, before Secunda did a Mickie and got in there first. It still seemed a bit much though, having to drive all the way to Birmingham, or wherever it was, when there were so many good singers already in London: Chris Farlowe, Rod Stewart, Stevie Marriott, lots of others like Terry that didn't have names yet. The boy in Free, he was good, too. But G said all the good ones were taken, reminding you that Stevie Winwood came from up there somewhere too, didn't he, so you never knew.

It was a Saturday night. G drove, you and Chris, who was still making up his mind, sitting in the back, smoking cigarettes and fearing the worst, that it would all be a big waste of time. Then you got there – another college gig. Small room at the back of the building, band called Hobbstweedle. Like something out of Lord of the Rings. *Then they came on and you really feared the worst. Bunch of dope-smoking yokels, doing covers, American hippy, old flower power stuff. Waste of time. But the singer, he was quite good, actually. Big bugger in a University of Toronto sweatshirt. Did a version of the Airplane's 'Somebody to Love' and really turned it on. A bit too good, perhaps. How come no-one had heard of him apart from Terry? And bloody Secunda?*

You were suspicious, didn't believe in gift horses. Either there was something wrong with him personality-wise or he was impossible to work with. It was the only explanation you could think of. But G, who hadn't come all this way for nothing, was more gung-ho. 'Invite him down for an audition, then decide,' he said. So you did and a few days later this big kid with big curly hair was standing at the door of the pad in Pangbourne, grinning. You had taken him in and made him a cup of tea, offered him a fag. Told him to skin one up if he wanted, offered him your stash. At first it had been awkward, you could tell the kid was nervous. A few years younger, he'd done a couple of things, made a couple of records, but no hits to speak of. The only people you had in common were Terry, who the kid didn't actually seem to know that well; Secunda, who was always too busy with The Move to make up his mind one way or the other, and Alexis Korner. But then every young kid you ever heard of had once sung or played in a band with Alexis.

Things warmed up when you started playing records. You told him about your idea for taking the Yardbirds and building on it, going in a whole new direction. The kid nodded along, 'Yeah, great', though it was fairly clear he didn't know any of the Yardbirds' songs – not from your time with them anyway. But you sat there on the floor together, letting him flick through your LPs, pulling out stuff by Larry Williams, Don and Dewey, the Incredible String Band, Buddy Guy and early Elvis. A mixture of stuff the kid – Robert – claimed to know well or admitted he'd never really heard before. When you put on 'You Shook Me' by Muddy Waters, then 'She Said Yeah' by Larry Williams, his face lit up. When you put on 'Babe I'm Gonna Leave You' by Joan Baez he looked puzzled. He was still nodding, still sitting there pulling on a joint and going, 'Yeah, man, groovy,' but you could tell he didn't really know what on earth you were on about half the time. He'd heard of Joan Baez, all Dylan fans had heard of Joan Baez, but what did she have to do with the New Yardbirds? He was just a big curly-haired kid with a big curly-haired voice from somewhere up there in the Midlands.

So you picked up your acoustic guitar, said, 'I've got an idea for this one', and began playing your own arrangement of 'Babe I'm Gonna Leave You', and slowly, slowly, it began to sink in. Not all of it but enough to get him started; get him thinking about it on the train back to Brum or wherever it was he came from. Then you said he could crash for the night if he wanted and he did.

'I really didn't know much about the Yardbirds,' Robert Plant would tell me. 'I knew what they had meant and that in their latter stages they'd made a lot of pop records, which were good. But they didn't . . . they were very much . . .' He struggles to find the right words but what he's trying to say is that he'd never actually bought any Yardbirds records, never been what you'd call a fan. He had certainly never seen himself being in a group like that. He and his friends saw themselves more as the English version of Moby Grape, if they saw themselves as anything. Or as he put it, 'I knew that Keith Relf had got the kind of voice that he'd got and I couldn't see where I'd fit in. But of course I didn't know where it would go ...'

Nearly thirty years after they broke up, Led Zeppelin is still a tricky subject for Robert Plant, full of 'grey areas' and things he doesn't want to talk about, particularly from the latter half of their career, when the drugs had taken over and the madness seemed to double with every stumbling, life-wrecking step the unruly giant they had created took. The early days are safe ground, though. In fact, by the summer of 1968, Robert Plant had all but given up on the idea of having a career in the music business. He'd sung in various groups since he was a teenager, coming closest to the spotlight in the Band of Joy, a bunch of Birmingham-based American West Coast wannabes specialising in covers by Love, Moby Grape and Buffalo Springfield, who'd got as far as some club dates in London before falling apart from lack of any real record company interest. After that, he'd sung and played briefly with Alexis Korner, but still no cigar. He'd even released a couple of solo singles – both flops. Now he was back home, working on a building site and singing part-time in the horribly named Hobbstweedle.

Looking back now though, he tends to idealise those days. 'I really just wanted to get to San Francisco and join up. I had so much empathy with the commentary in America at the time of Vietnam that I just wanted to be with Jack Casady and with Janis Joplin. There was some kind of fable being created there, and a social change that was taking place, and the music was a catalyst in all of that.' He gave a more accurate description of his circumstances back then, when in 1969, he told hippy bible, *International Times*: 'It was the real desperation scene, man, like I had nowhere else to go.' Even his old pal, John 'Bonzo' Bonham, was now doing better than him, earning £40-a-week drumming in American singer-songwriter Tim Rose's backing band. Forty quid a week! Robert could pretend he wasn't jealous but no-one believed him, let alone his pretty Anglo-Indian fiancée Maureen who he had met at a Georgie Fame concert two years before. As he later told me, 'For a while I was living off Maureen, God bless her. Then I did some road-making to earn some bread. I actually laid half the asphalt on West Bromwich High Street. But all it did was give me six shillings-and-tuppence an hour [31p], an emergency tax code and big biceps. All the navvies called me the pop singer ...'

Plant told me he actually 'ignored the telegrams' he'd received from

Peter Grant, inviting him down for an audition in the New Yardbirds, but it's hard to believe. He said he only really considered it after Grant had phoned and left a couple of messages for him at his local pub in Walsall, the Three Men in a Boat. (Grant had phoned the pub, he explains in an aside, because he didn't have a phone of his own and used the pub as his 'office'.) The fact, though, as he had told *IT*, was that 'everyone in Birmingham was desperate to get out and join a successful band … everyone wanted to move to London.' Nineteen-year-old Robert Plant was no exception. He may not have had the same yearning to go and live in 'the smoke', as the rest of the country still called its capital, but he was desperate to make a living out of his singing, a dream that had stubbornly refused so far to come true. Finally, he said, 'I went down there and then I met Jimmy, I didn't know whether or not I would get the gig but I was … curious.'

You bet he was. Paul Rodgers, then fronting Free, recalls seeing Plant perform in the summer of 1968. 'It was just before he joined Zeppelin,' he says. 'Free played up in Birmingham with Alexis Korner at the Railway Tavern, a blues club and Robert got up to jam with Alexis and he was the Robert Plant that we know and love today – full-on hair and tight jeans and everything, doing that "Hey babe!" [imitates Plant's trademark vocal]. Full on everything, you know? He was giving it large with Alexis who was playing an acoustic guitar, and people didn't quite get it. He really needed Bonham and Page behind him. We were staying at some hotel and afterwards he came back for a cup of tea. He said: "You know, I'm thinking of going down to London. What's it like down there?" I said, "Oh, it's pretty cool, you know, it's good." He said, "I've had a call from this guy called Jimmy Page, have you heard of him?" I said, "Oh yeah, everyone's talking about him, he's a big session guy down there." He said, "Well, he wants to form a band with me. They've offered me either thirty quid or a percentage." I said, "Take the percentage." Next thing I knew it was Led Zeppelin, right?'

Thirteen days after the final Yardbirds show in Luton, Plant packed an overnight bag and bought the cheapest train ticket available that would take him from Birmingham to Reading, and then onto the local stopping service to Pangbourne. He walked the rest of the way to Jimmy's, ignoring the disgusted looks of the distinctly middle-class denizens who mainly lived alongside the river. Trying not to look too impressed as Jimmy showed him in and went to put the kettle on, the wide-eyed would-be wild man was utterly overawed by his slightly older host. When they started putting on records and talking about music, there was more of a connection, he said, though it was Jimmy who did most of the picking and putting on.

'You can smell when people have had their doors opened a little wider than most, and you could feel that was the deal with Jimmy. His ability to absorb things and the way he carried himself was far more cerebral than anything I'd come across before and I was so very impressed. I don't think I'd ever come across a personality like it before. He had a demeanour which you had to adjust to. Certainly it wasn't very casual to start with . . .'

Nor would it ever truly become so.

2

Daze of My Youth

You had wanted to be a singer for as long as you could remember. You were fifteen-and-a-half the first time you went to Brum town hall to see a concert on your own. Your uncle had taken you when you were a kid but this was something different. It was February 1964 and you were there to see the great Sonny Boy Williamson. Stood there in his black bowler hat, a mockery of the strait-laced world he was sending up, his shoulders hunched over like a vulture's. Sonny Boy looked more dead than alive, more out than in: a ghostly black-and-white reflection of some hazy, distant world full of smoky bar rooms and laughing, painted ladies crossing and uncrossing their legs. The kind of place you had dreamed of as you sat on your bed, listening to the music and staring at the LP covers. Now here that world was – a small but significant part of it anyway – right in front of you, right here in Brum. You could hardly believe what you were seeing, up there on the town hall stage, so near to him you could hear the old blues master breathing into the mike, yet still so far away from your life in Kidderminster you may as well have been looking through a telescope at the moon.

Closer to home and much more believable, yet just as inspiring, also on the bill that night was the Spencer Davis Rhythm-and-Blues Quartet, and Long John Baldry's All-Stars, both of whom had singers – Stevie Winwood and Rod Stuart [sic] as he was billed on the posters outside – who couldn't have been much older than you. Winwood was even a local lad. If he could do it, then you could too, couldn't you?

What a great night that was. All your mates were there too and there were loads of birds. Not yet the dope-smoking hippy you would soon become, you were still Jack the Lad. When it came out after the show that Sonny Boy's bass harmonica had gone missing, everybody knew it was probably Planty that had 'had away with it'. What a prize it was! Like *getting your hands on an actual piece of the dream, a tiny bit of something to make it all seem more real.*

You'd been a teddy boy but now you were mad about the blues, everybody knew that. Not just Sonny Boy Williamson, but Howlin' Wolf, John Lee Hooker, Muddy Waters ... Then came that first show at the Wolverhampton Gaumont, the year before the Sonny Boy concert. A package bill starting with The Rattles, Mickie Most and The Most Men, Bo Diddley, Little Richard, the Everly Brothers and the Rolling Stones. You were sweating with excitement even before The Rattles came on. The star of the show was Bo Diddley. The Stones were good too but they had nothing on Bo Diddley! 'All his rhythms were so sexual,' you'd recall later, 'just oozing ...' It was after seeing Bo Diddley that you bought 'Say Man'. There was a sale on at Woolies and you'd got that and 'I Love You' by The Volumes, 'I Sold My Heart To The Junkman' by Patti Labelle and The Blue Belles, and 'My True Story' by The Jive Five, scribbling your name – Robert (not Rob, as your mates called you) Plant – in the corner of the labels.

After that came singles by Solomon Burke, Arthur Alexander, Ben E. King ... then your first LP, Muddy Waters' Live At Newport 1960 *... it used to be Elvis, now it was Muddy you sang along to, 'I've Got My Mojo Working' ... then came* Blues Volume 1 *on Pye International with Buddy Guy, Jimmy Witherspoon, Howlin' Wolf, Chuck Berry and Little Walter ... various EPs ... Chuck Berry's 'This Is ...', Howlin' Wolf's 'Smokestack Lightning' ... you kept finding more and more stuff, going right back to the original jook-joint guys like Charley Patton, Son House, Robert Johnson, Earl Hooker ... Folk Blues of John Lee Hooker was one of the greatest LPs ever made by anyone! And you could prove it. It was all in the book. The great book – Blues Fell This Morning by Paul Oliver – which you'd refer to in the way other people did the Bible, using it to help you choose which records to send off for. Real rare stuff, too, all the best gear by everyone from Hooker, Sonny Boy and the Wolf, to even less well-known American blues originals like Bukka White, Lightnin' Hopkins, Snooks Eaglin, Tommy McClennan, Peetie Wheatstraw ... all of them. The bloody lot! What a gang! Peetie was known as 'the Devil's Son-in-Law' and the 'High Sheriff of Hell'. Crazy, man!*

By the time you'd seen Sonny Boy at Brum town hall you considered yourself an expert. A proper connoisseur, able to trace stuff back to its proper roots, eventually all the way back to obscure collections of African roots music and field recordings. As anal as any trainspotter, you would file, catalogue and rate your ever-growing collection of treasures. Every week you bought Melody Maker, the only music paper which covered blues, folk and jazz as well as the pop scene, and sit there after school reading it cover to cover. On Saturdays, when you weren't at Molineux watching the Wolves, you were hanging around the record shops in Brum's Soho district, especially The Diskery, which only proper fans went in, fingering the racks, always on the lookout for something new. That is, something old. Best of all, something good that nobody you knew had ever heard before. You were ready for anything. One week it was 'Shop Around' by the Miracles. The next it was Chris Kenner's 'I Like It Like That', never heard singing like it. You were past all that now, though. A serious collector now, combing The Diskery for rare French RCA EPs by Big Bill Broonzy's harp player Jazz Gillum, or the original Sonny Boy Williamson LP with sleeve notes by Alexis Korner. Even some folk and jazz. You had to hear it all, to see for yourself what it was like. It was always the blues you came back to, though. That was the ideal. Pestering Mum and Dad for the money to buy it, then taking it home, putting it straight on the little cream and red Dansette, singing along while watching yourself in the bedroom mirror.

Mum and Dad said you were mad but you'd been that way since you were nine, singing along at the top of your voice to 'Love Me' by Elvis. Standing behind the curtains in the living room, flicking the baby quiff you'd perfected that Mum would make you get rid of soon after. That was the first time you realised you could actually sing – a bit. It was also the first time you cottoned on that Mum and Dad didn't actually share your love of this music, as if there was something funny about it. Didn't even like Johnnie Ray! Bloody 'ell! You felt a bit sorry for them, actually . . .

Before Terry Reid had suggested Robert Plant, Jimmy Page had been giving serious thought to inviting Chris Farlowe to join him in the New Yardbirds. Years later, Chris would sing on Jimmy's soundtrack for the *Death Wish II* movie, and again a few years after that on his 1988 solo album, *Outrider*. Twenty years before, however, Farlowe was busy building a solo career that had already seen him in the charts with his version of the Stones' tune, 'Out Of Time', which Page had played on as a session guitarist. Ultimately, Plant got the gig because he was the only decent vocalist who was available right away and willing to give it a go; the only decent singer Page could think of that didn't have anything better to do. Nevertheless, he still harboured doubts. 'I liked Robert,' he would later tell me. 'He obviously had a great voice and a lot of enthusiasm. But I wasn't sure yet how he was going to be on stage; what he'd be like once we actually got together as a band and started playing.'

What sealed the deal was the arrival into the story of a pal of Plant's from Brum, a drummer named John Bonham. Bonham and Plant had been in the Band of Joy together. According to Jimmy, 'The one I was really sure about right from the off was Bonzo.' Until then, Page's inclination had been to offer the gig to Procol Harum drummer B.J. Wilson, who he'd played with recently on the Joe Cocker session that had produced '(I Get By) With A Little Help From My Friends' – an ornamentally heavy treatment of what had originally been a lightweight Beatles tune sung by Ringo, and a rough template for the kind of guitar-heavy musical melodrama that Page had in mind to utilise in his own next project. But Wilson wasn't interested, understandably rating his chances of lasting success with Procul Harum – who had arrived with a huge splash the year before with the no. 1 hit, 'A Whiter Shade of Pale' – as infinitely better than the revival of a band that hadn't had a hit for two years.

Other drummers considered included Aynsley Dunbar; Mitch Mitchell, who'd been in the Pretty Things before joining Hendrix in the Experience, where it was whispered he was now falling out of favour; and Bobby Graham, Jimmy's old 'hooligan' session pal who'd never been tempted before to give up his hefty regular wage packet for the insecurity of a full-time post in a group. And not just any group, either, but the possible flogging of a dead horse. In desperation, Grant also invited out for lunch to 'discuss a new project' the similarly disinterested Clem Cattini, another old pal of Jimmy's from the session scene. But Clem was always so busy earning fortunes from playing on hits by Ken Dodd, Sandie Shaw, Dusty Springfield, Gene Pitney, P.J. Proby, Marmalade and countless others, he could never find the time to sit down with Grant, who simply refused to discuss it over the phone. 'I now had a family,' Cattini later recalled, 'and I thought – wrongly – that I'd found my niche as a session drummer.' Two years later, when Zeppelin was the biggest-selling band in the world, Clem recalled running into

Peter and asking him: '"That lunch date", was it to do with ... ?"
He just nodded.'

And so, at new boy Plant's urging, Page had gone to see his pal
John 'Bonzo' Bonham play with Tim Rose at the Country Club in
Hampstead, north London. It was 31 July 1968 and, Page told me, 'He
did this short five-minute drum solo and that's when I knew I'd found
who I was looking for.'

'Jimmy rang me up and says, "I saw a drummer last night and this
guy plays so good and so loud, we must get him",' Peter Grant would
recall. But Bonham, already rated as one of the best young drummers
in England, was not convinced. With a wife, Pat, and two year-old son,
Jason, to support, the regular weekly wage he was getting from Tim
Rose was not something he was about to just give up. Never one to
mince his words, the thought of joining the New Yardbirds hardly
thrilled him, either. 'When I was asked to join the Yardbirds, I thought
they'd been forgotten in England,' Bonham explained. '[But] I knew
Jimmy was a highly respected guitarist, and Robert I'd known for
years,' so he did at least finally agree to meet with Page and Grant. But
only after they had virtually begged him to do so. Unable to reach him
by phone because Bonzo didn't have one, at Page's urging Grant had
bombarded him with over forty telegrams – nearly all of which were
ignored. But with time running out and their options swiftly dwindling,
Grant had been even more persistent than usual. One day G and
Jimmy just turned up on John's doorstep, taking him for a pub lunch
where Page says he 'basically spelled out the whole deal. How this was
gonna be unlike any band he'd ever been in. That it was a once-in-a-
lifetime thing.' The fact that his mate Plant was also involved appears
to have swung the deal. That and the fact that there was no guarantee
Rose would take Bonham with him when he returned to America, or
that Bonham would have wanted to go.

Word was out on the drummer, though. Not only was he earning a
good weekly wage now, the Rose tour was the first time the name John
Bonham had been mentioned in the music press, when one of the
shows was reviewed favourably in *Melody Maker*. Chris Farlowe, whose
new album had been produced by Mick Jagger, now wanted to offer
him a job too, as did Joe Cocker. Page was abject at the thought of
being forced to stand by and watch yet again as someone he wanted
for the group appeared to be spurning him for what they felt would

be a better opportunity with someone else he knew. Which is when Plant says he stepped in. 'I went to Bonzo and said, "Hey, the Yardbirds!" And [his wife] Pat said to me, "Don't you even think about it! John, you're not going off with Planty again! Every time you do anything with him you come back at five in the morning with half-a-crown!" [12½ p] So I worked on it and worked on it. I said to Jimmy, "What can you offer him?" '

As a result, Plant told me, both he and Bonham were initially offered £25 per week in England; £50 per week in Europe and £100 per week for touring America. He chuckled as he recalled how Bonzo said '"That's not enough for me." He did some kind of deal with Peter Grant whereby he got an extra £25 per week for driving the van! Bear in mind that he never even had a driving licence. It was a bit like a Keystone cops chase half the time, constantly leaving the road and driving through hedges . . .'

Plant had first met Bonham four years before, at the Oldhill Plaza in Birmingham, where, as a seventeen-year-old, Plant had blagged a job as an occasional MC. That night, however, he'd also been singing there in his band, the Crawling King Snakes (after the John Lee Hooker song). He was actually on stage when he first laid eyes on him. 'I noticed this guy looking at me,' he said. 'He came up to me afterwards and said, "You're pretty good but your band's shit. What you need is somebody as good as me".' It was Bonzo, a name all his friends called him for no particular reason other than it fitted him so well. This big, beefy bloke who could hit a drum kit so hard he would literally smash it to pieces, and would do so for fun, especially to other drummers' kits. This larger-than-life, hard-drinking, outspoken absolute git of a bloke who could be as soft-hearted as a girl one minute and punch your lights out the next.

The whole thing really took off for you – the mad idea that the audience would actually 'take notice' of you as a drummer – when Dad took you to see Harry James at Brum town hall. Sod the trumpet. It was the drummer, Sonny Payne, who you couldn't take your eyes off. Sonny Payne, who would bounce the drumsticks off the skins and catch them behind his back! Fucking hell, look at that! That was when you knew for sure. You'd tell 'em: 'It's all very well to be playing a triple paradiddle – but who's going to know you're actually doing it? Being original is what counts.'

*You didn't need lessons, either. Buddy Rich never had lessons, did he?
No, he bloody didn't, mate. Much better to learn as you went along, that
way it stuck in your head and stayed there, no matter how many pints
you'd had that night. Better to suss out who the good ones were and stand
there and watch them, and listen. Knock on their doors if you had to. That
was how, when you were fourteen, you'd met Garry Allcock. Garry had
been playing drums since 1951. He was also mad about cars, which was
good too, sitting together in Garry's front room with your sticks and your
practice pads, nattering about cars when it got boring and having a fag.
Garry, who used to sit there frowning when you hit the snares too hard,
shouting: 'For Chrissakes, John, take it steady!' Gary, who used to tell you
to watch it or you were, 'going to knock it through the floorboards!' Gary
was a worrier but a good bloke, too. Knew his drums and his cars. Ace
geezer.*

*Then there was Bill Harvey, another good 'un who knew his drums,
who you'd met down the youth club when you were fifteen. Bill was in his
twenties, an older fella who'd been drumming for years. Bill had laughed
at you and called you 'a tiny lad' and told you to come back later. But
you weren't having none of that. So you kept on, turning up and pushing
him, letting him know all about it, and before long Bill was coming round
to your dad's caravan to give you 'clinics'. Dad would go mad at the noise.
'Not you two at it again – clear off!'*

*Once, when Bill had had a row with his band, the Blue Star Trio, and
fucked off in a huff, you offered to sit in for him. The band had laughed
but when you got up and started hitting them fucking skins they'd shut up
quick, like. When Bill came back later that night and saw you thumping
away on his kit he went all funny on you. But then you had a brainwave
and told him, 'Come on, let's do a solo together,' and you'd both got up on
the same kit. It was great! It went down so well Bill said you should make
a regular thing of it, like. From then on, whenever he played he'd pretend
to pull you, this kid, out of the crowd. Years later, you were still laughing
about it. 'Everybody went, "How did they do that?" They didn't realise we
had rehearsed it for hours.'*

*You and Bill became good mates in other ways too. Already fond of a
pint, you would get behind the wheel of your dad's Ford Zephyr convertible
and the two of you would go out on the lash together. No bloody breathalyser
in them days, mate, and the two of you would get paralytic. Them were
the days. But the best thing Bill ever did for you was introduce you to the*

*Dave Brubeck Quartet, whose drummer Joe Morello was famous for his
'finger control' technique – this weird bloody thing he did with his fingers,
tapping on the snare drum in a way that made it sound like a lion's roar
one minute, then doing something else that made it sound like a bow and
arrow the next. You couldn't get over the idea of using your bare hands on
the drums. You thought it was the best thing since sliced bread. Then Bill
showed you another 'great pattern' from a Humphrey Lyttelton recording
he had called 'Caravan', where the drummer played floor-toms with his
hands. You couldn't get over it and begged Bill to show you how it was
done. 'Forget it, you'll never get it,' he'd said. But you bloody well did,
mate. You bloody well fucking did!*

*At first, you'd shout and swear as you cut your hands and broke your
fingernails on the rims and cymbals but you were buggered if you were
giving up and eventually you got it. 'It wasn't so much what you could
play with your hands,' you'd say later, when they all came round to ask
you about it. 'You got a lovely little tone out of the drums that you couldn't
get with sticks. It hurts your hands at first, but then the skin hardens.' In
the end you got so used to playing drums with your hands you believed
you could hit 'em harder with your hands than with the sticks. And you
could, you bloody well could.*

*By the time you left school you were so determined to become a drummer,
you said, that 'I would have played for nothing. In fact, I did for a long
time. But my parents stuck by me.' And you stuck by them, joining the
family business as an apprentice carpenter. Brick-laying and hod-carrying
made you physically strong but getting up for work at six every morning
nearly fucking killed you, especially when you began playing in local pub
bands, waking up the next morning for work still pissed. But music was
becoming even more important than cricket. Once you cycled forty-eight
bloody miles to see Screaming Lord Sutch and get his autograph. And you
began building up your record collection. Not that you were fussy, like.
Johnny Kidd & The Pirates were all right, so were the Hollies and the
Graham Bond Organisation, whose drummer, Ginger Baker, you liked
better than anyone since Gene Krupa. The way you saw it, Ginger was
responsible for the same sort of thing in rock as Krupa had been in jazz.
'Ginger was the first to come out with this "new" attitude – that a drummer
could be a forward part of a rock band – not something that was stuck in
the background and forgotten about.'*

You didn't make a big thing of it but you were always learning, always keeping your eyes and ears open, even when you were pissed. When you were seventeen you'd go and see Denny Laine and The Diplomats whose drummer, Bev Bevan, was about the same age as you and a good bloke. He'd let you sit by his side during the gig sometimes, just watching what he did, seeing if there was anything you could nick. US soul and R&B was good too, especially once you'd worked out how to get that big, open drum sound all those records had. The trick, you reckoned, was to get your hands on the largest drums you could find, without the poncey dampers and mufflers, and just start hitting them, bashing them like bricks. You were determined, you said, to 'get that sound'.

It wasn't long after this that you finally got out of the pubs, when you got your first real break on what they called the Ma Reagan Circuit – the Oldhill Plaza, the Handsworth Plaza, the Gary Owen club, the Birmingham Cavern, all them sorts of places – playing in groups like Terry Webb & The Spiders, the Nicky James Movement, Locomotive and A Way of Life. You'd even drummed briefly for The Senators and got to play on a track, 'She's A Mod', that ended up on that compilation album, Brum Beat. It was 1964, you were sixteen, and if that didn't make you a real drummer you didn't know what bloody did, mate . . .

'Robert said you should really come along and see this drummer, he's working with Tim Rose,' Jimmy Page remembered. 'I was gonna find the singer first and then pull it together. But when I heard John Bonham, albeit in quite a limited experience compared to how everyone else knows his playing now, he had that sort of energy in his drumming that was inspiring, you could tell that straight away. I'd been used to drummers who were [very good] going right the way back to Neil Christian & The Crusaders. I mean, he was like the best drummer in London. He'd been a drum major and he was really, really *active* on the kit, bass drum independency and all that. And I'd been used to all of that, and in the studios [there] was Bobby Graham who did all the sessions, playing on Kinks and Dave Clark Five records. Bobby was a real sort of hooligan drummer as well. So I'd been used to all this sort of stuff. And I knew that because it was gonna rely on this three-piece, that the drummer had to be somebody who, basically, had an amazing intellect on the kit as well as all the power and the passion. But I'd never seen anyone quite like Bonzo.' As soon as Jimmy saw him play, 'That was it, it was immediate. I knew that he was gonna be perfect.'

Not just for what he calls the 'hooligan' stuff either, he said, but for 'this thing in my mind of employing dynamics and light and shade. I knew he was gonna be the man; that he could do all this.'

And yet it so nearly didn't happen. Bonzo seemed so disinterested when Plant first discussed it with him the singer furtively sounded out other local drummers. One such was Mac Poole, an old friend of Bonham's who had replaced him as drummer in A Way of Life after 'John lost them too many gigs for playing too loud'. Poole bumped into Plant at a Joe Cocker gig in Birmingham a couple of weeks after the singer had returned from Pangbourne, where 'Robert put it to me in a very kind of simplistic way,' Poole said. 'He just said, "I'm doing these sessions with a guy called Jimmy Page, and we're gonna put a band together and we're gonna call it the New Yardbirds – and we need a drummer". That was like asking me if I was free. That's how we did it in Birmingham, you sounded people out first, you didn't just say, "Do you want the job in the band?" But I just said, "Well, I've got my own band, Rob, we've got our own deal." '

Poole had, in fact, recently formed Hush, who had indeed just signed a deal. 'I said to Robert, "What's wrong with John?" He said, "He's touring with Tim Rose." Which he was and of course Tim Rose was paying regular money. And at that time anyone paying regular money was worth holding on to. Then Robert said, "OK, maybe I'll try Phil Brittle.". He was kind of running ideas past me.' Brittle was another Birmingham-based drummer who would later find fame locally in a band called Sissy Stone. 'He was a very good drummer,' Poole told me in 2005, 'and of course Robert wanted somebody that would probably do what he was told a bit more, you know. And probably wouldn't get drunk, cos I mean Robert knew John of old and that it might be a bit of a dangerous deal.' Less than two weeks later, however, Poole ran into Plant again – this time in company with Bonham. 'We met up in the room where we all used to meet up after gigs, at the Cedar Club. They were both together and I said, "Ah, don't tell me, he's joined your new band." And Robert said, "Yeah." They were still called the New Yardbirds, which I shied away from. I thought they were all gonna be wearing dickey-bows doing "Over Under Sideways Down". I thought, "Bloody hell, Bonzo ain't gonna last in that lot ... " '

When Jimmy finally persuaded him to give it a try, Bonzo had asked him what sort of drummers he liked 'and I played him a single called

"Lonnie on the Move" [by Lonnie Mac]. It's like "Turn on Your Love-light" as an instrumental, and it's got this drumming that's really super hooligan [and] I said, "This is the sort of angle that I'm coming in at".' Bonzo picked up on what Jimmy was talking about no problem at all. As Mac Poole points out, 'John had hammered his own style together well before Zeppelin. So when he joined Zeppelin it was easy, he just pissed all over the band. John was *always* an effective drummer; he was always determined to be part of it. And there was nobody that was gonna fucking put him at the back and tell him to sit there like a good little boy because that wasn't the man that you were dealing with.' He laughed out loud. 'Even in the early days, he was determined to be heard!'

Poole does concede that having to perform for a name musician of the calibre of Page did force Bonham to 'toe the line a lot more – certainly in the beginning. Jimmy was the one giving all the directions.' He talks about how he and Bonham and future ELP drummer Carl Palmer – another local lad destined to make good – were 'all in this melting pot with this equipment, smacking seven bells out of the kit just to be heard'. The advent of rock'n'roll 'changed the whole method of thinking, certainly on the drum kit. John would always be saying things like, I worked with such-and-such a group and the fucking guitarist deafened me! After that, just to make sure his bass drum was heard, he'd put silver paper in it so that it would project. John was determined not to be sunk down.'

It was an attitude, Poole said, which worked to his detriment in a lot of the early bands he played with – hence the reputation for being *too* loud. 'If the band wasn't gonna turn down, he sure wasn't. I know Dave Pegg [later bassist of Fairport Convention] had problems with him like that in A Way of Life. Every gig they did they got banned because John wouldn't play quieter. And through that he developed this whole attitude towards other musicians which was tantamount to war, you know? He was a good drummer, a good time-keeper. But whatever they call the X-factor, John had it. He didn't care about technique, it was like he was gonna try something new that he'd thought about in his head. And even if it didn't come off and it absolutely messed the band up, he didn't care, he'd play it anyway. Most drummers practise a new idea and come back with it perfected. John would perfect it on stage [and] when it fitted, it was a fucking stroke of genius. And that's where his innovating spirit came from – a complete disregard for the other musicians. Guitarists, all they had to do was turn up the volume control and they could be louder.' It was this same belligerence, said Poole that 'came through in Zeppelin and made the band what they were, musically. I think Jimmy immediately understood what he had and helped him harness it.'

It was towards the end of these approaches that the final piece of the jigsaw fell into place, again, quite by accident, or possibly destiny, depending on what you believe. In Jimmy Page's case, that meant it was almost preordained. Whichever it was, John Paul Jones came in 'late in the day,' said Page 'and all of sudden all the ingredients are now there. Like it was meant to be ... '

But while Page may insist he never had any doubts about how Bonham and Jones would work together as a rhythm section, the difference between their two personalities could not have been more stark. Like Bonzo, Jones was already married with children. But Jones was also a softly-spoken middle-class Southerner; Bonzo a raucous, working-class Midlander. Yet somehow the two hit it off immediately. Even later on when Bonham was on a drunken rampage, Jones was rarely the target for his ire. As he later told me, 'Musically, we were very proud of our capabilities as a rhythm section. We'd listen and leave space for ourselves. There was a great deal of mutual respect. We were always incredibly locked-in – phrasing the same and always coming to the same musical conclusion. The empathy we had when we played was always incredibly exhilarating. But then I was fortunate. I was playing with the best drummer I'd ever known, and I'd known most of them ...'

You'd been John Paul Jones for four years now and you still weren't any more famous than you'd been as plain old John Baldwin. What was the bloody point? How had it come to this, churning out nonsense for Harry Secombe and Des O'Connor? You may as well have stayed behind in the Home Counties and got yourself a proper job. The pay might not have been as good but the hours were the same and at least you'd feel like you were getting somewhere. More and more this felt like nowhere. This was nowhere. Not even a window to gaze out of. Just the four walls, the endless cigarette smoke, putting one out, lighting another, endless bloody cups of tea, watching the clock ticktocking by. Then coming home at night and complaining to your wife: 'I'm making money, Mo, but I'm not enjoying it anymore . . .'

How had it happened? You felt more like a pop star when you were seventeen than now at twenty-two. At least back then you felt like you were getting somewhere, your future opening up. Things had been groovy back then, touring the country with Tony Meehan and Jet Harris. Proper touring, not just wedding parties and youth clubs; proper gigs in front of proper audiences that had come to hear the hits . . . 'Diamonds', 'Scarlet O'Hara', 'Applejack' . . . sleeping in proper digs; guesthouses, bed and breakfast, then in the van again and off. Smoking reefer for the first time, chatting up the birds, the birds chatting up you. All that and thirty quid a week! Bloody heaven! Absolute bloody heaven! Then suddenly – it was all over. Just like that. Finito; gone. Even though Tony had tried to keep it going, it was never the same again after Jet's accident. Suddenly it wasn't about the hits anymore. It was about . . . something else. Something the punters didn't get or even like. Oh, there had been 'Song of Mexico' but who remembered that? 'I wanna try something new,' Tony had said after Jet had gone. Jazz and pop. You were up for it. Till you started getting booed off every night. Still plenty of reefer to smoke but no more birds to chat up or thirty quid a week to spend. Then Tony took the job as an A&R man at Decca and that was that. You were out on your ear.

You told yourself it was a good thing. Especially when Andrew Loog Oldham – Andrew Loog Oldham of the Beatles and the Stones! – said you could make it on your own. That you could be the New Jet Harris! And you believed him . . . almost. Putting out your own record – 'Baja' by John Paul Jones. Your new name on the sky blue Pye label. Not exactly an original tune but the part you wrote for it on the six-string Fender bass was. Quite nifty, in fact, even if you did say so yourself. Not quite nifty enough to turn you into the new Jet Harris, though.

It did introduce you to some important new people, though. Friends of Andrew's, what he called the Andrew Oldham Orchestra. Little Jimmy Page, Big Jim Sullivan and the rest. All playing easy-listening guff like 'There Are But Five Rolling Stones' and '365 Rolling Stones (One for Every Day of the Year)', all having a laugh – and getting paid. Then the LP: 16 Hip Hits. 'Come on,' said Andrew, 'You know classical,' after the original arranger, Mike Leander, got a better job at Decca, same as Tony. You laughed about it now. 'I wanted to arrange, Andrew wanted to produce and neither of us was very choosy,' you would say, sending the whole thing up. But you loved it really. 'I was allowed to write them nice, interesting little things, especially for woodwinds. We'd always have a couple of oboes or French horns.' The sort of thing you could play your mum and dad without making them groan too much. A laugh and getting paid, better than being stuck at home anyway. It wasn't like you saw it in the shops or heard it on the radio or anything.

Then the Shadows phoned up one day, looking for a replacement for their bassist, Brian 'Liquorice' Locking, and suddenly you were ready to chuck the whole thing in and join the Shads, you bet your bloody life you were! But nothing came of that either and that's when it began properly, picking up session work, well-paid session work, but still just session work, as and when it came up. It was never meant to last long. But it did. It never bloody ended, playing bass or Hammond organ. First there was Herbie Goins and the Night Timers. At least they played something you liked: bit of Tamla Motown, some James Brown, even a couple of 'originals' (white versions of let-me-hear-you-say-yeah, but you could dig it). When everybody else was into folk and blues you'd been listening to Otis Redding and jazz. You'd always loved 'soul'. Live was where Herbie really earned his corn though, the records just there to help sell the tickets really. That was all right too, playing the Hammond on their first single, 'The Music Played On', and their next single, too, 'Number One in Your Heart' which wasn't bad at all and actually got played on the radio. Not the proper radio but the pirates, which was still quite good, you know . . .

By 1968, as well as a bass player, John Paul Jones was becoming known on the London music scene as a reliable keyboardist and inspired arranger. It began, most spectacularly, with the Mickie Most-produced session for Donovan – the non-doctrinal British version of Bob Dylan – which produced 'Sunshine Superman', a No. 1 hit in the US in 1966. 'The arranger they'd picked really didn't know about anything,' Jones recalled. 'I got the rhythm section together, and we went from there. Arranging and general studio direction were much better than just sitting there and being told what to do.' 'Sunshine Superman' had also been one of Page's last high-profile sessions before joining the Yardbirds. Hence the story – apocryphal, as it turns out – that still circulates to this day about it being the Donovan session where Jonesy first approached Pagey about the possibility of joining the new band he'd heard on the grapevine that he was starting. 'We may have discussed something along those lines,' Jones would later tell me. 'But I don't think it was directly about what became Led Zeppelin. More a general sort of, "If you ever decide to do anything group-wise give me a call", sort of conversation. We were both still young and, I think, equally bored with being in the background. Not because of a craving for the spotlight, more just wanting to express ourselves as musicians. Do our own thing.'

After that Jones had arranged the orchestral strings on 'She's A Rainbow' from the cod-psychedelic Stones' album, *Their Satanic Majesties Request*, though he complained about having to wait around endlessly for them to turn up for the session: 'I just thought they were unprofessional and boring.' Presumably not as boring as the two days he spent working at Abbey Road in February 1968, along with the Mike Sammes Singers and a full orchestra, playing bass on and arranging two of the six tracks earmarked for Cliff Richard to sing as potential entries for that year's Eurovision Song Contest, including such mainstream monstrosities as 'Shoom Lamma Boom Boom'. By then, however, Jones was used to churning it out for what he calls the 'bow-tie brigade': Tom Jones, Englebert Humperdink, Petula Clark, Harry Secombe, Des O'Connor . . . there was apparently no shilling too greasy for the once promising 'new Jet Harris' to pocket.

Jimmy Page found himself in the same boat as the fad for guitar-oriented mainstream pop faded in the mid-Sixties and the fashion for horn-section and/or orchestral-led records took their place. Reaching a new low in his session career, one of the reasons Page surprisingly offered to help the Yardbirds out when Paul Samwell-Smith walked out was because he had recently found himself contributing to a series of recordings intended as background music for supermarkets and hotels. A decade later, Brian Eno would make an ironic virtue out of music for airports, but what Jimmy Page was playing on in 1966 was the real thing. A state of affairs so dispiriting that not even money could balm the creative cuts. Not entirely anyway.

Little wonder John Paul Jones was also now chafing at the bit to do something different. 'Slowly going mental' playing schmaltz during the most exciting, creative time in the history of popular music. Like Page, Jones was desperate to take part in what was going on in London and elsewhere, as epitomised by the Beatles, Pink Floyd, Cream, Hendrix and the rest. Unlike Page, though, he didn't know how to go about it; thought his chance may already have gone. 'It's getting too much,' he complained to Mo. But he showed no real determination to do anything about it. Even when she replied by showing him the story in *Disc & Music Echo* saying Jimmy Page was looking for musicians to join him in a new version of the Yardbirds, his first reaction was to dismiss it out of hand. 'I was fed up with playing sessions and my wife said, "Give him a call." I said, "Harrumph, it doesn't sound very good." But she said, "Give him a call!" So I did, saying, "I hear you need a bass player", and he said, "Yes, and I'm going to see a singer who knows a drummer" – who turned out to be Robert and John – "I'll give you a shout when I get back".'

Years later, Page would tell of a conversation he'd had with Jones during sessions in June 1968 for Donovan's *The Hurdy Gurdy Man* album. 'I was working at the session and John Paul Jones was looking after the musical arrangements. During a break, he asked me if I could use a bass player in the new group.' Jones, though, remembers things differently. 'It's possible we may have spoken about something like that,' he said when we discussed it in 2003. But as he was the one who booked the band, he points out that Page wasn't actually called in for that particular session (the famously hazy guitar parts provided by Alan Parker). If anything, he feels the story is probably based on 'a vague comment I might have made' at either the earlier Donovan session for 'Sunshine Superman', or more likely, an entirely different session around the same time that he and Page also worked on for the singer Keith De Groot, a rising star in the eyes of producer Reg Tracey who'd put together a suitably stellar band for the recording including Page, Jones, Nicky Hopkins, Albert Lee, Big Jim Sullivan, saxophonist Chris Hughes and drummer Clem Cattini. Sadly for De Groot, the ensuing album, *No Introduction Necessary*, was a flop. But it was here, perhaps, Jones suggests, that the seed of he and Page working together on something more permanent may have first been planted.

It wasn't until prodded by his wife to actually phone Page and confirm his offer of help that the idea suddenly became concrete and Jones spent the next few days waiting impatiently for him to call back. A laconic, slightly professorial figure, even in his early twenties, it wasn't his style to go overboard about anything. He admitted when we later spoke, though, that he 'sensed something good might be going on with Jimmy'. He'd played on Yardbirds' records before; worked with

Page in dozens of different contexts. As he said, 'I wasn't particularly interested in the blues. I was more interested in Stax, Motown, that sort of thing. But Jimmy promised something a little different from a regular, one-style blues band.'

'I jumped at the chance to get him,' Page would later recall. 'Musically he's the best musician of us all. He had a proper training and he has quite brilliant ideas.' According to another source, though, Page was also considering Jack Bruce, as well as Ace Kefford, formerly of The Move, who had also recently auditioned for the Jeff Beck Group as bassist/vocalist, in the wake of Rod Stewart and Ronnie Wood's departure for (eventually) the Faces. In fact, Ronnie Wood says now that he, too, had been approached by Page to become the bassist in the New Yardbirds. 'But I didn't fancy that at all,' he grimaces, putting out one cigarette by using it to light another. 'All that heavy stuff wasn't my bag at all. I knew where they were going musically because Jim had been to see us [the Jeff Beck Group] loads of times. Taking notes. It was pretty obvious too that they'd probably make it, especially in America where they loved all that. But I'd had my fill with Jeff. And I wanted to play guitar again. Joining Jimmy would have been like playing with Jeff, being stuck on bass. And anyway, there was only ever going to be one guitarist in a group like [Led Zeppelin] – and it wasn't going to be me.'

Ironically, when Wood left Beck, one of the latter's first thoughts was to recruit Jones as his replacement. John had played bass on 'Beck's Bolero' and organ on 'Old Man River' – both on *Truth*, Beck's first album, also released in 1968. But Jones knew Page was the better long-term bet. Jeff was moody and mercurial. Jimmy was self-confident and reliable. In the end the choice was made for him when Page phoned him back with a firm job offer. One of nature's born sidemen, John Paul Jones had just landed his dream gig. And not a moment too soon ...

As Page told me, 'I was absolutely convinced that all that was needed was for us all to get in a room. Cos I knew that the material that I had was really good. It's nothing that they'd ever really played before. Like Robert hadn't played anything like the sort of thing that we were gonna be doing, and neither had Bonzo. But I just knew, for example, that with the areas of improvisation, I *knew* this was going to appeal to them because of the calibre and quality of players. It was only a matter, really, of getting it together. I knew this was gonna work.'

On Monday 19 August 1968, the day before Plant's twentieth birthday, a first rehearsal was arranged to take place in a small room below a record shop in Gerrard Street, in London's Soho. 'We all met in this little room just to see if we could even stand each other,' recalled Jones. 'Robert had heard I was a session man, and he was wondering what was going to turn up – some old bloke with a pipe?' Plant was actually more concerned about what the seasoned session pro would make of such a studio greenhorn. 'I don't think Jonesy [had] ever worked with anybody like me before,' Plant said, 'Me not knowing any of the rudiments of music or anything like that, and not really desiring to learn them, but still hitting it off.'

'It was clear that it was going to work from that first rehearsal,' Jones would tell me. 'There didn't seem to be any fixed idea. We just sort of said, "Well, what do you know?" and we ended up playing "Train Kept A-Rollin'"', which had been an old Yardbirds number. Loads of people had done it, in fact. But we ran through it and the effect was immediate. The whole thing was quite stunning. I thought, is it just me or was that *really* good?' It wasn't just Jonesy. 'It was unforgettable,' said Jimmy. 'It was down in what's now Chinatown. The room was really quite small; just about got our gear in it. And we did "Train ..." and I don't remember the other numbers we did because it was so flipping intense. At the end of it, it was like, *"Shit!"*, you know? I think everybody just freaked. What it was with Zeppelin was it was like these four individuals, but this collective energy made this fifth element. And that was it. It was there immediately. It was so *powerful* that I don't know what we played after that. For me it was just like, "Crikey!" I mean, I'd had moments of elation with groups before, but nothing as intense as that. It was like a thunderbolt, a lightning flash – boosh! Everybody sort of went "Wow" ...'

When Jimmy phoned G the next day to tell him the news, he knew he would have to move fast. If the new line-up was half as good as Page said – and Jimmy wasn't one for exaggerating, which meant they must be bloody amazing – Grant knew he would have to stake his claim before the cat was out of the bag and Mickie got his hands on it like he had the Jeff Beck Group. Egged on by Page who was utterly determined not to allow Most to try and take control in the studio the way he had with Beck. 'I'd been an apprentice for years and I'd discovered things that someone like Mickie didn't have a clue even existed.' Grant made it his first port of call to tell his former mentor that his services would not be required in the New Yardbirds. In return, Grant would relinquish any control he had in the Jeff Beck Group.

To Grant's surprise, Most merely shrugged and wished his partner well. If anything, he was hard pushed to suppress a snigger. With hit singles and now an international hit album in *Truth* on the way, Mickie was more than happy to be the one holding onto the Jeff Beck Group while Peter threw his energies into whatever prospects the New Yardbirds might have. Displaying the same arrogance that had made him so successful as a music mogul and, ultimately, so limited as a producer, along with his usual breathtaking ability to rewrite history, Most would later refute any suggestion that he had, in fact, missed a trick the day he allowed Peter Grant to walk off with the band that became Led Zeppelin. How could it have been a mistake, he asked, when Beck and the *Truth* album was such a clear 'forerunner to Led Zeppelin'. *Truth*: 'A great album,' he declared proudly, 'which I made.'

G merely smiled and said nothing, for not to allow Mickie his victory would have been to jeopardise his own, much larger enterprise before it had even got off the ground. Now he had seen what it might entail, he wasn't about to do that. Let Mickie think and say what he pleased. As long as Peter was free of his tentacles at last, it wouldn't matter. In the long term, it would be the music that did the talking for Led Zeppelin – Peter Grant would make bloody sure of it.

Less than three weeks after that first rehearsal, the New Yardbirds played their first gig together at the Teen Club, a school gymnasium in Gladsaxe, Denmark. It was 7 September 1968 – exactly two months to the day since the old Yardbirds had played their last gig in Luton. The tour dates had been in the diary for months before that though. Rather than cancelling them, Jimmy and G saw them as the perfect opportunity to bed-in the new line-up and earn some money. Not that anyone was paying attention. The following night in Britain, the Beatles premiered 'Hey Jude' live on the David Frost TV show. The same week, John Peel became the first British DJ to play Joni Mitchell on his *Top Gear* programme on BBC Radio 1. And while the British pop charts were a typically provincial amalgam of cheesy pop hits (chart-toppers that year included 'Cinderella Rockafella' by Esther & Abi Ofarim and 'Congratulations' by Cliff Richard, interspersed by more qualitative successes such as the Beatles' 'Lady Madonna' and the Stones' 'Jumping Jack Flash'), substantive new albums had already been released that summer by Cream (*Wheels Of Fire*), Bob Dylan (*John Wesley Harding*), the Small Faces (*Ogden's Nut Gone Flake*), The Band (*Music From Big Pink*), the Kinks (*Village Green Preservation Society*), Pink Floyd (*Saucerful of Secrets*), The Doors (*Waiting For The Sun*), Fleetwood Mac (*Fleetwood Mac*), Simon and Garfunkel (*Bookends*), and – most significant of all from Jimmy Page's point of view – the Beck Group, whose debut, *Truth*, had not only picked up rave reviews but was now on its way into the US Top 20. Still to come before year's end were new, epoch-defining double-albums from the Beatles (*The White Album*) and Jimi Hendrix (*Electric Ladyland*), plus the much vaunted debut from Traffic (*Mr Fantasy*) and the best Stones' album yet (*Beggars Banquet*). This was the richly multifaceted back-drop against which Jimmy Page was determined to get his own new music noticed.

Meanwhile, 1968 was shaping up to be one of the most politically charged years of the decade, scarred by civil unrest, racial strife, student protest and encroaching social breakdown, as symbolised in America by the assassinations of Martin Luther King and then Robert Kennedy, the ensuing bloodbath on the streets of Chicago at that Autumn's Democratic National Convention, and the ominous arrival in November of Richard Milhouse Nixon as the thirty-seventh president of the United States. In response, Lennon rewrote 'Revolution', Jagger gave the world 'Street Fighting Man' and even the avowedly apolitical Hendrix was moved to write 'House Burning Down'. Not that any of this impinged too greatly on the consciousness of the four members of the New Yardbirds as they readied themselves for their first eight-date tour together. They were hardly alone in this. For whatever the history books tell us now of the counter-cultural 'revolution' apparently taking place in the mid-Sixties, the end of the decade found British rock still little more than a funhouse populated by weekend rebels whose heroes were far too busy accumulating country mansions, white Rolls-Royces, exotic girlfriends and expensive drugs to care about what was actually going on in the real world, no matter what platitudes they were spouting in their songs. As John Lennon memorably put it in *Rolling Stone* in 1971, when asked to assess the impact of the Beatles during this period, 'Nothing happened, except we all dressed up. The same bastards are in control, the same people are running everything. It's exactly the same.'

And so it was. Largely an American conceit, the onset of the so-called counter-culture may have led to the young political left in Britain attending protest meetings about the war in Vietnam or marching in London's Grosvenor Square – a protest that appeared to be as much against the capitalist stooges of the Labour Party than American involvement in a war Britain was not directly involved in – but it certainly hadn't lead to the much vaunted 'long-haired revolution' routinely ranted about by everyone from Allen Ginsberg and Timothy Leary to John Peel and Donovan. Young, largely middle-class British students may have been happy to turn out in their thousands for rock concerts and even poetry events, but when in 1967, a genuine French revolutionary named Guy Debord arrived in London to rally round 'the people' to the idea of actually seizing power for themselves, of twenty hardcore British revolutionaries who had agreed to meet him at a flat in Notting Hill Gate, only three actually turned up – and they had spent the evening getting drunk on beer and watching *Match of the Day* on TV.

While Debord returned home to Paris shortly afterwards, forming a student-based group named 'Les Enragés' (the same stridently political group behind the great Paris and Nanterre student riots of 1968, in which nearly six hundred students were arrested in fights with police in a single day, while almost ten million French workers went on strike in support), the so-called revolutionaries of London merely looked on from afar, more at ease smoking dope and debating the merits of Dylan's 'comeback' than actually taking to the streets in any meaningful way. The only fight they appeared to have any real stomach for was for free rock festivals; a spurious 'cause' that would lead to the unwelcome chaos of the 1970 Bath Festival, where ticketless Hell's Angels and French student 'radicals' demanded to be allowed in and start as many fights as they liked.

Ultimately, the only real confrontation of note between the British 'establishment' and its so-called hippy 'alternative' focused on whether a particularly priapic Oz magazine cartoon depiction of Rupert Bear was 'obscene' or not, a ridiculous situation that eventually led to the infamous Old Bailey trial in the summer of 1971, which culminated in all three Oz editors receiving suspended prison sentences, along with an unprecedented level of national fame from which two of the three – future *Private Eye* editor Richard Neville and multi-millionaire publishing magnate Felix Dennis – would benefit immeasurably in the years to come. As the astute political commentator Andrew Marr later put it: 'A teddy bear with a stiffy: it rather sums up Britain's answer to revolution.'

In Britain, 1968 was the first year that album sales outstripped those of singles, another fact that didn't register with Jimmy Page, who was far too wrapped up in the excitement of leading his own band at last to care about anything else that might be happening out there in the pretend real world. However, the healthy state of album sales would have an unmistakable impact on the fortunes of his New Yardbirds. Right now, however, Page was too busy putting together a set list bolted together from old Yardbirds numbers and blues covers – stuff that would, as he put it, 'allow us to stretch out within that framework'; the kind of musical 'freak-outs' he'd only occasionally come close to exploring fully in the Yardbirds but which he hoped the new line-up would allow him at last to develop. 'There were lots of areas which they used to call freeform but was just straight improvisation, so by the time Zeppelin was getting together I'd already come up with such a mountain of riffs and ideas because every night we went on there were new things happening.'

The others were certainly ready. 'Bonzo and I were already in the freak-out zone after the Band of Joy,' Plant told me, 'so it was quite natural for us to go into long solos and pauses and crescendos. I mean, I listen to things like 'How Many More Times' and it swings, and it's got all those Sixties' bits and pieces that could have come off a *Nuggets* album. For Jimmy, it was an extension of what he did, and for us, it was an extension of what we did.'

Page remained secretly unsure about how well his new singer would work out eventually ('It was obvious he could sing but I wasn't sure about his potential as a frontman'), but he became more convinced of his worth with every performance. So powerful was Plant's voice that when the amplifiers inexplicably shutdown during a show in Stockholm on 12 September, 'you could still hear his voice at the back of the auditorium over the entire group'. Besides, things were suddenly moving too fast to stop now. The same day, the US trade magazine *Amusement Business* reported that 'London session bassist John Paul

Jones and vocalist Robert Plante [sic] have been asked by Jimmy Page to join his New Yardbirds.'

One person who was paying attention at that first-ever show was Danish photographer Jorgen Angel, then a seventeen-year-old student, who later admitted: 'I didn't expect much. Not long before the concert actually began, there was still a lot of talking on whether they were going to play under the name of "The Yardbirds" or under the name of "The New Yardbirds", and how people would react. Because in the club magazine, they were billed as "The Yardbirds", with a photo of the Yardbirds, not of Bonham, Plant, Page and John Paul Jones. Plus, in those days, when you saw a band turning up with the word "New" in its name, you knew that something was murky, that it wasn't the same group anymore. Can you imagine a group called The New Beatles? Of course not, you would be disappointed even before hearing a single note. So before these New Yardbirds even went on stage, I remember I was annoyed. I wanted "the real thing". But, as soon as they began to play, I was hooked . . .'

Their second appearance later that same night at the Pop Club in nearby Bronby was reviewed by local newspaper *Glostrup Handelsblat*, which noted that while Robert Planto [sic] 'sang well' his 'dancing needed work'. At both shows, the band performed a forty-minute set including 'Train Kept A-Rollin'', 'I Can't Quit You Baby', 'You Shook Me', 'How Many More Years' and just one would-be 'original', 'Dazed and Confused', and even that, in fact, was a better disguised, less well-known cover that Page had been performing for over a year previously with the Yardbirds.

The final Scandinavian date was at the Stjarscenen club in Gothenburg on 15 September. Twelve days later, in London, they began recording their debut album, moving into Olympic 1, a popular eight-track studio in Barnes, housed in the town's old music hall – the same studio the Stones had made *Beggars Banquet* in and that a few months later Fairport Convention, featuring a young Sandy Denny, would record their third album in.

Page instructed the band to begin by simply laying down the live set they'd been hammering into shape over the past few weeks – including a couple of days rehearsing together at Page's Pangbourne boathouse – plus a couple of extra tracks, starting with 'Babe I'm Gonna Leave You', and 'You Shook Me', both recorded virtually live that same day.

All recording expenses were paid for by Page. Grant and Jones might have been expected to pick up some of the tab, too. They could both certainly afford it. But Jimmy didn't want that. This was his baby and he intended to keep it that way. Let the others leave the worrying and forking out to him. As long as they did what they were told and kept playing the way they had been, the guitarist was satisfied he'd get it all back later. As he said, 'I wanted artistic control in a vice grip because I knew exactly what I wanted to do with these fellows ... I knew exactly what I wanted to do in every respect.'

Nine days later, despite a total of just thirty hours in the studio, the album had been fully recorded, mixed and was ready to be cut onto a mastered disc. Total cost, including artwork: £1,782. This was extremely fast work, even taking into account how experienced and versatile session-vets like Page and Jones were – or the fact that all four had proved how remarkably well they gelled in the studio when they performed as backing band (with Plant on harmonica) on a P.J. Proby session in London arranged for them by Jones, just prior to leaving for Denmark (the track 'Jim's Blues', later released on the 1969 Proby album, *Three Week Hero*, consequently became the first studio track to feature all four members of the future Led Zeppelin).

They were also beginning to bond as people. Jimmy already knew Jonesy, of course, and he was already forming the basis of a friendship with Robert through their shared efforts at creating new material for the live set. As for Bonzo, that was trickier. As Jimmy said, 'The thing is, I don't drive a car. I didn't drive a car then and I don't now. So the fact that John lived in the Midlands, we didn't get to see each other as much as if he'd lived closer.' However, there was one incident in the early days that seemed to cement their friendship, when one night Bonham turned up unexpectedly on Page's doorstep. 'It was about two in the morning and he was just standing there with Pat and Jason, asking if they could stay the night. He had been kicked out of Pat's mum's house after a row and had nowhere else to go.' He laughed as he recalled how Jason – then just a two-year-old toddler – threw a record that happened to be an early Plant solo single called 'Our Song', off the balcony and into the river. 'I don't think Robert ever forgave him for it!' Jimmy laughed; then added: 'I was pleased that Bonzo came to me, actually. Obviously, he trusted me. And he came down and we had a laugh and we hung out, and that was really good.'

The other thing that really pleased Page was how astonishingly well the recording sessions had gone. With the emphasis on speed as much as quality, nine tracks had been recorded: a patchwork of originals, former Yardbirds material, covers and what most charitably might be described as 'disguised' covers – the latter of which continue to cause ripples of discontent, not least amongst the real authors of said songs, to this day.

3

Light and Shade

Opening with the rhythmic battering-ram that is 'Good Times Bad Times' – one of just three originals, and credited to Page, Jones and Bonham – the immediate impression one got from hearing the *Led Zeppelin* album for the first time was one of pure shocking power, its opening salvo summing up everything the name Led Zeppelin would quickly come to embody. A pop song built on a zinging, catchy chorus, explosive drums and, at exactly the right moment, a flurry of spitting guitar notes that don't stick around long enough to be called a solo. 'It's got quite a complicated rhythm, which Jonesy came up with,' said Page. 'But the most stunning thing about it, musically, is Bonzo's amazing kick drum. He's playing brilliantly on everything else but that is right out of the norm – playing with one kick drum and making it sound like two. People that know music, when they heard that they started to realise what he was capable of, and what it meant the band was capable of.'

If 'Good Times Bad Times' pointed the way forward for rock music in the Seventies, towards heavy-duty riffage and mallet-swinging drums, its counterpart on side two, 'Communication Breakdown', with its spiky, downstroke guitar riff and grafting of the *ostinato* from Eddie Cochran's 'Nervous Breakdown' – again credited to Page, Jones and Bonham – was proto-punk; the sort of speeded up, one-chord gunshot the Ramones would turn into a career a decade later. 'Your Time Is Gonna Come', the third of the three originals on the album, this time credited simply to Page and Jones, is something else again: a wonderfully understated pop song built in the fashion of the time around a Bach fugue, played by Jones on what sounds like a church organ, then swept into a completely different musical zone by Page's pedal steel guitar – an instrument he had literally picked up in the studio that day and begun to play.

The rest of the album, however, was a very different kettle of fish: equally impressive in the scope of its sonic architecture, but quite shamelessly unoriginal in its choice of material, as exemplified by its final track, 'How Many More Times'. It is credited to Page, Jones and Bonham but is a composition clearly based on several older tunes, primarily 'How Many More Years' by Howlin' Wolf, a number which Plant and Bonham had performed their own version of in the Band of Joy, inserting snatches of Albert King's 'The Hunter'. The 'new' Zeppelin version opened with a bass riff snatched from the Yardbirds' earlier reworking of 'Smokestack Lightning', plus more than a passing nod to a mid-Sixties version of the same tune by Gary Farr and the T-Bones also re-titled 'How Many More Times' (and produced by original Yardbirds manager Giorgio Gomelsky). There was even a lick or two appropriated from Jimmy Rodgers' 'Kisses Sweeter Than Wine' as well as, bizarrely, a slowed-to-a-crawl take on Jeff Beck's solo from the Yardbirds' 'Shapes of Things'. All of which the band might have gotten away with if so much else on the album didn't also take its cue from the work of others, largely without acknowledgement, then or now.

Indeed, of the other tracks on the album credited to various band members, all have subsequently had that contention challenged, with varying degrees of success. Beginning with 'Babe I'm Gonna Leave You', Page's dramatic reworking of the traditional song was first heard outside contemporary folk circles on a Joan Baez album. Although not unjustly credited on the original Zeppelin album as a 'Traditional' song, 'arranged by Jimmy Page', by the time of the 1990 release of the Zeppelin *Remastered* CD box-set the credit had been amended to include one A. Bredon, aka American folk singer Anne Bredon, who had recorded her own version in the Fifties. It is now generally acknowledged that the 'new arrangement' Page had first played for Plant on the acoustic guitar was, in fact, at least partly influenced by Bredon's earlier treatment.

Similarly, the track 'Black Mountain Side', an acoustic guitar instrumental in the exotic, modal style of Page's earlier Yardbirds-era showcase, 'White Summer', even down to the percussive accompaniment of the Indian hand drums known as tablas, provided in this instance by Viram Jasani. Where 'White Summer' had been Page's 'interpretation' of Davy Graham's famous version of 'She Moved Through the Fair', 'Black Mountain Side' was in fact Page's instrumental version of fellow Graham disciple Bert Jansch's 1966 recording of another traditional Gaelic folk tune titled 'Black Water Side' – one, coincidentally, almost certainly shown to Jansch by Anne Briggs, another Page favourite from the Sixties, who had herself been shown the tune by a characterful old folklorist named Bert Lloyd.

As a result, although Jansch's record company sought legal advice in consultation with two eminent musicologists and John Mummery QC (one of the most prominent copyright barristers in the UK at the time), it was decided not to pursue an action for royalties against Page and/or Led Zeppelin. As Nat Joseph, then head of Jansch's record company, Transatlantic, later explained: 'It had been reasonably established that there was every chance that Jimmy Page had heard Bert play the piece at a club or concert . . . or that he'd heard Bert's recording. However, what could not be proved was that Bert's recording in itself constituted Bert's own copyright, because the basic melody, of course, was traditional.'

Nevertheless, crediting 'Black Mountain Side' merely to Jimmy Page led Jansch to treat me to one of his famously wan smiles, as he says, 'The thing I've noticed about Jimmy whenever we meet now is that he can never look me in the eye. Well, he ripped me off, didn't he? Or let's just say he *learned* from me. I wouldn't want to sound impolite.' His dark, wrinkled eyes fix me with a beady glare, as if daring me to disagree. But then, as Page himself later admitted, 'At one point, I was absolutely obsessed with Bert Jansch. When I first heard [his 1965 début] album I couldn't believe it. It was so far ahead of what anyone else was doing. No-one in America could touch that.' Clearly, he was even more taken with Jansch's third album, *Jack Orion*, which contained not only 'Black Water Side' (also later recorded by Sandy Denny) but was full of the sort of sinister drones and fierce, stabbing guitar that Page would incorporate into his work throughout his subsequent career in both the Yardbirds and particularly Led Zeppelin.

Even the two acknowledged covers on the Zeppelin album – 'I Can't Quit You Baby' and 'You Shook Me' – would bring charges from the critics of a form of plagiarism. Not through lack of credit this time – both tracks were originally by Willie Dixon and are credited as such on the sleeve – but, in the case of the latter, that it was a rip-off of the version recently released on Jeff Beck's *Truth*. Some critics went further, pointing out the obvious similarities between *Truth* and the first Zeppelin album, from the line-up (two extrovert lead guitarists in Beck and Page in harness with two powerhouse vocalists in Rod Stewart and Robert Plant) to the concentration on light and shade, the reworking of Yardbirds material, even the inclusion of traditional folk 'interludes' ('Greensleeves' on *Truth* and 'Black Mountain Side' on *Led Zeppelin*). Most glaring of all, the respective covers of 'You Shook Me'. An irksome comparison, from Jimmy's point of view, that would continue to cast a shadow over Zeppelin's credibility, right up to the present day.

Taken from the same Muddy Waters EP that both guitarists had loved as kids (the same EP, coincidentally, that contained the track 'You Need Love', which would provide Page with yet more 'inspiration' when it came to the next Zeppelin album), Jimmy has always claimed that it was simply 'a coincidence' that the same song should end up on both albums; that he hadn't realised Beck had already recorded a version for his album, even though Peter Grant had given him an advance copy of *Truth* weeks before its release. Even if it were possible that Page had somehow neglected to afford the album even a cursory spin, it seems inconceivable that John Paul Jones would not have mentioned at some point that he had actually played Hammond organ on the *Truth* version.

In reality, Jeff Beck was the one who didn't know what was going on. The first he knew of his friend Jimmy's decision to record the same track with his new group was when he played it to him. According to Beck, 'He said, "Listen to this. Listen to Bonzo, this guy called John Bonham that I've got." And so I said I would, and my heart just sank when I heard "You Shook Me". I looked at him and said "Jim, what?" and the tears were coming out with anger. I thought, "This is a pisstake, it's got to be." I mean, there's *Truth* still spinning on everybody's turntable, and this turkey's come out with another version. Oh boy ... then I realised it was serious, and he did have this heavyweight drummer, and I thought "Here we go again" – pipped at the post kind of thing.'

Page merely shrugs when I mention it. 'It wasn't modelled on Jeff's band at all. For a start, Jeff had a keyboard player in his band. He was attempting an entirely different thing. The only unfortunate similarity

was that we both did a version of "You Shook Me". I didn't know he'd
recorded it until our album was already done. You know, we had very
similar roots but we were trying for a completely different thing, in
my opinion.'

Listening to both tracks now, forty years later, what is most striking
is the *lack* of similarity between the tracks. While the Beck version is
short and gimmicky, almost throwaway, the Zeppelin version is almost
three times as long, much more portentous, with swampy bottleneck
guitar more redolent of the original's swooning rhythms. Then Page's
guitar solo comes in and it is fluid, haunting, ancient-sounding and
mysterious, not bitty or showy like Beck's. It's then the thought strikes:
Page knew exactly what he was doing. Of course he'd heard the Beck
version. This was his hefty riposte. That when he played it to Beck, he
was saying: there you go, Jeff, that's how you do that one. Then
probably regretted it when he saw how badly his old friend took it.

*For you it wasn't about rebellion, it was about proving a point. You loved
your mum and dad, felt at ease in their comfortable world of net curtains,
untipped cigarettes and cups of tea. They never tried to stop you doing
what you liked; giving you the front room to play in every Sunday afternoon,
when Jeff would come over and you would muck about together on the
guitars. Mum would push back the chairs and say 'Give us a dance, Jim!'
Dad had the same name as you – James Patrick Page – and the same
sense of humour. When your driving test came up and it turned out you
had a session that day you'd jokingly told him to go in your place and he'd
just laughed with you and done it, so at least one of you could drive.*

*It was a different world to the one they'd grown up in but they didn't
seem to mind, as long as you were happy, and you were. You'd listen to
them telling stories about it. How during the war your dad had been a
wages clerk, then a manager giving the orders at the aircraft works in
Middlesex. Mum was another Patrick – Patricia Elizabeth Gaffiken – a
proper Irishwoman who'd worked at the doctor's surgery as a receptionist,
making the appointments, always smiling with a good word for everybody.
Well, nearly everybody. They hadn't been married very long when they
found out she was having you. That was when they lived in the old place
in Heston, the little gaff near Hounslow Heath. You were a war baby, they
said: born 9 January 1944, at the Grove Nursing Home on Grove Road,
just up the road from the house. They had you baptised cos that's what*

everyone did but they never made you go to church. Mum and Dad didn't believe in God – not really – and neither did you. Not the old chap with the long white beard, anyway. The only time you even said his name was when something went wrong. Oh, God! Oh, Christ! Oh, bloody hell!

Music wasn't important, either. There was the radio and later the telly but you never really knew what a record looked like until you were older. No brothers and sisters, either. You were 'an only child,' they said, who 'liked his own company' and who liked reading and drawing and collecting stamps; an only child who was 'very mature' for his age. 'Jimmy was fun,' your mum would say, looking back years later. 'But quiet fun, he wasn't a "screamer" sort of boy.' Or as you would put it: 'That early isolation probably had a lot to do with the way I turned out. A loner. A lot of people can't be on their own. They get frightened. Isolation doesn't bother me at all. It gives me a sense of security.'

After the war, when Mum and Dad moved from Heston to Feltham, on the other side of the Heath, the noise from London Airport was terrible. Jets would 'circle the airport. You could hear them going over all the time.' So Mum and Dad moved again, this time all the way to Epsom in Surrey, where Dad started his own business buying and selling cars – Page Motors. Epsom was where you eventually got your soft Surrey accent, living in the nice new house in Miles Road. It was great – posher than Heston. Nice house, lace curtains, nosy neighbours, playing football and cricket over the park. Summer holidays were best. You would go down to your great-uncle's farm in Northamptonshire. First time you ever went fishing. And you could muck about with the animals. You really loved the animals.

The rest of the time you were a Pound Lane Primary School pupil. A good boy until you got to twelve and discovered the guitar. Later, you'd boast how 'I had a really fine education from the age of eleven to seventeen on how to be a rebel and I learned all the tricks of the game.' But that was just boasting. Really you just liked to show off. You'd take the guitar in knowing the teachers would take it off you and not let you have it back till home time. It was only one of those old Spanish-type jobs with horrid steel strings but when you took it out to the playing fields after school and started strumming all the girls would stand around pulling at their hair, staring at you as though seeing you for the first time. You didn't even know how to tune it till another boy showed you. Then you got that Play in a Day book by Bert Weedon, but more out of curiosity. You soon forgot about it. Mum and Dad paid for some lessons, too, but that wasn't any good either.

You were always too impatient. There was what the tutor in Kingston asked you to practise and then there was what you were hearing when you played the records. Especially Elvis and 'Baby Let's Play House'. Gee whizz! It was so catchy you couldn't get it out of your head! No drums, just guitars and more guitars; pure excitement and energy, wanting to be a part of it. So you learned to play by ear, starting with the solos, usually Buddy Holly cos they were easiest, just chord solos like 'Peggy Sue'. Then Johnny Day, who played guitar for the Everly Brothers. 'Teaching myself was the first and most important part of my education,' you'd say later, when they asked you about those days. 'I hope they keep it out of schools.'

Sometimes it would take hours, days even, before you got it but you always got there in the end. After Buddy Holly it was Ricky Nelson. James Burton was his guitarist, you found out. 'Which was when it started to get difficult,' trying to do that bendy string style of solo. It was months before you realised 'you had to remove your traditionally coated third string and replace it with an uncoated one because it was physically impossible to bend otherwise'. No flies on you.

It was better after you'd got yourself the Hofner Senator, with the electric pick-up, bought with the lolly you'd saved up from your paper round. But it still wasn't what you called 'a proper electric guitar, which to me was one with a solid body', so you saved up some more and eventually swapped it for a Grazioso, sort of like a solid-body Strat, except made in Czechoslovakia. Like Hank Marvin from the Shadows with his Antori, sort of. Just plug it into the radiogram and go.

It was all about rock'n'roll. A-wop-bop-a-loo-bop … saving up your pocket money so you could run down to Rumbelow's in Epsom to buy 'The Girl Can't Help It' by Little Richard. Rumbelow's that sold washing machines and vacuum cleaners down the front and had a little record counter at the back, building up your own collection of 78s. Until then it had all been trad jazz, listening to the Light Programme and the Home Service. Now, all of a sudden, it was about Elvis and Gene Vincent, and before that Bill Haley and Lonnie Donegan. Lonnie was especially good. Skiffle! You loved that! But by the time you were fifteen and thinking about leaving school, it was Elvis and Ricky Nelson, the hard stuff. It was also around now that you first had a go at reading Magick in Theory and Practice *by Aleister Crowley. It wasn't till years later you really understood what it was about but that was the start. Mainly, though, it was all about the guitar and rock'n'roll, Scotty Moore and his Gibson Super-400 CES*

*semi-acoustic. Rockabilly chording, bent-note solos, the sort of tight inter-
woven riffing from the guitar and bass that made Elvis shout 'Yeah!'
Years later, you'd do your own version in your own group and call it
'Communication Breakdown' ...*

*Other stuff, too, like the jangly sound James Burton got from his Fender
Telecaster on 'Hello Mary Lou'; or Cliff Gallup and Johnny Meeks blasting
it out on 'Be-Bop-A-Lula'; or Carl Perkins, who called rock'n'roll 'a black
man's song with a country man's rhythm'. You didn't know about that till
later and by then you only had to listen to the way you played to know it
was true. The sort of thing that would never go away, so that it was still
all there when you came to do your solo on 'Heartbreaker' or the chunky
der-duh-der-duh riff to 'Whole Lotta Love'. It was amazing how one thing
led to another. How Lonnie Donegan's 'Rock Island Line' led to Leadbelly's
'Cotton Fields'; how Elvis led to Arthur 'Big Boy' Crudup and Sleepy John
Estes. How the more you listened and played along, the more it all fitted
together in your mind. It was obvious most of it, but no-one except you
seemed to know. Not even Mum and Dad ...*

*These were still the days when rock'n'roll was not really allowed. Not
in Surrey. These were the days when rock'n'roll were still dirty words;
forbidden fruit. Then all of a sudden it was the blues and your mate down
the road who had such an amazing stash of those LPs, always asking to
let you borrow them, promising to look after them. Blues was so far
underground it made even Elvis sound normal. You couldn't hear it on the
radio; you never saw it on telly. You couldn't even find it in the shops that
sold records; didn't even know the records existed until you held them in
your hands, could smell how old and strange they were. 'When I heard
those songs for the first time,' you'd recall, 'they really did send chills up
my spine.'*

*Of course they did. At first it was Robert Johnson, then Bukka White,
Mississippi Fred McDowell ... all the older stuff, just listening to the guitar.
Soon it was newer stuff. Muddy Waters, Freddy King, Howlin' Wolf. Even
wilder guitar! Hubert Sumlin, Howlin' Wolf's guitarist was the most! You
could play along to that stuff and make your own stuff up on top of it. 'A
good sketchpad,' you'd call it. And then you found it: where rock'n'roll
joined up with the blues. Chuck Berry, Bill Broonzy; the Chicago sound.
Everyone else at school was into Cliff and the Shadows, things that
'sounded like they were eating fish-and-chips while they were playing.'
Music for girls ...*

*

Jeff Beck may have got there first in his attempt to form his own band, but there's no mistaking Page's belief that he could do better. Speaking in 1976 to the writer Mick Houghton, Beck had had 'fantastic bands,' Page said. 'The early one with Aynsley Dunbar was a brilliant band, but it was his own temperament and the way he treated his musicians which was really outrageous. Sacking and rehiring ... purely at Jeff's convenience. You're never gonna get the right feeling within the band or the right chemistry when people feel they're not getting their just deserts. Jeff's his own worst enemy in that respect.' But if Page was keen to show he was better than Beck by beating him at his own game, it conversely had the opposite effect, making critics feel he was inferior. Routinely accused by critics, ever since, of taking his cue for Zeppelin directly from Beck's work on *Truth*, history has tended to afford Beck the mantle of 'true original' while Page has often subsequently been regarded as a mere copyist, or at best a musical arriviste. None of which was actually true. Page may have been permissive when it came to 'borrowing' material but the first Zeppelin album exuded the kind of production techniques and musical nous Beck could only hint at with his own, less stable group.

The most blatant steal on the first Zeppelin album, though, occurred on the track most people now remember best from it, and the number, ironically, destined to become one of the most closely associated with Jimmy Page: 'Dazed and Confused'. Although credited solely to Page, the original version of the song had been written by a twenty-eight-year-old singer-songwriter named Jake Holmes, who Jimmy had seen performing the song just a year before.

Holmes had already tried his hand at various branches of the entertainment industry – from comedy to concept albums – by the time he came to find himself and his two-man acoustic backing band opening for the Yardbirds at the Village Theater in New York's Greenwich Village one Friday night in August 1967. His solo album, *The Above Ground Sound of Jake Holmes*, had just been released that summer. Included from it in his set was a witchy ballad entitled 'Dazed and Confused'. Although acoustic, it included all the signature sounds the Yardbirds – and later Zeppelin – would appropriate into their versions, including the walking bass line, the eerie atmosphere, the paranoid lyrics, not about a bad acid trip as has long been suggested, says Holmes now, but a real-life love affair that had gone wrong. Watching him perform the song spellbound from the side of the stage that night in 1967 was Yardbirds drummer Jim McCarty, and standing next to him, Jimmy Page. McCarty recalls going out the very next day and buying a copy of the Holmes album specifically to hear 'Dazed and Confused' again. He claims Page also went out that day and bought his own copy of the album for the same reason.

Given a new, amped-up arrangement by Page and McCarty, with lyrics only slightly altered by Keith Relf, it quickly became a highlight of the Yardbirds' live show during their last months together. Never recorded except for a John Peel session for Radio 1 in March 1968 just before they left for that final US tour, a version that sounds almost identical musically to the number Page would take full credit for on the first Zeppelin album, but which on the expanded 2003 remastered CD version of the Yardbirds' *Little Games* album is credited to: 'Jake Holmes, arranged by the Yardbirds' – there was never any question in the rest of the band's minds over who the song had been written by. 'I was struck by the atmosphere of "Dazed and Confused",' McCarty recalled in a 2003 interview, 'and we decided to do a version. We worked it out together, with Jimmy contributing the guitar riffs in the middle.'

By the time Page came to record it for the first Zeppelin album, the only substantial change from the version he'd been performing with the Yardbirds just three months before was his own rewrite of the lyrics, including such darkly misogynistic ruminations as the 'soul of a woman' being 'created below'. Other than that, the song stuck to the original arrangement, up to the bridge, where even then the fret-tapping harked back to Holmes' original. The only other difference of note were the effects Page obtained from sawing a violin bow across the E string on his guitar, creating a startlingly eerie melody full of strange whooping and groaning noises; a trick he had first experimented with in his session days. As if to prove just how indiscriminate he was in his 'borrowing', Page followed up the bowing section of 'Dazed and Confused' with a series of juddering guitar notes – as Plant over-emotes in a blur of stygian yowls – lifted wholesale from an obscure Yardbirds' B-side called 'Think About It', exhibiting a tendency to recycle his own motifs and ideas as well as others'.

Speaking to Jake Holmes now, he says he wrote 'Dazed And

Confused' on a college tour just a few months before his show with
the Yardbirds. 'I didn't think it was that special. But it went over really
well, it was our set closer. The kids loved it – as did the Yardbirds, I
guess,' he remarks dryly. He says it wasn't until 'way later' that he first
became aware that Page had recorded his own version with Zeppelin –
and given it his own songwriting credit. 'Rock'n'roll was kind of going
into its second life when Led Zeppelin came along. I wasn't fifteen
years old anymore so I wasn't listening to that stuff. I was too busy
hanging out at clubs like the Night Owl with the Lovin' Spoonful,
Vince Martin and Cass Elliot.' So much so, he says his first reaction
was to be blasé. 'I didn't give a shit. At that time I didn't think there
was a law about intent. I thought it had to do with the old Tin Pan
Alley law that you had to have four bars of exactly the same melody,
and that if somebody had taken a riff and changed it just slightly or
changed the lyrics that you couldn't sue them. That turned out to be
totally misguided.'

Over the years, he says, he has 'been trying to do something about
it. But I've never been able to find [a legal representative] who was
aggressive enough or interested enough to really push it as hard as it
could be pushed. And economically I didn't want to be spending
hundreds and thousands of dollars to come up with something that
may not work. I'm not starving, and I have a lot of cachet with my
kids because all the kids in their school say, "Your dad wrote 'Dazed
and Confused'? Awesome!" So I'm a cult hero.'

In terms of royalties, he just wants a share of the credit, he says,
and 'a fair deal. I don't want [Page] to give me full credit for this
song. He took it and put it in a direction that I would never have
taken it, and it became very successful. So why should I complain?
But give me at least half credit on it.' The fact that 'Dazed and
Confused' was destined to become one of Led Zeppelin's great set-
piece moments, he points out, 'is partly the problem. [Page] is
gonna be so connected to that song by now, it's like if your baby is
kidnapped at two-years-old and raised by another woman. All these
years later, it's *her* kid. To confess or admit that it's not is tantamount
to admitting that you kidnapped a child. For [Jimmy Page], it's
probably more difficult to wrench that song away from him than it
would be any other song. And I have tried, you know. I've written
letters saying, "Jesus, man, you don't have to give it all to me. Keep

half! Keep two-thirds! Just give me credit for having originated it."
That's the sad part about it. I don't even think it has to do with
money. It's not like he needs it. It totally has to do with how
intimately he's been connected to it over all these years.'

Over the years, Page and Zeppelin's appropriation of other artists'
material was to become a longstanding criticism. Rightly so, one might
argue, when one considers just how many times they would be accused
of the offence over the course of their career. And yet, they are hardly
the only ones. David Bowie ripped off the Stones for 'Rebel Rebel';
the Stones ripped off Bo Diddley for 'Not Fade Away'; the Beatles
ripped off Fats Domino for 'Lady Madonna'; everybody ripped the
Beatles off for something. The Yardbirds were equally guilty. Tracks
like 'Drinking Muddy Water' – attributed to Dreja, McCarty, Page and
Relf – was an obvious rewrite of the Muddy Waters' tune 'Rolling and
Tumbling'. But then Waters' version was itself a patchwork of several
earlier blues numbers. The same went for the aptly titled 'Stealing,
Stealing', a song originally by Will Shade's Memphis Jug Band, but
with the Yardbirds again listed as authors.

One could argue that with the folk and blues 'traditions' based
almost entirely on tunes handed down over generations, with each
passing bringing its own unique interpretation, that Page and others are
as within their rights to claim authorship of their own interpretations of
this material as Muddy Waters, Davy Graham, Willie Dixon, Bert
Jansch, Blind Willie Johnson, Robert Johnson and all the other artists
Led Zeppelin would knowingly 'borrow' from over the years. In the
early part of the twentieth century, the legendary 'patriarch' of American country music, A.P. Carter, copyrighted dozens of songs written
decades before his arrival in the Appalachians, many of which had
their origins in ancient Celtic tunes from the British Isles. As a result,
to this day a venerable old masterpiece like 'Will the Circle Be
Unbroken' is still spuriously credited to Carter.

Similarly, Bob Dylan – widely considered the most groundbreaking
and original songwriter of the late twentieth century – accurately
described his first album as 'some stuff I've written, some stuff I've
discovered, some stuff I stole'. In that instance, he was talking mainly
about arrangements, such as his 'Man of Constant Sorrow', lifted
wholesale from Judy Collins' 'Maid of Constant Sorrow'. Or, most
brazenly, the steal of Dave Van Ronk's innovative arrangement of

'House of the Rising Sun', which Van Ronk resented hugely. But there are plenty of other examples from his career. 'Masters of War' is sung to the tune of 'Nottamun Town', which Dylan heard Martin Carthy sing on an early visit to the UK. While 'Bob Dylan's Dream' derives from the old English folk ballad 'The Franklin', and both 'Girl from the North Country' and 'Boots of Spanish Leather' are again based on hearing Carthy's take on 'Scarborough Fair'. None of these ever received any due credit on Dylan's album sleeves. The list goes on: the melody for 'Blowin' in the Wind' is from an old anti-slavery song, 'No More Auction Block'; the melody for 'Don't Think Twice, It's All Right' comes from a traditional Appalachian tune, 'Who's Gonna Buy Your Chickens When I'm Gone'. Even elements of Dylan's towering reputation as a lyricist can be traced back to certain jumping-off points such as his 'borrowing' from the opening lines of the epic ballad 'Lord Randall' for his own 'Hard Rain's A-Gonna Fall'. John Lennon believed Dylan's '4th Time Around' to be nothing less than a deliberate parody of 'Norwegian Wood'. Of course, one might point out at this juncture that Lennon's 'All You Need Is Love' was barely more than a modern re-reading of 'Three Blind Mice'. But the point holds true: Jimmy Page is hardly the only artist to find 'inspiration' from underneath his nose.

Jeff Beck wasn't above a bit of rule-bending either, of course. No songwriter, and consequently 'starved of material', *Truth* included more than one outright steal. As Beck revealed to Charles Shaar Murray, when discussing the remastered CD version of *Truth* in 2005, the track 'Let Me Love You' – credited on the sleeve to one Jeffrey Rod (i.e. Beck and Stewart) – bears an uncanny resemblance to an earlier Buddy Guy track of almost the same name. 'We just slowed it down and funked it up a little with a Motown-style tambourine,' admits Beck. 'There was a lot of conniving going on back then: change the rhythm, change the angle and it's yours. We got paid peanuts for what we were doing and I couldn't give a shit about anybody else.' Other Jeffrey Rod compositions on *Truth* included 'Rock My Plimsoul' – another 'sloweddown, funked up' version, this time of BB King's 'Rock Me Baby'; and 'Blues De Luxe', based entirely on BB King's 'Gambler's Blues'. Ditto the Jeffrey Rod credit for 'I've Been Drinking', from the Dinah Washington original 'Drinking Again'.

As far as Page was concerned, it was all grist for the mill. 'The thing is they were traditional lyrics and they went back far before a lot of people that one related them to,' he told writer Dave Schulps in 1977. 'The riffs we did were totally different, also, from the ones that had come before, apart from something like "You Shook Me" and "I Can't Quit You", which were attributed to Willie Dixon.' More to the point, as he has said more recently, 'As a musician, I'm only the product of my influences. The fact that I listened to so many various styles of music has a lot to do with the way I play. Which I think set me apart from so many other guitarists of that time.'

Nevertheless, the accusations of plagiarism would have a debilitating effect on Zeppelin's long-term credibility. It's one thing to 'assimilate' old songs, quite another to claim the credit for having built them from the bottom up. Even today when 'sampling' is the norm in the hip-hop world, woe betide any artist who omits to credit the original source. On a purely musical level then, while it would be churlish not to extend Page and Zeppelin the enormous credit they deserve for 'creating' epic rock moments like 'Dazed and Confused' – and so many others that would follow in a similar vein, from 'Whole Lotta Love' to 'Nobody's Fault But Mine' – history has been largely indifferent to their refusal to acknowledge the true originators of these ideas, and indeed their reaping of the huge financial rewards that resulted.

Even Jimmy Page's novel use of the violin bow – which became for him what the tremolo bar was for Hendrix, or the playing of the guitar behind his back was for Beck, that is to say, his signature gimmick – would eventually be called into question, with critics eager to point out that he wasn't the first guitarist to use a violin bow. Eddie Phillips, guitarist with The Creation (a mod outfit from London that Page was familiar with, who would climax their set by throwing paint on a canvas backdrop, action-painting style) scraped a violin bow across the fretboard on the group's two 1966 singles, 'Painter Man' and 'Making Time'. Shel Talmy, who produced those records, and who worked with Page on sessions for the Kinks and The Who, later insisted, 'Jimmy Page stole the bowing bit of the guitar from Eddie. Eddie was phenomenal.' There was also Kaleidoscope, a psychedelic five-piece from Pasadena, whose guitarist also embellished certain tunes with a violin bow. Page knew of them too. When I asked him, however, he insisted it was concertmaster violinist David McCallum Snr – father of the *Man from U.N.C.L.E.* star – who first suggested the idea as the two chatted during a tea break at a session in 1965. As a result, he had first experimented using a violin bow in the Yardbirds, on two tracks on *Little Games*: 'Tinker, Tailor, Soldier, Sailor' and 'Glimpses', the latter becoming an early violin-guitar showcase for him on stage, to be replaced during their final months by 'Dazed and Confused'.

Ask Page now for his thoughts on the first Zeppelin album and he'll talk about how it 'had so many firsts on it, as far as the content goes. Even though we were heavily involved in a sort of progressive blues thing, one of the most important parts was the acoustic input. Things like "Babe I'm Gonna Leave You", which had the flamenco-type bits in it. The drama of it – the light and shade – I don't think had been touched by anybody. With the acoustic input you had this sort of embryo, which was good.' But the first Zeppelin album was less a new beginning for Page than a culmination of everything that had gone before. All it really proved was that Zeppelin were great 'synthesisers' of existing ideas. That this was accomplished in an era when such notions were still considered outside acceptable bounds says something about fortune and the talent to influence it. With Jimmy Page at the helm, Led Zeppelin would have both.

In fact, the real innovations of that first album were in the advanced production techniques Page was able to bring to bear and the sheer weight of musicianship he had assembled to execute them. Being able to produce such power and cohesiveness from a line-up that was barely a month old was extremely impressive; to capture that energy on record, however, little short of astonishing; his previously unknown talent as a producer overshadowing even his dexterity as a guitar player. Not least in his innovative use of backwards echo – an effect that engineer Glyn Johns told him couldn't be done until Page showed him how – and what Jimmy calls 'the science of close-miking amps'. That is, not just hanging microphones in front of the band in the studio but draping them at the back as well, of floating them several feet above the drums, allowing the sound to 'breathe'. Or taking the drummer out of the little booth they were routinely shoved into in those days and allowing him to play along with the rest of the band in the main room. This would lead to a lot of 'bleeding' – the background sound of one track echoing in the background of another, particularly when it came to the vocals – but Page was happy to leave that in, treating it as one more 'effect' that gave the recording 'great atmosphere, which is what I was after more than a sterile sort of sound'.

As then star writer at *Melody Maker*, Chris Welch, recalls: 'One of the younger writers brought an early pre-release copy of the album into the office and played it on the office stereo – and it just sort of leapt out at you! I'd been a big supporter of Cream, had seen Hendrix and The Who perform several times, but I'd never – never! – heard anything so loud and overpowering coming off a record before. It really did feel like a great leap forward, in terms of the sound you could actually get on a record. And that was just the first track.' Or as Robert Plant later put it: 'That was the first time that headphones meant anything to me. What I heard coming back to me over the cans while I was singing was better than the finest chick in all the land. It had so much weight, so much power, it was devastating.'

The material may have been largely derivative, the 'light and shade' aspect not nearly so interesting or new as Page still insists – certainly not compared to the multifaceted aspects of the music then being made by the Beatles and the Stones, or even Dylan and The Who, all of whom had alternated between electric and acoustic instrumentation for years, playing not just with light and shade but helping shape the parameters of rock music as a creative genre – but it had never been done with such finesse and know-how, or quite so much determination to succeed at any cost. Indeed, the first Zeppelin album was an almost cynical attempt to outdo its immediate competitors – Hendrix, Clapton, Townshend, and of course the unwitting Beck – while at the same time demonstrating that the man at the back, lurking in the shadows – Page himself – had more up his sleeve than mere conjuring tricks. That this was a rock wizard with incredible mastery over his tools, one who had stood off to one side watching for long enough. Now it was time to do, to be, to overcome. If anyone was going to get credit for that achievement, it was Jimmy Page. When Glyn Johns, who had also worked with the Beatles, the Stones and The Who, and who Page had known since his days as a teenager playing in a local hall in Epsom, asked for a producer's co-credit, Page gave him short shrift. 'I said, "No way. I put this band together, I brought them in and directed the whole recording process, I got my own guitar sound – I'll tell you, you haven't got a hope in hell".'

One other omission that, in retrospect, appears glaring is that of any songwriting credit for Robert Plant. It's since been suggested that Plant was still tied up contractually to CBS and therefore unable to be listed as co-author of any of the material on the first Zeppelin album. However, in reality Plant simply wasn't contributing anything meaningful, either lyrically or musically, at this stage. 'I didn't know what he'd be like yet as a songwriter,' Page later told me. 'When I first saw him he was a singer first and foremost. I don't even know if he had written anything before.' It was, in fact, said Page, 'one of the things that still concerned me' about his new frontman. For the time being, however, what was most important was that the boy could sing, and in that regard there were no doubts whatsoever.

You were ten the first time you saw an electric guitar, watching Sunday Night at the London Palladium *on telly when suddenly Buddy Holly and the Crickets came on. You couldn't take your eyes off Buddy's Fender Stratocaster, something you'd later describe as 'an incredible symbol of what I hadn't got my hands on yet'. Not that you had any chance of getting your hands on one. Instead, you made do with learning how to play the kazoo, the harmonica and the washboard. Mum and Dad laughed, called you a skiffle singer. 'Hark at little Lonnie Donegan!' Lonnie was all right, 'My Old Man's A Dustman' always went down well at home. But for you it was mainly about Elvis. Not even Mum and Dad could argue about Elvis. It was through Elvis that you eventually discovered everything else. Loving Elvis meant loving all kinds of different music whether you knew it yet or not: blues, rockabilly, skiffle, R&B, on into country-and-western, folk, gospel, bluegrass, then over the hills and far away into Zydeco, vaudeville, Appalachian, jazz, hillbilly, eventually ending up at light opera and mainstream show tunes. Elvis was everything all rolled into one, everything you'd ever dreamed of before you'd even dreamed it. Elvis was King and you were his most faithful subject and one day all this would be yours, you just knew it, staring into the bedroom mirror and flicking your hair . . .*

You were in the fourth year at King Edward VI Grammar School in Stourbridge when you began singing in your first proper group: Andy Long and his Original Jaymen. Well, 'proper' in the sense that you actually rehearsed together. Mum and Dad hated it. To them, that sort of scene just didn't fit in with the life they'd made for you all in Hayley Green. Less to do with Birmingham and the Midlands, or so it liked to think, Hayley Green was the sort of stuck-up little town that aligned itself more with the posh parts of Wales, whose borders were less than eight miles away, or if not there then the gentrified parts of the West Country. Hayley Green didn't appreciate being reminded of its gritty, working-class Midlands origins and neither did your dad.

Once, Dad – a fully qualified civil engineer and proud of it, also named Robert – went mad and cut the plug off the Dansette after you'd sung along to 'I Like It Like That' about seventeen times in a row, standing in front of the mirror willing your hair to grow. The same Dansette him and your mum had given you as a surprise Christmas present when you were twelve. When you opened the lid you'd found a copy of Johnny Burnette's 'Dreamin'' inside, already on the turntable. As you'd later recall, 'It was a rocky journey with my parents.' They had tried but 'they just didn't understand it at all, any of it. In the beginning, they thought it would pass.' But of course it didn't, none of it. It just grew and grew, like your hair. The older you got, the longer it got, the worse the arguments with your dad got. He'd have bloody cut it off like the plug on the Dansette too if he could but you were getting too big for that and Dad would just have to put up with it.

Now that you'd left school though, it was less about rock'n'roll or doo-wop and more about the blues. Mostly, it was about Robert Johnson, the most legendary bluesman of all. It had begun when you'd bought the first ever LP they put together of his original 78s (the one with 'Preaching Blues' and 'Last Fair Deal Gone Down' on it and the gatefold sleeve with the picture of a sharecropper's shack on the front) out of money saved up from your paper round. Of course, you weren't the only English white boy back then to become obsessed with Robert Johnson. Eric Clapton, various Rolling Stones, and of course a certain Jimmy Page were all equally obsessed. But you didn't find that out until later. 'I was probably a year or two behind Keith Richards and Mick Jagger, but I went, "This is it!"'

Back then though, after seeing Sonny Boy at Brum town hall, you'd become more convinced than ever that the straight life wasn't for you. Nevertheless, after leaving school you had enrolled in the business studies course at Kidderminster College of Further Education – a compromise you'd agreed to with your parents. You weren't interested in getting a job and they weren't interested in seeing you just bumming around pretending you were a singer. The only thing Kidderminster was famous for was its carpets. So much so the college even had a Department for Carpet Technology. Bloody hell! Most of your friends had either already left school and started to earn a few bob or gone to Stourbridge Art School, the biggest

skive going and the place with all the best-looking birds. You found the
whole thing slightly depressing, though you still had your music – music
and clothes and the Wolves and Saturday nights out on the town. That
was when you really started to think about your singing. Anything to save
you from carpets and college and your dad moaning. According to your
mate Dave Hill, another bored local lad who would later become the
guitarist in Slade, until then you were just another 'local Mod with very
short hair'. It wasn't until you opened your mouth and started to sing that
anyone noticed there might be anything different about you, that anyone
really started paying any attention. And that, above all, was what you
liked best – attention. You liked it like that and wanted to keep it that
way . . .

With the album safely in the can, Peter Grant was ready to go out and
get a deal for the new band. However, experience taught him that it
would be a mistake for them to sit back and wait for that to happen.
He needed a 'buzz' to keep the momentum going, not just from a
commercial point of view but a creative one, too. Page was happy to
oblige. Inordinately proud of what he had already achieved on his own
without any help whatsoever from his former band-mates in the
Yardbirds, he couldn't wait to start showing off the new line-up. And
so gigs were arranged – still billed as the New Yardbirds – beginning at
the Marquee Club in London, on Friday 18 October, barely a week
after recording sessions were completed at Olympic.

There was a problem almost immediately when it became clear they
could no longer use the Yardbirds name. They have always claimed
since that the New Yardbirds moniker had simply been made 'obsolete'
by the excellence of the material the new line-up had now amassed.
'We realised we were working under false pretences,' Page would later
claim. 'The thing had quickly gone beyond where the Yardbirds had
left off. We all agreed that there was no point in retaining the Yardbirds
tag, so . . . we decided to change the name. It was a fresh beginning for
us all.'

In reality, however, the first Zeppelin album would almost certainly
have been the first New Yardbirds album had it not been for the fact
that Chris Dreja sent a lawyer's letter warning them to 'cease and desist'
on pain of legal action. According to Dreja, the contract McCarty and
Relf had signed when agreeing to allow him and Page to continue as

the New Yardbirds only covered the Scandinavian dates in September, as they had already been provisionally booked before the group officially split up. When Dreja then discovered that Page was now intent on keeping the name for a fresh round of UK dates in October and November – even a new record deal and album – he railed against the decision and sought legal advice. Forced to find a new name for the group, Page merely shrugged. So confident was he feeling about his new group he later claimed he wouldn't have cared if it had been called 'the Vegetables' or 'the Potatoes'. Instead, it was Grant who reminded him of Keith Moon's joke about going down like a Lead Zeppelin. Both men agreed it was a neat idea. Just one further snag: they would have to drop the 'a' from Lead. 'I played around with the letters,' said Grant, 'doodling in the office and realised "Led" looked a lot simpler – and it was all that light and heavy irony.' Page agreed, concerned that otherwise people might mispronounce the name, as in 'lead guitar'.

The new name was made official on Monday 14 October – just five days before their first show in London, still billed as the New Yardbirds. In an attempt to try and get the news out quickly, Grant rang round the London music press, managing to get a last-minute news item about the change of name squeezed into the 19 October issue of the weekly *Disc* magazine, while Page turned up personally at the offices of the biggest-selling music weekly, *Melody Maker*, then in Fleet Street, where he sat down with Chris Welch to help him pen a lengthier piece. 'I remember Jimmy looking over my shoulder at my notes and correcting me on the spelling,' says Welch. 'I had written "Lead" and he pointed out it was actually "Led".' Cajoled into going along to see the Marquee show that Friday night, Welch remembers standing next to 'a certain drummer from a fairly well-known group whose blushes I'll spare by not mentioning by name. But I remember he leaned over and said, "Christ, that drummer is so fucking *heavy* . . . " This guy more or less gave up drums after that.'

In the subsequent review, however, the *MM* still referred to them as 'the regrouped Yardbirds', adding that they were 'very much a heavy group' and that 'generally, there seems to be a need for Led Zeppelin to cut down on volume a bit'. Advice they did not heed. Instead, the more people complained of the 'noise', the more Grant encouraged Page not to pay any attention, to turn the amps up even more. Keith

Altham, then writing for the *NME* and later publicist for the Stones
and The Who, recalled seeing one of the earliest Zeppelin gigs at a pub
in London and leaving after the first three numbers because 'my ears
were ringing'. When Grant phoned him the next morning to ask what
he thought, Altham was honest and complained 'they were far too
loud'. Grant merely snorted with derision. 'Well, of course, every time
I saw [Grant] after that it was: "Well, my band's doing quite well,
despite what you thought of them". By which time they had become
the biggest band in the world.'

Playing its last gig with the old name at Liverpool University on
Saturday 19 October, the new band performed its first official date as
Led Zeppelin six nights later at the University of Surrey in Guildford.
It was a low-key occasion. 'I drove John and Robert to their first
engagement as Led Zeppelin in my Jaguar,' Reg Jones of Bonham's
former group, A Way of Life, would later recall. 'There was a huge
banner outside that read: "Tonight – the Ex-Yardbirds!" Underneath in
smaller lettering it said: "Led Zeppelin". After the gig, I couldn't start
the Jaguar and we all came home on the train.' Their second official
gig as Led Zeppelin occurred the following night at Bristol's Boxing
Club. 'It was a try-out for their big hype launch,' remembered Russell
Hunter of support act, the Deviants. 'The audience hated us and
despised them. When [they] came on, they got through a number and
a half until the fire extinguishers, buckets, bricks and everything was
being thrown at them.'

Undeterred, the band made their London debut as Led Zeppelin
with a show at the Middle Earth Club, held at the Roundhouse in
London's Chalk Farm on 9 November, where they earned their highest
fee so far, £150, and received their first encore. There were half-a-
dozen more dates after that, mainly club and university venues like
the Science and Technology College in Manchester (22 November),
the student union hall at Sheffield University (23 November), Richmond Athletics Club (29 November) and a return date at the Marquee
(10 December). They had been paid their highest fee yet in Manchester – £225 – but picking up decent UK dates was a slog. Grant
was having trouble getting top-drawer booking agents along to see the
group, and without them it was impossible to consistently get onto the
A-list concert circuit. He was also having problems getting them a
record deal. Received wisdom tells us now that the Grant masterplan

had always been to launch the band first in America. In fact, he spent the weeks between completing the album at Olympic and the start of November when they played their first London show as Led Zeppelin trudging around the major London record labels, trying and failing to land them a deal. Grant would later recall with bitterness being 'shown the door' by several major labels before deciding his best chance lay in America. 'Pye Records laughed me out of their office. I went to see their boss, Louis Benjamin, and asked for an advance. The figure was £17,500. He just said: "You've got to be joking".' Grant was even more chagrined when he received a similar reaction from Mo Ostin at Warner Bros., who at least knew Page well from all the session work he had done for the label over the years. Still no dice, though.

Reading the runes, Grant set off for New York in the first week of November 1968, armed with the nine tracks recorded at Olympic, plus some live tracks recorded off the mixing desk at various gigs. In his favour, he knew the name Jimmy Page meant more to the business in America than it ever had at home in Britain, something he'd first been made aware of during a Yardbirds tour. He and Page were strolling down Fifth Avenue one afternoon when a limousine screeched to a halt beside them, 'and out gets Burt Bacharach – white tuxedo and beautiful woman in the back – and greets Jimmy enthusiastically.' Bacharach remembered Page from sessions he'd done for him in London in the early Sixties, when the great composer was working on the *Casino Royale* soundtrack. 'All the important guys in the US biz knew about Jimmy Page,' boasted Grant.

As well as Page's reputation as a top-flight session muso, the Yardbirds had always been more commercially successful in America – where they had enjoyed five consecutive chart albums – than they were in their homeland. They were also seen as vastly more influential. 'By the end the Yardbirds were pretty tied in with that whole psychedelic scene in America,' says Dave Lewis, founding editor since 1979 of *Tight But Loose*, the ultimate Zeppelin fan mag (and now website) and a man who has spent a lifetime compiling data about the band. 'They may have meant next to nothing in Britain anymore but in America the Yardbirds were seen as innovators, right behind the Beatles and the Stones. There was clearly huge interest in whatever the members of the band did next.' The timing of Grant's visit was also fortuitous. The same month, Cream had completed their final US tour and were now on their way to London to perform their 'farewell' show at the Albert Hall, after which Clapton would announce the formation of another 'supergroup', Blind Faith with Stevie Winwood. Meanwhile, Hendrix was enjoying his greatest critical and commercial success with *Electric Ladyland*; his first album to be recorded and released first in America. Also, in November 1968, Joe Cocker replaced Mary Hopkins' 'Those Were the Days' at no. 1 in the UK charts with his funereal-paced 'With A Little Help from My Friends' – featuring Page on scintillating lead guitar. Clearly, for those with eyes and ears to notice, this was a great time for guitar-oriented 'progressive rock'.

Where Grant's managerial instincts proved particularly shrewd was in his targeting of Atlantic Records – the soon-to-be defunct Cream's US label – as the potential 'home' for Page's new group. He deliberately avoided EMI, the Yardbirds' label in London, and Epic, their US label, on the grounds that the former had done such a piss-poor job on the *Little Games* album, and that in the case of the latter, who had always rolled out the red carpet for the Yardbirds, he felt a certain amount of complacency had set in and that they would simply not be able to take the New Yardbirds, or their resultant offshoot, seriously enough. It was important, he felt, to begin with a clean slate. G didn't want business as usual. G wanted all systems go.

4

Going To California

According to Epic's then A&R executive in New York, Dick Asher, 'When we heard that the Yardbirds had split up and Jimmy had formed Led Zeppelin, we naturally assumed that the rights to Page would go automatically to Columbia [Epic's US parent company].' This cosy assumption was swiftly disavowed after a meeting with Grant and his American lawyer, Steve Weiss. Presiding over the meeting was Columbia president and legendary record man Clive Davis. 'It was Clive's first meeting with Peter Grant,' Asher recalled, 'and we talked and talked about all sorts of things. It just went on and on but there was no mention of Led Zeppelin. Finally Clive said, "Well, aren't we going to talk about Jimmy Page?" Grant replied, "Oh, no, we've already signed the Zeppelin to Atlantic".' At which point Davis lost his cool and went berserk. 'We were all stunned,' said Asher, 'especially after all we had done for them. It was a horrible, horrible meeting and I'll never forget it as long as I live.' Grant didn't bat on eye, just thanked them for their hospitality and told them he'd see them around, then strode leisurely out of the office with a big smile on his face. He'd been on the receiving end of bad news too many times in the past not to enjoy his moment of triumph.

Born in South Norwood, a nowhere south London suburb, on 5 April 1935, you were just four when the Second World War broke out. Your mum, Dorothy Louise Grant, had deliberately 'forgotten' to put your dad's name on your birth certificate because your dad, whoever he was, had buggered off long before you were born, and because she was Jewish and he wasn't. That left you with your mum's maiden name. You loved your mum and always took care of her, not that it was anybody's bloody business. You never talked about your childhood, in fact, because yes, seeing as you ask, it was just too bloody painful. You came from nothing, poor, illegitimate, a born bastard, what's it to you? Later, when Mum got diabetes then had to have her leg amputated, you were there for her. Not that that was anybody's business, either. When she finally snuffed it, you were going to go to her funeral alone, then at the last minute asked Mickie Most to come with you. You didn't have many friends but Mickie was one, you supposed.

You and mum had been together so long, just the two of you, it didn't seem right now she was gone. The two of you had moved to Battersea just before the war, a two-up, two-down terraced job down by the river. Mum got a job typing for the Church of England Pensions Board. Next thing you knew the Second World War broke out and you were evacuated to the country, six years old and no-one to turn to. The whole school ended up at Charterhouse. Charterhouse! Fuck all to eat but that's when you began to put on weight, a miserable fat kid missing his mum. The nobs at Charterhouse used to joke that even your name was big. 'Grant,' they sniggered, 'from the thirteenth-century Norman nickname "graund" or "graunt", doncha know, meaning large, or "a person of remarkable size".' Ha fucking ha! Top-hole, old chap! How you fucking hated it there. Bullied and looked-down on by a bunch of toffee-nosed public school cunts. It was at Charterhouse that you really developed your hatred for people like that, the ones for whom fortune came as part of their birthright, not something they'd worked hard for, worked as fucking hard as you would have to. It was at Charterhouse that you'd learned to fight. 'The scum had arrived from Battersea,' you'd remember. 'There used to be great battles and we'd beat them up.'

You were ten by the time you were finally sent home to London. You didn't cry when you saw your mum. You didn't cry and you didn't moan or complain. You just put the kettle on and made a nice cup of tea while she fussed around you, crying and laughing all at the same time. The next day you went back to your old school and hated it. You planned to leave as soon as you could, get out there and start earning your keep, the man of the house. But Mum told you no, hang on and get an education, get a good job, make something of yourself. Fat chance! The headmaster wrote in your final school report: 'The boy will never make anything of his life.' Fucking cunt! You'd show him!

You were fourteen, no qualifications, no nothing, but Mum didn't mind. Not really. You'd soon found a job anyway, working as a labourer at a *sheet metal factory in Croydon. Christ almighty! A month later you were looking for something else. Something a darn sight bloody easier that getting up at five in the bollocking morning and carrying great big sodding hods of bricks around thank you very fucking much. Sometimes it was like the world after the war was worse than it had been during it. You knew, though, that if you were to amount to anything more than just a glorified skivvy you'd have to use your brain as well as your brawn. You would need to duck and dive. Be ready for anything; which is how you got the job working for fifteen bob a night as a stagehand at the Croydon Empire. The Empire was great. You got all sorts down there. Singers and comedians;* 'revue' *shows like* Soldiers in Skirts. *Later, when the Empire became a cinema, you were properly cheesed off. But you went out and found something else, like you always did, working for tips as a waiter at Frascati's in Oxford Street, then as a messenger for Reuters over in Fleet Street.*

You'd always liked music, the good stuff though like Stan Kenton and Ted Heath, the big, noisy, swinging stuff. Rock'n'roll was all right too, for what it was, but it would never beat a good big band jazz orchestra. After working at the 2Is there had been other jobs, like working as the bouncer at Murray's Cabaret Club, the only geezer amongst all the showgirls. 'I wasn't married then,' you'd recall later, 'and what with me being the only man around and about forty girls backstage, it was all right.' Bloody right, mate. Then there was the time you filled in as a minder for Peter Rachman, the slum landlord. Not so bloody nice, but better paid and that's a fact. You didn't have to do much anyway, just stand over them and growl. They soon coughed up if they knew what was good for them. And if they didn't a good chinning soon sorted things out. There was even a job in the movies at last, a small part as one of the sailors in A Night to Remember. *You and Kenneth More, if you don't mind! A right laugh. You took Mum to the pictures to see that one; couldn't wait to see her face. You thought perhaps it would lead to bigger things but fat chance. Then suddenly out of nowhere you got the job working as a double for Anthony Quinn in* The Guns of Navarone. *Sweet as a nut, my son. That was when it started to look like it might become steady. There was even a bit of telly work. The dodgy barman in* The Saint, *even given a couple of lines to do with Roger Moore. Then the pantomime villain in* Crackerjack, *a walk-on in* Dixon of Dock Green *and a cowboy in* The Benny Hill Show. *Nothing very earth-shattering but the dough wasn't half bad: fifteen quid a day for the film stuff. Less for the telly but there was more of that and it got your face about, who knew where it might lead? Like being a bloody great Mace-donian guard in* Cleopatra.

And then you met Don Arden and that was when life changed again . . .

Jerry Wexler, the vice-president of Atlantic Records, didn't care much for long hair and loud guitars. But he had looked on with a mixture of bafflement and envy these past two years as his partner Ahmet Ertegun took the plaudits – and counted the profits – from the enormous success of Cream, a long-haired loud guitar group from England that Wexler would never have signed. Now Cream was over and Atlantic was in the market for a 'new Cream', Wexler wasn't about to make the same mistake twice. So when Peter Grant came to see him at his office at 1841 Broadway, Wexler was all ears. He may not have liked or understood this music but he sure as hell grasped its popularity. As well as Cream, Atlantic was then enjoying huge commercial success with Vanilla Fudge (one of the new breed of 'heavy' bands that rarely featured in the Top 10 yet whose albums nevertheless stayed glued to the charts for *months*) and Iron Butterfly, another pioneer of the latest lugubrious rock sound that had sold more than two million copies of their *In-A-Gadda-Da-Vida* album since it had been released that spring (becoming the first album in history to be awarded platinum status). The name Led Zeppelin even sounded similar to Iron Butterfly, and, to Wexler's ears, offered a similar-sounding musical proposition.

Using the same broad strokes to sell the group to Wexler, Grant argued that Zeppelin would outdo the Butterfly in the US in the same way the Beatles had overtaken the Beach Boys, their Capitol label-mates, back in 1964. What's more, there would be no further financial outlay, either in terms of production or recording costs. The album was a done deal, ready to go, go, go. Zeppelin, said Grant, delivering the *coup-de-grace*, would be the successors to Cream. Better still, there would be no farewell tours just as things were getting good, either. Jimmy Page may have been only twenty-four but he was already an old pro with a proven track record of reliability. What's more, unlike the other old Yardbirds guitarist, Jeff Beck, who Atlantic had missed out on when he chose to stay at Epic and who was now enjoying considerable Stateside success despite being unable to write a tune, Jimmy and his band had songs for days. Just listen to 'Good Times Bad Times', urged Grant. Or 'Dazed and Confused', or 'Black Mountain

Side'! Fast, slow, acoustic, electric, these kids had the lot! They even had a lead singer so good-looking Grant was tempted to stick a fuck into him himself.

Jerry went away still laughing at that one. When he came back he did so with a contract in his hand. And not just any contract, but one which came with the largest single advance ever offered to an unsigned artist: a five-year deal with a $143,000 advance for the first year, plus four one-year options, making the whole caboodle worth $220,000 – there on the table right now. G nearly bit his arm off. 'I was proud of the signing,' Wexler wrote in his autobiography, 'but as it turned out, I didn't really hang out with the group. Ahmet [Ertegun] got along famously with them (and Peter Grant).'

In fact, once he'd brokered the deal, Jerry would have little more to do with Zeppelin, and it was G's burgeoning relationship with Ahmet that would become one of the key factors in the band's gargantuan success over the next decade. The flamboyant, Turkish-born blues and jazz fanatic who had co-founded Atlantic Records with his brother Neshui twenty years before, Ahmet Ertegun prided himself on being one of the original record men: blessed with good 'ears' and an even better business sense. The son of a diplomat who travelled the world, the sort of smooth operator who spoke several languages and knew how to get along with everybody, from royalty to riffraff, Ahmet had the happy habit of never listening to what anybody else thought, unless they happened to agree with him already. Short, extrovert, bald, with a neatly trimmed goatee and a highly developed sense of humour, Ahmet was every musician's friend; every businessman's dream associate. A class act on every level.

As a result, early signings to his label had included other class acts like Ray Charles and Wilson Pickett. Even in the late Sixties, as the new album-oriented rock took over, Ahmet never lost his Midas touch. He was now middle-aged, fond of finely tailored suits and expensive wine, but he always knew where to find the good shit, signing first Cream, then Yes, Zeppelin, Crosby, Stills and Nash ... The list would grow longer and more impressive with each passing year. He was also good at signing the most talented executives to his label. One of the first things Wexler did after Ertegun brought him to Atlantic was to poach the then unknown Aretha Franklin from Columbia and make her a star through the not-so simple expediency of picking and

producing all her biggest hits himself. Ahmet Ertegun, said Jerry
Wexler, had allowed him to take someone like Aretha and 'put her in
the church'. Lately, he had been doing a similar job for England's
greatest female singer, Dusty Springfield, producing what is now recognised as her finest hour with the *Dusty in Memphis* album. (When
Dusty mentioned she had worked with John Paul Jones as an arranger,
and how highly she rated him, Wexler was doubly determined to sign
Zeppelin to the label.)

Two born hustlers from entirely different sides of the tracks, Ahmet
Ertegun and Peter Grant were made for each other. Jerry Wexler just
happened to be the one who helped bring them together, which is
where they belonged. 'As far as I know,' said Jimmy Page, 'we were the
first white band on Atlantic because all the earlier white bands had
been on Atco.' In fact, the Shadows had beaten Zeppelin to that
accolade by a good seven years. No matter, the fact that Zeppelin was
signed to the same label as Aretha Franklin and John Coltrane said it
all for Page. 'I didn't want to be lumped in with those [Atco-signed]
people,' he said, 'I wanted to be associated with something classic.'
There was no doubting, either, the extraordinary nature of the deal
Grant had negotiated for them. Signed to Zeppelin's production
company, Superhype, a partnership between Page and Grant formed
just two weeks before the manager arrived in New York, it was a
ground-breaking arrangement for the time that afforded the band
unusual levels of control over their own product, including all aspects
of production, artwork, choice of singles, photos, marketing procedures
for both vinyl and non-vinyl products and, most unusually, the option
of leasing back control over master-tapes. Anything, in fact, that might
one day bear the name Led Zeppelin. Jimmy would produce all the
records, G would be executive producer. All that was left for Atlantic
to do was manufacture, distribute and to some extent promote the
albums.

An utterly unique deal for its time – the Beatles had only that same
year managed to get EMI to re-sign them via their own newly formed
corporation, Apple, while the Stones would later borrow the outline for
their own distribution deal with Atlantic for Rolling Stones Records –
perhaps its most extraordinary aspect was that it was all done on a
handshake, before anyone at Atlantic had even seen the band play.
'Ahmet was the finest record man of all time,' Grant later declared.

'Every time we negotiated and he said, "Peter, shake on it", you knew it was done.' Interestingly, Grant also neglected to put into writing his management status with the band. He and Page had a contract for the co-ownership of Superhype but everything else was done on a purely verbal, non-legal level. 'We just had a gentlemen's agreement,' John Paul Jones told Chris Welch. '[Peter Grant] got the normal management fees and royalties from records as executive producer. [It was] all pretty above board, and as a result, it was a really happy band.'

When Grant returned to his room at the Plaza Hotel and picked up the phone to call Jimmy with the good news, he knew the real work would only begin now. But he also felt more sure of himself and what he was doing than he ever had before. As if to compound his newfound confidence, the band's first London show as Led Zeppelin at the Marquee on 10 December was a surprise sell-out. He recalled: 'I went out early afternoon from our office on Oxford Street to Wardour Street. And I thought, "Fuck me, what's this queue?" There were about two hundred already lined up.'

Three nights later they performed at the Bridge Country Club in Canterbury, which is where Jeff Beck caught sight of Led Zeppelin for the first time. 'Things went slightly wrong,' Beck remembered with a smile. An amp, which he later realised was actually one of his own 'borrowed' by Grant, blew up halfway through. What really struck him, though, was 'the potential. It was just amazing, blew the house down; blew everybody away.' Compared to the Jeff Beck Group, he conceded, '[They] had a better looking lead singer ... he had golden curly locks and a bare chest, and the girls fell in love with him. They also had Bonzo on drums, creating all sorts of pandemonium.' It was, he concluded, 'a much better package than I had ... I was blind jealous.'

By now the first part of the Atlantic advance had been banked and once Page had been paid back the money he'd already put in for tour costs and recording, plus a healthy dollop of cash on top to reward him for his endeavours, the rest of the band were delighted to be handed big fat cheques by Grant of £3,000 each. Plant and Bonham, in particular, were ecstatic. The most the drummer had ever received for playing had been the £40-a-week Tim Rose had paid him, while Plant still considered his £25-a-week stipend from Zeppelin a godsend. Bonzo immediately raced out and bought a brand new Jaguar XK 150.

Plant, who had married Maureen in November – a quickie ceremony at the local registry office, before jumping in the car and racing down to London for the band's gig at the Roundhouse that night (he almost didn't make it when his old jalopy broke down on the motorway) – used the money for a down payment on a large, ramshackle house in the countryside. Maureen had been heavily pregnant when they decided to get married and, partly for this reason, Plant invited several friends to move in with them in a sort of semi-commune over which he would preside – benignly, in his view, though ownership of the property was never in doubt – for the next few years. He reasoned that it would also be good for Maureen to have some company while he was away touring with the new band.

It was clear to everyone that knew them that a whole new chapter had begun in the lives of Robert Plant and John Bonham. 'We were both like, Christ, this is amazing!' Plant told me in 2005. 'Plus, we were playing great. Playing with guys who were leagues above and beyond anything we'd played with before. So we were being stretched and pulled and challenged musically. There was a lot of demand, which in the end kind of brought us together. Because we'd drive home from rehearsals from [Jimmy's house in] Pangbourne, together in Bonzo's mum's Anglia van – and we started communicating as the two guys from the Black Country who had a lot to take in. This was the first time we'd actually found something that was so substantial. It was musically amazing. And it was building around our own contribution, which made it even more amazing. Because we weren't coming along to replace anybody anymore, what was the Yardbirds was Led Zeppelin the minute we started playing. So we talked about a lot and we developed an affinity which was based on us being probably naïve. We were big fishes in a small pond up in the Black Country and suddenly we were in a kind of *world* situation, where we were sitting on planes together not knowing which cutlery to pick up.'

Mac Poole recalled bumping into Bonham around this time. 'He said to me, "We've just had some money in advance from the record company". I said, "That's handy", thinking he was gonna say, like, a hundred quid. But it was something ridiculous like two or three grand. I said, "What?" Bear in mind, he was living in a council flat in Dudley at the time. Three grand was like a new house in those days. I nearly fell through the floor. He said, "Yeah, our manager has got us this amazing deal.".. I think John was as amazed as I was, buying everybody drinks. He was throwing it around like it was nothing, cos it was the first time he'd ever seen any real dough. That's what made me think, bloody hell, they've landed this. And as soon as he played me the original demos I knew that the band was gonna do it.'

It was only down the road but Redditch was starting to feel like a million miles away to you now you'd got a bit of dough in your back pocket. Not that you'd ever forget where you were born: a small, shithouse of a town in the Black Country. Or when: 31 May, 1948, a Gemini, whatever the bloody hell that meant. You'd been due to arrive the day before, your mum said, but like one of those long, busy drum fills you liked to do, you'd left your entrance to the last possible moment. Always trying to get a rise out of everybody, your poor old mum had been in labour for over twenty-six hours before you let her have it. It nearly killed you, too. Later, they told her your heartbeat had suddenly stopped, by which point the drunken bastard of a doctor on duty that night had already staggered off home. Fortunately, a nurse was able to summon help in the nick of time, your mum said. The nurse told her it was 'a miracle' the baby had survived. You had to laugh though whenever she told that story. It tickled you to think of them all there, waiting for you to stick your head out the door, moaning and a-groaning.

Redditch had once been famous locally for its needle-making – that and its honking Batchley cheese. But by the time you'd come along it was just another part of Brum. Or near as buggery anyway – a bus ride away. You were named after your dad, who was named after his father: John Henry Bonham. Your mum was Joan and you were their first. A carpenter by trade, your dad – Jack to his mates – ran his own building company, J.H. Bonham & Son. Joan ran the corner shop, selling everything from bread and sweets to whisky and cigarettes. Then there was your brother Michael (Mick) born when you were three. There was a sister too, Debbie, but she didn't come along till you were fourteen and by then it was too late, you were off and running.

As a kid, you'd all lived in a small house in Hunt End, on the outskirts of town. You and Mick were always outside playing. Sometimes you'd go to one of the building sites your dad worked on and play there too. 'Careful, our John!' your dad would call out. 'You'll bloody get yourself killed jumping off that wall!' You didn't care. You liked everyone looking at you.

Even as a toddler you'd always been the centre of attention, always noisy, always climbing and fighting and shouting and breaking things. Always falling over and getting hurt then jumping up and doing it again. You loved hitting things harder and harder and harder. You were five when you started playing drums. Not proper drums, like, don't be daft. Like you said, 'I used to play on a bath-salts container with wires on the bottom, and on a round coffee tin with a loose wire attached to it to give a snare drum effect. Plus there were always my mum's pots and pans.'

Poor old Mum. She had her hands full with you. Then when Mick came along it was bloody havoc. Somehow she always coped, though. People did back then. Mum and Dad did anyway. Never short of a bob or two, either. Between the building business and the shop, they did all right. One of the first families in the street to own a car, one of the first to get a phone, you stuffing your pockets with sweets from the shop, you all did all right. You got a shock though when they started sending you and Mick to Wilton House, the local posh school. Parents had to pay to send their kids to Wilton and some right toffee-nosed bastards were there too. Not you and Mick but all the others. You knew Mum and Dad were only doing what they thought was best for you, but you bloody hated it there. Oh, the teachers were all right, most of them. But oh Christ, the uniform! You and Mick would look a right pair walking out the door each morning in your stripy brown, white and blue blazers and caps. Cos there was two of you it wasn't so bad. But then you'd have to walk right past St Stephen's, where all the other kids round where you lived went. Always the same, the bastards shouting after you: 'Got your pyjamas on?' Mick would look straight ahead and try to ignore them but you would get right fed up. 'Come on, our kid,' you'd say, 'let's have a bit of this!' and you'd run over to sort them out. 'There'd be ten of them!' Mick would recall years later. 'Either he couldn't count or he'd got bad eyesight because we used to get a kicking every time.'

So what? You didn't care. Fuck 'em if they can't take a joke, that's what you used to say. Big lads for your age, you and Mick were always getting into scraps anyway. 'Me and John were very much alike,' remembered Mick. 'Somebody would only have to look at you or say something wrong and then we wanted to fight the world.' Sometimes you'd even fight each other, just for devilment. You'd rip a page out of Mick's Eagle *annual, so he'd stamp on your watch, little bastard! That's when you'd get really angry and smash his poxy watch and he'd end up throwing a bloody*

carving knife at you! Mum would come in and see the knife sticking out
the door and go absolutely raving bloody mad! She'd call your dad in and
tell him to give you both what for but he was such a softy when it came to
stuff like that he never used to do anything, really. Just shout at you and
threaten to tan your bloody hides. He never did, though. Not really. Good
old dad, a great bloke. One year he bought a caravan and every summer
after that he'd take you all off to the seaside for your holidays. Then he
bought a boat and he'd take you and Mick fishing on the canal. He was a
bloody great bloke, your dad. Hands like shovels.

The only part of school you really liked was sport. Mick liked football
but you preferred the cricket, even after your nose was broken by a stray
ball. You hadn't even been playing that day, just standing by the boundary
chatting up a bird when suddenly the ball smacked you in the face. It was
a relief when you finally left Wilton for good and your mum and dad let
you go to the local secondary modern, Lodge Farm County, instead. Not
that you were much good at lessons there, either. When you left at fifteen,
the headmaster, a right stuck-up prat if ever there was one, told your mum
and dad you wouldn't 'even make a good dustman'.

But then, according to your brother, you were 'a rogue, there's no doubt,'
who was 'always getting the cane'. One of those sods who was 'always
into everything' and 'stood out like a sore thumb'. You didn't think you
were that bad, actually. Especially after you got into the drums, good and
proper, like. You were good at carpentry too – probably your dad coming
out in you – lending a hand to build the school greenhouse. Once the drums
came in though, that was it, you were off. Nothing else mattered anymore,
not really. You were ten when you talked your mum into buying you your
first snare; fifteen when you talked your dad into buying you your first
full-size kit; a second-hand Premier. 'It was almost prehistoric,' you'd
remember. 'Most of the metal had rusted.' So bloody what? You didn't
care. 'I felt nothing for any other instrument. Later I played a bit of acoustic
guitar, but it was always drums, first and foremost. I don't reckon with
that jack-of-all-trades thing.' Bloody right, mate . . .

The real turning point though was seeing The Benny Goodman Story
on the telly one Sunday afternoon. You couldn't believe it, watching the
drummer Gene Krupa doing 'Sing, Sing, Sing'. You'd never seen anything
like it – ever! Just brilliant! It was the first time you realised that drummers
didn't have to be stuck at the back, while the fellas at the front – the singers
and the guitarists and whatnot – got all the attention; that drummers could

be the stars of the show too. As you'd explain years later, chatting over a pint to Chris, the nice bloke from Melody Maker, *'Gene Krupa was the first big band drummer to be really noticed. He came right out into the front and he played drums much louder than they had ever been played before – and much better. People hadn't taken much notice of drums until Krupa came along.'*

With Peter Grant still holding out hope of putting together a separate deal in Britain, the first Led Zeppelin album – adorned with just the name of the band as its title, as was the fashion of the day – was scheduled for release in America on 12 January 1969. When that separate UK deal proved unrealistic, however, Grant hurriedly offered Atlantic the 'rest of the world' rights, which they gratefully snapped up for next-to-nothing, and the album would eventually see the light of day in Britain in March. Meanwhile in America the hype had begun in earnest, with the very first Atlantic Records press release, which was headed in capital letters:

ATLANTIC RECORDS SIGNS ENGLAND'S HOT NEW GROUP,
LED ZEPPELIN, IN ONE OF THE BIGGEST DEALS OF THE YEAR!

It went on, 'Top English and American rock musicians who have heard the tracks have compared the LP to the best of Cream and Jimi Hendrix.' Accusations of hype swiftly followed, not least when it emerged that Atlantic had signed the band without even seeing them play live: sacrilege in those musicianship-as-end-in-itself times. From there on in, even after the album was released and people could decide for themselves whether the music contained enough merit to warrant 'one of the biggest deals of the year', the American media embarked on a love them or hate them relationship with Led Zeppelin, with nothing in between; a situation which would endure long after the band itself had ceased to exist.

Nevertheless, with the disinclination of the music business in Britain to see the new band's commercial potential, it was now America that Grant and Page were counting on to provide the leg-up they badly needed if Led Zeppelin really was to become the new Cream. There was only one way to do that: to tour, not stopping until people forgot about the accusations of hype and had a chance to make up their own minds. That was the key, said Grant. Page agreed. The sooner the

better, too, he said. And so G went to work. With the aid of Frank
Barsalona, an old and trusted contact at Premier Talent, then one of
America's biggest booking agents, plus the five years he already had
behind him working the American concert circuit, Grant knew exactly
where to start. The Fillmores in New York and San Francisco; the
Boston Tea Party; the Grande Ballroom in Detroit; the Kinetic Circus
in Chicago; the Whisky A Go Go in LA ... within days Grant had put
together an itinerary that included more than twenty US cities. And
though in the future he would become legendary for driving an impossibly hard bargain with American promoters, he didn't waste time
haggling about fees either. Not for this tour. While the Yardbirds at
their height had been getting $2,500 a show in the US, with the first
Zeppelin album as yet unreleased, Grant was happy if he could squeeze
$1,500 a show out of promoters for that first US tour. Some nights,
they played for as little as $200 – less than a hundred pounds. Con-
sidering how much it would cost to send the band to America, the net
result would mean taking a bath financially. 'It was worth it though,'
reasoned Page, 'we didn't care. We just wanted to come over to America
and play our music.' The attitude was 'come over here, work as hard
as we can, give them all we can, and if it doesn't work we would go
back to England and start again. Mind you, no-one would have had us
back if we'd died. It was really up to us.'

There was only one snag: it would mean the band flying out over
Christmas. John Paul, Robert and Bonzo were married. Jimmy was
living with an American girl called Lynn that he had met in Boston on
the last Yardbirds tour. What the hell, reasoned Grant, they were
young and there would be many more Christmases for them to spend
with their birds. After they'd won the war, he told them, they could
do what they bloody well liked. But for now, they would have to do
what they were fucking well told. Like it or lump it back to where you
came from, he said, knowing none of them would want to do that.

Nevertheless, he hadn't looked forward to breaking the news to
them. But when, finally, he gathered them in his Oxford Street office
and gave it to them straight, he was taken aback at how well they all
appeared to take it. 'Through much of it,' he explained, 'you'll be
opening for Vanilla Fudge. Oh, and you'll be starting on Boxing Day ...'
Just in case they didn't get the picture, he added: 'That's the day after
Christmas. That means you've got to leave England on December

twenty-third.' There were mixed reactions to Grant's plan but nobody wanted to lose face by admitting they might be conflicted by the news. Plant, whose wife Maureen had just given birth to a daughter named Carmen Jane, was in the most difficult position. As if to hide it, though, he was the first to speak up in favour of the plan. 'Well, let's just do what we have to do,' he said. 'When does the plane leave?'

Having got the band excited about their imminent trip to the US, he gave them the other bit of news he'd been saving: he wouldn't actually be going with them. Not over Christmas anyway. Grant was a thirty-three-year-old family man who had already travelled around America many times; there was very little allure in the prospect of spending Christmas and New Year away from his wife Gloria and two-year-old son Warren with a bunch of still relative nobodies. Instead, for the first couple of weeks of the tour at least, the band would be in the charge of a new tour manager, a twenty-four-year-old master-at-arms from west London who already worked for Most and Grant: Richard Cole, or 'Ricardo' as he liked to be known. Disappointed but not unduly concerned – Page and Jones already knew of Cole – Plant and Bonham followed the others' lead and mutely nodded their agreement. Jones had first met Cole back in 1965 when he'd been touring with the Night Timers, the first group Cole had ever driven the van and humped gear for. Since then the former unskilled labourer had worked his way up the ladder as road manager for Unit 4 + 2, The Who, the Yardbirds (where he first met Page), the Jeff Beck Group, Vanilla Fudge, the Rascals, the Searchers, the New Vaudeville Band, and, latterly, Terry Reid, who he'd just finished touring the US with. With Richard already in Los Angeles, Peter ordered him to find the band suitable hotel accommodation and to be there with a car waiting to meet them when they arrived at LAX Airport on Christmas Eve.

There was one final show to do in England, on Friday 20 December, at the unpromisingly named Fishmonger's Hall – a small room above the Fishmonger's Arms pub in Wood Green High Road – where they were billed as 'Led Zeppelin (formerly Yardbirds)'. Three days later they reconvened at London Airport where, along with another roadie, Kenny Pickett, they boarded a plane bound for New York. From there they all took a connecting flight on to LA. All, that is, except for Jones, who had decided to ignore Grant's wishes and bring his wife Mo with him. Although Mo would not be joining the tour, Jones was loath to spend Christmas without her and had made alternative plans for them to spend the holiday in nearby New Jersey with the black American singer Madeline Bell, who Jones knew from doing sessions with her in London. He would, he casually informed them, make his own way down from New Jersey to the first show in Denver, where they would meet up again on Boxing Day.

'We had a soul Christmas, and it was brilliant,' Jones would recall years later. 'And then we had to go and see some other relatives. Wherever we went, there was another meal waiting for us. I've never eaten so much food in all my life. They were really wonderful people.' It was, however, the first clear-cut instance of John Paul Jones creating 'my own space within the band' as he puts it now. Never one to waste words or raise his voice unnecessarily, Jones was nevertheless quietly determined to do things his way, whenever possible. As long as he was there on time for professional engagements, what did it matter if he chose not to spend his time in the company of the others? With Page, already a hardened road veteran, more than happy to go his own way, and Plant and Bonham happy for the time being to stick together, none of the others felt any cause for complaint. If anything, they had no more desire for the company of their professorial bass player than he did for theirs. It was a pattern of behaviour that would persist throughout their years together.

Born in Sidcup, Kent, on 3 January 1946, just like Jimmy you are a Capricorn; that is to say, a born conservative; quiet and undemonstrative on the outside, stubborn and unmovable on the inside. And, like Jimmy, you are an only child: self-contained, happy within yourself, not especially interested in pleasing others. The rest of the world, it comes and it goes. You are simply you, 'take it or leave it'.

Still waters run deep, they say – a phrase that might have been invented to describe your personality. This means they misjudge you, seeing only the smooth surface. You know this but are unconcerned. Let others say and do what they will, what's it to you? Ideal material for 'unsung hero' status, over the years most people will see only the bass guitar you carry or the keyboards you sit behind. Even when they see you stoop to retrieve your acoustic guitar, or note on the album credits that you also play the mandolin, koto, pedal steel guitar, autoharp, ukulele, cello, synthesiser, recorder or any number of different instruments, they still won't quite get it. Well, that's up to them. Or not, as the case may be. What's it to you? Absolutely nothing.

Your father, Joe, was the same. A professional concert pianist and arranger with the Ambrose Orchestra, it wasn't just music he taught you. A serious face hiding a wonderfully dry sense of humour, when he wasn't performing pieces for the BBC's Light Programme by Rossini, Handel, Ravel and Offenbach, he was working part-time in a musical comedy duo with your mother, performing more popular hits of the day by Mario Lanza, Ronnie Hilton, Lee Laurence, Vera Lynn and Donald Peers. Sometimes they would bring in a 'popular' singer to front the duo, a pretty young girl named Kathy Kirby. How your father laughed when, years later, his son was hired as a session player to play on some of Kathy's hits. You and the well-known session guitarist Little Jimmy Page . . .

With your mother and father always busy, often away touring the provinces – no place for a child, even one as musically precocious as you – you were sent to board at Christ's College in Blackheath, south-east London, where you were able to formalise your classical music studies. Even though you felt sick at the prospect of living away from home, it would be a marvellous opportunity for you, Father said. You were very lucky. It was at boarding school that you learned to play the school's chapel pipe organ. It was also at boarding school where you learned to dislike organised games and discovered you were at your best when 'left alone to get on with it,' as you put it. To please your father, you also agreed to take up the saxophone, but it didn't last. The bloody thing set your teeth on edge.

Away from the classroom, however, it wasn't just the classical piano of Sergei Rachmaninoff you admired. You also approved of the unruly blues of enigmatic American music titans like 'Big' Bill Broonzy, Fats Waller and, later on, Jimmy Smith, 'Brother' Jack MacDuff, and Richard 'Groove' Holmes. It was also through the blues that you would eventually discover jazz, particularly the head-spinning freeform style of Charles Mingus. You began to lead a sort of musical double-life: devoted to your study of piano and classical music, increasingly intrigued by more contemporary forms. At fourteen, you were good enough to be the choirmaster and organist at the local church. The same year you persuaded your parents to allow you to buy your first bass guitar – a Dallas solid body electric – after becoming obsessed with the incredibly fluid playing of Chicago bassist and band-leader Phil Upchurch, whose 1961 dance instrumental, 'You Can't Sit Down', featured the first bass solo you'd ever heard. You'd tried restringing an old ukulele you'd found gathering dust on the family upright piano, but it wasn't the same. In the end, you talked Father into acting as guarantor on an HP agreement to buy the Dallas, which you cleverly fed through the rewired amplifier of an old telly and were immediately able to use to begin thrumming along to records like 'Freight Train', a skiffle hit by Chas McDevitt, though not too noisily, in case it disturbed the neighbours. Mainly, you'd just play along to whatever happened to be broadcast on the Light Programme.

Armed with your snazzy new bass, you began playing with other kids your age and older at the local church youth club that opened after Sunday evensong. A group formed without a drummer, it required you to develop an unusually percussive style focused on the lower frets. It was something you'd come up with yourself which you were quite pleased with actually. The group, nicknamed the Deltas, got quite good and started to get invitations to play at wedding receptions, street parties and summer fêtes. Father even joined in on piano at some of the engagements. Those of the group who were standing perfected the synchronised footwork of the Shadows, and you became adept at playing the hits of the day. By the time you were seventeen you were so good you even got the occasional booking at various US army bases, like the one in Dartford where a teenage Michael Jagger had a holiday job as a PE teacher. Like Michael, it was here that you got your first taste of the American records on the jukeboxes: a heady mixture of blues, country-and-western and pop. It was on one of those nights that you heard Tamla Motown for the first time and nearly flipped your lid, as they say. You simply could not believe the driving, triumphant sound of the bass. If you needed any further proof that it was the bass that really gave these records their shape, it was all there in the grooves of every single Motown recording those big old American jukeboxes pumped out at you.

No longer playing organ in the church on Sundays and interest in your classical music studies on the wane, your perspective changed dramatically over those two years. Until then you'd imagined yourself following in Father's footsteps and joining the orchestra; now whole new vistas of possibilities opened up in your mind. Not that you said anything to Mother and Father. You'd learned the hard way it was best to keep those sorts of ideas to yourself. When someone tipped you off that the ex-Shadows stars Tony Meehan and Jet Harris were holding auditions to find a bass player for their new group, you found yourself on the train up to London for an

audition at an upstairs function room at a pub in the West End. You were
bloody nervous because this was a proper group. They had just had a
no. 1 with 'Diamonds' (which, years later, you'd discover to your mutual
amusement, had featured Pagey on guitar) and now they were looking to
put together a touring outfit.

You didn't really expect to be offered the job. Not because you didn't
think you were good enough: you knew you were. You just couldn't picture
yourself actually in a group like that, performing in proper concert venues
packed with people, touring the country with them. But they did offer you
the job – on condition you got rid of the Burns electric bass you were now
playing (along with the enormous Truvoice amp and speakers that were
nearly as tall as you were) and replace it with a Fender like the ones they
played. You were never one of those people that needed to be told something
twice and you went out that weekend and bought yourself a much more
professional (and expensive) Fender Jazz bass – the same guitar you would
use, in fact, right up until 1975 . . .

Jones' absence certainly made life easier for Cole, who now had
only three far-from-home young players to babysit over Christmas.
Cole had booked them into separate bungalows at the Chateau
Marmont, off Sunset Boulevard: Bonzo and Plant in one together,
Page on his own. The Marmont was an infamous Hollywood movie
star bolthole. Jean Harlow had conducted her affair with Clark
Gable there. Paul Newman met future wife Joanne Woodward there.
Years later, John Belushi would overdose and die there. More recently,
the late Heath Ledger would be filmed there snorting a white
powder. In 1969, though, the Marmont had become the latest
rock'n'roll hang-out. The place had a louche atmosphere that made
it perfect for the sort of antics most bands Cole had worked with
liked to get up to. Earlier that year, Graham Nash had lived there
for five months. Before that, a drunken Jim Morrison had spilled
out of a second-storey window, injuring his back and legs. Now
Alice Cooper's roadies played football naked on the mezzanine. But
apart from a couple of tame food-fights, none of this new lot seemed
to get it – except for Jimmy, of course, and even he seemed unusually
preoccupied. Cole was perplexed. Having road-managed the Yardbirds on their final US tour just six months before, he felt he already
knew all about Jimmy Page. How between shows he liked to unwind

by collecting art and searching for antiques – or better still, chasing girls. All on-the-road pleasures Ricardo was happy to help him participate in – and fully expected to do so again once the tour got underway. The others he had yet to figure out, though. His first impression of Bonzo was of 'a congenial fellow with a rich sense of humour and a contagious laugh'. Robert, though, 'had an aura of arrogance around him – arrogance coupled with anxiety – that created a shell that was difficult to penetrate'.

In fact, Plant was suffering from a tremendous attack of nerves. That and the jetlag the long journey had left him with had turned him into a complete mess. The band's first show would be opening for Vanilla Fudge, in place of the original opening act that had been booked, the Jeff Beck Group, and Plant was almost paralysed with fear at the prospect. This was America, after all, a place he had fantasised about being in, performing in, for most of his life. Now he was here he was terrified he might blow it, might let the side down and crush the dream they all shared for Zeppelin before it had even got off the ground. He could tell Jimmy still harboured doubts about him, not as a singer, but as a performer, as someone fit to share the same stage as him. And he knew that in Jimmy's world singers came and went; that this wasn't the bloody Beatles, or even the Stones. That there was only one star of this group – and it wasn't him. Newly married, freshly minted from the Atlantic advance, his whole future spread out before him like never before, Robert should have been on cloud nine, he told himself. Instead, he had never felt so alone or so far from home. Never felt so downright freaked out, man.

Even his mate Bonzo wasn't much help. Unable to sense the turmoil going on inside his friend, Bonham had his own problems. Unlike Plant, he wasn't worried for his place in the band. Bonzo knew he was good; he didn't need some soft Southern ponce to tell him that. No. Bonzo just hated not being at home for Christmas. He missed Pat and Jason. The fact that the older, more worldly-wise Jonesy had somehow managed to wangle it to be with his wife over Christmas only made him feel worse. It wasn't fucking fair. But then, he'd taken the money, hadn't he? Bought the big flash car? Now it was time to get on with the job. And so he kept his mouth shut and did his best to get on with it. But he didn't like it, not one bit. As a result, without really comprehending the other's difficulties, Plant and Bonham huddled together in those first days like two shipwreck survivors clinging to the same driftwood. They not only shared a room together, they would refuse to turn out the light and go to sleep until they were both safely tucked up in bed. Page, too wrapped up in his thoughts, appeared not to notice, but Cole observed it all with a cold eye. They would learn.

When, on Christmas Day, Bonzo used the self-catering facilities in the bungalows to cook them all Christmas dinner, nobody was really in the mood to enjoy it. Besides, it was a blisteringly sunny day outside, too hot to be eating turkey and roast spuds. It just didn't feel like Christmas. Plant, barely able to keep his food down, simply gave up. 'I hate to dwell on it,' he sighed, 'but it's really shitty being this far away from my wife at Christmas.' Bonzo grunted his agreement but waited to see what Jimmy would say. He merely nodded. 'It's a sacrifice,' he agreed, 'but there's going to be a pay-off. This band has a lot going for it. Let's make the best of it.' He raised his glass in a toast which the others joined him in, but nobody was smiling.

After another sleepless night in the Plant and Bonham bungalow, the following morning Cole got them up early and drove them back to LAX, where they boarded a TWA flight to Denver. From there he rented a car and drove them straight to the Auditorium Arena, where Jones was already backstage waiting for them. It wasn't just Robert who was nervous now. They always were before shows but this was the worst they had ever been: Plant pacing up and down the tiny dressing room chain-smoking and compulsively running his long fingers through his tight blonde curls, Bonzo obsessively rat-tat-tatting with his drumsticks on some cardboard boxes he'd found, while Page and Jones, more experienced but no less anxious, stood around avoiding eye-contact with each other, smoking and quivering in silence together.

The first time they had opened the show for another, ostensibly more famous group, going on before Vanilla Fudge would see Zeppelin thrown in at the deep end. The Fudge were big time, famous for what the *International Times* had admiringly described as the 'molten lead on vinyl' of their slowed-down, heavy-laden recordings of pop hits like the Supremes' 'You Keep Me Hanging On' and the Beatles' 'Ticket To Ride'. Known for taking no prisoners, they had built their live reputation in America by opening shows for Hendrix, The Who, Cream and The Doors, often stealing the headliner's thunder, said reviewers. Zeppelin shared the same label, Atlantic, even the same New York attorney, Steve Weiss. And they had toured with the Jeff Beck Group, where Grant and Cole had treated them well. But that didn't mean the Fudge boys were going to give these British newcomers an easy ride. They had come up the hard way, just like Zeppelin were doing now. Now they were headliners they weren't about to cede ground to anybody, friend or foe. All this ran through Jimmy's mind as he stood there backstage, smoking and trying not to look the least bit concerned.

Finally, after what seemed like forever, the third act on the bill, Zephyr, finished their set and walked slowly off the stage. The four Zeppelin boys wondered how much longer they would have to wait for their turn. The answer was: not long. Barely fifteen minutes later, a booming American voice announced over the PA: 'Ladies and gentlemen, for their first American appearance, from London, England, please welcome . . . Led Zeppelin!' There was a steady trickle of polite applause as they made their way in single file down the concrete stairs towards the stage. To add to their anxiety, they were forced to perform on a revolving platform, something Jimmy had done before in America where the idea of playing in-the-round was popular, but not something he had ever enjoyed. Robert, barefoot, still nervous, repeatedly introducing the band by name through the opening numbers, became confused over where to address himself. He'd start a sentence and by the time he'd finished it be looking out at a completely different set of faces. It was easier for the others, who didn't rely on eye-contact with the audience. Jonesy stuck close by the drum riser, where Bonham was busy pummelling his kit into the ground. In the end, Robert merely closed his eyes and hoped for the best.

The opening numbers all went by in a blur . . . 'Good Times Bad Times' . . . 'Dazed and Confused' . . . 'Communication Breakdown' . . . Jimmy's violin showcase on 'Dazed . . . ' went down particularly well, as it always had on previous Yardbirds tours. But by the end of the set there was something else going on too. The band had conquered its nerves and was working its way into a solid groove, Robert throwing his arms around like Joe Cocker, Jimmy swinging the flashy 1958 Fender Telecaster that Jeff Beck had given him around his knees, the notes tumbling out like sparks from a campfire. On through 'I Can't Quit You Baby' . . . 'You Shook Me' . . . 'Your Time Is Gonna Come' . . . contracted to perform for forty minutes, in the end they played for just over an hour, the excitement amongst the crowd gradually building towards an unexpectedly deafening crescendo of applause when they finally took their bows and skipped off, trying not to stumble on the still revolving floor.

In the dressing room afterwards they were all delighted. Not least Plant, who was overjoyed. 'I loved it!' he kept saying over and over. 'I loved it!' Then turning to whoever was standing next to him and demanding: 'It was good, wasn't it? It was good!' It was. So much so, in fact, that in the headliner's dressing room down the corridor there was now consternation. According to Fudge drummer Carmine Appice, once they had become headliners, 'we always wondered who the band was that was going to come up and kick our butt – and it was Zeppelin.'

If it was Peter Grant's business acumen that ensured Led Zeppelin's debut US tour would take the band to all the right places, it was Jimmy Page's expertise as a live performer that ensured they would be remembered by everyone fortunate enough to catch them in those places. Although they only had one album – unreleased until three weeks into the tour – from which to draw material, the guitarist was happy to pad the set out with any number of crowd-pleasing cover versions. The giddy ascent of Dylan and the Beatles to the twin thrones of a newly established and highly elite rock aristocracy may have reinforced the idea that the most gifted artists performed only their own material, but this was still a time when international stars like Hendrix, the Stones, The Who, Joe Cocker and, yes, Jeff Beck, routinely covered songs, especially in a live setting. Certainly in the case of the Stones and The Who, both of whom had aspirations to emulate the Beatles as songwriters of serious repute, the covers would be carefully selected – Chuck Berry and Robert Johnson for the former; Eddie Cochran for the latter – in order to both reflect the impeccable tastes of the performers and to suggest a certain credibility-by-association genealogy.

Led Zeppelin had more in common with the Jimi Hendrix approach: capable of originating their own material but equally at ease appropriating the work of others, with or without giving credit. Or put another way, they would play anything and everything they could think of to get the audience off, from revved-up versions of their own stuff to equally over the top versions of old Yardbirds hits ('For Your Love' was still trotted out to huge applause) and other guaranteed crowd-pleasers like 'Tobacco Road' (originally by the Nashville Teens), 'Something Else' (by Eddie Cochran), 'As Long As I Have You' (Garnett Mimms), 'No Money Down' (Chuck Berry), 'Flames' (Elmore Gantry) . . . whatever worked, even if it included old chestnuts like Little Richard's 'Long Tall Sally' or unexpected excursions like the Beatles' 'I Saw Her Standing There'. 'There was the stuff that I had outlined in my mind,' said Page. 'Then there was stuff that was written, amongst all of us or some of us. Then there were numbers to make a full set. A few sort of dodgy versions of old Yardbirds things like "Over Under Sideways Down", to songs which the band would go off into all these other areas on, just making frameworks for jamming, really.'

Some of the covers – like 'As Long As I Have You', which Plant and Bonham had performed a more faithful version of in Band of Joy – would be so drawn-out and convoluted they would be stretched almost beyond recognition as the band used them as 'frameworks' to improvise around. Some, like 'The Hunter' (already a stand-out in the regular set of a new young London-based band called Free, who Jimmy admired but no-one in America had heard of yet) were more straightforward, if delivered at twice the normal speed as a moment of 'spontaneity' at the climax of 'How Many More Times'. Others, like 'Something Else', would be 'super hooligan', the brutal sound of the Sex Pistols ten years ahead of their time. It didn't matter where the songs came from, it was all 'just an excuse to let rip and show what we could do'.

Sometimes they would even purloin material from one of the other bands on the bill, as when Spirit joined the Vanilla Fudge tour for a few dates and Zeppelin took to incorporating into their set snatches of 'Fresh Garbage' from the debut, eponymously titled Spirit album. Page was also taken with Spirit singer-guitarist Randy California's use of a theremin, which he had mounted atop his amplifier or sometimes down by his foot pedals. A device invented in 1920 by a Russian physics professor named Lev Termen (aka Leon Theremin), the theremin's strange tone and single-note pitch would be achieved by moving one hand across an extra-sensitive antenna as the other hand adjusted the volume control. The result would be a series of ghostly wails and piercing sonic waves that became popular as tremble-tremble music in countless sci-fi epics of the post-war era. More recently, it had been used by the Beach Boys on 'Good Vibrations', no. 1 in the UK around the time Page was switching from bass to guitar in the Yardbirds. It wasn't until he saw Randy California using one that he decided he wanted one too, buying his first theremin in New York at the start of the band's second US tour later that year and initially using it to enhance the extended jam-section finale of 'Dazed and Confused', and later a more famous effect on the recording of 'Whole Lotta Love'. (Vanilla Fudge drummer Carmine Appice would later claim that Page also 'adapted' a section of another, less well-known Spirit number, 'Taurus', from their first album, for the first five trademark chords of 'Stairway To Heaven', an allegation we will return to in due course.)

Certainly, originality was low on the list of priorities, while at the top of it lay doing what Plant would later only half-jokingly describe as 'what we knew got more people back to the hotel after the gig', including another feature Beck would claim to have pioneered on previous tours with his own group: the call-and-response routine between guitar and vocal that Beck characterised as 'the Harold Pinter-like question-and-answer with Rod, which hadn't really been done before'. It was 'one of the things we got noticed for in America,' he insisted, and yet another trick Zeppelin would also put to good use when they arrived there a year later. Struggling some nights to keep up with Page's rococo improvisations, Plant, whose multi-octave spread allowed him to push his untutored vocal style in all sorts of unlikely directions, would often simply discard words altogether, yelping and screaming, using his voice as 'a fifth instrument'. It was an unfettered approach that worked incredibly well on long, showpiece numbers like 'Dazed and Confused' and later 'Whole Lotta Love', itself the end-product of extensive improvisatory onstage jams. 'Right from the very first live performances there were these stretched-out impro-visations,' said Page. 'There was always that energy, which just seemed to grow and grow.' As time went on, and the shows got longer as the tours got bigger, 'It could be almost trance-like some nights.'

The aim: to shock American audiences that were then in thrall to the post-psychedelic, more 'lateral' sounds of the West Coast scene and groups like Love, Moby Grape, the Grateful Dead and even The Doors, whose pursuit of the intellectualisation of rock was then in full meandering force. Along with the less commercial emergence of the new 'country rock' scene in LA, Zeppelin's music appeared to offer the antidote: a heady brew of ferocious hard rock and steamy blues, awash in lengthy improvisations built on snatches of Howlin' Wolf's

'Killing Floor', scraps of 'Fought My Way Out Of Darkness', and the soon to be famous line about squeezing lemons 'until the juice runs down my leg' from Robert Johnson's 'Travelling Riverside Blues', made all the more remarkable, claims John Paul Jones, as 'Bonzo and I weren't into the blues at all. I'd never heard of Robert Johnson or Willie Dixon before I joined Zeppelin, but it became an easy thing to jam around on. Jimmy and Robert used to come in with licks and words; they'd start things and we'd follow on.'

These were moments which would soon coalesce into the songs that became the second Led Zeppelin album, but were still then, on that first catch-as-catch-can tour, as yet unnamed, unplanned, just thrown out there with the sort of wild improvisatory abandon familiar to freeform jazz aficionados but still largely unknown to most mainstream rock fans. Far from merely following in the musical footsteps of the, in reality, much more conservative Beck Group, the nearest equivalent would have been the freeform excursions of Hendrix at his best – though even Jimi felt constrained by a need to do the hits, an idea he was already rebelling against but would not live long enough to fully abandon – or the sort of stretched-out, heavy-handed jamming Vanilla Fudge indulged in, where again it was a case of taking an established hit song and turning it inside out. For Led Zeppelin, the preoccupation when they played live was not nearly so contrived. With no hits of their own to speak of as yet, the idea was simply to lift an audience previously oblivious to their music as high and as fast as possible, leaving them utterly drained and spent by the end, giving whoever followed the band onto the stage an almost impossible task. And it worked. As a result, said Page, 'our word-of-mouth reputation spread like a wildfire'.

5

High in the Sky

There was far more, of course, to the appeal of a Led Zeppelin show than mere music. There was theatre, too. Jimmy Page's violin bow showpiece, in particular, now began to take on a life of its own. Standing there alone on the stage, the bow held aloft like a baton, or perhaps a magic wand, what had begun in the psychedelic heyday of San Francisco as a mildly diverting moment in the Yardbirds show (an effect achieved by rubbing rosin onto the bow so that the guitar strings vibrated loudly as it sawed across them, then conducting the ensuing squall with skilful use of wah-wah pedals and echo units) now evolved into one of the most captivating and hallucinatory highlights of the live Led Zeppelin experience; the sort of trippy set-piece the new far-out hippy kids adored, eventually stretching the song to more than half an hour in duration as Plant also began adding ad-libs, dropping in verses of 'San Francisco', 'Walter's Walk' and anything else that came into his fevered mind. Everybody else always left the stage once Jimmy pulled out the violin bow, though. This was always his magical, moon-bathed moment, stopping the audience in its tracks by flicking the bow in their faces like an angry cat swishing its tail.

In the Yardbirds the violin had been used during 'Glimpses'. 'I had tapes panning across the stage on this high-fidelity stereo sampler. It was quite avant-garde stuff for the time,' Page recalled. However, it was replaced by 'Dazed and Confused' long before the formation of Led Zeppelin. 'Some of the sounds that came out of it were just incredible, sometimes it would sound like that "Hiroshima" piece by Penderecki, and other times, it would have the depth of a cello.'

The opportunities for Jimmy to fine-tune his performance were coming thick and fast now. This was still entry-level touring though; the soon-to-be legendary days of private planes and luxury hotel suites were still some way off. On that first US tour in 1969, they flew Coach Class on commercial airlines and used TWA's 'Discover America' frequent-flyers plan to gain discounts wherever possible on planes and rental cars, travelling through the night wherever possible to save on hotels. Only when absolutely necessary would they check into Holiday Inns or airport motels. All four band members and their personal luggage would squeeze into the same car with Richard Cole at the wheel. Kenny Pickett would follow behind with all the equipment loaded into a three-ton, U-Haul truck. It's under such make-or-break circumstances that most bands either forge unbreakable bonds or go swiftly to the wall. Fortunately for Jimmy Page, who had staked so much – personally and professionally – on the success of the venture, in Zeppelin's case it was the former. Because of the uniformly excellent reactions they were getting to their shows each night, even when things went horribly wrong, they still, somehow, seemed to turn out right, although there were some close shaves.

In Cole's 1992 memoir, *Stairway to Heaven*, for example, he tells of a harrowing drive from Spokane to Seattle, where they were due to catch a flight to Los Angeles. An arctic blizzard meant that Spokane Airport was temporarily closed. It was New Year's Eve and the band was keen to celebrate it: not under eight inches of snow, but in the warmth of LA. They also had an important show to do at the Whisky A Go Go on 2 January. So Cole took the enormously risky decision to drive the band through the snowstorm to Seattle Airport, where he had been told planes were still being allowed to take-off: a two-hundred-mile journey through knee-high slush and towering snow-banks that 'started out bad' and quickly got worse. 'As we slipped and slid, the visibility became worse,' he wrote. 'And I was becoming more anxious. To try to calm myself, I reached into the backseat and grabbed a bottle of whisky. I handed it to Bonzo and said, "Open it! Quick! I need something to relax me!" We passed the bottle around, and every-one had a few swigs.'

Brimful of Dutch courage and his own bloody-mindedness, when they came across a roadblock patrolled by state police who ordered them to turn back, Cole simply ignored them, driving back onto the highway at the next turn-off and continuing unabated to Seattle. 'I felt victorious,' he declared. 'But after just a few minutes, I realised that maybe the cops had been right. Sheets of snow alternated with torrents of rain and hail. The winds were ferocious. We were the only car on the highway. Parts of the road were caked with ice, and the car was skidding from lane to lane. If conditions got any worse, I could have turned off the ignition and just let the car slide all the way to Seattle.'

Page, who was huddled in the backseat suffering with Hong Kong 'flu 'didn't have much energy to complain about anything'. Everyone else in the car, however, including Cole, 'was absolutely terrified'. Crossing a narrow suspension bridge they found themselves swaying sickeningly in the wind. 'We were so close to the edge – and to a drop of about 100 feet – that Bonzo and Robert became absolutely frantic. "Richard, you fuckin' asshole, you're about to get us killed!" Robert shrieked, grabbing the bottle of whisky from John Paul's hands. "Oh, my God!" screamed Bonzo. "Can't you pull over until this storm ends?" I shouted back, "Shut up, you fuckers, just drink some more whisky". In fear and frustration, I pressed the accelerator to the floor and the car bolted ahead. Within another minute, we were safely on the other side of the bridge.'

But the nightmare wasn't over yet. When Cole made a piss stop a mile or so further up the road, the car slowly began to slide backwards off the road towards a precipice. Diving back into the car, Cole turned the steering wheel in the nick of time, bringing it to a halt as the occupants all screamed at him at once. They eventually made it to the airport all in one piece, followed a little later by Kenny Pickett, who had also ignored the police warning, but had not been so lucky keeping his vehicle on the road, crashing through a perimeter fence into someone's front yard, before righting himself and continuing on. Page, whose 'flu made him largely oblivious, told 'Ricardo' he was a hero. Jones, who had been abject with rage, was so drained he could no longer speak. Bonham was laughing hysterically. Plant, who had dived headfirst into the driver's seat at one point to try and hit the brakes with his hands, felt Cole should have been fired for his outrageous actions. He would never entirely trust his road manager again.

Mum and Dad always wanted what was best for you. A nice respectable job sat behind a desk, the sort of thing that would provide the kind of security they themselves had dreamed of during the war years. You understood all that but it was different for you, why couldn't they see that? They just didn't understand. Even when you tried talking to them properly without losing your head and giving up halfway through, they just didn't listen. Dad said one thing, Mum said another. You said something else again. The arguments just went round and round. Going on and on about your hair. It wasn't even that long. No one had short-back-and-sides anymore, why should you? And when you weren't arguing you were barely speaking to each other, sitting at the table eating, hardly saying a word, Dad not even looking at you.

Years later, you would romanticise this bleak period of your life. 'I only dared go home at night because my hair was so long,' you'd smile. 'So I left home and started my real education, moving from group to group, furthering my knowledge of the blues and other music which had weight.' But it was never going to be that simple. By the time you'd left grammar school, you had a regular spot at the Seven Stars Blues Club, getting up and singing a couple of tunes if and when the regular turn, the Delta Blues Band, let you. Dad did at least agree to drive you there and back once a week. You dreamed he might hang around one night to hear you do your stuff – see you belting out 'I've Got My Mojo Working' or 'Route 66' – and change his mind, but no chance, mate. Even when you teamed up now and again with an acoustic guitar player in order to land a spot at a folk club, doing 'Corinna Corinna' or 'In My Time Of Dying' from the first two Dylan albums, stuff that had nothing to do with the Beatles or pop music, your dad still looked on it all as a complete waste of time.

Anyway, you didn't care what your dad thought, not really. By the end of 1964 the Mod cut had gone. In its place you now allowed a sort of bouffant to grow, constantly standing in front of the mirror combing it with one of those special barber's combs with the razor in it. If your mates had seen you they'd have called you a poof but you didn't care. It looked good and the birds loved it. By now your curly blond hair was creeping down to your shoulders. You would try disguising its length by slapping it down with Dippety-Do gel but you still got it in the ear from the old man. It wasn't just at home that you heard about it now, either. You'd get it out in the street now too, in the pub, on the bus. 'Get yer 'air cut!' was the most common. 'Bloody poof!' Or 'Fucking queer!' But instead of putting you off it just made you more and more defiant, playing up the effeminacy on stage, sashaying around, grinning whenever you caught the eye of one of the girls who would crowd down the front. Their boyfriends further back, with their work and school haircuts, would look on with disgust. Sometimes they'd even come up to you afterwards. Luckily you were tall and a good talker or there might have been even more disgruntled boyfriends coming up afterwards.

But you had to bite the bullet when Mum and Dad finally cornered you into going for an interview for 'a proper job' as a trainee chartered accountant: something to aim for, they said, for when you'd finished college. Sure enough, when you left college in 1965, you turned up and began work in that horrible, disgusting, boring bloody office. You weren't getting your hair cut, though. They could stuff that. You'd just slap the Dippety-Do on even heavier, hide the rest of it under your collar and tie. And you were still out most nights, singing or watching other singers, turning up for work the next day knackered, the adding machine figures swimming before your poor red eyes. You lasted in the job just two weeks before they took you to one side and told you they didn't think you were really suitable.

Good. Who cared what some old fool in a shiny suit thought about anything anyway? You only cared what the audience thought, them and the other musicians and singers you were now meeting and mingling with at night, lying about your age, your lack of experience, trying to fit in with a crowd that was hard to get to know unless you were somehow already one of them, and you desperately wanted to be. So you concentrated on your singing. Started to sound less like a nervous schoolboy and more like what you thought you should. Less mannered, more earthy and real; started to open your shoulders and really have a go at it. The more you did it, the more your confidence grew. You knew you weren't technically all that great, wouldn't have even known how to be without someone to show you, to teach you. But what you wanted to do you knew no-one could teach you, to growl like Howlin' Wolf, to wheeze like Bukka White, to croon like Elvis and holler like Little Richard. Your voice wasn't pure like theirs, you knew that; knew you couldn't hold a silver note the way Roy Orbison could – who could? But you knew what you were after and you were getting closer to it, you felt, every time you held your heart in your mouth and climbed up on a stage. Learning how to hold the mike, pushing it away from your mouth like so on the big choruses, pulling it back closer on the verses, seeing how a moan or a sigh could be as effective as a strangulated scream. How a strangulated scream could sometimes work better than anything . . .

*

'I had a long way to go with my voice then,' Robert Plant would say of his early days in Zeppelin. 'But at the same time the enthusiasm and spark of working with Jimmy's guitar shows through quite well. It was all very raunchy then. Everything was fitting together into a trademark for us. We were learning what got us off most and what got people off most.' By the time he and Zeppelin had returned to LA to play the Whisky A Go Go, word was out on the band even though the album still hadn't been released. FM radio was beginning to play advance copies of it, crowds were starting to form outside their dressing room each night, the pretty girls suddenly just as interested as the serious-faced boys who were now going into record stores and ordering their own copies of the album.

Although Los Angeles was not yet America's foremost record industry city – still ranked then a poor third behind New York and San Francisco – the Whisky was the first prestige venue of the tour. The band was booked for a five-night co-headline residency with Alice Cooper, during which the cream of the city's music biz insiders were expected to show up. Ironically, then, it was the first time on the tour when the band did not approach their task in an unusually nervous mental state. Aware of how important the run would be, they were nevertheless so charmed by LA itself – the glorious weather, the gorgeous girls, the generally laid-back ambience of the people and the place – playing the Whisky for five nights was seen almost as a mini-break; a warm-up for the even more arduous task of appearing in San Francisco that would immediately follow.

The venue itself only cheered them further. It was situated in a building on Sunset Boulevard that had once been a branch of the Bank of America – hence its industrial green paintwork – with alcoves where the safes and desks had once been refurbished to home a small stage flanked by outlandishly large speakers. The scene was topped off by a series of glass-enclosed cages into which gaggles of miniskirted girls would take it in shifts to dance the night away; the sort of place Zeppelin would have enjoyed going to even if they hadn't been performing there. As it was they would have five nights to enjoy themselves. Jimmy, in particular, who had played the venue before and always enjoyed himself in LA, was in his element, despite still suffering from the ravages of 'flu.

With the week stretching out before them, the band settled into the

Chateau Marmont and began to take in their surrounds. Not yet into the full-on, town-owning, party-head mode they would occupy in years to come, the band indulged in less careworn offstage activities. Drugs were not yet an issue. According to Richard Cole, there was 'plenty of marijuana' and 'occasionally a snort or two of cocaine'. But alcohol was still the only 'everyday indulgence' at this stage. 'John Paul liked gin and tonic. Robert would drink mostly wine and sometimes Scotch. Jimmy was attached to Jack Daniel's. But Bonzo and I weren't as fussy. From Drambuie to beer to champagne, we'd drink just about anything . . .' As a result, all four members, all so different in their various ways, were now becoming close in a way that would not have been possible under any other circumstances. This became most evident on stage when Plant, relieved at not having to be compared to anyone else on the bill anymore, began coming out of his shell at last. Walking on stage each night in bare feet, he may have appeared to have 'gone native'; in fact, he was simply doing what he could to try to relax himself and remember that he was, as he puts it now, 'still just a hippy from the Black Country', however much he felt out of his comfort zone elsewhere on the trip. 'As a performer I might have remained huddled, clutching the mike stand with a large "Excuse me" written over my head,' he said. But it was in LA, where they would be headliners in their own right for the first time in America, that 'things finally started coming together'.

Offstage, Plant and Bonham still huddled together. Both, in their own way, couldn't wait to get home: missing wives and children; freaked out by their first in-at-the-deep-end tour of America; holed-up together in what they were told was Burl Ives's usual bungalow, while Ricardo doubled-up in a bungalow with Page and Jones shared space with Kenny Pickett. 'It was a bit like being on a space shuttle, in a way,' Plant later told me. 'So we did grow together, although we were never really particularly similar. But we had common ground which we began to share and we realised as time went on that we had to make this thing work.'

The more experienced Page and Jones handled things better: both men adept at always keeping a little back for themselves, going their separate ways as soon as the band checked into a hotel; the unofficial senior partners of the foursome. 'There was also the North-South divide and a lot of friendly teasing going on,' remembered Jones. 'I think Robert was still slightly in awe of us. To him, session men were pipe-smoking, *Angling Times*-reading, shadowy figures. He never knew what to make of me and to an extent still doesn't.' But if some members appeared more equal than others early on, there was clearly only one member in charge. Usually, 'Jimmy used to have one room and all three of us would be in another!' Jones laughingly recalled. 'But we soon changed all that.' As the only one who'd toured America before, however, Page tended to cut a solitary figure, although he and Peter Grant spent quite a bit of time together, going out searching for antiques.

As such, though the Whisky shows all went well, the band's main memories now are of 'offstage looning around,' as Plant puts it. When asked later what his main memories of that trip to LA were, he simply laughed. 'Nineteen years old and never been kissed!' It was, quite simply, 'the first time I ever saw a cop with a gun, the first time I ever saw a twenty-foot-long car . . . there were a lot of fun-loving people to crash into. People were genuinely welcoming us to the country and we started out on a path of positive enjoyment, throwing eggs from floor to floor and really silly water battles and all the good fun that a boy should have.' It was, he accurately surmised, 'just the first steps of learning how to be crazy'.

From LA, the band flew to San Francisco for the first of three nights at the Fillmore West. Already waiting for them was Peter Grant – and Maureen Plant, who lovesick Robert had been allowed to fly in. Grant had been tipped off about Plant's insecurities and he needed him happy and at his best for these shows – San Francisco was the big kahuna. Plant was a typical Leo, preening in front of the mirror, sauntering around in that unself-conscious 'Black Country hippy' way. But when Leos are insecure they begin to fall apart and G was worried that Robert, who had repeatedly been told how important the San Francisco dates were, might blow it. Plant told me: 'Peter Grant had said if we don't make it in San Francisco, at the Fillmore West, up against the cream of American music, if you can't kick arse there, the band won't be able to tour again,' He chuckled somewhat sheepishly at the memory. '[Robert] did lack a bit of confidence,' said Grant, who admitted he used to 'hide all the negative reviews we had' from the singer.

The Fillmore West was also where they got to know the already legendary promoter Bill Graham: a man who would figure prominently throughout the Led Zeppelin story in America. Born Wolfgang Grajonka in Berlin in 1931, the only surviving son of a persecuted Jewish family, Graham had escaped from the Nazis when he was just ten years old, fleeing an orphanage in Paris to walk all the way to Marseille, from where he stowed away on a ship to New York. Accepted as a homeless European refugee who spoke little or no English, he was given the more 'American' sounding name of William Graham and left to fend for himself. A tough upbringing on the streets of Queens and Brooklyn led to him finding work as a waiter in the Catskills when he was still barely a teenager. He later recalled, however, that it was here he learned the value of good service. An insight that would much endear him to the concert-going public after he'd saved up for a Greyhound ticket to the northern Californian coast where he began holding his own 'evening entertainments'(although the musicians he often rode roughshod over didn't always see it that way).

In 1966, he began to preside over two of the most legendary live music venues of the era: the Fillmore Auditorium in San Francisco – dubbed the Fillmore West – and its similarly named East Coast equivalent in New York. It was as boss of the two Fillmores that Graham almost single-handedly revolutionised the rock concert industry in America. Before Graham, promoters were fly-by-nights, used-car salesmen in disguise who would book a hall, however unsuitable, and stock it with as many acts as possible, using low-rent sound systems and herding the kids in and out again like cabbages; the ringleaders of a cash-rich business that soon moved on. The first promoter to identify the emerging rock culture for what it was, seeing beyond its potential merely as a cash cow, Graham began producing the first of several benefits for the San Francisco Mime Troupe. He had a simple idea – high-end production values and top-quality entertainment – and it caught on quickly with the new anti-materialistic generation of concert-goers. Along with his similar-minded rival, Chet Helms of the Family Dog, Graham's venues were the first to popularise light shows and produce bespoke concert posters; the first to manufacture specifically tailored merchandising that could be sold inside his venues; and the first to attempt State-wide tours and large-scale events such as the soon-to-be-famous New Year's Eve extravaganzas with his favourite San Francisco band, the Grateful Dead.

Anyone, however, who misread these ventures and assumed him to be a proto-hippy, was in for a rude awakening. Like Peter Grant, Graham had come up in the 'wild west' days of the music biz and had the brawling, street-wise style to match. Most often seen either yelling into a phone or someone's face, he both terrified and repulsed many of his would-be clients. Not because he was a bully but because he was, as he said, 'a stickler for principles'. In fact, like Grant, this apparently thick-skinned hustler was a deeply insecure individual who took every perceived slight to heart and above all feared being found wanting, of being a failure.

Mac Poole recalled Bonzo telling him how some nights on the US tour he'd become accustomed to playing without proper amplification. He had even come to see it as a badge of honour: the drummer who hit so hard he didn't need to be miked up. Poole recalled Bonham telling how he had boasted to Graham: 'That's why I've got a twenty-six-inch bass drum, I don't need a mike!' To which Graham had replied sternly: 'Listen, son, if you don't get miked you ain't gonna be heard past the first three rows no matter how hard you hit the kit. Now go get a fucking mike.' Bonham did as he was told. The result, as Jones later recalled, is that the Fillmore became 'the first milestone. I remember when we started the show there were just a lot of people standing there thinking, "Who the hell are you?" We turned a very indifferent crowd into a lot of warm and receptive people.'

Country Joe and the Fish were the headliners, Taj Mahal the opener. Not that anybody remembered much the next day about either after Zeppelin had finished mangling the audience's minds. It would remain a cherished memory for them all. 'In some ways the earlier American shows we did at places like the Fillmore were more real for me,' Plant told me in 2003, 'because they were easier for me to understand. There the audiences were getting three nights a week where every group in town would get up and play, everyone from the Steve Miller Band to the Rascals and Roland Kirk. There was enormous flexibility and choice and you really had to stand up and be counted for what you were.' As Page observes: 'The early interest was partly caused by the fact that I'd been in the Yardbirds and a lot of Americans had liked that group and wanted to see what Jimmy Page had moved on to. But then when they saw what we had to offer . . . I mean, Led Zeppelin was frightening stuff! The concept of psychedelic music was about roaming and roving but never actually coming together. That's why Zeppelin succeeded: there was a real urgency about how we played. Everyone would be getting laid-back and we'd come on and hit 'em like an express train.' The Fillmore West was the moment 'when I knew we'd broken through. There were other gigs, like the Boston Tea Party and the Kinetic Circus in Chicago, which have unfortunately disappeared as venues, where the response was so incredible we knew we'd made our impression. But after the San Francisco gig it was just – bang!'

When you looked back, it was like you'd known Jeff forever. Which wasn't true, you didn't even live near each other as kids. But he was the first other guitarist you ever really knew who was the same age as you and into the same sort of things, like Gene Vincent's guitarist, Cliff Gallup, who was big and fat and must have been at least forty but was about the only one playing the really sharp, fast stuff back then. You and Jeff liked him a lot – him and Scotty Moore and James Burton. It was like no-one else had even heard of them until suddenly Jeff was there. Talking about them, the two of you trading licks together, showing each other how it was done.

It was Jeff's sister, Annette, who'd got you together. It was her who told you about her brother who'd made his own guitar. You'd say, yeah? Tell him to come round one day. Then suddenly one day he did, standing there at the front door with his homemade guitar. You thought perhaps he was a bit funny but once he started playing it he was actually quite good, knocking out the James Burton solo from Ricky Nelson's 'My Babe'. You joined in, playing along on the orange-coloured Gretsch, but not making a big thing of it, wanting to make him feel at home. It was a good laugh.

Jeff – Geoffrey Arnold Beck – was from Wallington, only a bus ride away from Epsom. Another softly spoken Surrey boy who'd sung in the local church choir. Then one day he'd borrowed a guitar from a school friend. When he finally gave it back the strings were all broken. He didn't have the ten bob to buy a new set so he restrung it with some old piano wire which he'd been using for flying his model aeroplanes. You laughed when he told you that. You'd never have dared do such a thing! Then when he told you he'd actually done some shows, playing at a fairground when he was fourteen, doing 'Be Bop-A-Lula', you looked at him differently. He wasn't in your league, obviously, but you could see him getting up there, giving it a bloody good go. Now he was at Wimbledon Art College, which is how you first heard of him. You were at the Art College in Sutton, where Jeff's sister went too. 'You gotta see Jimmy, this weird thin guy playing a weird-shaped guitar like yours,' she'd kept telling him.

When you told Jeff you'd already been in a working band, touring the country, he didn't know what to say. Asked you how ... when ...? You told him how when you were fourteen you'd been on the telly, on the talent show, All Your Own, *you and some mates from school, playing a skiffle tune you'd come up with called – don't laugh – 'Mama Don't Allow No Skiffle Around Here', followed by a proper tune from Leadbelly: 'Cotton Fields'. How Huw Wheldon, the stuffy host, had asked you afterwards if you played any other styles. 'Yes,' you'd told him, looking at him like he must be deaf or something. 'Spanish guitar.' It wasn't the right answer and the old boy asked if you'd be playing skiffle when you left school. 'No,' you'd told him, silly old duffer. What then? 'I could do biological research,' you'd said. Jeff laughed out loud at that. But it was true and you told him how when you left school at fifteen you did so with five 'O' levels, enough to apply for a job as a trainee lab technician.*

Music was more just a hobby then. After school, though, things began to change. You began to change. You lost your virginity 'one particular day in the summer' when 'this girl and I wandered hand in hand through the countryside. It was the first time I felt truly in love.' Now Jeff didn't know where to look, went back to noodling on his guitar. So you changed the subject and you talked about how you had both just missed doing National Service, abolished just a few days before your seventeenth birthday. Phew! Imagine that! How your first real group after school had been the Redcats, backing combo to Red E. Lewis, an older chap who did a regular weekly spot at Epsom's Ebisham Hall, which was the real start of everything, really. Until then you'd just been jumping up and playing with whoever would let you. You and groups like Chris Farlowe and the Thunderbirds, whose guitarist, Bobby Taylor, was the only English player you'd ever seen – apart from Hank Marvin on the telly – with a Stratocaster. The Dave Clark Five had also played there, but this was before 'Glad All Over' and you'd been in the support band. That was the night Chris Tidmarsh saw you. Chris was the leader of the Redcats – Red E. Lewis himself! Like Gene Vincent and the Bluecaps only not as good, obviously, but still really good. You were still waiting to hear back about the lab tech job when Chris offered to audition you in a function room above that pub in Shoreditch. You were still playing the Futurama but Chris said you were all right and actually offered you the job. Blimey, you said. The

Redcats didn't just play in Epsom, they played in London! There was even talk of them making records, though Chris had made it clear you wouldn't be needed for any of that, just the shows. You didn't mind. He even said he'd talk to your mum and dad first, which was terrific, telling them he'd keep an eye on you and not to worry about the lab job, you'd soon be making much more money playing in the group.

Then it all changed again when Chris decided the Gene Vincent thing wasn't working anymore and changed his stage name to Neil Christian, renaming the band the Crusaders. He said you should have a flash new name too so you became Nelson Storm. That was the first time you really began to feel it, what it might be like to really be a pop star. When the girls first started really paying attention and you felt the jingle-jangle of real money in your pocket for the first time. That was when it really began to feel really, really good. But reality soon started to sink in when you found yourself going up and down the country doing one-nighters, playing all over the gaff, doing Chuck Berry and Bo Diddley numbers, old blues things. Jeff looked at you with envy in his eyes as you told him about it but he didn't know what it was like. No M1 in those days, just a load of winding roads going nowhere, a load of flat tyres, flat batteries and flat beer. Playing to punters that just wanted dance tunes, who didn't know what the blues was. Getting changed in the bogs, sleeping in the back of the horrible old van, puking up pale ale as the others looked on and laughed. You were just 'the boy', the baby of the group, and though they knew you could play they would all take the mickey, bloody bastards. 'Then what?' said Jeff, still all goo-goo eyed. Then you'd had enough, you told him. Kept getting ill and just couldn't stand it anymore. Which is when you'd packed it in and went to art college instead. You still liked to play but you kept schtum about it at college in case they went on at you to whip the guitar out and play for them at lunchtimes. Sod that! But then you met Jeff, who became more like a brother than a best mate; a brotherhood for two boys who had no real brothers of their own. And your interest in the guitar began to soar again.

Now you'd met Jeff, suddenly it wasn't just about Scotty Moore or James Burton or Cliff Gallup or even Elvis, it was about all sorts of things, from classical to folk to blues. Especially blues. Otis Rush and 'So Many Roads': the sort of thing that would send shivers up your spine. LPs like American Folk Festival of the Blues *with Buddy Guy – unbelievable! Or B.B. King's fantastic* Live At The Regal. *Or anything by Freddie King and Elmore James, just knockout! Not forgetting Hubert Sumlin, who you especially*

*loved. Hubert Sumlin, whose guitar was the equal of Howlin' Wolf's voice,
always the right phrase at the right time . . . 'Killing Floor', 'How Many
More Years' . . . Blues was the connection to another world, different people,
more like you and Jeff. The first time you met Mick and Keith was at a
blues festival, somewhere up north. This was years before the Stones.
Sending off to America for records you couldn't buy in the shops, writing
off mail order to labels like Excello, Aladdin, Imperial and Atlantic. Long
before British labels like Pye would stick out a bit of Howlin' Wolf or
Muddy Waters as part of their so-called International R&B series.*

*It was the blues that brought you back into the music business. Art
college was all right but you'd only been there a few weeks before you found
yourself getting up and having a blow one night at the Marquee, sitting in
with Cyril Davies' new band, the All Stars. You'd first met Cyril after he
and Alexis Korner had been sacked from Chris Barber's jazz outfit.
Together they'd formed Blues Incorporated, which was basically Cyril on
mouth organ, Alexis on guitar and anyone else who fancied getting up and
having a blow. This was at that funny little club in Ealing between a
jeweller's and the ABC teashop. You got all sorts there, Charlie Watts,
Brian Jones, Ray Davies, Paul Jones, Dick Taylor . . .*

*Cyril had asked you to join his band after he'd broken away from
Alexis and that whole scene had started up again with a Tuesday night
residency at the Marquee. You fancied a bit of that but you were still with
Neil Christian at the time and, besides, the thought of leaving Neil to join
Cyril then getting ill again and letting him down was too much to bear.
Cyril was an older bloke and not the sort you wanted to let down. When
Mick Jagger went to him for harmonica lessons, Cyril had just glared at
him: 'You put it in your mouth and fucking blow!' It wasn't until you were
down the Marquee one night and Cyril told you to get up and have a go
with what they called the interval band – a load of Cyril's mates, basically –
that you finally ended up playing with him. Only for fifteen minutes here
and there – sometimes Jeff and Nicky Hopkins would get up too – but it
was after one of those that somebody came up and asked you if you'd like
to play on a record. Of course you did! And before you knew it you were
doing all these studio dates at night, while still going to college in the day.
Which is when the crossroads appeared and you were left with a choice.*

The day after the final show in San Francisco, the *Led Zeppelin* album
was released. None of the band could resist the opportunity to visit

record stores whenever they could just to see what it looked liked racked up on the shelves in the 'New Releases' section. Its arty sleeve featured a Warholian facsimile of a photograph taken of the Hindenburg airship that caught fire during a flight in 1937, resulting in the death of thirty-five of its ninety-seven passengers, the name 'Led Zeppelin' tucked unobtrusively into the left-hand corner, the Atlantic logo directly opposite bottom-right. An image that has been most often described since as 'phallic', a cynical reference to the band's non-intellectual status amongst culturally snobbish rock critics, for the people that actually bought the album, it was simply an action-packed image that reflected the 'explosive' nature of its contents, which was of course the intention.

George Hardie, who created the image from the original black-and-white photo, certainly interpreted it that way. A student at the Royal Academy of Art who had previously worked with the photographer Stephen Goldblatt on the *Truth* sleeve – 'I'd helped him out with some typography' – Hardie had originally suggested a 'multiple sequential image' of a zeppelin partly submerged in clouds 'based on a club design I had seen in San Francisco.' But Page didn't like it. He already had the image he wanted, showing Hardie the photo of the burning zeppelin from a library book and telling him to 'recreate it.' Hardie 'did it dot for dot' using a Rapidograph. (Hardie's rejected artwork eventually turned up, uncredited, as a motif of clouds and suns on the second Zeppelin album.) Hardie received a flat fee of £60 for his work: a pittance, in retrospect, for an album that would eventually sell millions. But it got him started in the business and he went on to work with Hipgnosis, the company that would become famous in the Seventies for the sleeves of albums by Zeppelin, Pink Floyd and several others. He now works as an illustrator and lectures at the University of Brighton. (Interestingly, as if to show they didn't bear a grudge, the clock-face photo of the band on the back of the sleeve was taken by Chris Dreja.)

With the album not due out in Britain until March, the band was eager to discover what America would make of their music now it was finally something they could take home and listen to at their leisure. The answer was a fairly even split between the general public, who loved the work, and the US music press, who most assuredly did not. The review that really got the bandwagon rolling was the one written by John Mendelssohn in *Rolling Stone*, which described *Led Zeppelin* as the poor relation to *Truth*, with the band offering 'little that its twin, the Jeff Beck Group, didn't say as well or better three months ago.' Going on to describe Page as 'a very limited producer and a writer of weak, unimaginative songs,' it characterised Plant's vocals as 'strained and unconvincing shouting', damned 'Good Times Bad Times' as 'a Yardbirds' B-side' and called 'How Many More Times' 'monotonous'. It concluded: 'In their willingness to waste their considerable talent on unworthy material the Zeppelin has produced an album which is sadly reminiscent of *Truth*. Like the Beck Group they are also perfectly willing to make themselves a two (or, more accurately, one-a-half) man show.'

Sentiments echoed by several early reviewers, if not quite as vehemently expressed, it was the accusation of following in Beck's footsteps that once again most stung Page, who had not anticipated their ability to pick up so readily on the 'shared influences' of the two albums, or to express such enmity towards the idea. As such, it was the beginning of a mutually acrimonious relationship between Led Zeppelin and the music press – and Jimmy Page and certain writers, in particular – that would last for the entire lifetime of the band, and beyond, to the present day. 'It really pissed me off when people compared our first album to the Jeff Beck Group and said it was very close conceptually,' Page was still complaining in an interview with the American magazine, *Trouser Press*, nearly ten years later. 'It was nonsense, utter nonsense. The only similarity was that we'd both come out of the Yardbirds and we both had acquired certain riffs individually from the Yardbirds.' But then, as John Paul Jones pointed out, it seemed as though most critics had made up their minds about Led Zeppelin before they'd even heard the album. They were all 'hype' and there was no more serious crime in the late Sixties. 'We got to America and read the *Rolling Stone* review of the very first album, which was going on about us as another hyped British band. We couldn't believe it. In our naïvety we thought we'd done a good album and were doing all right, and then all this venom comes flying out. We couldn't understand why or what we'd done to them. After that we were very wary of the press, which became a chicken-and-egg situation. We avoided them and so they started to avoid us. It was only because we did a lot of shows that our reputation got around as a good live band.'

As Jones suggests, it's impossible to overstate the importance of the band's live reputation at this stage, or the fact that Peter Grant had seen fit to put them out on tour in America so early on, before they even had a record out. Had he held back and waited for the critical verdict to come in first, it's feasible that Zeppelin might not have toured America at all that first year, or certainly with much less wilful abandon. Instead, the *Rolling Stone* review and others arrived just as the Zeppelin was already in its ascendancy. Concerts were going so well that other ostensibly better-known bands were now refusing to follow Zeppelin on stage, and a second headlining tour of the US was already in the offing for the spring, when Atlantic aimed to drive home the message by releasing the band's first single.

On 28 January they returned for their second date at the Boston Tea Party, a 400-seater club constructed from a converted synagogue. The big local FM radio station in Boston, WBCN, was now playing the album round the clock and the show was a sell-out with hundreds more squeezing in than should have. When the band walked offstage for the first time that night, having played for their usual hour-plus, the crowd was in such frenzy they were swiftly brought back out to play for another fifty-five minutes, twelve encores in all that induced several standing ovations, many in the middle of songs. But when the band did their bows and walked off for the second time, fans began clambering onto the stage and yelling even more furiously for them to come back. The band, standing shattered mere feet away, could only comply. Finally, having performed their usual set, plus improvisations, nearly two dozen encores and covers all the way through twice, they actually ran out of songs to play. A laughing, sweating Page could only cough into his cigarette and beg the others: 'What songs do you know?' He was greeted with shell-shocked faces and shaking heads. But the crowd simply wouldn't let them go. They stumbled back out and performed rough approximations of 'Good Golly Miss Molly', 'Long Tall Sally', segued into barely remembered old blues riffs they simply busked into something else. By the fourth hour they had given up trying to do anything original at all and were exhaustingly blasting out old hits by the Beatles, the Stones and The Who, and still the crowd stamped their feet and hollered for more, more, more. When they came off finally, after four-and-a-half hours, they found Grant, the big guy who had already seen it all fuck you very much, weeping with joy in the dressing room. 'Peter was absolutely ecstatic,' said Jones. 'He was crying, if you can imagine that, and hugging us all. [He] picked all four of us up at once.'

Still the critics weren't having it. Jon Landau described the Boston show as 'loud . . . violent and often insane'. However, he did acknowledge that Zeppelin was attracting a generally younger generation of rock fans than the one Landau belonged to, where the cultural and political epiphanies of earlier Sixties artists like Dylan and the Beatles had been so important they couldn't help but feel everything that came after needed to be considered in that context. Ironically, John Lennon, who unbeknownst to critics like Landau was about to leave the Beatles, was now leaning in the opposite direction, having exhausted the possibilities of the post-psychedelic rock he had once been such an advocate of in favour of a return to the 'more honest' evocation of good-time rock. 'There's nothing conceptually better than rock'n'roll,' he would lecture *Rolling Stone* editor Jann Wenner in December 1970. 'No group, be it Beatles, Dylan or Stones, has ever improved on "Whole Lotta Shakin' Goin' On" for my money.' Led Zeppelin, in many ways, would become the living embodiment of that sentiment. As Page would opine in a February 1970 *Record Mirror* interview, 'I feel that some so-called progressive groups have gone too far with their personalised intellectualisation of beat music. I don't want our music complicated by that kind of ego trip. Our music is essentially emotional like the old rock stars of the past. It's difficult to listen to those early Presley records and not feel something. We are not going out to make any kind of moral or political statement. Our music is simply us.'

But while Landau and his fellow beard-strokers may not have approved of the unencumbered-by-political-ideal excitement this new music was causing, he was astute enough to foresee that the coming of Led Zeppelin and the bands that would inevitably follow represented a musical and cultural phenomenon that simply no longer relied on what he or his contemporaries thought. 'Zeppelin forced a revival of the distinction between popularity and quality,' he would later write. 'As long as the bands most admired aesthetically were also the bands most successful commercially (Cream, for instance), the distinction was irrelevant. But Zeppelin's enormous commercial success, in spite of critical opposition, revealed the deep division in what was once thought to be a homogeneous audience. That division has now evolved into a clearly defined mass taste and a clearly defined elitist taste.'

Where he was mistaken, of course, was in the accusation that Zeppelin's speedily mushrooming popularity came at an artistic price: the condensing of their talent into a lowest common denominator designed to appeal to 'mass taste'. But with only that first bludgeoning album of hardly original material to go on, it's easy to see now how Neanderthal the screamingly libidinous Zeppelin live show of 1969 must have appeared to people like Jon Landau. At a time when both Dylan and the Beatles no longer even deigned to perform live and their closest followers were getting ready for the 'return to the garden' of Woodstock, the unbridled ecstasy of a Led Zeppelin performance must have seemed an irrelevance at best, an offence at worst. Still clinging to the ideals of a decade now skittering towards its bruised and battered end, they simply didn't get it. You only had to visit the former flower-power citadel of Haight-Ashbury and note how deeply the ravages of heroin addiction had now overtaken the mind-expanding adventurism of LSD to see how poorly the message of the rock medium had actually been received, even when transmission was at its optimum with bands like the Grateful Dead and Jefferson Airplane on hand to deliver it. Ultimately, in an age when the threat of being sent to burn in the hell-on-earth of Vietnam was the chief concern of American record buyers under the age of twenty-five, the music of Led Zeppelin spoke to them in a way no other artist was doing at that point. The more benighted the band appeared to the 'elitist taste' makers of the US underground press, the more beloved they became for the kids who were now beginning to buy the album in their hundreds of thousands. The critics may not have approved of their 'too loud' album, but rather than quashing the possible audience for Led Zeppelin, it had the opposite effect, reclassifying them as iconic rule-breakers for a younger, more thrill-seeking generation. Certainly, the new album-oriented FM radio stations then springing up all over America had no such objections to the music. As well as WBCN in Boston and KSAN in San Francisco, other FM stations in New York, LA, Detroit and Chicago were now also playing the album round the clock, focusing on 'Communication Breakdown', 'Babe I'm Gonna Leave You' and 'Dazed and Confused'. As quick as the critics were to put them down, their momentum was building faster than ever.

Jimmy Page in 1967. One of the best-known, best-dressed guitarists in London – and one of its least famous (*Getty*).

Master and pupil. Which one was which, though? Page and Beck onstage in the Yardbirds, 1966 (*Pictorial Press/Alamy*).

Yardbirds publicity shot, London, 1966 (*GAB Archives/Redferns*).

Just a Black Country hippy. Robert Plant (centre) and dope-smoking friends, Birmingham, 1967 (*GAB Archives/Redferns*).

The New Yardbirds take flight as Led Zeppelin. Early publicity shot, 1968 (*Getty*).

Page with tour manager Richard Cole, stepping off the plane in Honolulu, May 1969. And stepping off the bus with Peter Grant in Honolulu, a year later (both *Robert Knight/Redferns*).

The Starship on the tarmac, Oaklahoma City (*Neal Preston/Corbis*).

Hanging out with Sandy Denny on the day of the *Melody Maker* awards, September 1970. Within weeks she was invited to duet with Plant on 'The Battle Of Evermore' (*S&G/P.A Photos*).
Later that evening with Peter Grant (*Tom Hanley/Redferns*).

At home in the early Seventies. Plant
enjoys the sound of Billy Fury, while Page
favours the handy can and chunky jumper
look (*Anwar Hussein/PA Photos & Jorgen
Angel/Redferns*).

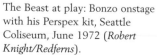

The Beast at play: Bonzo onstage
with his Perspex kit, Seattle
Coliseum, June 1972 (*Robert
Knight/Redferns*).

Classic Zep poster advertising
Southampton University show,
January 1973 (*GAB Archives/Redferns*).

G. 'When it came to Zeppelin, he could be very forthright indeed,' says promoter Freddy Bannister (*Neal Preston/Corbis*).

There was still one last tour highlight to come: their first appearances at Bill Graham's Fillmore East in New York - a two-night stint on 31 January and 1 February. They stayed at the Gorham Hotel on West 55th Street, which like the Marmont, came with kitchen-equipped suites, making it a cheap and cheerful stopover popular with visiting British bands since Who manager Chris Stamp had discovered it the year before. Arriving by car from Philadelphia early on the morning of 30 January, with three nights in New York to look forward to, the band settled in. It was important they relaxed. Like San Francisco, New York was a make-or-break date, maybe even more important. The home of the Atlantic top brass, the gigs would be full not just of other musicians, journalists, radio DJs and other scene makers, but the first chance Ahmet Ertegun and Jerry Wexler would have to see how their investment was working out.

The openers on a bill topped the first night by Porter's Popular Preachers and the headliners, Iron Butterfly, Grant managed to pull off a massive stroke when he took Graham aside during the soundcheck and asked him for 'a special favour': bumping Zeppelin up to second spot on the bill. 'Do it for an old friend,' Grant smiled, showing his tobacco-stained teeth. It was the band's first major date in New York – a huge occasion for them – and Grant wanted 'to see Zeppelin and Iron Butterfly perform back-to-back,' to see how far his 'boys' had come since arriving in the States six weeks before. Graham, who had noted the powerful reaction the band had received in San Francisco and liked the idea of Grant owing him a favour, merely shrugged and said, 'Sure, why not.'

Relieved, perhaps, at the prospect of not having to follow on to the stage a band whose reputation for leaving audiences sated was already well-known on the concert circuit, Porter's Popular Preachers seemed unaffected by the last-minute rearrangement. However, when Iron Butterfly learnt of the news, they were outraged. Having only recently graduated to the status of headliners themselves, and having heard how hard Zeppelin had pushed Vanilla Fudge, band leader Doug Ingle was so put out he threatened not to play at all. In a face-off with Graham they were bound to lose, they insisted that Zeppelin either be reinstated as show-openers or dropped from the bill completely. Graham, however, was not a man to be held to ransom and replied that if they didn't go on he would simply ask Zeppelin to play for longer, something he knew they were more than capable of.

It was a Mexican stand-off that was still going as Porter's Popular Preachers were packing up their gear and Zeppelin was getting ready to go on. At which point Grant chose to up the stakes even further by telling Jimmy and the boys exactly what was going on. They are scared of you, he sneered. 'Go out there and blow them out of this place!' The band hardly needed any encouragement to try and steal a show, but with Grant's voice still ringing in their ears they went out and ripped the joint apart. When they left the stage nearly ninety minutes later, the final chords of 'How Many More Times' still bouncing off the walls, the crowd began stamping their feet and chanting: 'Zeppelin! Zeppelin! Zeppelin!' In the audience that night was Paul Daniel Frehley (better known now as Kiss guitarist Ace Frehley), who told *Classic Rock* in 2007: 'That show at the Fillmore East changed my life . . . Between [Jimmy Page] and Robert Plant they destroyed.' The four members of Iron Butterfly were utterly distraught as they sat in their dressing room, listening to the chanting and feet-stamping. According to a gloating Richard Cole, 'The audience was still calling for more Led Zeppelin as Iron Butterfly began their set.'

When the band flew home to England the next day, they did so in the highest possible spirits. In just over a month and more than thirty almost back-to-back performances, they had been transformed from the revamped Yardbirds line-up that had departed London. They were now Led Zeppelin, a brand new entity that bore little resemblance to any of their pasts; the newest dicks on the block; hated by the critics, perhaps, but adored by the fans. In return, they would offer the best that rock music would have to offer in the coming decade. Of course, no-one was entirely sure exactly what that might be yet. No-one except perhaps for Jimmy Page, who had been convinced of the band's potential from the very first rehearsal in Gerrard Street just six months before, and of his own destiny long before that. All they had to do now, like they said in America, was to keep on keeping on. The rest would be easy meat, he felt sure.

Even Robert Plant, still so nervous and unsure of his place in the Zeppelin scheme of things, was starting to sense his destiny unfolding around him on stage. In 1973, relaxing by the pool of his hotel in New Orleans, he told *Creem*'s Lisa Robinson: 'I realised what Zeppelin was about around the end of our first US tour. We started off not even on the bill in Denver, and by the time we got to New York we were second to Iron Butterfly and they didn't want to go on! And I started getting this little light glowing inside, and I began wiggling me hips and realising that it was all a fantastic trip. I'm still not even really sure what it is that I've got to do, but I'm doing it.'

The *Led Zeppelin* album was at no. 90 in the US Hot 100 and rising steadily when the band boarded the plane to fly home from that first US tour. As a result, while Plant, Bonham and Jones couldn't wait to get back and tell their friends and family all about it, for Jimmy Page the arrival back in cold, wintry Britain was anticlimactic. With the album now on the schedule for a UK release, a more concerted countrywide tour had been booked, though the venues would remain modest. That wasn't enough to sate the growing hunger of the band's leader, though. If anything, he felt they had left America too early, just when they needed to be pushing on. However, Grant reassured him that they would be back in just a few short weeks and that this time they would be headlining. Now was the time to use the excitement of their breakthrough in the US to their best advantage at home, he argued. 'The return of the conquering heroes and all that codswallop,' he roared as the two of them sat sipping champagne on the flight home.

Instead of returning as heroes, however, the band's success in America led to yet more accusations of hype, albeit in a uniquely British way. They had obviously 'sold-out' to America, the music press raged, before 'paying their dues' by slogging around their own backyard in the time-honoured style. Neither the Beatles nor the Stones nor any other domestic artist, including Jimi Hendrix, an American, had left Britain till last to make their mark. The fact that Led Zeppelin had chosen to put America first was merely proof that they were little short of a 'manufactured' group, built purely for commercial success: a cardinal sin even today; virtually a capital crime in 1969. Jimmy could hardly believe what he was hearing. 'We just couldn't seem to do anything right as far as the critics were concerned,' he shook his head. 'At which point I think we all just sort of gave up on the idea of ever pleasing them.' Once again, it would be down to how well the band would be able to connect directly with their audience live on stage. Fortunately, this was a task they had already proved themselves supremely well qualified to accomplish.

Between 1 March and 17 April, they performed eighteen dates in
the UK. They also did some one-off dates in Denmark again and
Sweden. This time they had something to promote, although the
album – released the same month – again suffered from mainly indifferent reviews. There was one major exception: the review in Oz,
written by co-founder, Felix Dennis, which began prophetically: 'Very
occasionally a long-playing record is released that defies immediate
classification or description, simply because it's so obviously a turning
point in rock music the only time proves capable of shifting it into
eventual perspective.' In even more hyperbolic fashion, the review
went on to predict that album's impact would be akin to that of other
landmark releases such as Dylan's *Bringing It All Back Home,* The Byrds'
Younger Than Yesterday, Cream's *Disraeli Gears*, Hendrix's *Are You
Experienced?*, even the Beatles' *Sgt. Pepper.* 'This Led Zeppelin album
is like that,' it concluded. Page was pleased but not overly so. Even he
would acknowledge that *Led Zeppelin* was hardly in the same league
musically or culturally as *Sgt. Pepper.* Plant, however, was ecstatic. An
avid reader of Oz and like-minded fellow-travellers such as *IT* and
Friends, here at last was the kind of peer-to-peer recognition he'd
always dreamed of. It almost made up for the drubbing in *Rolling Stone.*
(Almost but not quite. That was one wound that would never entirely
heal.)

Unlike America, audiences were building slowly but the money
stayed low: sometimes as little as £60 against sixty per cent of the
gross; often only as high as a flat fee of £140. Compared to the sort of
relatively glamorous venues they had just been wowing in America,
the sort of venues the band found themselves playing back home were
hardly inspiring: the Van Dike club in Plymouth and the Wood Tavern
in Hornsey being about as far away, on every level, from the Fillmores
East and West as it was possible to get. Nevertheless, confidence
amongst them was running high. Mac Poole saw them play at the Farx
Club – a back room of the Northcoat Arms pub in Southall, west
London, on 30 March. Sitting with the band after the show 'over a
pint with the governor' he remembers Planty saying something about
having bought a house and needing some new carpets. 'I said, "I
wouldn't worry about carpets, Rob, I think you're gonna be moving
again." Even though I couldn't really hear John or Planty cos Jimmy
and John Paul were so loud that night it drowned out everything, there

was just something about that band, they had this incredible vibe, and I just knew these guys were gonna do some incredible business. I said, "I don't know why, I just think you're all gonna end up in mansions with this one." Rob said, "I hope you're right." '

Poole also recalled the impressive new maple-finish kit Bonham was playing on those dates. Afterwards, Bonzo showed him several extra-thick pairs of drumsticks that the Ludwig drum company had made especially for him after it became known how often he broke his sticks – sometimes two or three times a night. Vanilla Fudge drummer Carmine Appice, who Bonham had become close to during Zeppelin's stint with them, had personally called Bill Ludwig and suggested the company offer the young Zep drummer a similar endorsement to the one Appice already enjoyed the benefits of, including a large custom-made kit. Once Bill heard the album he agreed. The kit included two 26-inch bass drums – similar to the ones Appice played – that Bonham was especially thrilled about but which Page and Jones detested. Unlike Appice, Bonzo had a 'right-foot technique unlike any other drummer I've ever heard,' says writer Chris Welch, himself a drummer and expert on the instrument. 'He could already do with one bass drum what someone like Carmine – an excellent player in his own right but nothing on Bonham – would do using two drums.' Former Zeppelin roadie Glen Colson recalled setting up the kit the first time, and how Bonham 'did his nut on [it].' As a result, he said, 'Jimmy Page couldn't figure out what Bonzo was doing. There was so much drumming going on that he couldn't concentrate – he couldn't keep time. So Jimmy ordered me never to set up the double bass drums again. They freaked everyone out.'

In fact, Bonham would use the double-bass-drum set-up on several dates on the band's second US tour before an exasperated Page finally put a stop to it, though they would reappear sporadically. Appice insists Bonham later told him he'd used them on the recording of 'Whole Lotta Love', while Jones recalls Bonham sneaking them back in for sessions on the *Physical Graffiti* album until Page finally lost his rag and ordered the roadies to hide the second bass drum away – for good.

6
Cannons!

W hile the band was off the road in America, Atlantic sensibly decided the best way to keep them in the public eye was to release a single from the album, opting for 'Good Times Bad Times' backed with 'Communication Breakdown'. By the time Grant came to hear of it, several hundred promo copies (industry-only copies, not as yet distributed to general record stores) had already been pressed and mailed out to DJs all over the US, then standard practice in the run-up to a full-scale nationwide release. At the time, singles were not fashionable amongst 'serious' artists, although almost all were obliged to release and promote them heavily under the terms of their standard contracts. As Zeppelin's contract with Atlantic was far from standard, Grant was within his rights to restrain the label from releasing Zeppelin singles – an option he would exercise with force in the UK and the rest of the world.

However, America was always different. Not only was it the home of Atlantic, it was where Grant shrewdly judged Zeppelin's best chance of long-term success lay. There was also the financial side to consider. On a purely practical level, success in America would mean that, ultimately, it didn't matter whether the band caught on anywhere else in the world. Financially at least, they would be set for life. The phenomenal reaction from audiences to their first low-profile tour had been beyond even G's expectations. With a much higher profile second tour in the process of being finalised, it was crucial to try and keep the momentum going in any way possible. As a result, he not only approved Atlantic's decision to release a Zeppelin single in America, he insisted the label pay for the band to film a promotional clip of them performing it in case any TV stations wanted to use it while they were out of the country. Atlantic was happy to oblige. The result: an energy-packed film of the band miming to 'Communication Breakdown' against a white backdrop, Bonham stick-twirling as Page pretends to sing back-up vocals. Bizarrely, however, the only known broadcast of it in America wasn't until March 1995, during the ninety-minute Much-Music Led Zeppelin special, where a short clip was shown.

Everywhere else in the world, Page and Grant agreed, everything would rest on the success of the album as a stand-alone product, something no other major rock artist had ever attempted before but which Grant correctly reasoned would, in time, become a cause célèbre for the band. Moreover – and what really appealed to Jimmy – proof positive that Led Zeppelin was anything but some record company-manufactured hype. Let the critics stick that in their pipes and smoke it. Or as John Paul Jones told me in 2003, they were young and it was the era, but also, 'Page and I were fairly well experienced by then. We'd already played on a lot of hit commercial records as session musicians. We didn't benefit, in terms of celebrity or royalties, because we were very much behind the scenes. But we'd learned all about the art of compromise – in order to make a living. Which we were prepared to do, there's nothing wrong in paying the rent. But that wasn't the way I wanted to make my way in my own musical life. If I was going to join a band, it was to do music that I wanted to do and *not* compromise. The aim wasn't to be hugely successful. We felt fairly confident that we would be able to make a living by making music that we wanted to do without compromise. The fact that we were so successful couldn't have been planned. It was a lucky time as well. Album-oriented artists hardly even existed five years before we made our first record. There was the Beatles and the Beach Boys, and Dylan of course. But this was kind of a cultural step on even from that. I wasn't even listening to much pop or rock music, at the time. I had one Beatles album, *Revolver*, and *Pet Sounds* by the Beach Boys, but apart from that I was listening to jazz and soul music.'

As a result, while there would eventually be nine Zeppelin singles officially released in the US no Zeppelin single was ever officially released in the UK (with the sole exception of the 'Trampled Under-foot' seven-inch in 1975 – a much-trumpeted limited edition release, swiftly deleted). The immediate effect of the decision to block a single release in Britain was to ensure little or no radio exposure for the new band. The only Radio 1 DJ who went out of his way to regularly play any Led Zeppelin initially was John Peel, on his *Top Gear* show, aired on a Sunday afternoon and specifically directed at non-chart-oriented music, such as 'heavy' and/or 'progressive' acts like Zeppelin. Grant felt he had the solution to the lack of airplay when he arranged the first of four live sessions the band would record for the station that year, beginning with a behind-closed-doors performance at London's Playhouse Theatre on 3 March, and subsequently broadcast on the Peel show on Sunday 23 March. Radio was also a medium Grant felt he had some measure of control over (certainly more than TV where there were so few outlets for rock music in the late Sixties, unless you were a singles-oriented act), especially at the BBC, where production chief Bernie Andrews was someone he'd known since his days working with Bo Diddley, and felt he could trust. It was the start of a relationship with Radio 1 that would endure throughout the Seventies, when *Saturday Rock Show* presenter Alan 'Fluff' Freeman would always be the first British DJ to receive an advance copy of a new Zeppelin album.

Although they didn't realise it at the time, the BBC sessions were an important milestone for the band. John Paul Jones: 'We were very young and cocky at the time, very sure of ourselves. I don't think too many bands were doing the sort of improvising we were doing and the BBC, particularly the [later] *In Concert* live recordings, allowed us the scope to do that on the radio. This was in the days of restricted needle time so we were determined to make the best of every BBC radio opportunity.'

More reluctantly, Grant also allowed the band to undertake a handful of TV appearances throughout March 1969. With the advent of all-music satellite and cable channels, it's hard to imagine now how little opportunity there was in 1969 for live rock music to be broadcast on TV. Consequently, the band found itself performing at often ill-conceived productions such as the so-so guest-spot they made their television debut with, on 21 March, on a BBC1 pilot show intended as all-round family entertainment called *How Late It Is*, performing 'Communication Breakdown'. There were occasional highlights, like the thirty-five-minute live performance on Denmark's TV-Byen channel, filmed at Gladsaxe, on 17 March, where they steamed through 'Communication Breakdown', 'Dazed And Confused', 'Babe I'm Gonna Leave You' and 'How Many More Times', surrounded by a small but attentive studio audience seated cross-legged on the floor before them. The same month there was also a lip-synching performance of 'Communication Breakdown' on Swedish TV, and a somewhat self-conscious live performance on a short-lived commercial TV programme in Britain called *Supershow*, recorded in Staines on 25 March, where they noodled around on 'Dazed and Confused' for ten minutes. 'That was a mate of Jimmy's who buttonholed us into that,' said Grant. 'I wasn't that keen. I didn't even go to the filming.'

In the main, the band's attitude towards doing TV was bad right from the start. In the UK they weren't exactly spoiled for choice anyway. The only regular music show on British television in 1969 was *Top of the Pops*, a show specifically designed to reflect records in the Top 30 singles chart, which ruled Zeppelin out immediately. (Of course, a pop version of 'Whole Lotta Love' was later used as the theme tune for the programme, but Zeppelin, like The Clash, would go to their graves never having performed on the show.) Even with the arrival in 1971 of the album-oriented, late-night weekly BBC2 show, *The Old Grey Whistle Test* – filmed in a small back room studio entirely unsuited to the full-on Zep experience – they would steadfastly refuse to appear on TV. As Jones told me, 'Most other big-name groups had a lot of hit singles. Therefore, they did a lot of television and therefore had a lot of publicity, which we didn't. It was kind of our own fault, in a way. We decided we didn't have to do all of those pop shows if we didn't do singles. Some places in the early days you had to. Like Denmark, whose radio wasn't very good and that show was the only outlet they had for music like that. We were never really part of the pop scene, though. Doing pop shows on TV just wasn't us. It was never what Led Zeppelin was supposed to be about. Our thing was always playing live.' Or as Peter Grant memorably put it, 'Led Zeppelin was an in-person band.' Meaning: 'They weren't a band you saw on TV, they were the sort of band that to really appreciate you really had to see in-person, live on stage.'

However, one TV slot Grant was happy to give his blessing to was for a team to come along to the Marquee show on 28 March and film it for the BBC1 programme *Colour Me Pop*. Having talked it up to Jimmy as their best opportunity yet to get the real live experience of the band over to a huge potential audience, Grant's good mood on the night soon turned to embarrassment and then fury when nobody from the BBC bothered to show up or even have the decency to phone ahead to let him know they would not be coming. Having given it the big build-up, Grant now had the odious task of informing Page and the others he'd been let down without any explanation. He vowed then never to allow himself or Led Zeppelin to be placed at the passing whims of a TV company again, no matter how big or well known. It was a decision that would have fateful ramifications for Zeppelin's career that neither Page or Plant could have foreseen, not least the large degree of misunderstanding that would increasingly envelope their legacy as the years passed and more TV-friendly contemporaries like The Who and the Stones overtook Zeppelin in terms of both critical appraisal and historical importance, if not actual record sales. 'That's when I knew that we just wouldn't need the media,' said Grant. 'It was going to be about the fans.'

As with America, by tour's end in April the album had started to sell steadily. By the end of the year it would reach the 100,000 sales mark in Britain, reaching no. 6 in the national chart. But that was still some way off and when the band returned to America that spring they did so with a sense of relief. Where on the first tour they had been an opening act, often an afterthought not even included on the advertising for the gig, when they returned for their first show on 18 April at the New York University Jazz Festival, it was the start of twenty-nine shows in thirty-one days as co-headliners with Vanilla Fudge – the deal being whoever was biggest in any particular city going on last. With sales topping 200,000 and the album on its way to the Top 20, perception in America was now of a band on the verge of a major success.

The other change on this tour, as Robert Plant would note, was that 'people started taking an interest in the other members of the group, and not just Jimmy alone.' As the frontman, inevitably much of this new-found attention was centred on Plant himself. The fact that he hadn't written any of the material on the album was neither here nor there. Joe Cocker and Rod Stewart didn't write their own material either. And, like the latter, Plant didn't just sound great; he was tall, blond and looked good enough to eat, a veritable golden god shaking what he'd got – the perfect visual foil to Page's darker, more slender, slightly effeminate stage persona. With recognition came a resurgence of confidence, a quality Plant had never lacked in the past but was now rediscovering on a nightly basis. While Page was relieved to see his frontman visibly growing in stature on stage, off it the person who really felt the change was Richard Cole. Having already noted the singer's mixture of 'nervousness and arrogance', Cole recalls in his book that suddenly: 'He seemed intent on harassing me, at times seeming to even belittle me, making it clear who was the boss and who was the employee. When we were in hotels, he would call my room with requests like, "Richard, ring up room service and have them send up some tea and breakfast for me." I wanted to tell him to call the hotel kitchen himself. But he appeared to get a kick out of making me angry . . .'

And, of course, no-one could fail to notice Bonham's immense prowess as a drummer. While his rhythm partner, John Paul Jones, often looked and felt left out – a shadow on stage lingering by the drums while Plant and Page hogged the spotlight – no stage shadows were ever big or dark enough to contain Bonzo, not least when he went into his ever-lengthening drum solo, throwing the sticks down halfway through and pummelling the drums with his hands while cursing loudly. 'Cannons!' he would roar before bringing down the hammers. 'I yell like a bear to give it a boost,' he'd later explain. 'I like it to be like a thunderstorm.'

It was. Other musicians became particularly fascinated by Bonham's wildly untutored technique. Page told me a story about bumping into veteran drummer Ronnie Verrall on the second tour. 'Ronnie was from a previous era,' Jimmy explained, 'an amazing drummer who'd played in Ted Heath's band. Now he was playing in Tom Jones' touring band, along with Big Jim Sullivan, and we bumped into them at the Chateau Marmont. After saying hello he said, "Where's your drummer? I wanna talk to him." He wanted to know if Bonzo was using a double bass drum on "Good Times Bad Times".' When Jimmy explained that he wasn't, Ronnie was even more desperate to meet him. 'So I took him along to Bonzo and the first thing he said was, "How do you *do* that?" And I saw his face as Bonzo's showing him. Ronnie was like, "Fuck!" And here's a man who was like one of the tops, you know? I thought, wow, when you've got this level of musician paying attention to what this kid is doing, that's fabulous, you know?'

It wasn't just old jazzers paying attention, either. There was a whole new generation of rock'n'roll drummers coming along who were watching what Bonham was doing. Not least his old pal from Brum, Bill Ward, who was about to discover a similar level of success with Black Sabbath. 'Today's drumming masters can really lay down some hot shit and are full of tricks, aided by the amazing new technology that exists,' he told me. 'But I heard Bonham doing it on one bass drum when he was seventeen. The only guy I can think of who'd been laying it down close to that, before him, was Buddy Rich, who John was a big fan of. In fact, you have to really look back to the old timers to see that kind of work. Bonzo's feel and what he put into rock is so refined, he's the best model that any drummer could listen to. If you wanna know where to put a one, or you wanna know how to use syncopation then listen to the master, because Bonham was the absolute master even as a kid.' Or as Bev Bevan, another pal from Bonham's teenage days and later a star in his own right with first The Move and then the Electric Light Orchestra, later told me: 'What Bonzo could do on the bass drum with a single foot pedal was just *outrageous*. He certainly overtook me, in regards in sheer ability. It was just his over the top personality that people found hard to take sometimes.' Bevan said the fledgling Move originally considered offering the drumming job to Bonham, but thought better of it and asked Bevan instead. 'The Move didn't drink at all in their earliest days and they thought John might be too much of a loose cannon . . .'

By the time you met Robert you already knew you were good. It was at the Oldhill Plaza and he was dressed up like a poof doing the MC bit. Then he came on with his group, Crawling King Snake, in T-shirt and jeans. Group was crap and you told him so afterwards, but he was all right, actually. So you told him you'd do him a favour, offering to play with them. He looked at you and laughed and you thought he must be taking the piss and nearly chinned him. But it was obvious he could sing so you let him off just that once. One of them blokes who even looked like a proper singer and you didn't get many of them to the pound. You were both sixteen but you were always the eldest. And it was all right, doing regular spots at the Wharf, that pub in Worcestershire. You'd play with a pint of bitter at your feet, downing glass after glass. Never missed a fucking beat, though, doing things on the kit nobody else would. Hitting them cunts hard! Never mind the pretty boy singer, have some of that!

You were still living at home then, in Redditch, in the caravan at the back of your mum's shop in Astwood Bank. You'd already played with all sorts by then: Terry Webb & the Spiders, the Senators, now this lot. They'd either get rid of you for playing too loud – wankers! – or you'd get bored and just naff off. Tell 'em you had to have the drums cleaned, then once you'd got them back out of the van that would be the last they'd see of you. Ta-ta!

Crawling King Snake only lasted five minutes, too, before you got bored propping them up. Then there was the Nicky James Movement – great singer, no bloody songs – then Locomotive, then A Way of Life – another great group with no poxy songs of their own, none you liked anyway. Those were the ones you remembered anyway. Some you were in only lasted one night. Some wouldn't let you near them, had already heard of you. Dave Pegg, the bassist in A Way of Life, then later of Fairport Convention, used to say: 'If you were in a band with Bonham you knew you'd never get booked again. Often we only did the first half of the evening.' Yeah, all right, but it was like your mate Mac Poole said, you might have got the boot for being too loud or being too drunk or not turning up on time or missing a rehearsal or whatever the bollocking hell it might be. But you never got the sack for not being good enough, sticking silver foil in the bass drum to make it louder. The way you looked at it: I'm doing what I wanna do – you don't like it, fuck off.

The only thing you liked nearly as much as drumming was having a pint – or ten! It was like your other mate Jim Simpson from Locomotive always said: 'Time passed quickly in John's company.' Didn't stop the cunt sacking you though, did it? The first time, fair enough, cos you'd stood up on the drums and started taking your clothes off. But he was a gent was Jim, he'd always have you back again in the end. Especially when you'd bring him 200 Benson & Hedges or a bottle of whisky you'd nicked from the shop. Course, you'd end up helping him drink it but it's the thought that counts, innit?

Even the day before your wedding, you couldn't help but get pissed big time. You'd been to see Mac play, wearing your wedding suit, and you got on his kit and pepper-potted the skins. He yelled at you, 'Fucking leave it out!' But you'd just laughed. You never understood what the fuss was about drum kits anyway. You'd look at blokes like Mac treating theirs like gold dust and you'd pull a face. When the job was done and it was time to pack away the gear you'd just throw the bloody things off the stage and into the van. Mac said it was cos your dad had bought you your kit while

he'd had to pay for his own on the HP. Bollocks, you told him, you're only
fucking jealous.

There were some other things besides drums. Like the wife. You'd met
Pat Phillips when you were both sixteen, after a gig you'd done at the
Oldhill Plaza with Terry Webb. She'd asked you why you didn't wear a
lamé suit like Terry and you'd just looked at her and laughed. You and
your brother Mick would go out together with Pat and her sisters, Sheila,
Margaret and Beryl and it would be like Mick said, 'a party every night!'
It was only a few months later when Pat found out she was expecting, like,
and so you did the decent thing. Even though you were out of work again
at the time, you ordered a made-to-measure suit for the wedding from old
Robinson's in Redditch who allowed you to pay for it in instalments. Years
later, after you'd made your dough in Zeppelin, you paid him back good
and proper, going in and ordering a dozen different suits.

It was different when you were first wed, though. You'd set up home in
your mum and dad's fifteen-foot caravan. It was all right till the boy came
along – Jason – and the rows started about getting a proper job. That was
in July 1966. You'd do some work as a brickie for your dad but it never
lasted long. You were eighteen and there was no way in hell you were
gonna stop drumming completely. Instead, you offered to quit smoking to
help save some money. That never lasted either, though. You swore to Pat
you'd give up the drums if you had to but she said you'd be so bloody
miserable if you didn't drum you'd make life unbearable. Anyway, Dad
was always there with a few quid when you needed it.

Things got better when you moved into the council flat in Dudley – Eve's
Hill. You even got a part-time job at Osbourne's the men's clothing shop
in the high street and for a while things settled down a bit. You might have
been a tearaway but you always scrubbed up well, never went out without
a clean suit and tie on. And you never gave up on the drumming, drifting
from group to group, whoever paid the most, which is when you bumped
into Planty again . . .

The music was evolving at a faster rate on stage, too, with many of the
spontaneous jams of the first US tour now taking on a life of their
own, turning into fully fledged songs, which was just as well because
behind-the-scenes Atlantic was already pressing for a follow-up album,
ideally for release in the US that summer. G did his best to shield the
band from this extra pressure. Nevertheless, he could see the wisdom

of Ahmet's ways and encouraged Jimmy to take the band back into the studio as early as April, reconvening at Olympic in London for a few days with engineer George Chkiantz. One of the first numbers to emerge was a more elaborate, much heavier arrangement of Chicago bluesman Willie Dixon's 'You Need Love', retitled 'Whole Lotta Love', which had first surfaced on tour as part of an extended improvisation during 'As Long As I Have You'. There was also 'What Is And What Should Never Be', guitars making the most of the recent arrival of stereo with its flanged vocal effects and switching from left to right channel; and a shorter, bouncy rocker called 'Ramble On'.

'They were the first numbers written with the band in mind,' Page remembered. 'It was music more tailor-made for the units – the elements – that you've got. Like knowing that Bonzo's gonna come in hard at some point and building that in.' The songs were also the first on which Plant would be asked to contribute some of the lyrics. It had, he said, 'taken a long time, a lot of insecurity and nerves and the "I'm a failure" stuff' to produce the lyrics for the latter two. 'Whole Lotta Love' came from the tight riff Jimmy had come up with, 'Bonzo taking hold of the whole thing and making it work from the drums point of view.' Less concerned with specific lyrics, Plant's main preoccupation had been 'to try and weave the vocal in amongst it all, and it was very hard. Each song was experimentation . . .'

Their routine on the second tour was now well established. With the venues getting bigger, responsibility for road management was now split between Richard Cole and Clive Coulson. While Coulson oversaw the technical aspect of every show, taking charge of transporting and setting up the equipment, Cole took care of the band, driving them to and from airports in a rented station wagon, sorting out hotel reservations, airline tickets, gas for the car, and keeping them 'entertained' – a euphemism for getting them drunk and introducing them to willing groupies. What Ricardo wasn't so good at doing was keeping them fed or making sure they got enough sleep. Still travelling on commercial airlines, waiting in line like everybody else, this could lead to some tricky situations, most often for Plant who was still in the habit of going barefoot wherever possible, his hair now stretching down his back. Routinely spat at, yelled at and generally abused by anyone who objected to the sight of an obviously stoned hippy in their midst, instead of stepping in to save him, Cole, who was nursing a growing dislike for the cocky young singer, tended to look the other way. Plant's personal hygiene wasn't up to much either and he was often told to take a shower, wash his greasy hair and use some deodorant.

Other problems brought on by their growing popularity now included bootleggers and ticket scalpers. In Chicago, at a sold out Kinetic Circus, Grant discovered the hall manager selling tickets out of the back door and pocketing the cash. He and Cole grabbed the hapless swindler and forced him to turn out his pockets, confiscating all the spare cash. Still suspicious, they then dragged him into his office and pulled it apart until they discovered a waste bin filled with bogus ticket stubs of the wrong colour. Again, Grant and Cole forced the manager to turn over whatever illicit sums he had pocketed. Grant had seen it all before, you couldn't fool him. If God was in the detail, Grant was his winged messenger. The result was that Zeppelin would become the first major rock band that actually got to keep most of the money they made.

It wasn't just their music that was getting them noticed either. Ann Wilson, later of Heart, went with her sister Nancy to see the band at the Greenlake Aquatheater in Seattle, where they appeared on a bill with Sonny & Cher and Three Dog Night. 'The level of sexual arousal of the older girls in the audience was an eye-opener,' she told *Classic Rock*. 'This was no Three Dog Night show we were attending!' For Jimmy Page, twenty-five, single, and already highly attuned to the possibilities offered up by the permissive sexual nature of American groupies (certainly compared to their more staid British counterparts) from his years on tour with the Yardbirds, none of this was new, and he instructed Cole to offer backstage access to only the prettiest girls in the audience. But while tales abounded of Page's exploits – having Bonzo dress up as a waiter and 'serving' Jimmy on a room-service cart to a roomful of delighted young women – for the others this was a whole new world. One in which, despite their marital status, they would all take advantage of sooner or later. As Plant and Bonham's contemporary, Ozzy Osbourne, once told me, 'In them days in England, you'd still have to wine 'em and dine 'em before they'd let you near 'em. The first time bands like Sabbath and Zeppelin got to America, none of us could believe it. The chicks would just come straight up to you and go: "I wanna ball you!" None of us could resist that.'

In particular, Plant, who'd never been short of female admirers anyway, now felt overwhelmed by the attention he was getting. 'All that dour Englishness swiftly disappeared into the powder-blue, post-Summer of Love Californian sunshine, I was teleported ...' he told me. 'I was [twenty] and I was going, "Fucking hell, I want some of that and then I want some of that, and then can you get me some Charley Patton? And who's that girl over there and what's in that packet?" There was no perception of taste, no decorum.' However, when it came to groupies, the guilt he felt afterwards during the long car rides and plane journeys could be equally overwhelming. Feelings he would try to exorcise in the first song he would complete the lyrics for: a touchingly heartfelt, if somewhat disingenuous, ditty to his wife entitled 'Thank You'. 'It took a lot of ribbing and teasing to actually get him into writing,' said Jimmy, 'which was funny. And then, on the second LP, he wrote the words of "Thank You". He said: "I'd like to have a crack at this and write it for my wife." '

Even Bonham and Jones, both of whom had made a big show of turning down opportunities to frolic on the first US tour, would have their moments. As Jones later admitted, 'The touring makes you a different person. I realise that when I get home. It takes me weeks to recover after living like an animal for so long.' But while he tended to be discreet in any clandestine get-togethers with the groupie population, stories of Bonham's escapades – the drummer being egged on by Cole, with whom he had become regular 'boozing buddies' – would soon become almost as legendary as that of Page's. The most notorious being when Cole encouraged him to have sex with a notorious LA groupie known as the Dog Act, after her habit of always bringing her Great Dane with her to the hotel. Having tried and failed to get the Great Dane to perform cunnilingus on the girl by dangling pieces of fried bacon from her vagina, Cole dragged a drunken Bonham in to take the dog's place. As Cole would later tell writer Stephen Davis, 'So Bonzo's in there fucking her, and I swear he says to me, "How am I doing?" I said, "You're doing fine.". Then Grant walks in with this giant industrial-sized can of baked beans and dumped it all over Bonzo and the girl. Then he opened a bottle of champagne and sprayed them.'

As these youthful high-jinks are typical of the sort of thing that rock musicians, bored on the road and far from home, indulge in, the fact that at the same time as a naked Bonzo was having cold beans poured over him, Jimmy Page was in his room having himself photographed covered in offal, which another famous groupie, the GTO Miss Cinderella, pretended to eat off him, should shock no-one. Years later, however, when such incidents were related in awed tones in such laughingly prudish tomes as *Hammer of the Gods*, the shock they caused was enough to add several layers to the Zeppelin myth. In reality, of course, Elvis and the Beatles had been up to much worse long before Zeppelin crash-landed in America. Even in the mid-Fifties, before the so-called sexual revolution, Presley's former Memphis Mafia crony, Lamar Fike, told *Mojo*, 'Elvis got more ass than a toilet seat. Six girls in the room at one time ... when we left places it took the National Guard to clean things up.' Or as John Lennon later told Jann Wenner about the Beatles' on the road adventures: 'If you could get on our tours, you were *in*. Just think of [Fellini's film] *Satyricon*. Wherever we were there was always a whole scene going on. [Hotel rooms] full of junk and whores and fuck knows what.'

Even if the general public would remain ignorant of such antics a while longer, the fantasy of the rock star living the life of hedonistic abandon as some sort of entitlement had already been well established; an idea enhanced by such provocative images as that of a roomful of naked women used for the cover photo of Hendrix's *Electric Ladyland* album, or the famous bacchanal portrait photo of the Stones taken by Michael Joseph for the inside of the *Beggars Banquet* album, both released at the tail end of 1968. The new album-buying rock audience itself was hardly innocent, with movies of the period such as *Blow Out*, *Easy Rider* and, later, *Performance*, *Woodstock*, *Zabriske Point*, even latter-day Beatles films such as the acid-influenced *Yellow Submarine* and the downered-out ambience of *Let It Be* clearly reflecting the new sex-and-drugs consciousness evident in all aspects of the Sixties rock experience, certainly post-summer of love.

The GTOs were half-a-dozen groupie friends who became famous through the patronage of Frank Zappa, who had the idea of turning them into an actual group that would record for his own independent label, the aptly named Bizarre Records. GTO stood for many things: Girls Together Outrageously, Girls Together Only, Girls Together Occasionally, Girls Together Often, and any number of similar acronyms. There was Miss Cinderella, Miss Christine, Miss Pamela, Miss Mercy, and Miss Lucy (plus, at different intervals, Miss Sandra and/or

Sparky). Having proved themselves by appearing on stage at several Mothers of Invention shows as dancers and/or backing vocalists, in November 1968 Zappa put them on a weekly retainer of $35 each. As Alice Cooper, another notable signing to Zappa's label, later recalled in his autobiography, *Me, Alice*, the GTOs 'were more of a mixed-media event than musicians. People just got off on them. They were a trip to be with . . .'

As even an unashamed letch like the brutish Cole would acknow-ledge, groupies played an important role in the well-being of most working rock bands in America in the late Sixties. 'I don't think you will ever find an English musician who would ever put down those girls who were called groupies, cos those girls were not sluts or slags or whatever. They fucking saved my arse as far as patience goes, cos you're talking about twenty-year-old guys away from home. The girls took care of them and were like a second home. You could trust them. They wouldn't steal from you.' It wasn't just in Los Angeles or New York that the tribes gathered, either. 'There were quite a few of them,' Plant recalled with a smile, 'Miss Murphy, The Butter Queen, Little Rock Connie from Arkansas. Some of them are still around, too – but now they're teachers and lawyers.'

In Los Angeles, in 1969, there was no groupie more highly thought of or lusted after than the prettiest and best known of the GTOs, Pamela Ann Miller, aka Miss Pamela, aka Pamela Des Barres (as she became better-known in the mid-Seventies after marrying rock singer Michael Des Barres). Miss P, as she was also known, would sometimes babysit for the Zappas, make handmade shirts for her boyfriends, and was, she said, 'too romantic for one-night stands'. If she was with you, it was 'for the whole tour – at least, locally!'

Remembered by Alice Cooper as 'a smiling open-faced girl who looked like Ginger Rogers' with her strawberry blonde hair, freckles and goofy, flower-child smile, Miss Pamela was the epitome of the California Girl the Beach Boys had earlier eulogised. Although still only twenty years old, she already had a long history of 'hanging out' with rock stars before she met Jimmy Page, including Iron Butterfly singer Darryl De Loach, Jim Morrison, Noel Redding of the Jimi Hendrix Experience, Chris Hillman of the Byrds and actor-turned-country rock singer Brandon de Wilde. She had also met and spent time with the Jeff Beck Group.

When Zeppelin returned to LA to perform again at the Whisky A Go Go on 29 April, Miss Pamela was there. She later recalled how her friend and fellow groupie, Cynthia Plastercaster (of the Plastercasters of Chicago, famous for casting rock stars' penises in plaster), had warned her that 'the music was supposed to be fantastic, but they were supposed to be really dangerous guys, and you'd better stay away from them'. But she went anyway with fellow GTO Miss Mercy. Page looked frail and helpless, she thought, 'like Sarah Bernhardt.' Instantly smitten by what she perceived to be the guitarist's 'demure, almost feminine' persona, in her subsequent memoir, *I'm With The Band*, she breathlessly recalls Page wearing a pink velvet suit on stage, 'his long black curls stuck damply to his pink velvet cheeks. At the end of the set he collapsed to the floor, and was carried up the stairs by two roadies, one of them stopping to retrieve Jimmy's cherry-red patent-leather slipper.'

After the show, there was a party held for the band at LA's then most fashionable hang-out, a club called Thee Charming Experience, where Miss Pamela watched Zeppelin 'carousing at the darkest table at the back'. She was 'very proud not to know them' as she watched Richard Cole 'carrying a young girl around upside down, her high heels flailing in the air, panties spinning around one ankle. He had his face buried in her crotch and she was hanging on to his knees for dear life, her red mouth open wide in a scream that no-one could hear. It was hard to tell if she was enjoying herself or living a nightmare. Someone else was getting it right on the table.' Nevertheless, she found it hard to keep her eyes from straying towards Jimmy, who 'sat apart from it all, observing the scene as if he had imagined it: overseer, creator, impossibly gorgeous pop star'. Appalled, she fled the scene, despite having 'sticky thighs'. But she had been noticed and when the band next returned to LA, Page would send out his bloodhound, Cole, to find her . . .

While the band could not be held responsible for every strange or disturbing thing that happened to them out on the road (for example, when they arrived early one morning in Detroit, having flown over-night, they were greeted by the gruesome sight of a murdered corpse being carried out on a stretcher, a thick pool of blackened blood on the lobby floor where the victim had been gunned down), they clearly revelled in the chaos their mere presence seemed to cause everywhere they went. It was also in Detroit that *Life* magazine journalist Ellen Sander joined the tour. Sander had originally wanted to cover The Who, also touring the US that summer, but that had fallen through and so a story on the Zeppelin tour was hurriedly installed to replace it. It was her first assignment for *Life* and she was thoroughly looking forward to it, if a little disappointed not to be covering the much better-known Who. Noting her enthusiasm, Cole immediately organised a betting pool amongst the road crew on which member of the band would fuck her first.

For her part, Sander would characterise them accurately enough. Page was 'ethereal, effeminate, pale and frail'. Plant was 'handsome in an obscenely rugged way'. Bonzo 'played ferocious drums, often shirtless and sweating, like some gorilla on a rampage'. Jones was the one who 'held the whole thing together and stayed in the shadows'. She concluded that the band 'had that fire and musicianship going for them and a big burst of incentive; this time around, on their second tour, from the very beginning, they were almost stars'. Sander spent most of her time on tour with Page, not sleeping with him, as the boorish Cole had predicted, but quizzing him about the abuse she observed him dishing out to groupies. She quotes him: 'Girls come around and pose like starlets, teasing and acting haughty. If you humiliate them a bit, they tend to come on all right after that. Everyone knows what they come for.'

At the end of the tour, when Sander went to the dressing room to say goodbye, she claimed that: 'Two members of the group attacked me. Shrieking and grabbing at my clothes, totally over the edge.' Bonzo came at her first, she said, followed by 'a couple more ... all these hands on me, all these big guys'. Unable to identify them from the mêlée, it's not clear if these were actual members of the band or roadies. Terrified she was going to be raped, Sander says she 'fought them off until Peter Grant rescued me, but not before they managed to tear my dress down the back'. Furious at the offence, in retaliation Sander refused to write the planned *Life* article, thus denying the band what might have been important, perception-altering publicity on the grand scale later enjoyed by the Stones. She did, however, make her feelings felt in a subsequent book, *Trips*, in which she concluded: 'If you walk inside the cages at the zoo, you get to see the animals close up, stroke the captive pelts and mingle with the energy behind the mystique. You also get to smell the shit first-hand.'

When asked some years later about Sander's damning account of her experiences on tour with him, Page admitted, 'That's not a false picture,' adding only: 'But that side of touring isn't the be all and end all. The worst part is the period of waiting before going on. I always get very edgy, not knowing what to do with myself. It's the build-up where you reach a point almost like self-hypnosis. There's a climax at the end of the show and the audience goes away, but you're still buzzing and you don't really come down. That's when you get a sort of restlessness and insomnia, but it doesn't bother you too much if there's a creative stream coming through. Maybe it's necessary to that creative stream. What's bad is that it's not always a release. You build yourself to that pitch and the release doesn't come. There are different ways of releasing that surplus adrenalin. You can smash up hotel rooms – it can get to that state. I think we've learnt to come to terms with it. I've learnt to enjoy it and achieve something creative from it too.'

Ultimately, Led Zeppelin were neither saints nor sinners, certainly not in the context of rock history where outrageous offstage high-jinks and hyper-sexual-activity had been the norm for decades. They were merely one more cast of colourful characters on an already tilted stage. A fact Pamela Des Barres herself now vouchsafes: 'It wasn't just them. The Who were doing that stuff, and the Hendrix boys.' Although, as she adds: 'Zeppelin were a little extreme, they got a little rude sometimes. The girls would do anything to get near them and they sort of took advantage of that.'

Fucking groups, you'd known what they were like for a long time now. They'd always been the same, from the time you bought your first mini-bus when you were twenty-five and used it to drive the Shadows to gigs, to when you met Don Arden and he had you driving all these American cunts around on the package shows. The Everly Brothers, Little Richard, Brian Hyland, Chuck Berry ... didn't matter who they were, they all wanted something, expected you or someone else to provide it. When Chuck Berry complained his fee was three shillings and eleven pence short, he refused to go on until someone gave him the money. The crowd was going berserk but you only had to look at his little slit eyes to know the cunt meant it. You were only the driver but you realised that if someone didn't do something there would be a fucking riot. So you walked over to the cigarette machine, smashed it open and counted out the change until you had three shillings and eleven pence. Then gave it to him. Didn't even say thank you, just picked up his guitar and walked on . . .

Even when you started road managing for Don in '63, looking after Bo Diddley and Little Richard, it was the same old story. Bo was all right, give him his drink and his 'pretty womens' and let him get on with it. But Richard . . . Christ almighty! You needed eyes in the back of your arse. Except then you'd see all of them on the bed together in the morning, six or seven of 'em, that silly cunt sat there in the middle of it all reading his Bible. Punters loved him, though. You remembered how you'd had to flatten them sometimes to keep them off him. For their own good. They hadn't seen what you'd seen.

You learnt a lot from working with Don, though. He didn't take any shit off anybody. He'd go in hard, wallop, don't bother asking questions afterwards. He was smart, too, showed you how a tough reputation could be almost as effective as a good hiding. As Don used to say: 'If you don't like somebody, let 'em know from the first bell, baby.' Bloody good advice, you never forgot it. The other thing Don taught you was to always have a healthy respect for cash. That wad of notes at the end of the night that would go into your back pocket and stay there. Accept no substitute, not if you knew what was good for you.

Then came Gene Vincent. Gene and his gammy leg, standing there in the leathers Don bought him, looking at you like it was all your fault. Gene and his gammy leg and his whisky bottle and his gun and his wife and his girlfriends and all the other bloody palaver. Ladies and gentlemen – the King of Rock'n'Roll! What a cunt, made your life a fucking misery. But so good on stage, even you couldn't help look up to him when he was on form. And the crowds, they fucking loved him, couldn't get enough of the silly, drunken, curly-haired, miserable, moaning cunt. Screaming for bourbon on a Sunday afternoon in Doncaster. Screaming that he couldn't go on without it. You knew what to do. Grab the cunt by the throat and push him out there. Or if he was too pissed already, stick a tripod up the back of his jacket and strap him with gaffer-tape to the mike stand, wait for him to fall over and tell everyone he's suffering from exhaustion, poor fucking lamb. Sorry, no, no money back, he'd started the show, hadn't he?

*Not the boy's fault he's unwell. An old Don trick and a fucking good
one ...*

By the beginning of May, when the album had reached no. 10 (its
highest chart position), the vibe was now starting to spread back to
Britain, with the *NME*'s US correspondent June Harris reporting: 'The
biggest happening of the 1969 heavy rock scene is Led Zeppelin.'
Reaction to the group's latest American tour, she said, 'has not only
been incredible, it's been nothing short of sensational'. When, on 25
May, they appeared on the same bill as the Jimi Hendrix Experience
at the Santa Clara Pop Festival, in San Jose, Jimi told Bonzo, 'Boy,
you've got a right foot like a rabbit!' However, reviews in the US could
still be sniffy. Reporting on the final shows of the tour, two nights at
the Fillmore East in New York on 30 and 31 May, *Variety* ignored the
audience who were literally banging their heads on the stage and
instead wrote of the band's 'obsession with power, volume and melodramatic theatrics ... forsaking their music sense for the sheer power
that entices their predominantly juvenile audience.' Many of the band's
peers couldn't resist having a dig, too. Pete Townshend turned his
considerable nose up at 'solo-guitar-based groups' that did better in
America than in Britain. Keith Richards said Plant's voice 'started to
get on my nerves'. Even Eric Clapton said he thought Zeppelin were
'unnecessarily loud'.

After the second show, Atlantic held a party for them at the Plaza
Hotel in New York, where they were presented with their first gold
record for *Led Zeppelin*. Page could barely contain his delight. Such
sudden success, less than a year after forming the band, 'came as a
massive surprise – to be perfectly truthful, the shock didn't hit me
until a number of years later. We were touring until the day when we
were presented with a gold record. I thought, "My goodness! A gold
record!"' An occasion somewhat marred by the fact that it was here
they were informed they would need to pull their fingers out and get
the second album finished pronto if they wanted to catch the pre-
Christmas market that year. Stung into action, Jimmy ordered the
band back to the studio straight after the party.

While Page ploughed on in the studio with engineer Eddie Kramer,
seemingly oblivious, the studio workaholic, the others yearned simply
to go home. Bonzo was morose and homesick, Plant was loudly pro-

claiming to anyone who would listen how much he missed his wife, while Jonesy kept his head down as usual and said nothing. To try and keep their spirits up, Grant took the opportunity over the next few days to constantly remind them how well they were now doing. Not only were they in the US Top 10, they were making money from the tour. The first jaunt had cost them. This time around, with their nightly fees swinging from $5,000 to $15,000, they would be flying home quids in, he said. Even after all the agents, lawyers, accountants, roadies, hotels and travel expenses had been paid, they would be looking at splitting approximately $150,000 between them. And that was nothing, Grant said, compared to what they would make next time out. The third tour, already being set up, would pull in nearly half-a-million dollars, he announced – and for far fewer shows! Everything would be better soon, said G, the band nodding their heads resignedly.

In fact, the band had already begun serious work on the second album when they arrived back in Los Angeles in April, and spent their days off recording at A&M Studios. It was a pattern that would be repeated throughout the tour, studio-hopping whenever a small break in their itinerary allowed: as well as A&M, both Mystic and Mirror Studios were utilised in LA, as were A&R, Juggy Sound and Mayfair Studios in New York, plus a one-off stop at an eight-track 'hut in Vancouver' where Jimmy took Robert in to lay down some vocal overdubs and harmonica – a set-up so small they didn't even have headphones for the singer to wear.

Back in London in June, they flitted between engagements – miming 'Communication Breakdown' and 'Dazed And Confused' in Paris for a French TV show called *Tous En Scene*, which Grant said Page only agreed to 'so he could meet Brigitte Bardot' who never showed up anyway, and a couple more sessions for BBC radio, where the chief interest lay in an improvised rendition of 'Travelling Riverside Blues'. 'We were so organic at the time,' said Jimmy, 'that we used to make stuff up [on the spot].' Between times, sessions were booked at Morgan Studios, where they finished off 'Ramble On' and hurriedly recorded two additional filler tracks: 'Living Loving Maid (She's Just A Woman)', a lightweight, almost country-pop song about a groupie with 'a purple umbrella and fifty cent hat' dashed off by Jimmy and Robert as live in the studio, and 'We're Gonna Groove', an old Ben E. King number and one of the covers they routinely played live. It was hardly ideal – in the end they would use only one of the new Morgan tracks – but by then Atlantic was pressing hard for new product. So on-the-hoof were the recording sessions, in fact, that even the always self-confident Page was given to moments of private self-doubt. Seeing this, Jerry Wexler had at one point tried to smooth him out, telling him over and over that the new album was going to be 'a masterpiece'. Wexler wasn't just easing his pain, either. He firmly believed it to be 'the best white blues I have ever heard' – and that was after only hearing three tracks.

All of which only partially reassured the perfectionist guitarist, who worried that the second album may also be too different from the first, that they had 'overstepped the mark'. On the other hand, he was determined to show what he could do. As he told writer Ritchie Yorke during an earlier session in New York: 'Too many groups sit back after the first album, and the second one is a down trip. I want every album to reach out further – that's the whole point.' *Led Zeppelin II* certainly reached out further than its patchwork predecessor. Still essentially blues-, rock- and folk-based, this melded those forms into what, in retrospect, would become the foundation of a whole new genre in popular music: heavy metal; a reductionism that would eventually come to haunt the band that inadvertently did more than anyone to ultimately define its meaning.

Comprised of material built on ideas begun in motel rooms, tinkered with at soundchecks and rehearsals, and thrown into the creative furnace of live improvisations, *Led Zeppelin II*, as Page had already decided it would be called, was to become the speed-of-night Seventies road album *par excellence*, the sheer exuberance of the band at that time captured in the grooves which, forty years later, still virtually crackle with energy. The sound, although produced in so many different places, obtained a formidable three-dimensional quality unlike any achieved on record before – a feat made all the more remarkable considering the scattershot approach to its creation. The American engineer on the sessions, Eddie Kramer, who had worked the previous year with Hendrix on *Electric Ladyland*, recalled 'scrounging' recording time in any studio he could. Some of Jimmy's guitar solos were taped in hallways, he said. The end results of which would be mixed in just two days at A&R Studios in New York 'on the most primitive console you could imagine'.

And yet somehow it worked. As well as proving an invaluable ally in procuring the band studio time, Page credits Kramer with helping construct the famous psychedelic middle-section of 'Whole Lotta Love', in which Plant's howling lust-maddened vocal-improvs are mixed with an other-worldly cacophony of special effects, from the backwards echo of the slide guitar to the grinding sound of a steel mill, orgasming women, even a napalm-bomb explosion, and above it all, the eerie whining of Jimmy's recently acquired theremin, like something out of an old black-and-white horror movie. 'We already had a lot of the sounds on tape,' said Page, 'but [Kramer's] knowledge of low-frequency oscillation helped complete the effect. If he hadn't known how to do that, I would have had to try for something else.' For his part, Kramer compared working with Page to working with Hendrix. 'They were both very clear about what they wanted in the studio,' he later recalled. 'They also had a very clear vision and laser-like concentration in the studio – absolute laser-like concentration. It was amazing.'

As a result, while the guitarist may have had his reservations at the time about the ad-hoc way in which the second Zeppelin album came together – his famous ecstatically rendered solo, for example, on 'Heartbreaker', was 'an afterthought', recorded separately in a different studio to the rest of the song and 'sort of slotted in the middle' – even he now agrees the material as a whole displays a remarkable strength and consistency the band would rarely match in future recordings. This was Led Zeppelin at their most blood-and-guts elemental; rock music as bodily function. From the audible gasp with which Plant prefaces the monumental opening track, 'Whole Lotta Love', to the sinewy acoustic and harmonised electric guitars Page charms out of the speakers like snakes to transform otherwise straightforward rock moments like 'Ramble On' and 'What Is And What Should Never Be' into unbelievably subtle vessels of musical mayhem; to the stalking riffs of bones-into-dust headbangers like 'Heartbreaker' and 'Bring It On Home'; to Robert Plant purloining Robert Johnson in 'The Lemon Song' in what would become one of the most infamously derided yet joyously insouciant Zeppelin mission statements: 'I want you to squeeze my lemon ... till the juice runs down my leg ...' Then pretending to aim higher in 'Ramble On' and its 'days of old' Tolkien-esque references to 'the darkest depths of Mordor' where 'Gollum and

the evil one' slip away with his 'girl so fair'. Or, best of all, the
unflinchingly straight face with which he addresses his wife in the
almost unbearably sentimental 'Thank You', all chiming 12-string
guitars, melodramatic drums and swirling-fog organ. 'That was when
[Robert] began to come through as a lyricist,' Page told me. 'I'd always
hoped that he would.'

All trademark Zeppelin moments, all destined to become cornerstones in rock history; and all rooted in the same brooding, squalling
blues as white English contemporaries such as Savoy Brown, Chicken
Shack and early Fleetwood Mac, but reinvigorated with its original
down-and-dirty, walking-with-the-devil essence. Unlike the earnest
bluesologists then frequenting London's clubland, this was no respectful homage to the past. This was the primeval sex music of the future.
What Robert Plant would later characterise as 'a much more carnal
approach to the music and quite flamboyant'.

Even the obvious filler – and at 2 mins 39 secs, the shortest track on
an album with no real need for such things – 'Living Loving Maid
(She's Just A Woman)', which none of the band liked, or indeed would
ever perform live (although Plant would resurrect a version of it for a
solo tour in 1990), came straight from the top drawer; the sort of
direct hit to the body groups like T. Rex and Thin Lizzy would build
whole careers around in the decade to come.

The only real weak spot was the bone thrown to Bonham in the
shape of 'Moby Dick' – an exercise Page concocted from various
different takes in the studio in order to showcase Bonzo's usual drum
solo, known from the second US tour on, when it first began to feature
prominently in the set as 'Pat's Delight'. Derived from a riff Jimmy
had developed while playing a 'sleepy' John Estes song called 'The
Girl I Love She Got Long Wavy Hair', which the band performed
regularly throughout 1969, although drum solos were now becoming
de rigueur at rock gigs, only Cream had ever committed what was
essentially a drum solo as a track on one of their albums. A highly
condensed – 2 mins 58 secs of impressive percussive nous sandwiched
between some plodding riffage from Page and Jones – version of the
real thing, unlike its live counterpart which was a genuinely thrilling
spectacle, it's hardly a must-have moment. It's soon forgotten, though,
as it segues into the album's closing track and perhaps its best moment,
'Bring It On Home', based on the song of the same name that Willie

Dixon had written for Sonny Boy Williamson, but lifted onto a much higher musical plain by Page's own blazing riff and Bonham's shock-and-awe drums, both of which belonged only to Zeppelin.

The only other faults on an album that still sounds as cutting-edge today as it did forty years ago were, again, to do with how much of the material derives from other, deliberately uncredited sources. The most famous example being 'Whole Lotta Love', which, on closer examination, turns out to be one of Zeppelin's most thrillingly un-original moments ever. Not only is the basis of the song – certainly lyrically – taken from Muddy Waters's version of Willie Dixon's 'You Need Love', as would surface in 1987, when a belated plagiarism suit filed by Dixon's estate was settled out of court, but even the so-called 'new' arrangement they imbue it with is partially lifted from the Small Faces, who used to encore with their own highly energised version of 'You Need Love' in the mid-Sixties.

Recorded for their debut 1966 album where it was credited to vocalist Steve Marriott and bassist Ronnie Lane, former Small Faces' keyboardist Ian McLagan later admitted it was something 'we stole – or at least, the chorus was a steal. It was a nick Steve used to do because that's what was influencing him.' Zeppelin's version would also be 'a steal', except this time credited to Page, Plant, Jones and Bonham. There's no mistaking the similarity between the ferocious energy of Zeppelin's version and that of the Small Faces, not least in Plant's vocal phrasing that sounds uncannily like Marriott's. So much so, the latter would later claim that Plant had copied his vocals. 'We did a gig with The Yardbirds,' Marriott says in Paolo Hewitt's 1995 biography of the band. 'Jimmy Page asked me what that number was we did ... I said, "It's a Muddy Waters thing".' Plant 'used to come to the gigs whenever we played in Kidderminster or Stourbridge.' As a result, when Plant came to record 'Whole Lotta Love', 'he sang it the same, phrased it the same, even the stops at the end were the same ...'

Even the most memorable part of the song, that punchy B-D, B-D-E riff, was derived from the original guitar refrain of the Muddy Waters original. Nevertheless, Page insisted, 'As far as my end of it goes, I always tried to bring something fresh to anything that I used. I always made sure to come up with some variation. I think in most cases you would never know what the original source could be.

Maybe not in every case, but in most cases.' And while he does
laughingly concede that, 'We did, however, take some liberties,' he
now puts most of the blame for the subsequent plagiarism charges
down to Plant, saying that 'most of the comparisons rest on the
lyrics. And Robert was supposed to change the lyrics, and he didn't
always do that, which is what brought on most of our grief. They
couldn't get us on the guitar parts or the music, but they nailed us
on the lyrics.'

However, speaking in 1985, Plant seemed keen to shove the blame
back in Page's direction, when he joked: 'When we ripped it off, I said
to Jimmy, "Hey, that's not our song." And he said, "Shut up and keep
walking."' Five years later, he argued that in their appropriation of old
blues songs, Zeppelin was merely acting in the tradition of the form.
Nobody really knew where the songs came from originally. 'If you read
that book *Deep Blues* by Robert Palmer, you'll see that we did what
everybody else was doing. When Robert Johnson was doing "Preaching
Blues", he was really taking Son House's "Preacher's Blues" and remod-
elling it.'

Whichever way you looked at it though, there was no mistaking the
'origins' of tracks like 'The Lemon Song' or 'Bring It On Home'.
Musically, 'The Lemon Song' derived directly from Howlin' Wolf's
'Killing Floor', with flashes of Albert King's 'Crosscut Saw', while its
lemon-squeezing lyrical refrain also comes direct from source, in this
case Robert Johnson's 'Travelling Riverside Blues'. Again, however, the
songwriting credit given on the sleeve is shared squarely amongst the
four band members with no mention of either Chester Burnett (aka
Howlin' Wolf) or Robert Johnson. Over thirty years after his death,
whereas the work of the latter is now considered public domain, in
the early Seventies, Burnett's publishers Arc Music would sue Zeppelin
for copyright infringement; a suit the band was prepared to settle out
of court (with future pressings containing a co-songwriting credit for
Burnett). Similarly, 'Bring It On Home', which was based on an old
Sonny Boy Williamson track written by Willie Dixon but credited
simply to Page and Plant, was also later settled out of court at the same
time as the action against the band for 'Whole Lotta Love', with
Dixon also awarded co-songwriting credits for both songs on all future
Zeppelin products. Once again, though, Page was unrepentant. 'The
thing with "Bring It On Home", Christ, there's only a tiny bit taken

from Sonny Boy Williamson's version and we threw that in as a tribute to him.'

As Salvador Dali – another arch 'borrower' – once famously suggested, genius may steal where talent borrows, but Jimmy Page would continue to be more brazen about it than most. Ultimately, however, even taking into account the obvious plagiarisms in the songwriting, *Led Zeppelin II* was Page's record – easily his finest moment as a guitarist yet, certainly his most powerful statement as a producer, and a total vindication of his ambition to take the Yardbirds into truly new territory, even though he ended up having to do it alone with an entirely different line-up. As John Paul Jones was happy to vouchsafe, 'Any tribute [that] flows in must go to Jimmy.'

'The goal was synaesthesia,' Page said, 'creating pictures with sound.' Hendrix may have been the greatest guitarist ever, the Beatles the world's best songwriters and Dylan rock's most profound poet, but the panoply of gifts Jimmy Page brought to bear on *Led Zeppelin II* as producer, guitarist, songwriter and – not to be understated, band leader and musical director – proved him to be the ultimate sonic sorcerer. Speaking to me nearly four decades later, the pride in his voice was still there. 'You've got things like the light and shade aspect of "Ramble On" where I already know that if Bonzo's gonna come in and kick-in a chorus, that that's the way to have this song. And to be light on "What Is And What Should Never Be" then kick-in to the chorus. Because that's the way you're gonna get this dynamic. So all of these things are now actually designed, if you like, for [the band]. Having worked on the road with the band, it was starting to permeate into your inner being. I used to write stuff and hear Robert singing, and I knew the kind of thing John would be able to apply to it. His drumming on "Whole Lotta Love", for example, is just fantastic.'

He also stressed how 'ambient' the whole sound is. It's true. As he said, there is a certain way the band 'moved the air about the room' on those sessions that is clearly evident in the recording. For example, 'the middle part of "Whole Lotta Love", which is sort of what psychedelia would have been if they could have got there. That's what it is. It's also very organic. We always played together, that was an essential part of the overall thing: the acoustics of the room and how things are bouncing about. That was really important.'

Not that Page or the rest of the band would have much time to sit back and consider the enormity of what they had just done. Still only halfway through what would be the busiest year of their lives, the flight of the Zeppelin had only just begun.

7

Cracking the Whip

Atlantic had wanted the second Zeppelin album out in America by the summer and had fretted that momentum would be lost when Jimmy Page insisted on tinkering with the mix, pushing its release back to the autumn. But by the time *Led Zeppelin II* was finally made available on 22 October 1969, the band was already well on its way to becoming the biggest in the world.

In many ways, it might be said that Seventies-style rock arrived three months early with the release of *Led Zeppelin II*. With advance orders of 500,000 in the US, it debuted in the Top 40 at no. 25 in its second week of release. Two weeks later it was no. 2. Before the year was out, it was the biggest-selling album in America, deposing not only the final Beatles album, *Abbey Road*, from no. 1 but keeping the Stones' *Let It Bleed* from the top spot. Along with Simon and Garfunkel's *Bridge Over Troubled Water*, these were the three albums that summarised the epoch. *Led Zeppelin II* was also epochal, but not for the same reasons. The second Zeppelin album was the beginning of a brand new era. Released ten days later in the UK, it was a similar story, entering the chart on 8 November, where it began an unbroken 138-week residency, eventually climbing to no. 1 in February 1970. Within six months it had sold nearly five million copies worldwide. This at a time when a tenth of that figure was considered a major hit for most top-drawer artists.

Released a week after their fourth US tour began with a stunning brace of shows at New York's Carnegie Hall (the first rock shows there since the venue had banned the Stones after a riotous performance five years before), clearly a new order had arrived and with it a whole new chapter for the four Zeppelin members. 'Our whole lives changed, particularly me and Bonzo's,' Plant later told me. 'It was such a sudden change we weren't quite sure how to handle it. Bonzo was still in a council flat in Dudley, and he had a Rolls Royce at the bottom of the lift. Somebody keyed it one day and he couldn't understand why. It's a bit like that thing in *The Commitments* with the bloke trying to get a horse into the lift. It was a bit like that in parts of the Black Country, and still is.'

Chris Welch, who was at Carnegie Hall, remembers 'every musician that happened to be in town standing at the side of the stage during the show. I also remember the audience. It was the first time I had ever seen a New York audience and I couldn't believe how wild and noisy they were. They literally went completely mad the moment the band came on.' There was no party, as such, afterwards, 'just lots of drinking back at the hotel'. Although somebody in the band did send over some prostitutes with whips to his hotel room in the small hours. 'There was a lot of sniggering over breakfast the next morning as they awaited my reaction. But I just sent them away. I was a bit shocked actually.'

Reviews of *Led Zeppelin II* were generally supportive. In Britain, *Time Out* praised the album for being 'much looser than the group's first', adding that it was 'worth buying anyway for Plant's tortured voice and Page's guitar, which at times sounds as disturbing as car tyres screaming to a crash'. *Disc & Music Echo* pointed out that, 'It's difficult to capture stage excitement on record, but *Led Zeppelin II* comes very near to it.' Even *Rolling Stone* approved – at least superficially – calling it 'one fucking heavyweight of an album!' However, it soon became apparent again that John Mendelssohn was having difficulty maintaining a straight face. 'Who can deny that Jimmy Page is the absolute number-one heaviest white blues guitarist between 5'4' and 5'8' in the world??' he asked sarcastically. Adding, pointedly, that he'd been listening to the album 'on some heavy Vietnamese weed . . . mescaline, some old Romilar, novocaine, and ground up Fusion, and it was just as mind-boggling as before'. Followed by the *coup de grâce*, 'I must admit I haven't listened to it straight yet – I don't think a group this heavy is best enjoyed that way.' Ultimately, the message remained the same: two years after the Beatles had sung beatifically about only needing love here were the brutish Zeppelin threatening to give every inch of their love to anyone who came near enough for them to do so. The contrast could not have been starker. While the Beatles addressed us from somewhere up there in the cloudless blue sky; Led Zeppelin was the sound of voices writhing in the murky sprawl below; the black pieces on the chessboard to the Beatles' white.

Fortunately for the band, their fans' enthusiasm remained immune to such cartoonish characterisations. Elemental to its core, the music on *Led Zeppelin II* simply defied analysis, as gloriously impervious to criticism as the sound of a thunderclap on a stormy night. As Jimmy boasted in an interview just before the album came out: 'There is a tendency to return to some of the early rock'n'roll songs now almost as a reaction against the heavy, intellectual and analytical forms rock has been taking. It's very understandable to me – we play it when the mood takes us. It's the perfect balance – so simple. You can't read anything but what there is into songs like "I've Got A Woman". Some music has just got a little too complicated for the public.'

Known to fans affectionately as the Brown Bomber due to its sepia-tinted cover, it was essentially the *Led Zeppelin* sleeve in jaundiced silhouette. British designer David Juniper had just a few days to come up with a rough idea for it. Given nothing to work on, just told to come up with something 'interesting,' he hit upon the idea of doctoring a period photo of the Jasta Division of the German Luftwaffe, which had launched the zeppelins that bombed Britain during the First World War. Hand-tinting the photo, he crudely cut the four band members' faces from already much-used promotional shots and glued them onto the faces of four of the Jasta pilots. Page suggested Juniper also cut out headshots of Grant, Cole and Blind Willie Johnson and glue them onto four of the other pilots, as well as the blonde actress Glynis Johns, who had played the children's mother in the film *Mary Poppins*. It's since been assumed this was Page's joke on engineer Glyn Johns, who did not work on the album, although his younger brother Andy did. Others speculate it may have had something to do with the suggestion that the original Mary Poppins books by P.L. Travers mix fantasy with real-life magical events such as inanimate objects coming to life. Neither suggestion, however, seems likely on its own. What is now more mysterious is that close-ups of the cover shot, provided for this book by Juniper, naming each figure, look nothing like who they're supposed to – certainly not Cole or Grant, while the Blind Willie Johnson face is identified by the designer now as that of Miles Davis, though again it looks nothing like him.

As if to underline the band's own increasing sense of self-worth, the inside of the original gatefold sleeve – 'my entire idea,' says Juniper now – opened out to show a spotlight-swathed golden airship hovering over an ancient acropolis-type structure, beneath which are four coffin-like columns each bearing a band member's name. Again, the deeper significance of this has never been established, though themes of Ascensionism seem clear – the idea that a melding of science and religion is the next evolutionary step past the 'natural' human condition into immortality and beyond; the pyramid surmounted by a sun (see also the Masonic seal on the US dollar bill). Not that the album's most ardent supporters would necessarily have gotten all that from it, the inside of the sleeve seen mainly as a portable tray on which to roll joints. The rest was just pretty patterns, man . . .

Art college was all right. There were certainly a lot of nice birds there. And some crazy cats too. And you liked painting and drawing and mucking around all day. It could never really beat playing the guitar, though. You noticed that even the geezers the girls congregated around, the ones that could really paint and came on like Jackson Pollock, all cigarettes and sunglasses and paint-spattered Levis, you noticed how all that just . . . dissolved, man, the minute you whipped out your guitar and started strumming, lost in your own world, as if you didn't really notice the reaction you were getting from all that skirt. Even the other young cats tuned into you, even when they tried not to show it, even when they hated you for it. Take that, Picasso! But for all its grooviness, art college could never quite beat the power of the guitar – something you'd known about ever since the first time you'd stepped on a stage. Plus, you know, you'd already been out there, on the road, smoking and drinking and winking at all those pretty faces looking up at you, dirty cows. It was hard just going back to . . . normality. Dread idea . . .

So you went to the Marquee, always taking the guitar with you, not really knowing why, just that without it you'd be like all the others and who wanted to be like all the others? Not you. Bugger off! Next thing, there you are again, playing in the interval band, standing next to Jeff . . . When John Gibb from The Silhouettes came up to you afterwards one night and said, you know, blah blah blah, come and help, you'd hardly paid attention. But he seemed serious so you started to listen harder and he seemed to mean it and so you finally wrote down the address, and the time and when and where and bloody hell, what was all this then? A session, he said. You weren't so sure. There had been a time once before when Glyn Johns had said something similar, come on down, it'll be great, you can play and you'll get paid, it'll be great, come on down. But when you got there they stuck a sheet of paper under your nose. Oh, no! A row of dots, looked like 'crows on telegraph wires,' you'd joke later, but it wasn't so funny at the time. Bloody hurt that did, not knowing what the hell it all meant. Felt a right fool! It hadn't crossed your mind they'd want you to read music. You didn't have to read music when you were on stage, did you? No, you bloody didn't! Then they brought that other bloke in, some old sod, knowing you weren't up to it, giving you the poxy acoustic to play instead, your face red with shame. And it was so simple what he did, the other bloke. Just a simple poxy riff. Dah-dah-dah-de-dah! Any idiot could do that! Christ, you felt stupid. Stupid and angry. You wouldn't let that happen again ...

Now here was this bloke John Gibb, talking about EMI and Studio B and all this ... what if he stuck a sheet of paper in front of you, too? Fake it, you said to yourself. You could fake it. Why not? Just come up with something. It would be easy. Wouldn't it? Stood in the bar of the Marquee late that Tuesday night you'd said to yourself, 'Yeah ...' John smiled and you shook on it ...

When an edited-down version of 'Whole Lotta Love' reached no. 4 in the US singles' chart in January 1970, selling more than 900,000 copies along the way, the band's fate over the coming decade was sealed. Critics be damned, Led Zeppelin was it, baby. Next to them, the Beatles and the Stones seemed positively old-fashioned. That didn't stop Page being against the idea of the band's most famous *cri-de-coeur* being released minus over a minute of his greatest triumph yet as a producer, the psychedelic middle section. But he reluctantly accepted Atlantic's logic when some AM stations started making their own edits to the album track to fit the three-minute format. As a result, similar bite-size versions of the song reached no. 1 in Germany and Belgium. However, when Atlantic decided to repeat the process in the UK with an official release on 5 December, Jimmy insisted that G put his considerable foot down and veto the idea, much to the chagrin of Atlantic's recently appointed London chief, Phil Carson. This despite Page's previous announcement of the band's plans to release their first

UK single in an interview with *Top Pops* magazine in September. Would it be a deliberate effort to make a hit single, the magazine asked? 'Everyone says that they will not do that,' he had replied, 'but I suppose that is what we will be doing. But I don't see that we have to compromise our own standards. Jethro Tull managed to make a good-quality single,' he added, referring to 'Living in the Past', a no. 3 hit in Britain in the summer of 1969, though not included on any Tull album.

Similarly, the official press release Grant's office put out in early December explaining the decision not to release 'Whole Lotta Love' as a seven-inch didn't seem against the idea of singles per se, just not that one, explaining: 'Led Zeppelin had no intention of issuing this track as a single, as they felt it was written as part of their concept of the album.' Page was also quoted as saying: 'I just don't like releasing tracks from albums as singles. The two fields aren't related scenes to my mind.' The release went on to add that the band would release a special non-album track as their first UK single in the new year, though none ever emerged. According to Zeppelin archivist Dave Lewis, this was either going to be a finished version of 'Jennings Farm', a 'very catchy instrumental the band had worked up at a session at Olympic around that time' (which later resurfaced in altered form on their next album as 'Bron-Y-Aur Stomp') or possibly 'Baby Come On Home', a track left over from the original 1968 Olympic sessions when it was called 'Tribute To Bert Burns', which Lewis describes as 'very commercial, bluesy. The thing is, there was big pressure at that time for a single in the UK but they were totally against releasing "Whole Lotta Love" because Jimmy hated the fact it had been edited down. They may even have discussed an EP or a maxi-single, which Jethro Tull had done, or a special "stereo single", most singles back then still being mixed in mono for the two-inch speakers of transistor radios. Ultimately, it was all academic as they never released a single at all.'

Phil Carson, in particular, was convinced the band was wrong not to release the 'Whole Lotta Love' single in the UK. 'I went around to see Peter Grant,' he later recalled, 'and I tried to say, "Well, I'm the marketing genius around here, you know, and I'm telling you that if you want to sell albums, you've got to have a single." In the end, he convinced me that it shouldn't come out – in his own subtle way.' Grant was, he added, 'really insistent'. As it turned out, G was proved right, with the resultant publicity from *not* releasing a single helping *Led Zeppelin II* sell as fast as a single could sell in those days, with repeat orders of between three and five thousand units a day right through the busy Christmas period. After that, said Carson, 'I could never again say no to Peter Grant.'

Grant's trepidation about releasing singles in the UK was also based on his shrewd assessment of its chances of success – or lack of. Unlike America, where radio stations were at least fighting to play the track – some FM stations even ignored the single version to play the full-length album version, while still others took to flipping the seven-inch and playing the B-side, 'Living Loving Maid (She's Just A Woman)', which proved so popular it eventually got released in its own right as a US single, reaching no. 65 in April 1970 – Grant knew the BBC would be highly unlikely to playlist the song, however short the single version, on their conservative day-time shows. He thought the band would come out of it better by 'taking a stand' and not releasing singles, which is exactly what happened.

Led Zeppelin was certainly flying in Britain by then anyway. The previous summer had seen them consolidate their position at home with a short seven-date tour, the highlights of which were the opening date at Birmingham Town Hall on 13 June, which Jones remembers now as 'one of the first shows in Britain where we'd sold out a big venue and the crowd was all behind us' and a special occasion for both Plant and Bonham, their first time on stage at a hometown venue they had only experienced before from the other side of the footlights. Then, on 28 June, they appeared on the bill at the inaugural Bath Festival. Promoted by the husband and wife team of Freddy and Wendy Bannister, who had been involved in small club shows in London, Oxford and Bath for many years, the 1969 Bath Festival of Blues, as it was billed, was the first self-consciously 'rock' festival in Britain, and would later inspire another local West Country figure, Michael Eavis, to start his own copycat festival: Glastonbury, or 'son of Bath' as Eavis originally dubbed it.

Held at the Bath Pavilion Recreation Ground, above Zeppelin on the bill that day were headliners Fleetwood Mac, John Mayall's Blues-breakers, and Ten Years After. 'It went very well,' recalls Freddy Bannister, 'one of those wonderful eighty-degree days, everyone had just discovered dope so they were very placid.' Tickets for the all-day event were priced eighteen shillings and sixpence (approx 92p) and fourteen shillings and sixpence just for the evening (65p). Zeppelin's fee was just £200. 'Probably the least they ever got paid for an outdoor event,' muses Bannister, 'although Peter Grant did push me up to £500 before they signed the contract.'

However, it was their performance the following night that would cause the biggest splash of the tour: a show-stealing appearance at the finale of the Pop Proms at London's Royal Albert Hall. After short, tastefully restrained sets from Fleetwood Mac and folk quintet Pentangle (featuring two of Jimmy's favourite guitarists Bert Jansch and John Renbourn), Zeppelin's noisy, six-song set hit the stage like a hurricane, during which the crowd 'stormed the stage' according to Phil Carson, '[dancing] in the aisles and the boxes, and screaming so hard that the band did three encores'. Or as the subsequent review in *Disc* commented: 'When Led Zeppelin came on and played at a good ten times the volume of everyone else, the audience very nearly freaked completely.'

The first time Carson had seen Zeppelin on stage, he was blown away. When, just after 11.00 pm, the promoters turned on the house lights to signal the end of the evening, people reluctantly began heading toward the exits. But then Robert Plant suddenly returned to the stage and started blowing into his harmonica. Amazed audience members drifted back to their seats and the equally nonplussed promoters turned off the house lights again as one by one the rest of Zeppelin also returned to the stage. Unbeknownst to the organisers, they had arranged for some saxophonists (members of Blodwyn Pig and Liverpool Scene, the two bands that had supported them at the Birmingham Town Hall show) to join them for an extended jam on Little Richard's 'Long Tall Sally'.

Less than a week later they were back for their third US tour, built around a string of high-profile festival appearances, beginning on 5 July with the open-air Atlanta Pop Festival, followed the next day with an appearance at the famous Newport Jazz Festival, the first time an amplified rock band had been allowed onto the bill since Bob Dylan hijacked the show for a few numbers before being booed off four years before. In stark contrast to the Dylan fiasco, Zeppelin was warmly welcomed and applauded on and off the stage loudly. Grant, for one, would not have allowed them to go on stage had he not been sure of such a reception. This third US tour was all about profile. Nothing, he had decided, was going to stand in the band's way. He recalled telling them: '"Go out there and tear the place apart, take the roof or canvas off. I don't want to see you afterwards unless you succeed." That normally got the required response.'

In New York, on 13 July, they made another headline-grabbing appearance at the Schaefer Music Festival at Flushing Meadow's Singer Bowl, which *Cashbox* reviewed glowingly, describing Plant as an 'outstanding candidate for superstardom'. But what most of the 25,000 people there would remember best was the encore section of the show, featuring a mammoth nine-man jam between members of Zeppelin, the Jeff Beck Group, Ten Years After and Jethro Tull. They were in the middle of an extended 'Jailhouse Rock' when Bonzo suddenly took over the drums and altered the beat to that of 'The Stripper', then began ripping off his own clothes. According to Ten Years After drummer Ric Lee: 'Bonham, who had been drinking, took off his trousers and underpants. The police saw it and I saw Richard Cole and Peter Grant spotting the police. The number fizzled out and Peter and Richard ran on stage, each grabbing one of Bonzo's arms and you could see his bare arse disappearing as they carried him off. But they got his trousers on before the police arrived. Grant yelled at him: "What's wrong with you, John? Are you trying to ruin things for everyone?"' But then, as Beck later recalled: 'It was one of those riotous sort of days, everyone's energy level was 100 per cent and we were throwing things at each other on stage.' When the guitarist threw a plastic glass of orange juice at Ten Years After mainman Alvin Lee it stuck all over his guitar. 'It was just one of those animal things. Three English groups at the same place has to add up to trouble.'

Naturally, the fun and games weren't confined to the stage. Bill Harry, the band's newly appointed London-based PR who joined the tour for several dates, recalled hanging out after one show with that fast-becoming perennial double-act, Bonzo and Ricardo. After scaring the rest of the hotel guests by dancing on the tables, 'Richard went to the fridge and took out all the cans of lager, loading them up in a sack. "Let's go back to Bonzo's room." He was dragging this sack like Santa Claus. Then we stopped and looked out to the car park. We could see a bare arse moving up and down and it was one of the group with a girl in a car. We went up to the room and a detective followed us because we had a couple of girls with us. Richard slipped him a few dollars and he vanished. So we went into the room and one of the boys went to say something to one of the girls and he was sick all over her.'

It was a summer full of such vivid moments, culminating for Jones at the Dallas International Pop Festival on 31 August, where they received their largest fee for a single performance yet: $13,000. 'My wife was there for that one, and I recall that Janis Joplin taught us how to drink tequila with salt and lemon. There was just the three of us in her trailer – memories don't come much better than that.'

One festival appearance they declined to make that summer, however, concerned the now legendary free festival before an estimated 500,000 people that took place at Yasgur's Farm in Woodstock over the weekend that began on the morning of Friday 15 August, and ended in the early hours of Monday 18 August. Filmed for a 1970 movie and destined to become a sprawling multi-disc live album, Woodstock would go down as the most widely known rock festival in history; a profound moment in music history; the very apex of Sixties rock.

It had originally been announced that Zeppelin would be appearing on the night of 16 August, as would the Jeff Beck Group. In the event neither showed up. Why Grant took it upon himself to unilaterally decide that Zeppelin should pull out has never been fully addressed. The surviving members are vague on the subject, to say the least, but then they weren't really involved in the decision. On balance, it almost certainly had something to do with money. The thought of playing for free was anathema to someone like Peter Grant. The idea that someone other than the band would also profit from a movie and record album would certainly not have held appeal, either. Looking for assurances, and receiving none, that Zeppelin would get a slice of the pie, it appears G simply took a professional decision and decided to concentrate the band's attentions on more easily accessible streams of revenue, plumping for a brace of high-paying dates across the border in Canada that weekend instead. Twenty-five years later, Grant confirmed to Dave Lewis that Zeppelin had been asked to appear at Woodstock and that Atlantic was 'very keen', as was their US agent Frank Barsalona. For Grant though, 'At Woodstock we'd have just been another band on the bill.' Never mind that it might have changed critical perception of them; instead their absence only reinforced the idea of Zeppelin as quintessential outsiders.

The Beck Group would also have reason to view their no-show as a cause for regret. As Rod Stewart, then a rising star in America, says now, 'If we'd done it, I think we would have stayed together.' Instead, they broke up almost immediately after it, with Beck insisting to this day that it was the right decision. Stewart was 'on a power trip' and the band was 'disappearing up their bum'. Turning down Woodstock was his way of showing who was boss. Typical Beck, cutting off his nose to spite his face, others might say.

Not for the first or last time, the Led Zeppelin story appeared to be running parallel with more pressing events happening out there in the so-called real world. For in every other respect, 1969 would appear to have been rock's *annus horribilis*. A week before Woodstock, on the night of 9 August, as the band enjoyed a twenty-minute standing ovation for their headline show at the 8,500-capacity Anaheim Convention Center in LA, elsewhere in the city several drug-demented members of Charles Manson's self-styled 'family' burst uninvited into a house party at 10050 Cielo Drive, where they shot, stabbed and beat to death seven people, including a heavily pregnant Sharon Tate, actress wife of film director Roman Polanski. A bitterly frustrated musician who had tried and failed for years to get a record deal, despite the patronage of some of the biggest names in the business, including most famously Dennis Wilson of the Beach Boys, Manson, it transpired, had ordered the slaughter as part of his 'masterplan' to incite a race war, convinced that blacks would be blamed for the killings. He reasoned that once America's black population had won this unlikely conflict, Manson and his followers would take over, seizing the reins of power in America. Equally mind-boggling, Manson claimed to have taken his cue from the hidden meanings of several Beatles songs from the *White Album*, including 'Rocky Raccoon', 'Blackbird', 'Piggies', 'Helter Skelter' and 'Revolution 9'. The immediate upshot in LA was a massive overnight increase in private gun ownership and an instant reversal of the open-door policy that had existed until then in its lush valleys, certainly among its rock denizens. Suddenly everyone and everything was ultra-uptight. Love and peace was yesterday's news. Record company executive Lou Adler recalls how 'the Manson killings just destroyed us ... It was a very paranoid time, and the easiest thing to do was to get out of it.' Not in public, though, but behind locked doors. Suddenly places like the Whisky just emptied. As the LA writer and former groupie Eve Babitz put it: 'Everything had been so loose and now it could never be loose again.' Before the Manson murders, 'a guy with long hair was a brother – now you just didn't know.'

When, on 6 December, the Stones' free show at San Francisco's Altamont race track ended in the death of an eighteen-year-old black fan named Meredith Hunter, stabbed and bludgeoned to death by acid-crazed members of the Oakland chapter of the Hell's Angels as he pushed his way towards the stage – brandishing a revolver, they claimed – it looked like the game was truly up. Three other people also died at the same show, two as the result of a hit-and-run car accident and one by drowning in an 'irrigation canal', but the symbolism of Hunter's death was impossible to overcome: the moment when the Sixties died crystallised forever as the desperate, brutal and ultimately unnecessary murder of a fan, overexcited by the music his heroes made in a setting that became, in retrospect, the exact photonegative of everything both Woodstock and the Sixties was supposed to represent; the garden despoiled by blood, anger and the unprecedented cost of such alleged freedoms.

Once again, Led Zeppelin appeared to be living in an almost parallel dimension, flying ever higher above the earth just as everyone else appeared to be plummeting towards it in flames. Just as LA, in particular, was experiencing the seemingly self-inflicted psychic wounds of the Manson atrocity, Zeppelin were approaching the zenith of their relationship with the city they would increasingly come to regard as their spiritual home. 'That period was a major time for us,' Plant would later tell me. 'Ramshackle times when the music really was from the other side of the tracks. We often found ourselves in contretemps with the prevailing trend without even realising we had done anything. When we played it really did feel like we inhabited a parallel universe, quite apart from everything else, including the rock world of the times.'

On balance, perhaps there is no irony here, as Zeppelin's relationship with LA would be so utterly hedonistic and depraved that in many ways it could be argued that they, more than any other artist of the Seventies, came to embody the new, paranoid atmosphere dominating the new sleaze-mired culture of the city. For if 1969 was the year the party turned nasty, Zeppelin were very much the drunken gatecrashers.

Infidels storming the castle, daggers clamped between their teeth, intent on rape and pillage; master of the revels.

Certainly Jimmy Page was well on his way to becoming known as a bigger backstage legend amongst the groupie population than even Mick Jagger, not least because of his propensity since his touring days with the Yardbirds for carrying whips and handcuffs in his suitcase. 'He whipped me and it was great, it was beautiful, real good times,' claimed one of his conquests from those days. The rest of the band was no less rampant. This was the tour when Peter Grant would famously offer one hotel manager the cash to destroy one of his own guest rooms. 'The guy smashed the room to smithereens,' Richard Cole recalls in his book. 'And he came back, gave us the bill and we paid it [in cash].' These were the days when televisions routinely flew through windows, followed by refrigerators laden with champagne, young women's underwear and whatever else came to hand. One Holiday Inn manager looked like he'd spent the night in a haunted house after the band checked out the next morning. 'Five hundred pounds of whipped cream,' he jabbered. 'Who could possibly use that much whipped cream?' According to Cole: 'That was the fucking best time of my life. That [tour] was the one. We were hot and on our way up, but no-one was watching too closely. So you could fucking play.' He added: 'All the so-called Led Zeppelin depravity took place the first two years in an alcoholic fog. After that we got older and grew out of it. It became a realistic business.'

Well, almost. It was also on that third US tour in 1969 that what later became known as the famous 'shark' incident occurred. On 27 July, the band had appeared at the Seattle Pop Festival. Also on the bill that day were The Doors, who Zeppelin followed on to the stage, plus Chuck Berry, Spirit, Albert Collins, the Flying Burrito Brothers, Ike & Tina Turner, Vanilla Fudge, Bo Diddley and others. With the following day designated a rare day off, the band decided to spend it chilling out at the Edgewater Inn, an ocean-side establishment whose unique selling point was the opportunity it afforded its guests to fish, either by hiring boats or literally dangling a rented fishing rod from the balcony of their room. Returning to the hotel after the show, Cole was in full Ricardo mode as he joined Bonzo on the balcony of his second-floor room, where they sat till dawn, drinking heavily and fishing for sharks. When, by 4.00 am they still hadn't caught anything, a bored and drunken Bonham had begun pouring champagne over the bait. Almost instantaneously, he thought he had one. 'Grab the harpoon!' he yelled at Cole. But after they'd reeled it in amidst much whooping and mayhem, it turned out to be a red snapper. Over the next couple of hours they caught many more: snappers interspersed with a couple of mud sharks, which Cole inventively hung in a closet, threading coat-hangers through their gills.

The next day they were boasting of their exploits to the others. 'Charles Atlas couldn't have reeled in a couple of those suckers,' Bonzo told Plant and Pagey. 'So what are you going to do with them now?' asked Robert, holding his nose as he inspected the carnage in Bonham's room. 'We'll find something to do with them,' said Ricardo. Sure enough, that night they did. Entertaining a roomful of groupies, one of them, a tall, seventeen-year-old redhead named Jackie, idly enquired: 'Are you guys into bondage?' Not the sort of question one needed to ask Led Zeppelin but then they'd only just met. 'I really like being tied up,' she announced. 'I really do.' Jimmy licked his lips; Bonzo hooted, and Cole led the way as everyone lined up to take advantage of this propitious offer, inviting Jackie to strip off and lie naked on the bed, where he tied her hands and feet to the bedposts using rope ordered from room service. Then, with Mark Stein of Vanilla Fudge filming it on his Super 8 camera, Cole inserted the long nose of a dead red snapper fish into the hapless girl's vagina, followed by the head of a mud shark into her anus. 'What the hell is that?' she screamed. 'I'm putting this red snapper into your red snapper!' Cole cried jubilantly as the rest of the room fell about laughing. 'Smile!' cajoled Stein, getting in close with his whirring camera.

'It was just all in fun,' recalled Fudge drummer Carmine Appice. 'The chick was my groupie, I found her, we had a day off and she kept wanting to be on film with us.' Though he concedes that 'what actually happened, it was pretty disgusting, you know. It was pretty nutso.' The next day at the airport, Appice ran into Frank Zappa and told him the story. Zappa turned it into one of his most notorious songs of the period, 'The Mud Shark', released on his 1971 live concept album, *Fillmore East*. While such adventures have never been denied, nor Page's own less well-documented proclivities for whips and handcuffs, it's equally clear how little such tawdry scenes meant to him or the rest of the band. As Plant later told me, 'The thing people forget when they tut-tut about this stuff is what a laugh we were having. People have a tendency to look back on the band as this dark force spreading its wings when we were just young guys, having a good time. The main thing I remember most about those days now is the laughter.'

Nor was the American groupie scene in the late Sixties entirely down to one-night stands. Three days after the shark incident, the band was back in LA. This time the party at Thee Experience came before any gigs. Throngs of girls ran over to their table. But Jimmy wasn't there. Instead Cole grabbed the arm of Miss Pamela – who was there – and gave her Page's room number at the Hyatt House. 'He's waiting for you,' he told her. But, tempted though she was, she didn't go. Not straight away. 'That always made you seem intriguing to whoever it was,' she said. But Jimmy had gotten Miss Pamela's phone number and they hooked up the following night after their show in Santa Barbara, at the Earl Warren Showgrounds. Treated as not just another groupie but an honoured guest, she was immediately swept off her feet. Sitting next to Jimmy in the back of the limo after the gig, 'Whatever I did, it was just perfect: "Oh, Miss P, how could you say that, how could you do that? Oh my god, I've been looking for you all my life." And of course, years later, we found out he said that to all the girls . . .'

According to Des Barres, Page already had 'an evil reputation' as a 'heartbreaking, gut-wrenching lady-killer, wielding a whip and handcuffs, a concept that appeared to be in total contradiction to his perfectly poetic, angelic face.' However, that didn't stop her from becoming his LA girlfriend for the rest of 1969. On days off in August he would stay with Pamela, listening over and again to test pressings of *Led Zeppelin II* and taking 'reams of notes'. Robert, meanwhile, was spending time with one of Pamela's friends, Michele Overman.

On the night of the Manson murders, there had been a big party for the band after the Anaheim show but Jimmy and Pamela went to The Ex instead, got drunk and high on weed and wine, then retired to the hotel 'where we made exquisite love and crashed out'. Pamela had seen 'his whips curled up in his suitcase like they were taking a nap' but he had promised: 'Don't worry Miss P, I'll never use them on you.' Plainly, this was a side of Jimmy the girls he did whip never got to see. Instead, the guy Des Barres recalls now liked to go hunting for antiques and bought art, taking Pamela with him to buy some MC Escher prints (a typically shrewd Page purchase as Escher died shortly afterwards sending the value of the prints rocketing). Jimmy, she recalled, 'liked to be in control and didn't take many drugs or drink much alcohol. I think he believed his beauty was too important to tamper with. He was always in the mirror, primping on his splendid image, and putting perfect waves in his long black hair with a little crimping machine.' The next day they flew to Las Vegas together and sat in the front row of an Elvis Presley show, Elvis in black leather and looking sleek, à la his recent TV comeback. Afterwards, one of Presley's Memphis Mafia boys came out and asked Jimmy if he'd like to go backstage with his 'date' and meet the King. 'No, thank you,' said Page. 'I never quite got over it,' said Des Barres.

At the end of August, at Jimmy's invitation, Pamela joined the band in New York where they had a week off before their next show, a return date at Flushing Meadow's Singer Bowl. She stayed for three days and sat on Jimmy's amp while they played. Even Peter Grant, whose attitude to groupies was even icier than Cole's, took to her, bouncing her on his knee like a little girl, instructing Ricardo to make sure she didn't get lost in the seething mass of girls that now swarmed over the band after every show. Everyone in the band's entourage addressed her politely as Miss P, an endearment she 'accepted with slavish gratitude'.

When they parted at the airport, Jimmy bound for London, Pamela on her way home to LA, she was wearing his shirt and he was professing undying love. He had taken to introducing her to people as 'Mrs Page,' she said, and she was sure it was the start of something more than a 'one tour-stand'. But Zeppelin was back six weeks later for the start of their fourth US tour and by then Page's feelings had already cooled. He didn't even phone until he was in San Francisco for the band's three-night headline stint at the Winterland Ballroom between 6 and 8 November, the last dates of the tour, then welched on his promise to fly down to LA to see her. In the end she was forced to buy her own plane ticket and fly north to see him, but though he 'made a big display of being overjoyed to see me' it was clear he was 'slipping away from me'. Finally, he told her: 'P, you're such a lovely little girl, I don't deserve you, I'm such a bastard, you know.' Then he flew home to England and she was left alone again at the airport. As she puts it:

'Handed a one-way ticket to Palookaville.' Less than three weeks later, she was having a fling with Mick Jagger.

Back in England, with the band scheduled to take a break until after Christmas, Jimmy Page could look back over the past twelve months with unusual satisfaction. Bristling with even more self-confidence than usual, high on the speed of his band's giddy rise to the top in America, the huge transatlantic success of Led Zeppelin II may have taken certain critics by surprise, but the band saw it more as their just deserts. In the same year that Neil Armstrong would take his 'giant leap for mankind' onto the moon – 29 July, the day after the shark incident – the flight of the Zeppelin was arrowing ever deeper into the wide blue yonder.

A headline show before a packed Lyceum Ballroom in London on 12 October had also reconfirmed their growing status in Britain. Two weeks before Christmas, a special reception was held for them at the Savoy Hotel, where they were presented with two gold (for album sales worth one million dollars) and two platinum (for sales in excess of one million copies sold) records for both their albums. The event was presided over by the Hon. Mrs Dunwoody MP, who in her speech described them as 'not so much a Led Zeppelin, more a gas rocket' to Britain's export drive. Grant had been against the idea – 'too establishment,' he later announced – but this time Phil Carson got his way and the story made the papers the next day. More to the band's taste was a similar party held for them a few weeks later in Stockholm, which Grant insisted be held not at a posh hotel but a sex club. 'There's all of us getting the awards and on the floor are a couple having it away,' Grant recalled with a broad smile. 'The press didn't know what to make of that ...'

However, the press knew exactly what to make of the sold-out eight-date British tour they had completed in the new year, the highlight of which, a headline show at the Albert Hall on 9 January, would fall on Page's 26th birthday. There would be no support act on the tour, either, a trend they had decided would continue in America when they returned there in March, where the shows would be billed as 'An Evening With Led Zeppelin', allowing them to play for as long as they wished each night, setting entirely new precedents for spontaneous live performance no rock artist – not Cream, not Hendrix, not the Stones, no-one – had ever attempted before. 'I know it was corny,' said

Grant, who came up with the 'An Evening With ...' tag, 'but it was like the old Thirties stage line. I guess that was a by-product of my days as a fourteen-year-old stage hand.'

Grant had arranged for the Albert Hall show to be filmed documentary-style by the film-makers Peter Whitehead and Stanley Dorfman, their crew literally following the band onto the stage that night, where they clustered about them in such close proximity the surviving footage provides a splendidly candid representation of just how powerful and fully realised the Zeppelin live experience now was. The band had played over 140 shows in the preceding twelve months, the vast majority of them in the US, and it shows on the film footage, from the opening gunshot of Bonham's volcanic drums on 'We're Gonna Groove' to Plant's unfathomably vast vocal pyrotechnics, lion's mane of hair shaking as his hands pummel an invisible drum or guitar, to that huge but surprisingly nimble bass with which Jones effortlessly anchors the rhythm.

Page is, of course, the one you can't keep your eyes off, dressed down in his harlequin tank-top and skinny straight-legged jeans, skipping about the stage with the guitar at his knees, full of a savage intensity belied only by the way he peeps almost shyly out at the audience occasionally from behind the curtains of dark hair that smother his face.

'I look at the Albert Hall footage now,' said Plant, 'and the first thing I notice is how young we all are. I look like what I was: a Black Country hippy full of high ideals and low-cost living. I still couldn't quite believe where I was, everything had happened so fast for the group. Also, Jimmy's way of playing was very British, or rather not very American. If you listen to what were recognised as the big guitar records of the period just before Zeppelin – stuff by the Kinks and The Who – the solos are a much more tic-tack style of playing. Jimmy opened up the whole idea of having wonderful sustains amidst the chaos of the rhythm section.'

This was the voice that landed you your first proper gigs in bands like the New Memphis Bluesbreakers, the Black Snake Moan (after the Blind Lemon Jefferson song), the Banned ... nothing outfits that meant the whole world to you. All this and still your dad going on and on at you, life at home now so unbearable that some nights you preferred to sleep in the van than go home. Your hair was too long, your mouth was too big, your head full of too much nonsense. A contrary bugger, your dad called you. Contrary and ungrateful and for the high jump sooner or later, you wait and bloody see ...

Thank god for your mates. They were the same as you, most of them. You were all going to be pop stars or footballers. Not just worker-bees and drones like your mums and dads but rich and famous and creative and free, chuffing away on the good stuff, the birds all hanging around stroking your hair and gazing up at you admiringly. None of this get-a-boring-bloody-job rubbish. When you and Neville Holder went to Brum town hall that night and saw the Spencer Davis Group and was told the singer was barely older than you it was like the blanket being pulled off the budgie cage. Suddenly it was blindingly obvious what you should being doing with your life. Nev, a couple of years older than you, was the same. You both fancied yourselves as singers, though in Nev's case his mum and dad were all for it, encouraging him to practise his guitar and keep trying. Why couldn't your mum and dad be like that? All the same, if someone had told you then that you and Nev would both end up as singers in big rock bands – as stars – you'd never have believed it. Not of Nev anyway, god bless him. You thought you were doing him a favour when you let him become the driver of the van in one of your later bands, Listen. Even after he'd become the singer in the 'N Betweens with your other mate Dave Hill you never really saw it. But it was there that Nev and Dave met the rest of Slade, which just shows you how wrong you can be ...

It would be a long time before you learned that lesson though. Right now you were too busy living out your fantasy life as pop-star-in-the-making. A dream that came a step nearer when you smart-mouthed your way into becoming a regular at the Star and Garter in Halesowen, doing a bit of compering, playing fab gear Merseybeat covers in the Javelins. That was all right for five minutes. You eventually got your own way though when you persuaded them to play a 'farewell' gig – then returned the following week as the Crawling King Snakes (after the John Lee Hooker song – obviously!).

The Star and Garter was part of what they called the Ma Reagan Circuit. Mary 'Ma' Reagan was the best-known promoter in the whole of the Midlands. There wasn't a decent pub or club she didn't have the big say-so in. You were told to stay in with her if you knew what was good for you and you did. It wasn't long before you were bothering her to let you put on your own group at the Star, or the Oldhill Plaza, the other place you used to go regularly at weekends. By then you were also acting as part-time compere, introducing the bands, so it worked out all right. Crawling King Snake was one of the first you wangled in there. You thought you were the bloody bees-knees. And you were all right, actually, for what you were, a bunch of teenagers acting like they knew something about the blues.

That was when you learned how some of the best times were after it was over, sitting round drinking and smoking and having a right laugh about it. How it had gone, who did what, who didn't, who buggered it up good and proper. After hours on a Saturday night you'd all meet up at Alex's Fleur De Lys mobile pie stall, which would sit opposite the Albany Hotel, right in the middle of Brum. That's where you got to know them all. Danny King and his Mayfair Set, Carl Wayne and the Vikings, Johnny Neal and the Starliners, Gerry Levene and the Avengers, Mike Sheridan and the Nightriders ... A couple of wankers but mostly right good blokes, most of 'em. Later, after you'd had your pie and chips you might go off to the Elbow Room, or maybe the Rum Runner, or the Club Cedar or some other late-night joint. Which is when you first met Bonzo ...

Equally exciting amongst the Albert Hall footage is Bonham's jaw-dropping 'Moby Dick' drum solo, a work in progress that would eventually stretch to almost forty minutes some nights but is caught here at an earlier, more economical though no less overwhelming stage. 'Watching Bonzo now, being able to hear the detail, to actually see him close-up working, it's marvellous,' agrees Jones. 'That was the thing about the smaller gigs. Drums get fairly unsubtle through a large PA. But in a smaller place like the Albert Hall you can hear all the incredible detail he was always putting into his work. He was constantly varying, constantly changing all the time. He was just such an exciting musician to play with. Some musicians hate it if the drummer or one of the other musicians starts to diversify from the song, or go off into their own thing. But in Zeppelin that was the whole point, and John was magnificent at that. He really kept you on your toes as a musician and a listener. That's when the empathy becomes incredibly exhilarating. He was the best drummer I've ever played with, bar none.'

For Jimmy Page, the Albert Hall show would contain even more lasting significance. Watching from the wings that night was The Who's vocalist Roger Daltrey. Misunderstanding the lack of support act, he observed, 'I know why no-one wants to play with these guys. They're too good.' With him that night was his then girlfriend, Heather, accompanied by a friend, a young French model named Charlotte Martin. A slim, elegant blonde with perfect features, she was Jimmy's type and he made sure Roger introduced him to her after the show. Having dated Eric Clapton for a period in 1968, Charlotte was used to the attention of musicians, but Jimmy was different. Compared to most rock musicians she'd met he seemed quite sophisticated. Quietly spoken, undemonstrative, but confident and quite sure of himself. When she invited him back to her London flat, he agreed to go without a second thought, getting Cole to drive them.

When the band gathered at Grant's office four days later to begin the drive down to their next show in Portsmouth, Charlotte was still on Jimmy's arm. With Pat Bonham, Maureen Plant and Mo Jones also joining the band on the road for the UK tour, suddenly Charlotte became the new 'Mrs Page', the slot previously occupied by Miss Pamela. However, Jimmy's affair with Charlotte would remain in place a lot longer than his dalliance with the prettiest GTO. It was, in fact, the start of the first really significant love affair of the guitarist's life, and one he would remain true to even after the band had returned to the road in America. An almost unheard of sacrifice, even for the married men in the band, for Jimmy it was a sign of something much deeper.

The three-week, seven-country tour of the continent that followed the British dates was equally euphoric. Unlike America where, as Plant said, it was now 'a bit of a rant with cherry-bombs and firecrackers and blood-curdling whoops,' European audiences, though no less excited, tended to sit back and listen more, a quality that Plant, who often found himself, because of the long musical improvisations, forced to 'stand back and regard the band like another member of the audience' came to appreciate more as time went by. 'People talk now about the bombast and the dexterity,' he said, 'and while they were key ingredients, some of the most crucial elements in the performances were those indefinable moments inside the actual songs that were always going somewhere else. It was so subtle that it was something we didn't recognise at first. Then, once we did, we started really playing with it. There was a feeling of reaching and stretching for something that wasn't quite so evident on the records. Playing these things live was the real jewel in our existence, everybody had the capacity to take it and move it around until it took on whole new meanings. It was one of the most remarkable things about the life of the group. The travelling and the endless pressure to come up with the goods may have taken its toll some nights, but even then I defy anyone outside the band to ever know when that happened because the level we maintained was so high. On the right night, however, a Led Zeppelin show was a spectacular place to be.'

The only blemish was the opening show of the tour at the KB Hallen in Copenhagen on 21 February, which the band was forced to play under an assumed name after the Countess Eva Von Zeppelin, direct descendent of Count Ferdinand Von Zeppelin, who designed the prototype for the airship, threatened to sue the band for defaming the family name, giving a series of inflammatory local press interviews. 'They may be world-famous but a couple of shrieking monkeys are not going to use a privileged family name without permission,' she proclaimed haughtily. In a last-ditch effort to spare them from litigation and save the gig, Grant invited the countess to a private meeting with the band, which she surprisingly agreed to attend. There she was schmoozed by G and taken by the hand by Page who patiently explained that the band was immensely popular with people all over the world, none of whom, to his knowledge, had ever taken offence at the name. Suitably reassured, she seemed ready to be won over by the band's argument and readied to leave. Whereupon she spotted a copy of the first Zeppelin album that someone had left lying around. Horrified to discover the band was using a picture of the exploded zeppelin on its covers, she became upset all over again. There was no pacifying her this time, though, and as she stormed out Grant sat there groaning. 'This is the most ridiculous thing I've ever heard of,' he said, 'but that woman is angry enough to sue us.' Then he had a brainwave. The band would go ahead with the show – under another name.

Nobody thought this was a good idea but went along with it in the end after Grant spent the next couple of hours browbeating them about it, getting them to see it as having the last laugh over the hatchet-faced countess, rather than the pyrrhic victory it actually amounted to. So the show went on and the band played under the name of . . . The Nobs. Well, Bonzo found it funny. The band forgot their troubles later that night by visiting one of the city's numerous sex clubs, where

Bonzo felt moved to join one of the naked women on stage at one point, removing the batteries from her vibrator and announcing loudly: 'You girls gotta work for your pay!'

Back for their fifth US tour in March, it was business as usual as the band forged their way through what were now fervent Zeppelin strongholds – New York, LA, San Francisco – and on into newer territory in the American south like Memphis, Raleigh and Atlanta, where they were made to feel simultaneously both welcome and undesirable – a unique accomplishment even by the double-standards of the racially divided, sexually repressed American south. At the 17 April show in Memphis, the 'city fathers' awarded them the keys of the city. However, during the encores that night at the Midsouth Coliseum – the same venue where someone in the audience had thrown a cherry bomb at the Beatles in 1966 in the aftermath of Lennon's infamous 'bigger than Jesus' comment – the manager of the venue, one Bubba Bland, became so alarmed at the over the top reaction of the audience, he panicked and demanded Grant stop the show. When G just laughed in his face, Bland pulled a gun on him. 'If you don't cut the show,' he bellowed, 'I'm gonna shoot ya!' According to legend, Grant regarded Bland with disdain. 'You can't shoot me, ya cunt!' he is said to have roared back at him. 'They've just given us the fucking keys to the city!'

However, the only eye-witness to this event, in-house producer and co-owner of Ardent Studios in Memphis, Terry Manning, recalls things somewhat differently. A friend of Page's from Yardbirds days – they had met when Terry was the rhythm guitarist and keyboard player in Lawson and Four More, a local Memphis outfit hired to open the bill on one of Dick Clark's Caravan of Stars package bills that the Yardbirds were on – Terry had actually been another of the people sounded out by Jimmy in Zeppelin's earliest days as a possible member. Speaking from his home these days in the Bahamas, Manning recalls Page phoning to ask if he would be interested in coming to England, bringing the Lawson and Four More bassist, Joe Gaston, with him. 'He said, "I've got a great singer called Terry Reid, we'll get him in." I said, "Oh, I know Terry", because I had photographed the cover of his second album [Terry Reid].' The idea never developed beyond a phone call though. Reid turned Page down and Manning sensibly decided that with his own career now taking off as a producer for Stax Records,

working with artists like the Staple Singers, Otis Redding and Isaac
Hayes, 'It just didn't seem the wisest choice to give it all up to join the
New Yardbirds ... They weren't selling any records and it was almost
looked on in some circles as an afterthought.'

But they stayed in touch and Terry was a guest at many of the
earliest Zeppelin shows in the US. 'I saw maybe fifty or sixty shows,'
he says, 'including that night in Memphis.' He was standing with Grant
at the back of the stage when Bland drew his gun and aimed it at him
and recalls that far from facing his assailant with blind courage, Grant
was actually in fear of his life. 'He actually held Peter at gunpoint and
then pointed the gun at Robert Plant. Peter called Robert over to the
back of the stage and was yelling, "Calm them down! Stop the music,
no matter what! He's got a gun on me!" And Robert looks down, like
"Huh?" So Robert went back out and stopped the show. They were
playing "Whole Lotta Love" and everyone was on their seats and
they literally were going crazy. So they stopped, they brought the
houselights up, Robert pleaded with the audience, "Please everyone,
sit down, the show cannot continue. They've actually threatened us
back here, I need your help." And everyone finally did. Then Robert
said, "Everyone please stay seated, we're gonna finish this last song,
thanks for a great evening." Then rat-a-tat-tat, they went back into
"Whole Lotta Love" and everyone was right back up and people were
jumping again. But the houselights never went back down and finally
the show just disintegrated and we went backstage. There was Peter,
the four band members and me standing in the dressing room, and
Peter was cursing like you cannot believe. The band was so upset and
I'm standing there as a resident of Memphis Tennessee at the time,
saying, "Guys, I'm so sorry, I apologise. These people are cretins." The
thing is they had been shot at just the week before, leaving a gig in
Dallas. They were in the limo, on their way to the hotel and a bullet
grazed it. Someone shot at them and just missed. They said, "What is
it with the Southern US? We're never touring here again!" They were
just so upset.'

The weirdness didn't end there, either. Terry had arranged an Indian
meal for Jimmy back at his apartment that night – 'I knew Jimmy
loved Indian food and you just couldn't get it anywhere else in the
South back then' – so instead of leaving in the band limo, he and
Charlotte, who was also there, left with Terry in his Merc. On the way

out of the venue, however, fans spotted Jimmy and several took off after them in a car chase. 'All the way through the streets of Memphis with everybody screaming and yelling, "I know you're in there!" and he was just freaking out of course. While this was happening I had "Heartbreaker" panning back and forth on the car stereo. It was like a bizarre scene from hell . . . '

8

A Bustle in Your Hedgerow

What Robert Plant calls 'the craziness count' had definitely gone up since the band had last toured the States four months before. Bonzo, whose bouts of homesickness seemed to be growing in direct proportion to how successful the band became, began drinking more heavily and taking out his frustrations on hotel rooms. The show in Pittsburgh also had to be stopped when a bloody brawl erupted in the crowd. Elsewhere, cops hassled them at their own shows, blaming them for the uncontrolled antics of the audience. 'I don't think we can take America again for a while,' John Paul Jones told one writer at the end of it. 'America definitely unhinges you. The knack is to hinge yourself up again when you get back.' Plant suffered, too. 'More than anyone,' Richard Cole later noted, 'Robert seemed on the brink of collapse.'

As usual, they took refuge in LA. No longer staying at the Chateau Marmont – the Manson murders of the year before had thrown all of LA into a semi-permanent fug of paranoia and Peter Grant decreed the Marmont's spread of isolated bungalows too easy a target for any potential 'nutters', of which there were more than a few now following the band around on tour – the band had relocated to the Hyatt House, a few blocks up on Sunset. Or the 'riot house' as Bonzo and Plant now dubbed it, and for good reason. With a never-ending parade of girls finding their way up to the ninth floor where the band and its entourage were sequestered for a week, Richard Cole later recalled the limo for the shows being so weighed down by girls 'the trunk [had] become stuck on the riot house driveway, requiring a push off the curb . . . absolute madness'. Many were now routinely offering to be whipped by Jimmy, whose proclivities had become well known amongst the groupie community, while Cole and Bonzo devised ever weirder ruses to keep themselves entertained, including handcuffing groupies to the beds in their hotel suites until they returned from gigs. Cole would order them room service and leave a few joints for them to smoke. 'They never complained,' he recalled with a smirk. 'No handcuffs were needed to keep them around.'

Just as Zeppelin were reaching the height of their on-the-road notoriety, they were also on the cusp of making their most enduring music. That monumentally successful second album was only the beginning. In fact, in many ways, they only really began to make the great leaps forward musically that would cement their reputation as one of the all-time rock greats with what came next, starting with what was arguably their first proper album together: *Led Zeppelin III*. Written and conceived, in large part, in reaction to both criticism of their first two albums and their own frustrations at being forced to write and record so quickly and under so much pressure, although the third Zeppelin album would also eventually be hurried into pro- duction, the beginnings of the songs on the album – and indeed the album that followed – were undertaken in much less stressful circumstances. The end result would take everyone by surprise; the whole tenor of the album – acoustic-based songs, rooted in folk and country as well as their already well-established blues influences – the last thing anyone, including Jones and Bonham, who were largely excluded from the songwriting process, would have predicted at that point. Until then the question had been: how would they top the ecstatic thrill of that titanic second album? Would they be able to come up with another 'Whole Lotta Love'?

The answer was: they wouldn't even try to. 'People that thought like that missed the point,' Page told me in 2001. 'The whole point was *not* to try and follow up something like "Whole Lotta Love". We recognised that it had been a milestone for us, but we had absolutely no intention of trying to repeat it. The idea was to try and do something different. To sum up where the band was *now*, not where it had been a year ago.' And where the band was now – or where Page and Plant were anyway – was halfway up a mountainside in Wales.

Page seemed to be trying to put his personal life onto a more even keel, too. Back in LA in April 1970, when he bumped into Miss P and her new boyfriend, Marty, a dresser for rock stars from New York, Jimmy was friendly but distant. When they played on 13 April, it was

Plant not Page who invited her along and paid for her cab fare to the
show, adding kindly that he wouldn't go on till she got there. Leaving
Marty on his own at home, after the show she and Jimmy ended up
back at his suite at the Hyatt till five in the morning. All they did was
talk, though. He showed her pictures of Charlotte Martin – who
Pamela already knew about, having been tipped off by Miss Christine,
who had been in London with Todd Rundgren, where she'd seen Page
squiring his new love around town – and said he was 'being good'.
They parted friends but she wept all the way home.

With the final show of the tour cancelled when an exhausted Plant's
voice gave out, the band flew home from Las Vegas on 20 April.
Between their first show in December 1968 and their latest in April
1970, they had performed no less than 153 times in the US. They
were now playing for guarantees of up to $100,000 per show; they
would receive their first substantial royalty payments in 1970. Consequently, 1970 became the year when the band began to live large.
Twenty-four-year-old John Paul Jones bought himself a big new place
in Chorleywood, Hertfordshire, which he and wife Mo and their two
daughters moved into as soon as the band returned from America.
Twenty-two-year-old John Bonham finally moved out of the council
flat in Dudley he'd been living in since before the Atlantic advance
and relocated the family into a fifteen-acre farm in West Hagley, just
outside Brum. Plant – not twenty-two until August – had already paid
£8,000 the year before for a similar dwelling, Jennings Farm, near
Kidderminster. He now set about spending several more thousands
refurbishing it. Page kept the boathouse in Pangbourne but bought
Boleskine House – the home fifty years before of Aleister Crowley –
on the banks of Loch Ness.

But while Bonham and Jones immersed themselves in nest-building,
Plant was restless and began talking to Page on the phone about a
remote eighteenth-century cottage in Wales, which he recalled from a
childhood holiday. He told Jimmy how his father would pack the
family into his 1953 Vauxhall Wyvern and take them for a drive up
the A5 through Shrewsbury and Llangollen into Snowdonia. Places
with strange names, full of tales of sword and sorcery. The cottage,
named Bron-Yr-Aur (Welsh for, variously, 'golden hill', 'breast of gold'
or even 'hill of gold', pronounced Bron-raaar), had been owned by a
friend of his father's, and stood at the end of a narrow road just outside

the small market town of Machynlleth in Gwynedd. Plant further intrigued the guitarist by telling him of the giant Idris Gawr, who had a seat on the nearby mountain of Cader Idris, and how legend had it that anyone who sat on it would either die, go mad or become a poet; how King Arthur was said to have fought his final battle in the Ochr-yr-Bwlch pass just east of Dolgellau.

Page, who had only just begun to restore to its former glories the interior of his own new mythological abode – Boleskine – was equally taken by the idea of some time away from it all. Before committing full-time to the Yardbirds, he had been an occasional solo traveller, moving through India, America, Spain and elsewhere. Now, with Charlotte by his side and Plant talking of bringing wife Maureen and infant daughter Carmen and his dog Strider (named after Aragorn's alter ego in *Lord of the Rings*) with him, too, plans were laid for a sojourn together into the Welsh mountains.

Both men had also been very taken by the debut album two years before of Bob Dylan's former backing group, The Band: *Music from Big Pink*, famously named after the country house it was recorded in, in upstate New York. Jimmy and Robert weren't the only musicians newly influenced by The Band's ramshackle musical blend of rock, country, folk and blues. Eric Clapton had been so bowled over he had actually flown to Woodstock and asked to join the band, an overture they merely laughed at as they sat rolling another joint. George Harrison had also since flown out to hang out with them in LA, where they had fetched up to record their second album. Suddenly everyone, including all of Led Zeppelin, had beards, along with a new pastoral chic in sharp contrast to the blend of mod sharpness and pre-Raphaelite foppery which had dominated their look early on. There were other influences too, like Van Morrison's *Astral Weeks*, whose deeply spiritual, if somewhat bleak mix of folk and soul Plant was particularly taken with. Also Joni Mitchell, who Page now became besotted with, partly through her inspiring use of different acoustic guitar tunings, which were almost a match for his own in their range and obscurity, partly through her remarkably honest and clearly autobiographical songs – and, of course, her long blonde hair and aquiline features. The huge impact of Crosby Stills & Nash, who Plant had seen at the Albert Hall just before Zeppelin played there in January, had also been noted with intense interest by both men.

Above all, there was simply the desire to prove something about the band that neither the critics nor even the fans had picked up on yet, which was the fact that Led Zeppelin was not merely a one-trick pony. That there was more to Jimmy Page, certainly, than a growing collection of great rock riffs, not least his deep and abiding interest in the acoustic guitar. As soon as Robert suggested the cottage, Jimmy saw the potential. As he would later explain: 'It was the tranquillity of the place that set the tone of the album. After all the heavy, intense vibe of touring which is reflected in the raw energy of the second album, it was just a totally different feeling.'

You'd never seen yourself as a 'specialist' in the way that Eric obviously did. You loved the blues as much as anyone but you wouldn't have wanted to be lumbered with playing it forever the way he ended up doing. You'd always been too much into rock'n'roll – they didn't call Elvis the King for nothing. And then there was folk and classical, Celtic, Asian ... there would never be another James Burton or Scotty Moore. But there would never be anyone like Segovia or Julian Bream, either. You knew it didn't really fit together – or wasn't supposed to anyway. But in your mind it was all different sides of the same story. Same with someone like Manitas de Plata doing flamenco, just different approaches to the same thing really. Then there was Django Reinhardt and another completely different approach. Anything and everything you came across, you were able to digest and turn into something, especially if it involved new ways of playing the guitar, which is how you got into classical Indian music, wondering how on earth you played the sitar with its nine-strings, moveable frets and vibrating under-strings. Eventually buying one to try and find out ...

The guitar seemed to mirror your own personality. There was what you called your acoustic side – calm, quiet, meaningful but understated – and there was your electric side, the stuff that came out when you plugged your Gibson 'Black Beauty' in – loud, flash, attention-seeking, impossible to ignore. It wasn't about how good a player you were, it was about simple understanding. You didn't look upon yourself as particularly brilliant or gifted. You knew there were faster players than you. You knew there were technically better players than you. But there were few better all-rounders. Few who seemed to understand the importance of knowing more than one or two things at a time. That's why it was such fun playing with Cyril's interval band at the Marquee. They were bluesers but they could rock'n'roll

*too. Madmen, most of them, it was no surprise to you when they turned
up later in Screaming Lord Sutch's band.*

*It wasn't until you started doing sessions that you were forced to learn
the 'textbook' stuff. You never knew what you were going to be doing until
you got to there, which was good and bad. Sometimes it meant making it
up as you went along, almost telling them what to do. Others times, you
were so clueless you'd turn your amp off and just pretend to play along. It
wasn't like you'd heard it was in America, where you were meant to be a
specialist, brought in to do one specific thing, this one for soul, this one for
pop, this one for film music ... In London, the cats who got the gigs were
the ones who could do it all.*

*It was amazing how quickly things took off for you. First there was the
Johnny Howard and the Silhouettes thing, cheers for that Cyril. Then it
was Jet Harris and Tony Meehan and 'Diamonds', which Glyn Johns,
your old mate from Epsom who'd sung in The Presidents and was now
working as a tape op had recommended you for. When that went to no. 1
you couldn't believe it! So unreal, knowing you'd played on something that
was no. 1, yet no-one knowing it was you – except Jet and Tony, of course,
and the rest of the people behind the scenes. After that you got offered so
many different sessions it all turned into a blur. Some you never forgot, like
the time you were booked for the 'Goldfinger' session, playing in the John
Barry Orchestra for a day. Shirley Bassey turned up, threw her fur coat
on the floor, then strode up to the mike and just belted it out, perfect first
time – then fainted, spark out on the studio floor, everyone running around
like headless chickens trying to revive her. Some like 'Money Honey' by
Mickie Most and the Gear, you'd forgotten about practically the next day.
If someone had told you then how often Mickie the useless singer would
cross your path in the future you'd have thought they were bloody mad!*

*Even though you only read music 'like a six-year-old reads a book'
nothing seemed to hold you back. Before you, there had only really been
Big Jim Sullivan doing most of the sessions – him and Vic Flick and Alan
Parker, older geezers. Vic had played lead on the Bond theme with Big Jim
on rhythm. Now there was Little Jimmy Page to play rhythm while Big
Jim did the lead, like when you did 'My Baby Left Me' by Dave Berry
and the Cruisers. It was only a cover of Elvis's cover of Arthur Crudup's
song. But it got to no. 37 and you and Big Jim became quite matey after
that. You were both booked for the next Dave Berry single too, 'The Crying
Game', you strumming, Big Jim doing the obligato. Same thing when it*

came to stuff like 'Diamonds' and 'Hold Me'. Big Jim and Little Jimmy: you were the A team. Mostly, you were on your own, doing whatever came along, from the crud – 'Leave My Kitten Alone' by The First Gear, 'It Hurts When I Cry' by Sean Buckley and his Breadcrumbs – to big stuff like 'Hold Me' by PJ Proby, 'Walk Tall' by Val Doonican, 'The Last Waltz' by Englebert Humperdink, 'Little Arrows' by Leapy Lee, 'Tobacco Road' by the Nashville Teens – to the stuff that sort of fell in the middle like 'Baby Please Don't Go' by Them and 'Time Drags By' by Cliff Richard, so many you often didn't know you'd played on it till you heard it on the radio and recognised yourself. Sometimes not even that helped and you would swear blind you'd never been near the session. You didn't care. That is, you did and you didn't. As long as it all came with a nice fat cheque with your name on it what did it matter?

Except that it did matter. For your twenty-first birthday, you found yourself sitting in a circle with drummer Mickey Waller and a few other familiar faces, playing non-stop from ten in the morning till one in the afternoon on a Sonny Boy Williamson album. Four months later Sonny Boy died and somehow it didn't make sense. You playing on his last ever recording, but there it was. That's who you were now – a real pro. Such a pro, in fact, you were now playing on maybe half of all the records that were being produced in London, with Big Jim playing on the other half. The same year you even got to make a single of your own, a song you wrote in about ten minutes called 'She Just Satisfies', which – don't laugh – you even sang on! Yeah, well, so what? No-one would ever remember it anyway ...

Situated along a steep track that leads through a ravine, when Jimmy and Robert arrived at Bron-Yr-Aur in May they found a stone dwelling so derelict it had no electricity, running water or sanitation. Fortunately, as well as their respective partners, they had also brought Zeppelin roadies Clive Coulson and Sandy Macgregor with them, both of whom were now put in charge of domestic chores. 'It was freezing when we arrived,' Coulson remembered. He and Macgregor would be sent to carry water from a nearby stream and gather wood for the open-hearth fire, 'which heated a range with an oven on either side'. There were calor gas heaters but only candles to light the place. 'A bath was once a week in Machynlleth at the Owen Glendower pub. I'm not sure who got the job of cleaning out the chemical toilet ... '

Evenings off would also be spent at the pub, where they mingled with local farmers (from whom Page bought some goats which he had Coulson drive up to Boleskine House in a Transit), the local biker gang and some volunteers restoring another old house nearby. Invited to join in on 'Kumbayah' one night, Jimmy apologised and explained he didn't play guitar. Meanwhile, back at the cottage, where Page did play the guitar and Plant warbled on his harmonica, the songs began to come, sometimes just scraps, sometimes fully formed. Songs that would 'prove there was more to us than being a heavy metal band,' as Jimmy put it. Chief amongst them, 'Friends', built on some esoteric scales Page had brought back with him from a trip to India in Yardbirds' days laid over a conga drum that recalled the lumbering rhythm of 'Mars' from Holst's The Planets Suite, a big favourite; Plant's dreamy 'That's The Way'; and the rousting, misspelled 'Bron-Y-Aur Stomp'. There were also several begun there that would find a home not just on the next Zeppelin album but on their next four albums, including the bare bones of 'Stairway To Heaven', 'Over The Hills And Far Away', 'Down By The Seaside', 'The Rover', the similarly misspelled 'Bron-Y-Aur' and 'Poor Tom'.

Of the tracks that did make the third album, there was also 'Tangerine', with its nicely low-key, deliberate-mistake intro, originally begun at a disastrous final June 1968 Yardbirds session in New York as a song called 'My Baby', now reborn in Wales as a country-tinged, Neil Young-inspired dirge. As the Yardbirds had never copyrighted the piece, Page claimed authorship of the entire song, including the lyrics (even if they did smack of the classic flower-child-isms of Keith Relf). 'Bron-Y-Aur Stomp' had also begun life as another electric number, 'Jennings Farm Blues', laid down at Olympic the previous autumn, here transformed into a jugband hoedown dedicated to Plant's dog Strider. 'Walk down the country lanes, I'll be singin' a song,' Plant warbled cheerily, 'Hear the wind whisper in the trees that Mother Nature's proud of you and me . . .'

The song that really summed up the spirit of adventure at Bron-Yr-Aur was one that arrived almost unbidden late one afternoon as Jimmy and Robert traipsed through the surrounding flower-decked hills, then in full spring bloom. Stopping to smoke a joint and admire the view, Jimmy took the guitar he'd been carrying on his back and began strumming some random chords, half-remembered from Bert Jansch

and John Renbourn's version of the traditional arrangement 'The Waggoners Lad'. To Jimmy's delight, Robert began singing along in a much
more restrained voice than usual, ad-libbing the opening to what was
originally called 'The Boy Next Door' but later became 'That's The
Way'. Afraid to lose the moment, they pulled a cassette recorder out
of a knapsack and laid the rest of it down then and there. Afterwards,
they celebrated by sharing some squares of Kendal Mint Cake then
made their way back to the cottage where they sat before the fire
eating a fry-up and drinking cups of cider mulled by red-hot pokers,
listening back to endless repeats of the tape. Then they staggered off
to bed.

'We wrote those songs and walked and talked and thought and went
off to the Abbey where they hid the Grail,' Plant later told writer
Barney Hoskyns. 'No matter how cute and comical it might be now to
look back at that, it gave us so much energy, because we were really
close to something. We believed. It was absolutely wonderful, and my
heart was so light and happy. At that time, at that age, 1970 was like
the biggest blue sky I ever saw.'

Jones and Bonham were equally taken with the rough tapes of the
songs Page and Plant had returned with from Wales. Back in London
for a short stay at Olympic in early June, they struggled however to
recreate the atmosphere in the stale environs of a professional recording
facility. So they decided to decamp once again, this time for a dilapi-
dated mansion in Hampshire named Headley Grange, where with the
aide of the Rolling Stones' mobile studio, they hoped to have the
album finished before returning to the road in America in August.

Headley Grange had been found for them by Grant's secretary,
Carole Browne, through an ad she'd spotted in *The Lady*. Once again,
Page was attracted to the setting more by its history than its practical
application as a workplace. Known as Hallege in the Domesday Book,
the origins of Headley Village are even older than that, its landmarks
betraying its true age: Rectory Field, Long Cross Hill, Old Robin Hood,
Waggoners Lane, the Tithe Barn Pond ... Headley Workhouse, as it
was originally known, was a three-storey stone manor built for the
then substantial sum of £150 in 1795 in order to 'shelter the infirm,
aged paupers, orphans or illegitimate children of Headley' and nearby
Bramshott and Kingsley. Attacked by Swing rioters in 1830, it was still
known locally as Headley Poor when, in 1875, it was bought for £420

by a builder, Thomas Kemp, who converted it into a residence and renamed it Headley Grange.

With the advent of mobile studios – in the Stones' case, a bunch of recording equipment hot-wired together and loaded onto the back of a truck – and the Sixties fashion for 'getting it together in the country', the Grange began to be let out to rock groups by its widowed owner. Both Genesis and Fleetwood Mac had recorded there previously. With Page and Plant still enchanted by their newly consummated creative union, they were especially susceptible to their surroundings, and the austere, often bleak, mansion appealed to their same sense of adventure as the recent trip to Wales. 'It really looked to me as if it had been – not derelict, but it looked as if it had hardly been lived in,' said Jimmy. 'It had been a workhouse and it was quite interesting considering the tests we were going to put it to.' As Plant put it, 'We were living in this falling down mansion in the country. The mood was incredible.'

It wasn't all work though, with the band breaking for two weekends to play some dates. The first was two shows in Iceland on 20 and 21 June at a converted gymnasium in Reykjavic, from which they returned to Headley with a new, distinctly non-acoustic battle cry of a number called 'Immigrant Song', Plant solemnly intoning, '*We are your o-ver-looords . . .*' to chilling effect. The workers at the venue were on strike at the time so the local student body ganged together to help put on the show. 'The students took over,' Robert later told me, 'and got the whole thing going and it was just amazing. When we played there it really did feel like we were inhabiting a parallel universe, quite apart from everything else, including the rock world of the times.'

The following Sunday evening they were back for their second Bath Festival appearance, held not at the Recreation Ground this time but a much larger site in Shepton Mallet, ten miles away, where more than 150,000 people would eventually show up over the duration of the two-day event. The official line peddled by Grant to the press, via Bill Harry, was that the band was playing at Bath despite an offer of $200,000 to play in America that weekend – almost certainly Grant and Harry's shrewd attempt to drum up a bit of useful PR for the event. Nevertheless, it became another key moment in winning over the British music press.

B.P. Fallon, then working as PR for T. Rex but soon to become Zeppelin's publicist as well, was at Bath and remembers it well.

'Zeppelin had killed at the Bath Festival in 1970,' he says now from his home in New York. 'I was there as a punter, me and my girlfriend Eileen Webster, on acid in the VIP enclosure at the very front. The sunset was tickling the skies and this Led Zeppelin monster exploding into action yards away was like a fucking rocket going off and carrying us to Mars and beyond. Beyond brilliant, you know? But there was no strategic follow-up, not really. A bunch of small UK dates in spring 1971 and a month of concerts that autumn. I mean, Zeppelin were big but the focus had been on conquering the States. People in Britain knew that Led Zeppelin were doing very well in America but mostly they were lumped in with Ten Years After or Savoy Brown or Keef Hartley or whoever – this blues-based Second British Invasion Of America.' However, it was after Bath that Zeppelin began their rapid ascent in Britain to what Fallon describes now as 'full-on and on fire. They'd never done such an extensive UK tour – up and down the country for two months – and the press *en masse* finally got it as much as the fans. And after that, Led Zeppelin were treble-mega in Britain. Tick that box! Next!'

Also on the bill that year were Canned Heat, Steppenwolf, Pink Floyd, Johnny Winter, Fairport Convention, Jefferson Airplane, Frank Zappa and the Mothers of Invention, the Moody Blues, the Byrds, Santana, Dr John and nearly a dozen others. It should have been a landmark occasion but despite the eternal hippy ingénue Plant telling the crowd how 'really nice' it was 'to come to an open-air festival where there's no bad things happening', for its organisers, Freddy and Wendy Bannister, it became 'a vision of hell'. The problems began, says Wendy, 'when it suddenly became a free festival' after thousands of ticketless fans pulled down the two miles of chain-link fence the Bannisters had erected and just walked in. Freddy continues, 'Political militancy had grown enormously in just twelve months and there were all these "revolutionary" hippies from France there stirring things up. It was all, "Bannister is a bread-head." Of course, they never talked about how much money the groups all charged . . .'

Zeppelin's fee alone had risen from the £500 the Bannisters had paid them the previous year to £20,000 – 'enough for a house in Knightsbridge in those days,' as Wendy puts it. Grant insisted Zeppelin's name was double the size of anyone else's on the poster. 'As I'd already given my word to [Zappa manager] Bill Thompson that that wouldn't happen, he was very cross with me,' says Freddy. 'But Zeppelin were making it very big in America and we had to have Zeppelin. They were simply so enormous by then we knew that they'd bring in all the people.'

Intermittent rain throughout the weekend meant that by Sunday the only road leading to the site had become all but impassable. According to John Paul Jones, 'Peter Grant spent nine hours in a car getting down there.' Never one to walk when he could ride, Jones eventually hired a helicopter to ferry him to the site from nearby Denham Airport. 'Cheaper than a hired car, for some reason,' he recalled. The problem was they could only land in a field a couple of miles from the site. Fortunately for Jonesy, a posse of Hell's Angels offered him a lift through the mud on the back of one of their bikes 'It was a great entrance, I have to say. I was carrying a mandolin [and] I had a cowboy hat on – Peter Fonda!'

There were so many problems the only time Freddy Bannister went into the stage area throughout the entire weekend, he says, 'was to go and sort the Hell's Angels out. I'm not sure how tired or how stupid I was, but I did that on my own. I went and bought them off! I got them all backstage and I said, "Hey, this can't go on. You're being an absolute pain. I don't want you here, I want you to leave. I'll give you money".' The Angels took the £400 proffered by the stricken promoter and left without further trouble. 'Thank goodness they weren't like their American counterparts,' Freddy shakes his head, 'or I'd probably have been shot or stabbed.'

Also at the show that day was film-maker Joe Massot, who had directed the 1967 cult classic *Wonderwall*, shooting scenes on stage and off with his own 16mm camera. 'With the sun setting behind Robert's hair, the whole gig took on another dimension,' he recalled. However, the real scene-setter in this instance was Peter Grant, who – realising the sun was setting directly behind the stage – ordered Ricardo and crew to wade in and put a premature end to the band that was then in mid-set, a jazz-rock ensemble named The Flock. Which they did, unplugging cables and cutting off Flock violinist Jerry Goodman mid-cadenza, as Grant readied his charges into hurriedly following them straight on. 'I found out from the Met office what time the sun was setting,' Grant told Dave Lewis, 'and by going on at eight in the evening I was able to bring the lights up a bit at a time. And it was

vital we went on to match that. That's why I made sure Flock or
whoever it was got off on time.' As a result, Zeppelin's near three-hour
set began with a halo of sunlight descending into the horizon behind
their heads, the band dressed, as per their new pastoral mode, as
tweedy troubadours, heavily bearded, Page even sporting what looked
like a scarecrow's hat. 'I remember Jefferson Airplane and Janis Joplin
were also on the bill,' Plant once told me, 'and I remember standing
there thinking: I've gone from West Bromwich to this! I've really got
to eat this up. The whole thing seemed extraordinary to me. I was as
astonished as the audiences some nights . . .'

It was also at Bath that Page first met Roy Harper, destined to
become the titular subject of another of the songs on their next album –
'Hats Off To (Roy) Harper'. Rustic jester, folk troubadour, Harper
would exert an unusual influence on everyone he came into contact
with, including Led Zeppelin. Born in Manchester in 1941 but brought
up in Blackpool, Harper was a stereotypical English eccentric whose
formative years had seen him feign madness to get out of the RAF,
the result of which was five years in and out of mental hospital and
prison. He spent the early part of the Sixties reading poetry and busking
around Europe. Having washed up in London in 1964, he became a
fixture on the folk circuit, where Page had first noticed him, before
eventually recording his own albums, all quite distinct, all utterly
uncommercial.

Seeing Harper wandering around backstage at Bath, Jimmy, who
would make a guest appearance later that year on Harper's remarkable
Stormcock album, approached him and asked to be shown how he
played an instrumental from his first album, *Blackpool*. 'So I played it
for him,' remembered Harper, 'and he said, "Thanks very much". We
exchanged pleasantries and then he walked away. The only thing I
thought as I watched him leave was, "That guy's pants are too short
for him".' It wasn't until he saw Zeppelin perform that day that he
realised who Page was. 'During the second song, all the young women
in the crowd started to stand up involuntarily, with tears running down
their faces. It was like, "Jesus, what's happening here then?" In the end,
you knew you'd seen something you were never going to forget.'

Though he didn't know it then, it was also the start of a long
relationship between the two guitarists, with various members appearing at Harper shows and Harper opening occasionally for Zeppelin.

(Harper would fulfil a similar role for Pink Floyd, appearing on their 1975 opus, *Wish You Were Here*.) Nevertheless, he was taken aback some weeks later to discover his name on the next Zeppelin album. 'I went to their office one day and Jimmy said, "Here's the new record.". "Oh ... thanks," I said, and tucked it under my arm. "Well, look at it then!"' So Harper looked at it and twirled the little wheel around. 'Very nice and all that. So he went, "*Look at it!*" Then I discovered "Hats Off To Harper". I was very touched.' As he should have been. That one track would introduce the perennially unsuccessful Harper to millions of album buyers around the world over the next few years. 'As far as I'm concerned,' said Page, 'hats off to anybody who does what they think is right and refuses to sell out.' Or as Plant would later jokingly recall, 'Somebody had to have a wry sense of humour and a perspective which stripped ego instantly [and] we couldn't get Zappa.' Adding: 'That's not to say he didn't occasionally enjoy some of the Led Zeppelin by-products – like the occasional blow-job!'

Back at Headley Grange, they continued honing their new material. Eventually there would be seventeen near-complete tracks. To the acoustic-based material from Bron-Yr-Aur they now added 'Hats Off To (Roy) Harper', a piece of spontaneous combustion initiated by Page late one night inspired by some frenzied slide-guitar channelling of Bukka White's 'Shake 'Em On Down' (credited on the sleeve to Charles Obscure), and 'Gallows Pole', a rollicking reinvention of a centuries-old English folk song called 'The Maid Freed From The Gallows', a striking contemporary version of which Page remembered fondly from the B-side of a 1965 single by Dorris Henderson. A black American who'd arrived in London singing Appalachian mountain songs, Page first heard Henderson after she'd teamed up briefly with future Pentangle guitarist John Renbourn. Her debut single, a version of Paul Simon's 'The Leaves That Are Green', had sunk without trace, but the B-side, a new arrangement of 'The Maid ...' by Henderson that she'd dubbed 'Hangman' had stuck in Jimmy's mind. Credited on *Led Zeppelin III* as 'Trad arrangement: Page, Plant', it has since erroneously been cited as a derivative of the Leadbelly tune 'Gallis Tree', a version of which Bert Jansch also performed in the mid-Sixties. Page has subsequently claimed that the inspiration came from Fred Gerlach, an American acoustic pioneer whose album of Leadbelly covers, *12 String Guitar*, released in the late-Fifties on the Folkways label, also featured a version of the track. However, one listen to the age-old original confirms the truth, along with lyrics barely altered by Plant.

There were also a handful of electric, more obviously Zep-sounding tub-thumpers like 'Immigrant Song', 'Celebration Day' and 'The Bathroom Song' (so-called because everyone said the drums sounded like they had been recorded in the bathroom, but later changed to 'Out On The Tiles'), plus the foundation of what would become one of their finest ballads, the exquisite blues, 'Since I've Been Loving You'. Begun at Olympic during the same truncated sessions that produced the original electric 'Jenning's Farm', the band had already aired a shorter, tighter version live at Bath, but it wasn't until now that they tried to finish it. That said, the genesis of what was destined to become one of Zeppelin's most famous tracks can again be fairly clearly pinned down to an earlier, typically unaccredited blues jam by Moby Grape titled 'Never'. Located on the giveaway *Grape Jam* album that accompanied the band's official debut release, *Wow*, in 1968, as the Grape remain one of Plant's favourite San Francisco groups of the period, it's inconceivable the singer was not already acquainted with 'Never'. Indeed, the opening lines of 'Since I've Been Loving You' – 'Working from seven to eleven every night, it really makes life a drag, I don't think that's right' – are almost identical to those on 'Never', which go: 'Working from eleven to seven every night, ought to make life a drag, yeah, and I know that ain't right.' Plant also appears to echo Grape vocalist Bob Mosley when elsewhere he sings of being 'the best of fools' and complains his baby can't hear him crying.

There are also uncanny echoes in the music, both songs being extrapolations from a stately BB King-style blues, the main difference being Page's more coherent direction, working it up into a melodramatic musical statement with beginning, middle and end where the Grape working is more content to meander forth in the one-take jam style it was intended. With Plant also displaying his new Van Morrison and Janis Joplin influences on the scatted vocal amidst the sound of Bonzo's oil-free bass pedal squeaking, Jonesy's jazzy bed of keyboards, while playing the bass pedals of the Hammond organ with his feet, all that was needed to round it off was a typically spine-tingling guitar solo from Jimmy. The tape-operative at the session was a young former supermarket shelf-stacker named Richard Digby Smith. As he told *Mojo* in 2000: 'I can see Robert at the mike now. He was so passionate.

Lived every line. What you got on the record is what happened. His only preparation was a herbal cigarette and a couple of shots of Jack Daniel's ... I remember Pagey pushing him, "Let's try the outro chorus again, improvise a bit more."' He went on, 'There was a hugeness about everything Zeppelin did. I mean, look behind you and there was Peter Grant sitting on the sofa – the whole sofa.'

In an effort to try to complete the album, by now they had abandoned Headley for the more polished surrounds of Island's No. 2 studio at Basing Street in Notting Hill Gate. It was here that Page had demoed a guide solo for 'Since I've Been Loving You' – done with no real thought, just off the top of his head using someone else's amp. But try as he might, he just couldn't come up with the finished article. It was also during these sessions that the first rough recording of another new song, 'No Quarter', written by Jonesy, was etched out. But all other considerations went out the window as Page battled to come up with a suitably spine-tingling solo to finish off 'Since I've Been Loving You'. But by the time their next American tour began in Cincinnati on 5 August, the album still wasn't finished and Page was left with no option but to repeat the gruelling process that had characterised the previous summer's US tour, jetting off to the studio between shows. Fortunately, he was able to call on his old friend Terry Manning at Ardent Studios in Memphis for help. 'I'd pick Jimmy up at the airport and drive him straight to the studio to begin work. Peter always accompanied Jimmy too. No-one else, though. I think Robert came in for one day. Bonham came in for one. That was it.'

Manning remembers editing 'a lot' out of 'Gallows Pole' and Jimmy trying – and repeatedly failing – to find the right solo for 'Since ...' 'In the end Jimmy accepted that the demo solo done in England was not going to be bettered and so that was the one they eventually used. Listening back now, it's my all-time number one favourite rock guitar solo. We took three or four other takes and tried to put takes together and come up with something, and they were all great. But there's something magic about that one take [he did], that stream of consciousness.'

Page worked alone with Manning on the mix of the album. Manning says that the much looser approach – the tape-echo at the start of 'Immigrant Song', the wayward segue between 'Friends' and 'Celebration Day', the occasional voices you can hear in the background, what a quarter of a century later would be called 'lo-fi' – was 'all thought out, not accidental at all'. It was this aspect, he says now, that demonstrated to him what 'a *really* brilliant producer' Page was. 'Not to demean or cast any aspersions,' he adds, choosing his words carefully, 'but I think he harmed himself perhaps in a few ways later on. But at that particular time, the very early days, Jimmy was an incredibly insightful, true musical genius, in my opinion, and I've seen a lot of musical people. I would say that very little happened by accident. Yes, there would be the occasional take that you can't repeat so you go with that but it did take the insight to know that. He studied everything. When it says "produced by Jimmy Page" it *seriously* was. He asked me, "What do you think about leaving the beginning of the 'Celebration Day' thing on [referring to the moment when Bonham can be heard shouting 'Fuck!']? No-one ever seemed to pick up on it. But he said, "That's not why I wanna leave it, not cos that's cool. I like the sonic texture of everything. I like the feel that you're really there.". We really talked all that through.'

You had been writing bits of music almost since you'd begun playing the guitar. Then after playing on LP sessions and B-sides for the likes of Nico, John Mayall, Joe Cocker, the Kinks, The Who – endless, nameless – the whole thing was less of a mystery. If they could do it, well . . . especially when you found out how much money the writers of hit songs could actually make. When you were hired to play on a Burt Bacharach session you were flabbergasted to see him leaving in a chauffeur-driven Rolls Royce. Then someone started counting off all the hit songs he and Hal David had written and the light started to dawn in your eyes. You started writing songs and you started punting them around with all your contacts at the publishing companies in Tin Pan Alley.

Then you met Jackie DeShannon and things started to make more sense. Jackie was from Kentucky. The first American girl you'd ever really known, she was different. A professional songwriter who also sang, she'd been invited by the Beatles to come to London and make a single after they'd all fallen in love with her when she'd opened for them on a tour. And guess who got hired to play on the session . . . 'Don't Turn Your Back On Me, Babe' it was called and it was good, actually. She said 'It goes like this' and showed you the guitar chords. You got it first time and she said, 'That's fast! It usually takes them a long time to get it off in the States.' You didn't know if that was true but the way she looked at you when she said it, you knew what she meant. You ended up back at her hotel, writing songs together. Well, she did most of the writing, you just played along, coming up with a line or two here or there, a title perhaps, but by the end of it you had about eight songs – and you were in love. Weirdest of all, the songs you'd written together started getting picked up by people. Marianne Faithfull did one, P.J. Proby, Esther Phillips . . .

It was while you were with Jackie that you made your own first record: 'She Just Satisfies'. Your own song with you singing and Jackie on backing vocals. You were twenty-one and suddenly it was like you had the whole world by the arse. What a summer that was! You and Jackie, being seen out together around town, you in your navy blue donkey jacket, Jackie looking like the real deal – older, smarter, American, showing it all off in her tight skirts and big jewellery, holding your hand. Marianne Faithfull couldn't believe it when she saw you! No-one could! Jackie had written 'When You Walk In The Room', a hit for The Searchers, and she knew people and things you didn't. But you were on the scene in London and you could take her places she'd never been, too, show her stuff no-one else knew, her and her best friend Sharon Sheeley – another songwriter who'd been in the car crash that killed Eddie Cochran. Taking them to hip underground scenes to see 'recitations' by your favourite folk guitarists Bert Jansch and John Renbourn, showing them off, one to the other . . .

Even after Jackie went back to America, you kept writing and suddenly, just like that, probably because of the stuff with Jackie you'd already had placed, people started paying attention. 'Just Like Anyone Would Do' became a B-side for the Fifth Avenue; 'The Last Mile' which your new pal Andrew Loog Oldham did the lyrics for and became a B-side for Gregory Phillips; then there was 'Wait For Me', another B-side, this time for the Fleurs De Lys . . . You never really made any bread out of these things. Not like you did doing sessions. But it was a fair start and you began to divide the two things in your mind: session work that paid the bills – like the awful easy-listening instrumental LP you did called Kinky Music *– and what you were starting to see more and more as your own thing, like when you and Jeff sat down together and started busking together on Ravel's 'Bolero'. You never turned your back on guys like Big Jim though. They were the salt of the earth, the crème de la crème.*

Even so, for you it all came back to Davy Graham and his album, The Guitar Player, *the way he showed you and everybody else how to go from folk to jazz to baroque, blues, even Oriental and Asian. Davy and all the others that got there before you like Bert Jansch, Ralph McTell, Mick Softley, Jon Mark, Wizz Jones, all those weird-beards you'd go and watch play in smoky pubs full of ugly old men and surprisingly beautiful young birds. After Davy Graham, best of all were Bert Jansch and John Renbourn, whose album,* Bert and John, *you played again and again, figuring out the tunings, the fingerings, the whole weird whatchamacallit. They would play the Olive Tree in Croydon and Eric would also turn up. George Harrison was another who knew and dug the Eastern influence in their playing, who knew what was going on with John Mayer's Indo-Jazz Fusions and 'trance jazz' guitarist Gabor Szabo, the good gear like 'Krishna', 'The Search For Nirvana' and 'Ravi' . . . a 'salaam' to Ravi Shankar, the sitar player who'd done* Portrait of Genius, *which you and George argued over who'd heard first when you both knew it was Renbourn who'd been the first to find it, the first to turn you both onto it. Of course, Ravi was more interested in the fact that a Beatle was a fan of his music but even George knew the score there . . .*

What you liked best was that it wasn't meant to go anywhere, just digging the sound of the moment, spontaneous and seductive. McCartney found it 'boring' but what did he bloody know? Even Big Jim was into it, going out and buying his own sitar after catching a session by some Indian musicians at Abbey Road. When he used it on a new arrangement of 'She Moved Through The Fair' it blew your fucking mind! When Jeff persuaded the Yardbirds manager Georgio Gomelsky to use you on the session for 'Heart Full Of Soul', telling him you were good at coming up with 'weird sounds', you couldn't believe it when you turned up and saw the Indian musicians tuning up in the main room. Jeff had dragged you into the toilet where you both sat trying to come up with some gimmick to make the guitar sound like a sitar. Jeff finally came up with something and Georgio decided you and the Indian musicians weren't needed anymore. But you ran in and persuaded the sitar player to sell you his instrument – that and the bit of old carpet it was wrapped in, Georgio laughing as you walked out the studio with it under your arm, pleased as Punch . . .

It was also Terry Manning that Jimmy Page would ask to help master the album. With albums produced, mixed and largely made on computer these days, mastering a vinyl record is almost a lost art. Back in 1970, though, it was still one of the most crucial parts of the recording process. Using a lathe to transfer the sound from acetate onto vinyl, great care and an even greater set of ears were essential. Jimmy and Terry were well aware that many potentially marvellous albums had been ruined over the years because of poor technique at the mastering stage and they approached the task with great seriousness. That is, until the final moments, when adding the usual catalogue numbers that would be stamped onto the run-out groove of the finished record.

'Working with Big Star, we had added some messages of our own on there,' Manning says now. 'I mentioned this to Jimmy and said, "Anything you wanna write?" and he said, "Ooh, yeah ..."' Due to the enormous quantity of copies the pressing plant knew they would need to fill the advance orders alone on the next Zeppelin album, they had requested two sets of masters – not unusual for the biggest-selling American acts in those days. As a result, Page would come up with four separate 'messages', one per side of each master. Manning continues: 'We'd been talking about the Aleister Crowley thing, so he said "Give me a few minutes", and he sat down and he thought and he scribbled some things out and he finally came up with "Do What Thou Wilt Shall Be the Whole of the Law" and "So Mote It Be" and one other one which I've forgotten.' I suggest perhaps either 'Love Is the Law' or perhaps 'Love under Will', Crowley's other two most famous maxims, and Manning responds: 'I suspect the latter. Sounds the most familiar ...'

Did he share Page's interest in Crowley and the occult? He pauses. 'Well, I was always of a somewhat philosophical bent, of wonderment and experimentation, and what if and what other cultures think, and that sort of thing. So Jimmy's Aleister Crowley leanings were interesting to me. I didn't believe everything that Crowley ever wrote perhaps but it was interesting, I really wanted to study it more and see what it was all about. But [Jimmy] had a big love of all kinds of literature, and he had a definite interest in all things like that. I remember even before a show he would be sitting sometimes just reading things. Once he'd figured out what he wanted to say, I took this little metal pencil-like thing and wrote them very carefully, because if you drop that thing you've ruined your master. You can't touch the grooves, you have to lean over. Very difficult to do, that's why they don't really like you doing that. But we did it.' He recalls with a wry chuckle how: 'After we had written them we had the biggest laugh in the world. It was such a funny joke. We said, "Ha ha, maybe some day collectors will be trying to buy both sets so they can have everything. Ha ha ha! That's hilarious, no-one would ever do that!" '

He adds: 'By the way, when the first run of printed album jackets came from the printers, Jimmy found that they had left off my credit. He actually ordered all of those be destroyed and reprinted, with my credit included. That was not only expensive, but a very big thing to do and something I will of course always be grateful to Jimmy for. So I don't like to hear it when people sometimes say that Zeppelin in general, or Jimmy in particular, have failed to give credit where credit is due. In my experience, at least, the opposite was true. Jimmy went out of his way and spent extra money to be sure that credit was given.'

Released on 23 October 1970, two weeks after its release in America, *Led Zeppelin III* was already at no. 1 in the US album chart by the time it went on sale at home in Britain, where it would also top the charts. Nevertheless, it was destined to become one of their most overlooked collections, misunderstood and largely reviled by the critics even to this day. Even the fans seemed confounded, and though the album would eventually shift in its millions, it remains one of the comparatively weakest sellers in the Zeppelin canon. Indeed, by the start of 1971 it had all but disappeared from the charts, while its more popular predecessor maintained a steady presence in both the US and UK Top 40s. (Today, the album has sold more than six million copies in the US alone, an outstanding achievement for most artists, but still comparatively few when one considers that the first Zeppelin album has sold more than 10 million in the same market and the second more than 12 million, while its successor is now the fourth-largest selling album of all time with more than 22 million. Indeed, of the first six Zeppelin albums, *Led Zeppelin III* is still the lowest seller.)

As Terry Manning says now, the arrival of a mainly acoustic album from the recently crowned kings of heavy rock 'shocked both Zeppelin fans and people that weren't Zeppelin fans'. But if many were left nonplussed by the unexpected change in musical direction, the same critics who had previously attacked them for being shallow peddlers of roisterous clichés now accused them of daring to undermine such perceptions by singularly failing to repeat the trick. At best, they assumed the band had been unduly influenced by the recent success of Crosby, Stills & Nash, whose remarkable debut album had seen a seismic shift in critical opinion on where rock was – and should – be heading at the dawn of the new decade. This was a charge that Page, in particular, whose background in acoustic roots music was well-established long before it became the fashionable sound of Southern California, was furious over. 'I'm obsessed – not just interested, obsessed – with folk music,' he said, pointing out that he had spent many years studying 'the parallels between a country's street music and its so-called classical and intellectual music, the way certain scales have travelled right across the globe. All this ethnological and musical interaction fascinates me.'

But no-one was listening. Instead, the critics screamed betrayal. Under the headline 'Zepp weaken!' *Disc & Music Echo* typically enquired: 'Don't Zeppelin care any more?' There were occasional flashes of insight from the press. Lester Bangs – who had previously chastised Zeppelin for their 'insensitive grossness' – wrote in *Rolling Stone*: '"That's The Way" is the first song they've ever done that's truly moved me. Son of a gun, it's beautiful.' But the feeling persisted that Bangs, as was his wont, was simply swimming against the heavy tide of negative criticism the album was universally attracting, and Jimmy admitted he 'got really brought down' to the point where he refused to do any press interviews. According to Terry Manning, however, Page had anticipated such reactions. 'He was quite apprehensive but quite determined. We spoke of these matters as we were in the studio completing it. He would say, "This is so different, this is going to shock people." And it did.'

'I felt a lot better once we started performing it,' Page would tell Dave Schulps in 1977, 'because it was proving to be working for the people who came around to see us. There was always a big smile there in front of us. That was always more important than any poxy review.' Looking back now, Page still bridles at the rough ride the third album got from everybody. 'Even the record company said, "But there's no 'Whole Lotta Love' on it." We said, "That's right, there was never meant to be!" I think all of the albums were a reflection of what we were doing, how we were living, or where we were, at that point in time. I mean, geographically where we were as well as musically. So, basically, you've got the idea of what [the third album] was. We were living-in – first at the cottage, then at Headley Grange – and it was a question of getting up and kicking it off, getting the ball rolling, and getting the tape running.'

However, with an irate Page refusing to explain or make excuses to the press in 1970, it was left to Robert Plant to defend the album. 'Now we've done *Zeppelin III* the sky's the limit,' he told *Record Mirror.* 'It shows we can change. It means there are endless possibilities and directions for us to go in.' An entirely prophetic statement, as the next Zeppelin album would demonstrate in no uncertain terms. But that was still a year away and for now the band was forced to live through the first dip in what until then had been a steady upward surge in their commercial fortunes. By the start of 1971 'Zep to Split' stories were even beginning to pepper the British music papers.

But if the third Zeppelin album polarised opinion, in the long term it went a considerable way to cementing their reputation, confounding expectations and proving there was more to them than simply being the 'new Cream' they had started life as. Instead of more wall-shaking heavy rock classics, the third Zeppelin album should be looked at as the first convincing marriage of Page's fiery occult blues and Plant's swirling Welsh mists; the first serious proof of the band's ability to move beyond the commercial straitjacket that would eventually leave contemporaries like Black Sabbath and Deep Purple marooned in a creative cul-de-sac, churning out copycat hits until they finally ran out of steam, key members coming and going, their reputations sealed forever as second-rung niche acts, truly loved only by heavy metal fanatics.

Besides, with bands like Sabbath now doing the job for them – 'We used to lie on the floor of the rehearsal room, stoned, listening to the first two Zep albums,' Sabbath's Geezer Butler told me, confessing that the band's most famous song, 'Paranoid', 'was just a rip-off of "Communication Breakdown". I said, "We can't do that!" Guess who was wrong?' – the determinedly non-metallic direction of the new material was, in retrospect, not only a brave but exceptionally shrewd move.

As Terry Manning says, 'None of it was accidental. [Jimmy] knew they could not be more than the greatest heavy rock band if they didn't expand into new avenues, into more than just beating you on the head with a riff. You take a band like the Beatles, or Pink Floyd, the kind of bands that kids of fifteen love today as much as the kids of thirty or forty years ago, and they sound totally different from their first album to the middle of their career to the end of their career. And Jimmy knew that. He wanted to be more. The first two Zeppelin albums are quite different from the Yardbirds. He wanted to keep going, keep expanding. He would talk about rhythms, and people like Bartok, Karl Heinz Stockhausen or John Cage. He was totally into Indian classical music, Irish folk music, all sorts of things.'

This fact would become ever more clear on subsequent Zeppelin albums, where Page's fondness for such seemingly disparate musical bedfellows as funk, reggae, doo-wop, jazz, synth-pop and rockabilly would make themselves felt amidst the symphonic slabs of rock. For now, the third album showcased what he describes as 'my CIA'. That is to say, 'my Celtic, Indian and Asian influences. I always had much broader influences than I think people realised, all the way right through, even when I was doing [session] work. When I was hanging around with Jeff before he was in the Yardbirds, I was still listening to all different things.'

As if to add insult to injury, the gatefold sleeve of the third album was often more positively reviewed than the music therein. Designed by an old college pal of Jimmy's who liked to go by the name of Zacron, then a tutor at Wimbledon College of Art who had been asked to design something which reflected the less frenetic, more bucolic nature of the music, the end result consisted of a self-consciously 'surreal' collection of seemingly random images on a white background – butterflies, stars, zeppelins, colourful little smudges. The most striking element was a rotatable inner disc card, or volvelle, based on crop rotation charts which, when turned, revealed more indecipherable sigils and occasional photos of the band peeping through holes in the outer cover. The sort of thing that simply wouldn't be conceived of on a CD cover, it veered drastically away from what Page had actually asked for and was more to do with Zacron's own taste, rotating graphics being a signature of his work since 1965.

Speaking in 2007, however, Zacron recalled Page phoning him from New York to congratulate him on the job, saying 'I think it is fantastic.' But Jimmy told *Guitar World* in 1998, 'I wasn't happy with the final result.' Zacron had got far too 'personal' and 'disappeared off with it ... I thought it looked very teeny-bopperish. But we were on top of a deadline, so of course there was no way to make any radical changes to it. There were some silly bits – little chunks of corn and nonsense like that.'

Thankfully out on the road, things were less complicated, the band still going from strength to strength, whatever acoustic subtleties employed on their new album sacrificed in concert for all-out rock Götterdämmerung. With 'Immigrant Song' becoming another Top 20 single, reaching no. 16 during a thirteen-week run on the *Billboard* chart, their 1970 summer tour of the US was their biggest and most prestigious yet, topped off on 19 and 20 September with two sold-out three-hour shows at Madison Square Garden – their first time at New York's most famous venue, for which they were paid a guarantee of $100,000 a night.

The same month, under the heading 'Zeppelin Topple Beatles', they were voted Best Group in the annual Readers Poll of *Melody Maker*, the same music paper which had slated *Zeppelin III* for 'ripping off' Crosby Stills & Nash. The first act for eight years to oust the Beatles from the top spot in what was then the UK's most prestigious music magazine, the band returned to London for a special reception where they were also presented with yet more gold discs.

The band's profile at home was further boosted – if that's the right word – with the first appearance in the singles' chart of one of their songs. A year on from refusing to allow Atlantic to release 'Whole Lotta Love' as a single, Alexis Korner and Danish bluesman Peter Thorup took their own brass-heavy cover of it to no. 13, under the aegis CCS – for Collective Consciousness Society, another of Korner's short-lived but briefly successful outfits. (They would also do a less successful version of 'Black Dog' in 1972.) Taking their cue from the Johnny Harris Orchestra, who'd been specialising in jazzed-up orchestral versions of rock classics like '(I Can't Get No) Satisfaction' and 'Light My Fire' since the late Sixties, it was the CCS version of 'Whole Lotta Love' that would also become the theme tune for the next fifteen years to *Top Of The Pops*, Britain's enormously popular weekly TV show – a programme which, ironically, Zeppelin themselves would never actually appear on. (Dropped in the Eighties, the CCS version would be revamped into a techno-dance version and res-urrected as the show's theme tune in the Nineties.) 'It was pretty infectious, I suppose,' shrugged Jimmy, 'although its being on *Top of the Pops* every week killed it [in Britain], which was a drag.'

Another less successful attempt to cash in on the band's rapidly mushrooming fame had come from Screaming Lord Sutch, whose 1970 album *Lord Sutch And Heavy Friends* boasted much trumpeted 'guest appearances' from Jeff Beck, John Bonham and Jimmy Page, the latter also credited as 'producer'. When asked about it years later, Page sighed, 'It was a favour.' One he now appeared to regret. Or as Beck recalled years later, 'I loved Lord Sutch's act – it was fabulous. But when that record came out with [us] on it, I was surprised and annoyed . . . I vaguely remember recording it, in some sleazy studio up a side alley.' In fact, it was the product of several chance meetings between Sutch and whoever he could rope into the studio for a night. In the case of Page and Bonham, the meeting had occurred in LA at the start of the year when they had attended a three-night residency Sutch had somehow secured for himself at Thee Experience. Encountering the two sozzled Zeppelin members backstage after the show the recalcitrant frontman had no problem enticing them into the studio to 'guest' for him on 'a few tracks'. The subsequent album would remain an embarrassment for as long as it stayed on the radar of the music press, which fortunately for all concerned wasn't long.

Page was relieved. He had known David Sutch since he'd played on his 1964 single 'She's Fallen in Love with the Monster Man', a typically echo-heavy stab at a schlock horror movie soundtrack that fooled no-one. When it came to scary music though, Jimmy had left behind pantomime villains like Sutch a long time ago. He was now into the real thing . . .

PART TWO

The Curse of King Midas

'Nay! For I am of the Serpent's party;
Knowledge is good, be the price what it may.'

– Aleister Crowley, *The Psychology of Hashish*

9

So Mote It Be

The thing that dominated the room [was] a vast double circle on the floor in what appeared to be whitewash. Between the concentric circles were written innumerable words. Farthest away from all this, about two feet outside the circle and three feet over to the north, was a circle enclosed by a triangle, also much lettered inside and out. [The magician] entered the circle and closed it with the point of his sword and proceeded to the centre where he laid the sword across the toes of his white shoes; then he drew a wand from his belt and unwrapped it, laying the red silk cloth across his shoulders. 'From now on,' he said, in a normal, even voice, 'no-one is to move.'

From somewhere inside his vestments he produced a small crucible which he set at his feet before the sword. Small blue flames promptly began to rise from the bowl and he cast incense into it. 'We are to call upon Marchosias, a great marquis of the Descending Hierarchy,' he said. 'Before he fell, he belonged to the Order of Dominations among the angels. His virtue is that he gives true answers. Stand fast all . . .'

With a sudden motion [the magician] thrust the end of his rod into the surging flames . . . at once the air of the hall rang with a long, frightful chain of woeful howls. Above the bestial clamour [the magician] shouted: 'I adjure thee, great Marchosias, the agent of the Emperor Lucifer and of his beloved son Lucifuge Rofocale by the power of the pact . . .' The noise rose higher and a green steam began to come off the brazier. But there was no other answer. His face white and cruel, [the magician] rasped over the tumult: 'I adjure thee, Marchosias, by the pact and by the names, appear instanter.' He plunged the rod a second time into the flames. The room screamed . . . but still there was no apparition.

The rod went back into the fire. Instantly the place rocked as though the earth moved under it. 'Stand fast,' [the magician] said hoarsely. Something

else said, 'Hush, I am here. What dost thou seek of me? Why dost thou
disturb my repose?' The building shuddered again ... then from the middle
of the triangle to the northwest, a slow cloud of yellow fumes went up
towards the ceiling, making them all cough, even [the magician]. As it
spread and thinned [they] could see a shape forming under it ... it was
something like a she-wolf, grey and immense, with green glistening eyes. A
wave of coldness was coming from it ... the cloud continued to dissipate.
The she-wolf glared at them, slowly spreading her griffin's wings. Her
serpent's tail lashed gently, scalily ...

The above passage comes from *Black Easter,* written by James Blish.
Everyone who has read it since the book was first published in the late
Sixties has been immediately divided into two camps: those who
believed Blish had actually witnessed a genuine High Magick ritual, and
those who dismissed it as science-fiction. It's a debate that continues to
this day. For in the end, it comes down to belief, something you either
do or do not possess – or are busy, perhaps, trying to suppress. What
can't be denied is that such rituals do exist and are performed on a
regular basis – the essence of the Abra-melin ritual (one of the most
significant and difficult to achieve) is to 'Invoke Often' – and not just
in a few pockmarked villages in remote parts of the world. In fact,
there are hardly any major towns or cities in the UK that aren't home
to at least one secret society whose purpose is the study, practise and
performance of precisely such rituals. The people involved are not
simple peasants or social outcasts but some of the brightest, most
questioning minds most often drawn from the upper echelons of
society.

We are not talking about simple witchcraft of the type depicted in
a make-you-jump Stephen King novel or the broomstick abracadabra
of a Harry Potter movie (though many books, films and other famous
works of art do incorporate elements of genuine ritual magick). According to the nineteenth-century writer and magician Eliphas Levi, occult
knowledge – that is, the hidden knowledge of the ages, going back to
pre-Christian times, all the way to the Serpent and the Garden of
Eden – is a product of philosophical and religious equations as exact
as any science. Furthermore, that anyone able to acquire such knowledge and use it in the correct manner instantly becomes master of
those who are not. As an earlier proponent of the magician's art,

Paracelsus, wrote in the sixteenth century: 'The magical is a great hidden wisdom . . . no armour can shield against it because it strikes at the inward spirit of life. Of this we may rest assured.' Or as Aleister Crowley – after Merlin, now perhaps the most notorious occultist of all – put it in 1929 in *Magick in Theory and Practice*, the book that first alerted Jimmy Page to the possibilities of the occult: 'Magick is the Science and Art of causing Change to occur in conformity with Will.' (The 'k' was added to the word 'magic' by Crowley not only, as popularly understood, to distinguish what he was talking about from the simple tricks employed by conjurers, but for occult purposes too: the six-letter spelling of the word 'magick' balanced against the orthodox five-letter spelling being equal to the balance of the hexagram and the pentagram – 6 + 5 = 11, 'The general number of magick, or energy tending to change,' as he put it in his 1909 book, 777.)

The idea that rock music might also be related to occult practices hardly began, or indeed ends, with the long-held view that Page – and, ergo, Led Zeppelin – were dabblers in black magic and/or holders of so-called Satanic beliefs. Indeed, the most enduring myth about the band is that three of its members – the exception being the 'quiet one', John Paul Jones – entered into a Faustian pact with the Devil, signing away their immortal souls in exchange for Earthly success. Only someone who knew nothing about the occult could indulge in such an obvious fantasy, though. That is not to say that Jimmy Page has never been involved in occult practices; rather, the opposite – that Page's interest in occult ritual is so serious and longstanding it would be facile to suggest anything as feeble-minded as a pact with the Devil. As for involving anyone else in the band . . . that would have been like inviting them to co-produce the Zeppelin albums with him: a recipe for disaster that would only dilute and distort – completely ruin, in fact – what this master musician and would-be magician was attempting to do. Or as he would have put it back then – to invoke.

Even in 1970, the year Page's deepening interest in the works of the charismatic Crowley became public for the first time with the abbreviated inscription of his famous maxim, Do What Thou Wilt Shall Be the Whole of the Law, into the various run-out grooves of *Led Zeppelin III*, rock as devil's music was hardly a new idea. Even mama-loving, god-fearing Elvis stood accused early on of doing the

Devil's work with his dangerously gyrating rhythms and head-turning beats. While other stars of Presley's generation like Little Richard and Jerry Lee Lewis were so convinced of the intrinsic ungodliness of their music they would eventually give up years of their respective careers to wrestling painfully with the idea that what they'd been doing – inciting young people to utterly lose themselves in the wilful abandonment of rock'n'roll – was somehow wrong; not just subversive but fundamentally perverted; unfit for consumption by decent church-going folk. It was a notion compounded by the common-held belief that the blues – the forefather of rock'n'roll – was propagated by itinerant black men who, it was claimed, had been taught to play while sitting atop gravestones at midnight, or, in the case of Robert Johnson, from the Devil himself, encountered after dark at a certain crossroads. Such fanciful ideas were lent unsettling credence by the fact that so many early blues songs were built on notions of eternal damnation begun here on Earth, the outsider following his lonely doom-laden path, itself a perversion of the real roots of the music, which lay in preaching, the church, gospel and the praise of God, but which the blues now delivered unto the jook-joints, roadhouses and dollar-a-go brothels populated by gun-toting, fatherless men and evil, duplicitous women to whom it was a foregone conclusion a po' boy would surely lose his soul.

However, compared to the more intentionally subversive ideas being espoused just a decade later in the music of those flamboyantly attired, long-haired, album-oriented groups that took their cue from the Beatles and the Stones, what the original Fifties generation of rock'n'-rollers was up to is now seen as woefully innocent, quaint almost. The image of Aleister Crowley had already shown up at the personal request of John Lennon on the cover of Sgt. Pepper – glaring balefully out from between Mae West and one of George Harrison's Indian gurus – three years before a sniggering, stoned Jimmy Page instructed engineer Terry Manning to scratch Crowley-isms into the run-out grooves of the third Zeppelin album. And the Stones – influenced as much by Brian Jones' girlfriend Anita Pallenberg's enthusiastic but amateurish interest in the occult as by Mick Jagger's passing fascination with intellectual notions of good and evil and Keith Richards' more down-to-earth but steadily increasing use of cocaine, heroin and anything else that could take him to 'a different realm' – had released

Their Satanic Majesties Request while Jimmy was still scrabbling around on Dick Clark package tours with the Yardbirds.

But the Stones' flirtation with the dark side had come to an ignominious and bloody end when Meredith Hunter was murdered at Altamont, just as the band was reaching the climax of 'Sympathy for the Devil'. After that, whatever the Stones' involvement with the occult – from Jagger's brilliantly convincing portrayal of a degenerate rock star in the 1968 movie *Performance* (scripted and co-directed by Donald Cammell, son of Crowley biographer and friend, Charles R. Cammell) to his relationship with Crowley disciple, Kenneth Anger, whose 1969 underground film *Invocation Of My Demon Brother (Arrangement In Black & Gold)* featured the singer's specially composed synthesiser soundtrack – was rapidly curtailed, leaving the field open for less serious but more determinedly outré rock acts like Black Sabbath and Alice Cooper to base their entire acts on an ersatz but clearly signposted association with the occult, elaborating on the earlier pantomime shtick of self-styled tremble-tremble merchants like Screaming Lord Sutch (who would come on stage in a coffin) and Arthur 'God of Hellfire' Brown. Even on those occasions when these next-generation rockers showed a more serious interest in the occult, their basic lack of education in the subject left them as nonplussed as most of their easily shocked audience. Terry 'Geezer' Butler, bassist and chief lyricist of Black Sabbath, insists he had a 'genuine interest in the occult' when the band first started in 1968, but it was less to do with any serious reading of Crowley and his ilk and more 'an extension' of his fondness for 'science-fiction stories, horror films, anything that was kind of out there'. He also flatly denies that he or anyone else in Sabbath ever took part in any magickal rituals or spell-casting. 'I just had a morbid interest in it,' he told me. 'Everybody was reading up about it. All the love and peace thing had gone, the Vietnam War thing was happening and a lot of kids were getting into all kinds of mysticism and occultism.' His own interest ended abruptly after an incident which so frightened him, 'I just went off the whole thing.' Living in a one-bedroom flat that he had painted completely black, 'I had all these inverted crosses around the place and all these posters of Satan and all that kind of stuff. Then I was just lying in bed one night and I woke up suddenly, and there was like this black shape standing at the foot of me bed. And I wasn't on drugs or anything, but for some reason I thought it was the Devil himself! It was almost as if this thing was saying to me, "It's time to either pledge allegiance or piss off!"' He was so shaken he immediately repainted the flat orange. 'I took all the posters down, put like proper crucifixes in there, and that's when I started wearing a cross. We all did.'

For Butler, it was partly the era as much as anything else that led so many young musicians in the late Sixties to take an interest in the occult. In an age when drugs were still considered mind-expanding and sex was based on loving the one you're with, keeping an open mind on the subject of God and the Devil, and how the two might relate to the modern world, was clearly the more informed option. Hence, the slightly less frivolous antics of someone like Deep Purple guitarist Ritchie Blackmore, who in the Seventies was fond of using an Ouija board to hold séances in hotel rooms. The British writer, Peter Makowski, a confidant of Blackmore's back then, recalls an occasion he witnessed at the Château d'Herouville studios in France when 'Blackmore did this séance with an Ouija board. You never knew with Ritchie, though, how much was real and how much was just a wind up. He got the Ouija board out and started manipulating it himself, sending so-called messages from some malevolent spirit to this girl that was in the room, telling her she was gonna die and all this. She ended up screaming and running from the room and Ritchie just laughed.' He adds: 'You have to remember, there were no PlayStations in those days, no twenty-four-hour TV or internet. You had to make your own amusement.'

A fair point, yet a cursory flick through the pages of any well-known heavy metal magazine today will reveal an endless parade of ghost-faced, zombie-like creatures, their eyes glassy with contact-lens cataracts, their nail polish black; skin pancake white, trickles of fake blood crusting at the edges of grimacing mouths. Most simply enjoy the dressing-up, weekend Goths by any other name. Others, like Britain's Cradle of Filth, have claimed to be the real thing, while certain grisly Norwegian 'black metal' bands in the Nineties took to church-burning, drinking human blood, even murder in the case of former Burzum frontman, Count Grisnackh (real name: Kristian Vikernes), currently serving a twenty-one year sentence for the 1993 murder of Øystein 'Euronymous' Aarseth of rival Norwegian black metallists Mayhem, and the burning of three stave churches.

Hard rock and heavy metal had become self-consciously identified with notions of 'black magic' and 'devil worship' ever since the music itself became so ultra-commoditised in the Eighties that it became an entirely niche-driven pursuit, with groups like Iron Maiden – whose knowledge of Crowley's work, they were the first to admit, was limited solely to hearsay – having hits with intentionally headline-grabbing songs like '666 The Number Of The Beast', or Ozzy Osbourne's similarly uninformed album track from the same era, 'Mr Crowley', with lyrics by songwriter Bob Daisley, done purely for shock value, as befitting Ozzy's 'controversial' image in the Eighties.

It's not just hard rock and heavy metal musicians, either. Though he now plays down his former involvement, conspicuously wearing a crucifix around his neck, David Bowie famously dabbled in occult rituals and sang of being 'closer to the Golden Dawn, immersed in Crowley's uniform of imagery' in the song 'Quicksand' from his 1971 album, *Hunky Dory*. The 'golden dawn' being a reference to the Hermetic Order of the Golden Dawn, the secret nineteenth-century Masonic society based on the arcane rituals of ancient Egypt, that boasted such illustrious members as actress Florence Farr, writer Arthur Machen, chemist (and would-be alchemist) George Cecil Jones and the poet William Butler Yeats – and to which Crowley also became a leading light in 1898. But Bowie's interest, fuelled by mountainous supplies of cocaine and the first egocentric ravages of superstardom, tailed off in stupefied horror after the 1975 exorcism of the swimming pool at his Hollywood mansion. Present at the ritual – conducted in amateurish, coke-riven style by Bowie himself – was his then wife, Angie, who later claimed: 'The pool was definitely, absolutely, no doubt about it, bubbling with an energy for which there was no possible physical explanation.' When it was over, she said: 'On the bottom of the pool was a large shadow, or stain, which had not been there before the ritual began. It was in the shape of a beast of the underworld; it reminded me of those twisted, tormented gargoyles screaming silently from the spires of medieval cathedrals. It was ugly, shocking, malevolent; it frightened me.'

Jazz rocker Graham Bond was another unfortunate dabbler in the occult who insisted he was actually Crowley's illegitimate son, before hurling himself – or being hurled, depending on who you believe – under a London tube train in 1974. A decade later, Genesis P-Orridge,

founding member of Seventies electronic rock pioneers Throbbing
Gristle, led an outfit called Psychic TV which, he claimed, was a
musical art platform for a Crowleyan cult called the Temple Ov
Psychick Youth. Many other musicians – such as The Only Ones, who
in 1978 opened their debut album with the track 'The Whole Of The
Law'; Killing Joke, whose leader Jazz Coleman was rumoured to have
taken part in Crowley-esque rituals with Page in the early Eighties;
and, more recently, David Tibet, whose folk-rock outfit Current 93 are
said to be ardent occultists – continue to claim Crowley as an important
influence on their work. The fact remains, however, that for all their
public posturing very few really well-known rock musicians can boast
a truly encyclopaedic knowledge of the occult, be it of Pagan, Pantheist,
Kabbalistic, Masonic, Druidic, or any other esoteric origin. A major
exception to that rule, however, would be Jimmy Page.

No mere meddler he, I once asked Jimmy if the apparently mystical
aspect of much of Zeppelin's oeuvre – be it the music, the album
artwork, or simply the stage performances – was a product of the era
the band reigned over (like Sabbath *et al*) or whether it was to do with
a more longstanding personal interest. He replied: 'I was like that at
school. I was always interested in alternative religions.' He added with
a smile: 'These days it's alternative medicine, isn't it? But, yes, I was
always interested in mysticism, Eastern tradition, Western tradition. I
used to read a lot about it so consequently it became an influence.'
And, I wondered, as the Zeppelin phenomenon grew ever larger and
more unstoppable, did he feel he was tapping into something greater,
some form of energy more profound than just good-time rock'n'roll,
perhaps? He nodded. 'Yeah, but I'm reluctant to get into it because it
just sounds . . . pretentious. But, yeah, obviously, you can tell that from
the live things. It was almost a trance-state sometimes, but it just
sounds, you know . . .' He fell silent.

Page wasn't always so reticent to speak on the record about such
things, talking to writer Nick Kent in 1973 of the 'incredible body of
literature' that Crowley left behind and which involved 'a life's study'.
He went even further while being interviewed for *Sounds* magazine in
1976, describing Crowley as 'a misunderstood genius of the twentieth
century. Because his whole thing was liberation of the person, of the
entity, and [how] that restriction would foul you up, lead to frustration
which leads to violence, crime, mental breakdown, depending on what

sort of make-up you have underneath. The further this age we're in now gets into technology and alienation, a lot of the points he made seem to manifest themselves all down the line.' Asked to elaborate, he continued: '[Crowley's] thing was total liberation and really getting down to what part you played. What you want to do, do it ... In an Edwardian age that's just not on. He wasn't necessarily waving a banner, but he knew it was going to happen. He was a visionary and he didn't break them in gently. I'm not saying it's a system for anybody to follow. I don't agree with everything, but I find a lot of it relevant ...'

Or as he told *Circus* magazine in America the same year: 'I read Crowley's technical works. I read those a number of years back and still refer to them from time to time just because of his system ... The more I was able to obtain of his own, as opposed to what other people wrote about him, I realised he had a lot to say.' He denied trying to spread the word, however. 'I'm not trying to interest anyone in Aleister Crowley any more than I am in Charles Dickens. All it was, was that at a particular time he was expounding a theory of self-liberation which is something which is so important. He was like an eye into the world, into the forthcoming situation,' he added enigmatically. 'My studies have been quite intensive but I don't particularly want to go into it because it's a personal thing and isn't in relation to anything apart from that I've employed his system in my own day-to-day life ... The thing is to come to terms with one's free will, discover one's place and what one is, and from that you can go ahead and do it and not spend your whole life suppressed and frustrated.'

As Page said, it all began for him at school, when at the age of fifteen, he first read Crowley's magnum opus, *Magick In Theory And Practise*. However, it wasn't until Page was in his early twenties that he began to further his interest in Crowley and the occult: 'Reading about different things that people were supposed to have experienced, and seeing whether you could do it yourself.'

By the time Page joined the Yardbirds, he was already a frequent visitor to the studio flat in South Kensington where Brian Jones lived with Anita Pallenberg. Brian was into Paganism, Zen, Moroccan tapestries ... and drugs. Anita was an aspiring film star and model, into magick, sex, hanging out with rock stars ... and drugs. A small-time crook as a teenager, not only was Brian a gifted and successful musician, he was up for anything. He and Anita would hold séances at the flat using an Ouija board; or they would pile in the car and drive off to look for UFOs in the dead of night. Swinging by the Indica gallery and bookstore, buying the latest occult tomes, searching for 'Satanic spells to dispel thunder and lightning,' according to Winona, a mutual friend. When Jimmy bought his boathouse in Pangbourne he furnished it in a similar style to Brian and Anita's pad, except he took better care of his growing collection of rare books, paintings, rugs and antiques. And he began to take his 'studies' more seriously.

In 1966, when Jones was hired to provide the instrumental sound-track to a German film Pallenberg was appearing in called *Mort Und Totschlag* (A Degree of Murder), he rented out the same Olympic studio Zeppelin would later record in, playing sitar, banjo, dulcimer, harmonica, organ and autoharp. Ironically, the only instrument he didn't play was guitar. Instead he asked engineer Glyn Johns to hire Page (which he did, along with keyboardist Nicky Hopkins). The music was abstract but tinged with country-and-western, blues and soul, in places ghostly and dissonant, not least on the suitably spooky title track. Ultimately, none of it was ever issued on album and the film was never shown commercially outside Germany. Nevertheless, the experience left a huge impression on Page. Clearly, what Brian was doing lay outside the bounds of what the Stones would consider for one of their own albums, and Jimmy dug that – a lot. He even began wondering what it would be like to have a group that could, somehow, contain both elements: the rock *and* the experimental. Page was also on hand to witness the less palatable side of Jones's immersion in the dissolute, as over the next two years, first Pallenberg then the Stones abandoned him, rats fleeing a rapidly sinking ship. When Jones' messy departure from the band was made public in June 1968, around the same time as news of the Yardbirds' own break-up, Page's name was one of the first mentioned as his possible replacement. But there was simply no way. When he wasn't touring with the Yardbirds, Jimmy was one of the few old friends of Brian's who made a point of visiting him at Cotchford Farm, the lonely mansion on the edge of Ashdown Forest in East Sussex, which the increasingly desperate guitarist had retreated to and was eventually found dead at, floating face-down in the swimming pool.

Any suggestion that Jones' death may have had anything to do with his dilettante-ish interest in the occult was quickly brushed aside by

'I am a Golden God!' Plant in all his glory, Madison Square Garden, July 1973 (*David Redfern/Redferns*). And (below) Planty and Ricardo on a fur-covered double-bed on the Starship, during the band's three-night stint at Madison Square Garden, July 1973. Pretty ladies just out of shot . . . (*Getty*)

Earl's Court, London, 1975: Page in the famous Dragon Suit (*Dick Barnatt & Ian Dickson/Redferns*); Plant with infamous rocket in the pocket (*Ian Dickson/Rex*).

No way to go but down. Zeppelin at their zenith: Los Angeles Forum, March 1975.
Linda Lovelace introduced the show (*David Stratford/Redferns; Getty*).

(Clockwise from above) Crowley former abode, Boleskine House, on the shores of Loch Ness, 2005. After Page bought it, 'A few things happened that would freak some people out.' (*Topfoto*). Aleister Crowley, the self-portrait and the man himself – according to Page, 'A misunderstood genius of the twentieth century.' (*Corbis/Getty*). Page as The Magus: a still from the 'Dazed And Confused' violin bow/magick weapon fantasy sequence, *The Song Remains The Same* movie, 1976 (*The Kobal Collection*).

'I'm not really into solid foods very much.' Page onstage during the disastrous last tour of America, 1977 (*Richard E Aaron/Redferns*).

Page, just as it would be when, a dozen years later, the same suggestions would be made about the premature death of one of his own band. Instead, as the next few years flew by and Zeppelin began to take over from the Stones as the world's biggest rock band, Jimmy's interest in Crowley and the occult deepened to the point of almost complete immersion.

So who is Aleister Crowley and what is it about him that Jimmy Page – and millions of others around the world – still finds so compelling? And how much did the guitarist's interest in Crowley's occult teachings influence his own life and work? In order to answer that question, first we need to expose a few myths about Crowley. Famously once described in a magazine headline as the Wickedest Man in the World, while it's true that Crowley's influence proved to be the undoing of more than one of his many disciples – suicide, madness and death were recurring motifs for various wives and followers throughout his life – he certainly was not a Satanist. Nor did he practise 'black' magic. 'I did not hate Jesus and God,' he said, 'I hated the Jesus and God of the people I hated.' His main message, as he wrote in *The Book of the Law*, condensed as follows:

> 'There is no law beyond Do what thou wilt . . .
> It is a lie, this folly against self . . .
> I am alone: there is no God where I am . . .
> Every man and every woman is a Star . . .
> The word of Sin is restriction . . .
> Remember all ye that existence is pure joy;
> that all the sorrows are but shadows; they pass
> and are done; but there is that which remains . . .
> Love is the law, love under will . . .'

One also needs to consider the historical background of secret societies such as the Golden Dawn, which Crowley joined as a young man and which would exert a huge influence throughout his life, even after he'd resigned; the A.A. – aka the Great White Brotherhood, Crowley's own attempt at forming a secret magickal society; and, most significant today, the O.T.O. – the Ordo Templi Orientis, aka Order of the Temple of the East, aka Order of the Oriental Templar – that Crowley eventually became head of and to which it seems likely Page was invited to join in the early Seventies, and to which it is believed – as far as anyone can tell given the vow of silence that being an initiate inevitably entails – he still belongs today. Or as writer, filmmaker, Zeppelin fan and himself a member of the O.T.O., Dave Dickson says: 'I would be surprised, given his interest, if Page wasn't a member of the Order. I don't know for certain because it's not like there's a membership list. All I'm saying is, if you are interested in Crowley to the extent Page is, it seems almost inconceivable that he wouldn't be.'

As with all great sciences and religions, the teachings of the O.T.O. and other comparable 'brotherhoods' are full of arcane and dramatic rituals learned from ancient 'grimoires' (grammars of magic) handed down and rewritten from generation to generation, surviving the centuries despite the endless and ongoing attempts to erase them from history. Condemned by the Vatican as the worship of false gods, they are in fact the study of many different, more ancient 'gods'. Something the monotheist rule of Christianity in its myriad guises not unreasonably considers threatening. Hence the deliberate branding of such beliefs as 'heresy' and 'devil worship', and the systematic persecution of such 'diabolic' practices, from medieval witch-burning to simple modern-day ridicule. Yet every pre-Christian civilisation had its medicine man, its shaman or high priest who understood the delicate balance of the forces of nature and how one might invoke them to the greater good; gifted individuals whose potions and practices were passed down father-to-son; the magic they created the fundamental ingredient of all the most ancient religions; the aim, to see into the future and affect its outcome. Usually, this was for beneficial purposes, though curses were prevalent too.

The element of fertility was vitally important, with sex an integral part of many aspects of magic ritual – specifically, the controlled delay of orgasm, redirecting the sexual energy into ensuring that rituals are performed in properly 'exalted' circumstances. As practised by O.T.O. members of various higher degrees, these would include heterosexual magickal acts (adoration of the phallus as the microcosmic counterpart to the sun), masturbatory and autosexual techniques (referred to as the Lesser Work of Sol), and, at the highest level, anal intercourse techniques as sexual and magickal. Thus, ancient Eastern temples were filled with 'sacred prostitutes', an idea that went all the way back to ritualistic orgy and/or ritualistic human sacrifice and which Crowley almost single-handedly resurrected more than three thousand years later. Indeed, Ezra Pound once remarked that all religions could be boiled down to the single idea that copulation is good for the crops or that copulation is bad for the crops – with Christians coming out on the side of the latter, and Crowley (and, by definition, the O.T.O.) heartily endorsing the former.

Dave Dickson: 'The definition of magick is that it's a causation of a change in the physical universe by the application of will. What Crowley is saying is that sex is this huge motivating force, that when you're in that moment of passion, the feeling that you have, it's as if you are somehow connected to the whole of the universe. That every sense in your body is on fire ... and effectively that's what Crowley's use of magick was all about, using that [sexual] energy and that connectedness, not only for that intense feeling, but getting it to produce something beyond that, using that power to have some effect further down the line.'

Born in Leamington, in 1875, into a non-denominational Evangelical Christian movement called the Plymouth Brethren, Edward Alexander Crowley was the son of a wealthy brewing family; an extremely bright child who could read by the age of four and was studying Greek and Latin by ten. Able to quote passages verbatim from the Bible, it wasn't until the death from cancer of the father he was named after and adored, when he was just eleven, that young Edward began displaying the rebellious streak that would both mar and distinguish his later life. Let down by a god that had left him bereft and at the mercy of a mother he regarded with fear and suspicion, he now rejected his parents' religion wholesale and grew up to be vehemently anti-Christian.

Sent to board at a Brethren school in Tonbridge he decided to test the theory that cats possess nine lives by experimenting with different ways of killing them. Expelled, he was sent to Malvern where he was bullied for being fat. Having persuaded his mother to remove him by claiming he was being sexually abused, he was finally given a home tutor who, despite being a former Bible Society missionary, introduced him to such worldly pursuits as billiards, betting and cards. At fifteen, his domineering mother discovered her wayward son having sex on her bed with a chambermaid and loudly denounced him as 'a little beast'. Many of his later sexual fantasies were of his degradation at the

hands of cruel, domineering women; psychical and emotional equals –
priestesses – he dubbed the 'Scarlet Women'. His obsessive quest for
a dominant and sadistic mistress would remain the defining sexual
symbol of his life and it was not without irony that he later dubbed
himself the Great Beast – one of dozens of outlandish aliases he
adopted throughout his life, including Sir Aleister Crowley, Saint
Aleister Crowley (of the Gnostic Catholic Church), Frater Perdurabo,
Frater Ou Mh, To Mega Therion (also meaning 'the great beast'),
Count McGregor, Count Vladimir Svareff, Prince Chiao Khan,
Mahatma Guru Si Paramahansa Shivaji, Baphomet the Supreme and
Holy King of Ireland, and, after he had ascended to the level of a living deity in the O.T.O., Ipsissimus. He is chiefly remembered now,
however, as the Great Beast and/or the Beast 666. The '666' suffix,
he disingenuously told the judge in a libel case, 'means merely sunlight. You may call me Little Sunshine.'.

As a young man, he was a great prankster. One of his favourite
jokes was to write scandalised critiques of his own works, as with his
infamous prose poem *White Stains*, which he fixed a thunderously
straight-faced prologue to: 'The Editor hopes the Mental Pathologists,
for whose eyes alone this treatise is destined, will spare no precaution
to prevent it falling into other hands.' Then gave the author's name on
the title-page as George Archibald, a much loathed, real-life uncle.
His great literary 'discovery' in 1910 – a supposedly ancient occult
tome named *The Bagh-I-Muattar* [The Scented Garden] – was actually
all his own, quite brilliant work, including the English major he claimed
had translated it before dying heroically in the Boer War. Another
time, hearing that the authorities, scandalised by the size of the genitals
on Epstein's statue of Oscar Wilde had covered it with an extraneous
butterfly, he took it upon himself to forcibly remove the offending
object, then walk into one of London's stuffiest restaurants wearing it
over the crotch of his trousers.

There was a serious side to much of the hilarity, of course. For
example, the endless pseudonyms, which he later claimed a less
frivolous reason for, as he explained in *The Confessions of Aleister
Crowley: an Autohagiography*: 'I wanted to increase my knowledge
of mankind. I knew how people treated a young man from Cambridge ... Now I wanted to see how people would behave to a
Russian nobleman [Count Vladimir Svareff]. I must say here that I

repeatedly used this method of disguise – it has been amazingly useful in multiplying my points of view about humanity. Even the most broad-minded people are necessarily narrow in this one respect. They may know how all sorts of people treat them, but they cannot know, except at second hand, how those same people treat others.' Role playing, they call it now.

'Aleister' was a pseudonym, chosen in 1895 for its Celtic Druidic overtones. He was a student at Cambridge by then – reading moral sciences – where his insatiable appetite for all things immoral found him having illicit sex on an almost daily basis (mainly with other men) and enjoying his first taste of drink and drugs. When his hated mother died three years later he inherited £40,000 (approximately £5 million in today's money) and immediately left Cambridge for London without bothering to complete his degree. Instead, he moved to a flat in London's Chancery Lane, signing the lease under the name Count Vladimir Svareff. In 2006, when the building – now a four-storey office block – was being demolished for redevelopment, workmen arrived one morning to find a human skull perched amongst the rubble, illuminated by a single flickering candle, and beside that a pile of twigs arranged in the shape of a pentagram. The ghost of Crowley, perhaps? More likely a prank by one of his more ardent followers. For it was here, in an area of London full of medieval resonances, that Crowley first began experimenting with the occult. Having recently been initiated into the Golden Dawn, he now took the name Frater Perdurabo, meaning: Brother I-Will-Endure-To-The-End (he later changed it to Frater Ou Mh or Brother Not-Yet), and began learning of such secret arts as the invocation of angels and demons, invisibility, and astral travel.

The origins of the Golden Dawn are themselves shrouded in more mystery than even Crowley was able to unravel. Whatever system of belief holds the key, they are all based on the same ancient ideas traceable back to the tenth century BC and the rites of King Solomon, author of the most famous grimoire of all, *The Key of Solomon*. Based on the *Book of Enoch*, described by Dave Dickson as 'one of the great works of apocalyptic literature', according to Eliphas Levi it tells the story of 'angels who consented to fall from heaven that they might have intercourse with the daughters of the Earth [and which caused] the birth of Magic.' Hence the inclusion of 'Enochian calls' in many of the occult rituals practised up to the time of Crowley and beyond to the present day.

A collection of spells and incantations passed down through the centuries in various forms (its text to be copied out by hand for it to work properly) and the first to prescribe the casting of a magic circle on the floor (to contain demons and spirits that would otherwise wreak havoc before they were ritually banished) and many other details of ritualistic magick as practised here in the twenty-first century, from the instructions on how to hand-make robes, to the symbolic use of knives, swords, staffs, wands and other magical 'weapons', a Greek version of *The Key of Solomon* dating from the twelfth century AD, can still be found at the British Museum today, while official Vatican records show that in 1350 Pope Innocent VI ordered the burning of another version of the same book. It was also Solomon who first wrote of adepts entering trances in order to 'charge' themselves with magic energy, along with the use of pentagrams and other talismans. In another of Solomon's grimoires, known as *The Lesser Key of Solomon*, he provides incantations for invoking seventy-two principal demons, all of them named and described in exact detail.

Basically, what Crowley preached in his innumerable works – over a hundred published, at last count – was essentially the summation of all these ideas, along with ideas taken from the Knights Templar and their evolutionary offshoot, the Freemasons, and mixed them up with his own experiments with hashish, peyote, heroin, omni-sexuality, meticulous study of the Tarot and comparative religion, boiling the knowledge down to what he described as 'the quintessence of known methods'. The turning point came during a visit to Cairo in March 1904, when his first wife Rose fell into a trance and began murmuring phrases such as 'It's about the Child' and 'They are waiting for you', which led to Crowley discovering the name of his Holy Guardian Angel, Aiwass – 'dictating', he claimed, the whole of *The Book of the Law* to him over a three-day period. There followed a four-month period of 'insanity' walking through China as Crowley attempted to become the 'little child' Aiwass had spoken of. When he returned to England, he was ready to begin one of the most difficult magickal operations of all: the achievement of the Knowledge and Conversation of the Holy Guardian Angel; an invocation taking six months that requires expert magickal techniques, part of which involved being 'crucified' while swearing the following oath: 'I, Perdurabo, a member of the Body of Christ, do hereby solemnly obligate myself . . . and will entirely devote my life so as to raise myself to the knowledge of my higher and Divine Genius that I shall be He.'

It seems there was an evangelical aspect to Crowley's studies, too; certainly a desire to show off his knowledge. Partly in order to stop Crowley publishing their occult secrets in his bi-annual magazine, *Equinox* (published on the two days of equinox each year, 21 March and 23 September), in 1912 he became the English head of the O.T.O., where he was astonished to find that his 'new ritual' to invoke the Holy Guardian Angel was the O.T.O.'s most closely guarded secret. As he wrote in *Confessions*: 'I personally believe that if this secret, which is a scientific secret, were perfectly understood, as it is not even by me after more than twelve years' almost constant study and experiment, there would be nothing which the human imagination can conceive that could not be realised in practice.'

He abandoned his first wife Rose and their daughter, whom he had named Nuit Ma Ahathoor Hecate Sappho Jezebel Lilith, and who would die soon after. 'I was no longer influenced by love for them, no longer interested in protecting them as I had been,' he wrote. When the First World War broke out, he fled to America where he gave an infamous pro-Germany speech at the base of the Statue of Liberty. Returning to Britain in 1919 broke and saddled with a raging heroin habit, Crowley accepted a publisher's advance of £60 (roughly £3,000 in today's money) and promptly decamped to Sicily, where the cost of living was dirt cheap. With his new American mistress Leah Hirsig, a new baby daughter and her nurse, Ninette, who also bore Crowley a child, he set up home in a primitive hilltop villa which he named the Abbey of Thelema.

It was his adventures at the abbey in the early Twenties (bowls of heroin left around, children allowed to watch the grown-ups having sex, rituals involving animal sacrifice and a woman being penetrated by a goat *et al*) that led to the lurid headlines in *John Bull* magazine – the Wickedest Man in the World was swiftly followed by similar bold-type accolades such as The King of Depravity and A Man We'd Like To Hang and which finally brought Crowley to the attention of the wider British public. Meanwhile, a series of women attempted to personify his 'Scarlet Woman' ideal: as well as Leah and Ninette, there was Dorothy Olsen, another American; followed by a third wife, Maria Ferrari de Miramar; then a nineteen-year-old German mistress named Bertha Busch of whom he wrote: 'Instantly I got down on the scarlet woman. She pissed gallons. I tore off her clothes and we fucked and fucked.'

Clearly, involvement with The Beast came at a price. All three wives were eventually driven mad, with Hirsig actually committed to an asylum, while Busch stabbed Crowley with a carving knife before subsequently committing suicide. There were also a series of miscarriages and a suspicious death at the abbey – reputed to have been caused by drinking cat's blood – before Mussolini himself ordered Crowley out of Italy. He fetched up in North Africa, sleeping with young boys and prostitutes in every city he visited, before publishing an account in 1922 of his time at the abbey, the relatively mundane *Diary Of A Drug Fiend*, which the *Sunday Express* demanded be suppressed on the strength of its provocative title alone.

But the most heinous crime Crowley apparently admitted to – though never actually accused of in his lifetime – was that of human sacrifice, with the ideal victim, as he wrote in *Magick in Theory and Practice*, 'a male child of perfect innocence and high intelligence'. He claimed he had performed this rite an average of 150 times a year from 1912 onwards. Another typically bizarre Crowley joke, surely? Yes and no. For while it would surely have been impossible for anyone to carry out such an outlandish feat, let alone someone as in the public eye by then as Crowley, what he was actually referring to was the same 'scientific secret' he'd been experimenting with all those years – in essence, the formula of the Rose and Cross, the magick foundation that underpins all forms of religion; the 'sacrifice' Crowley spoke of to do with his successful invocation of his Holy Guardian Angel, Aiwass; the death done 150 times a year to the 'little child' within. That is to say, to Crowley himself, as well as – symbolically – Aiwass. A ritualistic act committed in that trancelike state where all the opposites are finally transcended, breaking down the barriers that separate Ego from one's True Self – and from the Universe. No wonder he considered himself a living deity at the end of it, for he had achieved godhead. He said.

Crowley spent his last years in and out of court, instigating futile libel actions or fighting actions taken out against him. After a minor heart attack he moved to a cheap boarding house in Hastings, where he breathed his last on 1 December 1947, aged seventy-two. It's said he lay screaming for morphine but the doctor attending him refused. Crowley howled with rage: 'Give me morphine – or you will die within twenty-four hours!' Still the doctor refused. Crowley died a few hours later, tears streaming down his cheeks. Reportedly, his final words were: 'I am perplexed. Sometimes I hate myself ...' Eighteen hours later, the doctor was dead too. Newspapers claimed that at the Great Beast's cremation in Brighton his followers conducted a Black Mass; in reality a Gnostic Catholic Mass, during which a priestess – yet another Scarlet Woman, presumably – took off her clothes (hence the lurid headlines). Afterwards, Crowley's ashes were whisked away to America. The local council passed an ordinance that no such 'heathen rites' would ever be tolerated in their town again.

How much of the legend one believes, there's little doubt that for all his 'rottenness', as he memorably described it to the American writer Frank Harris, Crowley was an accomplished mystic, yogi and devoted student of occultism. Amongst the detritus of his strange legacy were genuinely compelling works, such as his extraordinary treatise on yoga, *Book Four*, and his insightful *Gospel According To St. Bernard Shaw* (published posthumously and later re-issued as *Crowley on Christ*). And while W.B. Yeats would sum up most people's view when describing Crowley as 'indescribably mad' the facts are that he was also a record-breaking mountaineer (by 1901, he and fellow-climber, Oscar Eckenstein, held all but one of the world's climbing records between them). He was also a remarkable orator, portrait painter, muralist, big-game hunter and expert chess player. His influence was astonishingly wide-ranging during his lifetime and especially after it. Mentor to the illustrious Portuguese poet Fernando Pessoa, inspiration for both Somerset Maugham's 1902 novel, *The Magician*, and Malcolm Lowry's classic semi-fictional *Under the Volcano*, published the year Crowley died, James Bond author Ian Fleming also modelled one of his most famous super-villains, Bloefeld, on Crowley, who he'd gotten to know when Fleming worked for British intelligence during the Second World War. (Fleming suggested Crowley as interrogator for Rudolf Hess when the occultist Nazi leader mysteriously parachuted into Scotland.) It's claimed it was even Crowley who suggested Churchill's famous V for victory sign, a magickal gesture, he said, that would counteract Nazi use of the swastika.

After the war, one of Crowley's most ardent disciples was a young

Californian named Jack Parsons, who wrote a 'fourth chapter' of *The Book of the Law* and later became one of the masterminds behind the American space programme. Working alongside Parsons was L. Ron Hubbard, who later ran off with Parsons' mistress and founded the cult of Scientology. Parsons took up instead with his own Crowley-esque scarlet woman, the Beat artist Marjorie Cameron, who would later star in some of Kenneth Anger's films and was said to be the inspiration behind the Eagles' 'Hotel California'. Parsons, who died in a lab explosion in 1952, now has a crater named after him on the dark side of the moon.

Crowley's writings on drugs, too, are prescient; decades later, psychedelic gurus such as Timothy Leary would merely echo many of his earlier claims. He also influenced post-Beat counterculture (William S. Burroughs endlessly recycled Crowley's 'sex-magick' theories in his own writings), and became something of a patron saint to the original hippies of the late Sixties whose advocating of drugs and 'free love' again echoed much of the old master's teachings. It was now that the revival of interest in Crowley began in earnest, and has continued in a consistently upward curve ever since. Though as Dave Dickson points out, 'He became this kind of hippy hero, but this is hugely open to misinterpretation. Do what thou wilt shall be the whole of the law – basically, what that means is: each of us has a purpose in life. This was the Crowley philosophy. That we are each put on Earth to achieve certain goals. And the purpose of our being on Earth is to discover what that destiny is and to follow it no matter what – the idea of True Will. What it doesn't mean is: "Hey, you can do whatever you like, because you don't have to worry about the consequences.". That's a total misunderstanding of what Crowley was actually saying.'

Nevertheless, from the late Sixties on, Crowley's influence can be detected in all branches of the arts, including the occultism of such films as *Performance* and *The Devil Rides Out* (whose depraved character Mocata is another based on Crowley) and of course the life and work of Kenneth Anger, who became a higher-up in the O.T.O. Crowley's also been the model for various TV villains such as a murderous demonologist in Britain's *Bergerac* series, and name-checked in an episode of *Buffy the Vampire Slayer*, whose lead character, Buffy Summers, is named after another occult notable, Montague Summers. Yes, he fully believed that in the future Crowleyanity (as he called it) would ultimately displace Christianity. But his advocacy of the still undiscovered powers of the human mind put him a century ahead of what are now considered the most advanced thinkers of the twenty-first century. Meanwhile, his work is collected and studied with greater interest now than in his own lifetime, his influence on modern culture arguably as pervasive as that of Freud or Jung.

The question here is how much – if any – did Jimmy Page's own absorption of the works of Aleister Crowley influence either the music or the success of Led Zeppelin? Speaking with Nick Kent in 2003, Page said: 'I found that [Crowley's] system worked. Plus, all the aspects of ritual magick, talismanic magick – I could see that it worked.' And all that impacted on Zeppelin's music, Kent asked? 'As far as my involvement went, it did, yes,' said Page. He certainly offered up enough clues during the band's lifetime. For Page, music and magick were clearly linked. As he told me more than once, the music of Zeppelin was 'made by the four of us, to create this fifth element ... There was a definite telepathy between us, an energy we created that the audience picked up on and sent back to us. Really powerful stuff ...'

This 'fifth element' he refers to might as easily describe the penta-gram, the five-pointed star that is the ancient and powerful symbol of ritual magick. As Dickson points out: 'The only reason people get interested in magick is because they are interested in power. You use the skills you possess to improve your lot, everybody does. If one accepts that Page has learned about magick, it would be surprising to me if he *didn't* use that skill to basically forward his personal and/or group ambitions.' He pauses, then adds: 'Whether that eventually comes back to bite him or not is open to speculation. All I'm saying is if you've got a skill you tend to use it.' A 'skill' he suggests that would have been engaged numerous times. 'If you've got a toothache, you take an aspirin. If that doesn't work, you might take another one. If you say, I want a successful career, chances are that's not gonna come out of one ritual.'

Crowley, who believed that books and other works of art could be talismanic in themselves, was known for performing rituals to ensure the success of his own writings. As mentioned in his diaries between 1914 and 1920, where his editor Stephen Skinner counted as many as eighteen specific operations enacted by Crowley under the heading 'literary success' – for example, his Simon Iff stories ('for literary current'); certain magazine pieces (for 'success in Shaw article') and poetry (for 'poetic inspiration'). Were Crowley alive today and recording albums, it seems certain he would be doing the same for them too.

Or as Page pointedly told writer Chris Salewicz in 1977: 'You know, there are a thousand paths and [people] can choose their own. All I know is that [with Crowley] it's a system that works.' He added with a laugh: 'There's not much point in following a system that doesn't work ... When you've discovered your true will, you should just forge ahead like a steam train. If you put all your energies into it there's no doubt you'll succeed. Because that's your true will. It may take a little while to work out what that is, but when you discover it, it's all there.'

Certainly, Page's interest in Crowley and the occult really took hold during the early days of Zeppelin's success. With the money now to fully indulge his passions, he became a serious collector of Crowleyana, including first-edition books – some signed by the Beast himself – plus some of his hats, canes, paintings, his robes ... anything he could get his hands on. After his affair with Miss Pamela was over, he phoned from England one night asking her to search for some Crowley artefacts he had been told were for sale in Gilbert's Bookstore on Hollywood Boulevard: specifically, a typed manuscript with scribbled notes in the margin in Crowley's own hand. Page wired her $1,700 and she bought it and mailed it to him, special delivery. In thanks, he sent her an antique necklace of a turquoise phoenix, its wings spread, holding a large gleaming pearl. She immediately broke down in tears, filled with 'pain and delight'. For 'a handsome sum' he also bought a volume of Crowley's diary from Tom Driberg, the Fleet Street columnist, Labour MP and peer of the realm who had met Crowley as an undergraduate at Oxford in 1925. Bound in red Morocco leather and encased in baroque silver, it recorded his 'daily magickal and sexual doings'.

Page's most notorious purchase, however, was of one of Crowley's most infamous former abodes, Boleskine House, near Foyers, in Scotland, on the south-east bank of Loch Ness, across the water from the 2,000-foot snow-capped bulk of Meall Fuarvounie. Built in the late eighteenth century on consecrated ground – the site, it was said, of a former church burned to the ground with its congregation still inside – there was also a graveyard where the ruins of the original chapel still lay alongside a small watcher's hut, where relatives of the newly buried would spend weeks guarding against grave-robbers. Boleskine House's original owner was the Honourable Archibald Fraser, a relative of Lieutenant General Simon Fraser, Lord Lovat at the time. The Honourable Archibald apparently chose the site to build his house specifically to irritate the Lieutenant General, whose lands surrounded the property, in retribution for Lord Lovat's support of the English during the Jacobite Rebellion of 1745. The associations with the Fraser family can also be seen in the Gothic burial ground, with its crumbling, lichen-covered gravestones and vaults that sit loch-side across a single track road from the main house's front fence. There was also said to be a tunnel connecting the graveyard to the house.

Boleskine House remained in Fraser family ownership until Crowley bought it in 1899. A large, remote country pile facing north with close access to river sand – important ingredients in enacting magick rituals – Crowley later claimed to have invoked over a hundred demons during his years there, including the enactment of the Abra-melin ritual, his hurried abandonment of which it is reckoned lies at the heart of the house's disturbing atmosphere and the unusual manifestations that still occur there. But then Crowley also spent time at Boleskine shooting sheep, catching salmon, climbing the surrounding hills and scaring to death the locals who refused to go anywhere near the place after dark. A five-bedroom mansion with slate grey roofing and pale pink stucco walls, it's actually a very attractive-looking residence. Mock Greek columns, stone dogs and stone eagles stand guard on each side of the main door, the house sheltered by a screen of mature Douglas Fir and Cyprus trees and several handsome cedar and eucalyptus trees. Stone steps lead to fruit gardens and an orchard. However, having sold the place in the wake of his impoverished return to Britain after the First World War, Boleskine continued to lead a strange existence. Hollywood star and real-life gangster George Raft had been involved in a scandal involving selling shares in a piggery supposedly built on Boleskine's grounds – except there weren't any pigs in it. After the Second World War it was owned by another former Crowley disciple, an army major named Fullerton, who would later shoot himself with his own shotgun in 1965. Previous owners were said to have conducted a 'black magic' baptism on their child.

In 1969, Kenneth Anger, who had just finished his cult movie classic *Scorpio Rising*, heard it was back on the market and rented it for a couple of months. A year later Jimmy Page heard about it and promptly bought the house, installing an old school friend, Malcolm Dent, as live-in caretaker. 'Jimmy caught me at a time in my life when I wasn't doing a great deal and asked me to come up and run the place,' said Dent in 2006. When he arrived he found a magick circle, a pentagram and an altar in the dining room. It wasn't until later that he learned that Crowley had used the room as his temple. A six foot-plus Londoner and former commercial salesman, Dent didn't believe in things that go bump in the night. However, he had only been there a few weeks when one night he heard strange rumblings coming from the seventy-foot hallway. The noise stopped when he went to investigate but began again as soon as he shut the door. 'That's when I decided to find out what I could about the house,' he said. The rumbling in the hall, he discovered, dated back as far as the Battle of Culloden and was said to be the head of Lord Lovat, beheaded in the Tower of London. 'Above Boleskine there's a place called Errogie, which is supposed to be the geographical centre of the Highlands. Boleskine was then the nearest consecrated ground to Errogie and it's thought his soul, or part of it, ended here.'

He also experienced 'the most terrifying night of my life' when he awakened to hear what sounded like a wild animal 'snorting, snuffling and banging' outside his bedroom door. 'I had a knife on the bedside table and I opened the blade and sat there. The blade was small and wouldn't have done any good but I was so frightened I had to have something to hang onto. The noise went on for some time but even when it stopped I couldn't move. I sat on the bed for hours and even when daylight came it took lots of courage to open that door.' He added: 'Whatever was there was pure evil.' Another friend who spent the night there awoke 'in a hell of a state', claiming she'd been attacked by 'some kind of devil'.

Despite these and other hair-raising occurrences – chairs switching places, doors banging open and shut inexplicably, carpets and rugs rolling up on their own – Dent never considered leaving. 'Initially I thought I'd be coming for a year or so, but then it got its hooks in me. I met my then wife at Boleskine House. My children were raised there – my son Malcolm was born in Boleskine House. We loved living there in spite of the peculiar happenings that went on there.'

Page, meanwhile, began doing everything he could to return the

house to how it would have looked during Crowley's time. As well as
his growing collection of Crowleyana, he bought seven chairs from the
Café Royal, each with a nameplate back and front, including those of
Crowley, Marie Lloyd, Rudolph Valentino, drama critic James Agate,
Sir Billy Butlin, artist William Orpen and sculptor Jacob Epstein. Crowley's chair would be placed at the top of a large banquet table in the
dining room with three down both sides. Geese and peacocks roamed
the grounds and in a field beside the gardens a herd of goats grazed,
some from Bron-Yr-Aur. And he arranged for self-proclaimed 'Satanic
artist' Charles Pace to paint some Crowley-esque murals on the walls,
based on those later uncovered by Kenneth Anger under the white-
washed walls at the Abbey of Thelema.

It's fair to say that Page revelled in the rumours surrounding
Boleskine House. In a 1976 radio interview with Nicky Horne, he
boasted: 'I'm not exaggerating when I say that any people that have
gone to that place and stayed there for any length of time, by that
I mean a month, say, have gone through *very* dramatic changes in
their personal lives and whatever. It's quite an incredible place, and
yet it's not hostile. It just seems to bring the truth out of people in
situations ... people have had quite unusual experiences.' Asked
how the house had affected him personally, he gave a weak, druggy
laugh. 'The whole house has been filled with tales of people being
taken to asylums because of drunkenness, suicides, you name it and
it's there, you know?'

Helping Page with his hunt for rare Crowleyana in the early Sev-
enties was a new acquaintance, writer, antiquarian bookseller and
Crowley expert Timothy d'Arch Smith. Tim, a great cricket fan who
lives within walking distance of Lord's Cricket Ground in north
London, recalls Page first coming to see him 'at my little office just off
Baker Street, in Gloucester Place, in about 1970, sent, I suspect, by
Gerald Yorke, who was Crowley's disciple, because I was doing – and
I'm still doing – Crowley's bibliography. This chap with long hair came
down to the office, and I had a few Crowley things. We were being
redecorated and there was pop music going on – probably the Beatles,
I suppose – on a little tinny transistor that belonged to the painters.
And I said to Jimmy, "Christ, what a din!" and he said, "Well, actually
this is my business. I said, "Terribly sorry." I had no idea who he was

until I saw the cheque. He just came down to buy Crowley books from me.'

Were these rare texts? 'Well, at the time he bought an awful lot more because he didn't have so much. Now he's got almost all the printed books apart from *Snowdrops from a Curate's Garden* [1904], which nobody's got and really is a rare thing. It does exist, there's a copy in the Warburg Institute, and a bookseller friend of mine had another copy that he sold – it's in America now. But it really is terribly rare because I think they were all destroyed by the Customs, as opposed to the other two [rare] pieces, which were *White Stains* – which actually is a moderately common book – and *The Bagh-I-Muattar.*'

Tim adds: 'It didn't take me very long to realise how serious he was. He was always very charming. But the trouble with him of course was like all these really famous people, he was terribly difficult to get in touch with. And if you'd bought something for £250 in those days you couldn't really keep it in stock.' Consequently, 'I had some very nice things which he didn't get. Of course he was touring [and] there were no emails or anything like that. The other thing is that being Jimmy and being so rich, and this is true of a lot of rich book collectors, they always have it in the back of their mind that somebody's put a nought on the price.'

Page was also fascinated to learn that Tim had visited Boleskine when he was in the army in the Fifties. 'I was told if I was caught in the grounds [then owner] Captain Fullerton would set the dogs on me.' Instead, he and a friend 'climbed the hill behind Boleskine and took photographs. We could see Fullerton and the dogs padding around.' He later gave the photos to Page. 'They were only little snapshots but he was so pleased! We were up in the mountain that Crowley used to practise climbing on. But Jimmy said it would be good because they'd changed it so much and he was terribly pleased about it.'

Gerald Yorke, the epitome of the old-money English gentleman who had worked as Crowley's secretary for many years, and who later became the Dalai Lama's emissary, helping bring Tibetan Buddhism to the West, had told Tim that after Fullerton 'went mad' and shot himself, 'it was bought by a young man with a blind wife, a newly married couple. They'd only been in there a month and the husband walked out, leaving the woman wandering around blind. Gerald said, "Oh, it was an Abra-melin demon!" C.R. Cammell told me that that was really the cause of his [Crowley's] downfall. That he never banished the Abra-melin . . . that he was halfway through the ritual, and he went off [and] left the demons tramping about. There was a rather good book about a guy that did the Abra-melin ritual and Gerald asked me to get it for him, and I read it and said, "Gerald, this guy's telling me that on the sand of the temple there were actual hoof marks [of Satan himself]." And Gerald said, "I should bloody well hope there were!"' He roars with laughter. 'And then Jimmy bought it. Or it's roughly that sequence.' He never visited when Jimmy owned it, though. 'I did go past once, with some friends, we just drove past, and there was some thought of going in, but my friends weren't particularly interested. But somebody was telling me there were always strange number plates, he saw "Pan" on one, just a car with 'Pan' parked there.'

He feels that Page may also have been taken advantage of occasionally by those that led him to believe they had more occult knowledge than they actually possessed. For example, he says he 'didn't care for Charles [Pace]. I didn't like him at all. He came into the bookshop that I was working in and he was just a conjuror. He lit a match and put it under his hand. I mean, you know, you put your hand in some stuff before you go out . . . I was a conjuror as a boy which is why I know about these things. So I thought, no, I don't like this chap. He was a good artist. A sort of Crowley figure in a way, but I thought . . .' He pulls a dismissive face.

Tim claims he never openly discussed the O.T.O. with Jimmy, though it's the first thing he asks when I arrive. 'Are you a member of the Order then?' Nevertheless, Dave Dickson speculates that it was around the time Page first met characters like Anger, Yorke and d'Arch Smith that he would have been invited to join. 'In magick what's supposed to happen is that you meet [someone], almost by chance, in effect by destiny, the person who is going to instruct you.' Getting anyone to talk about it openly though would be impossible, even if Page wanted them to, says Dickson, because of the four main rules of the O.T.O.: To Know, To Dare, To Will and To Be Silent.

'To Know – you've got to study. You've got to find out about this stuff before you venture forth. To Dare – you've got have the courage to actually put what you know into practice. To Will – you have to have the mental capacity to actually carry it out, which is why you can practise magick and fall foul because your willpower simply isn't strong enough to resist the temptations. It is effectively a minefield that it's easy to get blown up on. And To Be Silent – meaning, shut the fuck up. Which is why Page may have mentioned it a few times or given passing reference to it but to my knowledge has *never* come out and said, okay, this is what I believe, this is my credo, here are my influences. Like I said, it's one of the rules, To Be Silent . . .'

Is there an evangelical aspect to the O.T.O., though? 'No. The whole object behind the magick is that the adherent finds it on his own, then the idea is that you will meet someone on that journey who can say, right, okay, you need to come along to this group, or whatever, that will further you along that journey. But you're not gonna find members of the O.T.O. out on the street trying to sign people up. It's invitation only.' So Jimmy Page wouldn't have been trying to spread the word, as it were? 'Not spreading the word exactly, no. He certainly seems to have deliberately offered some clues though.'

The reason for which, I would suggest, was more to do with his desire to indicate to the outside world that there was more to Led Zeppelin than meat-hook riffs and phallic imagery; that here was a musical entity created by someone whose reading and interests ranged far beyond the limited confines of the bovine metallists Zeppelin were still then routinely compared to. In which case, it's a sad irony that attempting to do so in this way only reinforced the idea over many years that Zeppelin had more in common with Black Sabbath and Alice Cooper than, say, Dylan or the Stones. That Jimmy Page and Led Zeppelin really were in league with Satan. As Timothy d'Arch Smith says with a wry smile, 'They always call it *black* magic, don't they? It's what they *want* to believe . . .'

10

All That Glitters

For all the band's public defiance, and the album's not inconsiderable sales, behind the scenes there was a palpable sense of disappointment when *Led Zeppelin III* slipped unobtrusively from both the UK and US charts within weeks of topping them; this at a time when *Led Zeppelin II* was still riding high around the world. Used to fighting fires, Peter Grant moved swiftly to reassure Jimmy Page that certainly no-one at Atlantic was perturbed by this disappointing downturn in events. The album had still sold more than a million copies in the US, and had gone gold (for advance orders of over 100,000) in the UK, the sort of figures they'd have been throwing lavish parties to celebrate a year before. The fact that the second album had sold more than five times that amount in the preceding twelve months was, if anything, a freak result, he argued, not the kind of thing one should expect every time Zeppelin released a new album.

Nevertheless, there *were* tensions over at Atlantic's Broadway offices. Relatively speaking, *Led Zeppelin III* had been a commercial failure. The feeling – politely disguised in earshot of Page, if not from Grant – was that the band had shot themselves in the foot by releasing something radically different from the winning formula established by their first two albums. In order to appease both sides, Grant suggested the band take the rest of 1970 off. That is, abort their previous plan to tour Britain over the Christmas period – and return instead to the studio to consider their next move. Though he was reluctant to spell it out to Page, Grant knew it was essential the band get another, hopefully more representative, album out as soon as possible. By going into the studio now, he argued, they would be in no rush this time, either. For once, the band would be able to sit back and take stock, really concentrate on what they were doing. It was time to unveil their masterpiece, he seemed to suggest. So concerned was he with getting the band back on track, Grant had in fact turned down an offer of a million dollars for a New Year's Eve concert to be performed in Germany but linked by satellite to a large chain of American cinemas. He said no, he later insisted, because 'I found out that satellite sound can be affected by snowstorms. The promoters couldn't believe it, but it just wasn't right for us.' In reality, he was more concerned for the band's long-term future as recording artists. Their next album, whatever else it turned out to be, would be make or break, he felt sure. For Peter Grant and Led Zeppelin there was much more than a mere million bucks at stake in whatever they did next; there was their entire future.

Fortunately for their beleaguered manager, the band bought his argument and returned home for a few weeks off before returning to the studio. Whether they were prepared to admit it or not – and to this day they most decidedly are not – even they were aware that something had to be done to get the mothership firing on all cylinders again. Whichever way they looked at it, it was, in any event, time for them to deliver something really special, if for no other reason than to prove the doubters and cynics wrong. The miracle was that they did just that, coming up with what is now fondly regarded as not just their greatest recorded achievement, but one of the greatest rock albums of all time.

With a number of tracks already either written or in a state of near-completion, confidence amongst the four was high as they re-entered Island's Basing Street Studios in December. 'We had little riffs here and there,' said Jimmy, 'certain constructions. And it was a question of really working on it and seeing how things came together. With direction, you know?' What emerged was a mellow Neil Young-influenced piece titled 'Down By The Seaside'; the semi-acoustic 'Poor Tom' and 'The Rover'; Jones' ghostly keyboard piece, 'No Quarter'; plus a lengthy instrumental track that Page had been tinkering with – no lyrics yet, just a nice chord progression building steadily towards a thrilling crescendo; something that would meld the acoustic and electric sides of Zeppelin into one overriding musical statement. 'I don't want to tell you about it in case it doesn't come off,' he had teased the *NME* as far back as April 1970. Using an eight-track studio he'd installed at the Pangbourne boathouse, he had been working on it, off

and on, ever since. It was, he told me, 'pretty much my baby, yeah'.
The idea: 'To have a piece with the sort of naked guitar starting off,
and then into a thing that would build up. And actually, this is another
one where you bring John Bonham in for effect, you know? Let the
thing go by and then bring in the effect.' He smiled. 'And that there
would be this great sort of orgasm at the end.'

Having demoed some of their new ideas at Basing Street, in January
they returned for two weeks to Headley Grange. They were in for a
shock. For all its dilapidations, back in the warm spring Headley had
taken on the form of a countryside idyll where they could play at being
gentleman rockers, Bonzo donning his gamekeeper's cap and tweed
jacket, striding through the woods on days off, aiming his shotgun at
squirrels. Now it was winter, 'cold and damp,' remembered Jones. 'We
all ran in when we arrived in a mad scramble to get the driest rooms.'
They were so cold one night Cole ripped a section of the bannister
from the stairs and threw it on the large open fire that occupied the
lounge. 'Actually, it had central heating but the boiler probably went
back to the 1920s,' said Jimmy. 'I remember they tried to get it going
and it was just fumes going everywhere, and it was abandoned. We
had a fire in the living room and that sort of thing but it was never
adequate. I remember actually in my bedroom – at the very top of the
stairs – the sheets were wet in there [from the damp]. It's lucky we
didn't all get bronchitis or pneumonia.' It's clear how much he enjoyed
the atmosphere though. As engineer Andy Johns later recalled, 'The
rest of us moaned about being cold, but Jimmy was more concerned
with creepy noises or flying fucking furniture.'

After a week spent writing and rehearsing the new material, Ian
Stewart (once the piano player in the Stones, now their tour manager)
and Andy Johns arrived with the Stones' mobile truck. Mike leads
were run through the windows of the drawing room, its walls sound-
proofed with glued-on empty egg cartons. All communications
between band and truck were conducted via closed-circuit camera
and microphone. Not ideal, yet the improvised setting encouraged a
freshness and spontaneity to the recording the band had rarely known
before. When Stewart unloaded the truck they found his piano in there
too. As a result he ended up adding his Johnnie Johnson eighty-eight-
key style to a handful of works-in-progress, including what Jimmy
called a 'spontaneous combustion number' called 'It's Been A Long

Time' – later re-titled 'Rock and Roll' – and another off-the-peg jam on Richie Valens' 'Ooh My Head', also later re-titled, in Stewart's honour, 'Boogie With Stu'.

Such sweet serendipity surrounded the making of the whole album. Another track – the one which would eventually open side one – based on a cartwheeling riff John Paul Jones had been 'inspired' to develop after listening to the similarly shaped 'Tom Cat' from Muddy Waters' 1969 album, *Electric Mud* (itself aimed squarely at the white rock market), was named simply 'Black Dog', partly in punning reference to the source material, but mainly after an old black Labrador that hung around the gardens and kitchen at Headley. 'He was an old dog,' recalled Page, 'you know when they get the white whiskers round the nose?' When he vanished one night, 'we all thought he'd been out on the tiles [because] when he got back he was just sleeping all day. And we thought, oh, black dog – cos we just called him black dog – he's been out on the razzle. And that was it. It just became a standing joke. Every time anyone went in the kitchen he was still flaked out ...'

So what sounds on the surface like a swaggering, psychosexual monster of a song is about being out on the tiles, I asked? 'No, no, it wasn't to do with that. It was just a working title that stuck.' Something Plant, who wrote the lyrics, contradicted when he later described 'Black Dog' to Cameron Crowe as a 'blatant let's-do-it-in-the-bath-type thing'. Jimmy is adamant, though, adding: 'Yeah, but you know the sort of subliminal messages that come across in songs. I know that Arthur Lee [of Love] wrote a song after that called "White Dog" cos he was really annoyed at "Black Dog". He thought that it was ... you know, people can take things on board in various ways.' He saw the black in 'Black Dog' as something negative? 'I guess so. Yeah, negative connotations,' he smiled and refused to say any more.

Arthur Lee was not the only one to pick up on the 'subliminal messages' – negative or otherwise – of 'Black Dog'. While musos stroked their beards appreciatively over the peacocking, lugubrious riff – originally all in 3/16 time, smirked Jones, 'but no-one could keep up with that!' – and Plant's accapella vocals, based on Fleetwood Mac's recent hit, 'Oh Well' – for those in the know about Page's obsession with the occult, it was assumed the title referred to some Baskerville-esque hellhound, a belief underscored by lines like, 'Eyes that shine, burnin' red/Dreams of you all through my head ...' But as the writer

Erik Davis points out, the burning eyes almost certainly belong to Plant himself, the song demonising not the sexual power of the 'big-legged woman' he's singing about but, as Davis puts it, 'the male's own lust, experienced as a possession from within'. By the final verse, unable to 'get my fill' the singer settles for a woman who's 'gonna hold my hand'.

Similarly, the track that would come next on the finished album, 'Rock and Roll', arrived out of thin air as the band was struggling to record something else. 'I've got a feeling now we were doing "Four Sticks", or "When the Levee Breaks",' Jimmy told me. 'I'm not quite sure which of the two it was. But it wasn't anything like the originals ... All of a sudden, between a take, John Bonham's started doing the opening of "Keep A-Knockin'" by Little Richard. And he did that, and where the band would come in I came in with the riff that you all know. Dead on, straight in – straight in! And so we went through like a twelve-bar and went, hold on, let's not do what we were doing, let's do this. And then we worked on it and we had it done in like no time at all.' It was, said Page, the sort of thing that could only have happened 'all working together under those circumstances and having the freedom to be able to do that, not having to look at the clock, having the time to work on it when you really felt like you were connected to the work ... never knowing quite what was round the corner.'

Plant's lyrics, made up as he sang along, referenced the Diamonds, the Monotones and the Drifters as he sought to get a cohesive theme going, while elements of Page's guitar solo date back to 'Train Kept A-Rollin''. But you didn't need to know any of that to pick up on the retro-yet-futuristic feel of a number that looked back while clearly running forward in headlong fashion.

The short-day/long-night atmosphere of Headley in winter also contributed to the wistful ambience of the two acoustic numbers on the album. The first, 'The Battle of Evermore' was something Page and Plant came up with huddled in front of the fireplace one night after the others had crashed out. 'I remember one night I came downstairs and Jonesy's mandolin was lying there,' Jimmy told me. 'He always had loads of different instruments lying around. I'd never played a mandolin before and I picked it up and started messing around with it, and I came up with all of "The Battle of Evermore". That would never have happened if we'd just been in a normal studio situation.'

Plant's lyric came from an idea he'd first had at Bron-Yr-Aur, based on his immersion in both *Lord of the Rings* and a military history of the Middle Ages – specifically in the case of the former, his mention of the Ringwraiths. Elsewhere, there were also references to the Battle of Pelennor Fields from *The Return of the King*, with the 'Queen of Light' as Eowyn, the 'Prince of Peace' Aragorn, and the 'dark Lord' almost certainly Sauron, while 'the angels of Avalon' were taken straight from Celtic mythology, in this context the border wars between Albion and its Celtic foes. Or as he told *Record Mirror*, in March 1972, 'Albion would have been a good place to be, but that was England before it got messed up. You can live in a fairyland if you read enough books and if you're interested in as much history as I am – the Dark Ages and all that.'

Later, when the band came to finesse the tracks back at Basing Street, Plant decided he needed another vocalist to act as his foil on the tune. Enter former Fairport Convention singer Sandy Denny in a beguiling cameo, her river-clear voice providing the perfect harmonic counterpoint to Plant's nursery-rhyme melody. 'It's really more of a playlet than a song,' Robert explained. 'So while I sang the events in the song, Sandy answered back as if she was the pulse of the people on the battlements. Sandy was playing the town crier urging people to throw down their weapons.'

Zeppelin already enjoyed a certain kinship with Fairport Convention. Their bassist Dave Pegg (a veteran who would go on to play with Pentangle, Nick Drake, John Martyn and many others) was an old mate of Plant's and Bonham's from Brum and the days when he played with A Way Of Life; the two bands had also jammed at the Troubadour in LA on Zeppelin's US tour the summer before. (Fairport were recording a live album there and the jam with Zeppelin was included, the band credited pseudonymously as the Birmingham Water Buffalo Society.) In September, they had also hung out together at the *Melody Maker* awards, and a month later during their lay-off, Jimmy and Robert had been to check out Sandy's new group Fotheringay when they opened for Elton John at the Albert Hall. For her part, Denny was knocked sideways by the energy of the session. 'I left the studio feeling slightly hoarse,' she told student journalist Barbara Charone in 1973. 'Having someone out-sing you is a horrible feeling . . .'

The other all-acoustic number that sprung from their time at Headley was yet another whose origins lay in Page and Plant's inspir-

ational stay at Bron-Yr-Aur, yet reflected their shared love and fascination for the place that would, as the Seventies unfolded, become
their second home in so many bittersweet ways – 'Going To California'.
On first hearing, an obvious paean to the genius of Joni Mitchell,
whose *Ladies Of The Canyon* album – a cornerstone of the emerging
Laurel Canyon 'folk-rock' sound exemplified by fellow-travellers such
as Crosby Stills & Nash (whose Graham Nash was then her live-in
lover), Neil Young (like Mitchell, a displaced Canadian, hypnotised by
the bucolic splendour of the canyon that lay, ironically, in the very
heart of the sleazy Hollywood glitz that it figuratively and metaphorically looked down on) and 'Sweet Baby' James Taylor (a junkie
LA troubadour whose saccharine tunes were belied by the impenetrable darkness of his harrowingly autobiographical lyrics) – had completely entranced both Page and Plant. 'Someone told me there's a girl
out there,' Robert sang, 'with love in her eyes and flowers in her
hair . . .' Or as he later put it: 'When you're in love with Joni Mitchell
you've really got to write about it now and again.'

Plant's Tolkien influence was also present on the album's most
overtly pop moment, 'Misty Mountain Hop', where the dancing foggy
slopes in question are again based on images from *Lord of the Rings*,
the singer appearing to draw allegorical ties between the hippy nation
he still saw himself as a devout member of and the mythological
eponymous heroes of *The Hobbit*. In fact, the lyric draws its chief
inspiration from a real-life drug bust, either in London or San Francisco,
and a consequent desire to flee to a place 'Over the hills where the
spirits fly . . .' The insanely catchy guitar motif was another that Page
'just came up with on the spot', which Jones developed early one
morning at the electric piano as the others slept.

There was only one track on which the band consistently struggled
and which they eventually came close to abandoning completely before
a suitably 'refreshed' Bonzo came to their rescue, and which they
consequently named after him – 'Four Sticks'. Based on Page's idea of
creating a riff-based song based on a trancelike Indian raga, fluctuating
between five- and six-beat meters, the band simply couldn't nail it
until Bonham – returning in the early hours from a night out in
London – downed a can of Double Diamond beer then picked up two
drumsticks in each hand and laid the track down in just two takes.
Jimmy recalled how, 'We'd tried the number and he'd been playing it

in a regular pattern. But we were gonna re-cut it [and] have another go at it. [Bonzo] had been to see Ginger Baker's Airforce and he came in and he was really hyped about it. He liked Ginger Baker but he was like, "I'll show him!" And he came in and he picked up the four sticks and that's it, we just did two takes of it. Because that's all we could sort of manage. But it's astonishing what he's doing. He'd never employed that style of playing before. I can't even remember what it was called, what the working title was. But it was sure as hell "Four Sticks" after that. Bonzo just took it into another stratosphere.'

The track everybody still remembers best from that fourth Zeppelin album, though, is 'Stairway to Heaven' – 'the long one' Page had been tinkering away at for nearly a year before finally taking the band through it at Headley. One of the first songs they actually had a crack at, Robert and Bonzo were sent to the pub the second night while Jimmy sat with Jonesy to write out the music for what would become the final version the band would begin to routine the next day.

Talking about it in 2001, on the thirtieth anniversary of its release, Jimmy's face still betrays his obvious pride in what is now regarded as probably Led Zeppelin's finest recorded moment. 'When I did studio work, and when John Paul Jones did studio work, the rule was always: you don't speed up. That was the cardinal sin, to speed up. And I thought, right, we'll do something that speeds up. But that, seriously, was another thing we always did in Zeppelin. If it started to move in tempo, don't worry, it's finding its own tempo. Don't worry, just all stay together. As long as you're all together on it, that's fine.'

As for the lyrics, written entirely by Plant, 'Jimmy and I just sat by the fire, it was a remarkable setting,' he recalled years later. 'I was holding a pencil and paper, and for some reason I was in a very bad mood. Then all of a sudden my hand was writing out the words, "There's a lady who's sure all that glitters is gold/And she's buying a stairway to heaven ..." I just sat there and looked at the words and then I almost leapt out of my seat.' The lyrics, he explained, 'Were a cynical thing about a woman getting everything she wanted without getting anything back.' Jimmy was pleased, too, that there was 'a lot of ambiguity implied in that number that wasn't present before'. In fact, he liked the lyrics so much they became the first ever to be reprinted on a Zeppelin album sleeve, 'so that people could really concentrate on it'.

Because he already knew the song was special? 'Yeah, I mean, there was a lot of stuff on there we knew was special. But "Stairway . . ." was something that had been really crafted. The lyrics were fantastic. The wonderful thing is that, even with the lyrics in front of you – you know how you listen to something and you might not quite get what the words are but you get your own impression? With this, the lyrics were there but you *still* got your own impression of what the song was about. And that was really important.'

More words would come the following day as the band worked their way bit by bit through the song's epic journey. 'I have an image of Robert sitting on a radiator,' recalled Richard Cole. 'He was working out the words to "Stairway . . ." while John Paul pulled out a recorder. Whenever they went into pre-recording, John Paul would come down with a carload of instruments, usually different acoustic instruments.' Things went reasonably smoothly except for Bonzo struggling at first to get the timing right on the twelve-string part before the electric guitar solo. Page recalled how, 'As we were doing all that, Robert was writing down the lyrics. They just came to him really quickly. He said it was like someone was guiding his hand.'

Assistant engineer Richard Digby-Smith remembered how: 'They ran up the stairs for the playback. Sounds wonderful. Bonham says, "That's it then!" But Pagey's quiet. He's a man of few words anyway. His hand's on his chin, he's going, "Mmm, hmm" – you never knew what he was thinking. So Bonham looks at him and says, "What's up?" And Page says he's convinced that they have a better take in them. Well, Bonham's not best pleased. "This always happens – we get a great take and you want to do it again." They go back down. Bonzo grabs his sticks, huffing, puffing, muttering, "One more take and that's it." He waits and waits until his grand entrance and, of course, when the drums come in, if you thought the one before was good this one is just explosive. And when they play it back, Bonham looks at Jimmy like, "you're always right, you bastard".'

The track's now celebrated crescendo – Page's goosebumps-inducing guitar solo – was attempted at Headley but after three hours of trying and failing to get it just so, Page finally gave up. Instead, he saved it for when the band were back at Basing Street. Rejecting his favoured Gibson Les Paul, he pulled out the battered old Telecaster that Jeff Beck had given him. Eschewing headphones, preferring to play the backing track back through speakers, as classical music soloists tend to, Digby-Smith recalled in *Mojo* seeing Page leaning against a speaker as he played, a cigarette stuck between the strings by the tuning peg. 'I winged that guitar solo, really,' Page later admitted. 'When it came to recording it, I warmed up and did three of them. They were all quite different from each other. I did have the first phrase worked out and then there was the link phrase. I did check them before the tape ran. The one we used was definitely the best.'

What not even Jimmy Page could have known was just how incredibly popular this one track would become. Now one of the best-known, most highly regarded songs in rock history, alongside such comparable cornerstones as the Beatles' 'A Day In The Life' – whose three-act, beginning, middle and arresting finale structure it draws on – and Queen's 'Bohemian Rhapsody' – which, in turn, clearly apes the epic grandiosity of Zeppelin's slow-build to a guitar-blazing conclusion – 'Stairway to Heaven' has become the national anthem of rock; a track whose fame now far exceeds its original context – despite the album itself becoming one of the biggest-selling of all time (second only to the Eagles' *Greatest Hits*). At last count, 'Stairway . . .' had been played on American radio alone more than five million times, despite famously never having been released as a single.

In fact, despite huge pressure from Atlantic to release 'Stairway . . .' as a single in America – to the point where advance promo singles were pressed up for US radio – the only track from the fourth album eventually issued in that format was 'Black Dog', an edited version of which was released (with 'Misty Mountain Hop' as its B-side) in the US on 2 December, eventually reaching no. 15. '"Stairway to Heaven" was never, ever, *ever* going to be released as a single,' Jimmy told me earnestly. 'Australia put it on an EP, with "Going to California" and "The Battle of Evermore" on it. They might have tried to slip out a single as well, but it was too late to do anything about it when we found out. But when [America] said "Stairway . . ." should be a single, I said absolutely not. The whole thing was we wanted people to hear it in the context of the album. Also, I said it will help the album sell because it's *not* a single. One thing I would never have entertained was messing around with that song. I knew that the minute it was a single, the next thing they would want it to be an edited version, and I wasn't having that, no way.'

Did Jimmy have any sense at all as he was recording it though that it would become so enormously popular and well known? 'Well, I knew that it was really good,' he said with a grin. 'I knew that it had so many sort of elements being brought in that were really gonna work, I knew it was gonna hold up as a piece of music. But I didn't ... I mean, obviously, I never expected it to ... I thought it would make a bit of a splash, so to speak. But, of course, one could have only hoped in your secret dreams that things could last the way that they did. I never really expected that, but I was always fully aware of how good our music was. Because of the way it was played.'

Is it the best song he's ever written; the best Zep song ever? 'It was certainly a milestone along one of the many avenues of Zeppelin, yes.' Did he wonder how he would ever top it? 'No, because that was never the intention. That's definitely not the thing to do if you want to keep creating great stuff. To try and top it would have been like chasing your own tail. There was never meant to be another "Whole Lotta Love" on the third album, nor was there meant to be another "Stairway ..." on [the album that followed]. In the context of Zeppelin, they [the record industry] were playing by the old rules, and we weren't doing that. The albums were meant to sum up where you were at at the time you recorded them.'

Since its release, however, there have been those who claim that 'Stairway to Heaven', like so many previous Zeppelin songs, was more closely based on the work of others. Most notably, a track from Spirit's eponymous 1968 debut album called 'Taurus', a short instrumental which does contain a brief passage that bears a passing resemblance to the opening guitar lines of 'Stairway ...' Unlike tracks like 'Dazed and Confused' or 'Whole Lotta Love', where the amount of 'borrowing' is clear for all to hear, the case for 'Stairway ...' being partly lifted from 'Taurus' is much weaker. If Page, who was a fan of Spirit – witness Zeppelin's performance of 'Fresh Garbage' from the same Spirit album on their earliest US tours, when the two bands shared bills – was influenced by the guitar chords on 'Taurus' what he did with them was the equivalent of taking the wood from a garden shed and building it into a cathedral, which somewhat wipes the slate clean. Equally, claims that Page lifted chords from a song by the Chocolate Watch Band – a band he had also shared a bill with in Yardbirds' days – called 'And She's Lonely' would seem to miss the point entirely, as do

suggestions that 'Stairway . . .' was based, structurally, on 'Tangerine'. Again even if this were the case, any suggestion that any of these songs in any way prefigured the existence of a landmark musical moment like 'Stairway to Heaven' is plainly ludicrous. Page was certainly a musical magpie – to put it mildly – and would continue to be so as the years blinked past like the lights of a passing train. And yes, of course 'Stairway to Heaven' didn't just arrive out of thin air. Jimmy once told me, in an interview for the BBC which they later shamefully 'misplaced', that for him the antecedents of his most famous musical creation lay in the same 'She Moved Through The Fair'/'White Summer'/'Black Mountainside' guitar showcase he had already spent years 'fine tuning' – but in this instance full credit needs to be given to the creator of what quickly became perhaps the grandest, certainly most affecting musical statement of his generation.

All that said, for many people the really big moment on what still remains the biggest, most seamlessly complete Zeppelin album, in every sense, was saved till last: 'When the Levee Breaks', an old 'Memphis' Minnie [McCoy] and 'Kansas' Joe McCoy tune the band re-imagined as a hypnotic, blues rock mantra. On paper, another Zeppelin 'original' (though uncredited on the album sleeve, the lyrics were originally performed on record by the husband-and-wife McCoy team, documenting the great Mississippi River flood of 1927, where the couple's manically twinned guitars mimicked the sound of rainwater lashing down) like 'Whole Lotta Love', 'Bring It On Home', 'Lemon Song' and others before, what Zeppelin did to 'When the Levee Breaks' so far exceeded the sonic parameters of the original it did in the end come very close to being an entirely new work – though not quite enough to warrant the misappropriation of the relevant royalties (an omission rectified in recent years with the addition of a co-credit for Memphis Minnie), particularly when it came to the lyrics, where Minnie's exhortations – 'Cryin' won't help you, prayin' won't do you no good/When the levee breaks, mama, you got to move' – formed the basis for Plant's own.

The big difference, in the first instance, was in the titanic drum sound. 'It was always an electric blues,' said Jimmy, 'but I never quite knew that the minute John Bonham had set his drum kit up in the big hall [at Headley] it would sound so fantastic.' Known as the Minstrels' Gallery, the hall at Headley, 'was three storeys high and so it was this

big cathedral-like hall. And [Bonham] just started playing this kit that had arrived, and it sounded so fantastic we went, hold on, let's do "... Levee Breaks". And we tried it and this incredible sound came out ...'

The sound was captured on tape by hanging two ambient Beyer MI60 mikes from the staircase and aiming them at where Bonzo was sitting at his kit, while Andy Johns sat in the mobile truck outside recording the sound through two channels he then compressed using an Italian echo unit called a Binson (belonging to Jimmy that used a steel drum instead of a conventional tape). A separate microphone would normally have been added to record the bass drum but Bonzo's unamplified kick sound echoing around the great hall was on its own so powerful there was no need. 'I remember sitting there thinking it sounded utterly amazing,' recalled Johns. 'So I ran out of the truck and said, "Bonzo you gotta come in and hear this." He shouted: "Whoa, that's it! That's what I've been hearing!"' (And what subsequent generations of producers and mixers have been hearing ever since, making it the most sampled drum sound of all.)

You were doing all right on the Ma Reagan circuit, singing and jumping around, sixteen years old and pulling a few birds. When Mrs Reagan employed you to be the MC at the Oldhill Plaza you even earned a few bob, going on stage in your suit, making all the announcements. One of the best times was introducing Little Stevie Wonder when 'Fingertips' was in the charts, they put down their pints and paid attention that night! No, it wasn't as good as being in the group but nearly, with everyone watching you, listening to what you had to say. Then jumping off and putting on a pair of jeans and a striped T-shirt and becoming a Mod, strutting about, showing off. And you still got to play sometimes.

It was after doing a twenty-minute set at the Plaza one Saturday night with Crawling King Snake when you noticed this beefy-looking bloke standing near the front with a pint in his hand, watching you. When you saw him walking over to the stage afterwards at first you wondered if it was going to mean trouble. That happened some nights, some bird got carried away wetting her knickers watching you, next thing you know her bloody boyfriend wants to have a go. But this bloke goes, 'I know who you are, you're pretty good but your band's shit. What you need is somebody as good as me.' To which you replied, 'Well, that's a good introduction,

*what's your story?' Said he was a drummer. Said, 'If you like, I'll come
and play with you and see what you think.' Same age as you, but he
looked older, more like someone your dad would knock around with, except
your dad wouldn't have knocked around with a yobbo like that.*

*So you said, yeah, okay, and he came along to the next rehearsal. And
bugger me if he wasn't amazing, fantastic, unbelievable – and loud. But
bloody good, you'd never heard a drummer like that before. But you
already had a drummer and this bloke ... well, he had a loud mouth too,
didn't he? Almost as loud as yours and you thought to yourself, 'Wait a
minute, this is gonna be a bit of a struggle here. This guy is a bit too
bolshie.' The sort of bloke who wasn't afraid to give you his opinion and
you weren't gonna have any of that. So when he told you where he lived
you said, 'Sorry, mate, it's way too far to come and pick you up,' even
though you and your mates only lived about ten miles away from him in
Kidderminster. He gave you his phone number all the same and you kept
it just in case.*

*Next thing you knew you were ringing it. Groups came and went so
easily in them days and decent drummers were bloody hard to find. So he
came along – you were hoping maybe he'd calmed down a bit but no
bloody chance – and you did a few gigs together, the Plaza, some pubs, all
the usual dives. Then you split up again, only this time it wasn't you
ditching him, it was the other bloody way around! Cheeky sod! But John
was always leaving groups in them days. Half the time you didn't even
know he was gone till he just stopped turning up for rehearsals or whatever.
The sod had this ploy where he'd say he had to have his drums out the
van and take 'em home to clean them. That was the sign for those that
knew. He wouldn't be back. It was quite funny, actually, he did it to
everyone, jumping like a big, fat burping frog from lily pad to lily pad. It
was quite funny as long as it wasn't you he was doing it to.*

*After that you'd run into each other from time to time, like you did
everyone on the circuit in them days. Except now he was married to his
girlfriend Pat Philips. You could hardly believe it, he was – you were! –
still only seventeen. But that was Bonzo; you never knew what was going
to happen next with that bastard. Next thing, he was a dad! Not that it
meant he'd settled down. Once, when he was just about to jump ship
again – this time from Nicky James & the Diplomats – you bumped into
him running down the street with a bass guitar under his arm. 'Quick,'
he said, 'I've got to put this in Pat's mum's coalhouse!' He hadn't just*

taken his drums back this time; he'd nicked the bloody bass too! Not that
he was a very good thief. The bass sat in Pat's mother's coalhouse on the
Priory Estate in Dudley for a few weeks. But everyone knew he had it and
eventually Nicky told him to bloody well bring it back or else, and he did,
just like that. Nobody said anything. Another time at the Cedar Club he
was swanning around in this expensive suede orange jacket he'd nicked
from somewhere which he ended up selling to about three different people
for a tenner each. 'Bloody hell, Bonzo!' you'd laughed. Sometimes you'd
just be walking down the street with him in West Brom and people would
cross the road to avoid him. You had to laugh. Laugh or cry . . .

Sometimes you were the one doing the avoiding. You always ended up
back together in the end, though. You got to know Pat and she was lovely.
And his mum and dad, who were lovely too, even though their son rarely
had a normal job and you were another one of the long-haired layabouts
he hung around with, nicking milk bottles from doorsteps early in the
morning. You were always so full of it, definitely a team . . .

With the drum track recorded, the band was left to roll freely on top
of the groove, Page's grinding slide guitar riffs building on the tension as
Plant's phased vocal wailed and vamped through the brutal, elemental
drone, the singer's harmonica solo helping create a whirlpool effect to
which Page then added a ghostly backward-echo – the whole thing
reputedly slowed down still further at the mixing stage – to create a
narcotic, blues rock colossus. 'I'll tell you what it was,' Jimmy said, 'it
was an attempt to have a really hypnotic riff, *really* hypnotic, hypnotic,
hypnotic, to draw you right in. Like a mantra, you know?'

By the end of January, safely ensconced back at Basing Street Studios
where they began working on overdubs, they had fourteen tracks in
various states of completion – all eight that would eventually be used
on the album plus loose ends like 'No Quarter' (which would have to
wait until their next album), and 'Boogie with Stu', 'Night Flight',
'Down By The Seaside', and 'The Rover', all of which would have to
wait another four years before being released. There was some discussion about perhaps releasing it all on a double album, or even, more
radically, a four-part series of EPs. Grant argued against such ideas,
though. After the ambivalent reaction across the board to *Led Zeppelin*
III, what was needed now, he knew better than most, was a tightly
conceived, well-executed, conventionally affordable single-format

album of music that Zeppelin fans would find inarguable. Listening to the band working on tracks like 'Black Dog', 'Rock And Roll', 'Misty Mountain Hop', 'When the Levee Breaks' and even the more complex 'Stairway to Heaven', Grant knew they had it in their hands. Nothing would fuck that up for them, he decided, and Page was happy to be 'talked out' of a double album.

On Andy Johns' recommendation, Page, Grant and Johns flew to Los Angeles on 9 February to begin mixing the tapes at Sunset Sound Studios. As the plane landed at LA, the city was in the midst of the Sylmar earthquake, whose impact reverberated around the whole State, cracking a dam in San Diego, a weird echo of the line from 'Going to California': 'The mountains and the canyons started to tremble and shake', and an omen perhaps for the difficulties awaiting them. For when they arrived that first morning at Sunset Sound, the studio Johns had worked in before (with a group called Sky) had been renovated and 'completely changed'. Forced to use another, unfamiliar room, the end results were less than promising.

'We should have just gone home,' said Johns, who would later admit that he had an ulterior motive for wanting to be in LA – a girl, inevitably. 'But I didn't want to and I don't think Jimmy did, either,' who never needed much persuading to spend time in LA. 'We were having a good time, you know?' When they returned to London a week later, however, and played the results back at Olympic to the others, 'It sounded terrible! I thought my number was up!' Jimmy was embarrassed and furious. 'Basically, Andy Johns should be hung, drawn and quartered,' he raged. 'We wasted a week wanking around.'

The plan had been to have the album ready for release in the spring, with a world tour already booked to back it up. Now those plans would need to be revised and – yet again – Page was forced to put the finishing touches to the album while on tour. Only the mix of 'When the Levee Breaks' survived from the Los Angeles trip, Jimmy later describing it as 'one of my favourite mixes', particularly the moment towards the song's climax where 'everything starts moving around except for the voice, which stays stationary'.

There was better news for Jimmy on the home front when he became a father for the first time with the birth in March of his daughter – conceived with Charlotte, he later realised, during his and Plant's working holiday at Bron-Yr-Aur the previous spring. Named

Scarlet Lilith Eleida Page; the 'Scarlet' after Crowley's Scarlet Woman; 'Lilith' after one of Crowley's own children. There was precious little time for celebrations, however, with the band now committed to their first UK tour in a year, culminating in a deliberately low-key yet intentionally profile-raising string of club dates at the end of March.

The idea of doing something different had been discussed while the band were down at Headley, with G suggesting unannounced appearances at unheard of locations like London's Waterloo Station or the headquarters of Surrey Cricket Club, Kennington Oval. In the end, a back-to-the-clubs tour was simpler and more in keeping with their desire to be seen as reconnecting with their roots. 'The audiences were becoming bigger and bigger but moving further and further away,' Page explained to *Record Mirror.* 'They became specks on the horizon and we were losing contact with people – those people who were respons-ible for lifting us off the ground in the early days.' So now they would be playing 'those clubs like the London Marquee for exactly the same amount as we did in the old days as a thank you to those promoters and the audiences alike. By doing this we will be able to tour the entire of Britain and not just those cities who are fortunate enough to contain large venues.'

A commendable idea but with one fatal flaw: with Zeppelin in far more demand than the relatively meagre success of their last album had indicated, instead of pleasing an influential cadre of fans (and critics) with their 'innovative' step backwards into smaller venues, the band succeeded only in upsetting and alienating thousands of fans who simply could not get into the venues – not that that stopped them turning up. The result: drunken fist fights, civil disturbance and bad headlines. Or as Jimmy later put it, 'We couldn't win, either way. First we were this big hype, now we were at fault for not playing places big enough for everybody to see us.'

For those who did obtain tickets, though, these were historic occa-sions, with the band starting the tour at Belfast's Ulster Hall on 5 March 1971. Outside that Friday night, the streets were ablaze as rioters·threw Molotov cocktails and set fire to a petrol tanker. Inside, however, Catholics and Protestants alike were able to enjoy the shared experience of witnessing new numbers like 'Black Dog', 'Going to California' and 'Stairway to Heaven' from the new, unreleased album performed live·for the first time. Page remembered reaction to the new material as 'a bit lukewarm, but it was all right, the reaction was fair enough – nobody knew what it was and *we* were still getting into it.' As can be heard on the 1998 *BBC Sessions* double-CD, which includes the band's *In Concert* performance recorded live at the Paris Cinema in London on 1 April 1971 and aired on John Peel's Radio 1 programme three days later: '"Stairway to Heaven" ', in particular, 'was a hard song to actually get right. Getting all these sort of movements right, and the tempo changes, without racing it, just keeping it right.' The first time Page had played a double-neck guitar on stage, it later became part of his trademark sound, 'the beginning of my building up harmonised guitars properly.'

Off stage, however, John Bonham seemed less concerned with musical time-changes as he was the closing times of various hotel bars. After their show at Dublin's Boxing Stadium (appropriately enough), he got into an altercation in the small hours when he broke into the hotel kitchen looking for food. With the chef brandishing a knife 'big enough to engrave initials onto a Brontosaurus' Cole hit Bonzo flush in the nose, breaking it and sending blood everywhere. 'You'll thank me for that when you sober up,' he told him but Bonzo never did.

Back at the drawing board, despite returning to Olympic in April and again in June, with sessions fitted in between European dates, the final mixes for the fourth album weren't delivered to Soho's Trident Studios for mastering until early July 1971 – six months after completing recording – with an extra set of lacquers being cut simultaneously at the Beatles' Apple Studios. By now they were performing most of the album live, including at the KB Hallen in Copenhagen on 3 May, their only known attempt at 'Four Sticks'. 'We'll try something we've never done before,' Plant told the audience. 'There's every chance that we will fall apart ...' A prophecy that almost literally came true at the final date of the European tour at the Vigorelli football stadium, in Milan, on 3 July, when riot police panicked at the sight of the crowd lighting fires and waded in with tear gas and batons, leaving dozens of audience members bloodied and beaten. 'Absolutely ghastly,' Page shuddered at the memory. 'The statement in the press the next day said that a bottle had been thrown [but] the police were just provoking the audience, and suddenly it went off like you couldn't believe. It was just pandemonium, and nowhere was immune from this blasted tear gas, including us. I was terribly upset afterwards.'

With the album still in the can, Atlantic were sceptical about the decision to go ahead with the band's seventh US tour in August – which began in Vancouver on the night of Plant's twenty-third birthday – with one exec calling it 'professional suicide'. But all the shows were sold out, the band was on fire, and they received a standing ovation at the LA Forum when they performed 'Stairway to Heaven'. 'Not all of the audience stood up,' Jimmy told me. 'It was about twenty-five per cent of it, and I thought hey, that's pretty good. They were really moved and I thought, this is wonderful, this is great. This is what we hoped for, that people would be that receptive to our new music, you know. Cos at that stage the album *still* hadn't come out ...'

With the mixes and mastering complete, the problem now, as Plant explained to the audience at Madison Square Garden on 3 September, was that they were 'trying to get a record cover that looks how we want it' – an allusion to mounting behind-the-scenes arguments with Ahmet Ertegun and his new chief lieutenant Jerry Greenberg over the 'concept' Page had for it: an album sleeve with absolutely no information on it whatsoever; a stubborn attempt to hit back at the familiar cry of 'hype' that had dogged them from the word go.

Finishing up with two shows in Honolulu on 16 and 17 September, the band enjoyed a few days off in Maui before flying to Tokyo for two shows at the Budokan, as part of a five-date tour, their first of Japan. The shows here were longer and more varied than any they had previously done, throwing in off-the-cuff covers of 'Smoke Gets in Your Eyes', 'Bachelor Boy' and 'Please Please Me'. 'We were taking the piss a bit,' Jimmy laughingly told me. 'It was such a shock to go out there and play to Japanese audiences. They are extremely respectful to what they're listening to [and] think it might be disrespectful if they make a noise, just in case you happen to go very quiet in the music, you know? There'd be applause at the end of each song and then it would just stop abruptly. We weren't used to all of this after coming from America where the whole show people were drinking and smoking joints and going nuts. In Japan, it was so quiet it was sort of eerie, and so we started just doing all these weird things, just goofing ourselves off and having a laugh. But we could have a laugh in Zeppelin. We did enjoy ourselves ...'

It didn't look like Robert and Bonzo were enjoying themselves very much though as they stood at the side of the stage that first night 'knocking six bells out of each other,' Plant told me. It was the end of the show and the band was debating what to do as an encore. But the singer, whose voice had given out during the latter part of the performance, was distraught. 'I said, "I can't do anymore, I've got no voice." Bonzo said, "It never mattered before. You're no good anyway. Just go out there and look good." So I bopped him! And then we had to go back on stage.' It was because they knew each other so well that they could fall out like that and still be friends, he insisted. 'There was never anything lasting.'

Perhaps not, but by then Bonham's increasingly erratic behaviour on tour was starting to become an issue. Taken by promoter Tats Nagashima to what he boasted was 'the most elegant restaurant in Tokyo', Bonzo grew fed-up with being served saké in tiny cups and demanded 'a beer mug or some buckets!' Later that night, they paid a visit to Tokyo's then famous Byblos disco where Bonzo showed his disapproval of the music by urinating from a balcony on the DJ. Bundling the drunken drummer into a cab, Cole finally gave up and left him to collapse on the street just feet from the entrance to the Tokyo Hilton where they were staying. The next day Bonzo and Cole both bought Samurai swords and, drunk again that night, began enacting a sword fight at the hotel, slashing and cutting at anything they could: chairs, curtains, mirrors, paintings. For an encore, they snuck into John Paul Jones' room and carried his still sleeping body out into the hall where he spent the rest of the night. (Hotel staff were too polite to wake him and placed screens around his prone body.) At the end of their stay, the Hilton banned Led Zeppelin for life.

The real enjoyment continued after the tour – at least for Page, Plant and Cole – when they decided not to join Jonesy, Bonham and Grant on their direct flight back to London. Instead, they relaxed into Pagey, Percy and Ricardo mode and decided on a zigzagging path home that took them via Thailand and India. Within hours of arriving in Bangkok, the trio had turned into trinket-buying tourists, visiting the Temple of the Emerald Buddha, where Jimmy bought a near life-size gold, glass and wooden Pegasus. Cole also bought a 'three-foot-high and three-foot-wide' wooden Buddha which he jokingly compared to Peter Grant. That night they visited Bangkok's renowned red light district where, at the urging of their driver Sammy, they spent the evening choosing girls by the number and enjoying endlessly revolving rounds of massages and sex. Or as Jimmy commented on the way home that night: 'They must have invented the term "fucking your brains out" here.'

From Bangkok they flew direct to Bombay, where they checked into the Taj Mahal Hotel, opposite the Gateway of India archway, and spent the next four days as they had in Bangkok, shopping for gifts to take back home (including a hand-carved ivory chess set for Page), visiting the red light district and hanging out at a local disco where Jimmy got up and jammed with some amazed local musicians on their Japanese-made guitars. However, the thrills came to an abrupt end when they insisted their hired guide Mr Razark take them for a meal 'where you go to eat' and all ended up with what Cole described as 'vicious cases of diarrhoea'.

Flying home to London via Geneva, there was a short break before their sixteen-date UK tour began at Newcastle's City Hall on 11 November – three days after the fourth Zeppelin album was released in the US and a week before it finally appeared in Britain. Untitled, fans simply assumed it was called Led Zeppelin IV. After all, none of the other Zep albums had a title either, just a number. What no-one understood until the reviews pointed it out was that the new album didn't even have a number – there was no lettering or information whatsoever included on the gatefold sleeve, not even the Atlantic logo. With the British tour now in full swing, it would be some time until the full significance of the new Zeppelin album sleeve became a subject for debate, at home and abroad, the only allusion to any sort of title the four hand-drawn symbols that elliptically adorned the brown inner bag, all of which were now reproduced as stage images, with Page even wearing a specially knitted sweater depicting his own symbol – what appeared to be the word 'ZoSo'.

Even more inexplicable than an album with no title, some fans found the introduction of a new acoustic set hard to swallow. It was a new section of the show first developed in the US, where they sat on stools weaving their way through 'Going To California', 'That's The Way' and 'Bron-Y-Aur Stomp'. Plant, who used the acoustic section as a chance to take a breather mid-set, was forced to yell at fans to 'Shut up and listen!' before adding a conciliatory: 'Give us a kiss ...'

The tour reached its climax with two landmark, five-hour shows at London's Empire Pool (now Wembley Arena) on 20 and 21 November. Dubbed 'Electric Magic', there was even a support bill for once, including Stone the Crows, plus Bronco on the Saturday night and Home on the Sunday. The festive atmosphere of both shows was completed by an array of novelty circus acts including performing pigs (with huge ruffs around their necks), jugglers and plate spinners. 'That wasn't my idea, the big circus show,' said Jimmy, 'it was probably Peter Grant's. And I don't really know how successful it all was. Electric rabbits out of an electric hat,' he smirked.

It was the sheer power of the music, though, that people took away with them from the Empire Pool. An entirely different proposition from the band that had tiptoed through their new material back in the spring, this was Zeppelin at full, unstoppable force. As Roy Hollingworth wrote in his *Melody Maker* review: 'Nothing, just nothing, was spared. This was no job. This was no gig. It was an event for all.'

A fortnight after the tour ended, the album sat at no. 1 in the UK charts, with demand for it so great that Richard Branson's newly established Virgin Records was forced to set up special stands to sell that album alone. In America, the album reached no. 2, where it stayed for five weeks, held off the top spot by Carole King's *Tapestry*. Six months later, aided by overwhelming airplay of 'Stairway to Heaven' (despite its steadfastly non-single status), it was still riding high in the US charts. It would be another three years, in fact, before the album would finally slip from the US Top Forty, on its way to its first 25 million sales, its astonishing influence on every subsequent generation of rock bands – unquantifiable yet unmistakable.

Not that any of the reviews it received at the time foresaw its eventual eminence. In Britain, *Sounds* called it 'a much overrated album' with 'Black Dog' lumbering around 'with all the grace and finesse of a farmyard chicken', while 'Stairway to Heaven' 'palls dramatically with repeated plays inducing first boredom and then catatonia'. *Disc & Music Echo* came closer to the truth but was still only lukewarm when it said: 'If *Zep III* gave the first indications that their music was by no means confined to power rock then this new album consolidates their expanding maturity.' For once, it was left to *Rolling Stone* to nail it, future Patti Smith guitarist Lenny Kaye describing it as 'an album remarkable for its low-keyed and tasteful subtlety' while applauding its 'sheer variety ... incredibly sharp and precise vocal dynamism [and] the tightest arranging and producing Jimmy Page has yet seen his way toward doing.'

Ironically, given their determination to escape easy pigeonholing by making the album sleeve as seemingly anonymous as possible, a great part of the Zeppelin myth is now rooted in public and private perception of its true 'meaning'. A framed photograph of a grizzled old hermit figure – stooped beneath the weight of a large bundle of branches he is carrying on his back – is tacked to a wall of badly peeling wallpaper which gives way, as we see when the outside of the gatefold sleeve is opened, to the crumbling wall, through which we sight a row of old-fashioned terraced houses beyond which rises a council tower block, the defining symbol of modernity in early Seventies Britain – and taken from a real photograph of the then new high-rise flats in Eve Hill, Dudley, where Bonham had recently lived with his young family, and which were eventually demolished in 1999.

'When I was living in Pangbourne,' said Jimmy, 'I always used to go down into the second-hand shops in Reading, getting furniture and bits and pieces. And Robert came down with me one day and he spotted the Hermit picture. It was there in a second-hand shop, in the corner. I'm not talking about an antique shop, I'm talking about a real dingy second-hand shop, stuff piled all over everything, you know. Robert spotted that, and he bought it. And well spotted, you know. The idea of using it on the album was to sort of show the progress ... It was done in quite a subtle way, really. The old being knocked down, the new buildings going up. They don't look so new now, do they? But they did in that time. And there was the old ways left on the wall.'

Of course, talk of a 'Hermit picture' depicting 'the old ways' inevitably leads to further speculation about what else attracted Page to using the picture. On the inside of the gatefold was 'a drawing that a friend of mine had done' in pencil and gold paint, of another, much more obviously occult Hermit figure, this time standing atop a steep mountain incline, his staff – or wand – in one hand, a burning lamp held aloft in the other, his face looking directly down the slope towards the tiny figure of a young man down on one knee, arms flung wide in supplication, and beyond him in the distance the zigzagging path he has taken from his home in a small, distant town with its church and barely visible steeple.

Although there is no acknowledgment on the album sleeve, the illustration was by a mysterious friend of Page's named Barrington Coleby (not 'Colby' as is usually reported) entitled *View in Half or Varying Light*. 'The illustration was my idea,' Jimmy told me. 'Some people say it has allusions to [Victorian painter] William Holman Hunt, but it hasn't. It actually comes from the idea from the Tarot card of the Hermit, and so the ascension to the beacon and the light of truth. The whole light, so to speak ...'

There are two points of interest here. The first concerns who exactly Barrington Coleby is. Extensive research unearths little or nothing about him or his work, save for just two other pictures, both in a remarkably similar style to 'The Hermit' of the Zeppelin sleeve. Perhaps he was not a career artist, then. A friend of Page's who now, it seems, resides in Switzerland – the ideal place, of course, for maintaining a profile so low as to be positively subterranean; some have speculated that either he has an alternate, possibly private, source of income – or that he may not exist at all. That 'Barrington Coleby' was no more than a pseudonym for the art school-trained Page himself. Certainly no-one from Zeppelin ever seems to have met Coleby. As Jimmy said to me, it was 'a drawing that a friend of mine had done, which I volunteered for the inside cover and everyone agreed'. So that was that.

Whatever the truth, the second and more important point about the illustration given such generous space on the fourth Zeppelin album sleeve is to do with its subject matter. As Page himself has pointed out, it is clearly based on the Hermit card in the Tarot – a symbol of self-reliance and wisdom. Hence, the remark about it being to do with 'the ascension to the beacon and the light of truth'. Might there be more to it though than this fairly pat explanation? In the O.T.O., the eighth, ninth, tenth, eleventh and twelfth degrees – i.e. the very highest levels of the Order, from Perfect Pontiff of the Illuminati up to Frater Superior (the level Crowley attained) – are known as The Hermit Triad. Some believe that the Hermit, in occult terms, is also synonymous with the Magus – or Master Magician. To quote from Crowley's *The Book of Thoth*: '... one of his [The Hermit's] titles is Psychopompos, the guide of the soul through the lower regions. These symbols are indicated by his Serpent Wand ... Following him is Cerberus, the three-headed Hound of Hell whom he has tamed. In this Trump is shewn [sic] the entire mystery of Life in its most secret workings.' In other words, The Hermit and The Magus are both guiding lights, spirits for lesser creatures – i.e. humanity. Therefore, would it be stretching the imagination to suggest that Page, self-confessed Crowley devotee, might be suggesting that the true path to knowledge – or at least the 'road he was on', to paraphrase 'Stairway to Heaven' – is via the occult beliefs of Aleister Crowley, Eliphas Levi and the rest, all the way back to King Solomon and indeed Enoch himself? Moreover, as Dave Dickson points out: 'If you hold the gatefold sleeve up to the mirror, it is possible to work out the figure of a black dog beneath the Hermit [which] appears to have two heads, even though Cerberus had three. So is it that big a leap to imagine that this black dog might have a third head that is less visible, perhaps pointing away from us?'

The occult resonances of the album sleeve – and indeed the album itself – don't end there. The original vinyl record came in a brown inner bag with the merest info on one side and the lyrics of 'Stairway to Heaven' on the other. The ornate typeface used for the lyrics was also Page's idea, taken from the nineteenth-century arts and crafts magazine *Studio*. 'I thought the lettering was so interesting I got someone to work up a whole alphabet.' In the left-hand corner there is a small picture of an Elizabethan-looking gentleman holding a book with some mystical inscriptions engraved behind him. No-one has ever been able to offer an explanation as to who this might be. Dave Dickson, however, believes it to represent Dr John Dee, court magician and astrologer to Queen Elizabeth I. According to *The Magical Diaries of Aleister Crowley*, edited by Stephen Skinner, Dee's 'system of Enochian Magic was one of the keystones of Crowley's practice. Both Dee and Crowley considered that spiritual practices should be recorded in as much detail as the laboratory notes of a research chemist or physicist, or even in more detail, as the grounds of magical practice are even more shifting than those of the physical sciences. It is ironic that Crowley claimed John Dee's amanuensis, Edward Kelly, as one of his past incarnations, showing a further kinship of spirit extending over three and a half centuries of occult practice.'

However, it is on the other side of the brown bag that the depth of Page's occult fascination is more obviously revealed, in the four hand-drawn symbols (or sigils) that sit atop the page: one for each member of the band. First introduced to the public via a series of teaser ads placed in the music press in the weeks leading up to the release, each depicting a particular symbol alongside a previous Zep album sleeve, as with all symbols, clearly there was a mystery here waiting to be unravelled.

Again, this was an idea of Page's that the band felt obliged to go along with, not really knowing what he was asking them. Arranged in magical formation, with the two strongest symbols – Page and Plant's – placed on the outside to protect the weaker two on the inside, each carried a very specific meaning. (Sandy Denny was also given a token symbol placed next to 'The Battle of Evermore' – three triangles, an ancient symbol for Godhead, almost certainly chosen for her by Page or Plant, semi-jokingly, to denote her guest appearance on the track.)

But while both Page and Plant came up with their own sigils, Jones and Bonham were content to browse through a book Jimmy had given them to choose from – Rudolf Koch's 1930 opus, *The Book of Signs*. Considering how apt the signs they chose were, it seems Page knew what he was doing. For Jones, the single circle intersecting three vesica-Pisces that he found on page 32 of Koch's book symbolises a person with confidence and competence (partly because of the difficulty in drawing accurately) – the very attributes, apart from his musicianship, that John Paul most embodied in Zeppelin. There was also an occult connection in that this sign also appears in various esoteric texts, such as the Rosicrucians'. Bonham's three intersecting circles – found on page 33 of the Koch book – symbolise the man-wife-child trilogy. Again, entirely apt, for as anyone who knew John would tell you, it was the home-loving, family-obsessed Bonham that lay beneath the beer-guzzling, room-wrecking Bonzo of tour legend. Like Jones' choice, Bonham's also had occult resonances, the three intersecting circles also evident in the Tarot, where it represents the three evolutionary ages of Osiris (past), Isis (present), and Horus (future) – another Crowley, O.T.O. tenet.

When Jones discovered that Page and Plant had actually designed their own symbols, he was not best pleased. 'Typical!' he blustered. But as Jimmy later told me: 'They might all have had a look in the book, me and Robert too. But it was like, if you want to design your own or put something else in that was fine, too.'

Positioned on the far right of the line, Plant's sigil – a circle with a feather in it – was chosen by him, he later explained, because it was 'a symbol on which all philosophies have been based. For instance, it represents courage to many Red Indian tribes. I like people to lay down the truth. No bullshit, that's what the feather in the circle is all about.' Whether Plant knew the encircled feather was originally the sign of Ma'at, Egyptian goddess of justice and fairness, and an occult emblem of a writer, remains unclear – though Page would surely have known. The original can be found in the book, *The Sacred Symbols of Mu* by the interestingly named Colonel James Churchward.

The only symbol that remained a real mystery was the one positioned at the start of the line on the left and chosen by Page – that one that appeared to read as 'ZoSo'. Although he never intended it to resemble a word, in the prolonged absence of any rational explanation for its meaning – the guitarist usually glaring silently at anyone rude or stupid enough to ask him outright for one – 'ZoSo' is what Page's sigil has continued to be called to this day.

Having always refused to talk about it, I was taken aback when one day, during a discussion about the fourth album's enigmatic artwork, I simply asked Jimmy outright what 'ZoSo' meant and he actually answered me. First, though, he explained that the original idea he had for the album was just one symbol. 'But that didn't seem to be fair.' From which I took it to mean he had intended his own ZoSo symbol. No, he said, 'It wasn't going to be any of the symbols that you know it to be. It was going to be like a tradesman's symbol. You know, they used to have those sort of like . . .' Like a seal? 'Yeah . . . It was gonna have something like that. But in the end we thought, well, no, that isn't quite right cos someone's not going to be happy. So in the end, we had the four.'

But why? Why not just give the album a conventional title? 'Originally, because they [the music press] were going on about Zeppelin being a hype, we wanted to put out an album with no information whatsoever on the cover. But I had to go in personally and argue with the record company about it. That's why the album took so long to come out, because they wanted to put a name on the cover. But I went in there with Peter, and I stayed in there even after Peter left, talking to them about it. I mean, I wouldn't do that now, but then – I just didn't want anything on the cover. Finally, it came down to, well, let's have a symbol on it. I don't know where that came from but I said, "You can't have one symbol, because no-one's going to agree on what it should be. Let's have four symbols, and everyone can choose their own.". And with the four symbols, that also made it "Zeppelin IV", so it was a completely organic process.'

And what did your sign mean? 'Well,' he sighed, 'let's just say we were breaking a lot of rules, and that was our intention.' A pause, and then: 'My symbol was about invoking and being invocative. And that's all I'm going to say about it.' A small chuckle: 'I take it you know what Robert's symbol is about?' Remind me. 'It's about American Indians and bravery. Though you might also say it's about a French maid tickling someone's bum. But I didn't say that ...'

'Invoking' and 'being invocative' – a sign with magickal power then. But to invoke what? Power? Well-being? Success? As Dave Dickson says: 'The only reason people get interested in magick is because they are interested in power. You use the skills you possess to improve your lot, everybody does.' Is that what the 'ZoSo' symbol is supposed to be doing for the fourth Led Zeppelin album then? Well, it certainly became their most successful album. But might there more to it than that?

The earliest appearance of what looks very much like the 'ZoSo' symbol was in the classical 1557 work *Ars Magica Arteficii* by a hermeticist named J. Cardan. Long out of print, a reproduction of the same symbol can now be found in the 1982 publication, *Dictionary of Occult, Hermetic and Alchemical Sigils* by Fred Gettings. On page 201, in the Planetary Symbols section, the sigil for the planet Saturn appears to be Cardan's 'ZoSo' symbol. As Page is a Capricorn, the astrological sign ruled by Saturn, this is unlikely to be mere coincidence (remembering also that Crowley taught that coincidence does not exist). The same symbol was also used by another renowned Capricorn, Austin Osman Spare, a psychic painter, Crowley disciple and another favourite of Page's. Spare was known by the magickal name of 'Zos'.

It's important to remember, though, that ZoSo is not a word or a name, but a magickal sign, a symbol, made up of constituent parts. Therefore we can be fairly certain that the 'Z' depicted thus ⟨ is a stylised representation for the Capricorn astrological symbol; while the o-S-o, shown as ⟨ is likely a reference to Crowley's 666. It's believed by occult observers to also have some relation to an obscure Crowley work entitled *Red Dragon*, another occult term for Kundalini energy, or downward travelling sexual energy, as opposed to upwards along the spinal column, to achieve immortality. Again, if Page was deliberately using this as part of his invocation, there can be little doubt that the fourth Zeppelin album is the one that comes closest to gifting him such 'immortality'.

Of course, many other such theories have been expounded over the years as to what 'ZoSo' really means. The o-S-o, for example, also appears quite similar to the alchemical sign for Mercury, the winged messenger of ancient myth, and therefore some believe 'ZoSo' to symbolise a near-death or Tantric sex ritual used to unify the worlds of the living and the dead – the light and the dark – and reveal the secrets of the universe. Others have postulated the theory that 'ZoSo' symbolises Cerberus, the three-headed guardian hound at the gates of hell, or that it has something to do with the pyramid of Zoser in Egypt. Some even say it is merely a joke taken from a character known as ZoSo in the children's book series *Curious George the Monkey*. But these are false trails, leading nowhere.

Ultimately, unless Jimmy Page ever decides to come out and discuss the matter more fully – exceedingly unlikely – we can never know for sure. But consider those words again – 'invoking' and 'being invocative'. Clearly, 'ZoSo' is an occult sigil. Make of that fact what you will, but Page wasn't joking when he chose it. As he told Nick Kent in 1973: 'What you put out, you get back again all the time. The band is a good example of that simply because there's an amazing chemistry at work there.' He added: 'Astrologically it's very powerful indeed.' Or as he put it to Chris Welch a year later in an interview for *Melody Maker*: 'There are powerful astrological forces at work within the band. I'm sure they had a lot to do with our success.'

Ironically, after its release, the main focus in attempting to unravel the album's occult connections was 'Stairway to Heaven', with the claim popular in the Seventies and the Eighties – i.e. before the advent of CDs – that if you spun the record backwards it would reveal a Satanic message – according to Pastor Jacob Aranza of Louisiana in his booklet entitled *Backwards Masking Unmasked: Backward Satanic Messages of Rock and Roll Exposed*, 'There's no escaping it. It's my sweet Satan!' Given Page's serious interest in the occult this rather unserious claim is plainly absurd.

Since then, however, certain religious fundamentalists have made much more detailed claims for the song's alleged 'Satanic' confluence.

The best example of this comes from American writer Thomas W. Friend, whose 2004 book, *Fallen Angel*, goes to inordinate length to 'prove' – via a detailed breakdown of the fourth album – that not only was Jimmy Page obsessed with the occult but that he had joined in a special pact with all three of the other members of Led Zeppelin in order to bring down Christianity and 'convert' the world's rock-buying audience to a devil-worshipping belief in Satan. Demonstrating an impressive – up to a point – grasp of the works of Aleister Crowley, as with all ultra-extreme views, there is a terrible plausibility to some of what Friend writes. Or at least there is for the few pages most people manage to wade through before giving up on the 600-page-plus tome after reading statements like the following one: 'Led Zeppelin are not the Devil's only messengers, but they are about the most powerful.' More powerful than political leaders who wage war? More powerful than dictators who would see their own people tortured and killed?

Yet what Friend has to say about the fourth album in general, and 'Stairway to Heaven' in particular, manages to stumble upon certain points that certainly carry resonance, given its principal author's pre-occupations at the time it was recorded. As Jimmy himself told me: 'There's lots of subliminal stuff there. [All the albums] were put together, there's a lot on them – a lot of little areas that you don't catch first off, sometimes not for a long time. But the more attention you pay to them, the more you get out of them. And they were meant to be that way, and that's good.'

Therefore when Friend writes of the fourth album's evocation of what he calls 'Aleister Crowley's bold Luciferian teachings', one sighs at the inference of 'evil-doing' yet cannot entirely dismiss the suggestion as so much else about the album plainly does allude to exactly that. Similarly, when Friend picks up on Page's comment to *Guitar World* in January 2002 that 'if something really magickal is coming through, then you follow it . . . We tried to take advantage of everything that was being offered to us', with Friend adding that Plant's 'channelling' of the lyrics put him in touch with malignant spirits, possibly Lucifer himself, and that Lucifer has 'a female consort in the form of light', hence the line in the song 'There walks a lady we all know, who shines white light and wants to show', it causes one to take a step back and think again. Does this seeming religious fanatic have a point?

Further references to Lucifer follow, says Friend, in the verse that goes: 'And it's whispered that soon, if we all call the tune, then the Piper will lead us to Reason/And a new day will dawn for those who stand long, and the forests will echo with laughter ...' arguing that Pan the Piper, aka the Greek God of the forests, was also characterised by Crowley as 'Lucifer the Piper, the maker of music', also citing the verse in Ezekiel chapter 28:13 that describes God creating Lucifer 'as the celestial composer of music, with celestial pipes'. In short, according to Friend, '"Stairway to Heaven" is nothing less than a song about "spiritual regeneration", or as he puts it: "born again Satanism", adding that the "reason" the Piper leads us to in the song, in Crowleyan terms at least, is nothing less than "a worship of Lucifer".'

At which point one fears he doth protest too much. It's interesting to note, however, that Kenneth Anger – Crowley acolyte, upper-echelon member of the O.T.O. and, at the time of the fourth Zeppelin album, personal friend of Page's – would himself later describe 'Stairway to Heaven' as Zeppelin's 'most Luciferian song'. Certainly, the lyrics seem to be concerned with a quest for a spiritual rebirth. While its unambiguously Pagan imagery of pipers, May Queens, shadows that stand 'taller than our soul', whispering winds 'crying for leaving', again, for anyone who knows anything about the occult, suggest a desire to get back to an older, lost world governed by older, more plentiful gods who can be directly appealed to and where personal transformation is still a tangible, achievable goal.

Or maybe not. As Dave Dickson says, 'I doubt that any but the most hardcore followers of Crowley would still say they want to destroy the Church. I think Page would fit in with the crowd that says, "Okay, I don't believe in that [the Church], can I just get on and do my own thing in my own way, and just be left alone."' Reading too much into Zep's music, he says, is too easy, like misreading the Bible. 'Whatever belief system you want to throw up, you can find it. So someone comes along and says "Stairway to Heaven" is actually a "Stairway to Hell", and if you're not very smart or you *want* to believe that, it must be incredibly easy to fall into that. Oh right, yes, of course, why didn't *I* know that? You've only got to look at Mark Chapman blowing Lennon away, or Manson previously, to see that people will read anything they like into songs or books or whatever they want. Charlie Manson believed the Beatles were talking to him personally. Were they? No, he was actually insane. "Stairway to Heaven" is a great song, but I would be very surprised if Robert Plant could put his hand on his heart and actually tell you what the lyrics are about.'

Nevertheless, it's a subject Plant would become increasingly agitated by over the years. Speaking in 1988, he told Q magazine how, despite his later equivocation about the song, at the time it was recorded, 'Stairway to Heaven' was 'important and it was something I was immensely proud of [and] the idea of the Moral Majority stomping around doing circuit tours of American campuses and making money from saying that song is Satanist and preaching their bullshit infuriated me to hell. You can't find anything if you play that song backwards. I know, because I've tried. There's nothing there ... It's all crap, that devil stuff, but the less you said to people, the more they'd speculate. The only way to let people know where you're coming from is to talk to the press, and we never said fuck all to anybody. We never made a pact with the devil. The only deal I think we ever made was with some of the girls' high schools in San Fernando Valley.'

Could it be possible though that Page had somehow planted the seed in the singer's mind? Had Jimmy ever discussed the occult with the rest of the band, Nick Kent asked him in 2003? 'I may well have had discussions with Robert about mysticism,' he replied somewhat disingenuously. But as Kent pointed out, Plant was always more focused on hippy ideals of peace and love, while Page's was the much darker presence. 'Whether I was attracted to the dark, or it was attracted to me, I don't know,' Jimmy replied typically enigmatically.

Whatever the truth, from here on in, nothing would ever be the same again for Led Zeppelin. 'My personal view is that [the fourth album] is the best thing we've ever done,' John Bonham told Melody Maker at the time of its release. 'The playing is some of the best we've done and Jimmy is like ... mint!' Page later told me he sees the fourth album as a culmination of all the band's best ideas. 'Consequently, you started to feel it was tangible – all the areas within the band. It was just a matter of tying it in. That's why an organic album like the fourth album was so good to do.' It demonstrated, he said, 'the difference of what Zeppelin was about – the calibre of the musicians. The four individual parts making this fifth monster, you know ...'

Some would argue that there were even greater albums to come, but it was their fourth resolutely untitled album that enabled Led Zeppelin to finally transcend their status as a 'heavy rock' band and transmogrify into something else entirely: a living, fire-breathing legend. From here on in, the story of Led Zeppelin entered a whole new category – epic, trangressional – where the real myth began to take hold, not just the one circulated amongst American groupies, but the stories that have continued to hold audiences spellbound ever since. Or as John Paul Jones once put it: 'After this record no-one ever compared us to Black Sabbath again.'

11

We Are Your Overlords

If the first four years in the life of Led Zeppelin had been about empire-building, the next four – from 1972 to '75 – would find them overseeing their kingdom with all the splendid pomp and inherent arrogance of Pharaohs. Self-made millionaires so famous they now hid behind armed guards, employed their own drug-dealers and flew by private jet, the same period also found them at their creative zenith, taking their music far beyond the bounds of most other rock groups. Indeed, only the Stones matched them at this time for musical promiscuousness, as both groups toyed, variously, with funk, reggae, country, West Coast ... Arguably, Zep went even further, allowing jazz, synthesisers, folk, doo-wop and Asian raga influences to seep into their signature sound. They went further in terms of on the road outrage too. Keith may still have draped silk scarves over his bedside lamps, carried guns and knives and shot up heroin, while Mick certainly kept the ladeez busy, but no-one was busting up rooms, cars, jaws like Bonzo, nobody was a bigger babe-magnet than rocket-in-my-pocket Plant, and not even Keef could keep up with nocturnal Pagey's non-eating, non-sleeping regime of smack, coke, Quaaludes, Jack Daniel's, cigarettes, weed, wine, whatever. Plus, Jimmy was the only one using whips and magic wands on any sort of regular basis. As the then new PR, BP Fallon, says now: 'Do you remember laughter? Mix in yarns of drugs a go go ... and fish. Coke? Smack? A red snapper? Was that most meticulous of musicians Jimmy Page at one point drifting too far from shore in the arms of Morphia? Whack in tales of darkened hotel suites and angels with broken wings and white feathers on the bathroom floor. And thus the seeds to some of the many mysteries of Led Zeppelin ...'

Still basking in the enormous success of the untitled fourth album, the band took the start of 1972 off. All except for Page who began working on a follow-up almost immediately, compiling demos of new ideas at his home studio. By late April, Zeppelin had hired the Stones' mobile unit again and begun recording at Jagger's country pile, Stargroves – where engineer Andy Johns had worked on the *Sticky Fingers* album – continuing later at Olympic, then Electric Lady in New York. Between times they had fitted in their first tour of Australia and New Zealand, a four-week schedule that saw them headlining 25,000-capacity venues like the Western Spring Stadium in Auckland and the Showground Stadium in Sydney. There had also been a large outdoor concert planned for Singapore but the band was refused entry by customs officials who objected to their long hair.

On their way back from Australia, Page and Plant stopped off in Bombay for a date Jimmy had arranged with the Bombay Symphony Orchestra, recording rough-and-ready versions of 'Friends' and 'Four Sticks'. 'The idea was to go there and to try and utilise some of the film people because we were told that they were the best musicians,' Jimmy explained. 'I had a contact via Ravi Shankar and was put onto somebody who got the musicians together. We went to a studio and all they had was a Revox [reel-to-reel tape recorder]. But the musicians were so fast! In fact, "Four Sticks" was difficult for them because there were lots of changes in the timings. But we also did "Friends" and that was astonishing. I had given them a sort of reward of a bottle of scotch after we'd done "Friends", cos all we were gonna try was the one number. And they'd all had a tipple and I think they fell apart a bit,' he laughed. 'It was purely an experiment to see how we would get on recording like that. One of the things that we always wanted to do was to actually go around doing concerts in places like that and Cairo, going all the way through Asia. Well, the closest we ever got to it was going to Bombay. George Harrison had done the things he did with the Beatles but no-one had actually worked with any of the musicians from India, got a proper orchestra together. It would have been great.'

The sixteen-date US tour that summer had again been phenomenally successful, including two blistering performances in LA at the Forum on 25 June and Long Beach Arena two nights later. Ticketwise, Zeppelin was now outselling the Stones (touring their *Exile on Main Street* album that year) by a ratio of 2:1. In terms of publicity, however, Zeppelin still came a poor second to Jagger and co. with their impossibly glamorous entourage that included Princess Lee Radziwell (sister of Jackie Onassis) and writer Truman Capote. As Jimmy moaned to the *NME*: 'Who wants to know that Led Zeppelin broke an attendance record at such-and-such a place when Mick Jagger's hanging around with Truman Capote?'

The new album – actually given a title this time, *Houses of the Holy* – should have been released in August but again there were problems with both the artwork and the mix and it was eventually put back until the start of 1973, by which time the band had completed their second Japanese tour and a long twenty-five-date jaunt around the UK, which began in December and continued to the end of January – the last time the band would ever tour their home country. They didn't know it then, though. Instead, this was seen as a triumphant homecoming parade.

Not that everything went smoothly. Bill Harry, the band's London PR, who had become used to 'walking into the Speakeasy and a plate of spaghetti comes flying through the air and lands all over your suit', quit his job after another such 'adventure'. Bill had been having a quiet drink at the Coach & Horses pub in Poland Street one afternoon when Bonzo walked in with Chicken Shack guitarist Stan Webb, both men ordering a concoction comprising measures from every bottle behind the bar all thrown together in one large glass. After drinking which 'they went berserk'.

Ordered by Bonham to fetch a couple of journalists for immediate interview, Harry tried to laugh it off. Interpreted as a snub, Bonzo 'leaned over and ripped the pocket off my trousers and all my money and keys went flying. He ripped my shirt as well and I was absolutely furious. I said, "I'm finished with you; I want nothing whatsoever to do with Led Zeppelin ever again. If I see you in the street, you'd better cross the road".' Grant later phoned Harry and apologised, advising him to 'go out and buy the most expensive pair of trousers you can find and send me the bill.' But Bill was not for turning, telling Peter, 'I just can't handle them anymore.'

Chris Welch, who had become pals with Bonham, even being invited up on stage in Germany on one tour to play bongos during 'Whole Lotta Love', witnessed the incident but insists 'John wasn't nasty, just very loud and boisterous. Because John, who was drunk, thought Bill was ignoring him, he grabbed him as he went past and ripped off his trousers.' Not nasty at all – unless they happened to be your trousers.

Bill's replacement was the younger, more flamboyant self-styled 'PR guru' B.P. Fallon, a young Irishman who'd made his name in Dublin as a teenage DJ, before becoming a photographer and writer. These days, Beep, as he became known, provides 'the vibe' for artists as diverse as U2, Boyzone and Courtney Love. When he began working for Zeppelin in 1972, it was his work with T. Rex that brought him to their attention. As he says now: 'Dig, the band and G were well aware of my work with Marc Bolan and T. Rex – and that had become the biggest rock'n'roll splash in Britain since the Beatles. Everyone knew that, including the Beatles themselves. So Peter phoned me and we had a meet in his office in Oxford Street and I said "Look, if this is going to work to the max, we all need to spend time together in a band situation to see how we get on, to see if we're digging each other." So they flew me out to Switzerland where they were doing a couple of gigs. They knew I loved rock'n'roll and in Montreaux at [promoter] Claude Nobs' house we bonded over some brilliant Gene Vincent and the Bluecaps French double LPs. Then at the afternoon soundcheck I was sitting on the stage on an amp of Jimmy's when I heard this thud and realised that in the middle of this very loud music all around me I'd managed to fall asleep – and landed on the floor still asleep. Years later, the band said they'd been impressed by my ability to do that! God! And they knew I was what some folk might call eccentric – for the first gig I turned up in my blue velvet cloak, eye-shadow a-go-go, nail varnish boogie, pushing it, you know, to see what'd happen. Bonzo wasn't sure what to make of it at first but I caught him smiling. And after the gig, which was spectacular, we had dinner up a snow-covered mountain in this ooh la la restaurant and I was sitting with Jimmy and when the bowls of cherries in Kirsch came I said to the Maitre D, "This is lovely but would you be so kind as to take it away and remove the cherries and bring it back with large glasses so we can drink it more easily, please?" And laughing like lunatics we all slid back down the mountain to the hotel and that was the beginning of Led Zeppelin being stuck with me on and off for seven years . . .'

But even Fallon fell foul of the band's growing reputation for attracting trouble. On Tuesday 3 December 1972, after the first of two shows at Greens Playhouse in Glasgow, the band refused to do an encore after their new PR was beaten up by fans outside the venue following a confrontation over forged tickets. 'I said, "Excuse me, there seems to be some confusion about the tickets you're selling". And they all jumped on me.'

Now the biggest-selling band in the world, Grant was boasting to anyone within earshot how the band would rake in 'over thirty million dollars alone this year'. The fact that the band might, if all went well, make even a tenth of that sum was unheard of in those days when promoters still ruled the roost, taking the lion's share of the gross with artists lucky to walk away with a small percentage. Grant was one of the first managers to stand up to such 'standard' practices. Having already faced down the record industry by demanding – and getting – the most lucrative signing-on deal in history, G now took on the promoters, demanding an unprecedented ninety per cent of gross receipts for every Led Zeppelin show.

'You have to understand the kind of man Peter Grant was,' said Plant, 'He smashed through so many of the remnants of the old regime of business in America [when] nobody got a cent apart from the promoter. Then we came along and Grant would say to promoters, "Okay, you want these guys but we're not taking what you say, we'll tell you what *we* want and when you're ready to discuss it you can call us." And of course, they would call us and do things on our terms, on Grant's terms, because otherwise they'd be stuck with Iron Butterfly.' As Plant later put it, he not only rewrote the rules, 'Peter Grant had written a *new* book. And we were right in the middle of it all. We were the kind of standard bearers, if you like, from which that kind of patent has been used so many times now, it's become the general way that people operate.'

Grant made the same demands on every aspect of the Zeppelin operation, starting with the record companies, agents and promoters, working his way down to the road crew, merchandise sellers, catering crews, even the audience some nights, even the band. 'We *were* being powered by the hammer of the gods, if you like,' said Plant. 'Somebody was banging that great big skin at the back of the boat and we were just following the rhythm of the whole thing. When Bonzo's saying, "Oh fuck, I wanna go home now", Peter Grant used to talk to him and say, "Look, you've only got a little way to go ..."'

By 1973, Grant's reputation preceded him on every level. 'I know some things have been said about Peter, some good, some maybe not so good,' says Terry Manning. 'But he was a truly brilliant manager. He was tough, he was crude on purpose at times, but he was in no way less than a brilliant person. He knew what he was doing and he was totally dedicated to Jimmy and to the band. He was really a part of the family. Seeing him at the moment, *in* the moment, making decisions and carrying them out – and I saw him backstage do things I don't know should go in a book or not, I saw him do things in coffee-shops that should *not* go in a book, it was a heck of a scene – but he was so for that band and it was so much a part of their success.' Or as Grant said himself: 'I don't care if they hate me, you've got to do what's right for your artist. Always remember: it's the band and the manager versus the rest.'

It all changed the night you went out after a Bo Diddley show in Newcastle with Jerome the maraca player and the two of you saw the Alan Price Rhythm & Blues Combo. This was your big chance, you knew it. Oh, there was already a local scumbag on the scene, Mike Jeffrey, but there always is with these nothing provincial mobs. You soon took care of him, told him you'd get them the Chuck Berry tour, just sign here, schmucko. Next thing you knew you weren't working for Don anymore, you were working for yourself. Well, you and Mickie Most, sharing the office in Oxford Street, sitting at the desks facing each other, always on the dog and bone, doing deals. People assumed he was the brains and you were just the brawn, maybe even Mickie too, sometimes. You had to hand him his due though, it was Mickie that recorded 'House Of The Rising Sun' with them and suddenly the Animals, as they were now called – much snappier than the Alan Price whatsits – were as big as the Beatles, nearly. Everything changed after that, especially when the bloody record took off in America as well. You couldn't believe your luck: a no. 1 record in Britain and America with your very first punt! Top of the world, ma!

You didn't really know what you were getting into when you went to America with them, but then neither did they so that was all right. Told them you'd been out in Hollywood with Gene when he was making The Girl Can't Help It. *Load of bollocks, of course, but you should have seen the looks on their faces. Followed you around like kittens they did, after that. Mind you, you could have got yourself killed when you sorted out that nutter with the gun in Arizona. Eric, the singer, said he'd never seen such bravery, not even in the shit-hole clubs of Geordieland. But you didn't feel very brave, just didn't know what else to do. You saw the cunt pull out a gun and just reacted. Talking to him softly, like on telly, until he'd calmed down and you could grab him and bend his fucking arm round his back till it nearly fucking broke. Cunt! That's when you decided you might have to get a gun of your own one day. Or hire someone to carry one for you. The band all loved you after that. They weren't so lovey-dovey, though, when you got back to England and you realised you'd have to read Eric the riot act. Just like the rest of them, the moment he'd had a bit of success his head had started to turn, insisting on driving himself to gigs in that flash new TR6 sports job. Well, all right, everyone likes to flash the cash once they've finally got some. But when he started turning up late for the sodding gigs, that's when you realised you'd have to sort him out good and proper.*

'Where the fuck d'yer think you've been?' you roared at him the next time it happened, the rest of the band standing there, watching. Eric had just shrugged, showing off to all the birds hanging around too. So what if he was a bit late, he'd driven there as fast as he could, he said. So you stepped up to him, pushed your gut up against the little shit and yelled: 'Well, you fucking leave earlier next time, you cunt!' Then picked him up and threw him across the room, watched him bounce off the wall and hit the floor. He was never late again. None of them were.

By the time you took the Animals back to America for the tour with Herman's Hermits you'd really got the hang of it, no messing, and the groups knew it. Knew how to deal with the cops with their guns, getting nervous when the girls started screaming a bit too loud, like they'd never seen a bloody Beatles concert or something, like the crowd was meant to sit there sipping mint juleps or some-fucking-thing. Knew how to handle the cowboys who hated these long-haired layabouts from Limey Land coming over and deflowering their precious virgins. Knew what to do when Eric got drunk and started screaming abuse at the Ku Klux Klan scum handing out their dirty little books outside the hall . . . Years later, standing backstage one night at a Zeppelin show, reading some little faceless cunt in some crappy American magazine describe you as 'an ex-rock errand boy', you just laughed but inside you wanted to explode. Get your own back on the little shit, all the faceless little shits with their glasses and their fucking typewriters that ever doubted you. 'Fucking great,' you'd smiled impassively. 'Fantastic.' Then strolled off to check on the takings, the taste of blood in your mouth . . .

*

It was now in 1973 that the feeling of invincibility that Grant had helped foster really began to take hold of the band. Of course, this was also the rock-fabulous age of colour TVs out of windows and white Rolls Royces in swimming pools that bands like Zeppelin, the Stones and The Who came to embody. But no Seventies guitar god represented the extreme Byronic sensibility in person quite like Jimmy Page. He may have begun cultivating this dark mystique as a way of concealing his, in reality, more introspective, quietly spoken, earnestly-watching-from-a-distance nature, but by 1973 things had started to change. For those that knew him, it was still just possible to tell the difference, but as the next few years skittered and jolted by, the mask would become harder and harder for him to peel off. While both Bonham and Plant invested in new farmhouse estates in the country – a hundred-acre pile in Worcestershire, for the former, which he employed his father and brother to help him develop into 'a home fit for a king', replete with livestock; a working sheep farm in the Llyfnant Valley on the southern fringe of Snowdonia for the latter, where he took Welsh lessons and pursued his fascination with Celtic mythology at the National Library of Wales in nearby Aberystwyth, naming his first son, Karac, born that year, after the legendary Welsh general Caractacus – Page flitted between his own newly acquired eighteenth-century manor in Sussex (another riverside abode named Plumpton Place, replete with moat and terraces off into lakes) and flying visits to Boleskine House, intent on furthering his 'studies' into Crowley and the occult. It was as though, having conquered this world, Page and Zeppelin now looked for dominion of the next.

Released in March 1973, *Houses of the Holy* again came with no writing on the sleeve but an inner bag with full lyric sheet for the first time plus attendant info, all in the same enigmatic typeface as used for the track-listing on the previous album, the album's title stencilled at the top of each page: back to front, as if in a mirror, for side two. There was also a paper band wrapped around the outer sleeve – a last-minute concession to Atlantic who rightly felt this album would need a little more help than their last in terms of hard-selling it – with group name, album title and record company details on it, to be taken off and binned after purchase. The image that adorned the outer gatefold sleeve, however, was their most arresting yet: a view from behind of eleven naked children – all apparently young blonde prepubescent girls – in various stages of ascending a cratered hilltop slope. While the inside appeared to depict a human sacrifice, viewed from a distance, one of the blonde girls being held aloft by what appears to be an older, naked male figure as the sun's rays begin to appear over the top of a prehistoric castle-like structure at the crest of the hills – an echo of Crowley's symbolic sacrifice of the inner child perhaps?

However, surprisingly few of the critics who discussed the sleeve picked up on the likelihood of any occult references this time, preferring to dwell on, as writer Mat Snow put it to Page nearly twenty years later, its 'naughty overtones . . . naked little girls clambering up a mountain, a sexual representation of pre-sexual people.' The guitarist was not amused. 'I wouldn't have looked at it that way at all,' he responded tetchily. 'Children are houses of the holy; we're all houses of the holy – I don't see how that's naughty.'

In fact, the *Houses of the Holy* sleeve was conceived by Hipgnosis designer Aubrey Powell, after Page had angrily rejected the original idea put forward by Powell's partner, Storm Thorgerson: a picture of an electric green tennis court with a tennis racquet on it. 'I said, "What the hell does that have to do with anything?"' Jimmy recalled. 'And he said, "Racket – don't you get it?" I said, "Are you trying to imply that our music is a racket? Get out!"'

Powell, who hadn't heard the music, put forward two ideas: one involving a photo-shoot in Peru; the other a trip to the Giant's Causeway, the famous rock formation on the north-east tip of Northern Ireland. Informed that both ideas would be extremely expensive, Powell recalled Grant exploding: 'Money? We don't fucking care about money. Just fucking do it!' Favouring the children climbing the mountain idea, lifted from novelist Arthur C. Clarke's 1953 sci-fi classic *Childhood's End*, which climaxes with the children of the story running off the end of the world, Powell promptly arranged a trip to Ireland with two child models, a camera crew and make-up artist.

Intended as a full-colour shoot, Powell revised his plans when it rained the entire week he was there, shooting 'in black and white on a totally miserable morning pouring with rain'. A collage of over thirty different shots in which the two children became eleven, Powell had planned for the models to be painted gold and silver but in the final hand-tinted images they appear pale pink, almost white. 'When I first saw it, I said, "Oh, my God." Then we looked at it, and I said, "Hang on a minute – this has an otherworldly quality." So we left it as it was.' The inside photo was taken at an ancient real-life Celtic castle nearby. The crew was 'so cold, and so freaked out because it wasn't working, that the only thing I could keep everybody together with was a bottle of Mandrax and a lot of whisky.'

The musical content of the album also had a certain colourfully 'hand-tinted' quality to it, the sound brighter and more effervescent than on any previous Zeppelin album. Opening with the ringing symphonic guitars of 'The Song Remains The Same', the first of four determinedly upbeat Page and Plant songs on which the album is built – part-sonic overture (its working title in the studio was alternatively 'The Overture' and/or 'The Campaign'), part-hippy dream – the overall feeling is one of joyous abundance, excitement at life, the sheer thrill of it all; Plant's vocals shrilly enhanced by Page speeding them up in the studio, the chiming guitars filched from the opening chords to the Yardbirds' *Little Games* track, 'Tinker, Tailor, Soldier, Sailor', originally credited to Page and drummer Jim McCarty, layering it to such extremes it begins to resemble the sound of a sitar or tambura, Plant's artificially accelerated vocals in such a high register they too begin to resemble the excitement of Indian reed and vocal music.

'The Rain Song', which follows, was originally going to be an extension of 'The Overture', but became a track in its own right after Plant had unexpectedly added verses to the latter, turning the former into a smouldering elegy to 'the springtime of my loving', an equally euphoric, if slowed down, sunburst of a song, John Paul Jones adding exotic texture with the swelling orchestral sound of his newly acquired mellotron, a kind of semi-mechanical synthesiser, using tape loops triggered by keyboards and a favourite effect until then of progressive rock groups like Genesis and the Moody Blues, unheard of previously on a Zeppelin album. Similarly fresh-sounding was 'Over The Hills And Far Away' – another resoundingly upbeat number, acting as almost a climax in a trilogy of crescendoing openers, its signature acoustic-electric dynamic traceable all the way back to 'Babe I'm Gonna Leave You' and 'Ramble On'. So, too, 'Dancing Days', a snake-hipped, long, hot summer of a song, inspired by a typically slouch-backed melody overheard during their stay in Bombay that finds the Page-Plant axis at its most delirious, all zinging guitars, bouncing drums and Plant's

voice bill-and-cooing like the lovesick hippy he still believed himself
to be.

However, it was the other four tracks that provided most of the
talking points, typifying the more ensemble feel of the album, beginning with the last track on side one, a band-composition titled 'The
Crunge', a taking-it-to-the-bridge funk parody that singularly fails to
deliver any laughs, despite a desperate last-ditch attempt by Plant who
can be heard at the end demanding, 'Where's that confounded bridge?'
A dance groove that you couldn't actually dance to, the great pity of
'The Crunge' is that it's so utterly unnecessary. Zeppelin had proved
they had the funk in abundance from the moment Bonham's hand-
grenade drums exploded over the intro to 'Good Times Bad Times';
had repeatedly demonstrated, in fact, with tracks like 'Whole Lotta
Love' and 'When The Levee Breaks', that white rock musicians could
do things with black funk music nobody else had even thought of.
Much better was 'D'Yer Maker' – a title filched from an old music hall
joke: 'My wife's gone to the West Indies.' 'Jamaica?' 'No, she went of
her own accord.' Boom, boom! – another band-composition that critics
assumed was another parody, this time of reggae, but was in fact an
innovative re-imagining of the form, replete with grafted-on doo-wop
vocals.*

The third band composition, 'The Ocean', which closes the album,
was another vertiginously upbeat number that contained their most
memorable guitar riff since 'Bring It On Home' and was so clearly a
crowd-pleaser in the most elemental sense – Bonham in full Bonzo
mode, growlingly counting the song's pulverising beat in, ('We've
done four already but now we're steady and then they went one . . .
two . . . three . . .' pow!) – it was already a part of the band's encores
long before it was finally released. The only studiedly 'down' track on
the album was the one begun three years earlier but never finished
until now: John Paul Jones' self-consciously creepy piano-synthesiser
opus 'No Quarter', an old pirate saying and Keith Moon catchphrase,
its chill ambience – 'Close the door, put out the lights' intones Plant
solemnly, his voice again filtered through distortion – utterly at odds

* The question in parenthesis at the bottom of the lyric sheet, 'Whatever happened to
Rosie and the Originals?' refers to singer Rosie Hamlin, whose 1960 hit, 'Angel Baby',
had never been followed up, but who was, by 1973, with the Blossoms, then working
as backing vocal group for Elvis Presley.

with the rest of the album, but an exemplary piece of work and another track destined to become a cornerstone of the live set, Jonesy's own personal showcase.

The message that ultimately comes across from the fifth Zeppelin album, as Dave Lewis says 'is of a band doing exactly what they want to do. The fourth album had huge economy with absolutely everything in its right place. *Houses of the Holy* was less about being perfect, more about letting loose and having fun. A hugely confident if underrated album.' A fact reflected in the exceedingly mixed reactions it drew from critics and fans. Similar to the fate that awaited *Led Zeppelin III*, for many *Houses of the Holy* was a let down after the monumental achievements of its predecessor. Where there was disappointment that the third album contained nothing of a similar stature to 'Whole Lotta Love' or 'Heartbreaker', the knee-jerk reaction to *Houses Of The Holy* was that it lacked something of a similar eminence to 'Stairway To Heaven' or 'When The Levee Breaks'. On reflection, however, it clearly signposted the way forward for a band now operating at its giddy peak. The days of grand statement albums like the first, second and fourth had given way to, as Lewis says, 'simple fun', an outlandish concept at a time when a band's artistic stature was still measured by how 'heavy' it was – musically, lyrically, metaphorically. In that sense, the fifth Zeppelin album was a relatively lightweight affair, and therefore, most critics argued, of not much importance either.

'Several tracks on this new Led Zep album are simply bad jokes,' bleated one typical review in America. Fortunately, not all reviewers were so blinkered. According to Jonh Ingham in *Let It Rock*, the album showed 'increasing diversity, humour, and richness, with only moderate self-indulgence.' Fans were equally divided, however, and while *Houses of the Holy* became the band's third album to top the British and American charts, selling more than three million copies in the US where it had symbolically replaced Elvis Presley's *Aloha From Hawaii* at no. 1, it slipped out of the UK charts after just thirteen weeks, soon overtaken by its still selling heavily predecessor. The obligatory single from the album in America – 'Over The Hills And Far Away', issued in May, also flopped, becoming their first not to reach the Top 50, though 'D'Yer Maker', released six months later, got to no. 20. (As usual, neither track was issued as a single in the UK.)

Publicly, the band, brimming over with confidence, saw the album as another triumph. Tracks like 'Whole Lotta Love' were 'just one colour in the rainbow of what we do and what we are intending to do in the future,' Plant billowed in *NME*. 'It's my ambition to write something really superb. I listen to people like Mendelssohn – "Fingal's Cave" – and it's absolutely superb. You can picture the whole thing and I'd like it to be the same way for us in time to come. I should think that we've got it under our belt to get something like that together.'

Sitting at home, drawbridge raised, Page, however, privately fumed at this latest example of critical misapprehension. Complaining on the phone to G, the manager decided it was time for a change of strategy; that the summer tour of the US that year would see a major change in the band's attitude to how they dealt with the media, beginning with the appointment, in time for their next US tour, of their first full-time American PR, Danny Goldberg of Solters Roskin & Sabinson. SR&S were best known for working with movie heavy hitters such as Frank Sinatra but had recently opened a music division, and with Goldberg having previously worked as a freelance writer for *Rolling Stone* – one of the magazines Page and Grant specifically wanted to woo – his inside knowledge made his appointment a done deal. Not that that changed things much, initially. 'Most of the journalists present seemed so shocked that we'd done this,' said Jimmy, 'One of them said: "My first question to you, Mr Page, is – why are you giving me this interview in the first place?' The answer lay in the band's determination to see their public image upgraded and moved onto the same footing as the Stones. 'Without getting too egocentric,' said Robert, 'we thought it was time that people heard something about us other than that we were eating women and throwing the bones out the window.'

This was a view apparently backed by the unprecedented numbers the band was now able to attract to its concerts. Their ninth American tour opened on 4 May with a huge outdoor show at the Atlanta Braves football stadium where a crowd of 49,236 paid a total of $246,180 to see them, beating the previous record of just over 33,000 set by the Beatles in 1965. The following night in Tampa, Florida, an even bigger crowd of 56,800 paid $309,000 to watch them perform – then the most lucrative single performance in show business history, again beating the Beatles' previous high of 55,000 (and a gross of $301,000) at Shea Stadium eight years before. As the limousine pulled up at the backstage gates, Plant turned to Grant and said, 'Fucking hell, G! Where did all these people come from?' Speaking with Jimmy in 1990, he recalled how, 'That was one of the most surprising times. We didn't even have a support act, and we thought, hey, what's going on? I mean, I knew that we were pretty big, but I hadn't imagined it to be on that sort of scale. In fact, even now I still find it difficult to take it all in, just how much it all meant, you know?'

Danny Goldberg made himself immediately useful, alerting the *Guinness Book of Records* armed with a quote from the local mayor, who called the Atlanta show: 'The biggest event to hit the area since the premiere of *Gone with the Wind*.' The mayor of Miami Beach retrospectively presented the band with the keys to the city – quite a turnaround considering Miami had once considered banning rock concerts altogether (following the infamous incident in which Jim Morrison pulled out his penis on stage during a Doors concert). As Plant said, 'This whole thing about playing the huge ballparks *on your own* – not as part of a festival bill with Janis and The Doors and the Airplane, but actually just going to Tampa and playing to however many people with no opening act … It was almost as if we had to go out and do that like some kind of study. We were wielding our art; we were moving it in the biggest, most gargantuan way, but without any press, without any promotion, without anything.'

Well, not quite. Goldberg's appointment had coincided with a total revamp of the way the band presented itself on stage. Learning from the Stones – who had quickly shoehorned the new 'glam' look of recent arrivals on the scene like Marc Bolan and David Bowie into the way they dressed on stage – the new Zeppelin show would be the first to feature a full-on professional lightshow, including lasers, mirror balls and dry ice, as well as a whole new set of stage costumes specially designed for each member – the most flamboyant being Page's now famous glittering moon-and-stars outfit, the buttonless, wide-lapelled jacket flapping open, his flared trousers boasting three symbols down the side of the leg, the top symbol, like an ornate '7' representing Capricorn, his sun sign, a bastardised 'M' representing Scorpio, his ascendant sign, and below that what looked like a '69' representing his moon sign. Even the normally spotlight-avoiding John Paul Jones had his own specially designed suit, a *commedia dell'arte*-type jester's jacket with little red hearts hanging from the frockcoat sleeves, while Robert became bare-chested, the lion in spring, his 'third leg' showing prominently through his ultra-tight jeans, his shoulders squeezed into a powder-blue puffed-sleeve blouse; even Bonzo was now done up in a black T-shirt with a big shiny star sequinned upon it, the hair now very long indeed, hemmed in by a darkly sparkling headband.

'We came across some people that made these fantastic clothes,' John Paul Jones later told me. 'They were very enthusiastic and we bought all this stuff – the outfit with the hearts that I wore and Jimmy's suit with the moon and stars. It just seemed like, why not? The lights were on us, we might as well have something for them to bounce off of! But the theatrical settings were all produced by the music. Visually, the real theatre relied more on the performances of Robert and Jimmy. They gave the band a visual presence it would never have had otherwise. But it was never contrived. That was just them being . . . them.'

'It's a work of art, that suit,' Jimmy told me. 'Originally, we saw the whole essence of our live performance as something that the audience listened to very carefully, picking up on what was going on, the spontaneity and musicianship. And you can't do that if you're running around the stage all night, or at least we couldn't back then.' By 1973, however, 'we were much more ambitious, in that respect. We really wanted to take the live performances as far as they could go.'

They now travelled by private jet, hired at a cost of $30,000 per tour and christened the Starship – a Boeing 720B forty-seater owned by former singer Bobby Sherman, one of the creators of The Monkees. When they picked it up at Chicago's O'Hare airport, it was parked next to *Playboy* boss Hugh Hefner's plane, the words 'Led Zeppelin' emblazoned down one side. Fitted with lounge-seats and dinner tables, a fully stocked bar and a TV lounge, there was also an electric Thomas organ which Jonesy would sometimes entertain the 'guests' with, and, in a rear cabin, a double bed covered in shaggy white fur that became one of the most popular compartments on the plane – though few ever slept in it.

Back 'home' in LA at the end of May, they had sold all 36,000 tickets for their two shows at the Forum within hours of the box office opening. The Saturday 30 May show had to be rescheduled for the following Wednesday after Page injured a finger on his left hand messing around climbing a wire fence at San Diego Airport, while the Sunday night show which went ahead as planned was delayed by half an hour due to 'traffic congestion'. In truth, neither show went as well as their two LA shows the previous summer, Jimmy clearly still struggling to play at the first show – visibly wincing with pain and dipping the injured digit into a glass of iced water between numbers to keep the swelling down – the band surprisingly ragged during parts of the second. Behind the scenes, however, everything appeared to be hurtling along at full throttle.

The first show happened to coincide with Bonham's twenty-fifth birthday. His present from the band: a new top-of-the range Harley Davidson motorcycle. 'He just tore up the hotel corridors and made an incredible mess, apparently,' said his old pal Bev Bevan, who had left The Move and now joined ELO. 'But he paid the bill the next day then told 'em – "Oh, and keep the bike." Unbelievable but that was John.' The Forum audience had also given him a birthday cheer during his twenty-minute rendition of 'Moby Dick'. 'Twenty-one today,' Plant had announced from the stage, and 'a bastard all his life'. Afterwards there was a huge party thrown for him at the Laurel Canyon home of a local radio station owner. Guests included George and Patti Harrison, Roy Harper, B.P. Fallon, Phil Carson, and the usual gaggle of dealers, groupies and hangers-on. Writer Charles Shaar Murray, who was also there, recalled 'Gallons of champagne, snowdrifts of cocaine, bayous full of unfeasibly large shrimp, legendary porn flick *Deep Throat* looping on a videotape player at a time when VCRs were hugely expensive luxury items available only to the stupendously wealthy.' George Harrison crowned Bonham with his own birthday cake. Bonzo chased the former Beatle and threw him and his wife into the pool fully clothed, followed by anybody he could lay his hands on. Jimmy, meekly complaining he couldn't swim, was allowed to walk into the pool in his new white suit with the 'ZoSo' symbol on the back. Harrison later claimed it was the most fun he'd had since the Beatles.

The LA music scene had moved on from the Laurel Canyon vibe the band had become so entranced by three years before. Just as in London and New York, the hip new sound of 1973 belonged to Bowie, T. Rex, Mott the Hoople, Alice Cooper and Roxy Music – glam rock. The complete opposite of the bewhiskered, down-at-heel ambience of the nouveau pastoralists, suddenly artists like Rod Stewart and Elton John were shaving their stubble and donning pink satin pants, stack-heeled boots and spraying their hair with glitter. The new cool hang-

out was Rodney Bingenheimer's English Disco on Hollywood Boulevard. Soon the walls of Rodney's office at the club were decorated in
pictures of him not just with Bowie *et al* but Phil Spector, Mick Jagger,
John Lennon and, eventually, Led Zeppelin, attracted to the club not
for the music but because of the teenage girls that packed the place
seven nights a week. Although the glam scene had a large gay following,
you'd never have known it sitting at Rodney's table. 'Rodney fucked
movie-star bitches you would not believe,' recalled Kim Fowley. 'He
got so much cunt that in his early thirties he had a stroke.' For which,
claimed Fowley, 'Led Zeppelin paid the hospital bill – a hundred
thousand dollars.'

When Zeppelin hit LA now, they practically owned it. No longer
content with booking the entire ninth floor at the Hyatt, they now took
over the eleventh floor too, just a few steps from the rooftop swimming
pool. They had permanently reserved tables at all the best-known Hollywood rock dives, not just Rodney's but at their other favourite new
hang-out, the Rainbow Bar & Grill, where they had their own special
half-moon tables roped-off at the back. With a fleet of limos waiting
kerbside, they also attracted star-name hangers-on such as Iggy Pop,
sitting cross-legged in the corner of Jimmy's suite, rolling joints as endless
platoons of gorgeous girls wandered in and out, happy to trade 'favours'
in return for access to the Zeppelin magic kingdom.

Rejected by the Laurel Canyon sophisticates – much to Plant's
chagrin – who were offended by Zeppelin's sleazy reputation, the band
simply took over Rodney's or the Rainbow and treated the places as
they did the Hyatt: to use and abuse at will. For many chroniclers of
the LA music scene, this was the beginning of its bleakest period. Nick
Kent, another visitor to Rodney's, claims he'd 'never seen anyone
behave worse [there] in my life than John Bonham and Richard Cole.
I saw them beat a guy senseless for no reason and then drop money on
his face.' Even Miss P – still on the scene but now reconciled to a
life without Jimmy, except for those occasions when he suddenly
remembered her number – would later tell writer Barney Hoskyns: 'As
much as I really loved Zeppelin, they kind of fucked things up in LA.
The magic really went out of rock'n'roll.'

None of which fazed Jimmy Page at all, who was entranced by the
city's dark side, boasting to Kent about 'one of his Hollywood girlfriends
[who] bit into a sandwich that had razorblades in it'. There was

also the city's strong connection with the occult. As Angie Bowie commented in her autobiography: 'Hollywood is very likely the most active occult area on the planet, and it's been that way for decades. The black arts are established to the point of being ingrained, and in the mid-Seventies they were thriving as never before or since. There were almost as many occult bookstores as health food joints.' Even Robert began to exult in 'the recklessness that for me became the whole joy of Zeppelin . . . ten minutes in the music scene was the equal of a hundred years outside it.'

Mostly though, LA was about the girls. Whatever feelings of fidelity Page had originally expressed for Charlotte Martin were long gone, and though they continued being live-in lovers – and parents – in England, it was now that Page began the most notorious of his on-the-road relationships, lavishing attention on a fourteen-year-old habitué of Rodney's named Lori Maddox. Tall, dark, skinny, with huge baby seal eyes, Lori and her friend Sable Starr were two of the best-known 'dancers' at the club. Having been turned on by pictures B.P. Fallon had taken of the young model the previous year, Jimmy once again ditched Miss P and turned his full attention to Lori. She later recalled being 'kidnapped' by Richard Cole one night, who drove her in a limo to the Hyatt, where she was taken to Page's top-floor candle-lit suite. 'I saw Jimmy, just sitting there in a corner, wearing this hat slouched over his eyes and holding a cane,' she said. 'It was really mysterious and weird . . . He looked just like a gangster. It was *magnificent*.'

But then, as B.P. Fallon says now: 'The whole world was different then. Better or worse? You choose. The end of the Sixties, much of the Seventies, it was freer then, less uptight, less censorious. For a while it seemed everything and anything was possible. For many young white people, anyway. And if you were a British band on the road in America – any band in America – it was, quite simply, sex and drugs and rock'n'roll. Didn't mean you were forced to partake but it was there on a plate – or a mirror – if you wanted it. There must be at least a couple of hundred old geezers dotted around Britain – and many more in the States – who for a few years had the time of their lives beyond their wildest craziest maddest dreams, travelling and playing rock'n'roll and having fun, fun, fun in what was still then the Promised Land. You'd be locked up if you did that stuff now. Underage sex? Forget it, baby. And now at the Hyatt House on Sunset Strip there are

screens over the balconies so you couldn't even throw a peanut out
the window. Ah, back then through the dented mists of time, rock'n'-
roll was a truly powerful potion! There were fresh enthusiastic girls
everywhere going completely mad for it and there wasn't the horror
of AIDS. And no-one much thought about the longer-term ramifications of doing hardcore drugs. You can see these anonymous old
codgers in a pub now somewhere, looking aged by more than time,
buying another round and saying "Did I ever tell you about these girls
in Detroit who called themselves The Nymph Five? It was 1971
and ..." Yeah, yeah, drink up ...'

He goes on in typically feverish fashion as he recalls what it was like
being part of the Zeppelin inner-sanctum. 'Well, Zeppelin were the
kings of the castle – the biggest and, if you could believe your eyes and
ears, the baddest – and they took it to a whole other level. You can
imagine The Rat Pack at their height in Vegas – Frank Sinatra and
Dean Martin and Sammy Davis Jnr and their mad mob – all chasing
women and going wild and being completely untouchable. Zeppelin
were like that, with the volume turned up. There were placid moments
but ... c'mon! Wonderful.

'The record sales, albums flying out of Atlantic as quick as Ahmet
can punch a hole into the middle of 'em. A bigger, flashier, more fun-
filled plane than President Nixon that whizzes these deities from city
to city where eager policemen on motorbikes with sirens blaring escort
this speeding convoy of black-windowed limos through red lights and
along highways that lead to yet another huge glowing stadium where
the faithful are ready to go mental again at the feet of their redeemers.
Golden hordes of nubiles allegedly ready to give themselves over body
and soul to these four electric horsemen of the apocalyptic now. Good
Lord! And the four cats themselves are more than interesting, if they
deign to let anyone in: Jimmy Page the magus, designer of this Led
Zeppelin combo and the root of this wild adventure, guitar-playing
sonic architect extraordinaire who's taking the blues and rock'n'roll
and folk music to thrilling uncharted territories as his luggage eyes
twinkle magnetic naughtinesses. Robert Plant, verily the golden god,
feral moans and wistful yearnings and a voice and presence from a
benign Valhalla. John Paul Jones enigmatic bass guitarist keyboard
maestro, weaver of mood and half of the most pugnacious yet precise
rhythm sections in rock'n'roll history. And on the drums, John Henry

Bonham! Fuck yeah! John was the powerhouse, magnificent, and when he played it seemed as if the drums were extensions of himself, he became so at one with his instrument. Rhythm. Bonzo, you were the king of rhythm and the engine-room of the band. Stir in Peter Grant, a figure literally larger than life. Stir in laughter. Whack in tales of darkened hotel suites and angels with broken wings and white feathers on the bathroom floor. And thus the seeds to some of the many mysteries of Led Zeppelin ...

'For all their offstage fun and frolics, Led Zeppelin were never anything less than 100 per cent on the ball when it came to their concerts. Oh, maybe once in San Francisco they left out a song or two so they could more quickly jet back to LA for more, um, relaxation but ... well, that saved half an hour! Cut Led Zeppelin's set in half and you've still got twice as much as what anybody else was delivering, not just in length but in terms of undeniable fuck-me power. The music was beyond amazing and the music's still here to hear, will be forever, thank God, this Led fucking Zeppelin. You have to dig it. And them. Thank you, gentlemen.' He pauses, at last, for breath.

It wasn't just in LA that the band enjoyed themselves. Out on the road, groupies and drug dealers were now everywhere. Three members may have been married but the concept of the 'on the road lady' was still a valid one in the Seventies. In New Orleans, they stayed at the famous Royal Orleans hotel and hung out in the French Quarter where Jonesy got embroiled in 'a spot of bother' with the local drag queens. They all now regarded cocaine as 'rocket fuel', though wary of attracting too much attention had begun to employ a full-time 'coke lady', a mysterious Englishwoman whose sole purpose was to administer cocaine with her index finger to members of the band then dab their noses with a pinch of cherry snuff and a drop of 1966 Dom Perignon. None of which was considered addictive, but rather sophisticated, even elegant.

Was that part of the buzz, I once asked Jimmy. That different rules applied? 'Sure, yeah, it was part of the reality of it. That's the point, it's part of the reality of it and that was exhilarating, yeah. But it was very apparent that we were right on the cutting edge of everything that was happening.' Did it make it hard, though, for life away from the stage to match that kind of excitement and intensity? 'No, I was still celebrating!' He grinned. 'No, because things were in a balance. There was the intensity and energy and creativity that was going on, that was the slot for that. The rest of the time was preparation or recovery. You know, most of it was so cocooned. We used to leave the stage, jump into the cars and get whisked off to the aeroplane, which would fly us to the next gig. Our feet never really touched the ground.' He paused. 'There was always a lot of theatre. There always is on rock'n'roll tours, though I think we might have pioneered a lot of it. In fact, I know we did . . .'

More seriously, although they didn't make it known until the tour was over, Page had also received death threats, some from out-and-out crazies, some of a more worrying origin. All were taken seriously by Grant, who doubled then trebled on-tour security, posting heavies at the elevator doors of the floors on which the band stayed at hotels and ordering Cole to help him keep an eye on the crowd each night. 'It was a lot more serious than I thought,' said Page, claiming someone had eventually been arrested. 'It was a real Manson situation and he was sending out waves of this absurd paranoia which a friend of mine got mixed up with . . . eventually this guy was tracked down and got carted away to hospital. He would have definitely had a try though.'

It wasn't just Led Zeppelin under threat from the new, drug-heavy, post-Manson atmosphere at rock shows. The Stones had been the first to suffer at the hands of their own image-making, with the debacle of Altamont. Now it was bands like Uriah Heep, whose singer David Byron complained that albums like *Demons and Wizards* and *The Magician's Birthday* had attracted 'people on another planet' to the band. 'It was a joke for a while, and then it just started to do us in.' Black Sabbath guitarist Tony Iommi recalls arriving at the Hollywood Bowl in 1972 to discover a large cross painted in fresh blood across their dressing room door. When Iommi, whose gear was playing up, became so irate on stage that night he kicked over a large speaker cabinet, it revealed a knife-wielding figure dressed in long black robes. 'He was about to stab me,' Iommi shook his head. 'But luckily the roadies tackled him to the floor. I mean, I did feel uncomfortable about it, but I think in them days we were doing so many drugs that it all just flowed into one.'

Of course, it could be argued that these rock stars invited such attention, not least Jimmy Page, whose occult interests were plainly – even to his least credulous fans – far more serious than his contemporaries. Might it be that, head swimming with the power he now contained quite literally in his fingertips, he saw Zeppelin concerts as themselves a form of magick ritual? Dave Dickson certainly thinks it possible, comparing the stage to an altar. 'There is more energy at a rock concert than the most intense evangelical church and it's all geared towards one group of people. That's why people always want to hear the greatest hits and why you feel a bit deflated when they play the new stuff, because you're not part of that ritual. The whole basis of ritual is that it's the same thing over and over again. When you get someone like Jimmy Page though, because he knows about magick, about the rituals, about the energy that can be garnered from that exercise, it's entirely possible that he would have gone off somewhere at a later date and harnessed that energy.' Speaking in 1976, Page certainly acknowledged there was 'a hell of a lot that's involved with the feedback between the group and the audience – an incredible energy that builds up, and you know it's euphoric for the audience'. He added: 'It's just something that's evocative and it's been invoked.' That word again – 'invoked'. Like Iommi though, he seemed remarkably unperturbed. 'There's a lunatic fringe,' he shrugged, 'whether they're Christian or Satanists or whatever . . . it's not a karmic backlash or anything like that . . . there have been lots of little magick happenings but nothing that has really perturbed me.'

More down to earth but no less worrying was the increasingly erratic behaviour of Bonham. At one point on the tour, Grant asked: 'What's wrong with you, John? Why are you trying to ruin things for everyone?' It was a question almost everybody who ever knew Bonham would ask at one time or another. The only answer everyone agreed on was that there seemed to be two sides to the drummer: Bonham the loving, generous family man who hated being away from home; and Bonzo, the drunken, drugged-up thug who took his frustrations out on whoever happened to be standing in his way at the time. A Jekyll and Hyde character whose personality was split most easily when he'd been drinking.

But then, as Page told me, 'Everybody around that point in time was drinking. I mean, that's how it was. It was hedonistic times, you know? Bonzo was definitely the guy who'd go down the pub and drink one more than everybody else – and not be sick. That's how the drinking tradition was in those days. But he *enjoyed* having a drink. And the thing is that his playing was always there. So you just think, well, that's it.' A long pause. 'There were a lot of people that liked to put it away at that point in time. So it didn't actually seem that much out of the ordinary – not at that age.'

'In general terms, he was a nice man, a very generous guy, too,' said Bonzo's old Brum pal, Mac Poole. 'But he could be obnoxious when he'd had a drink, a rotten bastard. He had a way with him where he'd belittle people, you know. And I used to sharpen my mouth against him at times. I said to him, "You wanna lay off the booze, John, because it's no good for ya." I mean, he went over the top and far away. He'd set up a whole kind of situation, buy everybody [so many] drinks they'd have to fly the bloody manager in to pay the bill! That was John, having such a gregarious character, people would take advantage. And of course he'd made such a name for himself; it was a bit like Moony, he almost played up to it.'

Back home in England, the money would be spent on gifts for his wife and son, family and friends. 'He was very dapper as well,' said Bevan. 'He used to love wearing three-piece suits and ties and stuff. And he used to spend a lot of money on cars. He always kept six cars.' One week it would be a Maserati, the next a Jensen Interceptor, an E-type Jag or maybe a Rolls Royce. At different times he also owned a Ferrari, a red AC Cobra and an Aston Martin. The Aston Martin had been a birthday present for Pat but she was so frightened when John took her for a spin in it – careering down country lanes at 100mph – she refused to ever step inside it again.

'There was a particular garage there that he frequented,' said Bevan. 'God, what a salesman's dream he was! If I saw him once a month, he'd still have the six cars but one of them would be different from what he'd had the last time I'd been there. The next month another one would be gone to be replaced by something else.'

He also bought an old two-door 1923 Ford Model T from Jeff Beck, which he turned into a hot rod with a massive seven-litre Chevrolet engine. 'It was a purple, sparkly thing that could do nought-to-sixty miles-per-hour in about three seconds,' said Bevan. Riding with Bonzo in the car was 'absolutely hair-raising. One time he parked it in the fast lane of a dual-carriageway and waited till he saw a car in the rear-view come screaming down the road at us at 70mph – then just floored it! The wheels started screeching and the front of the car reared up in the air. I couldn't speak, I was so terrified . . .'

*

*Planty was all right actually but like all singers there was always a ponce
inside him waiting to get out and in the end you'd had enough of his poxy
little group and fucked off. They weren't exactly going anywhere you hadn't
been already. You didn't need them to show you round the Ma fucking
Reagan circuit. Now you wanted in at hipper Birmingham dives like
Henry's Blues House and Mothers. The sorts of gaffs the really big boys
like Carl Wayne & the Vikings did. Which is how you ended up back in
A Way of Life, living in the caravan with Pat and the boy and running
round town at night with the chaps – Mac Poole, Bill Harvey, Bev Bevan,
Jim Simpson and the rest. The sort of blokes who liked a pint almost as
much as you did and didn't give you earache for playing too loud. Not
often anyway.*

*You'd all go round Mick Evans' drum shop in Brum, you and all the
other drummers like Mac and Mike Kelly, Carl Palmer and Bev, Cozy
Powell and of course Bill Ward. Mick Evans was a great guy, keeping the
place open for you all, even on a Sunday afternoon sometimes after the
pubs had shut. Hanging around, playing records and talking bollocks. It
was amazing how many of you ended up in proper bands, bands that
made it so you could pay the rent and own a nice motor and buy your
mates a fucking pint.*

*Then out of the blue one day Planty was back on the blower. Next thing
he's standing there outside the caravan talking to your mum and scratching
his crutch, scruffy cunt. You stood behind your mum pointing and mouthing
the words 'Stop doing that!' until the silly sod finally caught on. He was
in the Band of Joy by then and you were doing nothing so you joined in
too. All right it was as well, you were all going to be rock stars, poncing
around in your kaftans and your fucking beads. It was good though cos it
allowed you to do more with your drumming, more than just cha-cha-cha.
They were all into this trippy shit and would nod and smile when you
went off into one on the drums, doing your knitting, as you called it. The
only trouble was there was never enough money in it and that was never
going to fucking do, not when you've got a wife and kid.*

Out on tour Bonzo was now all but uncontrollable. He even had a new
nickname – La Bete (the Beast) – given to him by French record
company executive Benoit Gautier after watching him take such a
dislike to the food and drink backstage at a show in Nantes in March
1973 he destroyed all three trailers being used as dressing rooms. Later

the same night, he pulled apart Gautier's Volvo on their way back from a restaurant, prising off the lid of the trunk, smashing open the sunroof and sticking the heel of his boot through the dashboard. As with so many others, Gautier later observed how John could be 'the most generous guy and the worst guy. Bonzo would cry talking about his family.' Then the band or roadies 'would push him to do something and he'd go crazy'. Gautier also claimed Bonham once offered him cocaine – which turned out to be heroin. 'He thought that was the funniest thing. He would take a chance on killing you!'

Bonzo loved playing with the band, no question. His urgent need to 'bend the arrangements' each night spurred them into some stellar improvisations. Bonzo was also rightly credited for co-writing several of their best-known numbers. As Page said, 'With John you could just use the drums as an effect in the studio.' Plant recalled how Bonham exerted so much energy on stage he would 'roar like a bear' throughout the show. How when the show was over he was ready to 'get loose and blow off some steam'. More often than not, this might involve the sort of booze-swilling, coke-horning, groupie-bingeing, room-wrecking activity that constituted 'normal' behaviour for any self-respecting rock star in the early Seventies. He also had a deep-rooted fear of flying that caused him to be drunk on planes, a problem only exacerbated travelling in the Starship, where drinks would be served before the plane had even taken off.

He was also surprisingly insecure, so worried about letting the band down that Cole recalls him downing 'ten or twelve drinks a night' before a gig. 'It calms my nerves,' Bonzo told him. A big, tough guy on the outside, he would often be sick before he went on stage, stricken with nerves. 'There's no question that what you've got here is a super-sensitive guy,' Black Sabbath drummer Bill Ward told me. 'Although he hit the drums hard it was the subtlety in his playing too that made it, the sensitivity of it. I'm saying that because I saw that – without going into some of the private things that we talked about. He had enormous sensitivity, yeah, definitely.'

It was a side of him hardly anyone else saw though. Backed up by roadies ready to 'steam in' on his command, tanked up beyond repair in his eternal efforts to 'wind down' after a show, on tour Bonham was a ferocious, unstoppable figure. 'Bonzo used to like to put it away, it's true,' said Page. 'The thing is his playing was always there. You could actually feel the energy coming off him. After three hours of that, there's no way you come off stage and turn it off like a tap. It has to have its coming down period and so that's probably why he didn't sleep at night. It's very obvious when you relate it to the music. He also had a really, really strong sense of commitment to family. When you hear about Bonzo playing up on the road or whatever, the reality of it was that he was desperately homesick, and that's a real key to things. He didn't used to like to go to bed until it was daylight. He was really just ... lonely sometimes, I think. He really missed his family terribly.'

Now, however, Bonzo began falling out with the band. Chris Welch recalls how 'Robert would taunt John – offering him a banana at the end of his solo and calling him King Kong. At which point, John would explode, letting his fists do the talking.' According to another insider, things got so bad between Plant and Bonzo that Grant eventually sat Robert down and told him: 'It's got to stop. It's either you or Bonham and right now it looks like it's not going to be you.' Plant stopped the taunting, to Bonzo's face anyway. 'He didn't do it in front of me either,' Jimmy once told me. 'Or I would have told him to fuck off.'

Plant would admit they had their ups and downs. 'We did flare up at each other,' he told me in 2005. '[But] we had a margin, Bonzo and I, for the majority of the years ahead, which we could return to together. Even though we would then become individuals, we still only lived like six miles apart. As time went on, we did drift. Because Bonzo had his preoccupations with his cattle and farm and I was still in the middle of what I called hippy-build – taking ruined houses with a bunch of itinerants who'd just come back from Afghanistan and a truck load of dope, you know, some very nice rugs – and build a sort of rustic paradise. But we always managed to meet. We'd have football matches where my pub would play his pub. I've still got some video of it somewhere. My pub was the Queen's Head and his pub was called the New Inn. The New Inn's star left winger was a bloke with one arm who took the throw-ins. And if I played for the Wolves in some charity thing, Bonzo would come along and take the piss.'

Back on the road in the summer of 1973, the idea of doing some sort of feature-length 'concert film' – an idea they had been toying with since the decision not to do TV – was back on the agenda. Grant, who was loath to enter a world where his experience was virtually nil, had always played down the idea. Now with the tour reaching some sort of climax, he relented. On 14 July, less than a fortnight before the end of the tour, he phoned Joe Massot, who he had first met when Massot filmed the band at the 1970 Bath Festival, and instructed him to 'get your arse out here'. Massot duly arrived with a hastily assembled crew in time for the final week of dates in Baltimore, Pittsburgh and Boston, where he shot some backstage scenes, before arriving in New York for the finale of the thirty-three-date tour with three nights – 27, 28 and 29 July – at Madison Square Garden. Massot and his crew filmed the first two shows. At Bath in 1970, the footage had been dark and unusable. This time Massot was determined to capture the band in all their newfound, polychromatic glory.

'By the time we got to the Garden,' said Robert, 'the whole thing had taken on an entirely different aspect. It was such a big deal by then the feeling of freedom it gave out was tremendous. We were buccaneer musicians, ready to try anything and, for me, Madison Square Garden was a seminal moment. Until then, I don't think I could ever have imagined something like that, where there was so much energy coming and going between us and the audience. It was like having a dream come true that you never knew you had. Afterwards, I thought: now we know what happened to Judy Garland!'

Then, in the midst of triumph – disaster. After the final New York show it was discovered that somewhere in the region of $200,000 in cash had gone missing from the band's safety deposit box at the Drake Hotel, where they were staying. The money had been deposited in $100 bills by Richard Cole and band lawyer Steve Weiss the night before the first Garden show – an on-tour slush fund larger than usual in order to pay off the Starship and film crew after the final show. With only Cole and the hotel's own security team having a key to the safe deposit box, the finger of suspicion was pointed at the band's maverick road manager, who was promptly arrested and held for questioning. He was freed the following day after some fancy footwork by the band's lawyers and the voluntarily undergoing of a lie detector test – which he shocked the cops by passing with flying colours. Most of the band were told about the theft after the show, Jimmy being informed at the side of the stage during Bonzo's lengthy drum solo. Before he called the police, Cole had combed the band's rooms for drugs. But when the FBI became involved the press were alerted, sparking headlines around the world the following day. Grant lost his cool and slugged a reporter from the *New York Post* outside the Drake and found himself arrested and dragged off to the local cop station. Eventually Goldberg called a press conference to try and take the heat out of the situation. But G became riled again when another reporter from the *Post* asked him if the theft was a publicity stunt.

When the dust had settled, Grant pleaded guilty to harassment, and the case was adjourned contemplating dismissal; Cole, still under suspicion from the police and the press, later successfully sued the Drake, while the band flew home to England utterly exhausted. Charlotte was so freaked out when she saw the state Jimmy was in that she tried to get him checked into a sanatorium. But he baulked at the idea, though admitted he felt he belonged in a monastery. 'It was like the adrenaline tap wouldn't turn off.'

Amidst the hullabaloo, what was never fully addressed was the more pressing question: if neither Cole nor the hotel's own security had stolen the money, who had? It's well known now that the Mafia had begun to infiltrate the music business in the early Seventies. Grant's former mentor Don Arden told me the story of how just a few months after the Drake theft, Joe Pagano – head of one of the five Mafia families – had sent one of his henchmen, 'Big Waasel', to inform Don he was taking over the management of his own band, ELO, physically threatening him backstage at a show at New York's Palace Theater. It was only because Don stood up to them, he said, issuing his own counter-threats, that he was then invited to lunch with family head, Joe Pagano, who he then became firm friends with, thus averting the proposed ELO takeover. Could it be that the theft of Zeppelin's money from the Drake just a few months before was also in some way Mafia-connected? That perhaps a similar attempt to 'take over' Zeppelin from Grant had ended with a show of power from the mob? As Grant, nor anyone else from the Zeppelin organisation ever alluded to it, it now seems unlikely.

Which points the finger of blame back at either the hotel staff or the band itself: the former exceedingly unlikely as a hotel like the Drake relied so much on its reputation as a safe haven for high-rollers. Which only leaves the band. The question is: why, hypothetically, would they 'steal' their own money? One possible answer: in order to keep it. With Britain's Labour government then enforcing a draconian

ninety-five per cent tax rate on the country's wealthiest citizens, Led
Zeppelin were not the only internationally successful rock artists then
looking for ways around the problem, regarded as particularly unjust
as the average lifespan of a successful rock star back then rarely
exceeded two or three years. The simplest option, to become a tax
exile, would be taken up by several of Zeppelin's contemporaries
during this period, including the Rolling Stones, Elton John, Rod
Stewart, Eric Clapton, David Bowie, Status Quo and many others.
With the '73 US tour now at an end, could it be that Grant had
hatched a plan to squirrel away at least some of the wads of cash the
band would be bringing back with them, by making it 'disappear'?
Classic Rock editor, Geoff Barton, recalls Grant boasting over lunch
with him in the mid-Eighties of bringing 'false-bottomed suitcases'
stuffed with wads of cash back into Britain from various Zeppelin
tours. They could have been the idle boasts of someone enjoying a
particularly long lunch. Grant was well aware of his reputation by then
and liked to play on it. Or he might simply have been telling the truth.

At the time, the cloud of suspicion never fully lifted from Cole. The
only one of the Zeppelin inner circle from its earliest days not to be
transformed into a millionaire by the band's travails these past five
years, he would admit he suffered feelings of jealousy, even entitlement,
as the years passed and everyone got richer – except for him. Might
he have reached some sort of tipping point at the end of what was
then the most lucrative tour in music history? What was a couple of
hundred thousand dollars now to Led Zeppelin? Didn't he, Ricardo,
faithful servant, master-at-arms, confidante, quality-drugs-and-gro-
upies procurer par excellence, deserve a more substantial reward than
his monthly pay cheque? As we now know, lie-detector tests are not
infallible. And wouldn't he, a man used to being ice-cold under pressure, stand a better chance than most of beating the system? Or might
he simply have left the key lying around while he slept off another
long night's carousing? He says he had not been near the safety deposit
box since the first night at the Drake. Was it possible he had simply
looked the other way while someone else crept down there on his
behalf and did his dirty work for him?

All of this is pure speculation, and Cole and the band may be
entirely innocent – something Cole has repeatedly stressed. All we
know for sure is that the case was never solved, though the reper-

cussions for the band in America, where insurance companies would from now on view them with utmost suspicion, would be long term. Not that anyone from the band seemed overly concerned. Despite the theft, they would come home a reportedly $4 million richer. 'It had reached that point where we really couldn't care too much,' Page told the *NME* a couple of months later. 'I mean, if the tour had been a bummer, then that would have been the last straw, but it wasn't. I've had to deal with far worse situations than that on the road.' He mentioned cutting his finger in LA ('I had all manner of treatment and injections') and the fact that he had been labouring under death threats. 'It's things like that that tend to lessen the effect of having £80,000 [roughly the sterling equivalent of $200,000 in 1973] ripped off at the end of a successful tour.'

As was his wont, John Paul Jones also appeared to affect an eye-of-the-hurricane calm about these latest developments. But behind the Cheshire cat smile there was a growing concern over the way the band and its organisation conducted itself. Not on stage, where 'the feeling of satisfaction was enormous'. But offstage, as the groupies got wilder, the drugs got more expensive and the dreams grew ever more fanciful. By the end of the '73 US tour, in fact, he was ready to quit, joking to friends he was considering 'retiring' to become the choirmaster at Winchester Cathedral.

'I'd just had enough of touring,' he later told Dave Lewis. 'I did go to Peter and tell him I wanted out unless things were changed. There was a lot of pressure on my family what with being away so long. Funnily enough things changed pretty quickly after I'd seen him. We didn't tour in the school holidays as much and there was more notice given for when we were touring. Things had to change and they did, so it quickly blew over. I trusted Peter to put it right . . .'

Grant's way of 'putting it right' was to try and keep a lid on it, even from Plant and Bonham. 'I told Jimmy of course, who couldn't believe it,' he confided in Lewis. Jones was 'a family man' who had become rattled by the way the '73 US tour had gotten out of control, culminating in the robbery from the Drake Hotel. He was also worried about the death threats, which Grant admitted 'got very worrying'. In short, Jones had had enough. But Grant, shrewd as ever, felt a period away from the action was all that Jonesy would need to bring him round. In reality, however, it would take a great deal more than mere promises to persuade the ever-dependable Jonesy not to abandon ship, insiders now suggesting that to all intents and purposes he did, briefly, tender his formal resignation and that the start of 1974 found Page and Grant in a quandary over how best to proceed without him, keeping Plant and Bonham in the dark about how serious the situation was until they could figure out what to do.

The first time you really felt like a session pro was when you were booked for the Dave Berry session that produced 'The Crying Game'. You'd played bass on that and on the B-side, 'Don't Gimme No Lip Child'. You knew that was a proper session because Jimmy Page, a well-known session guy, was there too and the record was actually on the radio and telly and everything. Juke Box Jury. 'Our panel votes it ... a hit!' said David Jacobs. And it bloody well was too. Now you knew how someone like Jimmy Page felt, sort of. He'd played on loads of hits. Not that you'd know it when you spoke to him. Always very cool. Friendly, but very cool. Which is how you acted too. Bumping into each other all the time over the next couple of years, nodding and saying 'hi'. Smiling and saying nothing. Just plugging in and getting on with it. Thrumming away behind Lulu, Donovan, Herman's Hermits ... always very cool, never giving anything away.

Sometimes it didn't seem to matter who played what. Sometimes, like on Herman's million-selling 'Silhouettes', you knew it was your throbbing bass and Jimmy's colourful guitar that made it what it was as much as Peter Noone's gormless smile. The girls all screamed when he walked on stage but you knew that Mickie Most the producer knew who was really responsible for the record's success. Not that you ever said anything. The real guys like Mickie and Jimmy never did. They just got on with it, and so did you. The money was good too. Thirty quid a day some days, other days even more. If you wanted it, and John Paul Jones did. John Baldwin might have wondered what it was all about, what it was all eventually supposed to be leading up to, but he was boring. John Paul Jones was one of the boys, knew the score, what it was, making more money in a day sometimes than his dad would make in a week, a month. More money than seemed right somehow.

It wasn't all bad either, not by a long chalk. Playing bass on singles for young cats like Marc Bolan and Rod Stewart. Cats with talent who the world hadn't heard of yet. Young cats with no bread; just helping them out, cos you were a good egg. Even becoming known as an arranger; sorting out the strings on tracks for the groovy ones who could afford to pay like the Yardbirds, the Stones, Donovan . . . Coming in, sorting everything out for them, going away again, everyone grateful.

And you didn't always have to go straight home either. Hanging out, making the scene at places like The Crazy Elephant, the Roaring Twenties, the Scene, the Flamingo, or the less fashionable Marquee. Meeting and turning on young cats like Davy Jones. 'We went over to his flat. He had a huge room, with nothing in it except this huge vast Hammond organ,' David Bowie, as he would become better known, would later recall: 'I watched in wonder while Jonesy rolled these three fat joints. And we got stoned on all of them. I became incredibly high and it turned into an in-fucking-credible hunger. I ate two loaves of bread. Then the telephone rang. Jonesy said, 'Go and answer that for me, will you?' So I went downstairs to answer the phone and kept on walking right out into the street. I never went back. I just got intensely fascinated with the cracks in the pavement.'

Your real party pal was Pete Meadon, who was working as the PR for the Pretty Things when you first met him and was later manager, briefly, of The Who and Jimmy James and the Vagabonds. Pete was nuts – far out – and you loved it. It was with Pete that you once gate-crashed a coming-of-age party in Downing Street for Caroline Maudling, daughter of the Chancellor of the Exchequer, Reginald Maudling. You couldn't bloody well believe your eyes but Pete just talked you both through the door and right into the middle of the room, grabbing two glasses of champagne as he did.

It was also through Pete that you got into Preludin, an appetite sup-pressant that contained amphetamine sulphate. A really great pill. Pete was older, ultra-Mod, and always carried all sorts of pills in his jacket pocket, blue ones, purple ones, Preludin to get you up; barbiturates to help you down. 'Pop music was all pills in those days,' you would recall years later. French Blues, Black Bombers, Mandies, Purple Hearts . . . over, upwards, sideways, down . . . It was funny later on, after you'd made it in Zeppelin, how people always used to think of you as the Quiet One . . . Ha bloody ha said the clown . . .

12

The Golden Gods

Even without the threat of John Paul Jones leaving, the calamitous end of the 1973 tour had forced Page and Grant to sit back and take stock. The plan had been for October and November to be spent recording the next album. Instead, Zeppelin was put on hiatus as Jimmy and G considered their next move. In the works was the proposed tour movie – and accompanying live soundtrack album. Also looming on the horizon was the renewal of the Atlantic deal, the band's initial five-year contract now having run its course. With all five Zeppelin albums having sold well in excess of a million copies in the US alone, Ahmet Ertegun was happy to propose a five-year extension with attendant multi-million dollar signature advance. But Grant now demanded more. Having seen both the Beatles and Stones graduate to their own boutique labels, he and Page wanted the same for Led Zeppelin. Despite the disastrous outcome of Apple (where the lack of quality control led to more signings than anybody could properly account for) and the strange inertness of Rolling Stones Records (which, despite occasional one-off signings like Cuban rockers Kracker, and former Wailer Peter Tosh, it soon became clear that it was an outlet purely for the Stones themselves), the allure of owning your own label was strong: not just because it would mean an end to the protracted disputes over record sleeves, mastering, singles, release dates and etc that had persistently dogged them over the years with Atlantic, but because it was a sign that you really had made it; that you weren't just big, you were supernova; something that appealed greatly to both Jimmy's and G's vanity. Grant was also not slow to grasp that it would help offset some of the gargantuan amounts of tax the band would otherwise have been forced to pay. And so negotiations began for Zeppelin to have the autonomy of their own label, although under the distribution umbrella of Atlantic, thus guaranteeing no immediate shortfall in sales opportunities, distribution being the single most important thing giant corporate labels like Atlantic actually had to offer in the Seventies.

Both Page and Jones, meanwhile, embarked on what were essentially solo projects, with Plant also now thinking of making a Rod Stewart-like plunge into a parallel solo career. Despite denying it as soon the press had gotten wind of the idea, 'To go away and do a solo album and then come back is an admission that what you really want to do is not play with your band,' he said, feigning shock at the very idea, Plant was only talked out of proceeding with a solo album when Grant insisted it would be better to wait until the band's own label was in full swing before embarking on such a venture. In reality, G had no plans whatsoever to allow a Plant solo album, he merely wished to present as united a front as possible to Ahmet during the negotiations over Zeppelin's own label. Ertegun was well aware that the bass player might need replacing but it was a situation that could be managed; losing the band's singer, however remote the possibility, could not be.

Relieved to be out of the maelstrom of touring, Jones had begun producing and playing on an album for his old friend, Blue Mink singer Madeline Bell. Titled *Comin' Atcha*, he also performed live with Bell in December on the BBC 2 TV show *Colour My Soul*. Desperately keen to prove to himself that he still had a viable career outside Zeppelin if he so wished, he also appeared at the invitation of producer Eddie Kramer on the *Creatures of the Stre*et album by derided American glam rocker Jobriath. Fortunately for Zeppelin, neither album was a major commercial success; with Grant making suitably consoling noises, Jones indicated he'd be happy to return to the fold.

With no need for a solo album – Zeppelin albums were his solo albums – Page, nevertheless, had embarked on an intriguing side project which, while it never threatened to replace Zeppelin in his thoughts, would come shockingly close to derailing the future of the band in ways they could not have considered possible back then: to write the soundtrack for a film by Kenneth Anger, entitled *Lucifer Rising*.

Page had met Anger at a London auction of Crowley memorabilia in 1970. 'Anger had some money at the time and he and Jimmy were both . . . not really outbidding each other but I think there was a time when they were competing,' recalls Timothy d'Arch Smith, then acting

as Page's chief procurer of occult books, paintings and other memorabilia. 'I think it was for the *Bagh-I-Muattar*, actually. I said to Jimmy,
"I'm not bidding for it. I'm going to Paris." Because [Gerald] Yorke had
sent Anger in who always scared me to death. He never smiled.'

Described these days by the American Film Institute as 'the magus
of cinema', Dr Kenneth Anger, as he enjoys being addressed since
receiving an honorary doctorate in humanities a few years ago, long
ago reached the status of real-life Magus and is, according to Dave
Dickson, now one of the highest ranked members of the O.T.O. His
credentials for such a role go back to 1955 when he travelled to Cefalu,
Sicily, with Alfred Kinsey, the self-proclaimed 'sexologist', where they
unearthed a number of pansexual murals at Crowley's Abbey of
Thelema, later mimicked by Page at Boleskine with his Charles Pace-
commissioned murals. 'I never talk about it with people that aren't
magicians,' Anger told one reporter in 2006. 'Because they would think
you were a fucking liar. But, you see, I'm not a Satanist. Some people
think I am. I don't care ...'

Now seventy-eight, Dr Anger lives alone in his Hollywood apartment block, currently too ill to respond to requests for interviews,
although he continues to talk of new film and book projects. He is also
renowned, says d'Arch Smith, for a volatile temperament and 'for
putting curses' on anyone who crosses him. However, behind the
popular image of an almost Nosferatu-like character lies a clearly
visionary thinker, bitter perhaps at so consistently being misinterpreted
and misunderstood but whose work, lying so determinedly outside the
mainstream, ranks amongst the most innovative in cinematic history.

Born Kenneth Wilbur Anglemyer, in Santa Monica, California, in
1930, Anger began his career as a child actor, starring alongside Mickey
Rooney as the changeling prince in the 1934 Max Reinhardt production
of *A Midsummer Night's Dream* (also featuring James Cagney as Puck).
His own career as a filmmaker began in 1947 with *Fireworks*, a bizarre
short featuring sailors with lit candles for penises, and continued in
1954 with *Inauguration of the Pleasure Dome*, a gloriously ecstatic
exposition of Crowleyan ritual, followed in 1963 by *Scorpio Rising*, a
homosexual fantasy about leather-clad bikers intercut with images of
Christ, Hitler and the Devil, and a soundtrack comprised of thirteen
pop songs – an innovation that prefigured future cine-icons such as
Martin Scorsese and Quentin Tarantino in their use of 'found' music

for their films. Serious critics placed Anger's work in the same surrealist category as Luis Bunuel's *Un Chien Andalou* and Jean Cocteau's *The Blood of a Poet*; works that expanded the language of film. Most mainstream cinemagoers, however, remain utterly oblivious of his place in the canon. Instead, he became better known for his *Hollywood Babylon* books, a trio of tomes published over a forty-five-year period filled to bursting with scurrilous anecdotes concerning the sex and drug thrills of golden-era movieland stars such as Fatty Arbuckle, Gloria Swanson and James Dean, to name just a few.

The late Sixties found Anger in London, where he began a close association with the Rolling Stones, a period which saw the release of the *Their Satanic Majesties Request* album followed by the song 'Sympathy for the Devil', which Anger boasted was inspired by his conversations with Mick Jagger. He also became close to Keith Richards, who was now shacked up with Brian Jones' former girlfriend, the occult-curious Anita Pallenberg. 'Kenneth had a huge and very conscious influence on the Stones,' Marianne Faithfull told Mick Brown, explaining that Anger had initially considered Jagger for the title role in *Lucifer Rising* with Keith as Beelzebub, and how his kinship with the Stones soon led to 'a veritable witches' coven of decadent Illuminati, rock princelings and hip nobility'. But the Stones quickly began disassociating themselves from him after he freaked Keith and Anita out by somehow arranging for their front door to be painted gold one night while they slept upstairs, in preparation for a Pagan marriage ceremony they had agreed for him to preside over on Hampstead Heath, so upsetting them they backed out of the wedding.

Anger claimed that showing his films were magickal ceremonies in themselves, describing them as 'spells and invocations' specifically designed to exert control over people's minds. He often revised and updated his movies – he had been working on and off on *Lucifer Rising* for years before he met Jimmy – adding soundtracks by famous rock stars to some – as with Jagger's synthesiser contribution to *Invocation of My Demon Brother* in 1969 – and ELO to a later print of *Inauguration of the Pleasure Dome*.

Shot in England, Germany and Egypt, *Lucifer Rising* was to be based on the story of the Fallen Angel of orthodox Christian mythology, restored to his Gnostic status as 'the Bringer of Light' – an implicit part of Crowley's own teachings, as also depicted in Milton's *Paradise*

Lost, which ends with the angel, and his host, finding reconciliation with 'the Beloved' – and would include real-life Crowleyan occult rituals. As Page well knew, it's only in recent history that the name Lucifer has become synonymous with that of 'Satan'. In fact, Lucifer was originally a Latin word meaning 'light-bearer'; a Roman astrological term for the 'Morning Star' and a direct translation of the Greek word *eosphorus*, meaning 'dawn-bearer', while in Romanian mythology, Lucifer (from the Romanian word Luceafăr) was used for the planet Venus.

Anger experienced numerous problems with his much-cherished project from the start, leading to whispers that the film was – literally – cursed. His first attempt at getting it off the ground in 1967 had failed when its original lead, a five-year-old boy – another representation of Crowley's 'little child' perhaps – died in an accident before filming began. His place was initially taken by Bobby Beausoleil – aka Cupid, Jasper, Cherub, and other weird aliases – a former guitarist, briefly, with the group Love. Beausoleil had lived for a time with Anger in San Francisco, at a rambling old mansion on Fulton Street known locally as 'the Russian Embassy'. They fell out, however, when Anger threw Beausoleil down the stairs after discovering he'd hidden a large parcel of marijuana in the basement. Aggrieved, Beausoleil made off with most of the early footage, burying it in California's Death Valley. In revenge, Anger placed 'the curse of the frog' upon him, trapping a frog in a well. When, soon after, Beausoleil, now running with the Manson family, was arrested for the Tate- and La Bianca-related murder of music teacher Gary Hinman, he was sentenced to life imprisonment – trapped behind four walls, just like Anger's cursed frog.

Using what little footage he had managed to salvage from the Beausoleil episode, Anger had made *Invocation of My Demon Brother* using Jagger's soundtrack. But his intention had always been to return to what he felt would be his magnum opus, this time with Jagger as Lucifer, and Marianne Faithfull and Donald Cammell also in principal roles. When Jagger suddenly changed his mind, setting the production back yet again, Anger punished him by casting his younger brother Chris in the role. But the younger Jagger proved no less malleable and was dismissed after an on-set row. Eventually a Middlesbrough steel worker named Leslie Huggins was given the part, and filming finally began.

'I was already aware of Anger as an avant-garde filmmaker,' Page told *Classic Rock* writer Peter Makowski in 2007. 'I remember seeing two of his films at a film society in Kent – *Scorpio Rising* and *Invocation of My Demon Brother* [and] I was already aware of Anger because I had read and researched Aleister Crowley . . . [That] made him somebody I would like to meet. Eventually he came to my house in Sussex and I went to his flat in London.' It was during the visit to Anger's London flat that 'he outlined this idea for a film that became *Lucifer Rising*. It was then he asked me if I would like to take on the commission and do the music and I agreed to that.' It was a decision that would, quite literally, come back to haunt him.

According to Anger, he and Page had a 'gentleman's agreement' and never discussed money, as their collaboration was to be an 'offering of love'. The two of them would split the profits from the film, with Page taking all proceeds that were earned from the soundtrack. In response, Page set about creating his aural equivalent of Anger's film and with it the most imaginative, evocative, if ultimately lost, music of his career. It was, he said, 'an honour'.

Page now claims he was given no final footage to work with, pointing out that Anger had commissioned the soundtracks for both *Scorpio Rising* and *Invocation of My Demon Brother* on a similar basis. All he knew, he told Makowski, was 'that it was about the deities of Egypt'. And some of the characters: 'You have Isis who would correlate to the early religions. Isis is the equivalent of man worshipping man, which is now where we have Buddha and Christ and all the rest of it, like the three ages. And then the child is Horus, which is the age of the child. Which is pretty much the New Age as it was seen.'

Back in 1976, however, he told Mick Houghton he'd been given a twenty-five minute opening sequence to work with. He was nervous, he said, because 'the opening sequence is a dawning sequence which immediately brings comparisons with [Stanley Kubrick's] *2001* to mind. The film was shot in Egypt and I wanted to create a timelessness, so by using a synthesiser I tried to change the actual sound of every instrument so you couldn't say immediately, "that's a drum or a guitar". I was juggling around with sounds in order to lose a recognisable identity as such.'

Encouraged by the knowledge that unlike Zeppelin records, which were designed to appeal to the widest possible audience, 'This was going to be something which I knew was going to be shown in arts labs and underground cinemas and brotherhoods', he allowed his imagination to run wild. As well as running his electric guitar through an ARP synthesiser, his used a mellotron, his 12-string acoustic guitar, various keyboards, plus tabla drums and a tempura (an Indian drone instrument), all of which he played himself. For the climax he created a synthesiser effect: 'These great horns that sound like the horns of Gabriel. It was a good piece.'

The end result, as obtained from an extremely rare bootleg CD, is, as might be expected, an unsettling listening experience. Beginning with a loud, hypnotic drone which continues for several minutes, what few melodies there are – by turns portentous, forbidding, weirdly euphoric – meld into dissonant cadences that both repel and attract, like an electric current. About two-thirds of the way through, a thunderstorm erupts like a growling bowel movement into the aural mire, followed by Buddhist chants that sound like they might have been slowed down and corrupted, harmonic yet dense and ominous, at which point things appear to strive for some sort of staggered, juddering climax as another muted thunderclap is overheard in the distance. Ultimately, the feeling repeated plays imparts is one of dis-orientation. Not entirely morbid but a feeling nevertheless of being scattered, dizzy ... unhinged. Having played it all the way through several times, I have not been tempted to listen to it much since. Or as the eminent American music critic Juli Le Compte wrote: 'Haunting and disturbing, this piece is highly expressive of Page's strain of morbidity.'

Meanwhile, back in the so-called real world, the band's own movie was also still being shot. Enlarging on the original idea for a concert performance interspersed with interviews and offstage footage, Joe Massot – who found himself struggling to sequence the footage from the two shows he had shot – proposed they ditch the straightforward documentary idea and go for something more representative of who the band really were with each member, plus Grant, filmed in individual segments in which they would assume a character of their choice. Massot said: 'We wanted to show them as individuals, but not in the traditional way with interviews. They wanted more symbolic rep-resentations of themselves. All the individual sequences were to be integrated into the band's music and concerts.'

Not unlike the 1972 T. Rex movie *Born To Boogie*, which Marc Bolan pretentiously claimed was based on the dreamlike films of Fellini but had more in common with the self-consciously 'wacky' ideas first expressed in the Beatles' *A Hard Day's Night* – specifically Ringo Starr's brief metamorphosis into a tramp – and although hampered by the fact that none of them could act or would come up with suitably coherent ideas to sustain five consistently interesting depictions, what became known as the 'fantasy sequences' would, however inadvertently, reveal much about each of them. Thus Plant's incarnation in the finished film as a sword-bearing handsome prince, given to sailing, horse-riding and rescuing damsels-in-distress, relayed during the extended instrumental passage of 'The Rain Song'. Seen sword-fighting on the cobblestone floor of the Great Tower of Raglan Castle (a fifteenth-century ruin that stands between Monmouth and Abergavenny, and built by Agincourt veteran Sir William ap Thomas, 'the blue knight of Gwent') it was, however cringe-making it looks now, an idea which nonetheless clearly mirrored his self-image as the gallant, peace-making knight of the group.

Similarly, Jones' highwayman fantasy – played out during 'No Quarter' – of leading some subterranean mission through the impenetrable rigmarole of a weird cemetery scene, before whisking off his mask and returning in more familiar guise to his family – may have featured some of the most stultifying acting ever committed to the cinema but was also perfectly in keeping with his perceived role as the behind-the-scenes manic-mechanic of the group. While Bonzo's metamorphosis during 'Moby Dick' from red tractor-driving farmer to drag-racing daredevil clearly reflected the split-personality of the lives he led on the road with Zeppelin (dangerous, speedy, haphazardly flame-throwing) and off it with his family (both wife Pat and son Jason in tenderly glimpsed scenes under the protection of the husband and father only they really knew). Even Peter Grant and Richard Cole are given their own sequence, filmed earlier in 1973 on the Hammerwood Park Estate in Sussex (which the group were then considering purchasing and turning into their own recording and rehearsal facility, an idea later abandoned), in which they become cigar-chomping, machine gun-toting gangsters, laughing loudly as their bullets strafe a roomful of money-counting adversaries – obvious metaphor for the faceless 'suits' who run the music business.

Naturally, the sequence that drew the most comment – as it continues to today – is the one in which Page is seen climbing the steep slopes of some dark, craggy mountain at night, a full moon smudged by thin clouds. At the peak, he encounters the cloaked figure of the ancient Hermit, who stands head bowed, holding aloft his lantern, the light to which Page, the apprentice adept, is purposefully ascending. His visage, when revealed, then retreats backwards in time to reveal Page's own face through middle-age, adulthood, young man, teenager, child, baby and eventually embryo, forked by white lightning, before returning through the various stages back to that of the ancient Hermit – or Magus. The idea is given extra resonance when one knows that the mountain being climbed is actually Meall Fuarvounie, opposite Boleskine House – the same snow-capped peak Crowley liked to climb half a century before – and the fact that the sequence is intercut in the final version of the movie during Jimmy's violin bow showcase in the middle of 'Dazed And Confused', the bow melding into one clearly occult image as the Hermit/Magus waves his bow/wand in a slow arc through the air, left to right, its colours showing eleven (Crowley's 'general number of magick') shades of green, yellow, blue, red, gold and so on. It's as if the 'Barrington Coleby' painting from the inner sleeve of the fourth Zeppelin album has been brought to life, its visual metaphor obvious: the journey to occult enlightenment.

'I knew *exactly* what I wanted to do with that,' Page told writer Mark Blake upon the re-release of the film on DVD in 2007. 'I knew I wanted to do it at the house I had in Scotland, and I knew I wanted to be filmed climbing this escarpment, which I'd never actually climbed before.' The shoot had taken place on the night of the first full moon in December. 'I wanted the full moon to get a sort of luminescent quality,' he had told me previously. 'And I said it would be great if it snowed, too. And it did. Of course that meant it was freezing and when they asked me to do the climb again and again I did think, oh no, what have I let myself in for.'

The scene was intended as 'an interpretation of the Hermit tarot card,' he agreed. 'The Hermit standing there with his beacon of truth, you know the light and everything. And the attainer [sic] or whatever climbing up to try and reach it. But the fact being that when he reaches the Hermit the face starts to change, and the message being that the truth can be attained at any point but you may not have received it

and learned that you've received it or whatever.' Elaborating with
Blake, he added: 'It comes from the Rider [-Waite] deck, but that
particular interpretation has allusions to the work of [William]
Holman-Hunt, a pre-Raphaelite painter ... it was a statement about
what was going on in my life.'

Earlier in the film, he is pictured cross-legged by the lake at his
home in Plumpton, cranking out an ancient folk tune, 'Autumn Lake',
on a wheezing old hurdy-gurdy. In the background can be seen some
of the black swans he had populated the lake with. Then, as he looks
up and his eyes meet the camera, they glow a luminous red, as if
recalling the lines from 'Black Dog': 'Eyes that shine burning red,
dreams of you all through my head.' Not that he would say exactly
what it was supposed to mean, besides allowing for the generalisation
of 'My eyes being mirrors to the soul, that sort of thing ...'

When Massot presented a short rough-cut segment of the film at a
special screening for the band in early 1974, it was a disaster. 'They
finally came to a preview theatre to see the "Stairway to Heaven"
segment,' he recalled, 'and started to fight and yell when the film
began. They thought it was my fault Robert Plant had such a big cock.'

*With or without Bonzo you always knew you'd make it. You had the looks,
had the voice, the right ideas. You knew it, everyone knew it. As well
as Crawling King Snake there was also The Good Egg, The Tennessee
Teens ... the Teens were like The Who only better, or just as good, everyone
said so. Earned good bread, too, whenever they landed a gig. When they
changed their name to Listen and asked you to join full-time you thought
you'd cracked it. Bye, bye Snake boys, hello big time! Then CBS came a-
calling and you knew you'd cracked it. Only a one-off single deal but it
was obvious it would turn into something else, once the world got wind of
you. Still only seventeen, you had to get your mum and dad to countersign
the contract. Or would have done if they'd got round to posting it to you.
But that was all right. CBS was not the big deal it would become later,
not in England anyway. Still a proper record label from London though,
the Holy Grail ...*

*The A-side was 'You Better Run', a note-for-note copy of the American
hit by the Young Rascals, only much, much better. The B-side was an
original, 'Everybody's Gotta Say', which should have been the A-side
really, it was that good but you know what record companies are like,*

*man. Either that or the other one you'd all come up with which everyone
loved – 'The Pakistani Rent Collector'. It wasn't up to you, though, not
yet, so 'You Better Run' it was. You had to think commercially when it
came to singles and it was obvious it would sound good on the radio. None
of the pirates really picked up on it, though, which really surprised you. I
mean, come on, it was loads better than some of the old bollocks you heard
on there. You were told later that Radio London had played it a few times,
actually, but you didn't live in London so only found out about it when it
was too late, otherwise you'd have done something about it. At the end of
the day though it wasn't really a hit and you didn't really blame CBS
when they 'declined to pick up the option' on a second single. Bit of a
bummer but you'd have done the same if you were them. That's the way
the biz works, you know? It was still a bit of a blow though when Listen
sort of drifted apart after that. They could have made it if they'd stuck
around, cos they were definitely good enough. Everyone said so . . .*

*You weren't discouraged though. You just started making tapes and
posting them out to all the London record companies. In the end, good old
CBS stepped in and offered you a solo deal. Obviously the boys in Listen
weren't best pleased when they found out but that's the way it goes
sometimes, you know, those cats in London, what can you do, they just
really dug your voice. And what they were talking about was a little bit
different, your first solo single a translation of an Italian ballad called
'Our Song'. Some said it sounded a bit Tom Jones but they were only
jealous. Anyway, it did okay, you know, though you never got to hear it on
the radio again. But at least they went for a follow-up this time, another
cover, not bad this time though, called 'Long Time Coming', which definitely
was more your thing and got quite a good review in the New Musical
Express actually. It was just a shame the bloody radio gits didn't pick up
on it. But then you had to buy wankers like that off, the whole thing was
a rip-off, everyone knew that.*

*It wasn't long of course before you were singing in another group. It
was a stroke of luck CBS not wanting to make any more records with
you in the end cos this lot were even better than Listen, with a better
name and everything – the Band of Joy. No more R&B covers with this
lot. This was more West Coast, kinda like what came after the Animals
and the Yardbirds. The sort of thing you could really relate to, though
in fact you could actually sing and play a lot better than most of the
groups you were listening to. And it was cool cos the band's leader*

*Vernon Perara was related to your bird, Maureen, from Walsall. You'd
known Vernon since he'd been with the Stringbeats, the first white-and-
coloured group in the world from Stourbridge, who you'd also sung with
sometimes.*

*Vernon was the one in charge though and after a while it began to get
you down a bit so you left. Not left, just sort of stopped doing it for a while
to give you a chance to get a change of scene and check out the vibe. By the
time you came back the band had changed again. They'd kept the name
but Vernon was gone and you all went on stage with war paint on your
faces like Red Indians. Kind of like what Arthur Brown was into, only
better. Then you were doing the Rainbow Suite in Brum one night and got
carried away and jumped into the crowd, who all ran from you. That was
the last time you went on looking like a Red Indian. You kept the
make-up and stuff but made it more sort of mystical and far out, less
cowboy-ish.*

*When Band of Joy needed a new drummer in the summer of 1967, you
mentioned Bonzo. The sort of thing you were doing now – covers of Love
and Moby Grape and the Jefferson Airplane – was something different for
John but he soon got stuck in. Nothing fazed that fucker. The face paint
had given way to kaftans and beads and Bonzo was told to do his own
thing, too. So he got hold of a milkman's white jacket and dyed it mauve.
Next thing he had a bright green kaftan with beads and bells and he'd
grown a moustache. He told you that when he went to see Bill Harvey his
dad had said, 'Who's that poof?' He didn't give a stuff. He even got his
mum to make him a frock-coat out of old curtain material, getting on the
147 bus to Redditch with his hair all frizzed out like Jimi Hendrix. He
even came on that 'Legalise Pot' demo you organised hoping to get into the
papers, which you did. Then had to hide them at home in case your bloody
old man saw them . . .*

*In the end the Band of Joy became quite well known, playing all over,
opening for Terry Reid, Spooky Tooth, Keith West's Tomorrow, Aynsley
Dunbar's Retaliation. It was a happening scene. You even got a date at
the Speakeasy in London. You were unloading the old Comma van outside
the Speak when a Rolls Royce pulled up to let an old lady cross the road.
Suddenly a voice boomed from the grill, 'You'll have to move faster than
that, madam!' Nearly gave the poor old dear a heart attack. It was Keith
Moon in the car. You just stood and stared, wanting to laugh but not
knowing whether to. Then on stage that night, singing away, giving it loads,*

*bloody hell if there wasn't Long John Baldry standing there 'looking lovingly
into my eyes' as you later put it, Bonzo roaring at him to 'Fuck off!'*

The size of Robert's cock notwithstanding, so deeply disappointed was
Jimmy with Massot's work he instructed G to summarily fire him,
installing an Australian filmmaker named Peter Clifton in his place.
Viewing Massot's rough-cut, Clifton could only agree with the band's
view that it was 'a complete mess. There was no doubting Joe's talent,
but he was in deep waters with this filming attempt and he did not
have the strength to push the band members around. None of the
material he had captured on 16mm or 35mm actually created
sequences. There were a few good shots but they didn't match up,
there was no continuity, and no cutaways or matching material to edit
or build sequences.' Though Clifton agreed to try and salvage the film,
he felt that by then the spark had been lost and that 'the guys weren't
terribly into it' anymore. That it was now 'more Peter's idea' to
continue. As a result, it was another nine months before Clifton would
have anything new to show them, during which time they had all but
abandoned the idea in their minds – even G, who now began referring
to it only half-jokingly as 'the most expensive home movie ever made'.

However, one significant addition Clifton somehow managed to persuade everyone to agree to before the shutters totally came down was to
re-shoot the whole show on a soundstage in England in order to fill some
of the 'holes' left in the original footage. Jimmy rolled his eyes at the
memory. 'We were like, "Oh, no! How are we going to remember the
improvisations we did, how can we reproduce it?" But we booked into
Shepperton Studios and proceeded with it – miming to our own soundtrack and doing a variation of the one thing we'd always tried to avoid
doing – miming on *Top of the Pops*.' So unprepared were they for this
eventuality that John Paul Jones, who had recently cut his hair, was
forced to wear a wig to match the lampshade style of '73. 'The office
rang me up and asked if I needed anything for the Shepperton shoot. I
replied, "Well how about six inches of hair for starters!" ' he laughingly
recalled. 'So I had to use a wig which caused some laughs.'

But if the band film was becoming a pain in the arse, plans for their
own record label were now proceeding apace and by January 1974 a
deal was ready to be signed on a group-owned subsidiary label under
the Atlantic aegis – to be named Swan Song. Originally the title of an

Riding Caesar's chariot on the '77 US tour. According to one journalist, Jimmy 'sauntered unsteadily into the room on obscenely thin legs.' (*Richard E Aaron/Redferns*).

Oakland Coliseum, 23 July 1977. Later that night Peter Grant and his henchman would beat up a security man so badly they would be arrested by an armed SWAT team the following day (*both Ed Perlstein/Redferns*).

Knebworth: the official programme, 1979. The sunny blue sky was superimposed from a picture of the Texas skyline because the actual Knebworth sky was too grey. 'Knebworth's going to be different,' said Jimmy Page. It was, but not in the way he predicted (*GAB Archives/Peter Still/Redferns*).

Plant and Page onstage at Live Aid, July 1985. Jones (not pictured) was forced to play keyboards as he had not originally been included in the line-up and a bass player had already been added (*Lynn Goldsmith/Corbis*).

Onstage at the O$_2$ Arena, London, December 10, 2007 (*NME*).

Alison Krauss and
Robert Plant onstage
together, Manchester,
June 2008. 'There is
so much joy onstage
. . .' (*Jeff Kravitz/Getty*).

The reluctant Hermit. Page at the O$_2$ goes through his violin bow showcase one more time during 'Dazed And Confused' (*Getty*).

unreleased twenty-minute Page instrumental (also sometimes known as 'Epic', yet another theme developed out of his original 'White Summer' showcase) then also the working title of their next album, Page brushed off concerns about 'negative connotations' by explaining, 'They say that when a swan dies it makes its most beautiful sound.' Based on apocryphal tales of mute swans 'singing' just prior to death, swans in fact are not mute and do not emit any particular sound when they die. Original suggestions for a label name, however, had included less inspired suggestions such as Eclipse, Deluxe, Stairway, Superhype (the name of their publishing company) even Slut and Slag: 'The sort of name one would associate with us touring America,' joked Plant.

Unlike the Stones' label, said Page, Swan Song was not 'going to be an ego thing. We're going to be signing and developing other acts too.' Plant added: 'We didn't start Swan Song to make more bread. I mean, what are we going to do with any more bread?' First to be signed was Bad Company (initially only for America, as vocalist Paul Rodgers and drummer Simon Kirke were still under contract to Island in the UK as Free), followed by Maggie Bell (whose band, Stone The Crows, Grant had previously managed) and The Pretty Things, who Jimmy had known since his session days and whose 1970 album, *Parachute*, achieved the distinction of being the only album voted album of the year by *Rolling Stone* never to go gold in America. Roy Harper was also supposed to join the roster but eventually demurred. Plant, Page and Bonham had recently guested at his Rainbow concert in London, with Robert acting as MC. But Harper was privately dubious about the enterprise, fearing it would go the same way as Apple, and he remained with EMI.

Offices were opened in New York's plush Rockefeller Plaza in Manhattan, where US press agent, Danny Goldberg, was installed as vice-president. A London office, opposite the World's End pub in the King's Road, was also opened later that year – a delay caused partly by Grant using the new Swan Song deal as an opportunity to formally bring an end to the co-production deal he was still tied into with Mickie Most, and because for a time he had considered basing Swan Song's offices from his own sixteenth-century country manor house, Horselunges, in Hellingly, Sussex (famously built by architect, anti-quary and topographical historian Walter Hindes Godfrey). The split from Most also allowed Grant and Page to reorganise their publishing, forming Joaneline Music Inc to specifically publish all future Led Zeppelin songs. A sub-company owned by the group known as Cullderstead was also registered for Swan Song as a business name.

Once the new King's Road offices were established, Zeppelin initially turned to their UK PR man, B.P. Fallon, to head up the new company, but B.P. was a free spirit and didn't relish what he foresaw becoming a full-time desk job. So the job went to LA record exec Abe Hock. But he only lasted a few months before being replaced by Alan Callan, another acquaintance of Page's since Yardbirds days. Unlike their plush US offices, however, Swan Song's London base was remarkable for its shabbiness, kitted out with unwanted second-hand furniture from a nearby Salvation Army building. Outside there wasn't even a sign to let visitors know they had found the Swan Song offices, just grubby off-white walls with peeling paint and a plaque: 'Dedicated to the memory of Aileen Collen, MBE, who devoted so much of her life to the welfare of ex-servicemen and their families.' However, there was a sign in the Swan Song reception area that read simply: 'If you can't dazzle them with brilliance, baffle them with bullshit.'

An eye-catching logo was designed for the label, typically full of symbolism. Based on the painting *Evening (The Fall of Day)* by nineteenth-century symbolist artist, William Rimmer, completed circa 1869–70, the Swan Song logo is almost identical bar a couple of small details. The original painting depicts a winged-figure arching its back: a symbolic portrayal of the Greek mythological Sun God, Apollo, rising from the Earth at sunset. Similarly, the Swan Song logo, the only difference being that Rimmer's painting shows the winged-figure with his left arm bent backwards, his left wing a large dark mass (as the sun declines into shadow), while the Swan Song figure has both arms outstretched, his left wing more straightforwardly spread before him, as though greeting the sun.

Over the years, there have been many interpretations of both pictures. Many original observers of Rimmer's painting mistakenly took it to be a portrait of Icarus, who perished when he flew too close to the sun. In recent times, Robert Plant has also maintained that the figure on the Swan Song label is that of Icarus. When the logo was first revealed in 1974, however, many Zeppelin fans assumed it was actually a mythologised depiction of Plant himself – with wings. But the most popular and enduring myth surrounding the logo is that the figure is, in fact, Lucifer. Given that at the time of the label's launch Page was concurrently working on the soundtrack music for *Lucifer Rising*, it's understandable why such rumours might circulate, with the figure on the Swan Song logo appearing to be Lucifer returning to the Light. Certainly, Page would not have found fault with such an interpretation, though this time he chose to remain silent on the subject. (Interestingly, you can now buy Zeppelin T-shirts on the internet with the words 'Swan Song' over a picture not of the logo but the Rimmer painting. Meanwhile, the William Rimmer original currently resides in the Boston Museum of Fine Art.)

Officially launched in May 1974 with lavish, much publicised parties set a week apart in New York and Los Angeles, at the Four Seasons hotel in New York, where more than two hundred guests tucked into swan-shaped cream pastries, the food and drinks bill came to over $10,000. Everything went well until a furious Grant realised the 'swans' he'd paid to glide elegantly amongst the guests were actually geese. Bonzo and his ever-present accomplice Ricardo – suitably fortified by snorting coke off a plate from the buffet – chased the geese out into the street where two of them were killed in rush-hour Manhattan traffic.

Things went more smoothly at the second party at the Bel Air hotel in LA, where guests included Groucho Marx, Bill Wyman and Bryan Ferry. After the party the band repaired to their usual half-moon table at the Rainbow, where Jimmy rowed with his new LA main-squeeze, nineteen-year-old model Bebe Buell, who felt he was being unnecessarily cruel ignoring his other girlfriend there, sixteen-year-old Lori Maddox. 'The first time I heard Led Zeppelin was when this boy played their first album for me in his car as he was trying to get into my knickers,' Bebe later recalled. 'Everyone in my crowd was flipping out over them. There was a "who do you like better, Jimmy Page or Robert Plant?" thing. I thought Jimmy Page was the most beautiful man I had ever seen. He was angelic.'

It was also during this LA trip that the band finally agreed to meet Elvis Presley, who was appearing at the Forum. Organised by Jerry Weintraub, agent for both Zeppelin and Presley, Plant recalled: 'The King demanded to know who these guys were who were selling tickets faster than he was.' Whisked up to his top floor penthouse suite, Presley strode straight up to them, 'and the four of us and him talked for one

and a half, two hours. We all stood in a circle and discussed this whole
phenomenon, this lunacy. You'd have to go a long way to find someone
with a better idea of what it was all about. He was very focused – very
different to what you now read.' Elvis also had a request: would they
sign autographs for his six-year-old daughter, Lisa Marie? They would,
then stumbled from the room to the elevator, before a fit of the stoned
giggles got the better of them. *They* were signing autographs for *Elvis*?
Far fucking out, man …

The official UK launch of Swan Song occurred six months later on
31 October, Halloween night, at a party at Chislehurst Caves near
Bromley, ostensibly to launch the new Pretty Things' album *Silk
Torpedo*. Amidst the gallons of booze consumed, naked women reclined
before mock black-mass altars while strippers dressed as topless nuns
mingled with fire-eaters and conjurers. Not everything ran smoothly,
of course, and Bonzo had to be restrained after a *Sounds* journalist had
affronted him by saying he thought Bonzo was the greatest drummer
in the world, asking to shake his hand. 'I've taken enough shit from
you cunts in the press!' Bonzo screamed before launching himself at
the terrified journo, offering to 'give that horrible little fucker an
interview he'll never forget!'

Despite dire predictions in the press about the new label being little
more than a vanity project, in the short term Swan Song was a much
bigger success than even the egocentric Page and Grant could have
imagined. When the first Bad Company single, 'Can't Get Enough',
and album, *Bad Co.*, both hit no. 1 in America that year, it looked like
Swan Song really was more than an ego trip. Within a year all four
Swan Song artists – Zeppelin, Bad Company, Maggie Bell and The
Pretty Things – had albums in the US Top 100. Ironically, the Bad
Company album had been recorded at Headley Grange, using Faces'
bass player Ronnie Lane's mobile studio, in February 1974 during time
originally booked for Zeppelin, but which they were unable to take
advantage of, said Page, because Jones 'wasn't well'. The more likely
scenario is that Jones was still making his mind up about whether he
wished to continue with the band. At any rate, Grant was able to pull
another rabbit from the hat by sending Swan Song's first and most
prestigious signing down there instead. 'Grant suggested that we steam
in and use the gear to record a few songs,' Paul Rodgers says now. 'We'd
been rehearsing like mad and we went in and recorded the entire

album – banged it all down in one. It was just a great place, a great vibe, you know.'

With time on his hands and money to burn, Page turned his attention to adding to his growing portfolio of weird and wonderful properties when he paid the actor Richard Harris £350,000 – outbidding David Bowie along the way – for the famous Tower House, in London's Holland Park, which he still owns today. A neo-medieval structure designed by William Burges, completed just before his death in 1881, as his biographer, J. Mordaunt Crook, puts it, the Tower House was a 'palace of art' where the architect's 'magical, alchemical process [had] converted archaeology into art'. Page's interest in Burges and the whole pre-Raphaelite movement, he explained thirty years later, went back to his teens. 'What a wonderful world to discover.' Notable for the architect's trademark attention to detail, 'I was still finding things twenty years after being there, a little beetle on the wall or something like that.'

As with his earlier purchase of Boleskine, Page's intention was to return the Tower House to its original purpose, in this case an escapist fantasy retreat. A relatively small but architecturally imposing structure, not least because of its most striking feature, the tower, the walls and floors are as thick and solid as a fortress, exactly as the architect intended. It was to here that Burges was able to retreat, shutting out the world to revel in his own self-created fantastical visions. Small wonder Page took such a liking to it. Here he could be in the centre of London but, at the same time, a million miles away. Each of its eight rooms was given over to a particular theme. The master bedroom, which would have appealed to Page, had a colour scheme of deep scarlet, with convex mirrors on the ceiling that aimed to reflect the candlelight, appearing as stars in the sky above the bed. As Mordaunt Crook puts it: 'Menaced by reality . . . Burges fled into a dream world of his own creation.' As Burges so, too, Page. When, not long after its purchase, he surreptitiously invited Bebe Buell to the Tower House while she was in London with her official boyfriend, Todd Rundgren (Charlotte was blissfully unaware, living as she was at the country pile), she recalls in her book how she was awestruck at the bewitching surrounds she found herself in. 'Maybe it was his Satanic Edwardian quality, maybe it was the medieval Sir Lancelot vibe, I didn't know or care.' She recalls how they took mescaline together in the master bedroom, after which, 'I needed to pull myself together and realise that it was just an average-sized penis.'

There were also several hints at Burges's connections to the occult at the house, most notably in the library where there was a picture of him holding a large compass. Not pictured but as an architect almost certainly within his sight, too, would have been a set-square – the interlocking of set-square and compass, forming an 'A', an ancient Masonic symbol, the 'A' standing for the Great 'Architect', often mistakenly believed to be synonymous with 'God'. As a renowned architect and favourite of the country's richest man, Lord Bute, it is, as Dave Dickson says 'staggeringly unlikely that Burges had not been invited to join the [Masons'] ranks'.

Similarly, the ceiling of the entrance hall is decorated with astro-logical signs and other mythical creatures, sometimes minute, appear in the windows, the fireplaces, the walls and the furniture. The windows of the library are decorated with cartoons representing what Mordaunt Crook describes as 'allegories of Art and Science' but could as easily be six of the seven Masonic pillars of wisdom, namely Arithmetic, Music, Astronomy, Rhetoric, Grammar, Logic and Geometry. 'The representations here are slightly different,' says Dickson, 'but perhaps Burges simply thought his six better displayed his own pillars of wisdom'. But the most purely Masonic piece in the whole place is 'The Great Bookcase', whose panels are separated into two categories: the left side depicting Christian symbols with the right concentrating on Pagan ones, reflecting the fact that Freemasonry is a combination of Christianity, Paganism and the occult. Ultimately, what Burges constructed was a paean to the fabulous, the exotic, and the eccentric, incorporating his own interests in both Paganism and Christianity. That said, he only managed to stay there for three years before he died, his final visitors apparently being Oscar Wilde and James Whistler. Almost a hundred years later, the place had now come into the hands of someone else anxious to retreat from reality and indulge in a Pagan hideaway.

It was also around this time that Page acquired his own specifically occult bookshop, just a brisk walk from the Tower House, at 4 Holland Street. Named Equinox after Crowley's magazine, in the days before the internet, the most significant occult books were exceptionally hard to find. As Jimmy said at the time, one of the reasons he bought the place was because 'I was so pissed off at not being able to get the books I wanted.' Owning Equinox not only gave him access to its extensive library, it placed him firmly at the forefront of serious occult anti-quarians. Equinox would carry books on Tarot, astrology, and of course a large section devoted to Crowley's works, including several books signed by Crowley, plus his birth chart pinned to one wall, and a first edition set of Crowley's ten-volume work *The Equinox* priced at £350 – a substantial sum for a book now, a small fortune in the mid-Seventies.

Page also saw to it that Equinox published two books under its own imprimatur, including a perfect facsimile of Crowley's *The Book of the Goetia of Solomon the King* and *Astrology: a Cosmic Science* by Isabel Hickey. The latter is an expert explanation of how astrology can affect a person's spiritual development (as opposed to the fatalist 'predictions' of standard newspaper columns); the former essentially Crowley's interpretation of *The Lesser Key Of Solomon*, 'Translated into the English Tongue by a Dead Hand and Adorned with Divers [and] other matters Germane Delightful to the Wise. The Whole Edited, Verified, Introduced and Commentated by Aleister Crowley.' Along with the names, offices and orders of the seventy-two spirits with which Solomon was said to have conversed, together with the seals and characters of each, the text of the conjurations are given in both Enochian and English, as translated by Crowley. Both books are still available under new imprints today. Original Equinox editions are not too hard to find either, although much more expensive. According to Timothy d'Arch Smith, who sold an extremely rare copy of the original to Page, the Equinox version of *The Goetia* is 'exactly the same as the original, except it has hard covers and the original has soft. Apart from the one copy on vellum pages on which Crowley's actually painted the demons in the margin. It's in the Warburg Institute now but it was Gerald Yorke's. It's fantastic.'

Such a relief to be out of the session world. You still kept your hand in obviously, it was good bread, but you didn't rely on it anymore. And you were touring again, a hit act, lots of birds screaming and doing their pieces, lots of young geezers with beards asking you how it was done. You'd just smile and say nothing. Not to the blokes anyway. A really happening scene ... This was before the boathouse, when you still lived in Elsham

Road, round the back of Holland Park Road, near the tracks of the Metropolitan Line tube. Get up late, have a fag, maybe a joint, then go shopping for clobber, on your own or with your mate Jeff Dexter, the DJ from Middle Earth. Checking out Liberty's, looking for cloth that could be made into groovy new threads. Or the posh shops in Jermyn Street and Cordings in Piccadilly, who did absolutely the best socks. Carnaby Street was only for mugs and punters. Though 26 Kingly Street, which ran parallel to Carnaby Street, was hip to the trip. It was in Keith Albarn's gallery at 26 Kingly Street that you first met Ian Knight. Ian designed stages for Middle Earth, and it was you who got him working for the Yardbirds and, later, Zeppelin. You, the two Jeffs and Ian, all into the Buffalo Springfield vibe. Them and the Small Faces too, who were so basic and yet so cool. It made you think what you could do with some of that attitude in the Yardbirds. Keep the light shows and the little happenings, keep the good stuff, but add some balls to it. Make it a bit more hooligan, as Jeff called it . . .

You were always keeping an eye out for new things. You had to, there was so much to dig back then that was new. Like when you went to see the Ravi Shankar concert and there were no young people in the audience at all, just a lot of older blokes in suits from the Indian Embassy, their wives dragged along in evening dresses, all stifling yawns. This chick you'd been hanging out with said she knew him so afterwards you went backstage and she introduced you. A nice old cat, very mellow vibe, though still sweating buckets from the gig, like you do. You knew the scene and wanted to show you weren't just anybody so you told him how you had a sitar, but admitted you didn't really know how to tune it. You couldn't believe it when he sat down and wrote down the tunings on a piece of paper. Couldn't believe a nice old cat like that could be so cool, sitting there in his robes, writing it all down for you, like giving you his blessing. Different scenes you could learn from, man . . .

By the spring of 1974, Zeppelin was ready to reconvene for their third visit to Headley Grange, taking Ronnie Lane's mobile studio (cheaper than the Stones') and engineer Ron Nevison. With Jones having thrown his hat firmly back in the ring, though still antsy about having to put up with the increasingly wayward offstage proclivities of the others, G compromised on the living arrangements and had Cole book them all – bar Page – into the plush nearby Frencham Ponds hotel. 'Page stayed behind at Headley,' chortled Cole. 'He was quite happy in that fucking horrible cold house.'

Once they had finally begun work, new tracks were laid down quickly and relatively easily with the bones of eight lengthy new compositions rapidly emerging: 'Custard Pie', 'In My Time Of Dying', 'Trampled Underfoot', 'Kashmir', 'In The Light', 'Ten Years Gone', 'The Wanton Song' and 'Sick Again'. With final overdubs and mixes taking place as before back at Olympic in London in May, had they left things as they were they would have emerged with an album somewhere between the gritty sonic overload of their second album and the methodically applied brilliance of their fourth: that is to say, one of their three greatest works. As it was they took the decision to try and build on that remarkable achievement by adding a plethora of older tracks still sitting in the can from as far back as their third album in 1970: 'The Rover', 'Houses of the Holy' and 'Black Country Woman' from their various *Houses Of The Holy* sessions two years before; 'Down By The Seaside' from the December 1970 Basing Street sessions for the fourth album; 'Night Flight' and 'Boogie With Stu' from the January 1971 Headley Grange visit; and 'Bron-Yr-Aur' (spelt correctly this time) from the original June 1970 Basing Street sessions for the third album.

Thus, Led Zeppelin finally got the double album Jimmy had always craved. There were many reasons why he decided the time was finally right for it. To begin with, there was the simple fact of having such a large and impressive backlog of material. In the days before 'bonus' tracks and endless box-sets featuring 'previously unreleased' material became the norm, the likelihood was that any material leftover from previous albums would never see the light of the day. However, more pressing than that was the burning desire – as with the fourth album – to prove wrong the naysayers who had dared to question the worth of *Houses of the Holy*. Stung into pushing themselves to their limits with the follow-up, just as they had been after their third album, Jimmy wanted to nail the dissenters once and for all. This was also the age of the double album as Major Status Symbol. Much as with owning their own record label, in order to be considered in the same light as the Beatles, Dylan and the Stones, even Hendrix and The Who, all of whom had been praised for releasing momentous double albums – even career-defining in the case of *Blonde On Blonde, Electric Ladyland*

and *Tommy* – Page felt deeply that Zeppelin would also benefit from having 'a bigger palette' from which to paint their pictures. It was also the fashion now, with everyone from Elton John to Deep Purple, Yes and Genesis having released portentous double albums in the past two years.

Did it actually make for a better album, though? Certainly the fifteen tracks spread over two LPs created a textural and thematic breadth one could only stand back and admire. As such, *Physical Graffiti*, as it was to be called – an inspired title Jimmy had come up with at the last minute after viewing early drafts of the proposed artwork – is now regarded by many as the pinnacle of their career. The sheer variety of material – from stonking crowd-pleasers ('Custard Pie', 'Trampled Underfoot') to left-field acoustic enchantments ('Bron-Yr-Aur', 'Black Country Woman'), lighter pop moments ('Down By The Seaside', 'Boogie With Stu'), slinky, slit-eyed groovers ('The Rover' – remodelled from its acoustic blues origins – 'Sick Again') and, of course, lengthy body-dredged-from-the-river blues ('In My Time Of Dying', 'In The Light', 'Ten Years Gone') – it also gave the band their third hallmark track in 'Kashmir'. Of the same order of class as previous touchstone moments as 'Whole Lotta Love' and 'Stairway To Heaven' – that is, destined to transcend all musical barriers and become universally recognised as a classic – and another song that utilises Jimmy's signature DADGAD tuning to create a musical and meta-phorical drive toward some irresistible far-off horizon, 'Kashmir' encapsulated Zeppelin's multi-strand approach to making rock music (part rock, part funk, part Himalayan dust storm) as completely as 'Stairway . . . ,' but is arguably an even greater achievement. Certainly Robert Plant thinks so, even now. Especially now: 'I wish we were remembered for "Kashmir" more than "Stairway To Heaven",' he once said. 'It's so right – there's nothing overblown, no vocal hysterics. Perfect Zeppelin.'

Jimmy wouldn't go quite that far, though he agrees it's one of their finest moments. 'It was just Bonzo and myself at Headley Grange at the start of that one,' he explained. 'He started the drums, and I did the riff and the overdubs, which in fact get duplicated by an orchestra at the end, which brought it even more to life, and it seemed so sort of ominous and had a particular quality to it. It's nice to go for an actual mood and know that you've pulled it off.'

Of course, there were many different moods on *Physical Graffiti*, as well as the usual handful of 'borrowings'. The most notable case was 'Custard Pie', credited to Page and Plant, but its juddering intro recalling Blind Boy Fuller's 1939 recording 'I Want Some Of Your Pie' (later reworked by Sonny Terry and Brownie McGhee for their 1947 recording 'Custard Pie Blues'), while Plant relies for his lyrics almost entirely on Sleepy John Estes' 1935 recording, 'Drop Down Mama', while also lifting lines from 'Help Me' by Sonny Boy Williamson and 'Shake 'Em On Down' by Bukka White, before returning to Fuller's 'I Want Some Of Your Pie'. Arguably, Sleepy John Estes and Blind Boy Fuller should now be co-credited in the same way Willie Dixon and Memphis Minnie are on current Zeppelin CDs. Similarly, 'In My Time Of Dying', credited here to all four Zeppelin members but actually based on an original Blind Willie Johnson tune from 1928 called 'Jesus Make Up My Dying Bed' – the title of which Plant references in his own adaptation (along with a cry at the climax of 'Oh, my Jesus!' cheekily interspersed allegedly with 'Oh, Georgina!', the name of yet another on-the-road conquest) – and famously covered in previous years by everybody from Bob Dylan to Plant himself in pre-Band of Joy days. It's interesting too that Page uses the song to show off his chops on the slide guitar, one of the few occasions he would actually play one, an instrument Johnson himself famously excelled on.

Ironically, the one derivation they did try to credit the original source for – 'Boogie with Stu', actually an improvised reworking of 'Ooh My Head' by Richie Valens (itself little more than a reworking of Little Richard's 'Ooh My Soul') – resulted in the threat of a court action. As Page recalled: 'What we tried to do was give Ritchie [Valens'] mother credit, because we heard she never received any royalties from any of her [deceased] son's hits, and Robert did lean on that lyric a bit. So what happens? They tried to sue us for all of the song! We had to say bugger off!'

There were also some moments where cloaked references to Page's ongoing deep interest in the occult could be discerned: an obvious, cheesy reference to 'Satan's daughter' and 'Satan and man' in 'Houses of the Holy' and a less obvious but likely more accurate reference to having 'an angel on my shoulder, in my hand a sword of gold ...' in the same song. 'Kashmir', too, seemed to resonate with occult meaning with its images of 'Talk and song from tongues of lilting grace' –

Enochian calls? – and a 'pilot of the storm who leaves no trace, like thoughts inside a dream' – a Magus, perhaps? All pure speculation, of course. As is the fact that the title to 'Trampled Underfoot' appears nowhere in the song, but seems to hark back to something the occult writer V.E. Mitchell wrote some years before when he revealed that 'Whenever a Templar was received into the Order he denied Christ ... forced to spit on a crucifix and often even to trample it underfoot.'

Ultimately, though, none of these things are what made *Physical Graffiti* such an appealing Zeppelin album. The reason it's still revered now is for tracks like the sublime 'Ten Years Gone' – its woozy moonlit mood light years ahead of something as prosaic by comparison as 'Since I've Been Loving You'; the eerily affecting 'In The Light', with its supernatural drone intro and cathartic entreaty to 'find the road' (with Lucifer as 'light-bearer', no doubt); even sleazy tunnel-dwellers like 'Sick Again', the paean to teenage LA groupies with 'lips like cherries' and 'silver eyes' (specifically to Lori Maddox, in the line, 'One day soon you're gonna reach sixteen') which closes the album. All tracks so far beyond the wide-eyed blues rock of their early albums the word 'mature' barely covers it; so worldly you can almost see their noses dripping in the flickering candlelight, this was no longer the finely manicured, full-spectrum sound Page had meticulously contrived for the second and fourth albums and something much more brutal and uncompromising, everything presented as if done in one take – though no less dizzily exciting in its resolutely don't-give-a-fuck fashion.

In that respect, *Physical Graffiti* resembled the Stones' earlier double, *Exile On Main Street*, another ragbag collection made by a band now so far over the rainbow they felt they had nothing more to prove and now appeared more focused on keeping themselves entertained, be that with hard drugs, harder women or simply over-indulging their own musical fantasies, touching down on blues, country, funk ... wherever the stoned fancy left them crashed out on the floor, the whole thing working, nevertheless, to eerily stunning effect. Jimmy had, in fact, being hanging out with Keith and Mick off and on throughout 1974, bumping into each other at Tramp or the Speakeasy in London, before all going back to Ronnie Wood's rambling mansion, The Wick, in Twickenham, where Keith had practically moved in that year. One night in November Jimmy found himself embarked on an all-night jam with Keith and Ronnie on a song called 'Scarlet', named after Jimmy's two-year-old daughter. 'It started out as a sort of gentle folk ballad,' he later recalled. 'But then Keith suddenly decided, "Right, now it's time to add the reggae guitars."' Jimmy and Keith, whose mutual interests now extended far beyond music, were especially close, the Stones guitarist teasing the Zeppelin leader about Plant and Bonham, who he referred to as 'a couple of clueless Ernies from the Midlands'. So close were they at that point it was even rumoured that Jimmy would replace recently departed guitarist Mick Taylor on the band's 1975 American tour – before Ronnie stepped in.

The *Physical Graffiti* sleeve, designed by Mike Doud and Peter Corriston, would be another controversial talking point. Eschewing the usual gatefold design in favour of a special die-cut cover styled to look like a brownstone New York tenement through whose windows could be viewed an eclectic mix of famous faces including Buster Crabbe's Flash Gordon, Elizabeth Taylor's Cleopatra, Charles Atlas, Neil Armstrong, Jerry Lee Lewis, the Queen, King Kong, Peter Grant, Marlene Dietrich, Laurel and Hardy, the Virgin Mary, Rossetti's portrait of Proserpine, Judy Garland's breasts-strapped Dorothy and the cast of *Wizard of Oz*, plus the various members of Zeppelin dressed in drag – it was similar to the third album sleeve in its fiddly intricacy. The idea was actually lifted wholesale from the 1973 José Feliciano easy-listening album, *Compartments*, featuring an almost identical brownstone tenement with windows revealing its occupants, as well as a pull-out card and hidden pockets. Doud and Corriston used a photograph of a real-life New York apartment block at 97 St. Mark's Place for their version of the same idea. The band loved it, seeing it as another impressive example of their own increasingly ambitious attempts to place themselves above the confines of 'normal' rock bands, into a realm uniquely their own – or at least one shared only with the crème-de-la-crème and those who could afford such indulgences.

Released on 24 February 1975, in the middle of the band's tenth US tour, a riotous two-leg jaunt that would see them at their preening peak, *Physical Graffiti* was another chart-topper in both Britain and the US – entering the latter at no. 3 in its first week of release, an unprecedented feat at the time. It also attracted the best set of reviews any of the band's albums had ever received. In the UK, *Melody Maker* called it 'pure genius' while *Let It Rock* boldly predicted that 'by the end of the year *Physical Graffiti* will be beginning to exude as much of that nebulous "greatness" that clusters around the likes of *Blonde On Blonde, Beggars Banquet* and *Revolver'*. In the US, *Creem* was no less effusive: '*Graffiti* is, in fact, a better album than the other five offerings, the band being more confident, more arrogant in fact, and more consistent ... Equal time is given to the cosmic and the terrestrial, the subtle and the passionate.'

To compound the critical backslapping, it was also on this US tour that *Rolling Stone* put Zeppelin on its cover for the first time, with an article by their new, fifteen-year-old cub reporter, Cameron Crowe. Untainted by having been amongst the clique of original *Stone* writers who had routinely trashed the band, Crowe was clearly a real-life fan, and the band treated him to one of their most revealing interviews. Page even opened up about Boleskine House, dropping hints as to its hidden purpose by referring directly to 'my involvement in magic' and explaining how 'I'm attracted by the unknown ... all my houses are isolated ... I spend a lot of time near water ... a few things have happened that would freak some people out, but I was surprised actually at how composed I was'. How he doubted 'whether I'll reach thirty-five. I can't be sure about that.' But that he wasn't afraid of death. 'That is the greatest mystery of all.' Ultimately, he whispered, 'I'm still searching for an angel with a broken wing.' Then added with a grin: 'It's not very easy to find them these days. Especially when you're staying at the Plaza Hotel ...'

It was also at the Plaza in New York at the start of the tour that he set up a large stereo system to playback the music he had so far made for *Lucifer Rising*. 'I was on the sixth floor and there were complaints from the twelfth,' he said at the time. There had already been two private screenings of the first thirty-one minutes of film at the Museum of Modern Art in New York and at Berkeley University in LA where the reaction had been generally positive, and Anger now planned a full release by the end of the year, he said.

Meanwhile, the tour got underway under something of a cloud when Page yet again injured a finger on his left hand, just days before its official start at the Minneapolis Sports Center on 18 January. 'It happened when I was on a train in England, on my way to rehearsal,' he said. 'I must have grabbed at something, and the finger got caught in the hinge of the door. I was just totally numb – numb with shock. I just looked at it and said, "Oh, no".' The band ended up cutting 'Dazed and Confused' and doing 'How Many More Times' instead, while Page soldiered on by self-administering codeine tablets mixed with Jack Daniel's whisky to deaden the pain.

It was now that Danny Goldberg pulled off his biggest PR coup yet, when he arranged for William S. Burroughs to interview Page for a lengthy cover story in *Crawdaddy* under the heading: 'The Jimmy and Bill Show'. It may not have been Truman Capote writing about the Stones but it was damn close – better, in Jimmy's view, as Burroughs was another advocate of Crowley's sex magick, as famous for being a heroin addict as he was a writer of apocalyptic literature.

Burroughs wrote of seeing one of the band's three shows at Madison Square Garden in February, describing the audience as 'a river of youth looking curiously like a single organism: one well-behaved clean-looking middle-class kid' and compared the show itself to a bullfight. 'There was a palpable interchange of energy between the performers and the audience,' he noted. 'Leaving the concert hall was like getting off a jet plane.' The article also discussed how 'a rock concert is in fact a rite involving the evocation and transmutation of energy. Rock stars may be compared to priests.' And how the Zeppelin show, 'bears some resemblance to the trance music found in Morocco, which is magical in origin and purpose – that is, concerned with the evocation and control of spiritual forces.' Adding: 'It is to be remembered that the origin of all the arts – music, painting and writing – is magical and evocative; and that magic is always used to obtain some definite result. In the Led Zeppelin concert, the result aimed at would seem to be the creation of energy in the performers and in the audience. For such magic to succeed, it must tap the sources of magical energy, and this can be dangerous.'

The actual interview with Page, conducted 'over two fingers of whisky' at Burroughs' Franklin Street 'bunker' – a converted boys' locker room in downtown New York – was less interesting, with Burroughs doing most of the talking, Jimmy simply adding the occasional 'wow' and 'yeah'. Though Burroughs noted they had 'friends in common: the real estate agent who negotiated Jimmy Page's purchase of the Aleister Crowley house on Loch Ness [Boleskine]; John Michel, the flying saucer and pyramid expert; Donald Camell, who worked on *Performance*; Kenneth Anger, and the Jaggers, Mick and Chris ...'

Though Burroughs added: 'There are no accidents in the world of magic.' Page, he concluded, was 'equally aware of the risks involved in handling the fissionable material of the mass unconscious'.

'I pointed out that the moment when the stairway to heaven becomes something actually *possible* for the audience, would also be the moment of greatest danger. Jimmy expressed himself as well aware of the power in mass concentration, aware of the dangers involved, and of the skill and balance needed to avoid them . . . rather like driving a load of nitroglycerine.'

'There *is* a responsibility to the audience,' Page agreed. 'We don't want to release anything we can't handle.' He added: 'Music which involves riffs, anyway, will have a trance-like effect, and it's really like a mantra . . .'

Another memorable meeting Page had during the band's stint in New York was with David Bowie, then also heavily involved in his own cocaine-fuelled investigations into Crowley and the occult. Introduced by Mick Jagger, in town planning the next Stones tour, Bowie was curious to know more about Page's work on Anger's film. Tony Zanetta, then president of Bowie's management company, Mainman, later wrote in his book, *Stardust*, about how Crowley's beliefs encompassed 'promiscuity and the use of drugs like cocaine . . . It was another version of David's beloved Ziggy Stardust.'

Bowie was convinced that Page's study of Crowley had given him an especially strong aura – a magnetic sphere composed of three fields or bands of different colours that surrounds the body. He invited Page to the house he was then living in on 20th Street. 'Though he was his polite self, David was wary of Page,' writes Zanetta. 'Occasionally during the evening, the conversation touched on the subject of the occult. Whenever the power of the guitarist's aura was mentioned, Page remained silent but smiled inscrutably. It seemed that he did believe he had the power to control the universe.'

Eventually, Page's 'aura' so rankled Bowie he began to seriously lose his cool. 'I'd like you to leave,' he snapped. Jimmy simply sat there smiling, still saying nothing. Pointing to an open window in the room, Bowie hissed through gritted teeth: 'Why don't you leave by the window?' Again, Page merely sat there smiling, saying nothing, staring right at Bowie as though speaking to him telepathically. Eventually, Jimmy got up and strode out, slamming the door behind him, leaving

Bowie quaking in his boots. The next time they bumped into each other at a party, Bowie immediately left the room. Shortly after, claims Zanetta, Bowie insisted the house on 20th Street be exorcised 'because of the belief it had become overrun with satanic demons whom Crowley's disciples had summoned straight from hell ...'

13

The Devil in His Hole

On stage, the show had moved on considerably from the obvious glitz of 1973, towards a slicker, even more extravagant piece of theatre. Jones' onstage arsenal of instruments now included a Steinway grand piano, an electric Rhodes piano, a mellotron and clavinet. Bonham's drum kit was larger than ever and placed high on a rostrum, the stage straddled by large video screens and a neon sign which flashed the name Led Zeppelin up at the end of the show. A whirling umbrella of green lasers was used for the first time during Page's violin bow section of 'Dazed and Confused'. From the new album came panoramic versions of 'Kashmir', 'Sick Again', 'Trampled Underfoot', 'In My Time of Dying' and 'The Wanton Song'. The band still wore much the same stage gear as they had two years before, though Jimmy had a new, even more outrageous suit to wear, variously embroidered with dragons, crescent moons, blood-red poppies, spangly stars, the 'ZoSo' emblem, what appeared to be a stylised '666' and a Scorpio Rising sign.

Travelling aboard the Starship again, they had finessed their travel arrangements still further, now working out of 'bases' around the country. For the first leg of the tour, they used the Chicago Ambassador as their camp, jetting out to shows in surrounding areas before returning 'home' straightaway afterwards. Elvis may have left the building with the crowd still chanting his name; Zeppelin had taken off into the stratosphere long before anyone had even arrived. When Plant got 'flu, leaving them with four days to kill, they rode the Starship down to LA, Jonesy sulking because he'd wanted to go to the Bahamas. But Page had unfinished business in LA, as always, and the band was still Jimmy's baby. So LA it was ...

The Los Angeles concerts themselves – two nights at Long Beach Arena, three at the Forum – came at the finale of the tour, so LA was used as a base to fly back and forth to shows in Seattle, Vancouver and San Diego. They'd hurry back to LA, hitting the Troubadour in time for the late show from Bobby 'Blue' Bland one night, the Roxy for Suzi Quatro another night. As Jimmy told me in 2005: 'I was living it. It was what it was.' After playing for three hours a night 'you can't just switch off the adrenalin. For us, the way to wind it down was to go to a party. Before you know where you've been, you've missed a night's sleep. Then, two weeks later, you've missed a few nights' sleep because you've been having such a good time. I certainly wasn't the only musician on the road back then who stayed up for a few nights on the trot.'

But even Jimmy Page was now beginning to weary of the groupies who found everything he said 'far out'. Plant and Jones had gone as far as renting mansions away from the Strip for the duration of their stay. And while Page and Bonham were still happy to hang their hats at the Riot House – if on separate floors – Jimmy appeared to have entered a period of celebrity wife-swapping. Having enjoyed luring Bebe Buell away from Todd Rundgren, he now turned his attentions to Chrissie Wood – wife of Ronnie, then on tour with the Faces – who became his 'special friend' throughout the West Coast leg of the tour. Not special enough, though, to prevent him from also trying to woo Joni Mitchell, who he'd become infatuated with since meeting her at a party in London twelve months before. She had appeared more interested in Rod Stewart on that occasion – until her then boyfriend, drummer John Guerin, turned up and both Page and Stewart had beaten a hasty retreat. Guerin had 'a few hairs on his chest,' as Stewart put it. Six months later, however, Mitchell was back in London for a Crosby, Stills, Nash & Young show at Wembley. Afterwards, there had been another soirée at Quaglino's that all of Zeppelin attended, only to find Mitchell once again accompanied by her impressively hirsute boyfriend. Now, in LA, when Page found her alone at last with friends at the then fashionable Greenhouse Restaurant on Sunset, they sat and chatted together for half an hour before Mitchell got up to go. Jimmy tried to persuade her to stay but Joni politely refused.

Another night during the LA stay Jimmy treated writer Nick Kent and some other friends – 'seriously wired on the voluminous quantities of cocaine [and] heroin' – to an impromptu late-night showing in his suite of *Lucifer Rising*. 'The piece lasted for about half an hour,' recalled

Kent, 'and consisted of amateurish home-movie-style footage shot by Anger of an extremely stoned Marianne Faithfull in black robes silently stumbling down a staircase holding a lighted candle.' Viewing the film now, though, there's clearly more to it than an admittedly stoned Kent recalls. Far from looking 'extremely stoned' and holding a candle, Marianne Faithfull – in grey not black robes – casts a solemn, intriguing figure, as she wanders through the Egyptian deserts, dwarfed by the ancient monuments characteristic of the region. The rest of the film – a montage of visually arresting scenes and colourful images reminiscent of the 'surreal' early films of Bunuel – is even more intriguing, containing snatches of real-life depictions of magick ritual, though it has to be said that Leslie Huggins as Lucifer fails to cut a completely convincing figure; more *Carry On* than *Rising*. Donald Cammell is more in synch as Osiris, the God of Death – chosen for the role, Anger later claimed, 'because he was always threatening suicide. And finally he did it. He blew his head off.'

Page's original soundtrack also works surprisingly well; its dense, ominous tones lending an air of authority to the inevitably oblique imagery. As he explained at the time: 'The film's pacing is absolutely superb. It starts so slow, and after say four minutes it gets a little faster and the whole thing starts to suck you in . . . . There's a real atmosphere and intensity. It's disturbing because you know something's coming.' There is also reputedly a brief glimpse of Page himself, holding the Stèle of Revealing while gazing at a framed photo of Crowley. The Stèle is an ancient Egyptian funerary artefact that played a role in the creation of Crowley's Thelema religion as described in *The Book of the Law*. There are also extracts inscribed on it from the Egyptian *Book of the Dead*, specifically text 'to allow the astral form of the deceased to revisit the earth at will'. This curly-haired, bearded figure is glimpsed only for a few seconds, and then only in half-profile, so it is not possible to say with absolute certainty whether it is Page. There is certainly a strong resemblance – years later, facsimiles of this same scene were used to advertise limited edition bootleg copies of the Page soundtrack in California, clearly referencing it as a clip of Jimmy from the film itself – but if it is Page, it's a wonder Anger himself has never advertised the fact more, considering the added attention such a scene would bring his little-seen film. On the other hand, Anger is perverse enough to not wish to credit Page. Either way, it's an intriguing sidebar for those fans of Page's who revel in his clear associations with the occult in general and Crowley in particular.

As always, the real bad boy of the tour was John Bonham. At the start, it had been fun. Even though he was banned from driving in Britain, where he'd been caught speeding while 'under the influence,' in Texas he'd bought a customised 1966 Corvette Stingray for $18,000 (spending hours sitting in it with Keith Moon, now resident and permanently on the rampage in LA, the two of them just revving the engine). John also bought his nine-year-old son Jason a miniature Ludwig drum kit, which he would teach him to play. 'It wasn't so much that he wanted me to get involved in the music business,' Jason told me in a 1990 interview. 'I think he was more interested in giving me some understanding of what it was he was doing with his life. He used to get a kick out of watching me thump around. Like, "That's my boy!"' Plant told me one of his favourite memories was of Bonham 'standing over Jason with his little mini-kit positioned next to the jukebox. Bonzo with a lilac drape suit on, a fag sticking out of his mouth, going "Come on!" Then sticking the Isley Brothers on yet again until Jason got it right.' (In a *Melody Maker* article at the time, Bonham expressed doubts over whether Jason would follow in his father's footsteps. 'You can't teach him anything,' moaned Dad. 'He's got a terrible temper.')

However, back on the road it was the frustrated family man who was increasingly showing his bad temper, as once again he transformed into La Bête. Dressed on stage like a *Clockwork Orange* droog in white boiler suit and black bowler hat, acting like one off it, onlookers ceased to be amused and began to feel disgusted. By now the band's off-road requirements had been finessed down to intricate details: Jimmy insisted his suite always have the curtains drawn, whatever time of day or night it was, the place lit by scented black candles, the fridge stocked with vintage Dom Perignon champagne. Other members expressed preferences for certain oriental rugs hung from the walls, grand pianos and, in the case of Bonzo, a full-size pool table. Nothing else mattered to the increasingly errant drummer – most of it was inevitably hurled from his window anyway; he even attempted to smash a grand piano into small enough pieces to send it flying out of his suite in LA. Word spread and the New York Plaza now demanded a $10,000 deposit before they would even let Bonzo check in. On the flight to LA during

Plant's 'flu bout, a drunken Bonzo frightened even Cole and Grant who had to restrain him from forcing one of the Starship's pretty flight attendants into having sex with him. On a flight to Detroit, he grabbed the glasses off a startled Atlantic Records representative's face and crushed them with his hands, grinding the broken pieces into the floor, then got up and walked calmly to the back of the plane. However, one night at the end of the tour he got a taste of his own medicine when he drunkenly took on one of the bouncers at the Rainbow – an expert in karate who responded by sending Bonzo to the hospital emergency room for the rest of the night. Lesson unlearned, Bonzo wanted to press assault charges but was finally dissuaded by G, who sensed it might open the floodgates to similar complaints from everyone else who had suffered at the hands of La Bête over the years.

'It was the alcohol,' said Bev Bevan. 'The longer the tours went on, the more he drank.' With wife Pat now expecting their second child – a daughter, Zoë – Bonham missed being home more than ever and was swift to take out his frustrations on any unsuspecting passer-by. 'There's no doubt about it,' Mac Poole later told me, 'the success fuelled the disease – because he had nothing to stop him, nothing to make him pull back from booze or anything else. And he had no self-discipline. Unfortunately, John let booze and frivolity temper his life.'

It wasn't just the booze now. On stage he had begun holding a plastic bag containing an ounce of cocaine between his legs, reaching in and rubbing handfuls of the drug into his mouth and nostrils as he played. After each show the crew would carefully dismantle the kit and shake the drum mat over a plastic bag of their own into which large deposits of all the coke Bonzo had spilt would accumulate, which they would then share amongst themselves. Bryan Ferry, whose band Roxy Music were also in town, was with Bonham one night when he burst into tears, freaked out, he blubbed, by his own behaviour. Both Page and Grant even made sure their suites were on different floors of the hotel to those of Bonham's now, while the same scenes that had caused Jones to temporarily quit the band two years before now meant he did everything in his power to stay away from, as Cole puts it, 'the chaos and excesses that he may have seen bringing Led Zeppelin down'. Often on tour, Jones would sidle up to Ricardo and tell him: 'Here's the phone number where I'll be for the next forty-eight hours. Unless there's an absolute emergency, don't tell anyone – and I do mean *anyone* – how to reach me.' Grant would grow steadily more furious with these regular disappearances. But, as Cole says in his own published account, 'Perhaps Jonesy was smarter than any of us, keeping his distance while the rest of us were gradually sinking into the quicksand . . .'

Partly because of Bonzo's over the top antics, partly through Jimmy's reputation for being the devil in disguise, and partly through Plant's self-proclaimed status as 'a golden god!' as he boasted to Cameron Crowe on the Starship late one night, Zeppelin's reputation now preceded them wherever they went, a situation not helped by the growing thuggishness of the entourage now surrounding them.

'There were many times that Robert's dogs – whoever was looking after Zeppelin at the time – were ready to punch anybody's lights out the minute you went near the band,' recalled Mac Poole with a shudder. 'It got to be a very leery situation. You could see trouble coming.' What's more, the 'dogs' were now armed. According to Swan Song's Alan Callan, speaking in 1975, this was because of panicky insurance companies who, in the wake of the dubious theft of 1973 insisted on 'guards outside every hotel and dressing-room door . . . police escorts on the cars to and from gigs'. It wasn't just the hired heavies that were now packing heat, though. Both Cole and Grant were also said to carry not-so-concealed weapons on occasion, while Bonzo reputedly stuck a gun in Deep Purple bassist Glenn Hughes' back after drunkenly accusing him of sleeping with his wife Pat.

Aynsley Dunbar recalls Cole pulling a gun on him during the LA leg of the tour. Having achieved a certain measure of fame since his Jeff Beck days drumming with Frank Zappa, David Bowie and Lou Reed, Dunbar was now a founding member of soon-to-be American stars Journey, whose debut album was about to be released, and was staying at the same hotel as the band. 'It was very interesting,' he tells me over the phone from his current home in California. 'They were staying at the Hilton on Santa Monica and Wilshire and I had a suite there too and we used to hang around together and go to the parties afterwards. That was when [Cole] pulled a gun on me. He wanted me to leave but leave behind the two girls I was with. So I punched him in the balls. He turned round and goes, "That was fucking stupid!" I said, "No, the stupid part would be what you did. If you'd shot me in the head you'd have a lot of fucking explaining to do.". He was just jealous of the fact I had two chicks with me – we used to have threesomes in my suite. But Led Zeppelin at that point thought they were the kings, they had guns with them and everything else, you know . . . the whole thing was so bloody weird. Talk about gangland . . .'

But then these were witchy times. When, a few days before the band left LA, a skinny red-haired girl began bombarding Danny Goldberg's suite with phone calls, demanding to see Jimmy, who she said she had 'a warning for', claiming his life was in jeopardy, Goldberg placated her by asking her to write her 'visions' down on a note which he promised to pass on to the guitarist, then threw the note away as soon as she finally agreed to leave. Six months later, however, Page was rattled to be told the same girl could now be seen on TV, having been arrested for aiming a loaded gun at President Ford on the streets of Sacramento – she was identified as Lynne 'Squeaky' Fromme, a member of the Charles Manson cult.

It hardly mattered – by now the rot had set in anyway. I once asked Jimmy if it was true he had avoided Bonzo on tour by then. 'Well,' he said, 'I'm a very private person, and still am, so maybe people played that up into something else.' In other words, yes. What about the image – the bad man with the guitar in one hand and the bag of tricks in the other? True, too? 'Well,' he said again, 'there's no smoke without fire. I guess I'm a pretty complex person.'

Despite being at the very height of their commercial powers (as well as *Physical Graffiti*, all five previous Zeppelin albums had re-entered the US charts that spring), behind the scenes, even greater dramas were already beginning to unfold. According to Cole, the 1975 US tour was the first where heroin began to 'circulate freely'. Although not a subject the band has ever been willing to discuss openly, Page, Bonham, Cole and others in their organisation would succumb to various levels of smack addiction over the next five years. 'It was hedonistic times, you know?' said Page. 'We wanted to be on that edge, it fed into the music.' As he said in another 2003 interview: 'I can't speak for the [other members of the band], but for me drugs were an integral part of the whole thing, right from the beginning, right to the end.'

Maybe, but Cole complained that Page became even more mysterious and withdrawn on smack, while Bonzo, 'already unpredictable, became more volatile'. Of course, it's hard now to think of even one

major Seventies rock band that didn't see drugs as an essential part of
the kit. Indeed, the history of heroin in music goes much further back,
with the jazz giants of the Fifties famously falling for its occult allure.
In the case of Zeppelin, however, cocaine and heroin came to represent
their hubris; a symbol of their spectacular spiral to the ground over
the next five years.

Even Grant, who disdained junkies, had developed a not-so-secret
coke habit, holing up at Horselunges, his mansion in Sussex, for days
at a time when off the road, and spending increasing amounts of time
locked away in his hotel suite when on it. The band may not have
noticed anything radically different about their manager but those
employees working closest with him now began to notice serious cracks
in the previously thought impregnable demeanour. Chatting years later
with Richard Cole – who, ironically, was now babysitting the ailing
figure of Don Arden, Grant's former mentor – he told me his main
memory of Grant at this time was of his mentor and employer sitting
at home at Horselunges, like the Al Pacino character in *Scarface*, a
mountain of coke on the coffee table in front of him, spooning it into
his nose and bemoaning the fact that, as Cole put it: 'There was
nowhere left to go. They'd reached the top of the mountain. The only
way now was down ...'

Michael Francis, who later worked with Bon Jovi, later recalled the
bizarre circumstances of his first meeting with Grant after being hired
as a Swan Song band bodyguard. He told writer Phil Sutcliffe how,
after being driven down in Grant's Daimler from London to Sussex,
he was forced to sit waiting for hours. 'Then Norman [the chauffeur]
explained that Peter would not be able to see me today and that I was
to stay the night at the house.' He did as instructed, assuming Grant
had merely been 'called away on business'. Until later that evening
when 'the chef said he was taking Peter's supper up to him and I
realised he had been in the house all this time. When Peter met me
for breakfast, he offered no explanation. I later discovered that he
would often stay secluded in his upstairs quarters for days at a time,
taking cocaine.'

According to Alan Callan, however, it wasn't just drugs that were
G's undoing. His ten-year marriage was also now crumbling. To make
matters worse, when wife Gloria finally left him, she did so hand-in-
hand with the farm manager at Horselunges. 'If I had asked Peter about

mistakes he had made,' Callan later told Phil Sutcliffe, 'he would have
said, "Lots, we all makes mistakes. We all win sometimes too.". But if
I asked him about failures, I believe he would have said only one: his
marriage. He was a person who believed you married for life. I think
the break up and its aftermath had a huge impact on him.'

*After the Animals came the Nashville Teens, another Don Arden group,
who Mickie had produced their biggest hit for, 'Tobacco Road'. Everyone
was still getting a taste except you. But life was better in other ways now.
You'd met Gloria, this tiny, pretty little thing who had been a ballet dancer.
It was like Beauty and the Beast; you never knew what she saw in you. You
knew it didn't hurt not to be broke, but that was the same for any bird,
wasn't it? That doesn't mean they have to say yes when you ask them to
marry you, but Gloria did. Then gave you a gorgeous son, Warren, three
years later, and then, not so long after that, a beautiful baby girl, Helen.
Best of all, she didn't want to know about the shows and the whatnot, the
telly and the fucking lah-de-dah. She just wanted to be a mum and a wife.
Woe betide any cunt saying so, but you'd never been happier. A proper
family man at last, you'd found someone not just to go home to at night
but someone to look forward with as well.*

*That was when you knew you had to make it. Like Don, like Mickie,
like all the other smart-mouth cunts in their suits and ties and double G&
Ts. There was wonga to be made – big wonga – and you were going to get
your share, make fucking sure of it. For Gloria and the kids. So while
Mickie was striding ahead, producing Herman's Hermits, Donovan, Lulu
and the rest, you took a punt on The Flintstones – a right load of old crash-
bang-wallop that went nowhere – and a girl group called She Trinity –
from Canada. You got them signed to Columbia but despite their looks
you could never get the bloody thing off the ground. Three singles and not
a fucking tickle. 'Forget 'em,' said Mickie. 'Move on.'*

*So you did, signing the New Vaudeville Band – well, Geoff Stephens,
the songwriter and producer. Geoff would knock out some tunes in the
studio, you would get 'em played on the radio, and if it bit you'd help him
put a band together to tour. Geoff wrote the schmaltzy sort of thing your
old mum liked, but catchy and done with a twist, to make you laugh. You
could see it on the telly, like Kenny Ball and his Jazzmen or Freddie and
the Dreamers. Mickie laughed and took the piss but fuck me if it didn't
take off! 'Winchester Cathedral' was a hit all over the fucking place –*

number four in Britain and – ready? – number fucking ONE in
AMERICA!! Next thing you knew you were back in the States, doing Ed
Sullivan and whatnot, they couldn't get enough of it. 'This is it!' you told
Gloria. 'This will buy us our house!'

It bloody well did too. It also put you in touch with someone else who'd
stick by you through the years. A young lad who reminded you of you – or
what you might have been like if you'd been ten years younger. Richard
Cole, a former scaffolder from north London. A wild card but the best often
are. Not afraid to get stuck in, either, if there was trouble brewing, and
there nearly always was. Coley had fought as a boxer and knew karate.
A great fucking kid to have around, the sort you only had to tell once.
Gobby, too, which also reminded you of you. Like when you told him, 'If
you ever fucking repeat anything you hear in this office, I'll cut your fucking
ears off,' and quick as a flash the little cunt said back, 'If you're going to
point your fucking finger at me much longer I'm going to fucking bite it off!'
Funny little fucker, you sent him to work as road manager with Geoff and
the Vaudevilles and that was it, he never left your side again. Well, not till
the very, very end, but that was another story . . .

After the US tour ended in March – *Deep Throat* star Linda Lovelace
introducing them on stage for the final show of their three-night run
at LA's Forum – the band flew home via New York, where Grant broke
the news they had been warned to expect but had secretly dreaded:
on the advice of their stern accountants, all four band members plus
Grant were advised to become tax exiles, an increasingly well-trodden
path at this point in the mid-Seventies for a generation of British rock
artists. The good news: they would hold onto more than half their
huge multi-million earnings from their combined album sales and tour
receipts for 1975 – at that point estimated to reach in the region of
$40 million. The bad news: they would have to leave the UK almost
immediately, unable to return until April 1976 at the earliest. Most of
the ensuing period would be taken up touring the world, it was decided,
affording the band unusual opportunities to travel to territories they
had never been able to before – South America was seriously discussed,
as was India, Africa, and other previously thought out-of-the-way stops
on the rock'n'roll map. Grant would direct operations from a newly
established base, renting promoter Claude Knobs' house in Montreaux.

Jones received the news in his usual stoic fashion: the children could be left to board at school if necessary. Page and Plant were generally upbeat: both men viewing the forthcoming year as an adventure. 'I think it's time to travel,' Page had told Cameron Crowe, 'start gathering some real right-in-there experiences with street musicians around the world. Moroccan musicians, Indian musicians ...' He even talked fancifully of 'getting a travelling medicine wagon with a dropdown side and travelling around England. Just drop down the side and play through big battery amps and mixers and it can all be as temporary or as permanent as I want it to be.' Bonzo, though, was distraught, knowing what a long time away from home would in reality mean for him, even refusing at first to comply with G's proposals, until it was made abundantly clear to him just how much money he would be kissing goodbye: up to ninety-five per cent of his earnings.

Afterwards, Page and G stayed on in New York, making plans for Zeppelin's return to the US later that summer for some giant outdoor stadium shows. Meanwhile, back home in early May, a limited seven-inch single of 'Trampled Underfoot' b/w 'Black Country Woman' was issued as a precursor to what would be, they decided, the crowning achievement of the band's career in the UK so far: five sold-out shows at London's 17,000-seater Earl's Court arena. Grant had initially booked three nights – 23, 24 and 25 May– but they sold out so quickly that two more dates were added on 17 and 18 May.

The run would be an unparalleled triumph in the band's career. Then the largest indoor arena in Britain, the band had installed two 24 x 30-feet Ephidor video screens either side of the Earl's Court stage – an innovation. 'It was the first time anyone had used [the video screens] at a major rock show,' said Jimmy. 'I remember we had some lasers too. What would now be regarded as fairly cheap-looking beams of light – but it was the first time it had been done. I think we broke the rules using them, actually, because we really wanted it to be a show.' One in which the band consciously looked back on their entire career to date. 'Six-and-a-half years is a hell of a long time,' declared Plant from the stage the first night. 'We want to take you through the stages of six-and-a-half years of our relationship.' At which point the band bludgeoned into 'Rock and Roll' and the place erupted. As Peter Makowski – then the teenaged UK equivalent of *Rolling Stone*'s Cameron Crowe – who reviewed the show for *Sounds*, later recalled: 'One minute we were in the kingdom of Valhalla – all swirling dry ice and blinding lasers during "The Song Remains The Same" and "Trampled Underfoot"; the next revisiting "our travels in Morocco ... and the story of our wasted, wasted times" for "Kashmir"; then transported to a small cottage in Wales while Plant regaled the throng with tales of stoned nights putting together *Led Zeppelin III*.' Nor could Plant resist throwing in some sarcastic comments about the band's imminent tax-enforced departure from Britain, a subject made public just weeks before. 'Somebody voted for someone and now everybody's on the run,' he announced one point. 'You know, Denis [Healey, then Chancellor of the Exchequer] there'll be no artists in the country anymore ... he must be "Dazed and Confused" ...' While his final words before leaving the stage at the end of the last night were: 'This is our last concert in England for some considerable time. Still, there's always the Eighties.' Then added: 'If you see Denis Healey, tell him we've gone ...'

Each show was compered by a different DJ – respectively, Johnnie Walker, David 'Kid' Jensen, Nicky Horne, Bob Harris and Alan 'Fluff' Freeman – all then presenters of the best-known rock shows on British radio. After the first show there had been a private get-together at Blake's Hotel in Kensington where Robert had been in effusive mood, welcoming one and all and acting out scenes from the then recently released *Monty Python and the Holy Grail* film. Jimmy stayed in his room, 'discussing occultist theology with two sinister-looking characters,' recalled Nick Kent, 'and listening to a tape of murderer Charles Manson singing his creepy self-penned songs.'

The last of the five nights saw a much more lavish after-show party held in the bowels of Earl's Court, with pub rockers Dr Feelgood providing the entertainment for guests, including a large Swan Song presence in Maggie Bell, Dave Edmunds and all of Bad Company, plus Nick Lowe arm-in-arm with band PR and self-appointed 'entertainments manager' B.P. Fallon, whose handy phial of amyl nitrate and ever-ready supply of cotton wool balls made him the most popular man in the room after the band itself. Later, the party moved on to a more private gathering at Chelsea's St James Club, where Keith Richards and Ronnie Wood showed up. Though Led Zeppelin didn't know it yet, this would be the peak. They would go on to headline even larger venues, they would continue to sell many more millions of albums, but in every other respect this was the high watermark of their career; the point at which the mighty Zeppelin, which had soared so high these past six years, would begin its fiery descent.

Forty-eight hours after the last Earl's Court show, Robert and Maureen Plant set off on holiday with their two children for Agadir. Three weeks later they were in Marrakech, where Jimmy, Charlotte and their four-year-old daughter Scarlet flew out to meet them. Together they took in a local festival 'that gave us a little peep into the colour of Moroccan music and the music of the hill tribes,' said Plant. From there they journeyed thousands of miles by Range Rover down through the Spanish Sahara just as the Spanish-Moroccan war was breaking out. 'There was a distinct possibility that we could have got very, very lost, going round in circles and taking ages to get out,' said Plant. 'It's such a vast country with no landmarks and no people apart from the odd tent and a camel.'

A month later, driving up through Casablanca and Tangier, they arrived in Switzerland for a band meeting with Grant at his new base in Montreaux, and to spend a few days hanging out at the Montreaux Jazz Festival, then in full swing. But by the end of July Plant was getting itchy feet again, 'pining for the sun [and] the happy, haphazard way of life that goes with it.' It was then the idea of driving down to the Greek island of Rhodes came up. Plant arranged to meet Pretty Things vocalist Phil May and his wife, Electra, who had rented a house on the island from Roger Waters of Pink Floyd. Page, Charlotte and Scarlet followed in a second car, with Maureen's sister Shirley and her husband. On 3 August, Jimmy briefly left the party to fly to Sicily, to visit Crowley's old Abbey of Thelema, which Kenneth Anger had told him so much about and that he was now considering buying. The plan was to all meet up again in Paris a couple of days later where they would begin rehearsals for their next US tour, scheduled to begin with two sold-out shows on 23 and 24 August at the 90,000-capacity Oakland Coliseum in San Francisco.

The next day Maureen was at the wheel of the rented Austin Mini sedan – Robert beside her in the passenger seat, Karac, Carmen and Scarlet in the back – when it skidded and spun off the road, nose-diving over a precipice into a tree. Landing on top of Maureen, the impact shattered Plant's right ankle and elbow and snapped several bones in his right leg. Looking at Maureen, who was bleeding and unconscious, he thought she was dead; the children were screaming in the back. Fortunately, Charlotte and Shirley, in the next car, were there to summon help but it was still several hours before the family could be taken – via the back of a nearby fruit farmer's flatbed truck – to the local hospital, where it was discovered that Maureen had suffered a fractured skull, as well as a broken pelvis and leg. Four-year-old Karac had also broken a leg, while six-year-old Carmen had broken her wrist. Scarlet was the only one to escape with just a few cuts and bruises. Maureen had lost a lot of blood but due to a rare blood type could only take Shirley's blood for immediate transfusion. The process was painfully slow, with only one doctor on duty at the cockroach-ridden Greek hospital. Plant was forced to share a room with a drunken soldier who insisted on singing 'The Ocean' (from *Houses of the Holy*) to him.

That night a hysterical Charlotte phoned Richard Cole in London, begging him to do something to get everyone home. Cole flew into action, furiously phoning round until he had co-opted two senior physicians – Dr John Baretta, a Harley Street specialist who also acted as medical consultant for the Greek Embassy and spoke fluent Greek, and Dr Mike Lawrence, a prominent orthopaedic surgeon – into journeying with him to Greece immediately. It was still forty-eight hours before they arrived, though, and even then hospital officials refused to release the patients until a police investigation – searching for causes of the crash, specifically drugs – was completed, which might have taken weeks. Again, Cole saved the day, hiring a private ambulance and arranging for two station wagons to be parked at a side entrance, wheeling Robert, Maureen and the children – their IV bottles swinging besides them – down to the getaway cars in the dead of night. Hours later, they were in the sky heading back to London.

Their return home was delayed still further, however. This time, unbelievably, on the instructions of Swan Song's accountants, who, in the absence of direct orders from Grant, had insisted Cole delay the plane's landing by thirty minutes so as to avoid using up a precious day of Plant's allotted time in the UK. Circling at 15,000 feet, he reflected that while it may have saved Plant thousands of pounds in taxes, 'I still thought it was more important to save a life.' When the plane finally touched down, the Plants were transported via waiting ambulances to Guy's Hospital, where Maureen underwent immediate surgery. It would be several more weeks before she was well enough to leave, while the singer – who was placed in a cast that ran from his hip to his toes – also faced sobering news from the doctors. 'You probably won't walk again for six months, maybe more,' he was told. 'And there's no guarantee that you'll ever recover completely.' It was debatable who took the news most badly – Plant or Grant. 'This could be the end of Led Zeppelin,' G complained to Cole, 'This might be the end of the line.'

Page was also devastated by the news. However, like Grant, his main concern was for the future of the band. 'I was shattered,' he said. He had 'always felt,' though, 'that no matter what happened, provided he could still play and sing, and even if we could only make albums, that we'd go on forever.' Plant's fate, he had no doubt, was tied inextricably to that of the band's. 'Just really because the whole aspect of what's going to come round the corner as far as writing goes is the dark element, the mysterious element. You just don't know what's coming. So many good things have come out of that that it would be criminal to interrupt a sort of alchemical process like that.' He added: 'There's a lot of important work to be done yet ...'

To make matters worse, to preserve his new tax-exiled status, Plant would have to be moved out of the country again while his wife was still recuperating in hospital. Temporary accommodation was arranged for him on the island of Jersey – exempt from punitive British tax laws – at the mansion home of millionaire lawyer Dick Christian, who sent a limousine and an ambulance to meet Plant and his mini-entourage of Cole, Zeppelin soundman Benji Le Fevre, and Swan Song PA, Marilyn. Christian kindly offered his guest the use of his Maserati and Jensen Interceptor but a wheelchair-bound Plant would spend the next six weeks moping around the guesthouse, drinking beer and knocking back prescription painkillers. Occasionally he played the piano but mainly he just sat and stared, his mood desperate. 'I just don't know whether I'm ever going to be the same on stage again,' he repeatedly told Cole.

Eventually, it was decided that work was the best therapy. 'The longer we wait,' Page, who phoned every few days for progress reports, complained to Cole, 'the harder it's gonna be to come back.' With the band's ambitious touring plans put on indefinite hold, it was decided to get to work on the next Zeppelin album. By the end of September, Plant, his wheelchair and crutches were being boarded onto a British

Airways flight to Los Angeles, where Page was waiting for him in a
rented beach house in Malibu Colony. Like a reverse-negative version
of their stay at Bron-Yr-Aur five years before, the two planned to write
together. There were no peaceful, flower-strewn valleys to enjoy this
time, though, just the all-night lights of old LA beckoning them onto
the rocks, bewitching narcotic sirens to their hapless shipwrecked
mariners.

Robert's mood was still predominantly black but hanging out with
Jimmy, writing again, he now had good days as well as bad, taking
short, therapeutic strolls along the beach with his new cane. There
were also trips to see Donovan perform at the Santa Monica Civic, and
a catch-up with Paul Rodgers and Boz Burrell from Bad Company.
Jimmy also checked out the band Detective, offering them a deal with
Swan Song (the group was formed by Michael Des Barres, future
husband of Miss Pamela). Meanwhile, Robert turned up at the Renais-
sance Pleasure Fair in Navato, thirty miles north of San Francisco,
carried around in a sedan chair to great applause. However, there was
another factor about Plant's so-called Californian rehabilitation that
wasn't discussed, and was far less helpful, at least in terms of his
mental recovery: the plentiful supply of cocaine and heroin that Page's
presence anywhere now demanded. Also staying at the Malibu house
was a dismayed Benji Le Fevre, who told Cole they'd nicknamed the
place 'Henry Hall' – slang for heroin.

Having used up their backlog of material on *Physical Graffiti*, with
the exception of the riff to the unreleased 'Walter's Walk' which Page
now reused to create 'Hots On For Nowhere', songs for the new album
would have to be built from the ground up. One of the first to
take shape was 'Achilles Last Stand', the lengthy opus which would
eventually open the next album. Built on the sort of strident, all-hands-
on-deck guitar figure that Iron Maiden would later build a whole career
out of – Page attempting to create something, he said, that reflected
'the façade of a gothic building with layers of tracery and statues' –
'Achilles Last Stand' also featured the first of a string of intensely
autobiographical lyrics Plant now felt compelled to write. Originally
nicknamed 'The Wheelchair Song', the subject, in this instance, was
the enforced exile which had forced the band to become what Page
later described as 'technological gypsies' and led indirectly, Plant
seemed to suggest, to their current malaise – 'the devil's in his hole!'

he wailed balefully. Page later described his guitar solo as 'in the same tradition as the solo from "Stairway to Heaven".' In truth, few would now agree but, 'It is on that level to me,' he insisted.

Musically, 'Tea for One', the equally lengthy blues showcase which would close the album 'was us looking back at "Since I've Been Loving You",' Page told me in 2001, 'being in a very lonely space at the time and ... you know ... reflecting accordingly.' Lyrically, it found Plant metaphorically wringing his hands, the loneliness of his separation from his wife and children – Maureen being still too ill to travel – juxtaposed against the artificial luxury of his drug-fuelled life in Malibu. 'I was just sitting in that wheelchair and getting morose,' he recalled. 'It was like ... is this rock'n'roll thing really anything at all?' But that was as nothing compared to the venom he summoned up in 'For Your Life' and 'Hots On For Nowhere': the former a vicious attack on the LA lifestyle he'd once eulogised, railing against 'cocaine-cocaine-cocaine' in the 'city of the damned'; the latter directing his anger this time towards both Page and Grant, and their insensitivity to his situation, only concerned for their own futures, as he spits: 'I've got friends who would give me fuck all ...' Seemingly oblivious to Plant's ire, Page inadvertently colludes in the song's bitter denouement using the tremelo arm on the Strat he'd loaned from ex-Byrd Gene Parsons to produce a resounding twang in the middle of his solo.

Naturally, there was also the by now almost obligatory pillaging of the blues for a new cornerstone Zeppelin moment: another Blind Willie Johnson classic from 1928 called 'It's Nobody's Fault But Mine' – here shortened to 'Nobody's Fault But Mine'. Originally the story of Johnson fretting because his blindness prevented him from reading his Bible, thereby incurring the wrath of God, it became a useful metaphor for Zeppelin's own fiery descent from heaven, Plant adapting the lyrics to include some revealingly stuttering lines about having 'a monkey on my back' embellished by some suitably squalling harmonica. The only truly original parts were the strafing guitar lines Page concocted, again using the borrowed Strat, to which Bonzo would add his most mercilessly cannon-like drum-pummelling since 'When The Levee Breaks'. Even then, the overall arrangement owed much to Page's fascination with John Renbourn and his own 1966 version of the same song (which, like Page now, Renbourn would take credit for).

It wasn't all bleak, though. 'Candy Store Rock' – its genesis traceable back to live performances of 'Over The Hills And Far Away' where Page, Jones and Bonham would frequently drift off into a similarly paced improvisation – was a jolly enough romp, Page making a rare recorded return to his rockabilly roots, Plant cheerfully following suit, 'being Ral Donner,' as he put it, 'the guy who wanted to be Elvis'. 'Royal Orleans' was another deliberate attempt to lighten the mood, its pleasingly staccato rhythms enlivened by the jokey lyric: 'When the sun peaked through ... he kissed the whiskers, left and right,' and a jokey reference to talking 'like Barry White ...'

With most of the material finished by the time Jones and Bonham arrived at the end of the month, the time originally booked at SIR Studios in Hollywood for writing and rehearsal was used mainly to finesse what Page and Plant had already come up with. The work was described by Page as 'gruelling' as recently as 2004, because, he said, 'nobody else really came up with song ideas. It was really up to me to come up with all the riffs, which is probably why [the songs were] guitar-heavy. But I don't blame anybody. We were all kind of down.' In fact, neither Jones nor Bonham were given a chance to participate. As Jones told Dave Lewis in 2003: 'It became apparent that Robert and I seemed to keep a different time sequence to Jimmy. We just couldn't find him.' Adding that he 'drove into SIR Studios every night and waited and waited ... I learned all about baseball during that period as the World Series was on and there was not much else to do but watch it.' Even once recording on the album had begun, 'I just sort of went along with it all,' he shrugged. 'The main memory of that album is pushing Robert around in the wheelchair from beer stand to beer stand. We had a laugh I suppose, but I didn't enjoy the sessions really. I just tagged along with that one.'

Hence, the solitary co-writing credit Jones and Bonham receive on the album – for 'Royal Orleans'. Even when Jones did manage to contribute some solid ideas, such as the bass line he created with his distinctive Alembic eight-string guitar for 'Achilles Last Stand' and which he described to Lewis now as 'an integral part of the song', it went unacknowledged. 'What one put into the track wasn't always reflected in the credits,' he observed dryly. But it's clear this was not one of Jones's favourite Zeppelin albums. In truth, it would rarely become anybody's favourite Zeppelin album – except for Jimmy Page, who still stubbornly rates it one of their best. As Lewis says now: 'It was the first album all over again, with Jimmy in total control of everything and hardly anyone else getting a say. That's why there was no "Boogie With Stu" or "Hats Off To Harper" on that album, no mellotrons, acoustic guitars or keyboards of any kind – no Jonesy! It was all Jimmy. No-one else really got a look in . . .'

It wasn't until the Yardbirds that you really got a chance to put into practice everything you'd learned. Playing with Jeff was a revelation; you really thought you'd cracked it – for about five minutes. It could have been even better than the Stones – more solos and trading licks than the two-guitar rhythm thing – but Jeff just lacked . . . something. Discipline, they'd call it. But it was more than that. He just had something in him – some devil – that seemed to make him want to . . . mess things up sometimes. It was nuts. He could have been the best but he just didn't seem to care. Not like you. You cared about every last detail, always wanted it to be the best. Which is another reason why you hated working with Mickie Most so much. You'd be in the studio with the Yardbirds, expecting to change the world, and Mickie would treat it like one of your session gigs. 'Next!' he'd say, as soon as you came to the end of a take, without even listening back to it. You told him, 'I've never worked like this in my life,' not even at sessions. And he didn't even look at you, just said, 'Don't worry about it,' and that was it, you went onto the next number.

No wonder Jeff didn't give a shit anymore. It was a drag. This was when you were really getting into the Les Paul Black Beauty, a truly remarkable piece of kit. The sort of thing you'd dreamed of as a kid. You liked it so much the first time you saw it on the wall of the guitar shop in Dean Street you'd traded your Gretsch Chet Atkins for it. That was where the fuzz and the feedback came from, the Black Beauty. You'd actually heard Les himself doing it with his trio on 'It's Been a Long, Long Time'. He'd done it all on that one – not a foot wrong, from the tone to those fantastic introductory chords to the solo – multi-tracking, feedback, it all went back to the Les Paul Trio! And how long ago was that? Bloody amazing, when you thought about it, but then Les was into Reinhardt, wasn't he? So what do you expect? Eric was the first to get all that, when he was with the Bluesbreakers. Got himself one of the first Marshall amps and away he bloody well went! Really stirring stuff . . .

The closest you really got to going where you wanted to after Jeff left the Yardbirds was on 'Glimpses', which was the first time you really started using the violin bow for more than just tricks. They called it your gimmick but using the bow on the guitar was more than just a novelty to you. This was about making music, digging new sounds, as much as anything else you might have been able to do with it. You tried to show the others where it could all go, making up tapes with all these sound-effects on them, which you would play along with, improvising to the sound of the Staten Island Ferry, all these crunching noises and horns. You wanted to have some Hitler speeches on the tapes too but the others said you were going too far. Too far? No such thing. Try telling that to Keith after he's had a few, though. Or Chris, sitting there fiddling with his camera ... But to you, those nights at places like the Fillmore East, making the sky fall during 'Glimpses', that was where it was at, where it could be, where it should be going. Why couldn't the rest of them see that? You talked about using tape recorders that were triggered by light beams, with a go-go dancer doing her thing, making the lights flash and the music take off ... and they just looked at you and shook their heads like you were mad. Wankers. But you knew. One day everyone would be doing stuff like this. Lights and music and dancers. Rituals. Sex. Magic ...

One person blissfully unconcerned with the niceties of songwriting at this point was John Bonham, whose enforced year away from home was beginning to have the anticipated effects. One night during the SIR sessions, he arrived at the Rainbow where he sat at the bar and ordered twenty Black Russians – polishing off half of them in one go. Swivelling on his seat he espied a familiar face, Michelle Myer, long-time associate of producer and LA socialite Kim Fowley. Myer, sitting eating dinner, looked over and smiled. Bonzo did not smile back. Instead, he waded over and punched her in the face, knocking her off her seat. 'Don't ever look at me that way again!' he roared.

The band finally left LA at the end of October, Jimmy insisting they move at once following an unusually thunderous storm that erupted over the Malibu coastline, which he took as a bad omen. On the flight to Munich, where Musicland Studios had been booked for them to complete the album, Bonzo knocked himself out on several large G&Ts, a couple of bottles of white wine and champagne, causing so much disruption the other first-class passengers begged the steward not to wake him when the food was served. When he came to a couple of hours later, he had pissed himself. Shouting for Mick Hinton, his personal roadie, he forced him to stand in front while he changed his pants then made Hinton sit in his urine-drenched seat while Bonzo took Hinton's seat in Economy.

Situated in the basement of the Arabella Hotel, Musicland Studios were bright and modern, sparsely furnished, the accent firmly on the functional. Thin Lizzy had just been there recording overdubs for their *Johnny the Fox* album and the Stones were due in straight after Zeppelin. So tight was the scheduling squeeze, in fact, that the band had exactly eighteen days to work in. No Zeppelin album since their first eight years before had been recorded so quickly but Page was determined to make it work. In the event, he would find himself calling Jagger, begging for more time, a request the Stones' mainman was happy to acquiesce to – up to a point. He could let Jimmy have three extra days, he said. Hardly any time at all, in recording terms, but it was all Page needed to finish the job, laying down all his guitar overdubs in a frantic fourteen-hour session, including at least six for 'Achilles Last Stand', quitting only when his fingers ached so much he could no longer manipulate them properly.

Working round the clock, inside the studio it was permanent midnight, Jimmy staying up for three days at a time, sleeping on the floor of the studio. 'The band did the basic tracks and then went away,' he recalled, 'leaving me and [engineer] Keith Harwood to do all the overdubs. We had a deal between us: whoever woke up first woke up the other one and we'd continue the studio work.' As a result, Page remains inordinately proud of what at the time he initially referred to as simply 'the Munich LP', its final title undecided until the cover had been finalised. 'It was a very, very intense album,' Jimmy told me, 'Robert had had the accident, and we didn't know how he was gonna heal. He was on crutches and singing from a wheelchair.' Or as Plant said at the time, it was 'our stand against everything. Against the elements and chance ...'

However, the chief element aiding Page throughout his long 'intense' nights in the studio was much more prosaic. As Cole would later recall, 'One of our roadies ... pulled a bag of smack out of his coat pocket. "There's a lot of this junk here, and it's good," he said. With his help, I located a local drug connection within walking distance of the studio.' For Page – and soon Bonham and Cole too – heroin was ceasing to become a 'recreational' drug of choice and more of an addiction. For

Cole, the first signs of such occurred within weeks of the album's completion, during a meeting in LA, when Page complained privately to him of unusual aches and pains and a constantly runny nose – classic signs of heroin withdrawal. Then, at the end of the stay, sharing the drive to the airport, as Cole relates in his book, *Stairway to Heaven*, Page turned to him and said, 'Christ sakes, Richard, don't get into this shit.'

'What do you mean?' asked Cole.

'Heroin. I think I'm hooked. It's terrible.'

'Have you tried to stop?'

'I've tried, but I can't. It's a real bastard.'

It was the first open acknowledgement of the rapidly deepening darkness that was to cast its long shadow over the remainder of the band's career, even – some would argue – hastening its end. However, only once during the Munich sessions did the weird momentum Page had created threaten to unravel, when Plant, still in plaster – Bonzo rather unfunnily nicknaming him 'the Leaning Tower of Pisa' – pulled himself up from his wheelchair one afternoon to stretch, lost his balance and fell onto his bad leg, a horrifyingly loud cracking sound filling the room.

'Fuck!' he screamed. 'Not again! Not again!' First to reach him was Page, petrified the singer had broken his leg again. 'I'd never known Jimmy to move so quickly,' Robert later laughingly recalled. 'He was out of the mixing booth and holding me up, fragile as he might be, within a second. He became quite Germanic in his organisation of things and instantly I was rushed off to hospital again in case I'd re-opened the fracture.' So worried was Page that no more work could be done that day. Fortunately, a call later that night confirming no further injury to the singer found the guitarist back in the studio, putting in another all-nighter.

The album was finally finished on the day before Thanksgiving in America. The following morning while Page was still sleeping, a delighted and relieved Plant put an international call through to the Swan Song office in New York to give them the good news, even suggesting they call the album Thanksgiving. A week later the entire band was back on Jersey, where, on 3 December, Bonham and Jones made an impromptu appearance on stage with Norman Hale, resident pianist at local watering hole Behan's Park West. A former member of the Tornados, a week later the whole band joined Hale for a surprise forty-five-minute set at the club, where less than three hundred people watched as the band tore through their 'Eddie Cochran and Little Richard repertoire,' as Plant put it. 'I was sitting on a stool and every time I hit a high note I stood up but not putting any weight on my foot.' By the end of the set, 'I was wiggling the stool past the drums and further out. Once we got going we didn't want to stop.' In Paris three weeks later, celebrating New Year's Day, he took his first steps unaided since the crash five months before. 'One small step for man,' he joked, 'One giant leap for six nights at Madison Square Garden . . .'

January 1976 found the whole band in New York, staying at the Park Lane Hotel on Central Park South. While Page began tinkering again with the mix of the live soundtrack to the long-delayed 'road movie', Plant was hitting the town in the company of Benji Le Fevre and an English bodyguard named David. Although the plaster had now been removed, he still walked with a cane or crutch. Less conspicuously but more worryingly, Bonzo was also intent on getting the most out of his enforced stay in the city. When Deep Purple arrived in town for a show at Nassau Coliseum, a drunken Bonzo walked on in the middle of their set and, grabbing a free mike, announced: 'My name is John Bonham of Led Zeppelin, and I just wanna tell ya that we got a new album comin' out called *Presence* and that it's fucking great!' Then turned to Deep Purple's guitarist: 'And as far as Tommy Bolin is concerned, he can't play for shit . . .'

The album's eventual title, *Presence* – as irritatingly revealed ahead of time by Bonzo – was inspired by the sleeve it came in, a typically incongruous Hipgnosis creation, from an idea Storm Thorgerson, Aubrey Powell and friends Peter Christopherson and George Hardie (who had worked on the first Zeppelin sleeve), were already tinkering with. Reminiscent of the sleeve the same team had come up with the year before for Pink Floyd's *Wish You Were Here* (including images of two suited businessmen shaking hands, one of them on fire; a swimmer front-crawling through sand and others of that ilk), the front of *Presence* featured a photograph of a 'normal' family (Mum, Dad and 2.2 children) seated at a restaurant table. Positioned on the centre of the white tablecloth is not a candle, as might be expected, or some floral arrangement, perhaps, but a twisted black oblong shape mounted on a plinth, dubbed 'The Object' by Hardie and co. In the background to this central image, shot in a studio in Bow Street, London, are photographs from that year's Earl's Court Boat Show. The rest of the gatefold sleeve contains similarly contrived images: beginning with the back of the outer sleeve, where a schoolgirl (modelled by Samantha Giles, previously one of the children on the *Houses of the Holy* sleeve) is seen with her teacher and another pupil at a desk on which stands another image of The Object. Eight more similarly enigmatic images – many taken from the archives of *Life* and *Look* magazines – furnish the inner sleeve, while the bag containing the vinyl carried unvarnished images of The Object on its own.

Later copyrighted by Swan Song, the object in question was a twelve-inch black obelisk, designed by Hardie as 'a black hole' then completed by model maker Crispin Mellor. It was nicknamed 'the present', recalled Hardie, as 'a play on the fact that the actual object, a hole in fact, wasn't present at all, but absent'. Storm Thorgerson, who had first met Hardie while the pair were studying at London's Royal College of Art, described 'contaminating' the deliberately dated images with what he describes as 'the black obsessional object', which he maintained 'stands as being as powerful as one's imagination cares it to be ... we felt Zeppelin could rightfully feel the same way about themselves in the world of rock music.' According to Page: 'They came up with "the object" and wanted to call [the album] Obelisk. I held out for Presence. You think about more than just a symbol that way.' And of course, the acknowledgement of a 'presence' had more occult resonance than a mere 'object'. Unlike their previous two albums, however, this time they did allow for the band's name and album title to adorn the sleeve, albeit embossed within the white sleeve, similar to the Beatles' *White Album*. (The original UK shipment added a shrink-wrapped outer package, with title and band name in black with a red underlined border. In the US, the shrink-wrap also included a track-listing.)

To launch the album, Swan Song had a thousand copies of the obelisk made which they planned to place simultaneously outside a wide range of iconic buildings across the globe, including the White House, the Houses of Parliament and 10 Downing Street – again, not dissimilar to how Pink Floyd would a year later launch their *Animals* album by floating a giant pig over London's Battersea Power Station, another typically incongruous image taken from the

Hipgnosis-designed sleeve. But the idea was cancelled when *Sounds* magazine got wind and leaked the news. Instead, models of The Object were eventually gifted to various favoured journalists, DJs and other media people, and are now highly collectable artefacts. (Mancunian comic rockers Albertos Y Los Trios Paranoias later spoofed the 'object' in press adverts for their debut album.)

When *Presence* was released on 31 March 1976, it was another instant, no. 1 hit, going gold in the UK, platinum in the US, on advance sales alone, becoming the fastest-selling album in the Atlantic group's history. Reviews were generally good, too – Jonh Ingham in *Sounds* called it 'unadulterated rock and roll' and described 'Achilles Last Stand' as the song to 'succeed "Stairway To Heaven".' While Stephen Davis, in *Rolling Stone*, said it confirmed Zeppelin as 'heavy-metal champions of the known universe'. Adding the caveat: 'Give an Englishman 50,000 watts, a chartered jet, a little cocaine and some groupies and he thinks he's a god. It's getting to be an old story . . .' A more piercingly accurate comment than even the writer probably knew.

But sales soon tailed off, just as they had for *Led Zeppelin III* and *Houses of the Holy*, initial excitement failing to translate into wider general interest amongst non-partisan record buyers as what was correctly perceived as the album's generally depressing ambience became known. Even the more uplifting 'Candy Store Rock', released as a single in the US that summer, backed with 'Royal Orleans', failed to make any impression on the charts. Undeterred, Page and Grant dismissed the lack of a strong following sales wind for the album as a side-effect of the band's inability to promote it with a world tour. But the fact is, *Presence* remains one of Zeppelin's least satisfying musical confections; the story behind it of more lasting interest than the often rather turgid music that resulted, despite the fact that both Page and Plant regarded it as a personal triumph. 'Against the odds, sitting in a fucking chair, pushed everywhere for months and months, we were still able to look the devil in the eye and say, "We're as strong as you and stronger, and we should not only write, we should record",' Plant told a reporter from *Creem*. 'I took a very good, close scrutiny of myself, and transcended the death vibe, and now I'm here again, and it's mad city again.' Page's affection for *Presence* was more to do with fond reminiscences of the nights he spent alone with just Harwood for company, doodling away to his stoned heart's desire, than with the end product in itself. He was also doubtless thrilled that the end result had cost so little, certainly compared to all previous albums bar their first, and yet yielded so much – over the first few weeks of its bizarre half-life, anyway.

Not that Zeppelin's overall popularity was particularly affected. Promoters, eager to tempt the band back onto the road, told Grant that demand for Zeppelin tickets would be greater than ever – if and when the band decided they were able to return. In a presidential election year in America, the band also found itself in the invidious position of being publicly supported by both sides of the political divide, beginning with incumbent President Ford's daughter Susan announcing on the Dick Cavett talk show that Led Zeppelin was her favourite group. Not to be outdone, Democratic presidential nominee Jimmy Carter then reminisced publicly about listening to Zeppelin records during all-night sessions as governor of Georgia.

With time on their hands and interest in *Presence* quickly flagging, attention turned instead to the release of the movie, now provisionally titled *The Song Remains The Same*, and soundtrack album. Not that there was much for them to do as they waited for the editing process to be completed, so while Plant continued his physical rehabilitation in the company of Maureen and the kids, and Jones used the time to quietly forget about Zeppelin as he also attempted to make up for lost time with his family, Page and Bonham were left to get up to their by now all too usual tricks.

Bonzo had spent most of the summer in a rented château in the south of France with Pat and the children. Having sent them back to England with Matthew, his chauffeur, in time for the new school term to begin, he flew to Monte Carlo with Mick Hinton and his girlfriend, then had his own 'girlfriend' flown in from LA, the party also joined by Richard Cole. One night the gang was at Jimmy's, an expensive Monte Carlo nightclub. Drunk and stoned as usual, Bonzo lost his temper – as usual – with Hinton and pulled a gun on him. 'It was only a gas gun,' Cole recalled, but in a venue frequented by millionaire Arabs, Greeks, Corsican gangsters and members of the Italian Mafia – most of them surrounded by heavies armed with real guns – this was a deeply unwise move. Cole tried to intervene but Bonzo rounded on him, too. 'Shut up, you cunt, or I'll do you as well!' At which point Cole punched him in the face, knocking the drummer out of his seat and breaking his nose in the process. As the gun clattered to the floor Cole told Hinton's girlfriend to 'hide it, get rid of it' before the police arrived, which they duly did, arresting all three men who spent the next few hours in custody. Fortunately, recalled Cole, the police were so intent on finding the missing gun they overlooked the cocaine Bonzo and Cole had in their pockets.

Page, meanwhile, was locked up in his own dispute, concerning his much-touted soundtrack music to Kenneth Anger's *Lucifer Rising* film project. Anger, who had been working on editing down seventeen hours' worth of film he had so far shot into a manageable length, had spent the late spring and early summer working out of the basement of the Tower House, where Page had furnished him with the expensive editing equipment he needed to complete the job. Intrigued, Peter Grant even offered to co-finance the film when it was ready for release.

However, things came to a bad end when Anger was kicked out one evening, he said, by Charlotte Martin, who felt he was beginning to 'take over' the place, inviting people around she didn't know. Already frustrated and dismayed by what he saw as Page's flagging interest in the project, failing to deliver more than the twenty-five minutes or so of music he had initially come up with, despite persistent pleas from the director, Anger immediately went public with his grievances, announcing he had 'fired' Page from the project and claiming he had been locked out of the house, unable to collect his belongings, chief amongst them, besides the unfinished film, his cherished 'crown of Lucifer', studded with rhinestones from a dress once worn by Mae West.

Questioned for details on the fallout, Anger responded that the way Page had been behaving was 'totally contradictory to the teachings of Aleister Crowley and totally contradictory to the ethos of the film. Lucifer is the angel of light and beauty. But the vibes that come off Jimmy are totally alien to that – and to human contact. It's like a bleak lunar landscape. By comparison, Lucifer is like a field full of beautiful flowers.' Encouraged, he went further, voicing the opinion, so far unexpressed but increasingly held by those longstanding fans dis-appointed – at best confused – by Zeppelin's latest offering. 'I'm beginning to think Jimmy's dried up as a musician. He's got no themes, no inspiration and no melodies to offer. I'm sure he doesn't have another "Stairway to Heaven", which is his most Luciferian song.

Presence was very much a downer album.' He added, knowingly: 'On the one hand he's very into enterprise and hard work. But on the other hand he has this problem dragging him down. He's been acting like Jekyll and Hyde ...' Just in case anyone was left in any doubt as to what he was referring, Anger described Page as having 'an affair with the White Lady' – a clear reference to heroin.

Anger continued to badmouth Page at every opportunity. Trying to communicate with Page was like 'rapping on inch-thick plate glass,' he said. He had 'turned into an undisciplined, rich dilettante, at least as far as magic and any serious belief in Aleister Crowley's work was concerned.' A prime example of 'magic gone haywire, half understood, not under will'.

For the record, Jimmy now claims the row with Anger was sparked not by Charlotte but by his housekeeper at the Tower House discovering him 'giving some people a guided tour'. An argument ensued to which 'Kenneth took umbrage'. When Anger went public, 'the next thing I knew I started getting all this hate mail directed at [Charlotte] and myself'. More worryingly, the hate mail actually took the form of a 'curse' Anger now directed at both Page and Martin. 'He was a multi-millionaire miser,' a still furious Anger recalled in 2005. 'He and Charlotte, they had so many servants, yet they would never offer me a cup of tea or a sandwich. Which is such a mistake on their part because I put the curse of King Midas on them. If you're greedy and just amass gold you'll get an illness. So I turned her and Jimmy Page into statues of gold.'

'It was quite pathetic actually,' said Page, shrugging off any suggestion that Anger's actions may actually have exerted any power over him, explaining that the 'curse' mainly took the form of newspaper cuttings underlined in red ink. 'I did think about returning all his possessions in a hearse, but then I thought that might be a tad dramatic. Now I almost see it as being a bit sad. This [*Lucifer Rising*] was going to be a masterpiece, but he didn't manage to pull it off. All that remains now is the myth.'

Naturally, it's always been assumed that the curse Kenneth Anger placed on Jimmy Page didn't work. Yet it's interesting to note, in retrospect, how from that point on it was practically all downhill for Page and Zeppelin. Indeed, it could be argued that the 'curse of King Midas' – a metaphor for illness, or impotence, despite enormous wealth or fame – describes exactly what lay in store for both Page and Zeppelin over the next five years. It might even be said that the writing was now on the wall – underlined in red ink.

14
Caesar's Chariot

Sometimes when you looked back you simply couldn't get your head round it. You'd given yourself until you were twenty. You told everybody if you hadn't made it by then, you'd knock it on the head, find a proper job. But when the time came you weren't ready to quit. It was a close run thing, though - when Bonzo buggered off to Tim Rose's band you knew he wouldn't be back. Neither would you for forty quid a week. That was better than you were making on the building site. It nearly was you, too, when Alexis Korner stuck his head round the door at the Speakeasy gig. You hadn't worried about Bonzo or the others then, droning away about the blues to your new best mate, Alexis. When he suggested doing a couple of gigs together, just the two of you and his pianist Steve Miller, you nearly bit his arm off. When he suggested making an LP together you tried playing it cool but you couldn't contain yourself. 'This is it,' you told Maureen. 'Alexis wants me to go to London and do some stuff in the studio with him.' And off you went, sleeping on the couch at his flat in Queensway. 'Goodnight, Robert,' he'd say in that voice. 'Oh, by the way, it's the same couch that Muddy used to sleep on when he stayed here. And I don't know if we've changed the toilet bowl since Buddy Guy was here ...' Good scenes, hanging out, smoking dope and acting like this was nothing. Never did get round to doing the LP but you did record a couple of tracks together: 'Operator' and 'Steal Away'. Really good, you know, if you knew anything about the blues ...

You said goodbye and promised to keep in touch but never did, of course. No-one in the music biz ever did. Ships in the night, man ... Back in Brum, things went from bad to worse with the Band of Joy, you and Bonzo always scheming, trying to drum up cash. Lying to the others about how much you were getting paid so you could keep a bit back for yourselves. Pat and Maureen looking at you sitting there smoking and divvying it all *up, a right pair. 'We were like musical second-hand car dealers,' you'd tell the author, years later, still laughing.*

There was you, Bonzo, Kevin Gammond on guitar, Chris Brown on organ and Paul Lockey on bass. One of the greatest bands ever to come out of the Midlands, everyone said so, and you couldn't get a bloody deal. The tapes did get you a few tasty gigs here and there, opening for Fairport Convention, Ten Years After, Spooky Tooth, Mick Farren and the Social Deviants ... You took the music seriously, kind of psychedelic leaning heavily on West Coast stuff mixed with blues, the plan to take it on and keep extending the music so that it became almost just one long piece of music, just moving through various styles. Whether the world was ready for something like that yet, you weren't sure, you just knew it was the right way to go. The rest of the time, though, you had a right laugh. One time at Exeter University, supporting Mick Farren's lot, you'd both been on the cider and were so drunk Bonzo decided to drum standing up. The others hated it but you had to laugh. Then in the van coming back he had a flaming row with Kevin about his time-keeping. Neither of them knew what they were on about. Bonzo was out of his face and Kevin was playing so fast the pair of them had invented their own time-signatures. In the end, Kevin went bonkers and said he was leaving the band, made the van stop while he got out. You ended up doing the next gig in Scotland – the Victoria Hall, in Selkirk, if you please – with Paul playing lead guitar and Chris doing the bass with his left hand on the keyboard. Then it was your turn to have a row with Bonzo. Then got so drunk you fell asleep in a broom cupboard ...

It wasn't long after that you supported Tim Rose, which is how he heard Bonzo. You were furious when he said he was leaving but, fair play, he'd said, 'Look, I've got to go. We're broke. I've got a kid to support', and you knew where he was coming from even if you didn't agree with it. You knew it would be the end of the Band of Joy too and it was. That was in the spring and by the summer of '68, the summer of love long gone, you were back on the Ma Reagan circuit, working with the Irish navvies, digging up West Bromwich High Street by day and singing with Hobstweedle at the weekend, smiling and poncing about and making like everything was all going to plan but it fucking wasn't, none of it. Now and again something would crop up. Tony Secunda, the Move's manager, had asked you down to audition for his new label, Regal-Zonophone, but nothing came of it. Then there was talk of your old mucker Nev Holder making you second *vocalist of the 'N Betweens. But that was just the others having a go, they knew Noddy – as he was now called – preferred to go it alone at the mike.*

Your mum and dad had started up again now too, muttering to Maureen that it wasn't too late for you to resume your 'promising career' in chartered accountancy. You could feel the walls closing in. You were nearly twenty and you'd always said you'd knock it on the head if you hadn't made it by then and fucking hell you hadn't made it but you didn't want to knock it on the head, not to be a bloody accountant. You'd lie in bed some nights and you wouldn't be able to sleep. Fuck me, what were you going to do . . . ?

Then one day you got the telegram. You'd never received a telegram before, wondered what it might be about, thought maybe it was bad news, some bloody thing from your past catching up with you, something you'd done with Bonzo when you were out of it perhaps, something you couldn't even remember you were so stoned . . .

It was from someone called Peter Grant asking if you were interested in joining the New Yardbirds, said Terry Reid had put your name forward. You thought it was a joke, someone pulling your leg. You'd never heard of Peter Grant, didn't know anything about the Yardbirds, new or old, but you did know Terry Reid, who the Band of Joy had opened for once at the Boston Gilderdrome. Then they came up and you met Jimmy, who you'd never heard of either. But it seemed like they meant it, like something was going on. After so long, though, it just didn't seem real. You didn't even know if you really liked the Yardbirds. Didn't even know who Jimmy Page was. You'd heard of Clapton, obviously, and Beck, but not this bloke. But the money on offer seemed real all right.

Later on, your mate Austin Griffiths from the Stringbeats told a reporter: 'He was open-mouthed. "The Yardbirds want me", was all he managed to say.' It was true. The more you thought about it, the less you could believe it was happening to you. A few months later, after those first shows in Scandinavia and the band had changed its name, you were in a pub in Worcestershire one night, taking a piss, half cut, staring at the grubby white wall in front of you. When you'd zipped up, you took out a biro and wrote on the wall: ROBERT PLANT OF LED ZEPPELIN. Just to see what it looked like. Then you staggered back to the bar and ordered another round for everybody and forgot about it. A few weeks later, though, they told you, when someone pointed out to the landlord what he had on the wall of his bogs, he took some Sellotape and sealed it over the words. For posterity, he said . . .

*

With the swift passing of interest in the *Presence* album and still unable to tour, the latter half of 1976 was given over to finally releasing *The Song Remains The Same*, begun more than three years before. Backed with the simultaneous release of a double live 'soundtrack' album, the logic was simple: if Zeppelin couldn't go to the people, the film at least would enable the people to go to Zeppelin.

However, things did not get off to a promising start when Ahmet Ertegun dozed off during a private screening of the film for Atlantic Records' executives. Reactions elsewhere were of a similarly somnambulistic nature. Premiered in New York on 20 October 1976, where guests included Mick Jagger and Linda Ronstadt, critics unanimously panned it. It was the same two weeks later in Britain, where there were two premieres: in Birmingham and London. Arriving on screens just as the Sex Pistols were releasing their cataclysmic debut single 'Anarchy in the UK' – thus signalling the start of punk rock, a new musical 'movement' intrinsically antithetical to groups like Zeppelin – its timing could not have been worse. Not only did the film, with its mishmash of disjointed backstage scenes (usually involving Grant haranguing pirate merchandise sellers for 'ripping off Led Zeppelin' or some other unpardonable offence), live footage (of some uneven yet occasionally intoxicating performances) and 'fantasy sequences' (roundly condemned as the self-indulgences of a band clearly out of touch with reality) make Led Zeppelin seem dated, it made them one of the first major casualties of punk's ground-zero approach. On British television, Pistols singer Johnny Rotten claimed he'd 'fallen asleep' while watching the film, calling the band 'dinosaurs'. Sensing a trend, Paul Simonon of The Clash claimed, 'I don't have to hear Led Zeppelin. Just looking at their record covers makes me want to be sick.' More damagingly for the film's long-term prospects, in the US *Rolling Stone* critic Dave Marsh described it as 'a tribute to their rapaciousness and inconsideration. While Led Zeppelin's music remains worthy of respect (even if their best songs are behind them) their sense of themselves merits only contempt.'

Even the accompanying double live album came in for a drubbing, compared unfavourably to the many excellent Zeppelin bootlegs that already existed. As ever, Page staunchly defended the band against such criticism, insisting he considered the film 'successful, in so much as it is a frozen celluloid statement of an evening'. He did concede, however, that the soundtrack album 'wasn't necessarily the best live material we had but it was the live material that went with the footage so it had to be used. So, you know, it wasn't like A Magic Night. But it wasn't a poor night. It was an honest sort of mediocre night.'

Bonzo had his own way of dealing with things, too. When his ten-year-old son, Jason, got up and played drums at the after-show party for the premiere in Birmingham, John basked proudly in the spontaneous applause the boy's performance aroused. When the resident club DJ cut him short, though, by joking, 'If you think you're so good, let's hear you play this!' and put Sandy Nelson's 'Let There Be Drums' on the turntable, Bonham's eyes glazed over with fury, and he marched over and punched him in the face. According to onlooker David Hadley, the hapless DJ was then 'thrown into the canal' by a couple of 'heavy-looking blokes'.

Peter Grant was equally merciless when dealing with an errant photographer at the London premiere in Covent Garden, where guests included Paul and Linda McCartney, Lynsey De Paul, Lionel Bart and Joe Strummer. The photographer had been one of many snapping guests, Page recalled, 'and Peter said, "What are you doing there? Flying a kite or something?" Then somebody picked the guy up and threw him from the first floor balcony onto a car! Meanwhile, we were in there, trying to pull birds – heaven knows what else – and this sort of thing was going on, on the periphery.'

When *Sounds* magazine ran a jokey piece about the party in their gossip column, 'Jaws', including a picture of an elderly woman busker with a caption making punning reference to Peter Grant's mother, Grant predictably failed to see the funny side, not least because his real mother had recently died after a serious illness. Rather than instruct the band's PR to express his disquiet, typically, he decided to take matters into his own hands, phoning the editor, Alan Lewis, late one evening. It was the first serious blow in what would become an increasingly fractious relationship between the band and what had until then been one of its more reliable supporters in the British media.

Alan Lewis takes up the story: 'We used to often work late in those days but I was sitting on my own in the *Sounds* office this particular night, about nine or ten o'clock, when the phone rang and this growly voice said something like: "Is that the editor?" Yes. "That article in your paper today about Led Zeppelin, do you know my mum?" No. "Well, it's Peter Grant here, you know who I am." At which point, I realised what this was about and began to rehearse an apology in my head. But before I could speak he said: "Have you seen the film?" I said no. "Well", he said, "keep an eye on your door!" and hung up. I realised later he was alluding to the gangster sequence where he and his henchmen shoot up a room full of people. Of course, like most music papers back then, *Sounds* was quite outspoken and used to getting threats from record companies over something one of the writers had said. But this was of a different order. I'm not saying I lost sleep over it but I knew of Grant's reputation – everybody did – and I must admit there were quite a few occasions after that when I was alone in the *Sounds* office late at night, wondering if the door was going to burst open at any minute.'

The poor overall reaction to *The Song Remains The Same* meant the movie did only moderately well at the box office before quickly disappearing, not seen again outside cheap drive-ins in the American south or occasional late-night showings in the UK. Page and Grant took it all badly. Where in the past they had been able to shrug off poor reviews by merely pointing to the unprecedented level of success the band enjoyed, with the relative failure of the album, too – the Zeppelin fan-base huge enough to send it platinum in the US and gold in Britain but again, like *Presence*, unable to translate that partisanship into a wider interest from a music-buying market largely unimpressed by such second-rate fare – this was much harder to shrug off; their second relative failure in a row.

By now, Zeppelin appeared to be almost permanently at war with everybody, even the people they had made the movie with. So dis-illusioned had Peter Clifton become, he later described the band as 'the rudest, most arrogant people I ever encountered in my twenty-five years of filming music'. While Joe Massot, deemed a 'traitor' by Grant after he reacted to his firing from the project by describing the band in the press as 'bloody difficult, if not impossible', was forced to buy a public ticket to the New York showing of the movie, in spite of the fact that it consisted almost entirely of footage he had directed.

Most vociferous in their putdowns of Led Zeppelin were the new breed of punk rock bands, now using them for target practice in the press, despite Jimmy and Robert, at least, making apparently friendly overtures by turning up one night at the Roxy, then London's number one punk club, to see The Damned, who Jimmy thought were 'fantastic ... I was absolutely amazed by the power that was coming out of them' and whose Bonham-like drummer, Rat Scabies, he would later become pals with. Robert was also intrigued by the new music, so alien to the more technically adept Zeppelin mien, yet not so far removed from the original Fifties-style rock'n'roll he'd grown up on.

None of which impressed the leading lights of the punk movement one jot. 'When Robert Plant went down [to the Roxy] he had about five heavies with him, half the band and others,' sneered Johnny Rotten in *ZigZag*. 'There were about twenty of them. They like took a corner, posing and hurling abuse at people that walked by as if they were something special. Now if I go somewhere I either go on my own or with a couple of mates. I don't need all that heavy stuff.' He concluded: 'People shouldn't worship stars like Robert Plant ... These superstars are totally detached from reality. I've no doubt it's very difficult to keep in touch with reality once you get to that stage, but you should at least try. They don't seem to try at all. They let it overtake them.'

To his credit, though, Plant was the first to agree. 'Those accusations of remoteness, of playing blind, of having no idea about people or circumstances or reality, of having no idea about what we were talking about or what we were feeling, of being deep and meaningless and having vapid thoughts – there was a lot of substance in what was being said. People were quite right to say all that. It hurt at the time but I'd have to plead guilty.' Jonesy, however, was having none of it. He didn't agree with punk's suggestion that the band was verging on obsolescence, nor did he feel kindly towards the music of punk. His response, to largely ignore it: 'I must say I didn't like punk at first. It just sounded loud and horrible ... For us it was a case of just carrying on regardless.'

The end of 1976 found the band, Page in particular, doing exactly that, yet labouring under heavy manners. Down about the poor reaction to the band movie, which he could no longer even bring himself to watch, he was even more down, though refused to admit it, about the fallout with Kenneth Anger over his cherished soundtrack to *Lucifer Rising*. He now had to contend with evicting squatters from the Tower House: a bizarre couple, once friends, now no longer, who had taken to masquerading as he and Charlotte.

In January 1977, Jimmy finally got the news he'd been waiting for when Robert confirmed that he was ready to go back on the road – boasting of building up his leg strength by joining in on training sessions with his beloved Wolverhampton Wanderers football team. An equally delighted Grant began booking what would be their biggest US tour yet: 51 dates over a four-and-a-half month period, divided into three legs, which would see an estimated 1.3 million Zep fans snapping up tickets. A mix of multiple nights at arenas – including six nights at Madison Square Garden in New York and six nights at the Forum in LA, and huge outdoor stadiums in Chicago, Tampa, Oakland, Michigan – where they would set another attendance record at the Pontiac Silverdome (for over 76,000 fans, beating the previous best for a show there by The Who in December 1975) and single performance fee ($792,361) – climaxing at the JFK Stadium in Philadelphia where more than 95,000 people had bought tickets the day they went on sale. With the tour itinerary undergoing no less than six revisions before he was finally happy, this was to be the comeback to end all comebacks, Grant decided. It would be that, all right, though not for the reasons a relieved Jimmy and G envisaged as they laid plans and snorted coke together at Manticore, the west London rehearsal studio they had rented from Emerson, Lake and Palmer.

This would be Led Zeppelin out to prove themselves again, they decided: to the punks who disowned them, to the press who never lost an opportunity to put them down, to the fans that had stuck by them through the travails of the past two years, but most of all to themselves, their reward for hanging on in there, against the odds, as they saw it, before coming out the other side, more together than ever before, they decided. There were some marked differences, however, between the band that had bowed out in such splendour at Earl's Court in 1975 and the one about to reappear, as though nothing had happened, in 1977. First off, there was the music. While the set resembled the one of '75, there were some notable absences, such as 'Dazed and Confused' – though not the violin bow showcase, Jimmy merely taking a solo spot, coaxing all manner of eerie and grating effects from his green-lit Les Paul. Robert had also wanted to drop 'In My Time Of Dying', seeing it as one temptation of fate too many in the lead up to his and Maureen's accident, still as fresh in their minds as though it were yesterday. But he changed his mind halfway through the tour. And there were to be only two new songs from *Presence*: 'Achilles Last Stand' and 'Nobody's Fault but Mine'; almost an admission that the rest of the material on the album simply didn't measure up to the band's past. On the plus side, however, Jones unveiled his new triple-necked guitar, an exotic-looking instrument, built for him by guitar tech Andy Manson, which allowed him to play bass and rhythm guitar *and* help sustain the melody on numbers like 'Ten Years Gone' – performed live for the first time on this tour – emulating the multi-tracked guitars of the recording while enabling Page to take off in improvised flights of fancy on the lead. 'Rock And Roll' was also dropped as set opener, replaced by 'The Song Remains The Same', and the sit-down acoustic set was reintroduced to the American show for the first time since 1972. 'A unanimous group decision that Jimmy and I made,' joked Robert, who in reality needed the break to rest his still-damaged ankle and leg. There was also a new arrangement of 'The Battle of Evermore', with Jonesy singing the Sandy Denny parts. 'I'll never know how I agreed to that,' Jones later admitted. 'It was a case of: "Oh, Jonesy will do it", which happened quite a lot.' Page's old Yardbirds showcase 'White Summer' was also reinstated as a prelude to 'Kashmir', turning the entire set-piece into a twenty-minute epic.

The light show was much the same as before, though for the stadium shows there would now be the addition, as at Earl's Court, of the Ephidor video screens erected either side of the stage. The band's mode of transport also changed: the Starship had been grounded after one of its engines nearly came off mid-flight, so without telling the band why – lest it freak out its already jumpy passengers – Cole arranged for the hire of the private 707 owned by Caesar's Palace in Las Vegas, normally used to jet in high-rollers to the city's most lustrous hotel-casino. Named Caesar's Chariot, it had all the comforts of the Starship, with only one exception: no more Thomas organ. Nobody minded. The days of anyone from the band tinkling the ivories for the edification of whatever guests had been 'lucky' enough to find themselves on board their plane were long over. There were still many recreational activities to be enjoyed aboard Zeppelin's private plane, but no longer any half so innocent.

Other changes to the set-up would have more far-reaching consequences, notably the hiring of several new 'assistants'. Everyone would have one: Jimmy's would be his chauffeur and butler Rick

Hobbs; Robert's the former Maggie Bell roadie, Dennis Sheehan; John Paul's a qualified pharmacist and rugby player named Dave Northover; Bonzo's the rough-tough Rex King. Even Richard Cole now had a full-time second-in-command: Mitchell Fix, originally a member of the New York Swan Song team. The most noted of the new 'assistants', however, was Peter Grant's: a bit-part film actor – known for typecast hard-man roles in *Get Carter* and *Performance* – and real-life strong-arm merchant named John Bindon. Thirty-four-year-old 'Johnny' Bindon was a nasty piece of work who had been hovering on the fringes of the Zeppelin operation for some time; a shoot-first-don't-even-bother-asking-questions-later London 'face' who counted among his friends the Kray twins and Princess Margaret, and who would serve several prison sentences before being accused in 1979 of murdering another underworld enforcer named John Darke in a club brawl. Both menacingly intimidating and, apparently, hilariously funny, depending on his mood, Bindon's favourite party trick was to balance as many as six half-pint mugs on his erect penis. Bankrupt at the time of being hired by Grant, the only thing that assuaged his violent temper was the vast amounts of marijuana he smoked. With both Page and Plant now receiving death threats before the tour had even begun, G had decided he needed someone like Bindon along for if and when things got 'rough'. The trouble was, with someone like Bindon, things were likely to get rough sooner rather than later. As Alan Callan would observe, 'He certainly wasn't hired for his dinner conversation. He was Robert's bullet-proof vest. I believe Bindon would have actually taken a bullet for him.'

Speaking years later to Dave Lewis, Grant admitted that hiring people like Bindon was not, on reflection, a good idea. But as he said, 'It was hard for me really because I had to leave the kids and my divorce was starting. John Bonham was also uptight that year and we took Rex out to be his whipping boy.' Bindon was 'a friend of Richard's . . . an aide who ended up looking after Jimmy quite a lot.' He added: 'Jimmy's health was suffering. There were definite drug problems with one or two people, including myself.'

The immediate effect of so many 'cooks' on board the touring ship, Cole would later write, was 'multiple divisions . . . cliques were formed and a very tight organisation became fragmented'. Sometimes it was 'as though we were staying at different hotels from each other, not just down the hall'. Even when they did socialise 'streaks of hostility or maliciousness' poisoned each encounter. Even the once unstoppable Grant became more and more withdrawn, staying in his hotel room, snorting coke, issuing orders via Bindon or Cole. When the NME ran a gossip item claiming he had become a virtual recluse on tour, he flew off the handle yet again, insisting the paper print a hasty apology on pain of legal action – or worse.

The soft kernel at the centre of this increasingly hard outer shell was Plant himself. Able to walk again without a cane, his right foot was still swollen, the leg a long way from full recovery; he still had to take painkillers every day just to cope with normal activities. He was so nervous that the start of the tour – originally scheduled to kick off with a date in Fort Worth on 27 February – had to be put back, the official reason given as 'laryngitis'. How would he cope, he wondered, having to whirl and twirl and sashay about the stage as he had done in the past, the unremitting glare of the spotlight following his every move? Speaking just two days after the start of the tour in April, at the Memorial Center in Dallas, he confessed: 'I was petrified. For the ten minutes before I walked up those stage steps, I was cold with fright. Supposing I couldn't move around the stage properly because my right foot is permanently enlarged now? It was killing for the first two gigs. I had to be virtually carried back on one foot.'

Other nights on the tour, Plant could be seen visibly wincing in pain as he forgot himself momentarily and attempted a sudden twist or turn. Then there were the moments when he simply seemed lost, unable to project the kind of warmth and joie-de-vivre that had always been his stock in trade as a frontman. Conscious of the struggle the singer was going through, Page did his best to compensate, adding a little more physical exuberance to his own performance – at least on those nights when he wasn't so out of his head on cocaine and heroin that he began to seriously struggle himself. For this US tour would find Jimmy Page at his darkest. Forget Sid Vicious, for sheer cadaverous chic the Page of 1977 would take some beating: now sporting an all-white version of the famous dragon suit most nights, whip-thin, pinned pupils masked behind permanent-midnight sunglasses. He was now going three or four nights without sleep, and boasting of living on a liquid-only diet. 'I prefer to eat liquid food,' he explained with a stoned half-smile. 'Something like a banana daiquiri, which I can put powdered vitamin in. I'm not really into solid foods very much [but] I know I'll never turn down some alcohol, so a banana daiquiri, with all the food protein, is the answer.' To aide such special requirements, once again they'd hired their own doctor. A graduate of Harvard, he was a rock veteran whose first tour had been the notoriously out-of-control 1972 US trek by the Rolling Stones, as immortalised in the cult film, *Cocksucker Blues*. Jimmy vehemently denied the doctor was just there to provide the band with legal access to drugs. 'We had a doctor to look after all of us, period. It was a bloody long tour,' he later told writer Chris Salewicz. He also denied rumours that he was wheeled around between gigs in a wheelchair. 'I may have done that for a laugh – not seriously. No, no. That wasn't happening at all.'

The fact that such rumours did the rounds at all demonstrated how low Zeppelin's reputation had now sunk. During their four-night run at the gigantic Chicago Stadium, Page came on decked out in a decidedly punk SS Stormtrooper's cap, his long spider's legs disappearing into a pair of shiny black leather jackboots; no longer interested in concealing the darkness which he said had found him, not the other way around. On the third night, the show had to be abandoned halfway through 'Ten Years Gone' when Jimmy came down with 'stomach cramps', as the official explanation had it. Or 'technical difficulties' as another official explanation put it. In reality, according to one who was there but asks not to be named here, the show had to be called off because Page 'was so out of it he was trying to play twin-neck on the wrong guitar.' (Indeed, there is an infamous bootleg of the show called *China White* that appears to back this claim up. His playing, shaky throughout, simply stops halfway through 'Ten Years Gone'. 'Jimmy has got a bout of gastroenteritis,' Robert, doing his best to cover, tells the audience, 'which isn't helped by firecrackers, so we're gonna take a five-minute break'. They never came back out.) Another occasion on stage, 'he was so gone he couldn't even pull his own trousers up'. During the acoustic section of the next show he became so absorbed he leapt out of his chair towards the end of one song – unplugging his guitar in the process.

Speaking the next day to a writer from *Circus* magazine, Page blamed his inability to complete the show on 'food poisoning'; a mystery ailment, indeed, considering he wasn't actually eating any food at that point. He was dismissive about rumours that it was to be the band's last tour. 'Led Zeppelin is a stag party that never ends,' he declared unconvincingly. 'This is no last tour. It would be a criminal act to break up this band.' Perhaps, but his actions were now taking him perilously close to doing just that. As Dave Dickson points out: 'A rock star of the magnitude Page was by then, they live in a little bubble, there is no contact with reality. And there's so much pressure on you, the head guy of the biggest band in the world, if you find a release by doing heroin, because that just takes you away to some alternative place where no one can touch you, then you're gonna do it. The thing is, like Crowley discovered, it is eventually going to destroy you, because you become its slave. The heroin stops working for you and you start working for it.'

Page, however, remains almost blissfully unrepentant. Asked by Nick Kent in 2003 whether he regretted 'getting so involved in heroin and cocaine', he shrugged. 'I don't regret it at all because when we needed to be really focused, I was really focused. That's it ... You've got to be on top of it.' Clearly, though, there were exceptions to the rule and in 1977 they were becoming more frequent. A freak storm at Chicago's O'Hare Airport delayed the take-off of Caesar's Chariot. As a result, the next night's performance at the Minneapolis Sports arena was delayed by more than an hour. After the show, Jimmy got into an argument with the doctor when a phial of Quaaludes went missing from his black bag. When the doc cornered him in a bathroom about the missing drugs, Page was outraged. 'Accusing me!' he cried. 'Who the fuck does he think is paying his salary?'

American writer Jaan Uhelszki, who profiled the first leg of the tour for *Creem*, did his best to put a positive, if somewhat sceptical spin on things, quoting one unnamed source as follows: 'It was about 5:30 am, and I had finally managed to sneak away from all the carousing and carnage of the past 48 hours, and had successfully thwarted Bonzo from breaking down my door or dousing me with a wastebasket full of what I hoped was water. Bonzo was entertaining himself by going from room to room with a broken bedpost slung over one shoulder, demolishing as many rooms of Swingle's Celebrity Hotel in as little time as possible.' There was also a 'chilly' meeting with Page, who 'sauntered unsteadily into the room on his obscenely thin legs ... dressed in his regalia of the night before, which caused a passer-by in the hotel lobby to remark to her companion, "If that's not a rock star, he's a flaming wonder!" ' Travelling aboard Caesar's Chariot was more fun, though; the doctor 'threading his way through the cabin, passing out pre-"game" vitamins to all occupants of said cabin, regardless of whether you're one of the "players" or not.'

Cornering Plant to enquire where the band went from here, the singer answered sardonically: 'There are two paths you can take ...' When the writer corrected him: 'There are two paths you can go by, but in the long run, there's still time to change the road you're on,' Plant is taken aback enough to attempt a proper answer for once. 'I don't know,' he admitted, then added prophetically: 'I think it's an extension of what I'm doing but I don't think I'll be surrounded by so much hysteria. I think I will go to Kashmir one day, when some great change hits me and I have to really go away and think about my future as a man rather than a prancing boy.' A 'great change', though he didn't know it yet, sitting on Caesar's Chariot awaiting the next touchdown, was fast approaching.

In truth, there was a heavy atmosphere pervading all the shows now; a cold, black cloud that hung over the band even when they weren't on stage. Even the audience was starting to act up. At the next show, in St Paul, twenty-four fans were arrested for disorderly conduct as hundreds of ticketless fans tried to crash through the gates. There was a repeat performance five nights later at the Cincinnati Riverfront Coliseum, when over a thousand apparently crazed fans simply tried to gate-crash security and make their way into the building. This time local police made more than a hundred arrests. Then, in a surprisingly little-reported incident at the time, a fan tragically died during the second show in Cincinnati after accidentally falling from the venue's third level.

The first leg of the tour ended on Saturday 30 April, after their record-breaking show before 76,229 at the Silverdome in Pontiac, Michigan. The next day, Page flew to Cairo for a short break while the others flew home to England, Plant planning to spend his break horse-riding in Wales. Ten days later the whole band plus Grant attended the Ivor Novello awards at the Grosvenor Hotel in London to accept the 1977 award for Outstanding Contribution to British Music. Then, on 17 May, they flew to the US to begin the second leg of the tour with a swing through the South, beginning at the Coliseum in Birmingham,

Alabama, where Jimmy would include a snatch of 'Dixie' in his guitar solo spot.

Despite the near three-week break, when the tour reconvened, instead of lightening the atmosphere, if anything things became even more bleak. When the band found themselves sharing a hotel in Fort Worth, Texas, with Swan Song label-mates Bad Company, they invited guitarist Mick Ralphs up for a jam at their show that night at the Convention Center – bashing out a raggedy version of Jerry Lee Lewis's 'It'll Be Me' during the encores. Later on, back at the hotel, there was the inevitable 'party', during which damage to various rooms was so extensive and apparently systematic the local promoter likened it the next morning to 'a nuclear holocaust'.

The fun just never stopped. During their next stopover – a four-night run at the Largo Capitol Center in Landover, Maryland – G attended a specially convened dinner at the Russian Embassy – the first step, he hoped, in negotiations for Zeppelin to play behind the Iron Curtain. Afterwards, he invited a group of delegates to the show where he introduced them to the band, who for once were all on their best behaviour. Then, during the show itself, he arranged for John Paul to incorporate some Rachmaninov variations into his 'No Quarter' set-piece. 'It blew them away!' G cried afterwards, treating Jonesy to one of his bear hugs.

After the show at the Summit Arena in Houston on 21 May, overexcited fans again went on the rampage, causing an estimated $500,000 of damage. Police were called in and forty people were arrested on charges of disorderly conduct and drug possession. Two weeks later, when the outdoor show in Tampa – scene of utmost triumph four years before – had to be abandoned after just two numbers because of torrential rain, thousands of angry fans pelted the stage with bottles and fights broke out in the 70,000-strong crowd, aggrieved because tickets for the show mistakenly carried a 'rain or shine' pledge – something Grant had steadfastly refused to agree to since the death five years before of Stone The Crows guitarist Les Harvey, electrocuted on stage at the Swansea Top Rank after touching an unearthed microphone with wet hands.

As the band sped away from the stadium in police-escorted limos, forty more armed policemen in riot gear waded into the crowd to try and stop the commotion but only succeeded in escalating the violence as their billy clubs were met with fists and more bottles, until a full-scale riot was in progress. A stream of ambulances and police squad cars followed. More than sixty fans and a dozen cops were eventually hospitalised. Nineteen were arrested. The next day Grant ordered Concerts West, the promoters, to print a full-page apology in the local Tampa newspaper, absolving Zeppelin of any responsibility for the debacle. They meekly complied.

'I see a lot of craziness around us,' said Plant. 'Somehow, we generate it and we revile it. This is an aspect since I've been away from it which has made me contemplate whether we are doing more harm than we are good. That's very important to me. I'm not doing a Peter Green or anything. What I mean is, what we are trying to put across is positive and wholesome; the essence of a survival band, and almost a symbol of the phoenix if you will; and people react in such an excitable manner that they miss the meaning of it, and that makes me lose my calm, and I get angry.'

Not everyone took to the various changes that had been made to the set, either. While 'Stairway To Heaven' was still the ovation-demanding finale of every show, the set-list was even more gruellingly long than usual, Jonesy's 'No Quarter' now stretching to quasi-classical lengths of up to thirty minutes, while Bonzo's re-titled 'Moby Dick'/'Over The Top' drum solo clocked in some nights at almost forty minutes. Coming straight after equally self-conscious lengthy epics like 'Achilles Last Stand', for the first time ever at a Led Zeppelin show there would be intense fidgeting, some fans regarding these overindulgences as unofficial toilet breaks, wandering outside to the concession stands, waiting for the 'real' show to resume.

Three days after the Tampa fiasco, the band arrived in New York for their week of shows at Madison Square Garden, the first major highlight of the tour: six sold-out shows that would gross them over $2 million in ticket sales alone. Anxious to put on their best performances, all six Garden shows found the band operating at a new musical peak, the solos still as lengthy but reinvigorated, and with a couple more upbeat numbers added in, 'Over The Hills And Far Away' and 'Heartbreaker', neither of which had featured since 1973. The first night Robert jokingly dedicated 'In My Time of Dying' to the Queen: 'Tonight is the beginning of Queen Elizabeth the Second's Silver

Jubilee,' he announced, straight-faced, 'and that's a heavy one.' A pause and smile, and then: 'So we'll do this for Liz . . .'

Relatively incident-free, backstage was a friendlier place to be, too, with visitors including Mick, Keith and Ronnie from the Stones and actress Faye Dunaway, who also took pictures of the show from the photo-pit out front. The only blight was when Jimmy got hit on the hand by a firecracker and had to leave the stage. He was back a few minutes later, though, his mood, for once, undiminished. Between shows, the band could be seen out on the town, Jimmy hanging out with Keith and Ronnie at newly fashionable Trax disco, while Robert bought himself a new Lincoln Mark VI with plush red interiors, which he had shipped back to England. Plant even agreed to a few select interviews, something he had largely avoided until now. Talking to *Melody Maker* editor Ray Coleman, he said: 'It's been said these shows now are events more than concerts and I suppose that's true. But what's the option? I guess we must carry a bit of the legend with us.' Bonzo, meanwhile, made his presence felt in his own inimitable style, finally getting the band thrown out of the Plaza Hotel for good after he made so much noise throwing TVs and furniture off his balcony guests thought the hotel was under attack from Puerto Rican terrorists.

From New York they flew via Caesar's Chariot direct to the West Coast, for their six-night run at the Forum. It was in LA that Jimmy gave a series of fascinating interviews to Dave Schulps of *Trouser Press*. Describing Page as 'remarkably thin and pale, his sideburns showing a slight touch of grey, his skin exhibiting a pallor', Schulps said he 'found it hard to believe this was the same person I had seen bouncing around at Madison Square Garden a week earlier'. He also remarked on how 'Page spoke in a half mumble and whisper, which matched his physical appearance'. Nevertheless, and despite frequent interruptions stretching across several days, it was one of the most remarkably candid interviews Jimmy ever gave during Zeppelin days, tracing his career from wide-eyed start to pinpricked present.

The LA shows themselves were of a similar order to the New York ones, the band making a special effort to ensure that these performances at least would be remembered for all the right reasons. Highlights included an impromptu appearance on the third night from Keith Moon, who simply wandered on during 'Moby Dick' and preceded to join in, grabbing Bonzo's extra sticks and settling down for a genuinely exhilarating drum solo. An impression he then spoiled somewhat by coming back out and making a botch of introducing the encores. Then, after playing the kettle drums on 'Whole Lotta Love' and 'Rock And Roll' (during which the smoke bombs nearly blew him offstage) he wandered down to the front and tried joining Robert in singing Eddie Cochran's 'C'mon Everybody'. Page, Plant and Jones looked on and laughed. Well, what else could they do?

Offstage, however, what should have been a triumphal 'home-coming' and the culmination of the second leg of the tour, was again marred by the general 'bad energy' surrounding the tour. The night after his self-invited appearance on stage with the band, Moon, who had also booked himself into the band's hotel, joined Bonzo and the boys on a night-off visit to the Comedy Store, but the Who drummer was in melancholy mood and eventually got them thrown out for repeated – and unfunny – heckling. Bonzo didn't care. He was now so permanently out of it, day was colliding with night. Bev Bevan, in town with ELO, by then a huge US concert draw themselves, recalls inviting Bonzo over for a drink at his hotel. When he turned up, Bev was shocked by what he saw. 'I think he felt he had a reputation to live up to, like Keith Moon. For every one drink I had he'd order himself six Brandy Alexanders, just showing off, really, knocking them back one after another. Then he got up to play a tune with the house band – Stevie Wonder's "Superstition" – and he was awful! I was so embarrassed because I'd just been telling these guys, wait till you see him play, he's the best, but he could barely hold the beat. I don't think I actually saw him again after that.' The Bonzo who Bev had known in the old days had changed 'and it wasn't for the better. It's a shame but that's the truth. He was drinking so much it was terrifying, really.' Grant, meanwhile, was now so locked into his cocaine paranoia he arbitrarily ordered a full audit of the band's tour accounts, specifically the 'expenses' handled personally by Cole, where it was discovered that a total of $10,460 had apparently gone 'missing'. No less befuddled than Grant, Cole later admitted: 'I thought, what with all the drugs I may have made a blunder.' However, the 'discrepancy' was eventually traced back to $10,000 Cole was originally to have picked up from a Houston promoter, only to have arrangements altered at the last minute.

On the sixth and last night of the Forum run, Plant bid the audience

farewell with the words: 'Thanks to the badge holders of California' –
an in-joke reference to all the groupies backstage, now carefully delin-
eated by their own 'special' backstage passes, distributed by all the
various assistants – before Zeppelin roared through a medley of 'Whole
Lotta Love' and 'Rock And Roll'. Immediately afterwards, Cole did as
he always had and ushered the band – and their guests – into a fleet of
limos, waiting not to whisk them back to their hotel this time, however,
but direct to LAX airport and home. Exactly eight and a half years
since they'd made the same journey but in the opposite direction –
and in far less luxurious surroundings – Led Zeppelin's long, hot,
passionate, sometimes violent, always eventful love affair with the City
of Angels had come to an end. Though none of them, not even Jimmy
or G, knew it yet, they would never play there – in any sense – again.

The third and final leg of the US tour had begun in Seattle with a
sold-out show before 65,000 at the Kingdome, home of the Seattle
Sounders soccer team, on 17 July. It was a lacklustre resumption with
poor sound and another unruly crowd making for an unappetising
spectacle. 'It did begin to feel like a soundcheck in the dark,' said
Jonesy afterwards. 'The audience was so far away you could hardly see
or hear them.'

Six days later they arrived in San Francisco for the first of two festival
shows at the 90,000-capacity Oakland Coliseum. Intended as a festive
occasion, the band and all the main members of the crew, including
Grant, had flown their wives and children in. Also on the bill were
Rick Derringer and Judas Priest, both of whom would do their utmost
to try and pull the rug from under the headliners. Neither caused
Zeppelin as much embarrassment, however, as the new backdrop they
had specially constructed for the large outdoor shows – a mock-up of
Stonehenge (an idea that would return to haunt them in the post-
Spinal Tap age). Worse – much worse – was to follow at the end of the
first show though, and an event that would become the source of a
much deeper, more shameful stain on their reputation.

In his autobiography, promoter Bill Graham recalls the whole build
up to Oakland being pockmarked with unsavoury incidents – portents
of the gloom which would swiftly descend on all of them – beginning
with a phone call from Richard Cole the day before the first show,
demanding a $25,000 cash advance – 'drug money,' claims Graham.
He also noted the heavy atmosphere now surrounding the band. 'I

[had] heard about the ugliness of their security,' he wrote, 'how they were just waiting to kill. They had these bodyguards who had police records in England. They were thugs.' As if to prove it, when, in the build up to the first early-evening show, Jim Downey, one of Graham's regular stage crew made what Grant took as a disparaging remark about his weight – offering to help the stoned, tottering giant down some backstage steps – John Bindon stepped forward and punched him, causing Downey to bang his head on the concrete, knocking him out cold.

But that was small fry compared to what happened later during the show when another of Graham's staff, security man Jim Matzorkis, stepped in to prevent a young boy from removing a wooden plaque with the band's name on it from a backstage trailer door, explaining sternly they would need it for the following day's show. Unfortunately for Matzorkis, the boy was Warren Grant – G's son – and when Bonzo, who'd witnessed the incident, gleefully reported it to Grant – adding that Matzorkis had slapped the boy – the furious, spittle-flying manager grabbed Bindon and Cole and the four of them went looking for Matzorkis. 'You don't talk to a kid like that,' Grant told Matzorkis when he found him, and ordered him to apologise to Warren. As if to emphasise the point, Bonzo kicked him in the groin. Matzorkis ran for his life, hiding in one of the backstage production trailers. According to an interview Graham later gave *Rolling Stone*, in the tumult that ensued, his production manager Bob Barsotti was also hit on the head with a lead pipe. Grant then promised Graham there would be no further violence; that he just wanted to finish speaking with Matzorkis. So Graham reluctantly led him to the trailer where Matzorkis was hiding. 'I said: "Jim, it's okay, it's me", then I stepped in. I said, "Jim, this is Mr Peter Grant, the boy's father." Before I could finish the sentence Peter blasted Jim in the face.' Grant then had Bindon throw Graham out, closed the door, leaving the pipe-wielding Cole to stand guard outside as he and Johnny went to work on the terrified Matzorkis. The beating was so savage the trailer began to rock from side to side. Matzorkis only escaped, he later said, after Bindon had tried gouging out his eye. A horrified Graham had his still bleeding staffer rushed straight to East Bay hospital.

At the second show the following night, Zeppelin took the stage over ninety minutes late, waiting while a lawyer, hastily drafted in by

Grant, arrived backstage and informed Graham he would have to sign
a letter of indemnification, absolving the band and/or its employees of
any responsibility for the previous evening's atrocities – or the band
would not perform the second show. Not wanting a riot on his hands,
Graham signed. However, he did so safe in the knowledge that the
letter would have no influence on Matzorkis' own options. Robert,
who had always admired Bill, did his best to try and affect some form
of reconciliation – even thanking him publicly as the band left the
stage that night – but Graham wouldn't even look at him, let alone
speak. The show itself was a surprisingly good one, including an
impromptu acoustic version of 'Mystery Train'. But Page was distraught
throughout and did almost all of the show that night sitting dis-
consolately, with his guitar, on the lip of the stage.

The matter did not rest there, however. Determined to regain control
of the situation, Graham planned to fly twenty-five of his own armed
men into the next show at the New Orleans Superdome. Before he
could give the go-ahead, however, Matzorkis had beaten him to it by
going to the police. The morning after the second Oakland show, the
band's hotel was surrounded by an Oakland SWAT team as officers
went in, weapons drawn, and formally arrested Grant, Bindon, Bonham
and Cole on charges of assault. They were taken and held in an open
jail for several hours before being released on bail.

*The 155 Oxford Street office – above Millets – with Mickie became
legendary, the joint stuffed with music biz knocking shops, pen-pushers
churning out 'certain' hits for any dodgy publisher or record company dick
willing to give them the price of a pint or two. Chrysalis on the first floor;
Island Music and Mike Berry on the second. The only downside for you
was that your office was on the sixth floor. There was a lift but if some
fucker left the gate open the bloody thing wouldn't work. Mickie would just
run up the stairs. Not you. You taking the piss? Naw, when that happened
you'd simply turn on your heel and fuck off down the pub, or just go home.
It was even worse in winter, waiting for the cunts in the shop downstairs
to put the heating on, freezing your bollocks off trying to make a phone call.
In the end you'd go in there and grab the manager and tell him straight:
'If you don't put that fucking heating on, I'll put you in the fucking boiler!'
After that the cunts never turned the radiators off again, not even in
summer.*

You had a temper, course you did. You had to stick up for yourself in this business or they'd walk right over you. When you got really annoyed you'd kick the front panel out of your desk. You knew it'd been a stinker that day if the desk ended up in pieces on the floor. Usually you'd get it off your chest just by shouting and swearing, though. Give some deserving cunt an earful on the dog. But sometimes it took more than that. Sometimes you just wanted to break something . . . somebody . . .

It was at the Oxford Street gaff you met Bill Harry. One of the chaps, Bill was. A scally with the gift of the gab to prove it; you had him doing the PR for the New Vaudeville Band and later on Led Zeppelin. Lucky to have him too, they were. Bill had been to school with John Lennon, started Mersey Beat magazine and knew them all: the Beatles, the Hollies, the Kinks, Pink Floyd, Ten Years After, Jethro Tull . . . loads of 'em. It was Bill who switched you onto the pirate radio stations, chatting to him over a fag one day, setting the world to rights together. Next thing you knew there was you and Mickie in a fucking boat full of records, you driving, setting off from Clacton trying to get to Radio Caroline, Radio London and the rest. Not knowing what the fuck you were doing, Mickie trying to throw the records on board these big bastard ships, the records sailing off into the sea. You didn't know whether to laugh or piss yourself. Turn left at the Thames Estuary, Mickie said, and don't look back! The DJs all shouting, 'Never mind the records, throw the Scotch!' You sitting there, fucking miserable and starving. 'Don't worry,' Mickie would say, 'when we get to Southend, we'll have fish and chips.' Piss-taking cunt . . .

No-one ever forgot you, though, which was even more important than the records, in the long run. People didn't say, 'Let's go and see RAK Management,' they said, 'Let's go and see Peter and Mickie . . .' and it all came good eventually. Once you had four LPs in the Top 20! Take that, you bastards! Then came the Yardbirds. A bit of what you really fancied. Mickie was all over them like a cheap suit but you knew they'd need you too – a band like that didn't want to be in the studio all day, they wanted to be out there, earning, putting on the clobber and pulling the birds.

It was also through the Yardbirds that you got to know Pagey and Jones again. Pagey everyone knew, of course, from his sessions. And Baldwin, as he still was to you, was another face from that same scene that Mickie pulled in to do some work on the Little Games LP. By now it was all about LPs, the hippies had taken over. It was all dope and acid now and hey man you can fuck my girlfriend. But there was loot in it, and plenty of it if you only knew how, and you weren't gonna let it get away from you even if it meant growing what was left of your hair. Mainly, it was all about America. You'd had the Animals of course but it wasn't you that saw the money from them, it was Mickie and that cunt Jeffrey. God bless the New Vaudeville Band, they'd made a few bob for you over there but they weren't exactly fashionable. They were old men compared to this Yardbirds mob. You talked it over with Mickie but mainly he had his eye on the guitarist, Jeff Beck – well, good luck with that … But you reckoned if you played your cards right these Yardbirds could be like a cross between the Animals and the New Vaudvilles, successful and cool. You sat there at the broken desk, having a fag and thinking about it. First though, you'd have to get them back over to America, see the lie of the land for your own eyes …

You rang up Richard Cole and told him he could come too, be your assistant. You had a feeling you'd need all the help you could get. Sure enough, there were times when you wondered what the fuck you'd got yourself into. Like that rotten State Fair in Canada that winter, driving through the pissing rain and snow, lorries jack-knifed all over the highway. Then when you got there you were so late you'd missed the first show. Next thing you know these two Mafioso wankers are standing there saying they're gonna kill ya cos we'd cost them money and blah blah blah. You were sitting in the back of the bus when they pulled out their guns. You were so tired and fucked off you didn't give a shit, just stood up and waded into them. They pushed their guns into your guts but you just kept on coming. 'You're gonna do WHAT?' you screamed into their faces. Little cunts started laughing like a pair of schoolgirls. That's when you realised they were even more scared than you were. One look at you and everyone was always more scared than you were. That was the idea anyway …

It all came to a sticky end though when the band didn't want to know anymore. You know you're onto a serious loser when you can't even dangle money in front of the cunts. A club date in the States – flat fee, $5,000. A lot of fucking spondulicks. Jimmy, no fool, said yes, and so did Chris, but the others didn't wanna know. Big row. In the end you drafted out a letter giving Jimmy the rights to the name, which they all signed, so at least he could do the gig, pick up the bread. He was a good kid, Pagey. Quiet until you got to know him, but solid as a fucking rock when it came down to it. Better than Beck, who could play and had the looks but never knew

*whether it was Tuesday or fucking Selfridges. With Pagey you were solid
gold all the way. He was like you, wanted the copper and the kettle. When
he said he wanted to form his own mob you were ready to put the house
on it. In the end you would put that and a whole lot more. 'Just remember,'
you would tell people, 'if the ship starts to sink Jimmy is the first one in the
fucking lifeboat, get it?' Gloria heard you say it so often she used to say
you loved Jimmy more than you loved her . . .*

Speaking to Nick Kent in 2003, Jimmy said his main memories of
Oakland are that 'It was particularly ugly' all round, not just backstage
but, again, amongst the crowd itself. During the second of the two
shows, 'All I could see were people getting pulled over the barriers and
beaten up, and it was horrible to play in front of that. There was a very
nasty, heavy energy about the whole day. I don't know what arguments
had gone on between Peter and Bill Graham but I know it was getting
very ugly behind the stage. Our people beat up one of Graham's
security guards. It was a scandal, just abhorrent, but it was going on
out front all the time so it was "like attracting like" in a sense.'

He felt that Grant had been 'very, very affected by his divorce'
and, by implication, that his judgement was seriously impaired. 'A
lot of the violence that went on was kept away from the group, so
we rarely knew anything. It was only near the end that I saw it truly
manifesting itself. It had got very heavy by then and it was so far
removed from what the true spirit of the band was about. The bad
elements in the organisation grew out of all control and it became
a terrible misuse of the power of the band. It was people around us
abusing our power.'

Six months later Grant, Bonham, Cole and Bindon would file joint
pleas of *nolo contender* (I will not plead guilty) to the assault charges.
All four were found guilty and given fines and suspended jail sentences.
Matzorkis would also file a $2 million civil suit against the band, but
as none of the four had been required to appear personally in court,
the civil suit was never heard. Graham was outraged at such lenient
sentences but there was little the promoter could do other than
condemn them publicly. 'I could never in good conscience book them
again,' he said. Years later, Grant admitted he deeply regretted the
Matzorkis incident. So upset was he by Graham's account in his
autobiography, he openly wept in front of his friend, Dire Straits'

manager Ed Bicknell. 'I don't want to be thought of as a bad person,' he told him. But it was too late; much too late.

Typically, Jonesy was the first out the door after the Oakland shows. As he later told Dave Lewis, 'I actually had all the family over and was due to travel to Oregon the next day. I'd rented a motor home and I had it parked outside the hotel. We heard the police were on the way and they were swarming around the lobby. So me and my family went down this service elevator out the back, through the kitchen and into this motor home – which I'd never driven – pulled out of the hotel, onto the freeway and away from the trouble.' Adept at staying out of trouble, his philosophy: 'If it was fun you joined in, if it wasn't you didn't. I was often in another part of the hotel I guess. But that sort of stuff got a bit tedious after a while. Things were getting a little crazy with Richard Cole and the likes of John Bindon.' He added, pointedly: 'Every band was doing the drugs thing at the time – we didn't really worry much about it – but by then it was getting a bit out of control.'

And it was about to get worse. The band had only just arrived at the Maison Dupuy Hotel in Louisiana – where the governor planned to make them 'honorary colonels' – when Robert received a desperate phone call from Maureen in England saying that their five-year-old son, Karac, was seriously ill with a viral infection. Two hours later, Maureen called back with even more shattering news: Karac was dead. Details were hard to come by – Karac had been diagnosed with a respiratory infection; within twenty-four hours his condition had worsened so alarmingly Maureen had dialled 999 and an ambulance was sent, but it was too late and Karac had died in the ambulance on his way to the hospital. As Plant put the phone down, his world collapsed. So did what was left of Led Zeppelin's. All remaining shows on the tour were cancelled.

Cole, Bonham and Dennis Sheehan accompanied Robert on his journey home. A private jet met them at Heathrow to fly them up to the Midlands, where a limo was waiting to speed the singer home. They all stayed with him for the funeral in Birmingham, the only members of Zeppelin's inner circle to attend. Page, Jones and Grant were all still in the US, G busy dealing with the repercussions of having to cancel the remaining seven dates. Why neither Page nor Jones made the trip back for the funeral, neither man has ever explained fully, not even to Plant. Hurt the others hadn't showed up, he told Cole, in

Stairway To Heaven: 'Maybe they don't have as much respect for me as I do for them. Maybe they're not the friends I thought they were.'

'I just couldn't believe it,' said Jones. 'I was up in Oregon. Somewhere in Oregon I called in to New Orleans – I was going to stay with Tommy Hullat from Concerts West. It was quite a time for him, what with the Zeppelin tour being cancelled, and then Elvis died a couple of weeks later and he had to sort that out too. Anyway, Robert had gone home with Bonzo and I drove on to Seattle. It was a very strange time. We just knew we had to give him time.'

For Robert Plant, 1977 was 'the year it all stopped for me. Nothing could make it all right again and nothing ever will.' Through it all, he told me nearly thirty years later, Bonzo never left his side. 'During the absolute darkest times of my life when I lost my boy and my family was in total disarray, it was Bonzo who came to me. Him and Pat, they were the people who I'd been dealing with all over those years who were there. The other guys were in the South and probably because they didn't have the same social etiquettes as we have up here, Bonzo could actually bridge that very uncomfortable chasm between . . .' He paused, swallowed hard, '. . . with all the sensitivities that would be required . . . to commiserate and console.'

The press, however, were in no mood for consolation and instead began writing about a Led Zeppelin 'jinx'. A London tabloid quoted a 'psychic' predicting more troubled times ahead for the band, while a radio DJ in Chicago announced that 'if Jimmy Page would just lay off all that mystical, hocus-pocus occult stuff, and stop unleashing all these evil forces, Led Zeppelin could just concentrate on making music.'

It may have been crudely put, but it summed up the secret thoughts of many who had more than a passing acquaintance with Page and Zeppelin. Did such thoughts ever infect Plant, though? It's hard to believe that, in his grief, he didn't at some point allow himself to wonder if Page's occult connections hadn't in some way impacted upon the band's collective karma. Plant certainly believed in karma – as did Page – in good vibes and bad, in reaping what you sow. More likely, however, as with so many parents in similar situations, he merely blamed himself. The drugs, the groupies, the excuses to friends and loved ones and, ultimately, to oneself . . . how could it not all eventually end in tears?

There was more fuel to add to the karmic law bonfire though when, in September, a drunken Bonzo crashed his car while driving home from the pub one night. Going far too fast as usual, he spun off a bend and hurt himself badly, the car ending up in a ditch. Not willing to call the police or even a doctor, he had the wreck privately towed back to his farm and when he did finally agree to see a doctor – after suffering such pain he was having difficulty breathing – he was diagnosed as having broken two ribs. News eventually got out and the word 'jinx' was all over the papers again.

Jimmy was understandably touchy on the subject of bad karma. Speaking upon his return from America that year, he scowled: 'It's just the wrong term to ever use, and how somebody can level that at us shocks me. The whole concept of the band is entertainment; I don't see any link between [Karac's death] and karma, it's nonsense.'

Ultimately, what Robert Plant, as grieving father, needed was to be left in peace; for time to work its miracle and at least scab-over wounds that would never fully heal. The future of Led Zeppelin would simply have to be put on hold – again. There would be no daily phone calls from Page checking on his progress this time, either. He and Grant had already decided at a private meeting in London that they would give Robert 'three months or three years, whatever he needed,' as Grant put it. 'I felt quite remote from the whole thing,' said Robert, looking back many years later. 'I wasn't comfortable with the group at all. We'd gone right through the hoop and, because my hoop was on fire, I didn't know if it was worth it anymore.'

Drugs were also now an issue. After Karac's death, Plant would view cocaine and, particularly, heroin, in a very different light – along with those that used them, like Page. 'Addiction to powders was the worst way to see yourself, a waste of your time and everybody's time,' he said. 'You make excuses to yourself why things aren't right or about what's happening to your potential. You lie to yourself first and rub your nose later. It was time,' he concluded, not unreasonably, 'to get out . . .'

15

The Outhouse

After Karac's funeral, Robert Plant left Led Zeppelin far behind and simply, as he later put it, 'went away for a year ... when you've gone through something like that and come out the other end, all the godhead shit and the affectations of a rock star pale away. You tend not to take yourself too seriously.'

Speaking in 2005, it's a wonder, I said, he actually came back at all. 'Yeah, well ... as you get older, your shoulders get broader and you have to be prepared to go into territories that you've never been before for the sake of the people you love.'

Yes, I say, but you weren't really 'older' then, you were just twenty-nine.

'That's right, yeah. But it was me that seduced Bonzo to join the Yardbirds, and it was he that brought me back to go down to Clearwell Castle to piece together something that became *In Through the Outdoor*. And it was he that played so beautifully on [it]. So he worked on me, saying it was ...' He faltered as the memories came flooding back. 'You know, all I was doing was just parading around with a shotgun and a bottle of Johnnie Walker, trying to shoot at the press.'

It was Bonzo talking to you that got you past that? I asked.

'Well, yeah. I didn't want to leave my family, you know? I didn't want to leave Carmen and Maureen. And also I didn't know whether it was worth it, to be honest. John came over and nuanced all the reasons why it was a good idea. And then fell asleep on an Afghan cushion and was woken up twelve hours later!' He paused. 'I think it was just ... at no detriment to anybody who was around me then, it's just that he had the history with me outside of the success.'

It wasn't just Plant who found the aftermath of Karac's death difficult to get through, of course. With his beloved Zeppelin once again put on hold, this time possibly for good, Jimmy Page was left with nothing but time on his hands – a disastrous circumstance for someone with a raging heroin habit and all the money he needed to regularly keep it fed. Aware of the mire he was slowly sinking into, Jimmy booked a two-week holiday in Guadeloupe, in the West Indies, for himself, Charlotte and Scarlet, inviting Richard Cole along too, who he suggested join him in trying to get off smack by staying drunk on white rum for the duration of their stay. Miraculously, as a makeshift cure it worked – temporarily, at least. Back in England in September, relatively 'straight' though still drinking heavily and snorting coke, Jimmy tried to keep his mind off the heavy gear by staying active, performing for a kids' charity called Goaldiggers and working in his home studio, sifting through endless hours of Zeppelin live tapes going all the way back to the Albert Hall in 1970 for a prospective 'chronological live album' he'd convinced G would be just the thing to plug the gap while they waited for Robert to put his life back together.

But it all came to nought as the weeks and months dragged by, and by Christmas 1977 the project was no longer a talking point as he slipped back into a serious funk, taking heroin again and doing . . . not very much at all. When, not long after that, Grant had to be taken to hospital late one night after he'd suffered a minor coronary or 'heart scare' as he put it to the band and anyone else that needed to know ('all down to pressure,' he explained dismissively, conveniently over-looking the ruinously large amounts of cocaine he was still ingesting on a daily basis), it seemed there was no point fighting it. Despite the 'Zeppelin To Split' stories that were again now doing the rounds, Page had no choice but to sit back and bide his time, filling the void that opened up before him each day with drugs and drink. Even his occult 'studies' no longer interested him in the same way. He still had Bole-skine and all his treasured Crowley artefacts; he still read the books, drowsing over them into the small hours most nights. He just no longer had the outlet to somehow make it all make sense.

By spring 1978, however, Maureen was pregnant again and the healing process of the Plant family was finally underway. It was also around this time that Roy Harper gave an interview to a farming magazine, mostly about the sheep he kept on a small holding, but in which he also mentioned he'd been working with Jimmy Page, helping write lyrics for the next Zeppelin album. When Robert, who in his guise as gentleman farmer happened to subscribe to the magazine, read the article he was furious, phoning Jimmy for the first time in months and demanding an explanation. Taken aback, but not entirely displeased as it showed how deeply his singer still apparently cared about his role in the band, Jimmy denied the story but suggested that maybe it was time the band did finally get back together, just to see each other again, see how it felt. Robert, who had also had John Bonham working on him, dutifully obliged, agreeing to a meeting at Clearwell Castle, an eighteenth-century neo-Gothic mansion in the Forest of Dean, near his home on the Welsh borders.

Reputedly haunted by a mischievous female ghost who would mess up locked rooms and sing lullabies to her ghost child on the landing at night while playing a tinkling musical box, the vibes surrounding Zeppelin's brief visit were not promising. Taking over the basement, the band tentatively jammed for a few days, playing anything Robert felt comfortable singing along to, but despite Jimmy's constant urging and Grant's forcedly avuncular encouragement, sparks steadfastly refused to fly and the band went their separate ways again.

John Paul Jones, who had filled in the previous nine months building up his own newly acquired farm in Sussex, 'cooling out' with his wife and daughters 'and just taking stock,' found the Clearwell get-together decidedly 'odd,' he said. 'I didn't really feel comfortable. I remember asking, "Why are we doing this?" We were not in good shape mentally or health wise.' The only positive benefit from his point of view was that he became closer to Plant. 'If I was a little down Robert would try to cheer me up, if he was down I'd do the same and pull ourselves through ... It's not that we didn't have a laugh at Clearwell, it just wasn't going anywhere.'

Two months later Robert Plant finally stepped on a stage again, his first time since the nightmare of Oakland a year before. Not with Led Zeppelin at some enormous sold-out stadium though, but with an unknown local band called the Turd Burglars before a nonplussed audience of a couple of hundred at a small pub in Worcestershire, performing 'Blue Suede Shoes' and a handful of similar covers. A few weeks later, while holidaying with the family in Ibiza, he also got up at a club called Amnesia and sang with his old chums in Dr Feelgood – again, not Zeppelin songs but a clutch of storming R&B covers. A month after that, he repeated the trick, this time with fellow Swan Song artist Dave Edmunds, at a concert in Birmingham.

Slowly but surely, Plant was feeling his way back onto the boards. Watching from afar, cautiously excited, was Jimmy Page. The band did not meet again until September, though, when they all attended Richard Cole's wedding reception in London – a lavish party co-hosted by Bad Company drummer Simon Kirke who had also got married that day. Still, no-one broached the subject of getting the band back together directly with Robert for fear of frightening him off. But for the first time in over a year, positive feelings were beginning to emanate from the Swan Song offices in Chelsea. Then things turned weird again when Who drummer and long-time Bonzo cohort Keith Moon died after attending a party at the Coconut Grove in London hosted by Paul McCartney to celebrate the release of the movie *The Buddy Holly Story*. Word was that Moony had taken an accidental overdose of a drug he had been prescribed to help him combat his alcoholism, wound-up by being unable to join in with the revelry of the other party guests. Whatever the truth, Richard Cole, who had hung out with Moon at the Grove was shaken when, at the funeral, Pete Townshend came up to him, demanding 'What the fuck is going on? Keith is dead and you're alive ...'

Once again, the 'Zep to Split' stories started circulating, helped along by suggestions that with Keith Richards facing seven years in jail for his now infamous drug bust in Toronto and Zeppelin apparently in abeyance as Robert considered his future, Jimmy was being lined up to tour with the Stones. Whether he would have, or how that would have worked, being a raving junkie himself at the time, is not known. Clearly, things were starting to acquire a desperate edge. Zep chronicler Dave Lewis, who had first begun visiting the Swan Song offices in 1978, recalls 'a very weird vibe at the time, everything was very inconclusive. Peter was never around, no-one could get hold of him, and it was just ... strange. Here you were, at the headquarters of the biggest band in world and there was just nothing happening at all.'

Despite taking off like a rocket, the Swan Song label also began withering on the vine as the tangled personal lives of its owners saw them lose interest. Apart from Bad Company, only Dave Edmunds (Robert's old mucker from Rockfield, signed in 1976) enjoyed success, scoring UK hits with the singles 'Here Comes The Weekend', 'I Knew

The Bride' and 'Girls Talk'. Page's old drug buddy Michael Des Barres' short-lived band, Detective, was also signed but disbanded after just two albums: *Detective* in 1977 and, a year later, *It Takes One to Know One*. 'Once we were signed we never saw any of Led Zeppelin for two years,' said a disillusioned Des Barres.

Even Page's cherished Equinox shop closed down after the lease expired and he could no longer rouse himself to renew it. 'It obviously wasn't going to run the way it should without some drastic business changes and I didn't really want to agree to all of that,' he shrugged when asked about it. All he had ever wanted was for 'the shop to be a nucleus,' he said, for his own occult studies. Timothy d'Arch Smith believes the truth behind Equinox's closure was more prosaic. 'He had problems with the manager; I think that's what he told me. And it all went really rather wrong. They reprinted a couple of things but I think it was really rather a disaster.'

It wasn't until November 1978, sixteen months after the death of his son, that Robert Plant finally felt able to go back to work with Led Zeppelin. The first priority, it was decided, should be a new album. It had been nearly three years since they'd last released a collection of new material. A lot had changed since then, both for Zeppelin and the music world in general. It would be important to come back with a strong musical statement. But when they arrived at a rehearsal room in London, it soon became clear that the musical ideas cupboard was embarrassingly bare. Worse, Page, to whom they had always looked for direction, was so untogether now, the long months of inactivity with just his heroin habit to keep him company having sapped whatever creativity he had left. It quickly became apparent to John Paul Jones that with the band's principal songwriters both having been incapacitated this past year – albeit for very different reasons – it would be up to him to take up the slack and at least try to get the ball rolling again with some ideas of his own. Fortunately, Jonesy had been storing up ideas of one sort or another for years. That they weren't all necessarily ideal for a Led Zeppelin album hardly mattered; at this point, the important thing was to get something going, and quick, before the other three members of the band – now all so fragile in their various ways – took off in different directions again.

With Abba's Polar Studios in Stockholm booked for December, the band was ready to try anything. As with the Musicland sessions three years before, work proceeded extremely quickly. It wasn't Page cracking the whip this time though, it was Jones. Indeed, of the seven lengthy tracks which eventually emerged from the sessions as 'keepers', only five would be co-credited to Page – the first time any Zeppelin album would feature original material not at least part-credited to Jimmy – while all but one would be co-credited to Jones; another first. The only one not credited with any input at all was Bonham, which seems harsh as his drums are one of the few consistently good things about what would be the last, and least impressive, Zeppelin album.

The other change under Jones' stewardship was that they kept more regular hours. Page was still a creature of the night, nothing was going to change that, but instead of waiting for him to show up, or even Bonzo on those days he wanted to sleep it off after a heavy night on Sweden's extra-strength chemical beer, Jones and Plant simply cracked on, in charge of the sessions with everyone else's implicit if unvoiced blessing. 'There were two distinct camps by then,' Jones told Dave Lewis, 'and we were in the relatively clean one. We'd turn up first, Bonzo would turn up later and Page might turn up a couple of days later.' He and Robert, he said, 'spent much of the time drinking pints of Pimms and waiting around for it to happen. So we made it happen.' Says Lewis now: 'By then Jonesy and Robert ruled the roost. With Jimmy immersed in his various problems, someone needed to take charge of the music and that was Jonesy. Meanwhile, anything Robert wanted he got, everyone was walking on eggshells around him.'

While Page would still be credited as producer, in reality Jones and to a lesser extent Plant were now calling the shots there, too. Hence, the over-reliance on certain tracks of Jonesy's new toy: a Yamaha GX-1 synthesiser, which had just then come onto the market, anticipating the Eighties move towards electronic studio-generated sounds over the organic natural-talent-will-out musicianship epitomised by Zeppelin's generation of bands. Page was also becoming obsessed with this new technology and favoured a much more treated sound to his guitars throughout the album, which he chose to layer to unusual degrees even by his own intricate standards.

Every Friday afternoon the band would fly back to London where they would be met by four separate limos waiting to whisk them home. Every Monday morning the journey would be repeated in the opposite direction. Not even Richard Cole, still scuffing around for heroin (and finding it with a dealer living literally across the road from the studio in Stockholm) could get anyone interested in a party. When the new workmanlike approach succeeded – as it did most spectacularly on the track that would open the album, the desolate yet weirdly majestic 'In the Evening' – it seemed possible the band might actually have found a way through the emotional and spiritual morass of the past few years, discovering a new realm in which their music might still find meaning. However, the weaknesses in the new approach – above all, Page's apparent abdication of his role as band leader, his presence so subdued as to be positively ghostly – were all too plain on obvious filler tracks like Jones' and Plant's second-rate Elton John-style romp, 'South Bound Suarez', or the lightweight country hoedown parody cooked up by Page and Plant, 'Hot Dog'. Even its other cornerstone track, 'Carouselambra', was a let-down, Jones's parping synths ladled over everything like gravy disguising the lack of meat on the plate, swamping whatever drive and energy the original idea possessed until it became an inky vacuous dirge . . .

You'd first met Grant back when you were touring with Tony Meehan and Jet Harris, and Peter was tour-managing Gene Vincent for Don Arden. Apart from the fact he was a big chap, there was nothing that struck you that was particularly special about him. It wasn't until you started doing regular sessions for Mickie that you got to see the other side of his partner, sitting there at the Oxford Street office shouting the odds down the phone. There was Peter and Mickie and an accountant whose name no-one knew cos he was never introduced to people and Irene the receptionist, who was wonderful. Peter and Mickie liked to come on like the tough guys of the music biz but Irene ran both of them! Peter was managing the New Vaudeville Band and Mickie was doing so many things you couldn't keep up with him.

It was through Mickie you met Jimmy Page properly too. You were quite surprised when he actually rang you back about the New Yardbirds gig. But when you got to that first rehearsal at that pokey little room in Chinatown, you took one look at the other two he'd invited down and knew you'd never fit in with that lot. You just turned up and did what was required, quietly and efficiently, made sure you got paid then went home afterwards, alone . . .

But you plugged in and started playing, like you always did, and . . .

something happened. It was really quite odd. You'd never been into blues or rock or any of that stuff, though you did like Cream but that was different, they could actually play and had more in common with jazz, really, if you listened. But you plugged in as you always did and actually began to feel what was going on, feel it way down inside. It was the drummer. He was one of those who played loud – bloody loud! – but he didn't just do it for effect. It wasn't, wait till you hear this, it was wait till you hear us. You realised he was actually listening to what you did, that he was actually leaving space for you. On a basic level, you were both just doing a rhythm, but there was something about the way you phrased the bass line that led to something about the way he would play. Next thing you knew you were both just locked into it – together. It didn't matter what the name of the song was or even whether either of you knew how it went. You just listened to the drummer listening to you and crikey it just exploded!

And that was just that first rehearsal. You thought, blimey, if we can keep this up, we'll be able to do it with our eyes closed. This bloke's great! 'My name's John,' you said, holding out your hand, during the break. He sat there on his drum stool, smoking a cigarette and sweating, looking you over. Then he took your hand and shook it. 'Me, too,' he said, and smiled, and you noticed he had an accent.

The only one co-credited on all seven tracks was Plant, whose lyrics are the most consistently intriguing aspect of the entire album, clearly dealing as they do – unsettlingly explicitly on occasion – with the tragedies he has been through since the death of his son. 'I hear you crying in the darkness,' he sings-screams on 'In the Evening', 'Don't ask nobody's help, ain't no pockets full of mercy baby, cause you can only blame yourself ...' 'Fool in the Rain', one of the album's better moments with its lilting piano riff, nice Spanish guitar, and unexpected excursion towards the end into full-blown samba – replete with whistles, kettle drums and handclaps – also contains unveiled references to tragedy and altered perspective. While 'Carouselambra', with its off-puttingly self-regarding shape, seems to specifically target Page in its plaintive cries of: 'Where was your helping, where was your bow?' Even the clearly dashed off 'South Bound Suarez' contains nagging references to having 'feet back on the ground'.

The most moving moment though – musically, lyrically, emotionally – was the second of the two songs Page had nothing to do
with: Jones' and Plant's 'All My Love'. Built around a swooning synth
figure that – unlike other moments on the album – fits the mood of
mourning and hoped for redemption all too well, Bonham's sometimes
too brutal drums are restrained and understated, as ceremonious as a
guard of honour, Page's layered acoustic and electric guitars equally
tastefully applied, while Plant simply opens up his broken heart and
cries, as if directing the entire piece to his beloved son. 'Yours is the
cloth, mine is the hand that sews time,' he sings, the sob in his voice
all too detectable, 'his is the force that lies within. Ours is the fire, all
the warmth we can find. He is a feather in the wind . . .' Even the neo-
classical synth solo in the middle – soon to be a cliché of the Eighties'
over-fondness for synths-as-orchestral-magma – doesn't spoil the
mood. Page would later disparage 'All My Love' as something 'I could
just imagine people doing the wave and all of that . . . I wouldn't have
wanted to pursue that direction in the future.' But it was, with 'In the
Evening', one of only two tracks of sufficient quality to have graced
any of the earlier, much greater Zeppelin albums.

The final track on the album, 'I'm Gonna Crawl', was of a similar ilk,
though more of a musical pastiche, its echoing vocals and cartwheeling
guitars redolent of Elvis at his most melodramatic, the echo of footsteps
down an alley after the swelling river of keyboards that usher the song
in. Page's coruscating blues solo – excavated from some dark corner of
his smacked-out soul – almost makes up for his lack of ideas elsewhere
on the album, while Plant's heart-rending lyrics are directed this time
not to his lost son but to his wife, newly with child and the key, he
seems to suggest, to their escape from a pain that can never truly leave,
but can, perhaps, be better understood, with time. And love.

Three other tracks were also recorded during the Stockholm sessions
but left off the final running order of the album: two of which, 'Ozone
Baby' and 'Wearing And Tearing', were cringe-making attempts to
reinvigorate the classic Zep sound with the ripped-and-torn energy of
the new wave which so despised them. The former, full of the 'ain't's
and 'don't wanna's that were the lingua franca of early Brit-punk, finds
Plant actually trying out some inept punk phrasing while the others
do their best to keep it tight. The latter, which Page and Plant were
both so pleased with they considered releasing it as a stand-alone

single – once considered sacrilege; now the prerequisite of legitimate anti-album punk – was an overworked revamp of 'Train Kept A-Rollin'', and again found the band bending over backwards trying to rein in their natural inclination to stretch out and groove while Plant croaks away, his voice sounding horribly shot. The third track, 'Darlene', was the best of a second-rate bunch, and harked back to an earlier, more easy-fit, pre-punk era, when rockers rolled unself-consciously and girls were actually called Darlene and really did dance with their 'tight dress on'.

Ultimately, *In Through the Outdoor,* as it was jokingly and unhappily prophetically titled, was an unsatisfying mishmash of half-baked ideas and barrel-scraping make-do. Instead of making some grand statement that would both see off the punks and underline the band's continued creative health, as it was clearly intended to, it did as Page had once said he hoped all Zeppelin albums would and showed precisely – in this case, painfully – where the four individuals members were at, at the time it was written and recorded: down in the dumps. Even its best material – 'In the Evening', 'Fool in the Rain', 'All My Love' – sounded wan and elegiac; the party over but nobody quite wanting to leave just yet. 'I don't think it was really a Led Zeppelin record,' Plant told me in 2005. 'It was the four of us but I don't think it was as Led Zeppelin as it might have been, for a myriad of different reasons.'

It was certainly Jimmy Page's least impressive outing on a Zeppelin album, his playing to an expectedly high standard, but displaying remarkably few interesting new ideas, almost as if he were back to playing sessions – on his own album. There wasn't even the until now almost obligatory blues rip-off. The nearest he came was the recycling of some of the themes from his precious soundtrack to *Lucifer Rising* for the eerie instrumental intro to 'In the Evening' (with Plant stealing its first line, he later confessed, from 'Tomorrow's Clown' by Marty Wilde). As producer, Page was even less impressive, the sound on *In Through the Outdoor* being conspicuously atrocious in places; the appallingly bad vocal mix on 'In the Evening' being its most glaring offence, just when it most needed help too, Plant's voice now showing the wear and tear of his years on the road, as well as the side-effects of so many drugs and cigarettes and – yes – tears.

'It was a transitional period,' argued Jones, not unjustly. 'It was a chance to see what else we could do. The next album would have been even more interesting had we followed that direction.' Speaking about the album at the time, Page was typically more gung-ho. 'It's not like we've felt we had to change the music to relate to any of the developments that have been going on,' he said, conveniently ignoring the laboured attempts at updating the sound on 'Ozone Baby' and 'Wearing and Tearing'. 'There's no tracks with disco beats or anything . . .'

With mixes for the album completed back in Stockholm after the Christmas break, the only thing holding back the release of *In Through the Outdoor* was general agreement on how best to promote it. With Plant still antsy about the thought of embarking on any long tours – refusing point-blank to even contemplate returning to America – Grant bided his time before making any definite plans. Logistically, there was still a lot to do first anyway; decisions still needed to be made regarding the sleeve – with Hipgnosis brought in again to suggest ideas – and whether or not to release a single. Plant was strongly in favour of releasing 'Wearing and Tearing' with either 'Ozone Baby' or 'Darlene' as a possible B-side, while Page thought it a better idea to simply release all three tracks as an EP – another retro concept back in favour with the New Wave crowd. In the event neither suggestion would be pursued as attention turned instead to the idea of the band making their second 'comeback' in two years with a brace of enormous outdoor shows in England – at Knebworth Park – an idea suggested by the man who had promoted the two Bath Festival appearances and who had helped launch the band in Britain a decade before: Freddy Bannister.

Bannister had begun the by now annual Knebworth Festival in 1974, which Grant had originally agreed to Zeppelin headlining that year before a leaked news item in the music press led to a row with Bannister, who he wrongly blamed for deliberately leaking the story, and the immediate withdrawal from the project of the band. Bannister had been trying unsuccessfully every year since to lure Zeppelin back. 'But the timing was never right,' he says. 'So we'd always end up going with someone else.' Over the years, 'someone else' had included Pink Floyd, Genesis and the Rolling Stones. His original plan for '79 had been The Eagles, then at the height of their popularity. He had also been considering the possibility of another appearance by Pink Floyd. 'But then all these stories started appearing in the music press about

Zeppelin releasing a new album, their first for three years, and I thought: why not? Let's give it another go . . .'

In an attempt to grab Grant's attention, Bannister wrote to him suggesting Zeppelin do two consecutive Saturday shows – on 4 and 11 August – something that had never been done at Knebworth before, reinforcing the idea that Zeppelin was the biggest band in the world. He also decided to double all his previous financial offers. Grant phoned him a couple of days later. With G still at a loss as to how best to promote the new Zeppelin album without being able to send the band on tour, Freddy's offer was well timed for once and the two agreed to meet at Horselunges later that same week. Bannister recalls being taken aback at the security cameras and floodlights that had been installed since his last visit a few years before. Grant liked the idea of two weekends but thought the promoter's offer still too low. G wanted £1 million, he said. Freddy demurred but eventually agreed that a higher than normal ticket price of £7.50 (two pounds more than had been charged for Genesis the year before) might make it 'manageable' – assuming, of course, that both shows were a sell-out. With Bannister estimating the 36.4 acre Knebworth site capable of holding approximately 4,000 per acre – or roughly 290,000 people in total over two weekends (an overgenerous estimate, as it turned out) – Zeppelin's huge fee, plus VAT, equipment hire, fees for two full support bills, plus agent commissions, site rental to David Lytton Cobbold, whose family owned Knebworth Palace, plus the salaries of the numerous site staff that would be required both weekends and various other sundries (advertising, catering, transport, hotels, etc) – there would still be enough left over 'to make my own cut at the end of it reasonably attractive'.

What had not been taken fully into consideration was that no Knebworth bill had ever attracted more than the approximately 100,000 paying customers that had attended the Stones show in 1976. The chances of Led Zeppelin beating that figure appeared good when one considered it would be their first British appearance since the Earl's Court shows four years before and their first anywhere in the world since the debacle of Oakland in 1977. Whether they would be able to do so over consecutive weekends remained to be seen. Eager as he was to commit Grant to the shows, Bannister was savvy enough to get him to agree to the outlandish fee 'strictly on the understanding' that they would only go ahead with the second show if the first was a guaranteed 145,000 sell-out. Hence the decision, later regretted, to initially advertise only one show. As was normal with Grant, the deal was sealed on a handshake. Something else Bannister would later bitterly regret.

On the surface, at least, 1979 had begun more positively for the members of Led Zeppelin than any year since 1975. In January, Maureen Plant gave birth to another son, named Logan Romero, and with the announcement of a new album in the can and two mammoth comeback shows looming on the horizon, despite a predictably sceptical reception from the punk-obsessed UK music press ('The manner in which old superfart Led Zeppelin have consistently presented themselves has made the band's name synonymous with gratuitous excess,' blared the *NME*), Page was back in London giving interviews for the first time in four years. Drinking beer and chain-smoking Marlboros, he sat in the Swan Song offices and boasted of receiving letters from New Wave fans who 'got interested in the actual musical content and wanted to go one step further, which is how they discovered bands like us'; and how the new album had moved the band on musically 'sufficiently to be able to see the next horizon'; but that Knebworth would be 'far more important' because 'the LP's a frozen statement which can be always referred to, but Knebworth's going to be different'. There would be further concerts to come after Knebworth, he was quick to assure everyone, though 'not necessarily in England'. Instead, in an echo of the now-abandoned plans of 1975 to tour 'new stops on the map', they were now considering 'playing Ibiza ... just so we've got a chance of trying out new ideas and new riffs and arrangements and songs'.

In an attempt to underline his own right-on credentials and deflect attention away from the long period of drug-induced indolence that had followed the disastrous end to the 1977 tour, Page also went to some length to discuss his involvement with community politics in Scotland, where he had lent support to the utilisation of raw materials to build a harbour wall as part of a local job recreation scheme, attending the unveiling ceremony. He admitted, however, to voting Tory in the 1979 general election that would bring Margaret Thatcher to power – a veritable act of treason in the politicised punk world of the late Seventies – though he insisted it was 'not just for lighter taxes –

I just couldn't vote Labour. They actually stated that they wanted to nationalise the media – so what possible criticism of them would you be able to have?' The fact that the Tory Party then held effective control of the British print media anyway seemed lost on him. But then, as he also revealed, as a young multi-millionaire entrepreneur he had voted Conservative at the previous election too.

Meanwhile, plans for the Knebworth shows in August were not proceeding nearly as smoothly as either Peter Grant or Freddy Bannister had envisaged. Despite the first Knebworth show being announced by Bob Harris on *The Old Grey Whistle Test* (then the most respected album-oriented weekly music programme on British TV), followed a week later by blanket coverage in the music press, initial demand for tickets was so much lower than Bannister had anticipated it now looked unlikely that a second show would be feasible after all. There was also a tortuous twenty-six hour negotiation with Grant and Showco chief Jack Calmes regarding the budgeting for sound, lights and other necessities – such as the lasers Jimmy wanted, which would need to be flown in from the US – with Grant 'keeping himself going with long lines of cocaine plus the occasional Mogadon to maintain the balance,' Bannister recalls.

The promoter also experienced unexpected problems booking support acts. 'No-one, it seemed, wanted to play with Led Zeppelin. It was at this point, rather belatedly, that I began to realise just what a reputation the band enjoyed for their egotistical behaviour.' Turned down by J.J. Gale, Little Feat, Roxy Music and Ian Dury and the Blockheads, in the end Bannister settled for, in ascending order, Chas and Dave, the New Commander Cody Band, South Side Johnny and the Asbury Jukes, and Todd Rundgren's Utopia. Hardly the most scintillating bill, even by Seventies standards, but it was the best Bannister could do. (Grant had suggested Fairport Convention, who agreed but could only do the first show.)

The band was kept in blissful ignorance about the unexpected difficulty in selling tickets. Indeed, Page still believes now that Knebworth was a great success; proof that the band was bigger than ever. 'Everyone said, "Oh, they're bigger in the States than they are in England", and all of that,' he told me in 1999, adding that he never doubted for an instant they would sell out both shows. 'Actually, I was always confident. Everyone else said that we didn't have the following [anymore], but I knew we did, there was no doubt about that.'

In fact, there was now considerable doubt. By the first week of July, just over 115,000 tickets had been sold for the first show; far short of the 150,000 Bannister had viewed as the bare minimum needed to trigger the announcement of a second show. But Grant was adamant; he had told the band they would be doing two shows; he was not prepared to tell them that would no longer be the case as they could not sell enough tickets to do so. It was a matter of face – about all Grant had left at this precarious stage of the game. As a result, Page still maintains, as he told me, that 'there was more there than what there were officially [declared]' and that, as a consequence, 'we were partially paid ... Peter Grant told me and the rest of the band that Freddy Bannister reneged on it.'

In fact, in a last-gasp attempt to stimulate more interest, Bannister announced that the first show was now sold out but that a second show had been scheduled for the following weekend to deal with the 'extra demand'. To try and kick-start sales for the second show, he took 15,000 ticket applications for the first show – leaving just 100,000 paid for tickets for the first show – and sent them tickets for the second show along with a letter guaranteeing refunds if they could not attend. Unfortunately, a large swathe of disappointed fans did demand a refund. 'What we hadn't allowed for was that so many people had already booked their holidays,' he says now. Fearing the worst, Freddy plucked up the courage and phoned G with the news that they would have to cancel the second show. But G wasn't having it. Promising to 'see you all right' he persuaded Bannister to go ahead with the second show – which the promoter took to mean a renegotiation of their fee. Grant also promised to line up his own 'big attraction' to help generate ticket sales for the second show, which turned out to be the New Barbarians, the part-time band fronted by Ronnie Wood and featuring Keith Richards.

A few weeks before the first show, Richard Cole phoned Bannister to say the band wanted to inspect the site. Specifically, Page wanted to view the memorabilia of Bulmer Lytton, the novelist, also known for his interest in the occult, and one of Knebworth owner David Lytton Cobbold's forebears. During the visit, they had their photograph taken for the festival programme by Storm Thorgerson. 'Next to him, posturing for all she was worth, was a naked young woman obviously placed there by Storm to make the band less conscious of the camera,' recalled Bannister in his memoir, *There Must Be a Better Way*. 'Rumour has it that amongst the many photos taken that day is an interesting one of Jimmy Page minus his trousers, but regrettably I have never been able to confirm this.' The photos were later touched up because the sky was cloudy, superimposing a sunny blue Texan sky.

The plan had been to release *In Through the Outdoor* prior to the Knebworth shows. But delays over the cover – yet again – forced the release date back to 15 August, four days after the second show. Designed again by Hipgnosis, the album would come in no less than six different sleeves: all variations on the same New Orleans bar scene, featuring a boater-hat, suit-and-tie wearing man looking wasted at a seedy bar, being served drinks by a tattooed, vest-wearing bartender. In the background an older black man sat at a piano, a middle-aged black woman laughing and holding a drink and, over by the slatted window, a younger mulatto tart-with-a-heart in figure-hugging dress, a look of utmost indifference on her face. Each sleeve was sepia-tinted with a slash of colour daubed across it like a brush stroke – 'like you were looking inside the bar through its dusty window and the smear was where you'd wiped the pane with your sleeve to peer through,' explained Storm Thorgerson. The inside paper bag holding the vinyl contained two black-and-white line drawings – before and after scenes – of a shot glass, an ashtray, a cigarette and a lighter, which changed colour when water was added to them, an idea Jimmy had gotten from one of his daughter Scarlet's colouring books (though thankfully not one present on the modern CD version). Perversely, the finishing touch was to put each sleeve in a plain brown paper bag, the band name and album title added like a postal stamp. Conceived, ostensibly, as a way of preventing the buyer from knowing which of the six sleeves they were purchasing, it was also an in-joke on Thorgerson's part, who was 'fed up,' he said, 'with the band and the label telling us that it didn't matter what we put on the cover because a Led Zeppelin album would sell anyway. Peter Grant said we could put it in a brown paper bag and it would sell anyway. So we did and he was right!'

Indeed, *In Through the Outdoor* sold over a million copies in the US within forty-eight hours of going on sale, going straight to no. 1 in Britain and America. Over the next few months it would sell more than five million copies in the US, where senior industry figures were now quoted as saying it had 'almost single-handedly saved the American music industry', which was then experiencing a serious drought in record sales after the deluge of much more niche-oriented New Wave signings made by all the major record labels in the preceding eighteen months. In the words of writer Stephen Davis, in America at least, punk and the New Wave was 'for losers and nerds', while Zeppelin still represented, as fellow American scribe David Owen put it, 'a vague continuum of big money, fast cars and prestige'.

Back in Britain, reviews of *In Through the Outdoor* were as eloquent but much more damning. Even *Sounds*, along with the *Melody Maker* the only music paper left still regularly giving positive coverage to hard rock and heavy metal, now brought the hammer down on Zeppelin. Under the heading, 'Close The Door, Put Out The Lights', resident rock expert Geoff Barton's damning two-star review of the album concluded, somewhat sadly, if prophetically: 'I'm not proud to say it, but the dinosaur is extinct.' Grant, predictably, was furious. Having already banned *Sounds* from having their own tent at Knebworth, he now ordered the record company to pull all its advertising from the magazine's pages. But as then *Sounds* editor, Alan Lewis, now recalls: 'That generation of bands were now so out of favour, it didn't really mean much to us anymore. These days you'd crawl over broken glass for a Jimmy Page interview, but they were past their peak in '79. By then we had bands like AC/DC and Blondie setting the pace, in terms of what we put on the cover. We certainly wouldn't have lost any sleep over Zeppelin.'

The Knebworth shows themselves were strange, forcedly triumphal, occasionally brilliant, more often ramshackle occasions, ultimately eventful for none of the reasons the band had hoped they would be – and the cause of enormous hype both then and even more so in the decades that have followed. Fondly recalled now as two of the most successful, best-attended festival shows of the Seventies, with wildly inaccurate estimates of how many people attended; in reality, while the first show attracted a decent, if unspectacular by previous Knebworth standards, turnout of approximately 104,000, the second show was an unmitigated disaster, with barely 40,000 people in attendance on a day full of heavy rain and even heavier vibes.

Following two small warm-up shows in Copenhagen, the band had helicoptered into the first show so rattled by nerves that they could barely speak to each other, let alone any of the other acts appearing that day, or even their own backstage guests. With only two new numbers added – 'In the Evening' and 'Hot Dog' – to the set they had been trawling around America two years before, it wasn't the performance in itself that made them nervous, it was the heavy gravity of history they now felt dragging them down and slowing their steps. Not only was the crowd hyped up beyond reason at the prospect of seeing the first Zeppelin show on British soil for four years but so was everyone behind the scenes too. Seated in a special area at the side of the stage for all Grant and the band's guests was Ahmet Ertegun. Truly, it felt like their future was in the balance. Robert Plant, for one, no longer felt sure the band was strong enough to tip that balance their way. 'I didn't believe there was anything I could do that was really good enough to fulfil people's expectations,' he said afterwards. 'It took half the first show to get over the fact that I was there, and over everything that was going on. My voice was all clammed up with nerves.'

The day had begun badly for Freddy Bannister when a 'rather embarrassed-looking' Richard Cole had walked into the production office that morning and 'insisted' he sign a waiver for the film rights to the event. Still smarting over the critical backlash to *The Song Remains The Same* three years before, and painfully aware that if Plant carried through his threat never to tour America again a promotional Plan B might need to be activated at some point, Grant had hired director Mike Mansfield – whose weekly *Supersonic* pop show had become commercial TV's answer to the BBC's long-running *Top of the Pops* – to film Knebworth for a new feature-length film the band planned to make. As such, Bannister had agreed to allow more than a dozen cameras and crew to position themselves strategically around the site. As Knebworth promoter, Bannister might have expected some sort of royalty or fee from any resulting commercially available film. However, he was not, in principle, against waiving his rights – for an appropriate 'consideration'. When Cole told him he would be doing so for the princely sum of 'one shilling' (five pence) Bannister was outraged, not just at the insultingly derisory offer but the offensive manner in which it was made. 'Get lost!' he told Cole. 'No fucking way!' But Cole insisted, pointing out that the offer came from Grant and that 'with the mood Peter's in these days you really don't need the aggravation'. Bannister duly signed, in the knowledge, he says now, that 'Grant's meanness' would also be his undoing. 'If he had given me £250, the agreement would have been quite legal. However, the only way someone signs their rights away for five pence is under duress, as I was, and this, I was told sometime afterwards, totally invalidates the contract.'

Opening with 'The Song Remains The Same', and finishing more than three hours later with 'Stairway To Heaven', which Plant mucked up the lyrics to – deliberately, some speculated – no-one in the crowd could have guessed at the tensions whirling about the stage like the giant pyramid of green lasers surrounding Page during his violin bow showcase – now used as the prelude to 'In The Evening'. Jonesy's bass wasn't even switched on for the first three numbers (due to a technical fault that took time to repair). And when Plant launched into a garbled speech halfway through the first show, concluding, 'We're never going to Texas anymore ... but we will go to Manchester,' he did so while eyeing Grant at the side of the stage. 'He was in a difficult frame of mind,' said G.

For Jimmy Page, though, this was a great occasion. 'The first one was very special,' he told me in 1999, 'I remember the audience singing "You'll Never Walk Alone" [as the band re-emerged for the encores]. And I mean, that was a very ... an extreme emotional moment, you know? It really was incredible, a wonderful feeling and very emotional. There was tears in the eyes, believe me ...' Another fond memory, he said, was of John Bonham's then thirteen-year-old son, Jason, sitting at his father's kit bashing away on the drums during the soundcheck. 'We were doing "Trampled Underfoot" and I was playing along, con-centrating on the guitar, and I looked round and there was Jason on the drums! It was so John could go out front and listen to his sound balance. I remember Jason playing and John just standing there laughing.'

Mingling backstage in the VIP area were members of the same punk groups that had spent the past three years slagging bands like Zeppelin off: Steve Jones of the Sex Pistols, Mick Jones of The Clash, Chrissie Hynde of the Pretenders ... Not that Jimmy said he noticed. 'To be honest with you, I didn't mix with anybody. I spent most of my time being on my own, vibing up for the show. Even the other bands that were on, like Keith and all of that ... I mean, I love Keith, but I remember I didn't even get to see him.' Also in the crowd was a teenage band from Sheffield named Def Leppard, who saw the first show and decided, as guitarist Steve Clark later told me, 'That we'd just witnessed the Second Coming,' then drove back to Sheffield and signed their first record contract with Phonogram Records the very next day. Years later, Robert Plant would look back on Knebworth and sigh. 'Although we were supposed to be the arch criminals and the real philanderers of debauchery and Sodomy and Gommorah-y, our feet were much more firmly on the ground than a lot of other people around. But you wouldn't have believed that to see us swaggering about at Knebworth because Knebworth was an enormous, incredible thing. I patrolled the grounds the night of the first gig – I went out with some people in a jeep – and people pushed the stone pillars down, with the metal gates attached, because they wanted to get in early. Those gates had been there since 1732 and they just pushed them over. It was a phenomenally powerful thing.'

More, however, was expected from the second show a week later. But it was not to be. Reneging on his promise to see Bannister 'all right' over the lack of ticket sales, Grant now demanded the band be paid in full – on the basis that, as Grant's accountant Joan Hudson, told the promoter, 'you did have 250,000 last Saturday at the first show, so of course there will be plenty over to pay the band in full for the second show.' What's more, G wanted the money now, in advance of the second show. Aghast, Freddy and his wife and business partner Wendy demanded a meeting with Peter in person, which was duly arranged for the following day at Horselunges. But with Grant behaving 'rather like a character in a Tarantino film', the meeting quickly degenerated into threats of violence – and worse. Convinced the Bannisters were lying about the number of fans at the first show – Freddy insisting there were no more than 104,000 tickets sold, G sticking to his claim of 'a quarter million' – and Wendy 'close to tears', Grant suddenly 'jumped up and began waving his fist in her face. "Don't get smart with me," he yelled.'

The Bannisters, now frightened for their lives, got up and left immediately. But worse was to follow. The next day an American purporting to represent Grant and Zeppelin, turned up at their home. Clad in a 'black suit, black shirt and dark sunglasses', he looked

like 'a typical Mafia bully boy,' says Freddy. 'Although I think he was
probably just a private detective, there was all this talk of "people from
Miami". Then afterwards he just sat outside the house in this big black
car with tinted windows. It was very upsetting.' Accompanied by
'a rather seedy-looking Englishman introduced to me as a former
Metropolitan Police superintendent,' the pair claimed to have aerial
photographs of the first show that had been analysed by NASA
scientists, 'proving there were a quarter of a million people there'.
Seated now over lunch at a smart Chalk Farm restaurant, Freddy
laughs at the memory. 'I mean, really! What rot! Even if it were true,
how on earth would we have fit a quarter of a million people into
thirty-odd acres? They would have to have been standing on top of
each other.'

Again, the matter didn't rest there, and the following day – forty-
eight hours before the second show – Grant turned up at the Bannisters'
home in person, accompanied by the American and 'a great bull of a
man' introduced as their driver but clearly there, in Freddy's view, 'to
add an air of intimidation'. However, Grant was more amenable than
before, and while insisting that he still didn't believe there were less
than a quarter of a million people at the first Knebworth show, he told
them he was prepared to reduce Zeppelin's fee for the second show,
in order to allow the rest of the bands on the bill to be paid off. There
was, however, one proviso: he would be taking over the running of the
show from the Bannisters and putting his own 'people' on the gates.
Freddy was 'furious' but agreed. 'I didn't see that we had much choice,'
he says now, 'and frankly I'd had enough by then anyway. I just wanted
the whole thing to be over.'

Even though the crowd, by Freddy's estimation, was 'roughly a
third' what it had been a week before, Zeppelin's second show should
have been better, technically, the band having overcome some of their
nerves. However, the performance was desultory by comparison, the
mood far less buoyant than it had been at the first show. As Jimmy put
it to me years later: 'It wasn't horrendous, the second show. It was a
very fine show, but the first one had the edge on the second, definitely.'
There were also strange vibes front and back. It rained heavily and the
New Barbarians reputedly refused to go on until they had been paid,
causing a long delay. When, late in the afternoon of the second show,
Joan Hudson confirmed that the total number of tickets sold for the

event came to no more than the 40,000 Freddy had predicted, 'rather than lightening the atmosphere [it] seemed to make it worse', Grant furious no doubt to be so starkly confronted by the awful truth. The years that had elapsed between those five sold-out Earl's Court shows and these two undersubscribed Knebworth events had taken their toll, not just in terms of personal cost, but in the sheer weight of history. The world had not hung on for Robert Plant's leg to heal or his heart to mend; nor had the world shown patience while Page, Grant and Bonham got deeper and deeper into their own personal drug hells. Most of all, rock music had shown that it was quite prepared to move on with or without Led Zeppelin. Far from being the glorious comeback Jimmy and G had envisaged, Knebworth sounded the first sombre toll of the death knell for the band. From here on in it would be downhill all the way . . .

'It was all such a shame,' says Freddy Bannister now, 'and all so unnecessary. When I first knew Peter, as well as his natural astuteness and innate charm, he had judgment and taste that belied his humble origins. I am sure that he would have been successful in almost anything he undertook, not just in the music business, but also as an international art or antique dealer. But he changed over the years. Drugs changed him, success changed him. If I'd have known this I wouldn't have done the last Knebworth shows . . .' He breaks off into a sigh.

It's a remarkably philosophical attitude from someone whose dealings with Grant and Zeppelin, he says now, 'basically put us out of business'. The Zeppelin Knebworth shows were his and Wendy's last as promoters. A month later, the American had demanded another meeting, this time at the Dorchester Hotel in London, where he asked Freddy to sign a pre-typed letter – later reproduced in a page advert in *Melody Maker* – absolving Grant and the band from responsibility for any ill-effects of the Knebworth shows. News of some of the bad feeling backstage had begun filtering out and, as Bannister later wrote, after the suspended jail sentences Grant, Bonham and Cole had received for their part in the Oakland debacle, 'it wouldn't be that easy for them to obtain American work permits and if I made too much fuss about the way I had been so unjustly treated, it would probably aggravate an already delicate situation.' In fear of his life – 'By this time Peter Grant was in such a terrible state, both mentally and physically, we thought he was on the way out and would be delighted to take us with him' – he reluctantly signed the statement.

The final twelve months of their existence were far from good ones for Led Zeppelin. Just two months after Knebworth, a nineteen-year-old photographer name Philip Hale died of a heroin overdose at Page's Plumpton mansion. The matter made the British papers briefly; had it happened five years before, when the group was at the zenith of its popularity, this would not have been the case. Now, at the fag end of the decade they had once ruled, they were so far off the media radar it barely rated a mention outside the provincial press. An inquest was held in Brighton, at which Page was required to give evidence: the outcome a verdict of 'misadventure'. The hearings happened to coincide with the *Melody Maker* Readers' Poll Awards, which the band had been invited to attend, having swept the board. The band may not have been popular enough to sell out two nights at Knebworth but there were still more than enough fans to vote for them. The *MM*'s trendy young staff were not best pleased, but the *MM*'s readers – the kind that could be counted on to vote in such polls – were not like those of the much more punk-radical *NME* and still liked their rock gods to be long-haired and exceptionally good on their instruments. As if to rub it in, all of the band bar Page attended the ceremony; the first time they had done so since 1971. Plant driving himself in his Land Rover; Bonzo and Jonesy turning up in a chauffeur-driven Rolls Royce; the latter in a witty Rock Against Journalism badge (ha, yeah . . .). Dave Lewis, who was also there, recalls 'they told everyone that Jimmy was on holiday in Barbados, but the truth was he was at the inquest for Philip Hale. Jimmy definitely got away with that one . . .' At the party afterwards, a drunken Bonham staggered around yelling that The Police should have won the Best Band Award and began singing 'Message In A Bottle' at the top of his voice. As ever, Bonzo saw to it that nobody would forget him in a hurry. On 29 December that year, all but Page appeared at the UNICEF charity show, Rock For Kampuchea, at London's Hammersmith Odeon, Jimmy's absence again explained as being on 'holiday'. And again, nobody from the press batted an eye, nor cared overmuch either way . . .

There was to be one last hurrah when, six months later, the band, seemingly out of the blue, embarked on a three-week tour of Europe, beginning with the modestly-sized Westfallen Halle in Dortmund, Germany, on 17 June. Informally dubbed by the band as the 'Cut The

Waffle' tour, gone were the lasers, big screens, smoke bombs and lights, in their place a stark black backdrop, a greatly reduced PA and the decision to drop lengthy show-stoppers like 'Dazed and Confused', 'No Quarter', 'Moby Dick', even Page's violin showcase: anything that might be construed in the post-punk world as 'waffle'. Even the venues were scaled down; the smallest theatres they had performed in since 1973. The clothes the band now wore on stage also reflected their painful attempts to contemporise their image; out went the flared jeans and open-necked jackets and shirts; in came straight-legged trousers and regular shirts, even the occasional 'skinny' tie. And they had all had a haircut. All of which had the converse effect. Instead of making them look young and trendy, suddenly, Led Zeppelin looked very, very old.

The problems that still surrounded them were also not new. Despite reports now claiming he was in fine form musically, three numbers into the show in Nuremberg on 27 June, Bonham collapsed behind his kit and the rest of the show had to be cancelled. He only just about made it through the rest of the tour. According to Cole – whose own heroin habit was now so out of control Grant had omitted him from the tour – Bonzo was taking smack right up to the start of the tour. Could it be he was still withdrawing when he collapsed in Nuremberg? The band have never confirmed nor denied the stories. Plant later told me, in fact, that Bonzo played beautifully on that tour.

He wasn't well, though, was he, I asked Plant in 2005? 'No. He collapsed . . . I don't know what happened. I know he had to eat fifty bananas immediately. He had no potassium in him. You see, the only reason that we ever had a doctor around [on tour] in Led Zeppelin was to get some Quaaludes. So we never had anybody checking us up saying, "Oh man, the blood test says you're really low in minerals." I mean, every day now I have omega 3 oil for my joints so that I can play tennis and [perform well]. But we had no thought about that then. It was a very, very large Jack Daniel's and Coke – and on and on and on.'

Bonzo was joined on stage for the penultimate show of the tour at the Olympiahalle in Munich by Simon Kirke of Bad Company, who jammed with him on 'Whole Lotta Love'. Kirke recalled: 'The last time I saw [Bonzo] he was packing up little dolls he had collected from different countries for his daughter Zoë, wrapping up these little

dolls, one from Austria, one from Switzerland ...' The final show of
the tour was at the Eissporthalle in Berlin on 7 July, the band responding
to punk's accusations of obsolescence by cutting down on the more
'improvisational' aspect of what till then was regarded as the quintessential, over-the-top Zeppelin live experience, in favour of a more
down-to-earth approach that saw Page bantering with the audience
and – unheard of till then – actually introducing songs personally from
the stage.

'The state of mind was this,' Jones told Dave Lewis, who followed
the tour in person, 'let's sharpen up, cut the waffle out, take a note of
what's going on and reinvent ourselves ... it did that seem Robert and
I were holding it together, while the others were dealing with other
matters. The thing was it seemed to be such a shame to let it go down
the toilet.' For Robert, it was all about showing they'd 'learned a hell
of a lot from XTC and people like that. I was really keen to stop
the self-importance and the guitar solos that lasted an hour. We cut
everything down and we didn't play any song for more than four-and-
a-half minutes.' Or as he told me years later, 'By the late Seventies,
everything had become so overindulged, not just with the drugs, which
it was, but the music itself. It had gone from this tremendously exciting
burst of energy at the end of the Sixties, to this overindulgent monster
looking for a place to die.' Something he still wanted to save Zeppelin
from doing.

The other thing he was still trying to avoid on that 1980 tour was
the decision to return to America that he knew the others were
desperate for him to agree to. On the way home from the European
dates, he finally relented and within days Grant had already formulated
the next US campaign, giving it the working title: 'Led Zeppelin: The
1980s Part One'. Plant did, however, lay down some strict deal-breaker
conditions: no tour should take him away from his family for longer
than a month; the band would play a maximum of two shows back-
to-back followed by a day off; and, as with the European tour, Super-
domes were out, more modest venues in; the aim to re-establish
'contact' with the audience (and, by definition, themselves). Grant
and the others wearily complied. 'I reckoned once Robert got over
there and got in the swing of things he'd be okay,' said Grant.

Scheduled to open in Montreal on 17 October, there would be a
further twenty shows climaxing with four nights in Chicago in

November. 'Europe was "Let's please Robert cos he won't go to America," ' says Dave Lewis. 'Once he agreed to do America, though, everything kicked up a gear again.' He recalls talking on the phone to a delighted Bonham and being in the Swan Song office while Jimmy was there looking at a model of what was to be the new American stage show. 'After all the incoherence of the past few years, it was like all systems go again.'

Well, almost. Behind the scenes, Bonham was the one now panicking at the thought of returning to America. Whether it was the prospect of leaving home again which depressed him is unclear, but according to insiders, he had now kicked his heroin habit and was taking a pill called Motival, a mood-altering drug designed to reduce anxiety. He was, however, still drinking heavily. It was in this state of mind that he told Plant on the eve of rehearsals for the US tour: 'I've had it with playing drums. Everybody plays better than me. I'll tell you what, when we get to the rehearsal, you play the drums and I'll sing.'

The first day of rehearsal was scheduled for 24 September – just another day to Rex King, who drove Bonham down the M4 from his farm to the Old Mill House, Jimmy's new mansion (by the river) in Windsor, purchased earlier that year for £900,000 from the actor Michael Caine. Rex later recalled Bonzo telling him to stop off at a pub, where he downed four quadruple vodka-and-oranges and quaffed a couple of ham rolls. 'Breakfast,' he called it. When John got to rehearsals that day he wasn't feeling any brighter, moaning about how long they would be away in America. He continued drinking until he literally became too drunk to play; unheard of in his heyday. He then downed at least two more large vodkas before crashing out on the sofa at Jimmy's place, where everyone was staying, at around midnight. He was then half-carried, half-dragged to bed by Jimmy's assistant, Rick Hobbs, who had seen this movie many times before. Hobbs laid the comatose drummer out on his side supported by some pillows. Then turned out the light and left Bonzo to sleep it off.

When, the following afternoon, Bonzo still hadn't risen from his lair, John Paul Jones and Benje Le Fevre both went to rouse him. But there was a bad smell in the room, Bonzo's inert body unresponsive to touch and they realised with mounting horror that he was dead. An ambulance was summoned but it was already too late. The police also showed up but reported no suspicious circumstances. Paramedics deduced he'd probably been dead for several hours. Robert Plant immediately drove to the Old Hyde Farm to console Pat, Jason and Zoë. John Paul Jones went home to his own family, 'terribly shocked'. Jimmy Page stood inside his house – the second time someone had died under his roof in less than twelve months – watching at his window as a gathering group of Zeppelin fans arrived to hold a silent vigil outside his gates. The news was already on the radio and his phone was ringing non-stop but he didn't answer it.

In Los Angeles, eight hours behind England, Bonzo's old mate from Brum, Black Sabbath drummer Bill Ward, woke that day with a terrible hangover from 'a bender the night before' and 'junked out' – withdrawing from heroin. Bill, who had walked out on Sabbath some weeks before and would spend 'the next year staying in my bedroom getting high' was given the news of his friend John Bonham's death by his drug dealer. 'The dope dealer came around every morning with the allotted amount of stuff for the day. And one morning she came round and she was absolutely in bits, crying her eyes out because she was a major Led Zeppelin fan. I thought, "Oh, man, what's going on?" She said, "Bonham's dead". The very first thought I had was a selfish one, and it was: "I'll be next." Like, "I'm right behind you, Johnny. I'm right behind you . . . "'

As you lay there, the room spinning, your mind wandered off again . . . back to where the Worcestershire countryside blossoms, to the big ranch-style name board at the bend in the road and the twin white fences either side of the long, straight driveway to the farmhouse, where your dad did all the wood-panelling and your brother Mick helped build the extensions, surrounded by a hundred acres of sheep and cattle and trees and fields, to your beloved Pat and Jason and Zoë, to the bloody cats always under your feet and your cars, your pride and joys, all lined up in the converted barn, to your drum kits and your pub jukebox and your ale and your fags . . . to home. No way had you ever intended ending up a bloody farmer but then you'd seen this place, seen the look on Pat's face and bought it.

Planty was just a few miles up the road, too, with his flaming goats that ate everything, old boots, you name it. Not that you saw much of him when you weren't working. Your real mates were people like Bev and his wife Val, getting dressed up and going to each other's houses for dinner and a few bottles of wine. You liked getting dolled up in a nice suit and tie.

None of that hippy shit when you were out for the night with Pat. She'd be in her gladrags too, and you'd both jump in the car and drive over to Redditch to take your mum and dad out down the working men's club in Evesham and buy everybody a drink. You did it once in the white Rolls you'd bought after you'd first made a bob or two, and when you came out some fucking skinheads had smashed the bastard up, kicked in the windows and gobbed all over it, little cunts. You didn't make that mistake again but you did like to turn up looking nice in a smart motor. All your jewellery and everything, Pat on your arm in her diamond earrings and princess shoes, looking like a million bucks, your mum and dad so proud of you at last.

They knew it was all shit, what they wrote about you in the press. They knew you weren't anything like the cunt in the bowler hat that used to roar like a bear on stage, not really. That was all just for show. They knew you only used to drink like that cos you hated being away from them all, hated all the bullshit that went with it. They knew that wasn't really you in those pictures in the magazines; that you never went near groupies or took drugs or any of that other shit they accused you of. They knew you'd never do anything to hurt them, that you loved your wife, loved your kids, loved who you were and what you'd become, what you'd achieved, how you'd done it all for them and no-one else, never ...

An inquest was held on 8 October 1980 at East Berkshire Coroner's Court, which recorded a 'death by misadventure' verdict, concluding that John Bonham had died from choking on his own vomit while asleep, 'due to consumption of alcohol' – in the region, they calculated, of forty measures of vodka. As a result, he had suffered a pulmonary oedema – a swelling of the blood vessels – due to an excess of fluid and begun vomiting. It was death by 'accidental suicide', they said. John Bonham was thirty-two.

Inevitably, stories of the 'Zeppelin jinx' began to rear their head again, the *NME* scooping the prize for most tasteless speculation when under the heading: 'Bonzo's Last Bash', it openly suggested that Bonham's demise was somehow connected to Page's interest in the occult. The London *Evening News* also got in on the act, splashing with the headline: ZEPPELIN 'BLACK MAGIC' MYSTERY and quoting an unnamed source as saying: 'Robert Plant and everyone around the band is convinced that Jimmy's dabbling in black magic is responsible in some way for Bonzo's death and all those tragedies.' Others whispered it was surely more a case of 'bad karma'; an accusation Jimmy was still bridling at when I broached the subject years later. 'To blame something like that on bad karma makes me angry,' he said. 'It's ridiculous and disrespectful to the families involved.' Or as he told Nick Kent in 2003: 'I do believe in karma, very much so. But in life's journey whatever comes at you, you've got to deal with. It doesn't mean to say that you've generated the karma yourself.'

The funeral took place two days later at Rushock Parish Church in Worcestershire; his body buried in the same churchyard he is seen speeding past in his car in *The Song Remains The Same*. Over three hundred mourners attended, including Grant and the rest of the band. Tributes were also received from Paul McCartney, Cozy Powell, Carl Palmer and Phil Collins. The band shunned reporters but by then they were hardly speaking to each other. Robert seemed to take it the hardest. First his own tragedies, now this, his friend from home, from teenage years, from that time before Zeppelin; a place he knew he would never now be able to return to. Bev Bevan told me he heard about Bonzo's death on the radio. 'I tried to phone Robert and I tried to phone Pat but we just couldn't get through to anybody. It was just very difficult to come to terms with. The thing I do remember very well is the funeral. That was horrible. Unfortunately, I've been to a lot of funerals now. But that, I think, was the most horrible funeral I've been to. The church was absolutely packed with people – all his friends and family. I went with Jeff Lynne and Roy Wood. We got into the church but we were right at the back and we just about squeezed in somewhere. But it was just one of the saddest occasions. Unusually for a lot of the funerals I've been to, there was a lot of absolute weeping and wailing going on. People really were just hysterical. Just out of control, sobbing and weeping – screaming almost. It was just not a nice place to be. It was very moving – extremely moving. And what it did prove, even though it was unpleasant at the time to witness it, was just how much he was gonna be missed. It was just incredibly intense. You get upset yourself, obviously. I'm quite an emotional person so it doesn't take much to get me crying but I just burst into tears. It was horrible.'

Sitting in the basement kitchen of the Tower House in 2005, Jimmy Page absolutely refused to discuss that day. Instead, he ran his fingers

through his hair, puffed out his cheeks, and pointed out merely that it
was 'a desperate time, for me and for his family. It was also a great loss
in the musical world, this chap who was so inspirational in his drumming. He was a young man, yeah. But then again what a body of work
he left behind.' What about the night he died: was there anything at
all that could or should have been done to save him? Jimmy eyed me
uncomfortably. 'The thing is it wasn't new to us to see Bonzo drink
and pass out. I knew a lot of people who used to do that. Maybe in
this day and age it might ring alarm bells. But in those days it was the
norm within the sort of people that you knew. So one day – and this
is all I'm gonna say about it – he goes to sleep and he's had a lot to
drink that day, and he's collapsed and he goes to bed – and then he
doesn't wake up. I mean, that's something that, you know, you just
couldn't believe would ever happen.'

A few weeks after the funeral, the band met up with Grant at the
Savoy Hotel in London, where Plant, speaking for them all, said simply:
'We can't go on without Bonham.' There had been some suggestion
that they might continue, as The Who had done after Moon's death.
Carmine Appice, Cozy Powell and Bev Bevan – all old friends of
Bonzo's – were all said to be in the frame. But it was never really an
option. As Robert put it to me in 2003, 'There's always been this deal
about, "Oh well, everybody else does it." I mean, Jesus Christ, how
you ever gonna weave that magic that was there? If you look at the
DVD now and you watch things like "Achilles Last Stand", from
Knebworth, it's frightening! That is Bernard Purdy meets Buddy Rich
meets a brave new world that nobody's ever heard of! Even if certain
chemicals got the better of us here and there at that later stage, I still
don't think I've ever heard a rhythm section in a rock group do that.
Who you gonna bring in to make that happen again?' Or as Bevan said,
'God, if I had of been offered the job, I think I'd have been terrified
because I couldn't have replaced Bonzo. I can't think of anyone who
actually could.'

As Jimmy later admitted to me: 'It could have been any one of us
that [was] lost, at that point. And I know if it had been any of the
others we wouldn't want to have continued. We couldn't just replace
somebody; it wasn't that sort of band. You can't teach somebody,
especially in a live situation. You've either got it or you haven't, and
nobody else has got what John had.'

Peter Grant had reached the same conclusion before the band had even said a word. He told Dave Lewis that at the Savoy meeting, 'They all looked at me and asked me what I thought. I said it just couldn't go on because it had always been the four of them, and they were all relieved.' Getting a replacement 'would have been totally out of character'. Zeppelin had always needed all four members to make the magic happen. 'Now one of them was gone.'

On 4 December 1980, Peter Grant's office released an official statement confirming the break up of Led Zeppelin. It read: 'We wish it to be known that the loss of our dear friend and the deep respect we have for his family together with the sense of undivided harmony felt by ourselves and our manager, have led us to decide we could not continue as we were.'

That Bonham's early death would add lustre to the Zeppelin legend could not have been foreseen, said John Paul Jones. 'There is always that James Dean quality to it,' he told me. 'The real tragedy was that John was doing fine at the time he died. He'd been through a bit of a dark period, but he'd come through it and was full of enthusiasm again. Working together, we had new energy again and so when he died … I remember it with a lot of sadness but a lot of anger too. Kind of, what did he have to go and do that for? Not just because of the band but because it was just such a waste of life. In bereavement counselling they teach you that anger is often the emotion in close friends of someone who dies relatively young. But I was angry with the situation too. It was an accident that so easily could have been avoided.'

'It was such a different time, Mick, that's all,' said Robert. 'Because after John passed away, there was no more Led Zeppelin. No matter what anybody would think about replacing John. I mean, he and I played together from when we were fifteen. I couldn't walk away, feel bad, and then turn around and look for somebody else. It was not the issue. There was no need. What did anybody need to do that for?'

And yet … if Bonzo had died after the second album or even the fourth, there seems little doubt that Led Zeppelin would have kept going. If John Paul Jones hadn't changed his mind about leaving in 1974 they surely wouldn't have broken up. No, John Bonham's death – tragic though it was – didn't on its own also mean the death of Led Zeppelin. The band had been slowly dying long before that. Bonzo's drastic, shoddy demise simply made the whole thing more terrifyingly –

irredeemably – real. The song might have remained the same but nothing else ever did. No matter how much Jimmy Page, with his occult knowledge, all useless in the end, might have willed it.

16

To Be A Rock . . .

Y ou are Jimmy Page and in the summer of 2008 you are one of the wealthiest, most admired and famous guitarists in the world – and one of its most conflicted. Everyone says your band is the best in the world. The awards people at Mojo, the awards people at GQ, the awards people give you just so with their words, everywhere you go, saying you should get back together, that it would be great; that it would be the best; that it would be like the Second Coming. Everyone, everywhere, all the time. The only one who doesn't say it is Robert Plant. It's a drag. You and Robert should have been out there touring with Zeppelin this summer. That was the plan. Instead, you get up and guest onstage at a Foo Fighters concert in London, you go to dinner at Nobu and drink alcohol-free beer and wonder why everyone always expects you to pick up the bill. Your picture still appears in newspapers and on the cover of magazines and people still offer you millions to tell your story – the real story – which of course you turn down, never having been remotely interested in telling the real story, why would anyone want to do that? You turn up backstage at Aerosmith and White-snake shows, then leave when you start to get pestered by drunks with camera phones, all wanting the same thing, talking to you like they know you when they know nothing, you just smiling along, trying to be the good guy now the bad days are long gone. You ride on a red double-decker bus in Beijing, gurning your way through 'Whole Lotta Love' with X Factor winner Leona Lewis and wonder why not everyone thinks it's a great idea. Well, what are you supposed to do? The truth is, you don't know. Or do you? When someone who's supposed to know suggests you simply find yourself another singer, for the first time in years you're tempted. Why not? Queen did it, didn't they? Freddie's dead but John Deacon isn't and he's not part of it, either, yet no-one holds that against them, do they? No. And if Robert doesn't like it, let him say so. Let him come back and say he'll do

it instead. It worked before, didn't it, when you were with David Cover-
dale? And if it doesn't again this time, that stuff you've always said about
'chemistry', how it wouldn't work without all the components. Yeah, well,
blame Robert. Unless he comes back, of course, then you'll have all the
chemistry you could ever want again . . .

Although the story of Led Zeppelin ostensibly ended that bleak day in
September 1980 when it became clear that John Bonham's pale, inert
form would not be roused again, in reality new chapters have been
added to it on a regular basis ever since. The first – the posthumous
release in 1982 of the odds-and-sods *Coda* album, onto which was
bundled a ragbag of rejects, from the three unreleased *In Through the
Outdoor* tracks plus the leftovers of their earliest albums – was originally
meant to have closed the book. Instead, its comparatively modest sales
(a million in the US, compared to seven million for *In Through the
Outdoor*, and only 60,000 in the UK, where *Outdoor* had sold over
300,000) reflected how much interest in the Zeppelin legacy had
waned by the early Eighties. 'I wanted to do a live album, too,' Jimmy
told me as far back as 1988. 'Picking tracks from different eras. But we
could never get it together.' And nobody really cared anyway. Not right
then anyway.

Instead, the immediate period following Bonham's death was 'the
worst time in my life'. For the best part of two years, 'I didn't even
touch the guitar. I was shattered. I lost a very, very close friend.' The
guitar 'just related everything, you know, to what had happened . . . the
tragedy that had happened.' The days had passed slowly but the years
had 'flashed by'. He wanted to come back, to 'do something again'.
But to begin with, the omens had all been bad. 'I called up my road
manager one day and said, "Look, get the Les Paul out of storage.". But
when he went to get it the case was empty! I think somebody took it
out and never put it back. They shouldn't have and it eventually
reappeared. But when he came back and said the guitar's missing, I
said, "That's it, forget it, I'm finished." But it turned up again some
time later and thank God it did, otherwise . . .' He paused, took a drag
on his cigarette. 'Otherwise you wouldn't be here today?' I finished
the sentence for him. 'That's right,' he said softly.

One of the few people to visit Jimmy during those dark days after
Bonzo's death was Timothy d'Arch Smith. 'I went down to sort out

all his books and some days it was very, very gloomy,' he says now. 'You knew he was there. The books would arrive on the ground floor. And that sort of made me think, "I wonder why I'm not allowed upstairs?" And then other days he'd sit and talk but it was obviously ... difficult. I said "Are you going to start again?" and he said, "I can't, you know, the chemistry. It was telepathic between Bonham and me." Scarlet would come back from school and play the piano and the French woman [Charlotte] she was always very nice.'

In fact, it's said that Charlotte was nice to almost everybody that ventured near the house in those woebegone days, going so far as to invite fans inside sometimes, especially those who had travelled all the way from America, or even further afield. 'There are stories of Charlotte inviting people in and ordering them Chinese takeaways,' says Dave Lewis, 'which may not always have been wise.' He is referring to the fact that several high-quality Zeppelin bootlegs appeared in the early Eighties, many rumoured to have originated from Page's own collection of live tapes, pilfered by ungrateful houseguests. Jimmy, meanwhile, would lounge around upstairs in his dressing gown, barely leaving the house for weeks at a time. He was convinced Zeppelin would have carried on 'as normal' had Bonham not died. 'We were going to go to the States on tour and then we would have been revitalised,' he told me. 'Because that would have been the first really big tour we'd have had for quite a while. I'm sure that would have been enough stimulus to get us in the studio and probably doing ... who knows what? Every album was so different from the previous one. That was one of the best things about the band: that it was always in a state of change.'

None of which took into account the fact that Robert Plant was deeply conflicted over his continued role in the band and was already hankering for a life after Zeppelin; not just a solo career, which he would surely have pursued at some point with or without Bonzo, but to get away from the bad drugs, bad management and – yes – bad vibes. Peter Grant had also 'just had enough' as he later admitted. He told Dave Lewis: 'By 1982 I just wasn't up to it. Mentally and everything ...' Swan Song was already on the slide long before the final Zeppelin album. In order to preserve the myth and build the legend, the best thing that could have happened to them, arguably, was to split up exactly when they did. Certainly there appeared to be little room in the Eighties – a time when the Seventies had never seemed so far away – for a bloated old rock giant like Led Zeppelin.

Instead, Jimmy Page's rehabilitation was slow and painful, beginning with a half-hearted soundtrack album for director Michael Winner's *Death Wish II* movie: a hodgepodge of recycled ideas – 'In the Evening' reborn as the title track; Chopin's 'Prelude No. 3 in G#' re-jigged for the electric guitar as merely 'Prelude'; and several 'mood pieces' made up of swooping drones that harked back to *Lucifer Rising*. Neither film nor soundtrack won many plaudits and it would be another two years before Page was heard from again, coming on to play an instrumental version of 'Stairway to Heaven' at the 1982 ARMS charity concert at the Albert Hall, at the behest of his old mucker, Eric Clapton. Dave Dickson says it was during the making of a video for the charity that he met Page 'and he couldn't get a coherent sentence out of his mouth he was that far gone. You could see it in his face; his eyes were revolving in different directions. He was pale, so thin, like a walking skeleton. It was obvious he was still deeply into the heroin at the time.'

There had been some low-profile dates 'keeping my hand in' playing in Roy Harper's band, but it wasn't until he teamed up with former Free and Bad Company vocalist Paul Rodgers – who he had reconnected with on the US leg of the ARMS tour the following year – that Page really began to discover a musical life for himself after Zeppelin, finally shrugging off the heroin habit that had dogged him for so many years, in order to make the trip to the US. (He reportedly told friends it had only taken four days to do so, in which case he must really have been using some strong magic. The likelihood is it took considerably longer but he was loath to admit it, always having denied, as he continues to even now, that heroin had a seriously detrimental effect on his life or his career. That said, it's notable that Page has steered clear of the drugs ever since.)

With Rodgers also 'still recovering' from the loss of his own superstar outfit, 'Paul was one of the few people that could probably relate to what I was going through,' said Jimmy. The result: The Firm, a four-piece (also featuring ex-Uriah Heep drummer Chris Slade and former Roy Harper bassist Tony Franklin) that critics complained was neither fish nor fowl, but that Page said 'saved' him. The Firm would allow him and Rodgers to simply 'get out and play and just really enjoy

ourselves'. However, both men refused to perform any material from
their former bands, relying solely on the much blander, funk-tinged
sound of the new outfit, although the closing track on their self-
titled debut album in 1985, 'Midnight Moonlight', was a revamped
unreleased Zeppelin number – another variation on the lost 'Swan
Song' epic of the mid-Seventies – which Plant had reputedly refused
to sing. A second Firm album, *Mean Business*, was issued in 1986, but
neither release troubled the charts for long, despite the band becoming
a huge concert attraction in the US. By which time, Page was now
harbouring secret plans to put Zeppelin back together. If only Robert
Plant would agree.

Plant, however, had well and truly moved on by then, the thought
of resurrecting the behemoth he had spent so long escaping from
utterly abhorrent. The death of John Bonham appeared to have
affected him more than Page or Jones, but the death of Zeppelin had
freed him from the dark clouds he had operated under since 1975.
Even so, it would be a while before he would be able to step out from
the long shadow of the band's legacy and begin to forge a musical
identity of his own, his first tentative post-Zep steps an otherwise
anonymous five-track mini-album of R&B covers called *The Honeydrippers: Volume One*, and featuring both Jeff Beck (on two tracks) and
Jimmy Page (on one). A more decisive leap forward was the release in
June 1982 of his first bona-fide solo album, *Pictures at Eleven*. The last
recording to be issued on the Swan Song label, it was a transitional
work, never straying far from the sound he was then best known for.
In ex-Steve Gibbons Band guitarist Robbie Blunt, Plant had clearly
found someone he felt comfortable writing with. Inevitably, though,
the best tracks were the most Zep-like. Not least 'Burning Down
One Side', featuring portentous drumming from Phil Collins in his
misguided attempt to fill Bonzo's almighty shoes; 'Slow Dancer', a
rather too obvious attempt to create a worthy successor to 'Kashmir';
and 'Moonlight In Samosa', which sounds like 'Stairway to Heaven'
minus the successful ascent to the summit. Co-written, sung and
produced by Plant at a time when Page was still hiding away reclusively,
licking his wounds, it was the first encouraging glimpse fans would
have of what the post-Zep future might look and sound like. As a
result, it did much better in the charts than even Plant had dared hope;
reaching no. 3 in America and no. 2 in Britain.

Before the album was released, Robert took a tape of the basic tracks to the Old Mill House to play to Jimmy. 'It was very emotional,' he later said. 'We just sat there and I sort of had my hand on his knee. We were just sitting through it together. He knew that I'd gone, that I was off on my own with the aid of other people and just forging ahead, and all I wanted was for him to do the same.' Ultimately, he said, he was still only thirty-four and 'I didn't want to be written off as an old fart'. When, a year later, the second Plant solo album, *The Principle of Moments*, was released – preceded by the fanfare of a big hit single in the wonderfully evocative ballad Plant had written with Blunt and keyboardist Jezz Woodroffe, 'Big Log', with its Latin lilt and glossy synthesisers and voice that found a new, more snug fit beyond the howls and moans of Zeppelin – it was a dream come true for the singer, and the confirmation of a new nightmare for the guitarist who had set him on his path so long ago.

John Paul Jones, being the 'sensible one', did what he always did and simply got on with things . . . quietly. Never any question of joining another group – as he put it, 'Who could I have joined that was as good as Led Zeppelin?' – he now became simple John Baldwin again, retreating to the Sussex farmhouse he had owned since 1977, spending time with his wife and daughters. When he did finally emerge from his shell, however, his various credits as musician, producer, arranger and songwriter began cropping up all over the place, as he began to collaborate in various guises with artists as diverse as R.E.M., Heart, Ben E. King, La Fura dels Baus, Brian Eno, Karl Sabino, the Butthole Surfers . . . He also worked with Paul McCartney, who had invited him to help out on the soundtrack of his semi-autobiographical musical film *Give My Regards To Broad Street*. He also fulfilled his earlier ambition of working on film soundtracks, beginning with Michael Winner's 1986 film *Scream for Help*, which also featured Jimmy Page on two tracks. He followed that two years later with the more conventional – and much more successful – production of *Children*, the third and best album from Sisters of Mercy offshoot Goth-outfit, The Mission, from which came the band's biggest hit, 'Tower of Strength'. 'We couldn't believe our luck, getting John as our producer,' recalled Mission mainman Wayne Hussey. 'We kept muttering under our breath, "Look out, Led Zeppelin guy! Led Zeppelin guy!" ' In 1990, he produced an album for his eldest daughter, the singer Jacinda Jones –

a less successful but 'even more wonderful' collaboration.

It didn't really become clear how much he still missed Led Zeppelin until July 1985, when the three surviving members took to the stage at the JFK Stadium in Philadelphia for their part in the Live Aid concert. While their playing that day – augmented by the more than capable former Chic drummer Tony Thompson, but ruinously distorted by the unrehearsed arrival halfway through of Phil Collins – was unarguably sloppy, and the sight and sound of the crowd (which I was fortunate enough to observe from the side of the stage) reacting with uncontrolled hysteria was something none of us who were there will ever be able to forget. In over thirty years in the music business, I've never seen anything like it. Even the people working backstage stopped what they were doing and stood, mouths agape, watching the giants walk again. Jimmy was clearly revelling in it, Robert, too, though both men would feel obliged to play it all down afterwards. 'We virtually ruined the whole thing because we sounded so awful,' said Plant. 'I was hoarse and couldn't sing and Page was out of tune and couldn't hear his guitar. But on the other hand it was a wondrous thing because it was a wing and a prayer gone wrong again – it was so much like a lot of Led Zeppelin gigs.' Or as Jimmy told me: 'My main memories, really, were of total panic.' Initially, the idea had been for Page and Plant – both then touring America separately, the latter with his solo band, Page with The Firm – to play together as the Honeydrippers. 'But it sort of snowballed,' said Jimmy, 'To where John Paul Jones arrived virtually the same day as the show and we had about an hour's rehearsal before we did it. And that sounds a bit of a kamikaze stunt, really, when you think of how well rehearsed everybody else was. But it was, under the circumstances, certainly the right time to get together again, because of the reasons for having Live Aid . . . I mean, our spirit was there as much as everybody else's was.' (Tellingly, the current DVD of Live Aid doesn't include Zeppelin's perilous performance. Rumour has it they refused to allow the footage to be used because the performance was so bad.)

John Paul Jones was also left with mixed feelings but for entirely different reasons. 'I had to barge my way into Live Aid,' he later told *Classic Rock* writer Dave Ling. Only finding out about Page and Plant's intention of playing together the week before the show, by the time he had 'barged' his way into the reckoning, Paul Martinez, from Plant's solo band, had been confirmed as bassist, forcing Jones to take the only available option left open to him and play the keyboards. It was an ignominious way to make one's return to the big time and naturally Jonesy took it badly. 'It was Plant again, you see,' he told Ling. 'Basically, I had to say to them, "If it's Zeppelin and you're gonna be doing Zeppelin songs, hi I'm still here and I wouldn't mind being a part of it." Plant went, [adopts Black Country accent] "Oh, bloody 'ell!" But I elbowed my way in.' He added: 'It's all about Robert and what he wants.'

In fact, Plant had been moved enough by the reaction at Live Aid to begin to consider the previously thought impossible. 'The rush I got from that size of audience, I'd forgotten what it was like. I'd forgotten how much I missed it ... I'd be lying if I said I wasn't really drunk on the whole event. The fact that they were still chanting for us fifteen minutes later and the fact that there were people crying all over the place ... odd stuff. It was something far more powerful than words can convey ...' So much so that when, ten days later, Page joined him on stage again, this time at one of his solo shows at the Meadowlands arena in New Jersey, jamming on the old blues classics 'Mean Woman Blues' and 'Treat Her Right', they agreed to 'get back in touch and have a cup of tea' when the tour was over – and this time bring Jonesy too.

This led directly to what was very nearly a full-on Led Zeppelin reformation, the first of what would become several such occasions over the next twenty years. Rehearsing in Bath, away from prying eyes in London, with Tony Thompson taking Bonzo's place, 'The first day was all right,' reckoned Jones. 'I don't know if Jimmy was quite into it, but it was good.' However, over the course of the next two weeks, tiny cracks in the relationship between the three principal members began to fissure into caverns, Robert moaning about how long it took Jimmy – who had gotten off drugs but was now drinking heavily – to set up and generally concerned that things were slowly sliding out of his control again. Then Thompson was involved in a minor car accident, being driven back from the pub one night, and it was seen as an omen, certainly by Plant. 'What I recall is Robert and I getting drunk in the hotel and Robert questioning what we were doing,' Jones told Lewis. 'He was saying nobody wants to hear that old stuff again and I said, "Everybody is waiting for it to happen." It just fell apart from then – I suppose it came down to Robert wanting to pursue his solo career at the expense of anything else.' Says Lewis now: 'I think what happened was Robert said to himself, one moment I've got a successful solo career, the next it's back to car crashes and bad karma, I don't need this.'

Watching from afar was the unhappy figure of Peter Grant. As the executor of John Bonham's estate, there was a period immediately after the drummer's death when G was involved in helping settle the family's affairs. He also negotiated Plant's five-album solo deal with Atlantic. But with both Page and Jones retreating from the spotlight, once Swan Song's affairs had been wrapped up, Grant retired to Horselunges with just his children, Warren and Helen – who he had won custody of – for company and a couple of roadies now employed as domestic servants. Virtually his last act on behalf of Led Zeppelin and/or Swan Song was to oversee Page's soundtrack album for *Death Wish II* – 'another nightmare' he called it – and the release of Plant's debut solo album. Then he had 'a bit of a falling out' with the singer and that was that. Even Jimmy became a stranger to him.

Still heavily involved with drugs, he stopped taking phone calls – even from the band – and refused invitations to go out. 'Why did he take cocaine? Because he was totally depressed,' said Dire Straits manager Ed Bicknell, who later became close to Grant. 'He felt responsible for John Bonham's death in the sense that he felt he should have been there and could have saved him. Swan Song had gone belly up because he couldn't cope with it and his empire was gone.' Every day he'd send a minion out to the local supermarket for a sack of sandwiches and several bowls of trifle: comfort food for the twenty-stone hermit. 'You'd phone him and he'd be in the toilet,' recalled his old partner, Mickie Most. 'But he'd been in the toilet for three days! It just meant he didn't want to speak to anybody.' The only person left Grant would still take phone calls from was the only friend left from the old days who never rang him – Page. Friends say Jimmy never forgave G for putting Plant on the path to a solo career; the final nails in Zeppelin's coffin, as he saw it. As former Sex Pistols manager Malcolm McLaren, who at one point was poised to make a film about Grant's life, later wrote: 'Grant needed the camaraderie of hard, dangerous men who gave him a sense of power. The harder they were, the tougher he felt, and only then was his desire for control satisfied.

It all fell apart when Grant aped the lifestyle of Jimmy Page, who then ostracised his biggest fan.'

When writer Howard Mylett visited Horselunges in 1989, he wrote that Grant was 'living in a flat above the garage because the house was in a state of disrepair. The stairs were rotten and there was an air of neglect. He weighed eighteen stone, he had diabetes and he was living on water tablets.' Eventually, like Plant and then Page, Grant did pull himself together, though it took a heart attack to finally make him do it, going into self-imposed withdrawal, locking himself away and drinking pure orange juice by the gallon. He took what was left of his cocaine – nearly three pounds of it, according to one friend – and flushed it down the toilet. His roadie assistants were aghast, complaining they could have got him 'a refund' if they'd known. When he emerged from his cold turkey four days later, he was a changed man. With his new sober eyes, he was astounded at the squalor he had allowed himself to fall into.

By the time I got to know Peter, briefly, in the mid-Nineties, in discussions for writing his official biography, he had changed almost beyond recognition. He was older, of course, than one recalled from the movie clips and music press cuttings, but the main thing was the weight had gone. He looked like a somewhat severe but strictly aboveboard businessman – an antiques dealer perhaps – certainly not someone who had first-hand knowledge of rock'n'roll management at its very height. He had had heart problems but was still smoking like a trouper, although he liked to go for long walks along the seafront at Eastbourne. And he still knew how to make you laugh. By then he had sold Horselunges and bought himself a 'bachelor's apartment' in Eastbourne, and begun rebuilding his collection of Tiffany lamps and William Morris glass – old passions abandoned once the coke took over in the Seventies. He was even invited to become a local magistrate at one point. He turned it down, claiming, he said with a grim smile, 'It wouldn't look very good on my CV.' He also became friendly with an eccentric local aristocrat named Lord John Gould, who shared Grant's passion for vintage American cars. Gould occasionally hired out one of his vehicles – allegedly once owned by Al Capone, including a compartment on the front passenger side door to fit a Thompson machine gun – for local weddings and on more than one occasion would act as chauffeur on the big day with G tagging along as his assistant. Little did the newlyweds know that the man opening the car door for them was once the most feared and powerful manager on planet rock.

He had found the whole Live Aid spectacle 'a bit distasteful really,' he said. 'It was so obviously unrehearsed, so rushed and thrown together, I couldn't see the point. Either do it properly or not at all.' He was even less complimentary about the band's next brief reunion in 1988, performing live in New York at the televised 40th anniversary celebration for Atlantic Records – this time with twenty-two-year-old Jason Bonham on drums. But then everyone agreed that was, as he said, 'a shambles' – if for very different reasons to Live Aid, the band apparently responding to the invitation to turn up and play at their former label's party by putting on an even worse performance than in Philadelphia three years before, with Jimmy in particular, appearing disaffected and playing spectacularly badly. What 'really upset me though,' he said, was not actually being invited to the party. Certainly Ahmet Ertegun – who once told Peter he had 'mourned too long' for John Bonham – would liked to have seen his old sparring partner there. But the label's old London chief Phil Carson had told him G was too ill to attend. Which may have been correct, but as Grant observed: 'I may not have gone but that's not the point.'

I first met Jimmy Page early in 1988, seven years after Led Zeppelin put out their official announcement confirming they'd split up. I'd been invited by his new record company, Geffen, to film a series of interviews with him for a promotional package to accompany the release of his first solo album, *Outrider*. We met at his recently acquired recording studio, Sol, in Cookham, Berkshire. Being acquainted with the legend, I wasn't sure what to expect of the reality but, as it turned out, the man I met was quietly spoken, friendly, happy to help in any way he could. Over the next few weeks of working together we got to know each other. Surprisingly talkative, always very friendly, if anything he struck me as a somewhat lonely, out of touch figure, asking me nearly as many questions as I asked him, curious about the rock scene, who was who, what was going on. He even volunteered to be a guest on a weekly TV show I used to present for Sky TV. His first TV appearance ever, as far as I could tell, it happened to coincide with my thirtieth birthday and he turned up for the morning taping with a large tray of beers on a bed of ice, even though by then he was mostly sticking to the alcohol-free stuff.

Inviting me up to the Old Mill House one day – the same house in which John Bonham had died – he showed me around. Here was his mother, a lovely old lady with smiley white hair and jaunty vibe, and his pretty young American wife, Patricia, also very smiley and busy feeding their baby son, Patrick. Here was his jukebox and interesting posters and a sprinkling of gold and platinum records and . . . 'Do you like this sort of thing?' he asked, pushing at a button on a control panel placed in the arm of a couch. The wall opposite the couch began sliding back to reveal another wall behind, from which hung three or four large oil paintings. 'What do you think?' he asked. I peered at them, not knowing what on earth to think. A best friend had been an art teacher; an old girlfriend had been an art student. I felt I knew not much but a little about the subject. I walked over and had a better look. Thick polychromatic splodges of oil on dark, brooding canvas; what appeared to be a series of bodies twisted in torment, as though in hell. Rather like Hieronymus Bosch, but much less lucid, more fiery and out of control. Like Goya, perhaps, gone mad – or even madder. 'Weird,' I said. 'Heavy . . .' I turned to him, waiting for some explanation but he merely stood there smiling, saying nothing. Then he leaned over, pushed another button on the arm of the couch and the paintings disappeared again as the outer wall slid back into place. I felt I had failed some sort of test. 'Come outside,' he said. 'I'll show you the river . . .'

Another time, he leaned over and showed me a ring he was wearing. 'What do you think of this?' he asked. It appeared to be a serpent swallowing its own tail. Having no idea of the occult significance of such a thing I merely smiled and passed some complimentary inanity. These days, I might have remarked on how the image of the serpent eating itself goes all the way back to the Book of Genesis and is a symbol synonymous with 'evil' throughout all conventional religions, the image of the serpent eating its own tail also cropping up in various guises in many cultures, symbolic of the circle of life. And how, in occult lore, the snake was originally an angel called Serpent, with arms, head and legs but who forfeited them for tempting Eve, and though he remains immortal, is doomed to suffer the pain of being born and dying, or, as it were, devouring his own tail . . .

But I didn't and again I felt I was not responding sufficiently knowledgeably. The conversation soon returned to more prosaic matters –

namely, my interest in the story of Led Zeppelin: how it had been, what it all meant. I hadn't really expected him to respond in any depth but to my surprise he seemed eager to chat. He didn't like to go into what he called 'the messy details' but he was still 'immensely proud of everything we achieved'. And then there was that other question: 'Would you ever consider getting the band back together, Jimmy?' I asked as innocently as I could one day. 'I mean, even for just one album, or some shows?' He looked at me and shook his head like an indulgent parent with a particularly wearisome child. 'You think I haven't thought about that?' I was perplexed. What was he waiting for then? He tutted, 'Robert has got a solo career which is working very certainly, so who knows?' As the years passed, however, the same old question would keep coming up whenever we met, and each time it would come down to the same old answer. As Jimmy said when we did a live interview for Radio 1 backstage at the Monsters of Rock Festival in 1990, just before he went on stage to jam with Aerosmith: 'You'll have to ask Robert.' Listening to a recording of it now, in the background you can hear his entourage yucking it up as he says it. 'It's true though, isn't it?' Jimmy insists above the guffaws. 'I mean, I'd love to, I love playing that stuff. It's a part of me, you know, a great big part of me, and I love playing it. But, you know . . .'

I knew all right. Or at least I was starting to get the picture.

It first became plain to the wider world what a gulf there now existed between Jimmy Page and Robert Plant at the disastrous Atlantic anniversary show, where Plant's now famous refusal to sing 'Stairway to Heaven' – later rescinded, under huge pressure – became a symbol of the psychic tussle that had developed between its authors over the years. On the *Outrider* tour that year, Jimmy had concluded the show each night with an instrumental 'Stairway to Heaven' which, in the absence of Robert ('The only singer I would ever play it with') the audience invariably, and rather touchingly, sang for him as tenderly as if they'd written the words themselves. Plant, having spent the Eighties trying to live down his former image as a self-proclaimed 'golden god', was increasingly loath to be associated with the song and everything it had come to represent post-punk. When, the night before the Atlantic show, he called Page and told him he didn't want to sing it the next day it sparked resentment and bitterness on both sides.

'Well, that was awful,' Page frowned, when I broached the subject with him more than a decade later. '[Robert] came together with Jason [Bonham], Jonesy and me in New York, where we were rehearsing, and started singing "Over the Hills and Far Away". And it sounded really brilliant, actually. Then we rehearsed "Stairway ... " and that sounded great, too. Then the day before the show he called me up that evening and said, "I'm not gonna sing it." I said, "What are you talking about? You're not gonna sing 'Stairway ...'? But that's exactly the one thing that everybody expects to hear us do!" He said: "I don't want to do it."'

Had Robert explained why he didn't want to do it? 'Oh, you know, he was like: "I wrote it when I was young and it doesn't feel right to sing it. I can't relate to the lyrics anymore." I thought, oh, what's he doing? What *is* this all about? To be honest, I didn't really sleep that night. I was jet-lagged anyway cos my son had just been born in England and I'd left within a few days of that. And I was really on a roll from that, you know, the high that you're into after the birth of a child. And all of a sudden, I plunged to the ground! Like, what the hell am I doing here? In the end, he said, "Well, I'll do it, but I'll *never* do it again!" I thought, "God, what is this really all about?" [Where is] the spirit of why we're supposed to be here? I don't need this. Unfortunately, by the time we got on – about three hours late – I'd just totally peaked. It was unfortunate because I was due to start my own solo tour soon afterwards and people looked at it [on TV] and went, "Oh, he can't play anymore." It was the only time it ever got to me. But it did that time. I just thought, it's a birthday party, let's all have a good time. Not start putting up barriers. Robert's probably got a perfectly adequate and eloquent reason for all of that but ... I don't know.'

As chance would have it, just a few months after that conversation, I found myself sitting with Robert Plant listening to 'Stairway to Heaven'. We were in the basement of Momo's, one of his favourite London restaurants, getting ready to film an interview for yet another promotional package, and he had put the CD on himself. Not of Led Zeppelin though, but of Dolly Parton, who had recorded a perfectly charming country version of the song. 'What do you think?' he asked. 'I really like it,' I replied. 'It's actually very good.' He nodded. 'Yes, even though it's not a song I'm particularly fond of ...'

Why is that, I wondered? Because it signified the wrong perception of who Robert Plant is, at this point, perhaps? 'Oh, no,' he smiled. 'No, no. I got round that one a few years ago. No, it's a great song. It's just that it's not appropriate for me. My headspace just doesn't allow for it. Ninety-nine per cent of the other stuff I did with Zep is absolutely spot on.' He pointed out that as a solo performer he still did 'an amazing version of "Celebration Day" on stage, which is stunning. And there's a version of "Four Sticks" which is totally removed from what Jimmy and I did. It's really cool and it breaks down into all these little passages. And we do a version of "In the Light" that's pretty smoky, because it's trippy . . .'

But not 'Stairway . . .'? 'No! Not that one!' Not ever? 'No, no. It's nothing to do with the construction of the song. The construction of the song is a real triumph, especially if you think about how it [recording] was then.' Why then? Because of what it became in people's minds? 'Partly what it became and the turning point, from what it became to what it has become now. It's . . . some good things just go so far round and round and round that in the end you lose perspective of what they really had. Because in the next incarnation, they don't really work. I mean, I don't think that Jimmy can ever be distressed with his contribution to the band, or Jonesy, or Bonzo, for that matter – because they're playing it. But some of the lyrical . . . I mean, I was a kid, you know?' He paused. 'I mean, those were different days. The intentions were really good. Songs as sort of fey as "Going to California" were basically just joining in with Neil Young's vibe. Like, you know, "Everybody Knows This Is Nowhere". For me, I was back over there in that sort of environment where harmony was the answer to everything, to create harmony and to promote . . . the brotherhood of man.' He smiled shyly.

Ultimately, he said, he simply wanted to move on. Not to forget about Led Zeppelin and 'Stairway to Heaven' but to leave it behind; let it rest in peace. He was a boy when he did that stuff. He was a man now. 'I think I'm fortunate because lots of parts of my life are in place, and I don't feel bad about chronology, time passing or anything like that, nor should I. I went to the doctor a while back and he said, "It doesn't matter what happens to you now, you've had the life of three men." He said, "You shouldn't even think about being ill – you shouldn't be alive!" I said, no, that wasn't me, I always went to bed early . . .'

Their most famous song notwithstanding, by then there had been numerous occasions when it seemed the spectre of Led Zeppelin might actually take flight again. In January 1991, their reputation freshly bolstered by the release three months before of the acclaimed, best-selling 4CD *Remasters* box set, Page, Plant and Jones were back together sitting around a table discussing the possibility of a money-spinning reunion, albeit on a strictly temporary basis. Much to his chagrin, Jason Bonham – who had played on Page's *Outrider* as well as the Atlantic show – was excluded from these deliberations, with Plant now pushing for the more fashionable Faith No More drummer Mike Bordin to be offered the job. Once again, however, the plan started to unravel almost as soon as it was decided upon, with Plant getting cold feet when the others began to express reservations about using the young, dread-locked FNM drummer. 'What you've got to remember,' an insider told me, 'is that Robert is used to having his own way now. He can't bear to go back to the days when Jimmy and Jonesy made all the major decisions about the music.'

Instead, Page resumed work on a second solo album, but Geffen Records had other ideas, suggesting he team up with label-mate and former Deep Purple singer David Coverdale in the short-lived but surprisingly invigorating Coverdale/Page. Ironically, Coverdale's post-Purple band Whitesnake had found fame in America with poor-man's Zeppelin numbers like the 1987 hit single 'Still of the Night'. But in the absence of the full-on Zeppelin reunion which Page no longer made any secret of craving, working with Coverdale was the next best thing. Certainly the eponymously titled album they released together in 1993 was the closest to Zeppelin Jimmy had got since the break-up, a fact reflected in its Top 10 status in the US. With Coverdale also clearly inspired, on titanic blues-rock workouts like 'Shake My Tree' and 'Absolution Blues', it was not long before a publicly smug but privately piqued Plant – whose solo album, *Fate of Nations*, released the same year had sold considerably fewer copies, barely scraping into the US Top 40 – was on the phone to Jimmy suggesting something similar . . . but different.

Officially, the spark had been an invitation to the singer from MTV in 1994 to participate in their then popular 'Unplugged' series. In truth, with Plant's solo career flagging – he had cringed to find himself opening for Lenny Kravitz on tour the year before – and Page clearly still hankering after Zeppelin, the chance to combine forces again was simply too good to miss. Page would have been happy to go for the full-on Zeppelin reformation. Plant, however, was still against the idea, arguing shrewdly that the pair could enjoy all the kudos of being back together without any of the nagging problems of using the Zeppelin name – unwieldy comparisons with the past; the odious spectre of being regarded as heavy metal – by deliberately not inviting John Paul Jones to the party, as proved to be the case. Yet despite the fact that the resulting October 1994 televised concert, and subsequent *No Quarter* album, was built almost entirely on the Zeppelin back catalogue, the judicious addition of an eleven-piece Egyptian ensemble, plus four brand new numbers, partly recorded in Marrakech – along with the shameful exclusion of Jones – successfully obscured the fact that this was a virtual Zeppelin reformation in all but name.

Jones, however, noted with disdain the posters for the subsequent Page & Plant tour which boasted the slogan: 'The Evolution of Led Zeppelin'. 'I felt that was a bit too close for comfort,' he said. He was also miffed that the title given to the accompanying album, *No Quarter*, was taken from one of his own Zeppelin songs. Touring with Diamanda Galás at the time, he found himself being asked for his reaction 'constantly, and it did hurt to have to deal with it. It was a great shame, particularly after all we'd been through together.'

Out on tour, however, where audiences had clearly come to hear the classics, the illusion of this not being a quasi-Zeppelin reunion was harder to maintain, and a new enmity between the two was slowly but surely brewing when Page found himself on the wrong end of Plant's wriggling insistence on not reigniting the Zeppelin flame when again he simply refused to sing 'Stairway to Heaven'. 'All I do know is that when we were in Japan,' Jimmy told me, 'we were on a TV talk show and we did a bit of it then, which was unusual. We just did a little bit of it, the opening part of it . . .'

There were warmer moments. Headlining London's Wembley Arena on 25 and 26 July, in a show of public reconciliation, Peter Grant was also invited to Wembley, where Plant paid tribute from the stage and the cheers of recognition from the audience were fulsome. The slimmed-down giant, now sporting a cane, held court at the mixing desk after the show, signing autographs and joking with fans. It was an almost-happy ending to a less than perfect story. One of the most lucrative tours of the year, word was they had earned more money even than in the days of Zeppelin. But arguments between the two now punctuated the tour. By the time they were back headlining two nights together at Madison Square Garden in October, scene of so many classic Zeppelin nights, personal relations were at a new low.

Back in London, Peter Grant was an honoured guest at the first International Manager's Forum dinner at the Hilton Hotel, where he was inducted into the Roll of Honour. Seated at a table with his former Swan Song colleague Alan Callan, friend Ed Bicknell, Simply Red manager Elliot Rashman and Queen guitarist Brian May, as he went up to pick up his award, people climbed onto their tables and cheered. Elliot Rashman shouted, 'Congratulations Peter, none of us could have done it without you!' Grant replied by telling the audience: 'I've been very lucky in my life, probably never luckier than at this moment when all of you people are honouring me. But the truth is that luck comes from the great fortune of being able to work with great talent. It is the great talent that allowed me to be successful.' Afterwards it was announced that future IMF Management Awards would be given in his name as the 'Peter Grant Award' to recognise 'Excellence in Management'.

Two months later, on 21 November 1995, G was travelling home in his car with son Warren by his side when he succumbed to another, more severe heart attack. He died later that same night. He was sixty. Jimmy Page and Robert Plant were still on tour when they received the news. The funeral was held on a cold, dark morning in December at St Peter and St Paul's Church in Hellingly, the East Sussex village where G had once lived in his grand mansion. In his address, Alan Callan said: 'His greatness was that he was a man of many parts. He was as adept at the ominous glance as he was at the disarming remark. He could engage you in the greatest conspiratorial friendship and you would know that through thick and thin he would fight with you all the way, unless of course he thought you might appreciate the humour of a sudden change of plan ... Wherever Peter is going now, I hope they've got their act together.'

At the funeral were a bevy of familiar names and faces from the past: Page, Plant and Jones plus the Bonham family, Jeff Beck, Paul Rodgers, Simon Kirke, Boz Burrell, Phil Carson, Chris Dreja, Jim McCarty, Phil May and Denny Laine. Others who couldn't attend but were there in spirit included Ahmet Ertegun – in frail health – and

Mickie Most, who wanted to attend but was told, mysteriously, that it was 'family only'. As the mourners left the church, no Zeppelin song was played. Instead, Grant had asked for Vera Lynn singing 'We'll Meet Again'. 'I just loved the guy for that,' smiled Callan. The wake was at Worth Farm, Little Horsted, a small wooden-beamed barn where Grant had once housed his vintage cars, the buffet table in front of Lord John Gould's famed 'Al Capone' car. It was an unhappy, brooding occasion, though, cold and silent. Jimmy Page was the first to leave, walking out and slamming the door loudly behind him. Only Jeff Beck seemed happy to chat, moving amongst the guests with a word and a smile for everybody.

Of the official statements issued, Robert Plant's said it best. Grant, he said, 'rewrote the rulebook. He did so much for us that in 1975 he had to turn around and say, "Look, there's nothing else I can do. We've had performing pigs and high wire acts. We've had mud sharks and all that – there's no more I can do because you really now can go to Saturn." I owe so much of my confidence to the way he calmed and nurtured and cajoled all of us to be what we were. He was larger than life. A giant who turned the game upside down. Fierce, uncompromising, with great humour.' Page's statement was briefer and to the point: 'Peter was a tower of strength as a business partner and a friend. I will miss him and my heart goes out to his family.'

There was a second Page/Plant album in 1997, the disappointing *Walking into Clarksdale*, but by now the writing was already on the wall. Inducted into the US Rock and Roll Hall of Fame the previous year, the Zeppelin flag was flying higher than ever, and more ludicrously rich pickings were to be had from the second Page/Plant world tour. There was even now a whisper that John Paul Jones – who had put in such a convincing performance with his old band mates at the brief Hall of Fame show – might be brought in at some point. But Plant bailed out yet again before that possibility could be explored, walking out on the eve of an Australian tour at the start of 1999, claiming disingenuously, as he told me, 'I didn't know how many more English springs I would see.' A furious Page turned instead to American blues-rockers The Black Crowes, who he successfully toured America with later that year with a set built solidly around the Zep catalogue. The resulting album, *Live at the Greek*, released initially via the internet, was not only a bigger hit than *Walking into Clarksdale*, it was simply a much more enjoyable album. 'I jumped for joy when they told me how many it was selling,' Page told me.

The odd collaboration aside – very odd, in the case of the 1998 performance ('I sent it down the phone line') on Puff Daddy's rap version of 'Kashmir' – Jimmy Page has mainly spent his post-Zeppelin career concentrating on keeping the flame alive, from producing the excellent *Remasters* box set to personally overseeing the ground-breaking twin-release in 2003 of the superlative six-hour *DVD* collection – his long-cherished dream of a chronological live history of the band writ-large, beginning at the Albert Hall in 1970 and ending with extracts from the 12-camera Mansfield shoot at Knebworth almost a decade later – and double-live CD, *How The West Was Won* (recorded in LA in 1972). Since then there have been at least two more occasions when Page and Plant have set aside their differences long enough to discuss the possibility of performing together again as Led Zeppelin. The first time was in preparation for the release of both *DVD* – which quickly became the biggest-selling music DVD in history – and *How The West Was Won*, which entered the US charts at no. 1 in 2003; a plan to undertake a brief but intensely lucrative US summer tour was scuppered, say sources, when Plant became more interested in the coincidental release that year of his *Sixty Six to Timbuktu* solo compilation. The second time was in 2005, when a brace of shows at Madison Square Garden was mooted to mark the 25th anniversary of Bonzo's death. The plan was scrapped when Plant couldn't decide whether it would be a good thing to do or not.

John Paul Jones, meanwhile, continued to be the odd man out. In 1994, he recorded and received co-billing on the excellent Diamanda Galás album, *The Sporting Life*, where his multi-instrumental embel-lishments on tracks like 'Devil's Rodeo' added depth to the poet-diva's songs of lust and decay, later also joining her for a spectacularly well-received world tour. Playing with the feisty songstress was 'the most fun I'd had since Zeppelin'. He recalled how when, at a concert in Chicago, somebody shouted out 'The song remains the same!', she had shouted back, 'No, it doesn't, motherfucker!' He also set up his own recording studio, which he dubbed the Sunday School, and where he recorded his first solo album, *Zooma*, released in 1999. An instrumental tour-de-force, on tracks like 'Tidal' and the thunderous title track itself, Jones created tumultuous pieces full of avalanching rhythms and eerie, sonic soundscapes, using a battery of four-, ten- and twelve-string basses. Other tracks, like 'Bass 'N' Drums' (inspired by his daughter Jacinda introducing him to drum'n'bass, the UK club sound of the mid-Nineties), showed both his sense of humour and his willingness to explore new musical terrains, while 'The Smile of Your Shadow' demonstrated he had not lost his ability for conjuring up suitably dry-iced atmospherics, either.

Two years later he was back with the follow-up, the equally adventurous but more accessible *The Thunderthief*, on which he played practically everything except the drums. It also, somewhat remarkably, included his debut as a solo vocalist on the witty, punk-derived 'Angry Angry' and the more traditional-sounding folk ditty, 'Freedom Song'. Mostly though, it was the driving rhythms of tracks like 'Down the River to Pray' that impressed. Emboldened, he put together his own touring band and gave concerts based on his solo work at home and in America and Japan. No Zeppelin songs, though, 'except one or two occasionally, for a laugh'. In 2004, he also toured as part of the group Mutual Admiration Society, along with Glen Phillips (previously best known as singer of Toad the Wet Sprocket) and various members of the band Nickel Creek.

In more recent times, he seemed to have gone back to his habit of simply turning up on other people's albums, such as the Foo Fighters' *In Your Honor*, where he played on two tracks (mandolin on 'Another Round' and piano on 'Miracle'). Foos frontman Dave Grohl later described working with Jones as the 'second greatest thing to happen to me in my life'. He also made a belated return to production: on latter-day recordings like The Datsuns' 'old-school heavy rock' album *Outta Sight, Outta Mind* in 2004 and, a year later, on Uncle Earl's critically acclaimed, neo-country collection, *She Waits For Night*. He has also completed more soundtrack work, including the theme tune to *The Secret Adventures of Tom Thumb*. Would he still consider strapping on his old fender bass, dusting down his mellotron and striding the boards under the Led Zeppelin banner, though? Of course he would. As he told me in 2003, as I compiled the sleeve notes for *DVD*, 'There's definitely the feeling of unfinished business about the band. Even though it's unimaginable, in one sense, to try it without Bonzo, we had hoped to do to the Eighties what we did to the Seventies. I still very much regret that we never got that chance.' What he hadn't told me and which only came out later was that Plant had also recently apologised to him – literally gone down on his knees, according to Dave Lewis – not just for excluding him from the Page/Plant collaboration, but for all the snide comments made at the time, too, along the lines of the 'he's just parking the car' comment at the first press conference when someone asked where Jonesy was.

And yet with neither Plant nor Jones choosing to join Page on the rostrum at the televised induction into the UK Hall of Fame in 2006, it seemed that the only person left in Led Zeppelin who would still countenance some form of reunion, however temporary or turbulent, was the band's original creator. Or so it seemed, anyway, right up to the announcement barely six months later that Led Zeppelin was to reform – with Jason Bonham taking his father's place on drums again – officially to commemorate the life of Ahmet Ertegun, who had died the previous winter, aged eighty-three, after a fall backstage at a Rolling Stones show in New York; unofficially as part of Jimmy Page's never-ending quest to get the band back together again.

Whatever the reasons, it could hardly have been a coincidence that the performance, originally scheduled for London's O2 arena in November 2007, would be accompanied by the release of a new Zeppelin compilation CD, *Mothership* – an unsatisfactorily unbalanced collection of the 'hits' with just one acoustic number, 'Babe I'm Gonna Leave You' – and, more interestingly, a DVD version, along with all the usual 'extras': deleted scenes, up-to-date interviews etc of their once-maligned, now regarded as historic 'home movie', *The Song Remains The Same*, along with a remixed, digitised version of the live album, with its own extras in the form of a handful of 'bonus' tracks.

One of the last times I spoke to Jimmy about getting Led Zeppelin back together he told me: 'There might have been a couple of occasions where we could have got it back together. I thought we had at least one good album left in us, put it like that. But I just presented scenario after scenario to him and ... Robert wasn't interested. He just didn't want to know. He said he doesn't want to sing Led Zeppelin numbers. But I love playing Led Zeppelin music. For me, they were one of the best bands ever and they made some of the best music ever and we should be out there playing it. But I don't see that it's ever going to happen again. Not now ...'

No-one should have been surprised when they did finally announce their comeback. At a time when everyone from The Police to Genesis, Pink Floyd and The Who have been reaping the rewards of their 'classic' status, from sold-out shows where ticket prices averaged out at £150 a throw, to a rejuvenated back catalogue selling better than ever – *Mothership* alone would sell more than 600,000 copies in the UK over the Christmas 2007 period – even Robert Plant could now see the benefit of a reunion, especially one so – apparently – brief. With the band committed to performing a full two-hour show for the first – and last, they insisted – time in twenty-eight years, it would, Plant said, be Zeppelin's chance to 'say farewell properly'. The implication: that, after the embarrassments of Live Aid and the Atlantic show, a proper send-off was only right, surely? And with a significant chunk – no-one spelled out exactly how much – of the 'net' proceeds going to Ertegun's charity – the Ahmet Ertegun Education Fund, which funds university scholarships in Britain, America and Turkey – the public lapped it up. Meanwhile the press was filled with stories of the official website selling tickets for the show – at £135 a pop – being brought down due to the huge demand, up to 25 million hits within the first twenty-four hours of going online, if the stories were to be believed. As part of the build-up, BBC Radio 2 held an auction for two tickets plus the chance to watch the soundcheck and meet the band, all proceeds going to Children In Need. Listener Kenneth Donell from Glasgow won with a bid of £83,000. Online reseller websites like Seatwave and Viagogo also had a field day selling single tickets for an average of £7,425. What was less known to the public was that corporate ticketing was also being conducted on a more discreet basis, with private twenty-eight-seat boxes plus full food-and-drink hospitality package available for the right price. At least a couple of thousand tickets were also held back purely for the band's 'friends and family' – and as many famous faces as they could fit in. The majority of people applying for tickets may well have bought them via the website, the money raised from these sales going to charity, but this was not an opportunity to be missed, either, in terms of reinforcing the Zeppelin legend.

Planning was meticulous, with all the remixing of the new DVD and CD of *The Song Remains The Same* and track sequencing and artwork for *Mothership* completed by May. Unlike the *DVD* and *How The West Was Won* package of 2003, where Page was in charge of every aspect of production, this time Plant took the helm. Kevin Shirley, the talented young South African producer who had worked with Jimmy on *DVD* and *How The West Was Won* and now found himself working with Robert on the re-jigged *The Song Remains The Same*, recalls how 'Jimmy wasn't that bothered this time around it seemed but Robert was really insistent on being there with me. When we came to that bit on "Stairway to Heaven" when he ad-libs, "Does anyone remember laughter?" he winced and asked if we could delete it. I said, "No, you can't erase that, it's what people remember, part of history!" So he very reluctantly allowed me to keep it in. There were a couple of other smaller ad-libs that I did take out for him here and there – a few of the baby, baby, babys – just to keep him happy.'

Once the job was done, a month was set aside for rehearsals. Meanwhile, all three surviving members were spotted at the O2 checking out shows that summer by Snow Patrol and Elton John. Behind the scenes, however, things were as fraught as ever. All three members had an equal say in the running order of the show, but as always some members were more equal than others. Ultimately, it all came down to what Robert wanted. He laid down several conditions. Specifically, that the music wasn't 'too heavy metal'. That meant no 'Immigrant Song', which Page and Jones could live with, and no 'Achilles Last Stand', which the others were put out by, particularly Jimmy, as he still considered it one of his finest moments. As for 'Stairway to Heaven' – the others held their breath – he *would* be prepared to sing that, he said, but not as any sort of finale. Instead, it would be performed in the middle of the set and with no great fanfare. Jimmy and John Paul had no choice but to agree. On a general level, the other condition Plant laid down was that there be no extended jams, as of days of old. Never mind Jimmy's talk of 'telepathy', improvisation was no longer in vogue; the numbers would be as close as the band could get them to how they sounded on album. Again, neither Page nor Jones were happy with that but there was little they could do about it. It was take it or leave it and both Jimmy and John Paul wanted this too badly not to take it.

Though the significance of its appearance could not yet be fully understood, there would also be one other, as it turned out even more important, release coinciding with the O2 date: that of a new Plant album, this time a collaboration with renowned American bluegrass singer Alison Krauss. A precocious young talent from Illinois who had signed her first record deal at thirteen, Krauss had spent the past two decades building up a sizeable reputation as the most recognised face in contemporary bluegrass and modern country music, winner of several awards and a seasoned collaborator. She had first performed with Plant at a concert celebrating the music of Leadbelly the year before. Thirty-five when she met him and therefore too young to have experienced Zeppelin first-hand, Alison had been a Def Leppard fan in her teens. Plant, for his part, had spent years as a solo artist bringing elements of world and roots music into his sound. When it was suggested he might like to collaborate with Krauss on some recordings, see how it went, he jumped at the chance. The fact that this coincided with the unexpected resurrection of the Zeppelin monolith was incidental – to begin with anyway.

The results of their collaboration, overseen by veteran musician, songwriter and producer T. Bone Burnett (best known for his soundtrack to Oscar-nominated movies *O Brother, Where Art Thou?* and *Walk The Line*, and production of albums by Tony Bennett and k.d. lang), turned into the album *Raising Sand* – an inspired collection of esoteric covers chosen by Burnett, combining a luxurious-sounding mix of modal blues, country soul, rockabilly and old-fashioned balladry. Even so, nobody was quite prepared for the glorious reception it received when it was released in October, just a month before Zeppelin's O2 date. *Rolling Stone, Vanity Fair, The Sunday Times* (who later made it album of the year), the *New Yorker, Entertainment Weekly, Mojo, People, USA Today* ... everybody fell over themselves to praise the album with the sort of career-defining reviews neither artist had ever experienced before. As a result, it entered the US album chart at no. 2. A week later it was no. 1. A month after that it was certified gold, then platinum. Sales in Britain were slower to kick in but once the ball was rolling, *Raising Sand* replicated its US success and, at time of writing, has now sold more than half a million copies in the UK – almost double-platinum. Robert Plant couldn't believe his luck. 'When we got seventy-five per cent of the way down the line,' he commented, 'I realised we'd created something that I could never have dreamt of.' Krauss was equally blown away. 'There's so much romance in contrast,' she said. 'It was a real life-changing experience.'

It certainly was. But not for Jimmy Page or John Paul Jones, both of whom appeared to regard the arrival of the *Raising Sand* album as a form of intrusion into their own long-awaited party. As Jimmy once told me, 'Whenever we do anything with Led Zeppelin these days, Robert always seems to have a solo album on the go at the same time.' The suggestion: that wily old Plant knows the value of publicity. Yet when Robert gave Jimmy and John a white-label pre-release copy of the CD, he was bitterly disappointed that neither man passed any comment on it, either for or against, something he was still smarting over nearly a year later, when, chatting to Kevin Shirley in LA in June 2008, he told him how neither man had 'even acknowledged that he had it'. Adding: 'You know, it's my work, I'm proud of it and they're my people that I'm with, and that they don't acknowledge what I'm doing is valid is, you know, it's joyless.'

There's little doubt, though, that the timing of the release of *Raising Sand* so close to the original O2 date of 26 November had a huge bearing on its success. With the world's media clambering for Led Zeppelin interviews, the proffering of the band's singer for a chat about his new solo project was snapped up by literally everybody, leading to such previously unexpected sights as Plant and Krauss appearing together on the BBC's flagship TV arts programme *The Culture Show*. Of course, everybody was extremely polite, asking about *Raising Sand*. But all interviews ended the same way: with a question about the Big One. Which naturally Plant would bat away with some mumbled inanity. It was a situation that also led to such clearly misleading magazine cover lines as the ROBERT PLANT ON LED ZEPPELIN heading that adorned the cover of *Q* magazine at one point, when in fact the feature was actually an interview with Plant and Krauss about *Raising Sand*, or *Mojo* co-opting a Plant/Krauss interview as part of a larger Led Zeppelin cover story. So heavily did the media spotlight fall on Plant and his new musical collaborator that when it was announced that the O2 date would have to be put back two weeks because Jimmy Page had broken a finger, cynics speculated that the delay had more to do with the fact that Plant was too busy promoting *Raising Sand* in America to rehearse thoroughly with Zeppelin and that a nervous Page – absolutely determined the show would wipe the slate clean of all the bad memories of Live Aid and the cursed Atlantic show – had made the story up in order to buy the band more time to rehearse when Robert returned. Something Page vehemently denies, of course.

As it turned out, nobody should have been worried about the Plant/Krauss album taking anything away from the Led Zeppelin reunion. The days and weeks leading up to the show found the band splashed all over every newspaper and magazine, from high-minded editorials from Germaine Greer in the *Telegraph* to the usual mindless tabloid waffle in the *Sun*, with photo agencies offering millions of dollars for the right to take and sell exclusive pictures of the show.

The show itself was a strangely cold affair, inside and out. Positioned at the centre of a concentric circle of shops, bars and restaurants, wandering around outside the O2 on an icy evening in December had an air of unreality about it, about what everyone was there for. Unlike most rock audiences, who are easy to spot from their typical jeans-and-T-shirt garb, this one was clearly made up of a much broader cross-section of society, though the majority appeared to be middle-class and middle-aged, dressed far too young. Inside, the O2 proved to be the perfect purpose-built venue for such a crowd, such an event. The security staff were all preternaturally friendly, seats large and comfortable with appendages for holding your drinks, the concessions a vast array of food and drink stalls where you could buy anything from chips to sushi; beer to champagne, coke or cappuccino.

The show started exactly on time, at 9.00 pm. Preceded by the same short clip as can be seen on the revitalised new edition of the *The Song Remains The Same* DVD – a TV news report from the record-breaking Miami show of 1973, and then suddenly – bam! – the band was pounding into 'Good Times Bad Times'. By far the most exciting moment of the night, once they were actually on stage together, it suddenly felt all too real: Jimmy in sunglasses and long black coat over crisp white shirt and dark trousers, his hair ghostly white; Robert more studiedly casual in open-necked shirt over dark jeans and boots, his most distinguishing feature no longer his hairless chest or huge todger but a new Colonel Sanders beard. Despite the fact that the house lights were kept unnaturally bright to accommodate the film crew who were recording the event – reputedly for a future DVD release – they looked amazing. However, the sound was appalling. It wasn't until about five numbers in that they finally started to sound as they should, by which time the mystique had well and truly worn off and one was left to gaze at the vast wraparound screen behind them onto which a variety of live stage shots and impressively arranged abstract gobbledegook – courtesy of the Thinkfarm design company – was displayed. Dragging one's eyes back to the clearly nervous figures on stage, Robert seemed in complete control, the perfect professional. Jimmy, who didn't seem able to shift his gaze from Robert for the first half of the set, also seemed relatively at ease, though huddled far too close to the drums. A month away from his sixty-fourth birthday, it would have been wrong to expect him to put on the kind of shape-throwing show of old. Nevertheless, to me he looked like what he was: an older man playing at a younger man's game. John Paul Jones looked as he always did: anonymous, a workman happy left to fiddle with his toolbox, nothing to see here. Jason Bonham was a revelation: bald, bearded, super fit-looking (a fact confirmed by his karate instructor, who I sat next to). That he was filling his father's shoes so convincingly was a tribute both to his talent and his courage, knowing that every single drummer in the audience – and there were many, from Dave Grohl of the Foo Fighters to Chad Smith of the Red Hot Chili Peppers, to name just two – would gladly have taken his place.

Mostly, though, the attention rested with Robert and Jimmy – in that order. Robert's voice helped by the general tuning down of the entire set, it was his gargantuan presence that really came across. I had half expected a somewhat smug, doing-us-a-favour figure, cracking in-jokes at Page's expense. Instead he gave every appearance of taking the event as seriously as the most devout Zeppelin fan, becoming very much the star of the show. Jimmy, though less obviously self-confident, was playing better than anyone had heard perhaps in over thirty years. Better, certainly, than the horrible US tour of '77; better than most of Knebworth; and certainly better than at any point in the nearly three decades that have somehow passed since Zeppelin crashed face-first into the ground.

They played mostly must-haves – 'Black Dog', 'Trampled Under-foot', 'Nobody's Fault But Mine', 'No Quarter', 'Since I've Been Loving You', 'Dazed and Confused', 'Stairway to Heaven', 'Kashmir'; plus a handful of less expected treats: 'Ramble On', 'In My Time Of Dying', 'The Song Remains The Same', 'Misty Mountain Hop' – and one they'd never played before in 'For Your Life'. The encores, of course, were 'Whole Lotta Love' and 'Rock And Roll'. Nobody got all their favourites but that was always going to be the case. It was still dis-appointing though not to have had the mini-acoustic set. So much for

Jimmy's much-cherished 'light and shade'. And of course there was very little improvisation, the songs, as Robert had insisted, all sticking as far as possible to the original template recordings. If that meant a much shorter than of old guitar solo on 'Dazed and Confused', then so be it.

When it was over the crowd stood and clapped and cheered and stamped their feet for a minute or two, then filed out politely, the ever-helpful venue staff wishing us all a 'good night, safe journey home'. There was no real sense of elation or sweat or danger or fascination; only a pleased it was all over feeling; the reality, as always, falling as flat as a burst balloon compared to the dreadful hype. I wondered what I actually made of it and had to conclude, ultimately, that whatever I'd just seen, it wasn't anything like the Led Zeppelin of the Seventies, or even Live Aid in 1985. Certainly not as vividly exciting as the *DVD* of 2003. I felt like I had just been taken on a very detailed tour of the pyramids. Fascinating stuff, even if I did find myself yawning and stealing glances at my watch as the second hour wore on. How different it must have been, though, in the actual days of the Pharaohs, back when giants walked the earth ...

The only moment when it truly felt like something momentous was actually happening, when some of that old telepathy had been rekindled, at least between the Magus and his adepts, was during the violin bow showcase, when Jimmy, bathed in that other-worldly pyramid of green light, proved he could still suspend time with his Penderecki-esque posturing and spirit-dragged-screaming-from-the-host anti-chords. The least convincing moment, oddly, was 'Stairway to Heaven', begun with no introduction, a grand old lady robbed of her dignity, Robert's voice so obviously detuned, emotionally as well as musically, it seemed ... unseemly somehow. Not least as Page's solo sounded better, every note perfect, than at any time since he actually recorded it. 'We did it Ahmet,' Plant said at the end but it verged, for the first and only time, on condescension and struck the evening's only real bum note.

After the show there was a VIP party for 700 people in a room that held 200, among the guests Mick Jagger, Paul McCartney, Priscilla and Lisa-Marie Presley, Jeremy Clarkson, Richard Hammond, Chris Evans, Jeff Beck, Liam and Noel Gallagher, Marilyn Manson, Def Leppard vocalist Joe Elliot, Pink, actresses Rosanna Arquette and Juliette Lewis, supermodels Naomi Campbell and Kate Moss, and many, many others. In the papers the next day – all of which, from earnest chin-scratching pieces in the broadsheets to vacuous tittle-tattle in the tabs, ran acres of coverage of the show and the endless lists of all the famous people that were there. How many of them would know their *Houses Of The Holy* from their *In Through The Outdoor* was debatable. But that, of course, was no longer the point. Because of the scarcity of public appearances, being seen at the Led Zeppelin show carried more cachet than being seen at even the Stones shows in the same venue earlier in the year, more even than any of the twenty-one nights Prince had done there just a couple of months before. More even, at this point, than anyone.

From overheard conversations it seemed no-one at the O2 believed this would be the only Zeppelin show. 'Would you go again?' someone I didn't know but who clearly assumed we were all now brothers asked me. I pondered for a moment then answered honestly. 'Probably not, no.' He looked at me, aghast. Everyone was asking the same question though the next day in the press and on the radio, in internet reports – pictures of the show posted live on the net as the show was actually taking place – and on TV. And I remembered something Robert Plant had said the last time we spoke, before either of us knew what was about to happen. I looked it up to see if I remembered correctly. We were talking about a reformation and, in a disgusted voice, he said: 'There's always been this deal about, "Oh well, you know, I don't know why they don't do it, get back together, everybody else does it." I mean, Jesus Christ, how you ever gonna weave that magic that was there?'

At the O2 we'd got our answer: you can't. Speaking in the *Guardian* six months later, Plant put it better when he described the show as 'a very humbling experience' and said he was 'in tears' afterwards. 'Because it really did work, whatever "it" was, for what it was. A great feat of engineering – social engineering, mostly. The trouble is now . . . it gets so big that it loses what once upon a time was a magnificent thing, where it was special and quite elusive and occasionally a little sinister and it had its own world nobody could get in.' Pressed on whether he had subsequently turned down the chance to get Zeppelin back together permanently, he said coyly: 'I don't hold the keys to any decision by anybody to do anything.' Zeppelin, he said, 'were always pushing it and manipulating music history – it had to be absolutely right'. Similarly, he did things now because 'I want to be excited and I want to be risky'. Something, he seemed to suggest, a reformed Led Zeppelin without John Bonham would clearly not be.

Instead of touring the world with Led Zeppelin, as had secretly been the plan, Robert Plant has spent much of 2008 touring Britain and America with Alison Krauss, promoting the still selling *Raising Sand* album. Having won the Grammy in February for 'Best Pop Collaboration with Vocals' for the single 'Gone Gone Gone (Done Moved On)', the couple are expected to rake up even more awards at the ceremony in early 2009 when the album will still be eligible for the 2008 awards. There are now plans for the couple to make a follow-up album at some point, ready for release in 2009, maybe even writing a few of the tracks together this time, once again with T. Bone Burnett overseeing production. There is also a return UK tour planned for October 2008, which record company executives admit privately they expect to take the album's UK sales alone to more than 800,000, a staggering figure for a member of Zeppelin to achieve without the band. Referring to Krauss pointedly on stage as 'the most gifted musician I know', Plant has made it clear he is exactly where he wants to be, in his life and career. Even if that still means performing a handful of Zeppelin songs – including 'Black Dog', 'The Battle Of Evermore', 'Black Country Woman' and 'When The Levee Breaks' – in his new guise with Krauss.

There is still talk behind the scenes of a semi-permanent Led Zeppelin reunion, probably in 2009. But when it comes to Robert Plant, not even Jimmy Page – one might say especially not even Jimmy Page – can ever say for sure what will happen. Kevin Shirley, who caught the Plant and Krauss show when it reached LA in June, tells me, 'The show he's doing with Alison is magnificent. It's like there's no ego on the guy at all. And they've obviously worked really hard, singing harmonies, getting everything right. When we spoke afterwards he said, "There is so much joy on stage." I said, "Well, it shows, it sounds fantastic. But you know the O2 show was great too." He said, "It was exactly the opposite getting there, though. It was joyless [but] everything is so joyful now." And he also said another thing which I thought was very telling. He said, "I'll be sixty soon and I'm so pleased to have found this in my life because I was really worried that I would not have anywhere to go. Those guys [Page and Jones] want me to run around the world with them but it's inane." He never said, "I'm not gonna do it" and he never said it won't happen. But I don't think he'll do it. He recognises the magnitude of it and I think it's difficult to stop the machine because it's so huge and he knows there's a billion dollars in it and that there's a year's worth of stadiums out there. And when he plays the Alison songs, every time they do a Zeppelin song the crowd just erupts that little bit more. So the legacy has obviously got its significance for him. But I think he would be just as happy if it actually stopped and died down now. He has made ten solo albums, he moved on with his career in 1980. So I think he's had enough of that.'

And apart from the money – of which he already owns a sizeable fortune, the Zeppelin catalogue alone still guaranteeing him an income of several million every year – what else can Zeppelin now offer Robert Plant that he doesn't already have? He now has a solo career that comparable artists in his position like Mick Jagger, Roger Daltrey and even Paul McCartney could only dream of, including Jimmy Page, having accomplished something none of them has yet managed: a second life with an album that has not only sold in its millions but been uniformly recognised as one of the key moments in our present musical epoch.

For a sixty-year-old former lemon-squeezer who has spent nearly half his life trying to live down his past, the dream really has finally come true. Why go back now when it can surely only spoil things? Will there be another Led Zeppelin show in the future? As long as Jimmy Page draws breath that likelihood will always remain. How tragic though that he is the one no longer in control of Zeppelin's destiny. The one who envisaged and created the whole thing, the one without whom none of it would have been possible or be so well remembered now, in many ways Led Zeppelin was a dream Jimmy Page once had that everyone else shared in. Has it now become a form of nightmare? The last time Jimmy Page released an album of new music was over a decade ago, with *Walking Into Clarksdale*, an album so thin it makes *In Through The Outdoor* look like the musical break-through John Paul Jones still kids himself it was. The truth is, Page should take a leaf out of Plant's book and move on. Instead he appears to be sitting at home, alone, still waiting for Robert to make up his mind whether he's going to agree to a few more reunion shows, still waiting for the call, a reluctant hermit, as rich in money and fame and as impotent in musical deed as the golden statue of Kenneth Anger's curse. Whether Plant goes back now is almost immaterial. Either way, as Peter Grant told Dave Lewis all the way back in 1993, 'You've got to realise Robert always wanted to be the boss of the band anyway. He finally got his own way.'

Timothy d'Arch Smith says that Jimmy sent him a pair of tickets for the O2 concert, 'But I gave them to my godson. I thought, when I get to heaven, St Peter's going to say, "Well, there was *one* thing that you did ... "' When I mention that I noticed Jimmy still had the ZoSo symbol on his amps at the O2, Tim smiles and says, 'Yes, it is interesting. I did hear that he'd given the whole thing up once, the whole Crowley thing. I think maybe that's why I didn't quote him things for a long while. It must have been quite a serious thing, somebody told me. Maybe he did and then took it up again. Some dark night of the soul or something like that ...'

He says that one of the last times he saw Jimmy he was talking about Boleskine House again, which he sold in 1991. 'He said he was thinking of buying the whole thing back and doing a great sort of ... making it a museum or something. He said it is so over-restored now, though, that nothing remains at all. Jimmy said it's just been torn to pieces. The end of the conservatory where the Abra-Melin demons were, that's all been torn down. But I bet whoever's got it is still being plagued. Well, not plagued ... but demons would still be there.'

One suspects that, for Jimmy Page they always will be.

Gone, Gone, Gone . . .

In the nearly two years that have passed since the O2 show, the legend of Led Zeppelin may have continued to grow exponentially, but the possibility that the band might reconvene in some very tangible sense – so fervently hoped for by Jimmy Page, John Paul Jones and Jason Bonham – has now all but disappeared. At least for the foreseeable future. And yet it should all have been so different; certainly as far as Page was concerned. For him, the O2 concert had proved 'that the essence of it, the energy, was still there'. But for Robert Plant, things were clearly less easily defined. 'Bear in mind that we're old guys now and we're not supposed to be hip-shrugging teenage idols,' he joked in an interview with *Uncut*. 'It was pretty – I'm not sure "sincere" is the right word. But it was as real as you're going to get. And Jimmy was on fire at times.'

It was not enough, however, to deflect him from his new, more compelling musical mission with Alison Krauss. Within weeks of the O2 show, the Plant and Krauss world tour was announced. Still, though, Jimmy clung to the vain hope that Robert might have a change of heart once he'd got his latest solo venture out of his system. In Japan, the following January, to promote the new *Mothership* and *The Song Remains The Same* releases, Jimmy had told a packed press conference in Tokyo how delighted he'd been by the O2 show. That what was 'so thrilling' was 'to come together after all this time and find that there was so much chemistry and so much electricity involved in these four characters'. He continued in hopeful fashion: 'We'd all agreed to take it very, very seriously and have a really good time at the same time. We worked out the songs we were going to play, and it was exhilarating, it was fantastic. Every week was a week to look forward to. I can assure you the amount of work that we put into the O2, for ourselves rehearsing and the staging of it, was probably what you [would] put into a world tour.'

However, when pressed on the exact nature of the band's possible future plans, Page could only comment: 'Robert Plant has a parallel project running and he's really busy with that project, certainly until September, so I can't give you any news.'

So there it was in nutshell: Jimmy wanted to, Robert didn't. Not while he had his 'parallel project running'. The mention of September was also telling. Plant, keeping his options open as he always did, far more shrewd than the happy-go-lucky figure he liked to present to the world, had successfully negotiated enough space for himself to embark on a world tour which, right then anyway, would take them up to September. Maybe after that he would be willing to get back together with Jimmy in a full-on, or even a nominally one-off series of O2-alike shows. Maybe . . .

The media remained undeterred and kept the pressure up whenever it could, sensing the story wasn't over yet. In April 2008, four months after the O2 show, both Q and *Uncut* magazines again ran Zeppelin on their covers, even though in the case of Q, the interview they had was with Robert Plant and Alison Krauss, with barely a mention of Zeppelin from the crinkle-eyed singer, and then only in the vaguest possible terms. Meanwhile, in *Uncut*, all three former members were quoted on where they thought the O2 show had left the group. Plant, true to form, appeared to be leaving as many doors open as possible. 'Hopefully one day we could do it again for another really good reason,' he said. 'Our profit is metaphysical,' he added gnomically. 'I'm not too sure about anything at the moment; I've got no idea what's going to happen. But I'd certainly like to play with Jimmy again,' said Jones, doing nothing to dispel the notion that he was along for the ride, wherever it took him. 'If you're talking about a tour, other dates, recording together – there's only one thing that's going to be a common denominator with that and that's commitment,' said Jimmy.

It was a familiar theme he would return to. Until the *Raising Sand* album's unforeseen multinational success, Plant had given every indication to his old boss that the O2 would be a stepping stone to much longer-term 'commitment'. But *Raising Sand* was continuing to sell in large quantities, and tickets for the Plant/Krauss world tour, announced in the spring, were fast selling out. Robert knew he'd quashed Jimmy's dreams but, hey, that's showbiz, even if he did want to at least be polite about it in public.

Describing his relationship with Page in the wake of the O2, Plant said: 'There's unfinished business definitely. And I don't think there's any need for it to be finished. There's going to be something to do some time.' Really? But then what else could he say? Plant, in particular, could not escape the question wherever he went. When, in January 2008, he turned up at a Knicks vs. Sixers basketball game at Madison Square Garden, cheerleaders danced to 'Rock and Roll' as the singer sat uncomfortably courtside, smiling sheepishly. Introduced at halftime for a televised interview, a female sportscaster from MSG TV asked him: 'Do you think you'll be back here with your bandmates?' He played the usual straight bat in his reply: 'Oh, I don't know. I'm getting ready for a tour with Alison Krauss and that's what I'm focusing on.' Did he have any plans beyond that, though, she persisted? 'Not really,' he said, 'It was just great to play with those guys again.' And if he had to pick one song to perform right now, 'to knock this crowd off its feet, what would it be?' Again, straight bat, usual answer: 'A song called "Kashmir" from the *Physical Graffiti* album. I'm most proud of that one.'

Meanwhile, when he wasn't accompanying Jimmy on a round of awards shows – *Mojo* in June; GQ in August – Jones was now turning up all over the place in a series of 'guest' appearances, not least a two-song bash with Page through 'Rock and Roll' and 'Ramble On' at a Foo Fighters show at Wembley Stadium that summer. He also agreed to produce a solo album in Nashville for Nickel Creek singer Sara Watkins, and in February 2009 was a 'surprise' guest at the BBC Folk Awards in London, where he presented the Lifetime Achievement Award to John Martyn. He also performed with Martyn on two of his own old Seventies' classics, 'May You Never' and 'Over the Hill', playing mandolin. Asked in an online interview about the future of Led Zeppelin, he would only say that they had 'had a meeting' but that 'none of them knew what was going to happen'.

A week later, he appeared in LA at the Grammy Awards alongside the Foo Fighters, where he 'arranged and conducted the orchestra' for a special performance of their hit, 'The Pretender'. In May, he could be found attending the Bergen Music Festival in Norway, where he

performed with Robyn Hitchcock and Patti Smith. He also attended a
pre-festival press conference performing two songs with Robyn, again
on mandolin. The event was dwarfed as a news story in Britain by the
'revelation' in the *Sunday Mirror* that Robert Plant had 'reportedly
turned down a $200 million deal to revive the legendary band for a
world tour'. The story went on, quoting a 'source' claiming that the
deal 'did not come down to money'. Although Page had 'enjoyed the
concert in December enough to want to tour again', feeling they 'still
had something to offer', Plant 'wanted to leave last year's concert as
their legacy. They had proved they could still do it and that was
enough.'

Certainly, Plant had never seemed happier than when on tour
with Alison Krauss. The master of having his cake and eating it too,
among the selections from *Raising Sand* that the duo performed live
when the tour began at the Palace Theater in Louisville on April 19
were a number of Zeppelin tunes, including 'Black Dog', 'Black Country Woman', 'Hey, Hey What Can I Do', 'When the Levee Breaks',
and even 'Battle of Evermore', with Krauss now taking the vocal part
Sandy Denny had made famous. Still, though, rumours of a full-on
Zeppelin tour continued to surface. In May, Whitesnake were the latest band to be said to be in contention for one of the opening slots on
the tour, joining previous contenders The Cult, Velvet Revolver and
the Stone Temple Pilots. Coverdale was quick to quash the story,
telling Classicrock.com, 'What fucking world tour, we ask ourselves?'
Indeed. But then the same week in June that Page and Jones had appeared at Wembley Stadium with the Foo Fighters, it was reported in
the *Daily Telegraph* that Page had told one interviewer after the show
that Zeppelin were ready to reunite and perform at more live events,
but that fans might have to wait until Autumn 2009 as band members
(i.e. Robert Plant) had to tie up individual projects first.

Speaking to XFM radio the week after that, in the wake of yet another awards show, Jimmy replied to a question about whether he'd
tried to persuade Robert to rejoin the band by saying, 'I'm not going
to persuade anyone to do anything. It's just like the O2; you do it in
the spirit of your heart, don't you? You either do it or you don't.' He
also took the opportunity to pour cold water on the rumours, still circulating, that the 'broken finger' which had delayed the O2 show by
three weeks was merely a ploy to buy some more much-needed re-

hearsal time, to cover for the fact that Plant had spent longer in the US promoting *Raising Sand*'s release than any of them had anticipated. 'Broken finger?' he said. 'Damn right! It broke here,' he said, showing XFM the now-repaired digit. 'This one that looks like a knuckle on the end. It seriously was, it was broken in three places.' Three weeks was an awfully short time for it to heal, though, wasn't it, they persisted? 'I gotta tell you, that was the kind of focus that there was on behalf of everybody towards that O2 gig.' In fact, he said, the finger hadn't fully healed by the time of the gig: 'But my personal focus was that broken finger. It didn't matter [about it]. It was just steering ahead. It didn't get better in three weeks; it's just that I played in three weeks.' He also stated that he remained positive that the O2 gig would eventually see the light of day on DVD, the first real public acknowledgement of the fact that the original plan had been to have a DVD of the O2 ready for sale when the Zeppelin tour proper kicked-in, originally intended for the summer of 2008, now postponed indefinitely.

Plant, meanwhile, was a world away, figuratively and metaphorically. The UK and European dates with Krauss had been overwhelmingly well received; the US tour was going even better. In June, the same month Jimmy was talking of tentative future Zeppelin plans, Plant and Krauss received three nominations in the prestigious annual Americana Music Honors and Awards Show in Nashville: for Album of the Year, Song of the Year (for 'Gone Gone Gone'), and Duo or Group of the Year. *Raising Sand* was also one of the 12 albums nominated for the 2008 Mercury Music Awards. It was around this time that they also offered the biggest hint yet that not only would Plant not be considering a return to Zeppelin any time soon, but that he and Krauss were seriously considering a second album together. Quoted in the US music industry bible, *Billboard*, Robert said pointedly: 'I'm in no hurry to go anywhere. I want to stay very close [to the project with Krauss and T-Bone Burnett]. This is a font of knowledge, and I'm sticking as close to it as I can.' Alison was also quoted, saying: 'We're all having a wonderful time, and I hope and I think all three of us are hoping to continue this and that it go on and on.' Though, perhaps out of politeness, she did add that the duo's association shouldn't bring the curtain down on any of their other projects. 'That doesn't mean we've lost any love for whom we've played for and play with,' she said. 'The guys in [her previous outfit] Union Station, that's like home. So I hope to continue this and go back home, too.'

Producer T-Bone Burnett also confirmed in a separate interview, 'I feel like we're just starting to know what we can do with it. The two of them [Plant and Krauss] are so incredibly good that I would hate to not continue to work with both of them.' Plant put the icing on the cake when he added that performing the album's rootsy music along with the revamped versions of various Zeppelin songs had 'become quite an illumination, really. What has been created with the chemistry between the three of us has its own kind of genre, really. I'm a very fortunate man. I couldn't wish for anything better than this.'

The tour, meanwhile, was now extended into October, with follow-up UK dates added. *Raising Sand*, released a full year before, had now sold 1.03 million copies in the US, according to Nielsen SoundScan, and more than 600,000 copies in the UK. According to data from 17 shows reported to Billboard Boxscore, nine of which were sell-outs, the US tour alone had also now grossed more than $5.2 million, drawing more than 77,000 fans.

Returning from his farcical appearance with *X Factor* winner Leona Lewis at the Olympics Closing Ceremony in Beijing, Page finally seemed to acknowledge that his wait for Robert to return from his 'one-off' project with Alison Krauss was not likely to end any time soon and he quietly began making plans behind the scenes to do what had previously seemed unthinkable: re-launch Led Zeppelin without Robert Plant at the helm. Suddenly new rumours began circulating about a possible launch show at Cardiff's Millennium Stadium, apparently pencilled in for some time in 2009, with a Wembley Stadium show to follow. Then, on August 26, Jason Bonham gave an interview to a Detroit radio station that seemed to confirm the new plans. He talked of having been working in the studio recently with Page and Jones, helping them come up with new material. He confirmed, however, that Plant had yet to show any interest in the project. 'At the moment, all I know is, I have the great pleasure to go and jam with the two guys and start work on some material,' Bonham was quoted as saying. 'When I get there [in the studio] I never ask any questions. If I get a phone call to go and play, I enjoy every moment of it. Whatever it ends up as, to ever get a chance to jam with two people like that, it is a phenomenal thing for me. It's my life.' Pressed on details of a possible album, he stressed that 'lots of politics [would need to] get ironed out first before an album could be considered. But that was clearly the idea.

How would Plant react to this latest development? In the past, it was thought by insiders that Page's re-emergence with former Free and Bad Company frontman Paul Rodgers in The Firm had been the spur for Plant expressing interest in the first, later aborted Zeppelin reformation, in the wake of Live Aid. It was also no coincidence, surely, that Plant had again extended an olive branch Page's way – though not for a Zeppelin reformation but the nearest thing to it in the Nineties with the short-lived but hugely profitable Page/Plant project – after Jimmy's success with his *Coverdale/Page* album with the former Whitesnake and Deep Purple singer. Would Page openly discussing going ahead with a Zeppelin reformation without Plant now work in the same way – force the recalcitrant singer to curtail his extracurricular outing with Alison Krauss, or at least make some sort of longer-term commitment to a Zeppelin project, perhaps for 2009 or after?

The answer came all too quickly for Jimmy's liking: no, it would not. In an official statement released via robertplant.com on 29 September 2008, Robert stated unequivocally at last that he had no intention of touring with anyone 'for at least two years'. In case anyone still didn't get it, the statement went on to say that, 'Contrary to a spate of recent reports, Robert Plant will not be touring or recording with Led Zeppelin. Anyone buying tickets online to any such event will be buying bogus tickets.' Plant was quoted directly as saying: 'It's both frustrating and ridiculous for this story to continue to rear its head when all the musicians that surround the story are keen to get on with their individual projects and move forward. I wish Jimmy Page, John Paul Jones and Jason Bonham nothing but success with any future projects.'

So that was it. If Jimmy bringing in a replacement singer for Plant had been some kind of bluff, Robert had now very publicly called it. Attending the Mercury Prize gala in London on 9 September, although *Raising Sand* eventually lost out to Elbow's *The Seldom Seen Kid*, Plant – who had not attended Jimmy's Living Legend award at the *Classic Rock* awards the previous December, nor Zeppelin's Best Live Band award at the *Mojo* awards in June – said that this was the sort of award he was proud to be nominated for. 'This record has provided me with two of the happiest years of my career. Then again, I can't remember much of what I did before.' Ouch. He added: 'I've loved working with Alison and the rest of the band, and it's provided me with so much freedom. It's great to get this recognition.'

Six days later, he and Alison joined Levon Helm of The Band on stage in Nashville, where they performed 'In the Pines', the song they first performed together for the Leadbelly Tribute where they had first met two years before. The concert was part of the Americana Music Honors and Awards that were held the next day. Taking place at the Ryman Auditorium in Nashville, a beaming Plant and Krauss stepped up to receive Album of the Year for *Raising Sand*, then again a short while later for Duo of the Year. Robert was one of the 'surprise' performers for the evening, singing with Buddy Miller on 'What You Gonna Do Leroy'. (Robert and Buddy had actually recorded this new song just a few weeks before in a dressing room in Toronto during the *Raising Sand* tour; a version later included on Miller's next album, released in March 2009.) Plant and Krauss also found themselves nominated for an award at the 42nd Annual Country Music Association Awards; broadcast live on national American TV from the Summit Center in Nashville on 12 November. The category: Musical Event of the Year, for their performance of 'Gone Gone Gone'. Alison was also nominated for Female Vocalist of the Year.

Page, stoic in public but privately seething, was now determined not to be outdone. With the ever-faithful Jones and Bonham still in tow, he began auditioning new singers in London, veering from the tried and trusted to comparative unknowns, even those, it was said, who had at one time sung in Zeppelin tribute bands. A fact confirmed by John Paul Jones when he appeared at the Manson Guitar Weekend in Exeter, in October, and took part in a question and answer session. Talking about the possibility of a full Zeppelin tour he said: 'As you probably know, Jimmy, Jason and I are actually rehearsing and we've had the odd singer come in and have a bash. As soon as we know – which we don't – we will let you know. But we really hope that something is going to happen soon because we really want to do it and we're having a lot of fun, actually, just rehearsing. Jason is actually tremendous . . . And what we've done so far sounds absolutely fantastic. When it does come, it will come, and you'll know about it.'

But what of Plant? 'We really want do something and Robert doesn't want to do this, at least for the moment,' replied Jones. 'I don't really know what his plans are. He really doesn't want to make loud

music anymore. We do. I mean, I love acoustic music, but it doesn't
stop me from turning something up.' Jones also brought up the idea
again of a DVD of the O2 show being released, possibly in time with
any tour. In an interview with BBC Radio Devon, he added: 'We are
trying out a couple of singers. We want to do it. It's sounding great and
we want to get on and get out there.' What they were hoping to avoid,
however, he said, was 'a replica of Plant. It's got to be right. There's no
point in just finding another Robert. You could get that out of a tribute
band, but we don't want to be our own tribute band. There would be
a record and a tour, but everyone has to be on board.'

The best-known singer to try out for the spot was Aerosmith's
Steven Tyler, who flew into London the same month for two days of
intense rehearsals with the trio. A long-time Zep-o-phile and well-
known friend of Jimmy's since the guitarist guested with Aerosmith
on some UK dates in the early Nineties, on paper Tyler was one of the
few established rock vocalists who might just have delivered a plausi-
ble performance in a revamped Zeppelin line-up – certainly live. But
Tyler appeared to be suffering from a heavy cold and his voice was
not in its best shape the first day, forcing the rehearsal to be curtailed.
When they reconvened the second day, however, according to insiders Tyler made the bold suggestion that the new material Jimmy and
Jonesy had been working on didn't yet contain any recognisable hits.
Trying to be helpful but fatally misjudging the situation, Tyler then
suggested they might like to try out some of the new songs he'd been
working on with his co-writer Marti Frederiksen. A well-known gun-
for-hire musician, producer and songwriter whose prowess as a hit-
maker for rock artists like Aerosmith, Def Leppard, Mötley Crüe,
Ozzy Osbourne and others has made him a 21st-century music industry star, Frederiksen was not the kind of behind-the-scenes worker-
bee likely to appeal to Jimmy Page. As a result, according to one
insider who does not wish to be named here, 'Jimmy never said a
word when Tyler came out with this stuff, just told his staff to get
him a plane ticket home. And that was the end of that.'

The closest anybody came to actually landing the job was a little-
known American singer-guitarist named Miles Kennedy, until then
the 39-year-old frontman of US band Alter Bridge, the band formed
by former Creed guitarist Mark Tremonti. According to Twisted Sister vocalist Dee Snider, who was the one who let the cat out of the

bag, speaking on his syndicated US radio show, Kennedy had landed
the gig and, with him on board, the band would shortly announce
what was to be the first Led Zeppelin tour since 1980, commencing in
the summer of 2009. With any official denial markedly not forthcoming, rumours reached such a pitch it became a topic of open discussion in numerous newspapers, magazines and other media outlets.
While everyone had been prepared to jump on the bandwagon of a
full-on Zeppelin reformation, no one, it seemed, was keen on the
prospect of a Zeppelin tour without Plant at the helm.

As former Zeppelin promoter Freddy Bannister pointed out: 'I can
see that Jimmy might be doing it because he really wants to play with
that band again. But from a promoter's point of view, I don't think
they would be quite the attraction they would be without Robert. Because Robert and Jimmy were the band – the focal points. I really
can't image the band as just Jimmy.' Page's old guitar mentor from his
session days, Big Jim Sullivan, was equally sceptical: 'Robert was another instrument in himself. To replace him with someone of equal
standing and experience will be very difficult. Anyone can sing a song,
but not the way he did. I can see it happening without him, but I can't
see it being successful.' Or as former Rolling Stones manager Andrew
Loog Oldham put it:'Led Zeppelin touring without Robert Plant? It's
like the Stones without Prince Michael of Kent.'

Page, himself, however appeared sanguine at the prospect, explaining: 'I've been writing music over the last few years. I've got
various "vehicles", and they can be used and employed in various situations. I'm ready to present the stuff that I've got. I've done a number
of projects but not an album . . . I've got enough new music to make
it tantalising.' Maybe so, but as veteran Scottish rock DJ Tom Russell
says, 'If Jimmy Page, John Paul Jones and Jason Bonham want to go
off and make music with a new singer then I say good luck to them.
Just don't call it Led Zeppelin.' Without that magic three-syllable
name, though, where would be the hullabaloo; the hundreds of millions of dollars that went with it?

Even one of both Page and Plant's staunchest former champions,
O2 promoter Harvey Goldsmith, weighed in with some very public
advice of his own. Speaking to BBC News music reporter Ian Youngs,
he said: 'I certainly don't think they should do a big tour because I
can't see the point of it.' He added there may be 'some opportunities'

for a reunion with Plant in the future. But any plans for attempting such a re-launch without him were surely doomed to failure. 'I just think it's a lot of talk, I think it's wishful thinking. Whether they all come together and do something in the future, they may. I think some of the band really want to go out and do it and other parts of the band need to understand why they're doing it, and if there's no compelling reason to do it, then they shouldn't do it.' He went on: 'I don't think a long rambling tour is the answer as Led Zeppelin. It's a question of whether they want to do it, and you've got to want to do it. Otherwise it's done for the wrong reasons, and when things are done for the wrong reasons, they don't work.' Speaking at the MusExpo music conference in London, Goldsmith said he would 'hopefully' be involved in any comeback.

Page was said to be so furious at Goldsmith's words that he pulled out of attending that year's *Classic Rock* awards when he learned the promoter would also be in attendance. Instead, the evening was notable for a completely unprovoked attack on Zeppelin by no lesser a presence than that of former Cream bassist and vocalist Jack Bruce. Picking up the Classic Album gong for Cream's *Disraeli Gears*, he gave an extraordinary after-show interview to the magazine's writer, Dave Ling, during which he launched into a bitter anti-Zep tirade, comparing their one-off O2 show unfavourably with Cream's own, much lengthier full-scale tour comeback in 2005. 'Everybody talks about Led Zeppelin,' he said, 'and they played one fucking gig. One fucking lame gig – while Cream did weeks of gigs; proper gigs, not just a lame gig like Zeppelin did, with all the [vocal] keys lowered and everything. We played everything in the original keys.' Increasingly agitated, he went on: 'Fuck off, Zeppelin, you're crap. You've always been crap and you'll never be anything else. The worst thing is that people believe the crap that they're sold. Cream is ten times the band that Led Zeppelin is.' When a clearly disconcerted Ling responded by describing Bruce's outburst as 'a bold opinion' the legendary bassist spat back, 'What? You're gonna compare Eric Clapton with that fucking Jimmy Page? Would you really compare that?' Ling: 'To be fair, they're different kinds of player, aren't they?' Bruce: 'No! Eric's good and Jimmy's crap. And with that I rest my case.'

In the end it was left to Kennedy himself to bring this sorry state of affairs to an end, possibly prompted by Page and Jones. Interviewed by Eric Blair of *The Blairing Out with Eric Blair Show* at the National Association of Music Merchants show in January, Kennedy said, 'I am not singing in Led Zeppelin or any offshoot of Led Zeppelin, but I did have a great opportunity and it was something that I'm very grateful for. But Alter Bridge will go on, and that's that.' When asked what it was like performing with his childhood heroes, Kennedy replied, 'Surreal. It was great.' He refused, however, to discuss the new material he had been asked to play with Page, Jones and Bonham or to elaborate any further on the situation. 'I'll tell that story some day. But for now, it was a good experience, and I'm still pinching myself, let's put it that way.'

But why hadn't it gone any further than 'jamming'? Speaking so close to the events, insiders are hugely reluctant to go on the record. Speaking off the record, however, the feeling was that the benefits of having someone like Kennedy taking Plant's spot – as one put it, 'Someone young who'd been a fan of the band and would do exactly what he was told by Jimmy,' including all the songs Robert wouldn't do – were ultimately outweighed by the sheer body of negative opinion against the idea of returning to life as Led Zeppelin without Plant. Plant may 'still drive him mad' but even a hugely frustrated Jimmy now sees that to try and continue without him could damage the long-term credibility of the band. Or as an earlier report on Rolling Stone.com put it, quoting another insider in the Page camp, 'Whatever this is, it is not Led Zeppelin – not without the involvement of Robert Plant'. Once that reality sank in, it seems, Jimmy's enthusiasm for the idea sank with it. If he'd wanted to put a 'new' band together he could have done it at any point over the past 30 years. He didn't want to start a new band; he wanted to revive Led Zeppelin. Even with Jonesy and Bonham's only son by his side, without Robert, it simply wasn't going to be possible. The world simply wouldn't allow it.

It had been touch and go for a while there, though. As recently as January 2009, Page's personal manager Peter Mensch still appeared to be talking up the inclusion of Kennedy and/or some other singer in a revised Zeppelin line-up, when he told *BBC 6 Music* the following: 'People don't really understand it. Jimmy Page has been playing guitar professionally since he was sixteen years old. Jimmy Page likes being a musician. That's what he does. He doesn't want to be a race car driver or a solicitor.' As a result, he and Jones and Bonham 'decided that if they could find a singer that they thought would fit their bill – whatever their bill was at this stage in their career – that they'd make a record and go on tour. That's what Jimmy Page does.' He added: 'I can't comment on any rumours right now. It's gonna be a long and difficult process. And we're not soliciting people. So don't call me about it!'

However, only days later came this story, via the *MusicRadar* website: another interview with Mensch, where he now stated categorically that, 'Led Zeppelin are over! If you didn't see them in 2007 [at the O2], you missed them. It's done. I can't be any clearer than that.' He did confirm that once that Robert Plant made it known he was continuing his partnership with Alison Krauss and had no intention of returning to Led Zeppelin, replacement vocalists were auditioned to possibly record and tour with Page, Jones and Bonham. 'They tried out a few singers, but no one worked out,' said Mensch. 'That was it. The whole thing is completely over now. There are absolutely no plans for them to continue. Zero. Frankly, I wish everybody would stop talking about it.' Pressed on what new projects Jimmy Page might now be involved with in 2009, Mensch said, 'Fuck if I know. I'm waiting to hear.'

And that, more or less, is how things remain in the summer of 2009. Of course, Jimmy keeps himself busy, pottering about with various projects: for example, the imminent release of the guitar documentary *It Might Get Loud*, in which he features alongside White Stripes frontman Jack White and U2 guitarist The Edge. A documentary directed by Davis Guggenheim, best known for his directorial role for the Academy Award-winning *An Inconvenient Truth*, it was well received when screened late in 2008 at the Toronto International Film Festival. Described by Sony Pictures Classic, its distributor, as 'a music lover's dream', the film covers three generations of guitar players 'and our plan is to attract the three generations of fans when we open the film [in the US in the summer of 2009]. We are pleased to be in business with director Davis Guggenheim and producer Thomas Tull, whose obsession with the subject has brought so much to the high quality of the film.' The spokesperson added, however: 'There is no news of a European release date as yet.'

In April 2009, Jimmy officially inducted Jeff Beck into the American Rock and Roll Hall of Fame during a celeb-heavy bash at Cleveland Ohio's Public Hall. He also got up and performed with Beck and

his band during a poignant version of 'Beck's Bolero'. Beck invited
Page up to the stage by introducing him to the audience as 'a big
chunk of Led Zeppelin, right here . . .' They also performed a rousing
version of 'Immigrant Song' with Beck playing the vocal lead on his
trademark white Stratocaster. Later in the evening Jimmy joined Jeff,
plus Metallica's Lars Ulrich, James Hetfield and Kirk Hammett, Aerosmith's Joe Perry, Ronnie Wood from the Stones and Red Hot Chilli
Peppers bassist Flea for an all-star jam of 'Train Kept a Rollin''. It was
a great moment, and Page's life now appears to consist of a string of
such moments, whether they be with the Foo Fighters, Jeff Beck or
whoever else he next chooses to jump up on stage with. But is that all
there is to his career now: a series of guest appearances?

Plainly, Jimmy would like to think not. But without Robert Plant to
front a Led Zeppelin revival, he still seems markedly reluctant to take
on any big new musical projects. Which is a great pity, for as his one-
time collaborator, Whitesnake vocalist David Coverdale, says, 'It breaks
my heart to see him frustrated like this. I can't tell you what it would do
to me if someone said I can't do Whitesnake. It's who you are. What
you do and he should be allowed to do it. But if he can't, what I said to
him was why doesn't he do like a Carlos Santana and get a whole load
of different vocalists in? He and John Paul Jones have probably written
some amazing new stuff, and why shouldn't they? They're both amazing musicians. And I think it's absolutely right and proper that they
should want to bring Jason in on drums too. He's family. And if Robert
doesn't want to do it, fair enough, ask some other people that would be
only too happy to come in and lend a hand. I've said that me and [Def
Leppard vocalist] Joe Elliot would be there in a shot . . .'

It's a good idea, one his old pal Jeff Beck certainly seems to have
embraced in recent times, too. Talk is that Beck – now sixty-five and
Jimmy's closest living contemporary – plans to retire at seventy, and
in the meantime intends to 'make the most' of the next few years, including a star-studded series of shows around the world like the special Fourth of July concert he put on at the Albert Hall this summer,
where he was joined on stage by a special guest star in the form of
Pink Floyd's Dave Gilmour. Why couldn't Jimmy Page do something
similar? And if Plant changes his mind at some point and agrees to do
some shows as Led Zeppelin, all to the good. Just put less all-or-
nothing emphasis on it . . .

So far, though, Page simply refuses to entertain the possibility. So far . . .

Elsewhere, both Jones and Bonham appear to have accepted that they will not be touring the world as Led Zeppelin any time soon. Indeed, Bonham has recently announced that he has rejoined Airrace, the group he helped form to no particular success back in the Eighties. He also played on some sessions for the forthcoming solo album from former Guns N' Roses guitarist Slash, and even joined tribute band Led Zepagain during their 77 Tour Revisited set at LA's House of Blues in March, coming up for the encore of 'Rock and Roll'.

Jones, of course, continues to potter around on various low-key projects, like the collaboration in April 2009 with Seattle alt.rock legends Sonic Youth, an original musical piece entitled 'Ninety Ninety', for the Merce Cunningham Dance Company, which they later performed together in Brooklyn Academy of Music, along with co-composer, mixed-media 'sound sculptor' Takehisa Kosugi. It was part of Merce Cunningham's ninetieth birthday celebrations, a four-day festival dedicated to the choreographer's work and influence. (Later in the year the show travelled to Madrid, Champaign-Urbana, Paris, Berkeley, and London.) And then there was the release of the debut solo album from Nickel Creek's Sara Watkins which Jones produced. In an interview for noted Zep fan-site *Tight But Loose*, Jones told TBL founder Dave Lewis, 'The really great thing about the whole process of making the album is that we achieved exactly what we set out to do. As for myself as producer, the entire vision I had for this record came to fruition. I'm really pleased with it. I wanted her voice to be really to the fore with a sparse accompaniment. It was a real throw-back to the old days of recording.'

As ever, the only former member of Led Zeppelin who continues to really capture the wider public's imagination is – no coincidence surely – the same one who is no longer interested in being involved in the group: Robert Plant. Awarded a CBE in the Queen's 2008 end-of-year honours list, 'for services to music', Plant continues to work his own idiosyncratic, stubbornly individualistic groove. As well as one-off appearances, variously, on stage with Fairport Convention last year, for their special Cropredy concert in memory of the 30th anniversary of the death of Sandy Denny, where he duetted on 'Battle of Evermore' with Kristina Donahue, so far this year he has recorded a duet with fellow West Midlands singer Scott Matthews, for a track, '12 Harps', on his latest album, *Elsewhere*, and, more recently, put in a surprise appearance on stage at the Womad Festival in Abu Dhabi, where he joined Strange Sensation guitarist Justin Adams and the West African riti (a one-string violin) master Juldeh Camara. Plant's last-minute inclusion on the bill was seen as a coup for the Abu Dhabi Authority for Culture and Heritage (Adach) and for Womad, whose director, Chris Smith, said: 'The fact is that Robert Plant only does things that he wants to do [and] he was excited by the thought of performing at a free festival in Abu Dhabi.' He added: 'Robert is a lovely guy who is very keen not to steal the thunder from the others.'

Jimmy Page might have something to say on that subject, of course. But for now, the last word continues to go to Robert, who told reporters at the festival: 'This is so straightforward, without any big production deals or anything like that. It's where music came from. And as time goes on, the less the hassle and the more the adventure, the more stimulating it is for me. This is just another one of those moments along the way.'

Indeed. Though not quite as important, perhaps, as the five Grammy awards he and Alison Krauss won at the 51st ceremony in Los Angeles, in February 2009, the highest tally of any act on the night. 'When we started this together it was all a mystery,' Plant said from the stage of the Staples Center in Los Angeles, where the awards ceremony was held. The five awards comprised: Best Contemporary/ Folk Americana Album Award for *Raising Sand*; Best Country Collaboration With Vocals Award for the track 'Killing the Blues'; Best Pop Collaboration With Vocals Award for 'Rich Woman'; Record of the Year Award for 'Please Read the Letter'; and Album of the Year Award for *Raising Sand*.

Plant also took the opportunity to reveal that 'Please Read the Letter' was 'an old song that me and Jimmy Page wrote together and been given that Nashville touch, and it feels pretty good'. In accepting the night's biggest award, Album of the Year, for *Raising Sand*, he said: 'I'm bewildered. In the old days we would have called this selling out, but it's a good way to spend a Sunday.' He and Alison then performed a medley of 'Rich Woman' and 'Gone Gone Gone'.

Backstage, Plant, Krauss and their producer T-Bone Burnett were jubilant. 'Yes, we're doing another record!' Burnett yelled. While Robert had a curt reply to the journalist who asked if Led Zeppelin would ever tour again. 'How old are you, man?' Plant snapped, while still maintaining a semblance of a smile, 'because you look older than me.' When that got a chuckle he lightened up again. 'You try to do "Communication Breakdown" in these pants!' The following week, *Raising Sand* had shot back up the US charts from Number 69 to Number 2, selling 77,000 copies in the days immediately after the Grammys.

Speaking to Ben Jones of Britain's Absolute Radio digital network in the week of the Grammys, Robert interrupted a pre-production session on his second album with Alison Krauss, to say: 'For me, well, I don't have a career, I just have a bunch of great events in my life and a few dips and troughs. I don't think I've ever had a career. I think when Led Zeppelin . . . when we lost John in 1980, I was desperate to not reinstate but do something for myself, free from the kind of shackles of people's expectations. And from that moment on, along the line, of course it would be great to get a reflection of your work, but "career" . . . it's not something I think about.'

As for Led Zeppelin, he sighed and said: 'I guess I . . . well, you know, the thing is, look at it like this, the reason that it stopped was because we were incomplete, and we've been incomplete now for twenty-eight years. And no matter what you do, you have to really guard the discretion of what you've done in the past and make sure that you have all the reasons in the right place to be able to do something with absolute, total conviction. I mean, if my great reward is to do this, then I don't want to do anything where we challenge what we did in the first place by just going back and visiting it without having a new, fresh makeover start. I mean, you only get one shot at these things, and if they're spectacular on day one, if on day ten they aren't so good . . . As Alison said, when we cut out, started to make *Raising Sand*, we gave ourselves a deal about if we don't get anything going in three days, let's just go out for lunch and say see you later. And I think the thing about it is really, is that to visit old ground, it's a very incredibly delicate thing to do, and the disappointment that could be there once you commit to that and the comparisons to something that was basically fired by youth and a different kind of exuberance to now, it's very hard to go back and meet that head on and do it justice.'

And for Robert Plant, it seems, it just gets harder every day . . .

NOTES AND SOURCES

The foundations of this book, in terms of quotes and the facts of the story so far as I have gleaned them, are based on my own original investigations, beginning with the various interviews and conversations over the years I have enjoyed with Jimmy Page, Robert Plant, John Paul Jones, Jason Bonham and many others, some of whom for reasons of privacy do not wish to be named.

Other voices that have provided me with invaluable information and insights over the years, often from personal anecdotes or even chance remarks, include Jason Bonham, Peter Grant, Richard Cole and again others who do not wish to be named here. I have also spent a great deal of time over the years compiling as much background material as possible from as much published – and, in a few cases, unpublished – material as there is available, including books, magazine and newspaper articles, websites, TV and radio shows, DVDs, demo-tapes, bootleg CDs and any other form of media that contained useful information, the most important of which I have listed here.

However, extra special mention should also go to a handful of books and articles that proved especially helpful, in terms of adding to my own insights and investigations. First and foremost, the series of excellent books and articles by renowned Zeppelin historian Dave Lewis of *Tight But Loose* fame; also my old mate Chris Welch, who has also written great books on Peter Grant and John Bonham; Richard Cole, whose own memoir remains insightful and wincingly honest – a great achievement; Stephen Davis also, whose *Hammer of the Gods* is well known, rightly so; Ritchie Yorke for his many articles and book; Pamela Des Barres whose *I'm With The Band* was essential reading; Stuart Grundy and John Tobler's first class *The Guitar Greats*; Alan Clayson, heroic author of many invaluable tomes on the Yardbirds, Brian Jones and others; Nick Kent, for his always excellent articles back in the Seventies for *NME* and more recently, in *Q*; Steve Rosen, similarly, for his unique take on things; Dave Schelps, whose trilogy of in-depth articles for *Trouser Press* in 1977 were magnificent; the 2003 Q Zeppelin special, which was especially helpful; and Brad Tolinski and Greg Di Benedetto, whose look back on all the

Zeppelin albums in *Guitar World* in 2004 was also illuminating.

There were many others, too, which I have endeavoured to list below, all of which deserve praise and acknowledgement for the role they played in helping shape the direction of this book. I extend my thanks and would urge readers to seek them out. Most of these articles I purchased either when they were first published or via a back-catalogue resource. Many, however, I now discover are available via the internet. If you can get hold of the originals though, I would recommend it for there is nothing quite like holding a vintage *Rolling Stone* or similar from the late Sixties or early Seventies, if just for the special smell of the now yellowing paper. As such, there are many titles I did not take direct quotes from that were also helpful in terms of background, cultural insight and – no other word for it – vibe. Titles such as *Street Life, Friends, Cashbox, National Rock Star, New York Rocker, Pop Swap,* and so many others, it will be years before I find a place to file them all.

Again, my utmost thanks to one and all.

BOOKS

A History of Modern Britain by Andrew Marr (Macmillan, 2007)

A Pictorial History of Magic and the Supernatural by Maurice Bessy (Spring Books, 1964)

At The Heart of Darkness: Witchcraft, Black Magic and Satanism Today by John Parker (Sidgwick & Jackson, 1993)

Backstage Passes, Life on the Wild Side with David Bowie by Angie Bowie (Orion, 1994)

Bill Graham Presents: My Life Inside Rock and Out by Bill Graham with Robert Greenfield (Doubleday, 1992)

Black Easter, or Faust Aleph-Null (After Such Knowledge; in Three Volumes) by James Blish (Faber & Faber, 1969)

Blues Fell This Morning: The Meaning of the Blues by Paul Oliver (Cassell, 1960) *Brian Jones* by Alan Clayson (Sanctuary, 2003)

Brum Rocked On! by Laurie Hornsby (TGM Ltd, 2003)

Call Up The Groups! by Alan Clayson (Cassell Illustrated, 1985)

Celebration by Dave Lewis (Omnibus, 1991)

Celebration II by Dave Lewis (Omnibus, 2003)

Dazed and Confused: The Stories Behind Every Song by Chris Welch (Carlton, 1998) *Dazzling Stranger: Bert Jansch and the British Folk and Blue Revival* by Colin Harper (Bloomsbury, 2000)

Deep Blues: A Musical and Cultural History of the Mississippi Delta by Robert Palmer (Viking, 1981)

Dictionary of Occult, Hermetic and Alchemical Sigils by Fred Gettings (Routledge & Kegan Paul, 1982)

Eliphas Levi, History of Magic: Including a Clear and Precise Exposition of Its Procedure, Its Rites and Its Mysteries by Eliphas Levi, translated by Arthur Edward Waite (Unknown Binding, 1969)

Fallen Angel, The Untold Story of Jimmy Page and Led Zeppelin by Thomas W. Friend (Gabriel Publications 2002)

Hammer of the Gods: Led Zeppelin Unauthorised by Stephen Davis (Sidgwick & Jackson, 1985)

I'm With The Band: Confessions of a Groupie by Pamela Des Barnes (Helter Skelter, 2005)

In the Houses of the Holy: Led Zeppelin and the Power of Rock Music by Susan Fast (Oxford University Press Inc, 2001)

Jeff Beck: Crazy Fingers by Annette Carson (Backbeat Books, 2001)

Jimmy Page: Magus, Musician, Man, An Unauthorised Biography by George Case (Hal-Leonard, 2007)

Jimmy Page: Tangents Within A Framework by Howard Mylett (Omnibus, 1983) *John Bonham: A Thunder of Drums* by Chris Welch and Geoff Nicholls (Backbeat Books, 2001)

John Bonham: The Powerhouse Behind Led Zeppelin by Mick Bonham (South Bank Publishing, 2005)

Led Zeppelin IV by Barney Hoskyns (Rodale, 2006)

Led Zeppelin IV by Erik Davis (33 1/3 publishing, 2005)

Led Zeppelin, The Press Reports by Robert Godwin (Collector's Guide Publishing, 2003)

Led Zeppelin: The Definitive Biography by Ritchie Yorke (Virgin, 1999)

Led Zeppelin: The Story of a Band and Their Music 1968-1980 by Keith Shadwick (Backbeat Books, 2005)

Lennon Remembers by Jann S. Wenner (Verso, 2000)

Magick In Theory And Practise by Aleister Crowley (Book Sales, 1992)

Me, Alice: The Autobiography of Alice Cooper by Alice Cooper (G.P. Putnam's Sons, 1976)

The Psychology of Hashish: An Essay on Mysticism Aleister Crowley (Holmes, 2001)

Peter Grant: The Man Who Led Zeppelin by Chris Welch (Omnibus, 2002)

Rebel Heart: An American Rock and Roll Journey by Bebe Buell with Victor Bockris (St. Martin's Press, 2001)

Rhythm and the Blues: A Life in American Music by Jerry Wexler with David Ritz (Alfred a Knopf 1993)

Small Faces: The Young Mods' Forgotten Story by Paolo Hewitt (Acid Jazz Books, 1995)

Stairway To Heaven: Led Zeppelin Uncensored by Richard Cole and Richard Trubo (Simon & Schuster, 1993)

Stardust: The David Bowie Story by Henry Edwards and Tony Zanetta (McGraw-Hill, 1986)

Stoned by Andrew Loog Oldham (Becker & Warburg, 2000)

The Aleister Crowley Scrapbook by Sandy Robertson (Quantum, 2002) *The Book of Signs* by Rudolf Koch (The Limited Editions Club, 1930)

The Book of the Goetia of Solomon The King, translated by Aleister Crowley (Facsimile edition, Equinox 1976)

The Book of the Law: 100th Anniversary Edition by Aleister Crowley (Red Wheel/Weiser; Centennial Edition, 2004)

The Books of the Beast by Timothy d'Arch Smith (Mandrake Press, 1991)

The Confessions of Aleister Crowley: An Autohagiography by Aleister Crowley (Law Book Co of Australasia; New Edition, 1979)

The Guitar Greats by Stuart Grundy, John Tobler (BBC Books, 1983)

The Hit Men: Power Brokers and Fast Money Inside The Music Business by Frederic Dannen (Random House, 1990)

The Hurdy Gurdy Man by Donovan (Century, 2005)

The Magical Diaries of Aleister Crowley, edited by Stephen Skinner (Jersey, Neville, 1979)

The Origin of the Species: How, Why & Where It All Began by Alan Clayson (Chrome Dreams, 2006)

The Times Deceas'd by Timothy d'Arch Smith (Stone Trough Books, 2003)

The Yardbirds by Alan Clayson (Backbeat Books, 2002)

There Must be A Better Way: The Story Of The Bath & Knebworth Festivals 1969 – 1979 by Freddy Bannister (Bath Books, 2003)

Trips: Rock Life in the Sixties by Ellen Sander (Scribner, 1973)

Truth: Rod Stewart, Ronnie Wood and the Jeff Beck Group by Dave Thompson (Cherry Red, 2006)

Unknown Legends of Rock and Roll by Richie Unterberger (Backbeat Books, 2000)

Waiting For The Sun: Strange Days, Weird Scenes and the Sound of Los Angeles by Barney Hoskyns (Viking, 1996)

NEWSPAPERS AND MAGAZINES

Live review, *Melody Maker*, 24 October 1968

Plant interview, *International Times*, Spring 1969

Review first album, John Mendelssohn, *Rolling Stone*, 15 March 1969

Review first album, Felix Dennis, *Oz*, March 1969

Page interview, Keith Altham, *Top Pops*, 13 September 1969

Page interview, *Record Mirror*, February 1970

Page interview, Keith Altham, *Record Mirror*, 27 February 1971

Plant interview, *Record Mirror*, March 1972
John Bonham quote, *Disc*, June 1972
Plant interview, Lisa Robinson, *Creem*, 1973
Review, Houses, *Phonograph Record*, May 1973
Review, Houses, Jonh Ingham, *Let It Rock*, June 1973
Article, Charles Shaar Murray, *NME*, 16 June 1973
Plant interview, Charles Shaar Murray, *NME*, 25 June 1973
Page interview, Nick Kent, *NME*, 1 September 1973
David Byron interview, Tony Stewart, *NME*, 8 September 1973
Page interview, Steven Rosen, *Los Angeles Free Press*, December 1973 Page
    interview, Chris Welch, *Melody Maker*, 23 March 1974
Page and Plant interviews, Cameron Crowe, *Rolling Stone*, 13 March 1975
Groupie article, *Phonograph Record*, March 1975
Page interview, Chris Salewicz, *Let It Rock*, May 1975
Physical Graffiti review, Chris Salewicz, *Let It Rock*, May 1975
Physical Graffiti review, Jaan Uhelszki, *Creem*, May 1975
Page interview, William S. Burroughs, *Crawdaddy*, June 1975
John Bonham interview, Chris Welch, *Melody Maker*, 21 June 1975
Page interview, Lisa Robinson, *NME*, 1975
Page interview, Jonh Ingham, *Sounds*, 13 March 1976
Presence review, Jonh Ingham, *Sounds*, 10 April 1976
Presence review, *Rolling Stone*, Stephen Davis, 1976
Plant interview, Chris Charlesworth, *Creem*, May 1976
David Bowie interview, Cameron Crowe, *Playboy*, September 1976
Page interview, Mick Houghton, *Circus*, 12 October 1976
Joe Massot quote, *Rolling Stone*, 13 January 1977
Plant interview, Roy Carr, *NME*, January 1977
Page interview, Chris Salewicz, *GIG*, May 1977
Johnny Rotten interview, Kris Needs, *ZigZag*, June 1977
Page interview, Steven Rosen, *Guitar Player*, July 1977
Article, Jaan Uhelszki, *Creem*, July 1977
Three-part Page interview, Dave Schulps, *Trouser Press*, 1977
Page interview, Chris Salewicz, *Creem*, November 1979
Beck interview, Steven Rosen, *Guitar World*, July 1986
Plant interview, Tom Hibbert, *Q*, 1988
Plant interview, Mat Snow, *Q*, May 1990
Plant, Jones, Mat Snow, *Q*, December 1990
Malcolm Dent interview, Nick Hunter, *Sunday Mail*, 24 March 1991
George Hardie quote, *Rolling Stone*, July 1991
Aubrey Powell quote, *Rolling Stone*, July 1991
Page interview, *Guitar World*, 1991

Bill Graham obit, Ben Fong-Torres, *San Francisco Chronicle*, 3 November 1991

Plant interview, *Mojo*, May 1996

Bebe Buell interview, *Mojo*, May 1996

John Paul Jones interview, Mat Snow, *Mojo*, December 1997

Page interview, Mat Snow, *Mojo*, December 1997

Peter Grant interview, Paul Henderson, *Classic Rock*, 1999

John Paul Jones interview, Dave Ling, *Classic Rock*, August 1999

Article, Phil Sutcliffe, *Mojo*, April 2000

Article, Jon Hotten, *Classic Rock*, December 2001

Article, Dave Lewis, *Classic Rock*, April 2002

Carmine Appice quote, Led Zeppelin, Q *Special*, March 2003

George Hardie quote, Q *Special*, March 2003

Jerry Wexler quote, Q *Special*, March 2003

Pamela Des Barres quote, Q *Special*, March 2003

Page interview, Nick Kent, Q *Special*, March 2003

Article, Phil Sutcliffe, Q *Zep Special*, March 2003

Storm Thorgerson quotes, Lois Wilson, Q *Zep Special*, 2003

Joe Massot quote, Peter Doggett, Q *Zep Special*, March 2003

Ian McLagan, Small Faces: The Darlings of Wapping Wharf Launderette E1, issue no. 24, a fanzine, 2003

John Paul Jones interview, Dave Lewis, *Tight But Loose*, December 2003

Jeff Beck and Jimmy Page interview, Charles Shaar Murray, The Guv'nors, *Mojo*, July 2004

Page interview, Brad Tolinski with Greg Di Benedetto, *Guitar World*, 2004

Article, Brad Tolinsky, Black Magic, *Guitar World*, April 2004

Plant quote, Nigel Williamson – *Uncut*, 2005

Plant interview, *The Guardian*, 14 October 2005

Article, *Word*, January, 2006

Lamar Fike quote, Elvis cover, *Mojo*, May 2006

Article, Nick Kent, *Mojo 70s Special*, June 2006

Plant quote, *Record Collector*, Dave Lewis, June, 2006

Plant quote, Mikal Gilmore, *Rolling Stone*, July 2006

Kenneth Anger interview, *Bizarre*, Mark Berry, 2006

Page interview, Peter Makowksi, *Classic Rock*, 2006

Malcolm Dent interview, Calum Macleod, *The Inverness Courier*, 3 November 2006

Ace Frehley quote, *Classic Rock*, December 2007

Ann Wilson quote, *Classic Rock*, December 2007

Eddie Kramer quote, *Classic Rock*, December 2007

Ric Lee quote, *Classic Rock*, December 2007

Richard Cole quote, *Classic Rock*, December 2007
Roy Harper quote, *Classic Rock*, December 2007
Zacron interview, *Classic Rock*, December 2007
Page interview, Mark Blake, *Mojo*, December 2007
Plant interview, Sylvie Simmons, *Guardian*, 16 May 2008

SOME USEFUL WEBSITES

www.cuttingedge.org
www.darklinks.com/doccult.html
www.furious.com
www. golden-dawn.com
www.inthelight.co.nz/ledzep/zososymbol.htm
www.ledzeppelin.com
www.members.aol.com/lzhistory/index.html.
www.news.bbc.co.uk
www.oto-uk.org
www.ratso.net
www.robertplantalisonkrauss.com
www.rocksbackpages.com
www.simoniff.com
www.stryder.de/symbole.html
www.tblweb.com
www.terryreid.com
www.victorian.fortunecity.com
www.youbettershutandlisten.com

OTHER MEDIA

Behind The Mask, Radio 1 series, 1985
Led Zeppelin: The Classic Interviews CD, Chrome Dreams CIS 2006
Sleeve notes, Truth CD, Charles Shaar Murray, February 2005
Jimmy Page interview, Nicky Home, Capital Radio, 1976, repeated Planet Rock, 2007
The Song Remains The Same DVD, Warners 2007
Led Zeppelin: DVD, Warner Music Vision 2003
Jimmy Page Audio Interview, Steve Rosen, Rock's Backpages, April, 1977

INDEX

A.A. (aka Great White
Brotherhood), 217
A&M Studios, 145
A&R Studios, 145, 146
Aarseth, Øytein
'Euronymous', 212
Abbey of Thelema, 223–4,
231, 302, 342
Abbey Road, 153
Abbey Road studio, 43, 196
Aberystwyth, 275
*Above Ground Sound of Jake
Holmes, The*, 62–3
Abra-melin, 208, 229,
232–3, 450
'Absolution Blues', 433
AC/DC, 402
'Achilles Last Stand',
345–6, 347–8, 350,
354, 367, 374, 415,
441
Adler, Lou, 163
Aerosmith, 418, 430
Agadir, 342
Agate, James, 231
Ahmet Ertegun Education
Fund, 440
Airforce, 242
Aiwass, 222, 224
Aladdin, 115
Alan Price Rhythm & Blues
Combo, 273
Albarn, Keith, 320
Albert Hall, 76, 160, 169,
170, 172–3, 181, 240,
387, 421, 437

Albertos Y Los Trios
Paranoias, 354
Alexander, Arthur, 30
Allcock, Garry, 35
'All My Love', 394, 395
'All You Need Is Love', 66
All Your Own, 113
Aloha From Hawaii, 279
Altamont, 164, 211, 288
Altham, Keith, 73–4
Amboy Dukes, 399
Ambrose Orchestra, 92
America
and Yardbirds, 5
social and political unrest,
48
Grant seeks record deal
in, 75–6
first tour, 88–91, 94–104,
107–12, 115–16,
118–23
Led Zeppelin released in,
115–17
success of records in, 123,
157, 198, 235, 244,
256, 279, 336, 354,
401–2, 419
second tour, 130–1,
135–42, 144–5
singles released in, 126–7,
244
third tour, 160–9
fourth tour, 153–4, 168
fifth tour, 169–70,
175–80
sixth tour, 202

seventh tour, 253
Led Zeppelin IV tapes
mixed in, 250
eight tour, 269
ninth tour, 280–8, 293–7
tenth tour, 325, 326–36
launch parties for Swan
Song, 315
plans for next tour, 340,
342
Page and Plant write
together in, 345–7
band visits to record
Presence, 347, 349–52
politicians in, 355
eleventh tour, 366–79,
382–3
1980 tour planned
410–11
reunions in, 423–5, 428,
430–1
brief references, 1, 13, 26,
223, 225, 273, 274,
381, 433, 438, 442
see also names of places
American Film Institute,
302
*American Folk Festival of the
Blues*, 114
Amusement Business, 50–1
Anaheim Convention
Center, LA, 163
'Anarchy in the UK', 362
Andrew Oldham
Orchestra, 41–2
Andrews, Bernie, 128

'And She's Lonely', 245
Angel, Jorgen, 51
'Angel Baby', 278
Anger, Kenneth, 211, 226,
    229–30, 231, 233,
    265, 301–5, 326, 327,
    332, 342, 356–8, 365,
    450 see also titles of
    films
'Angry Angry', 438
Animals, 353
Animals, The, 273–4, 310,
    338, 381
'Another Round', 438
Antonioni, 6
Appice, Carmine, 98, 100,
    125, 166, 415
Apple, 82, 300, 313
'Applejack', 41
Apple Studios, 252
Aranza, Pastor Jacob:
    Backwards Masking
    Unmasked, 263
Arbuckle, Fatty, 303
Arc Music, 150
Arden, Don, 16, 17, 19, 20,
    21, 22, 23, 80, 142,
    143, 273, 295, 337,
    338, 392
Ardent Studios, 175, 193
Are You Experienced?, 124
ARMS charity concert, 421
Armstrong, Neil, 169, 325
Arquette, Rosanna, 446
Asher, Dick, 77
'As Long As I Have You', 99,
    135
Astral Weeks, 181
Atco, 82
Atlanta, 175, 281
Atlanta Braves Football
    stadium, 280
Atlanta Pop Festival, 160
Atlantic Records
    targeted by Grant, 76
    record deal with
        Zeppelin, 77, 80–3, 88
    and Zeppelin's Fillimore
        East appearance, 121
    releases singles, 126, 244

and Led Zeppelin II, 134,
    146, 153
presentation of gold disc,
    144
Grant opposes release of
    single by, 157–8
and Led Zeppelin III, 235
and Led Zeppelin's
    seventh American
    tour, 253
and Houses of the Holy,
    275
and Led Zeppelin's own
    record label, 300–1,
    312
screening of band's film,
    362
Plant makes solo deal
    with, 426
40th anniversary
    celebration show, 428,
    430–1, 433
brief references, 17, 96,
    115, 118, 162, 202,
    334, 354
Atlas, Charles, 325
Auckland, 269
Auditorium Arena, Denver,
    96–8
Australia, 244, 268–9
'Autumn Lake', 309
Avengers, the, 172

'Babe I'm Gonna Leave
    You', 12, 25, 51, 55,
    68, 120, 128, 277, 439
Babitz, Eve, 164
'Baby Come On Home',
    158
'Baby Let's Play House', 60
'Baby Please Don't Go', 184
Bacharach, Burt, 75, 194
'Bachelor Boy', 253
Bad Co., 316
Bad Company, 313,
    316–17, 341, 345,
    373, 389, 409, 421
Baez, Joan, 25, 55
'Baja', 41
Baker, Ginger, 36, 242

Baldry, Long John, 29,
    312
Ball, Kenny, 338
Baltimore, 294
Band, The, 48, 181
Band of Joy, 13, 26, 32, 50,
    55, 99, 291, 310–12,
    359–60, 361
Bangkok, 254–5
Bangs, Lester, 199
Banned, The, 170
Bannister, Freddy, 20,
    159–60, 188, 189,
    396–8, 399, 400, 401,
    403–4, 405–6, 407
    There Must Be a Better
    Way, 401
Bannister, Wendy, 159, 188,
    405, 407
Barber, Chris, 115
Bardot, Brigitte, 145
Baretta, Dr John, 343
Barnes, 51
Barsalona, Frank, 89, 162
Barsotti, Bob, 378
Bart, Lionel, 18, 363
Bartok, Béla, 201
Barton, Geoff, 296, 402
Basing Street Studios, 193,
    236, 237, 240, 243,
    249
Bassey, Shirley, 183
'Bass 'N' Drums', 438
Bath, 425
Bath Festival, 49, 159–60,
    187–90, 294
'Bathroom Song, The' (later
    called 'Out on the
    Tiles'), 192
Battersea, 78
'Battle of Evermore, The',
    239–40, 244, 367, 448
BBC, 128, 130, 145, 159,
    246, 403, 443
BBC1, 128, 129
BBC2, 129, 301
    Light Programme, 92, 93
    Radio I, 47, 63, 127–8,
        252, 430
    Radio 2, 440

BBC Sessions, 252
Beach Boys, 80, 99, 127, 163
Beatles, 10, 18, 21, 43, 69, 75, 80, 82, 98, 105, 118, 119, 120, 123, 127, 138, 151, 154–5, 157, 175, 194, 200–1, 202, 210, 265, 280, 300, 321, 380
  albums, 10, 48, 124, 163, 353
  films, 138, 307
  songs, 10, 32, 47, 48, 65, 96, 99, 163, 244
Beausoleil, Bobby, 304
'Be-Bop-A-Lula', 61, 112
Beck, Annette, 112, 113
Beck, Jeff
  and Yardbirds, 5, 6, 7, 349
  and Jimmy Page, 5, 6, 14, 57–8, 62, 112–13, 114, 115, 195, 196, 201, 348, 422
  and 'Beck's Bolero' session, 14, 15–16
  and *Led Zeppelin*, 55, 57–8, 62, 117
  use of other artists' material, 66, 98
  impressed by performance of Led Zeppelin, 83
  and call-and-response routine, 100
  and Led Zeppelin's third US tour, 161, 163
  and Sutch, 203
  brief references, 9, 45, 67, 80, 290, 361, 381, 392, 435–6, 446
  see also Jeff Beck Group
'Beck's Bolero', 14, 15, 45
Beggars Banquet, 48, 51, 138, 326
Bel Air hotel, LA, 315
Belfast, 251–2
Belgium, 157
Bell, Madeline, 91, 301

Bell, Maggie, 313, 316, 341, 368
Belushi, John, 94
Benjamin, Louis, 75
Bennett, Tony, 442
Benny Goodman Story, The, 87
Benny Hill Show, The, 79
Bergerac, 226
Berkeley University, 326
Berlin, 410
Berry, Chuck, 30, 61, 98, 99, 114, 142–3, 165, 273
Berry, Dave, 183, 298
Berry, Mike, 379
Bert and John, 196
Bevan, Bev, 37, 132, 283, 290, 291, 334, 376, 412, 414, 415
Bicknell, Ed, 20–1, 383, 426, 435
'Big Log', 423
'Big Waasel', 295
Billboard, 202
Bindon, John, 368, 369, 378, 379, 382, 383
Bingenheimer, Rodney, 284
Birmingham, 24, 26, 27, 31, 34, 37, 38, 172, 291, 359, 362, 363, 383, 389 *see also* names of locations in Birmingham
Birmingham, Alabama, 372–3
Birmingham Cavern, 37
Birmingham Town Hall, 29, 159, 171
Bizarre Records, 138
'Blackbird', 163
'Black Country Woman', 321, 322, 340, 448
Black Crowes, The, 436
'Black Dog', 202, 238–9, 244, 250, 251, 256, 309, 445, 448
Blackmore, Ritchie, 212
'Black Mountain Side', 55–6, 57, 80–1, 246

Blackpool, 190
Black Sabbath, 132, 200, 211, 234, 267, 288, 292, 412
Black Snake Moan, 170
'Black Water Side', 56
Blake, Mark, 308, 309
Blake's Hotel, Kensington, 341
Bland, Bobby 'Blue', 331
Bland, Bubba, 175, 176
Blind Faith, 76
Blish, James: *Black Easter*, 207–8
Blockheads, the, 399
Blodwyn Pig, 160
Blonde On Blonde, 321, 326
Blondie, 402
Blood of a Poet, The, 303
Blossoms, the, 278
'Blowin' in the Wind', 66
Blow Out, 138
Blow Up, 6
Blue Belles, The, 30
Bluecaps, the, 113, 271
Blue Mink, 301
Bluesbreakers, 13, 159, 349
'Blues De Luxe', 66
Blues Incorporated, 115
Blue Star Trio, 35
'Blue Suede Shoes', 388
Blues Volume I, 30
Blunt, Robbie, 422, 423
'Bob Dylan's Dream', 66
'Bohemian Rhapsody', 244
Bolan, Marc, 271, 281, 298, 307
Boleskin House, 180, 181, 185, 228–31, 232–3, 275, 302, 308, 326, 327, 387, 450
Bolin, Tommy, 352
Bombay, 255, 269
Bombay Symphony Orchestra, 269
Bond, Graham, 213
Bonham, Jason, 33, 52, 95, 134, 307, 333, 363, 404, 412, 428, 430, 433, 439, 445

Bonham, John 'Bonzo'
life and career before Led
  Zeppelin, 26, 33–7,
  85–8, 132–4, 247–9,
  291, 311, 312,
  359–60
and formation of band as
  New Yardbirds, 11, 13,
  32, 37–40, 45, 50, 52,
  393
and Led Zeppelin, 54, 55,
  57
receives first large
  cheque, 83, 84–5
and first American tour,
  90, 91, 94, 95–6, 97,
  103, 104, 108, 111,
  123
new drum kit, 125
in promotional film clip,
  127
drumming tecnique,
  131–2
and Led Zeppelin II, 135,
  148, 149, 151
and second American
  tour, 136, 137, 141,
  144
and girls, 137, 141, 166,
  178–9
and UK tour, 159
and third American tour,
  161, 165–6
and fourth American
  tour, 153–4
and Albert Hall show,
  170, 172
and continental tour, 174,
  175
and fifth American tour,
  178–9
and Led Zeppelin III, 179,
  186, 192
relocates family, 180
and Sutch, 203
at Headley Grange, 237,
  246–7, 322
and Led Zeppelin IV, 239,
  241–2, 243, 246–7,
  260, 266

wild and aggressive
  behaviour, 252, 254,
  270, 283, 284, 289–90,
  291–3, 315, 316,
  333–4, 335, 349–50,
  352, 355–6, 363, 371,
  375
in Japan, 254
and Bill Harry, 270
buys farm in
  Worcestershire, 275
and Houses of the Holy,
  278
stage costume, 281
and ninth American tour,
  283, 284, 286
cars, 290
and film of band, 307
at launch parties of Swan
  Song, 315, 316
and Physical Graffiti,
  322
and tenth American tour,
  330, 331, 333–4, 335
and tax exile, 340
and Presence, 346, 347,
  352
proud of son's drumming,
  363
and eleventh American
  tour, 368, 371, 374,
  375, 376, 378, 379,
  382
arrested, 379
found guilty of assault
  charges, 382
and death of Plant's son,
  383, 384
car crash, 385
helps Plant towards
  recovery, 386
and In Through the
  Outdoor, 391, 394
at Knebworth, 404
at Melody Maker awards,
  408
and European tour,
  409–10
death, 411–13, 415
funeral, 414

end of Led Zeppelin
  follows death of,
  415–17, 419
Grant acts as executor of
  estate, 426
brief references, 74, 89, 99,
  101, 257, 268, 271,
  272, 297, 298, 313,
  325, 336, 337, 351,
  388, 407, 422, 428,
  448
Bonham, Mick, 85, 86–7,
  134, 412
Bonham (née Phillips), Pat,
  33, 34, 52, 95, 134,
  173, 248, 249, 290,
  307, 334, 335, 355,
  359, 384, 412, 413
Bonham, Zoë, 334, 409,
  412
Bon Jovi, 337
'Boogie With Stu', 238, 249,
  321, 322, 323, 348
Book of Enoch, 221
Book of the Dead, 332
'Boots of Spanish Leather',
  66
Bordin, Mike, 433
Born To Boogie, 307
Boston, 294
Boston Tea Party, 89, 112,
  118–19
Boston Gilderdrome, 361
Bowie, Angie, 213, 285
Bowie, David, 65, 213, 281,
  283, 284, 296, 299,
  317, 328–9, 335
Boxing Club, Bristol, 74
Boyzone, 271
Branson, Richard, 256
Bream, Julian, 182
Bredon, Anne, 55
Bridge Country Club,
  Canterbury, 83
Bridge Over Troubled Water,
  153
Briggs, Anne, 56
Brighton, 225, 408
Bringing It All Back Home,
  124

'Bring It On Home', 147,
    148–9, 150–1, 246,
    278
Bristol, 74
Brittle, Phil, 38
Bronby, Denmark, 51
Bronco, 256
'Bron-Y-Aur', 185, 321, 322
'Bron-Y-Aur Stomp', 158,
    185, 255
Bron-Yr-Aur, 180–1, 184,
    185, 191, 239–40,
    241, 250
Brooksmith, Maria, 224
Broonzy, Big Bill, 31, 61, 92
Brown, Arthur, 211, 311
Brown, Chris, 360
Brown, James, 42
Brown, Mick, 303
Browne, Carol, 186
Bruce, Jack, 45
Brum Beat, 37
Buckley, Sean, 184
Buddy Holly Story, The, 389
Budokan, Tokyo, 253–4
Buell, Bebe, 315, 317–18,
    331
Buffalo Springfield, 26, 320
Buffy the Vampire Slayer,
    226
Bunuel, Louis, 303
Burges, William, 10, 317,
    318
Burke, Solomon, 30
Burnett, Chester see
    Howlin' Wolf
Burnett, T.Bone, 442, 448
Burnette, Johnny, 71
'Burning Down One Side',
    422
Burrell, Boz, 345, 435
Burroughs, William S., 226,
    327–8
Burton, James, 60, 61, 112,
    114, 182
Burzam, 212
Busch, Bertha, 224
Butler, Terry 'Geezer', 200,
    211–12
Butlin, Sir Billy, 231

Butter Queen, The, 139
Butthole Surfers, 423
Byblos disco, Tokyo, 254
Byrds, The, 124, 139, 188
Byron, David, 288

Cader Idris, 181
Caine, Michael, 411
Caesar's Chariot, 367, 371,
    372, 375
Caesar's Palace, Las Vegas,
    367
Café Royal, 231
Cage, John, 201
Cagney, James, 302
Cairo, 222, 269, 372
California, Randy, 99, 100
Callan, Alan, 314, 335,
    337–8, 368, 435, 436
Calmes, Jack, 399
Cambridge, 221
Camel, C.R., 232–3
Cameron, Marjorie, 226
Cammell, Charles R., 211
Cammell, Donald, 211,
    304, 327, 332
Campbell, Naomi, 447
Canada, 162, 381
'Candy Store Rock', 346–7,
    354
Canned Heat, 188
Canterbury, 83
'Can't Get Enough', 316
Capitol, 80
Capote, Truman, 270
'Caravan', 36
Cardan, J.: Ars Magica
    Arteficii, 262
Carnegie Hall, New York,
    153, 154
'Carouselambra', 392, 393
Carson, Phil, 17, 157, 158,
    159, 160, 169, 283,
    428, 435
Carter, A.P., 65
Carter, Jimmy, 355
Carthy, Matin, 66
Cashbox, 161
Casino Royale, 75
Cassidy, Jack, 26

Cattini, Clem, 32–3, 44
Cavett, Dick, 355
CBS, 70, 309, 310
CCS, 202
Cedar Club, Birmingham,
    38, 249
Cefalu, 302
'Celebration Day', 192,
    193, 194, 432
Chapman, Mark, 265
Charles, Ray, 81
Charone, Barbara, 240
Charterhouse, 78
Chas and Dave, 399
Château d'Herouville
    studio, 212
Chateau Marmont, LA, 94,
    108, 131, 178
Chicago, 48, 89, 112, 120,
    136, 282, 366, 371,
    384, 410, 437
Chicago Ambassador, 330
Chicago Stadium, 370
Chicken Shack, 148, 270
Chien Andalou, Un, 303
Children, 423
Children In Need, 440
China, 222
China White, 370
Chislehurst Caves, 316
Chkiantz, George, 135
Chocolate Watch Band,
    245
Chorleywood, 180
Christian, Dick, 344
Christian, Neil, 5, 37, 114,
    115
Christine, Miss, 138, 180
Christopherson, Peter, 352
Christ's College,
    Blackheath, 92
Chrysalis, 379
Churchill, Winston, 225
Churchward, Colonel
    James: The Sacred
    Symbols of Mu, 261
Cincinnati, 193
Cincinnati Riverfront
    Coliseum, 372
Cinderella, Miss, 138

'Cinderella Rockafella',
47
Circus magazine, 215, 370
Clapton, Eric, 5, 7, 69, 71,
76, 144, 173, 181, 182,
273–4, 296, 349, 361,
421
Clark, Dick, 175, 211
Clark, Petula, 43
Clark, Steve, 405
Clarke, Arthur C.:
Childhood's End, 276
Clarkson, Jeremy, 446
Clash, The, 129, 362, 404
Classic Rock, 122, 136, 296,
305, 424
Clearwell Castle, 386, 388
Cleopatra, 80
Clifton, Peter, 312, 364
'C'mon Everybody', 376
Coach & Horses pub, Poland
Street, 270
Cobbald, David Lytton,
397, 400
Cochran, Eddie, 54, 98, 99,
195, 352, 376
Cocker, Joe, 32, 33, 38, 76,
98, 130, 194
Cocksucker Blues, 370
Coconut Grove, London,
389
Cocteau, Jean, 303
Coda, 419
Cole, Richard (Ricardo)
and first American tour,
90, 94–5, 96, 103–4,
108, 122
and second American
tour, 131, 135–6, 137,
140, 141
on role of groupies, 139
and third American tour,
161, 162, 165–6, 167,
168
and fifth American tour,
178–9
and Bath Festival, 189
and Headley Grange,
237, 243, 320–1
in Dublin, 252

in Tokyo, 254
visits Thailand and India,
254–5
and ninth American tour,
284, 285, 288, 294,
295, 296
and Bonham's drinking,
292
and theft, 294, 295, 296
and film of band, 307
and Swan Song launch
party, 315
and tenth American tour,
334–5, 335–6
and Grant, 339, 381
and Plant's accident, 343,
344
on Page's drug use, 350–1
in Monte Carlo, 355–6
has full-time assistant,
368
and eleventh American
tour, 368–9, 376, 377,
378, 382
arrested, 379
found guilty of assault,
382
returns to England with
Plant, 383
in Guadeloupe with Page,
387
wedding reception, 389
at Moon's funeral, 389
and Knebworth shows,
400, 403–4
on Bonham's drug habit,
409
brief references, 17, 155,
173, 337, 391–2
Coleby, Barrington, 258,
308
View in Half or Varying
Light, 258
Coleman, Jazz, 214
Coleman, Ray, 375
Coliseum, Birmingham,
Alabama, 372–3
Collins, Albert, 165
Collins, Judy, 65
Collins, Phil, 414, 422, 424

Colour Me Pop, 129
Colour My Soul, 301
Colson, Glen, 125
Coltrane, John, 82
Columbia, 77, 81, 338
Comedy Store, LA, 376
Comin' Atcha, 301
'Communication
Breakdown', 54, 61,
97, 120, 126, 127, 128,
129, 145, 200
Compartments, 325
Concerts West, 374, 384
'Congratulations', 47
Convention Center, Fort
Worth, 373
Cookham, 428
Cooper, Alice, 94, 107, 139,
211, 234, 283
Me, Alice, 139
Copenhagen, 174–5, 252,
402
'Corinna Corinna', 105
Corriston, Peter, 325
Cotchford Farm, 216
'Cotton Fields', 61, 113
Coulson, Clive, 135, 184,
185
Country Club, Hampstead,
33
Country Joe and the Fish,
111
Covent Garden, 363
Coverdale, David, 433
Crabb, Buster, 325
Crackerjack, 79
Cradle of Filth, 212
Crawdaddy, 327
Crawling King Snake, 34,
132, 133, 171, 172,
247, 309
Crazy Elephant, The, 299
Cream, 7, 8, 10–11, 12, 43,
48, 69, 75–6, 80, 81,
88, 96, 119, 124, 148,
393
Creation, The, 67
Creatures of the Street, 301
Creem, 123, 326, 354,
371

Crickets, the, 70
Crosby, David, 13
Crosby, Stills and Nash, 81,
    181, 199, 202, 241
Crosby, Stills, Nash &
    Young, 331
'Crosscut Saw', 150
Crowe, Cameron, 238, 326,
    335, 340
Crowley, Aleister
    and Boleskine House,
    180, 228, 229, 230
Page's interest in, 197, 209,
    214–15, 227, 228–33,
    259, 262, 275, 301–2,
    305, 319, 332, 333,
    357, 387, 450
life and ideas, 209,
    217–25, 227–8, 259
people interested in and
    influenced by, 210,
    211, 213–14, 225–7,
    327, 328
and Led Zeppelin IV, 262,
    264, 265
and Anger, 301–2, 303–4,
    356, 357
brief references, 211,
    308, 371
Writings:
The Bagh-I-Muattar, 232,
    302
Book Four, 225
The Book of the Goetia of
    Solomon the King,
    319
The Book of the Law, 3,
    217, 222, 226
The Book of Thoth, 258–9
The Confessions of Aleister
    Crowley: an
    Autobiography, 220–1,
    223
Diary Of A Drug Fiend,
    224
The Equinox, 319
Gospel According to St
    Bernard Shaw (later
    reissued as Crowley on
    Christ), 225

Magick in Theroy and
    Practice, 60, 209, 215,
    224
The Psychology of Hashish,
    205
Red Dragon, 262
Snowdrops from a Curate's
    Garden, 232
White Stains, 220, 232
Crowley, Rose, 222, 223
Croydon, 79, 196
Croydon Empire, 79
Crudup, Arthur, 61, 183
Cruisers, the, 183
'Crunge, The', 277–8
Crusaders, the, 5, 37, 114
'Crying Game, The', 183,
    298
Cullderstead, 314
Culture Show, The, 443
Current 93, 214
'Custard Pie', 321, 322, 323
'Custard Pie Blues', 323
Cyril Davies All Stars, 14,
    115

Daily Mirror, 20
Daisley, Bob, 213
Dale Martin Promotions, 19
Dali, Salvador, 151
Dallas, 176, 369
Dallas International Pop
    Festival, 162
Daltrey, Roger, 15, 172–3,
    449
Damned, The, 365
'Dancing Days', 277
d'Arch Smith, Timothy,
    231–3, 234, 301–2,
    319, 390, 419–20, 450
Darke, John, 368
'Darlene', 395, 396
Dartford, 93
Datsuns, The, 438
Dave Brubeck Quartet,
    35–6
Dave Clark Five, 37, 113
David, Hal, 194
David Frost TV show, 47
Davies, Cyril, 14, 115

Davies, Ray, 115
Davis, Clive, 77
Davis, Erik, 239
Davis, Miles, 155
Davis Jnr, Sammy, 286
Davis, Stephen, 137, 354,
    402
Day, Johnny, 60
'Day in the Life, A', 244
'Dazed and Confused', 51,
    62–5, 67, 68, 80, 97,
    100, 102, 120, 128,
    129, 145, 245, 308,
    327, 330, 366, 409,
    445, 446
Dean, James, 303
Death Valley, 304
Death Wish II, 31, 421, 426
Debord, Guy, 49
Decca, 41
Dee, Dr John, 259
Deep Purple, 200, 212, 322,
    335, 352, 433
Deep Throat, 283, 339
Def Leppard, 405, 442, 446
De Groot, Keith, 44
De Loach, Darryl, 139
Delta Blues Band, 105
Deltas, the, 93
Demons and Wizards, 288
Denmark, 47, 50, 51, 124,
    128, 129
Dennis, Felix, 50, 124
Denny, Sandy, 51, 56, 240,
    260, 367
Dent, Malcolm, 230
Denver, 91, 96–8, 123
De Paul, Linsey, 363
Derringer, Rick, 377
Des Barres, Michael, 139,
    345, 390
Des Barres, Pamela (aka
    Miss Pamela; Pamela
    Ann Miller), 138,
    139–40, 142, 167–9,
    173, 179–80, 228, 284,
    345
I'm With The Band, 140
De Shannon, Jackie, 194–5
Detective, 345, 390

Detective, 390
Detroit, 89, 120, 140–1
Deviants, the, 74
Devil Rides Out, The, 226
'Devil's Rodeo', 437
de Wilde, Brandon, 139
Dexter, Jeff, 320
Diamonds, the, 239
'Diamonds', 41, 94, 183, 184
Dickson, Dave, 218, 219, 221, 226, 227, 233–4, 259, 262, 265–6, 289, 302, 318, 371, 421
Diddley, Bo, 30, 65, 114, 128, 143, 165, 273
Dietrich, Marlene, 325
Digby-Smith, Richard, 192–3, 243, 244
Diplomats, The, 37, 248
Dire Straits, 20, 382–3, 426
Disc, 73, 160
Disc & Music Echo, 44, 154, 199, 256
Diskery, The, Birmingham, 31
Disraeli Gears, 124
Dixon, Willie, 56, 65, 67, 101, 135, 148–9, 150, 323
Dixon of Dock Green, 79
Dodd, Ken, 32
Dog Act, 137
Domino, Fats, 65
Don and Dewey, 25
Donegan, Lonie, 60, 61, 70
Donnell, Kenneth, 440
Donovan, 42, 44, 49, 298, 299, 338, 345, 392
'Don't Gimme No Lip Child', 298
'Don't Think Twice, It's All Right', 66
'Don't Turn Your Back On Me, Babe', 194
Doonican, Val, 7, 184
Doors, The, 48, 96, 100, 165, 281

Dorchester Hotel, London, 407
Dorfman, Stanley, 170
Dortmund, 408
Doud, Mike, 325
'Down By The Seaside', 185, 236, 249, 321, 322
Downey, Jim, 378
'Down the River to Pray', 438
Drake, Nick, 240
Drake Hotel theft, 294–7
'Dreamin'', 71
Dreja, Chris, 8, 9, 24, 65, 72–3, 116, 435
Dr Feelgood, 341, 388
Driberg, Tom, 228
Drifters, the, 239
'Drinking Again', 66
'Drinking Muddy Water', 65
Dr John, 188
'Drop Down Mama', 323
Dublin, 252
Dudley, 134, 154, 180, 257
Dunaway, Faye, 375
Dunbar, Aynsley, 13, 32, 62, 311, 335–6
Dunwoody, Hon. Mrs, 169
Dury, Ian, 399
Dusty in Memphis, 82
DVD, 437, 438, 441
'D'Yer Maker', 278, 279
Dylan, Bob, 10, 48, 49, 65–6, 69, 98, 105, 119,120, 124, 127, 151, 160, 181, 234, 321, 323

Eagles, the, 226, 244, 396
Eaglin, Snooks, 30
Ealing, 115
Earl's Court, 340–2, 366, 407
Earl Warren Showgrounds, Santa Barbara, 167
East Berkshire Coroners Court, 413
Eastbourne, 427

Easy Rider, 138
Eavis, Michael, 159
Ebisham Hall, Epsom, 113
Eckenstein, Oscar, 225
Edgewater Inn, Seattle, 165–6
Edmunds, Dave, 341, 389
Egypt, 305
Eissporthalle, Berlin, 410
Electric Ladyland, 48, 76, 138, 146, 321
Electric Lady Studios, 269
Electric Light Orchestra, 132
Electric Mud, 238
Elizabeth II, Queen, 374–5
Elliot, Cass, 64
Elliot, Joe, 446
ELO, 283, 295, 303, 376
Emerson, Lake and Palmer, 366
EMI, 76, 82, 157, 313
Empire Pool (now Wembley Arena), London, 256
see also Wembley Arena
Eno, Brian, 43, 423
Enragés, Les, 49
Entertainment Weekly, 442
Entwhistle, John, 14, 15
Epic, 76, 77, 80
Epsom, 59, 60, 113
Epstein, Brian, 21, 22
Epstein, Jacob, 220, 231
Equinox, 223
Equinox bookshop, 318–19, 390
Errogie, 230
Ertegun, Ahmet, 80, 81, 82–3, 121, 253, 300, 301, 362, 403, 428, 435, 439, 440
Ertegun, Neshui, 81
Escher, M.C., 168
Estes, Sleepy John, 61, 148, 323
Eurovision Song Contest, 43
Evans, Chris, 446

Evans, Mick, 291
'Everybody's Gotta Say',
    309
'Everybody Knows This Is
    Nowhere', 432
Everly Brothers, 30, 60, 142
Excello, 115
Exeter University, 360
Exile on Main Street, 269,
    324
Experience, the, 32

Faces, the, 45, 316, 331
Fairport Convention, 39,
    51, 133, 188, 240, 360,
    399
Faith, Adam, 18
Faithfull, Marianne, 195,
    303, 304, 332
Faith No More, 433
Fallon, B.P., 187–8, 268,
    271, 283, 285–7, 314,
    341
Fame, Georgie, 26
Family Dog, 110
Family That Plays Together,
    The, 99
Farlowe, Chris, 24, 31, 33,
    113
Farr, Florence, 213
Farr, Gary, 55
Farren, Mick, 360
Farx Club, Southall, 124
Fate of Nations, 433
FBI, 294
Feliciano, José, 325
Feltham, 59
Ferry, Bryan, 315, 334
Fike, Lamar, 138
Fillmore East, 166
Fillmore East, New York,
    89, 110, 121–2, 144,
    349
Fillmore West, San
    Francisco, 109–10,
    111–12
'Fingertips', 247
Fireworks, 302
Firm, The, 421–2, 424
First Gear, The, 184

Fishmonger's Hall, Wood
    Green, 90
Fix, Mitchell, 368
'Flames', 99
Flamingo, the, London,
    299
Fleetwood Mac, 48, 148,
    159, 160, 187, 238
Fleetwood Mac, 48
Fleming, Ian, 225
Fleurs de Lys, 195
Flick, Vic, 183
Flintstones, The, 338
Flock, The, 189, 190
Flying Burrito Brothers, 165
Folk Blues of John Lee
    Hooker, 30
Foo Fighters, 418, 438, 445
'Fool in the Rain', 393, 395
Ford, Sarah, 355
Ford, President, 336, 355
Fort Worth, 369, 373
Forum, Los Angeles, 253,
    269, 282–3, 315, 330,
    339, 366, 375–6,
    376–7
'For Your Life', 346, 445
'For Your Love', 6, 99
Fotheringay, 240
'Fought My Way Out of
    Darkness', 101
Four Seasons hotel, New
    York, 315
'Four Sticks', 239, 241–2,
    252, 269, 432
'4th Time Around', 66
Fowley, Kim, 284, 349
Francis, Michael, 337
Franklin, Aretha, 81–2
Franklin, Tony, 421
'Franklin, The', 66
Frascati's, Soho, 79
Fraser, Archibald, 229
Fraser, Lieutenant General
    Simon, Lord Lovat,
    229, 230
Freddie and the Dreamers,
    338
Free, 24, 27, 99, 421
'Freedom Song', 438

Freeman, Alan 'Fluff', 128,
    341
Freemasons, 222, 318
Frehley, Ace (Paul Daniel
    Frehley), 122
'Freight Town', 93
Frencham Ponds hotel, 320
'Fresh Garbage', 99, 245
Friend, Thomas W.: Fallen
    Angel, 264–5
Friends, 124
'Friends', 185, 193, 269
Fromme, Lynne 'Squeaky',
    336
Fuller, Blind Boy, 323
Fullerton, Major, 229, 232

Gable, Clark, 94
Galás, Diamanda, 434, 437
Gale, J.J., 399
Gallagher, Liam and Noel,
    446
'Gallis Tree', 191
'Gallows Pole', 191–2, 193
Gallup, Cliff, 61, 112, 114
'Gambler's Blues', 66
Gammond, Kevin, 360
Gantry, Elmore, 99
Gaston, Joe, 175
Garland, Judy, 325
Gary Owen club,
    Birmingham, 37
Gautier, Benoit, 291–2
Gear, the, 183
Geffen Records, 428, 433
Genesis, 187, 277, 322,
    396, 397, 440
Gerlach, Fred, 191–2
Germany, 157, 236, 408–10
Get Carter, 368
Gettings, Fred: Dictionary of
    Occult, Hermetic and
    Alchemical Sigils, 262
Giant's Causeway, 276
Gibb, John, 156–7
Giles, Samantha, 353
Gillum, Jazz, 31
Ginsburg, Allen, 49
'Girl Can't Help It, The', 60
Girl Can't Help It, The, 273

'Girl from the North
    Country', 66
'Girl I Love She Got Long
    Wavy Hair, The', 148
'Girls Talk', 390
Give My Regards To Broad
    Street, 423
'Glad All Over', 113
Gladsaxe, Denmark, 47,
    128
Glasgow, 271
Glastonbury Festival, 159
'Glimpses', 68, 102,
    348–9
Glostrup Handelsblat, 51
Goaldiggers, 387
Godfrey, William Hindes,
    313
Goins, Herbie, 42
'Going To California', 241,
    244, 250, 251, 255,
    432
Goldberg, Danny, 280, 281,
    295, 313, 327, 336
Goldblatt, Stephen, 116
Golden Dawn, Hermetic
    Order of the, 213, 217,
    221
'Goldfinger', 183
Gomelsky, Giorgio, 55, 196
'Gone Gone Gone (Done
    Moved On)', 448
Good Egg, The, 309
'Good Golly Miss Molly',
    118
Goodman, Jerry, 189
'Good Times Bad Times',
    54, 80, 97, 117, 126,
    131, 278, 298, 444
'Good Vibrations', 99
Gorham Hotel, New York,
    121
Gothenburg, 51
Gould, Lord John, 427, 436
Graham, Bill, 110–11,
    121–2, 377–8, 379,
    382
Graham, Bobby, 7, 32, 37
Graham, Davy, 11, 55–6,
    65, 195–6

Graham Bond
    Organisation, 36
Grande Ballroom, Detroit,
    89
Grant, Gloria, 90, 338, 339,
    382
Grant, Helen, 338, 426
Grant, Peter
    life and career before Led
        Zeppelin, 17–19,
        77–80, 142–4, 273–4,
        338–9, 379–82
    and formation of band as
        New Yardbirds, 8–9,
        13, 16, 23, 24, 27, 32,
        33, 34, 361
    reputation, 19–21
    management style, 20–3,
        272–3
    becomes manager of Led
        Zeppelin, 46–7
    arranges first gigs, 72
    and name of band, 73
    difficulties in getting onto
        concert circuit, 74
    seeks record deal, 74–6
    record deal with Atlantic,
        77, 80–1, 82–3, 88
    and first American tour,
        88–90, 98, 109,
        118–19, 121, 122,
        123
    and release of single,
        126
    and concentration on
        albums, 127
    arranges live sessions for
        Radio 1, 128
    and TV coverage, 129–30
    and Led Zeppelin II, 134–5
    and second American
        tour, 136, 137, 141
    opposes release of single,
        157, 158–9
    and Bath Festival 160,
        187, 188, 189–90
    and third American tour,
        160–1, 162, 165, 168
    and reception at Savoy
        Hotel, 169

    and Albert Hall show,
        170
    and Countess Von
        Zeppelin, 174
    and fifth American tour,
        175, 176, 178
    and Led Zeppelin III, 235
    and Led Zeppelin IV,
        235–6, 250
    and departure of Bill
        Harry, 270
    and appointment of B.P.
        Fallon, 271
    and Houses of the Holy,
        276
    and ninth American tour,
        280, 293–4, 295, 296
    increases security after
        death threats, 288
    and Bonham's behaviour,
        289
    and bad relations
        between Plant and
        Bonham, 293
    and film of band, 293–4,
        306, 307, 312, 362,
        364
    and theft of cash, 295,
        296
    faces possible departure
        of Jones, 297–8
    and negotiations for
        band's own record
        label, 300, 301
    publishing reorganised,
        313–14
    and launch of Swan Song,
        315
    and first band signing
        with Swan Song, 316
    and recording of Physical
        Graffiti, 320
    and tenth American tour,
        334, 335
    and drugs, 337, 426, 427
    breakdown of marriage,
        337–8
    and tax exile, 339, 340
    based in Montreaux, 340,
        342

and Plant's accident, 344
threatens *Sounds* editor,
  363–4
and eleventh American
  tour, 366, 368, 369,
  373, 374, 376, 378,
  379, 382–3
hires Bindon, 368
attends Ivor Novello
  awards, 372
assaults Matzorkis, 378
arrested, 379
found guilty of assault,
  382
cancels rest of American
  tour, 383
decision to give Plant
  time to recover, 385
suffers minor coronary,
  387
and Knebworth shows,
  396, 397, 398, 399,
  400, 403–4, 405, 406,
  407
and *In Through the
  Outdoor*, 401, 402
plans 1980 American
  tour, 410
at Bonham's funeral,
  414
and end of Led Zeppelin,
  415, 416
life after end of Led
  Zeppelin, 420, 426–8,
  434, 435
death and funeral, 435–6
brief references, 52, 57,
  145, 155, 193, 251,
  254, 256, 261, 286–7,
  325, 346, 354, 355,
  356, 388, 392, 409,
  450
Grant, Warren, 90, 338,
  378, 426, 435
Grape Jam, 192
Grateful Dead, 100, 110,
  120
Greenberg, Jerry, 253
Greenhouse Restaurant,
  LA, 331

Greenlake Aquatheatre,
  Seattle, 136
'Greensleeves', 57
Greens Playhouse, Glasgow,
  271
Greer, Germaine, 444
Griffiths, Austin, 361
Grisnackh, Count (real
  name Kristian
  Vikernes), 212
Grohl, Dave, 438, 445
Grosvenor Hotel, London,
  372
Grove Nursing Home, 58
GTOs, 138–9
Guadeloupe, 389
Guardian, 447
Guerin, John, 331
Guildford, 74
Guinness Book of Records,
  281
Guitar Player, The, 195
Guitar World, 201, 264
Guns of Navarone, The, 79
Guy, Buddy, 25, 30, 66,
  114, 359
Guy's Hospital, 343

Hadley, David, 365
'Ha Ha Said the Clown', 5
Haight-Ashbury, 120
Hale, Norman, 351–2
Hale, Philip, 408
Halesowen, 171
Haley, Bill, 60
Hamlin, Rosie, 278
Hammer of the Gods, 138
Hammersmith Odeon, 408
Hammerwood Park Estate,
  307
Hammond, Richard, 446
Handsworth Plaza,
  Birmingham, 37
'Happening Ten Years Time
  Ago', 5
Hard Day's Night, A, 307
Hardie, George, 116, 352,
  353
'Hard Rain's A-Gonna Fall',
  66

Harlow, Jean, 94
Harper, Roy, 190–1, 283,
  313, 387, 421
Harris, Bob, 341, 399
Harris, Frank, 225
Harris, Jet, 41, 93, 183,
  392
Harris, June, 144
Harris, Richard, 317
Harris, Wee Willie, 18
Harrison, George, 7, 10,
  181, 196, 269, 283
Harrison, Patti, 283
Harry, Bill, 161, 187, 270,
  380
Harvey, Bill, 35–6, 291, 311
Harvey, Les, 373
Harwood, Keith, 350, 355
Hastings, 224
'Hats Off To Harper', 190,
  191, 348
Hayes, Isaac, 176
Hayley Green, 70–1
Headley Grange, 186–7,
  191, 199, 237, 238,
  239, 240, 242, 243,
  246–7, 251, 316–17,
  320, 321, 322
Healey, Denis, 341
Heart, 136, 423
'Heartbreaker', 61, 147,
  177, 279, 374
'Heart Full Of Soul', 6, 196
Heath, Ted, 79, 131
Hellingly, 435
'Hello Mary Lou', 61
Hell's Angels, 164, 189
Helms, Chet, 110
'Help Me', 323
'Helter Skelter', 163
Henderson, Dorris, 191
Hendrix, Jimi, 8, 10–11, 12,
  32, 43, 48, 67, 69, 76,
  88, 96, 98, 101, 123,
  124, 138, 144, 146,
  147, 148, 151, 321
Henry's Blues House,
  Birmingham, 291
'Here Comes The
  Weekend', 389

Herman's Hermits, 7, 274, 298, 338, 392
Hermetic Order of the Golden Dawn, 213, 217, 221
Hess, Rudolf, 225
Heston, 58, 59
Hewitt, Paolo, 149
'Hey Jude', 47
Hickey, Isabel: *Astrology: a Cosmic Science*, 319
'Hi Ho Silver Lining', 6, 14
Hill, Dave, 72, 171
Hillman, Chris, 139
Hilton, Ronnie, 92
Hilton Hotel, London, 435
Hilton Hotel, Santa Monica, 335
Hilton Hotel, Tokyo, 254
Hinman, Gary, 304
Hinton, Mick, 349–350, 355
Hipgnosis, 116, 276, 352, 396, 401
Hirsig, Leah, 223, 224
Hobbs, Rick, 367–8, 411
Hobbstweedle, 24, 26, 360
Hock, Abe, 314
Holder, Neville, 171, 360–1
'Hold Me', 184
Hollies, the, 12, 36, 380
Hollingworth, Roy, 256
Holly, Buddy, 60, 70
Hollywood, 284–5
Hollywood Bowl, 288
Holman-Hunt, William, 258
Holmes, Jake, 62–5
Holmes, Richard 'Groove', 92
Home, 256
Honeydrippers, The: Volume One, 422
Honolulu, 253
Hooker, Earl, 30
Hooker, John Lee, 30, 34, 171
Hopkins, Lightnin', 30
Hopkins, Mary, 76

Hopkins, Nicky, 14–15, 44, 115, 216
Horne, Nicky, 231, 341
Horselunges, 313, 337, 338, 397, 405, 426, 427
Hoskyns, Barney, 186
'Hot Dog', 392, 403
'Hotel California', 226
'Hots On For Nowhere', 345, 346
Houghton, Mick, 12, 62, 305
House, Son, 30, 150
'House Burning Down', 48
'House of the Rising Sun', 66, 273
'Houses of the Holy', 321
Houses of the Holy, 269–70, 275–80, 321, 353, 354
Houston, 373
Howard, Johnny, 183
How Late It Is, 128
Howlin' Wolf (Chester Burnett), 30, 55, 61, 101, 106, 115, 150
'How Many More Times', 50, 55, 99, 117, 122, 128, 327
'How Many More Years', 51, 55, 115
How The West Was Won, 437, 440
Hubbard, L. Ron, 226
Hudson, Joan, 405, 406
Huggins, Leslie, 304, 332
Hughes, Chris, 44
Hughes, Glenn, 335
Hullat, Tommy, 384
Humperdink, Englebert, 43, 184
Hunky Dory, 213
Hunter, Meredith, 164, 211
Hunter, Ray, 18
Hunter, Russell, 74
'Hunter, The', 55, 99
Hurdy Gurdy Man, The, 44
Hush, 38
Hussey, Wayne, 423
Hyatt House, LA, 178, 180, 284, 285

Hyland, Brian, 142
Hynde, Chrissie, 404

IBC studios, 14
Ibiza, 388
'(I Can't Get No) Satisfaction', 202
'I Can't Quit You Baby', 51, 56, 67, 97
Iceland, 187
Idris Gawr, 181
Iggy Pop, 284
Ike and Tina Turner, 165
'I Knew The Bride', 389–90
'I Like It Like That', 31, 71
'I Love You', 30
'I'm Gonna Crawl', 394
'Immigrant Son', 187, 192, 193, 202, 441
Imperial, 115
In-A-Gadda-Da-Vidda, 80
Inauguration of the Pleasure Dome, 302, 303
In Concert, 128
Incredible String Band, 25
India, 254, 255, 269
Ingham, Jonh, 279, 354
Ingle, Doug, 121
'In My Time of Dying', 105, 321, 322, 330, 366, 374–5, 445
Innocent VI, Pope, 222
International Managers' Forum, 435
International Times (IT), 26, 27, 96, 124
'In the Evening', 392, 393, 394, 395, 403, 404, 421
'In the Light', 321, 322, 324, 432
In Through the Outdoor (eighth album), 386, 390–2, 393–6, 401–2, 419, 449–50
Invocation Of My Demon Brother, 211, 303, 304, 305
In Your Honor, 438
Iommi, Tony, 288

Ireland, 276
Iron Butterfly, 80, 121–2, 123, 139, 272
Iron Maiden, 213, 345
'I Saw Her Standing There', 99
Island, 313, 379
  Basing Street studios, 193, 236, 237, 240, 243, 249
Isley Brothers, 333
'I Sold My Heart To The Junkman', 30
'It Hurts When I Cry', 184
'It'll Be Me', 373
'It's Been a Long, Long Time', 348
'It's Nobody's Fault But Mine', 346
It Takes One to Know One, 390
'I've Been Drinking', 66
'I've Got My Mojo Working', 30, 105
'I've Gotta Woman', 155
Ivor Novello awards, 372
'I Want Some Pie', 323

Jack Orion, 56
Jacobs, David, 298
Jagger, Chris, 304, 327
Jagger, Mick, 33, 48, 71, 93, 115, 165, 169, 210, 211, 268, 269, 284, 303, 304, 324, 327, 328, 350, 362, 375, 446, 449
'Jailhouse Rock', 161
James, Elmore, 114
James, Harry, 34
James, Jimmy, 299
James, Nicky, 248, 249
Jansch, Bert, 56, 65, 160, 185–6, 191, 195, 196
Japan, 253–4, 270, 438
Jasani, Viram, 55
Javelins, the, 171
Jay, Peter, 12
Jaywalkers, 12, 13
Jeff Beck Group, 16, 45, 46,

47, 48, 83, 90, 95, 97, 101, 117, 139, 161, 162, 163
Jefferson, Blind Lemon, 170
Jefferson Airplane, 24, 120, 188, 190, 281, 311
Jeffrey, Mike, 273, 381
Jeffrey Rod (Jeff Beck and Rod Stewart), 66
Jennings Farm, 180
'Jennings Farm', 158, 192
'Jennings Farm Blues', 185
Jensen, David 'Kid', 341
Jersey, 344, 351
'Jesus Make Up My Dying Bed', 323
Jethro Tull, 158, 161, 380
JFK Stadium, Philadelphia, 366, 423–4
Jimi Henrix Experience, 139, 144
Jimmy's nightclub, Monte Carlo, 355–6
Jim's Blues, 52
Jive Five, The, 30
Joaneline Music Inc, 314
John, Elton, 240, 283, 296, 322, 441
John Barry Orchestra, 183
John Bull magazine, 223
Johnny Harris Orchestra, 202
Johnny the Fox, 350
Johns, Andy, 155, 237, 247, 250, 268
Johns, Glyn, 68, 69, 155, 157, 183, 216
Johns, Glynis, 155
Johnson, Blind Willie, 65, 155, 323, 346
Johnson, Robert, 30, 61, 65, 71, 98, 101, 147, 150, 210
John Wesley Harding, 48
Jones, Brian, 7, 115, 210, 215–16, 303
Jones, George Cecil, 213
Jones, Jacinda, 423, 438
Jones, John Paul
  life and career before

formation of Led Zeppelin, 14, 40–4, 91–4, 298–9, 392
on Peter Grant, 22, 83
and formation of band as New Yardbirds, 44–5, 46, 50–1, 52, 392–3
and Led Zeppelin, 54, 55, 57, 117
and first American tour, 90–1, 94, 96, 97, 101, 104, 108–9, 111, 119, 123
does not wish to compromise on his music, 127
and BBC sessions, 128
and TV, 129
and second American tour, 137, 141, 145
and Led Zeppelin II, 151
and Birmingham Town Hall show, 159
and third American tour, 162
and Albert Hall show, 172
and fifth American tour, 178
and Led Zeppelin III, 179, 186, 192
buys new home in Chorleywood, 180
and Bath Festival, 189
writes 'No Quarter', 193
and Led Zeppelin IV, 236, 238, 242, 243, 260, 267
at Headley Grange, 237
in Japan, 254
and Houses of the Holy, 277, 278
stage costume, 281, 282
and ninth American tour, 281, 282, 286, 287
considers leaving the band, 297–8, 316
works on two albums without Led Zeppelin, 301

Jones, John Paul—*contd*
and film of band, 307,
312
and recording of *Physical
Graffiti*, 320
and tenth American tour,
330, 331, 334–5
and tax exile, 340
and *Presence*, 347–8
and punk, 365
and eleventh American
tour, 367, 368, 373,
374, 377, 383, 384
and death of Plant's son,
384
at Clearwell, 388
and *In Through the
Outdoor*, 390, 391,
392, 394, 396
at Knebworth, 404
at *Melody Maker* awards,
408
and European tour, 410
and death of Bonham,
411, 412, 416
life and career after end of
Led Zeppelin, 423,
424–5, 430, 432–3,
434, 436, 437–9, 441,
443, 445, 450
brief references, 82, 89,
125, 131, 149, 209,
300, 352, 355, 380
Jones, Mick, 404
Jones, Mo, 41, 44, 90–1,
173, 180
Jones, Paul, 115
Jones, Reg, 74
Jones, Steve, 404
Jones, Tom, 43, 131
Jones, Wizz, 196
Joplin, Janis, 26, 162, 190,
192, 281
Joseph, Michael, 138
Joseph, Nat, 56
Journey, 335
Judas Priest, 377
Juggy Sound Studios, 145
Juke Box Jury, 298
Julie Felix TV show, 11

'Jumping Jack Flash', 48
Juniper, David, 155, 156
'Just Like Anyone Would
Do', 195

Kaleidoscope, 67
'Kashmir', 321, 322, 323–4,
330, 341, 367, 422,
437, 445
Kaye, Lenny, 256–7
KB Hallen, Copenhagen,
174, 252
Keef Hartley, 188
'Keep A-Knockin'', 239
Kefford, Ace, 45
Kelly, Edward, 259
Kelly, Mike, 291
Kemp, Thomas, 187
Kennedy, Robert (Bobby),
8, 48
Kenner, Chris, 31
Kent, Nick, 214, 227, 263,
266, 284, 331–2, 341,
371, 382, 414
Kenton, Stan, 79
Key of Solomon, The, 221–2
Kidd, Johnny, 36
Kidderminster College of
Further Education, 71
'Killing Floor', 101, 115,
150
Killing Joke, 214
Kinetic Circus, Chicago, 89,
112, 136
King, Albert, 55, 150
King, BB, 66, 114, 192
King, Ben E., 30, 145, 423
King, Carole, 256
King, Danny, 172
King, Freddy, 61, 114
King, Martin Luther, 48
King, Rex, 368, 411
Kingdome, Seattle, 377
King Edward VI Grammar
School, Stourbridge, 70
Kinks, the, 14, 37, 48, 67,
170, 194, 380
Kinky Music, 195
Kinsey, Alfred, 302
Kirby, Kathy, 92

Kirke, Roland, 111
Kirke, Simon, 313, 389,
409–10, 435
'Kisses Sweeter Than
Wine', 55
Klein, Allen, 22
Knebworth Festival, 396–8,
399–401, 402–7, 408,
437
Knight, Ian, 320
Knights Templar, 222
Koch, Rudolf: *The Book of
Signs*, 260
Korner, Alexis, 25, 26, 27,
31, 115, 202, 359
Kracker, 300
Kramer, Eddie, 144, 146,
147, 301
Krauss, Alison, 442, 443,
444, 448
Kravitz, Lenny, 433
'Krishna', 196
Krupa, Gene, 36, 87–8
KSAN, 120
Kubrick, Stanley, 305

Labelle, Patti, 30
Labour, 295–6, 399
Ladies of the Canyon, 241
'Lady Madonna', 48, 65
La Fura dels Baus, 423
Laine, Denny, 37, 435
Landau, Jon, 119–20
Landover, 373
Lane, Ronnie, 149, 316, 320
lang, k.d., 442
Lanza, Mario, 92
Largo Capitol Center,
Landover, 373
'Last Fair Deal Gone
Down', 71
'Last Mile, The', 195
'Last Waltz, The', 184
Las Vegas, 168, 180, 286,
367
Laurel and Hardy, 325
Laurel Canyon, 241, 283,
284
Laurence, Lee, 92
Lawrence, Dr Mike, 343

Lawson and Four More, 175
Leadbelly, 61, 113, 191,
    442
Leamington, 219
Leander, Mike, 41
Leary, Timothy, 49, 226
'Leave My Kitten Alone',
    184
'Leaves That Are Green,
    The', 191
Le Compte, Juli, 306
Ledger, Heath, 94
Led Zeppelin
    formed as New Yardbirds,
        6–16, 23–8, 31–4,
        37–40, 44–6
    management *see* Grant,
        Peter
    name, 15, 72–3
    and social unrest of the
        Sixties, 48
    Scandinavian tour, 47,
        50–1
    use of other artists'
        material, 55–8, 62–5,
        66–7, 149–51, 245–6,
        346–7
    first gigs under new name,
        74
    Grant seeks record deal
        for, 74–6
    record deal with Atlantic,
        77, 80–3, 88
    success of UK gigs, 83
    first American tour,
        88–91, 94–104,
        107–12, 115–16,
        118–23
    performances after return
        to UK, 124–5
    release of single in
        America, 126–7
    album-oriented, 127
    radio exposure, 127–8
    and TV, 128–30
    second American tour,
        130–1, 135–42, 144–5
    UK tour, 159–60
    third American tour,
        160–9

    resistance to release of
        single, 157–9
    fourth American tour,
        153–4, 168
    growing success in UK,
        169
    Albert Hall show,
        169–70, 172–3
    tour of continent, 175–6
    fifth American tour,
        169–70, 175–80
    performances in Iceland,
        187
    at Bath Festival, 187–90
    voted Best Group by
        Melody Maker readers,
        202
    and the occult, 209, 214,
        227, 234, 257–66
    tour of small UK venues,
        251–2
    more European
        performances, 252–3
    seventh American tour,
        253
    in Japan, 253–4, 270
    sixteen-date UK tour,
        255–6
    tour of Australia and New
        Zealand, 268–9
    eighth American tour,
        269
    last UK tour, 270, 271
    ninth American tour,
        280–8, 293–7
    film, 293–4, 306–9, 312,
        362–3, 364
    cash stolen from, 294–7
    Jones considers leaving,
        297–8
    own record label, 300–1,
        312–15, 316
    meeting with Presley,
        315–16
    tenth American tour,
        325, 326–36
    advised to become tax
        exiles, 339–40
    Earl's Court shows,
        340–2

    and punk, 364–5
    eleventh American tour,
        366–79, 382–3
    and 'jinx', 384–5,
        413–14
    rumours about split, 387,
        389
    and Knebworth shows,
        396–8, 399–401,
        402–7
    and *Melody Maker*
        awards, 408
    tour of Europe, 408–10
    1980 tour of America
        planned, 410–11
    end of, 415–17
    reunions and discussions
        about reunions, 423–5,
        428, 430–1, 432–3,
        433–4, 438–9, 439–47,
        448–9
    see also names of band
        members; titles of
        songs and albums
Led Zeppelin (first album),
    51–2, 54–8, 62, 63,
    68–70, 88, 115–17,
    120, 123, 124, 130,
    144, 174, 198
Led Zeppelin II (second
    album), 134–5, 144–5,
    145–51, 153, 154–6,
    159, 167, 169, 198,
    235
Led Zeppelin III (third
    album), 179, 186–7,
    191–4, 196–202, 209,
    235, 249, 279, 341,
    354
Led Zeppelin IV (fourth
    album), 235–47,
    249–50, 252, 253, 255,
    256–67
Lee, Albert, 44
Lee, Alvin, 161
Lee, Arthur, 238
Lee, Leapy, 184
Lee, Ric, 161
Le Fevre, Benji, 344, 345,
    352, 411

'Lemon Song, The', 147, 150, 246
Lennon, John, 10, 48–9, 66, 119, 138, 175, 210, 265, 284, 380
Les Paul Trio, 348
Lesser Key of Solomon, The, 222, 319
Let It Be, 138
Let It Bleed, 153
Let It Rock, 279, 325–6
'Let Me Love You', 66
'Let There Be Drums', 365
Levene, Gerry, 172
Levi, Eliphas, 208, 221, 259
Lewis, Alan, 363–4, 402
Lewis, Dave, 75, 158, 162, 189, 279, 297, 347, 348, 368, 383, 389, 391, 408, 410, 411, 416, 420, 425, 439, 450
Lewis, Jerry Lee, 210, 325, 373
Lewis, Juliette, 446
Lewis, Red E. (Chris Tidmarsh, later known as Neil Christian), 113–14 see also Christian, Neil
Life magazine, 141
'Light My Fire', 202
Lincoln, Paul, 18, 19
Ling, Dave, 424
Listen, 309, 310
'Little Arrows', 184
Little Feat, 399
'Little Games', 15
Little Games, 63, 68, 76, 277, 380
Little Richard, 19, 30, 60, 99, 106, 142, 143, 160, 210, 239, 323, 352
Little Rock Connie, 139
Little Walter, 30
Live Aid concert, 424–5, 427–8
'Live At Newport 1960', 30
Live At The Greek, 436
Live At The Regal, 114

Liverpool Scene, 160
Liverpool University, 74
'Living in the Past', 158
'Living Loving Maid (She's Just A Woman)', 145, 148, 159
Lloyd, Bert, 56
Lloyd, Marie, 231
Llyfnant Valley, 275
Loch Ness, 180, 228, 327
Lockey, Paul, 360
Locking, Brian 'Liquorice', 42
Locomotive, 37, 133
Lodge Farm County School, 87
London, 49, 313, 314, 343, 362, 389, 391 see also names of locations in London
London Evening News, 413–14
Long, Andy, 70
Long Beach Arena, LA, 269, 330
Long John Baldry's All Stars, 29
'Long Tall Sally', 99, 118, 160
'Long Time Coming', 310
'Lonnie on the Move', 39
'Lord Randall', 66
Lord Sutch and Heavy Friends, 203
Los Angeles
  and first American tour, 89, 90, 94–6, 107–9
  and second American tour, 139, 140, 145
  and third American tour, 163–4, 167
  Manson murders, 163–4
  and fifth American tour, 175, 178, 179–80
  Led Zeppelin IV tapes mixed in, 250
  and seventh American tour, 253
  and ninth American tour, 282–5, 287, 297

Swan Song launch party, 315
  Presley meets band members in, 315–16
  and tenth American tour, 330–1, 335–6, 339
  Page and Plant write in, 345–7
  and eleventh American tour, 366, 375–7
  brief references, 8, 101, 103, 120, 181, 203, 240, 349, 412
Louisiana, 383
Lovat, Lieutenant General Simon Fraser, Lord, 229, 230
Love, 26, 100, 304, 311
Love, Courtney, 271
Lovelace, Linda, 339
'Love Me', 31
Lovin' Spoonful, 64
Lowe, Nick, 341
Lowry, Malcolm: Under the Volcano, 225
Lucifer Rising, 301, 303–6, 315, 326, 331–4, 356, 357, 365, 395, 421
Lucy, Miss, 138
Ludwig, Bill, 125
Ludwig drum company, 125
Lulu, 298, 338
Luton College, 9
Lyceum Ballroom, London, 169
Lynn, Vera, 92, 436
Lynne, Jeff, 414
Lyttelton, Humphrey, 36
Lytton, Bulmer, 400

Mac, Lonnie, 39
McCallum Snr, David, 67–8
McCartney, Linda, 363
McCartney, Paul, 10, 196, 363, 389, 414, 423, 446, 449
McCarty, Jim, 63, 65, 72, 277, 435
McClennan, Tommy, 30
McCoy, 'Kansas Joe, 246

McCoy, 'Memphis' Minnie, 246, 323
McDevitt, Chas, 93
McDowell, Mississippi Fred, 61
MacDuff, 'Brother' Jack, 92
McGhee, Brownie, 323
Macgregor, Sandy, 184
Machen, Arthur, 213
Machynlleth, 181, 184
McLagan, Ian, 149
McLaren, Malcolm, 426
McTell, Ralph, 196
Maddox, Lori, 285, 315, 324
Madison Square Garden, New York, 202, 253, 294, 327, 366, 374–5, 434–5, 437
Mafia, 295
Magician's Birthday, The, 288
'Maid Freed From the Gallows, The', 191
'Maid of Constant Sorrows', 65
Mainman, 328
Maison Dupuy Hotel, Louisiana, 383
'Making Time', 67
Makowski, Peter, 212, 305, 340–1
Malibu, 345, 346
Malvern, 219
'Mama Don't Allow No Skiffle Around Here', 113
Manchester, 74
Manning, Terry, 175–7, 193–4, 196, 197–8, 199, 200–1, 210, 272–3
'Man of Constant Sorrow', 65
Mansfield, Mike, 403
Manson, Andy, 367
Manson, Charles, 163, 265, 288, 336, 341
Manson murders, 163, 164, 178

Manson, Marilyn, 446
Manticore Studio, 366
Ma Reagan Circuit, 37, 171–2, 247, 291, 360
Mark, Jon, 196
Marmalade, 32
Marquee Club, London, 72, 73, 74, 83, 115, 129, 156, 182, 251, 299
Marr, Andrew, 50
Marrakech, 342, 434
Marriott, Steve, 13–14, 15, 16, 24, 149
Marseille, 110
Marsh, Dave, 362
Martin, Charlotte, 173, 176, 180, 181, 250, 285, 295, 317, 342, 343, 356, 357, 387, 420
Martin, Dean, 286
Martin, Vince, 64
Martinez, Paul, 424
Martyn, John, 240
Marvin, Hank, 60, 113
Marx, Groucho, 315
Mary Poppins, 155
Massot, Joe, 189, 294, 306, 309, 312, 364
'Masters of War', 66
Matzorkis, Jim, 378, 379, 382
Maudling, Caroline, 299
Maudling, Reginald, 299
Maugham, Somerset: The Magician, 225
Maui, 253
May, Brian, 435
May, Electra, 342
May, Phil, 342, 435
Mayall, John, 13, 159, 194
Mayer, John, 196
Mayfair Set, 172
Mayfair Studios, 145
Mayhem, 212
Meadon, Pete, 299
Meadowlands arena, New Jersey, 425
Meall Fuarvounie, 228, 308
Mean Business, 422

'Mean Woman Blues', 425
Meehan, Tony, 41, 93, 183, 392
Meeks, Johnny, 61
Mellor, Crispin, 353
Melody Maker (MM), 31, 33, 69, 73, 88, 202, 240, 256, 263, 266, 325, 333, 375, 402, 407, 408
Memorial Center, Dallas, 369
Memphis, 175, 176–7, 193
Memphis Jug Band, 65
Memphis Minnie, 246, 323
Mendelssohn, Felix: 'Fingal's cave', 280
Mendelssohn, John, 117, 154
Mercy, Miss, 138, 140
Mersey Beat, 380
'Message In A Bottle', 408
Miami Beach, 281
Michel, John, 327
Middle Earth Club, 74, 320
'Midnight Moonlight', 421–2
Midsouth Coliseum, Memphis, 175
Midsummer Night's Dream, A, 302
Mike Sammes Singers, 43
Milan, 252–3
Miller Pamela Ann see Des Barres, Pamela
Miller, Steve, 359
Milton, John: Paradise Lost, 303–4
Mimms, Garnett, 99
Mingus, Charles, 92
Minneapolis Sports Center/Arena, 326, 371
'Miracle', 438
Miracles, The, 31
Mirror Studios, 145
Mission, The, 423
'Misty Mountain Hop', 241, 244, 250, 445

Mitchell, Joni, 47, 181, 241, 331
Mitchell, Mitch, 32
Mitchell, V.E., 324
'Moby Dick', 148, 172, 283, 307, 374, 375, 409
Moby Grape, 25, 26, 100, 192, 311
Mojo, 138, 192, 244, 442, 443
'Money Honey', 183
Monkees, The, 282
Monotones, The, 239
Monsters of Rock Festival, 430
Monte Carlo, 355–6
Montgomery, Alabama, 8
Montreal, 410
Montreux, 271, 339, 342
Jazz Festival, 342
Monty Python and the Holy Grail, 341
Moody Blues, 188, 277
Moon, Keith, 14, 15–16, 73, 278, 311, 333, 375–6, 389, 392, 415
'Moonlight in Samosa', 422
Moore, Roger, 79
Moore, Scotty, 60–1, 112, 114, 182
Mordaunt Crook, J., 317, 318
More, Kenneth, 79
Morello, Joe, 36
Morgan Studios, 145
Morrison, Jim, 94, 139, 281
Morrison, Van, 181, 192
Mort Und Totschlag (A Degree of Murder), 216
Mosley, Bob, 192
Moss, Kate, 447
Most, Mickie, 5, 6, 7, 8, 9, 12, 13, 14, 18, 19, 21, 23, 30, 42, 46, 47, 78, 183, 273, 298 313, 338, 339, 348, 379, 380, 381, 392, 426, 436
Most Men, The, 30
Mothership, 439, 440, 441

Mothers of Invention, 139, 188
Mothers, Birmingham, 291
Mott the Hoople, 283
Move, The, 24, 25, 45, 132, 283, 360
'Mr Crowley', 213
Mr Fantasy, 48
MTV, 433
MuchMusic Led Zeppelin special, 127
'Mud Shark, The', 166
Mummery, John, 56
Munich, 349–50, 351, 409
Murphy, Miss, 139
Murray, Charles Shaar, 66, 283
Murray's Cabaret Club, 79
Museum of Modern Art, New York, 326
Music From Big Pink, 48, 181
Musicland Studios, 349–50
'Music Played On, The', 42
Mussolini, Benito, 224
Mutual Admiration Society, 438
'My Babe', 112
'My Baby', 185
'My Baby Left Me', 183
Myer, Michelle, 349
Mylett, Howard, 427
'My Old Man's A Dustman', 70
'Mystery Train', 379
Mystic Studio, 145
'My True Story', 30

Nagashima, Tats, 254
Nantes, 291–2
Napier-Bell, Simon, 23
Nash, Graham, 12–13, 94, 241
Nashville Teens, 99, 184, 338
Nassau Coliseum, New York, 352
National Library of Wales, 275
Navato, 345

'N Betweens, 171, 361
Neal, Johnny, 172
Nelson, Ricky, 60, 112
Nelson, Sandy, 363
'Nervous Breakdown', 54
'Never', 192
Neville, Richard, 50
Nevison, Ron, 320
New Barbarians, 400, 406
Newcastle, 273
City Hall, 255
New Commander Cody Band, 399
New Jersey, 91, 425
Newman, Paul, 94
New Memphis Bluesbreakers, 170
New Musical Express see NME
New Orleans, 287, 384
Superdome, 379
Newport Jazz Festival, 160
New Vaudeville Band, 90, 338–9, 380, 381, 392
New Yardbirds
formation, 6–16, 23–8, 31–4, 37–40, 44–6
Grant becomes manager of, 46–7
and social unrest of the Sixties, 48
Scandinavian tour, 47, 50–1
album *see Led Zeppelin*
name changed to Led Zeppelin, 72–3
New York
Grant seeks record deal in, 75–6
and first American tour, 89, 121–2, 123
and second American tour, 144, 145, 146
and third American tour, 161, 168
and fourth American tour, 153–4
and fifth American tour, 175

and ninth American tour,
  294–6
Swan Song office in, 313
Swan Song launch party
  in, 315
and tenth American tour,
  326, 327, 328–9
Bowie's meeting with
  Page in, 328–9
band members stay in,
  352
film of band premiered in,
  362
and eleventh American
  tour, 366, 374–5
anniversary celebrations
  for Atlantic, 428,
  430–1
brief references, 62, 120,
  268, 339, 340, 439
see also names of venues
New Yorker, 442
New York Post, 295
New York University Jazz
  Festival, 130
New Zealand, 269
Nickel Creek, 438
Nicky James Movement,
  37, 133
'Night Flight', 249, 321
Night Owl club, 64
Nightriders, the, 172
Night Timers, the, 42, 90
Night to Remember, A, 79
Ninette, 223
Nixon, Richard, 48
NME (New Musical
  Express), 74, 144, 236,
  269, 280, 297, 310,
  369, 398, 408, 413
'Nobody's Fault But
  Mine', 67, 346–7, 367,
  445
Nobs, Claude, 271, 340
No Introduction Necessary,
  44
'No Money Down', 99
'No More Auction Block',
  66
Noone, Peter, 298

'No Quarter', 193, 236,
  249, 278–9, 307, 373,
  374, 409, 445
No Quarter, 434
North Africa, 224
Northover, Dave, 368
Norwegian 'black metal'
  bands, 212
'Norwegian Wood', 66
'Nottamun Town', 66
'Not Fade Away', 65
Nuggets, 50
'Number One in Your
  Heart', 42
Nuremberg, 409

Oakland, 366
Oakland Coliseum, San
  Francisco, 342, 377–9,
  382
O Brother, Where Art Thou?,
  442
'Ocean, The', 278, 343
Ochr-yr-Bwlch, 181
O'Connor, Des, 40, 43
Ofarim, Esther & Abi, 47
Ogden's Nut Gone Flake, 48
'Oh Well', 238
Old Grey Whistle Test, The,
  129, 399
Oldham, Andrew Loog, 18,
  41, 195
Oldhill Plaza, Birmingham,
  34, 37, 132, 134, 172,
  247
Old Hyde Farm, 412
'Old Man River', 45
Old Mill House, 411, 422,
  429
Oliver, Paul: Blues Fell This
  Morning, 30
Oliver Tree, Croydon, 196
Olson, Dorothy, 224
Olymiahalle, Munich, 409
Olympic Studio, 51, 75,
  135, 158, 186, 192,
  216, 250, 252, 269,
  321
Only Ones, The, 214
'Ooh My Head', 238, 323

'Ooh My Soul', 323
'Operator', 359
Orbison, Roy, 106
Oregon, 383, 384
Orpen, William, 231
Osbourne, Ozzy, 136, 213
Ostin, Mo, 75
O.T.O., 217–18, 219, 223,
  226, 233–4, 258, 260,
  265, 302
'Our Song', 52, 310
O2 concert, 439, 441, 442,
  443, 444–7, 448, 450
'Out of Time', 31
Outrider, 31, 428, 430, 433
Outta Sight, Outta Mind,
  438
Overman, Michele, 167
'Over The Hills And Far
  Away', 185, 277, 279,
  347, 374, 430
'Over Under Sideways
  Down', 9, 38, 99
Oz, 49–50, 124
'Ozone Baby', 394–5, 396

Pace, Charles, 231, 233, 302
Pagano, Joe, 295
Page, Jimmy
  life and career before
  formation of Led
  Zeppelin, 5–6, 13–14,
  15, 16, 42–3, 58–61,
  112–15, 156–7, 182–4,
  194–6, 319–20, 348–9
and formation of band as
  New Yardbirds, 6–9,
  10, 11–12, 13, 16, 21,
  23, 24–5, 27–8, 31–2,
  33–4, 37–8, 38–9, 40,
  44–5, 45–6, 50, 53,
  392
and Scandinavian tour,
  47, 50
and Led Zeppelin, 51, 52,
  54–5, 56, 57–8, 62, 63,
  64–5, 68–9, 116, 117,
  124, 144
use of other artists'
  material, 55–8, 62, 63,

Page, Jimmy—*contd*
  64–5, 66–7, 149–50,
    150–1, 245–6, 323,
    346–7
  use of violin bow, 67–8,
    102
  on Plant as songwriter, 70
  and change of band's
    name, 72–3
  name known in America,
    75
  and Atlantic record deal,
    80, 82, 83
  and first American tour,
    88–9, 94–5, 96, 97, 98,
    99, 100, 101, 102, 103,
    104, 107, 108, 109,
    111–12, 118, 123
  on absence of moral or
    political statement,
    119
  and concentration on
    album, 127
  and TV, 129
  and second American
    tour, 131, 136, 138,
    140, 141, 142, 144
  and *Led Zeppelin II*, 135,
    137, 144, 145, 146,
    147, 148, 149–50,
    150–1, 152, 154, 155
  and girls, 136, 138, 140,
    165, 167–9, 178, 285,
    315
  and veto of single release,
    157–8
  and third American tour,
    165, 166, 167–9
  and Albert Hall show,
    170, 172
  relationship with
    Charlotte, 173
  and Countess Von
    Zeppelin, 174
  and Manning, 175
  and fifth American tour,
    176–7, 178, 179–80
  and *Led Zeppelin III*, 179,
    185–6, 191, 192, 193,
    194, 196, 197, 198,

    199–200, 201–2, 235
  buys Boleskine House,
    180, 228, 230
  time in Wales, 181–2,
    184–6
  and Headley Grange,
    187, 237, 238, 320–1
  and Harper, 190–1
  interest in the occult,
    197, 209, 210, 214–15,
    217–18, 227, 228–34,
    258, 259–60, 261–3,
    264, 265, 266, 275,
    288–9, 318–19,
    323–4, 341, 384,
    412–14
  and Sutch, 203
  and Brian Jones, 215,
    216–17
  and *Led Zeppelin IV*,
    236–7, 238, 239,
    240–1, 241–2, 243–4,
    245–6, 246–7, 249,
    250, 255, 257, 258,
    259–60, 261–3, 264,
    266
  birth of his daughter
    Scarlet, 250–1
  and tour of small venues
    in UK, 251–2
  and continental tour,
    252–3
  and seventh American
    tour, 253
  in Japan, 253
  visits Thailand and India,
    254–5
  at Empire Pool, 256
  and Bombay Symphony
    Orchestra, 269
  character, 275
  buys Plumpton Place, 275
  and *Houses of the Holy*,
    276, 277, 280
  and appointment of
    American PR, 280
  stage outfit, 281, 282,
    370
  and ninth American tour,
    281, 282, 283, 284,

    285, 286, 287–8, 297
  death threats, 288
  on Bonham's behaviour,
    289–90, 292–3
  Charlotte concerned
    about, 295
  faces possible departure
    of Jones, 297–8
  and band's own record
    label, 300, 313, 316
  project for Anger (*Lucifer
    Rising*), 301–2, 305–6,
    332–3, 356–7, 365
  and film of band, 308–9,
    312, 362–3, 364
  publishing reorganised,
    313–14
  buys Tower House,
    317–18
  acquires occult bookshop,
    318–19
  and *Physical Graffiti*, 321,
    322, 323–4
  hangs out with Rolling
    Stones, 324–5
  on tenth American tour,
    326–7, 330, 331–3,
    334, 335, 336
  and drugs, 336, 337, 351,
    371, 387
  and tax exile, 340
  and Earl's Court shows,
    340
  holiday, 342
  and Plant's accident, 344
  and *Presence*, 345, 346–7,
    348, 350–1, 353, 354,
    355
  cursed by Anger, 357–8
  and punk, 364–5
  and eleventh American
    tour, 366, 367–8,
    369–70, 371–2, 373,
    375, 379
  and death of Plant's son,
    383
  decision to give Plant
    time to recover, 385
  in period after death of
    Plant's son, 387

Harper claims to be working with, 387–8
suggests meeting of band at Clearwell, 388
rumours about, 389
closes Equinox bookshop, 390
and *In Through the Outdoor*, 390, 391, 392, 393, 394, 395, 396, 401
gives interviews, 398–9
and Knebworth shows, 399–400, 404–5, 406, 407
and death of Philip Hale, 408
and European tour, 410
and death of Bonham, 412, 413–14, 414–15
and end of Led Zeppelin, 415, 417
life and career after end of Led Zeppelin, 418–19, 419–20, 420–2, 422–3, 424, 425, 426, 428–31, 432–3, 434–5, 436–7, 439–40, 441, 443, 444, 445, 446, 448, 449–50
Page, Patricia, 428–9
Page, Patrick, 429
Page, Scarlet Lilith Eleida, 250–1, 342, 343, 387, 401, 420
'Painter Man', 67
'Pakistani Rent Collector, The', 310
Palace Theater, New York, 295
Pallenberg, Anita, 210, 215–16, 303
Palmer, Carl, 39, 291, 414
Palmer, Robert: *Deep Blues*, 150
Pamela, Miss *see* Des Barres, Pamela
Pangbourne, 8, 24, 27, 51, 180, 216, 236
Paracelsus, 209

Parachute, 313
'Paranoid', 200
Paris, 49, 110, 145, 342, 352
Paris Cinema, London, 252
Parker, Alan, 44, 183
Parker, Colonel Tom, 21
Park Lane Hotel, New York, 352
Parsley, Sage, Rosemary & Thyme, 48
Parsons, Gene, 346
Parsons, Jack, 226
Parton, Dolly, 431
'Pat's Delight', 148
Patton, Charley, 30
Paul, Les, 348–9
Payne, Sonny, 34
Peel, John, 47, 49, 63, 128, 252
Peers, Donald, 92
Pegg, Dave, 39, 133, 240
'Peggy Sue', 60
Pentangle, 160, 240
People, 442
Perara, Vernon, 311
Performance, 138, 211, 226, 327, 368
Perkins, Carl, 61
Pessoa, Fernando, 225
Pet Sounds, 127
Philadelphia, 366, 423–4
Phillips, Eddie, 67
Phillips, Esther, 195
Phillips, Glen, 438
Phillips, Gregory, 195
Phillips, Pat *see* Bonham (*née* Phillips), Pat
Phonogram Records, 405
Physical Graffiti (sixth Led Zeppelin album), 125, 320–4, 325–6, 336, 345
Pickett, Kenny, 90, 103, 104, 108
Pickett, Wilson, 81
Pictures at Eleven, 422
'Piggies', 163
Pink, 447
Pink Floyd, 43, 48, 116, 188, 191, 200–1, 342,

352, 353, 354, 380, 396, 440
Pirates, The, 36
Pitney, Gene, 32
Pittsburgh, 178, 294
Plant, Carmen Jane, 90, 181, 342, 343, 386
Plant, Karac, 275, 342, 343, 383–4, 385
Plant, Logan Romero, 398
Plant, Maureen, 26, 84, 90, 109, 173, 181, 311, 342, 343, 344, 346, 355, 359, 361, 383, 386, 387, 398
Plant, Robert
life and career before Led Zeppelin, 26, 27–31, 70–2, 104–6, 170–2, 247–9, 309–12, 359–61
and formation of band as New Yardbirds, 13, 24–8, 31–2, 33, 34, 37, 38, 45, 46, 50, 52, 361
and Scandinavian tour, 50, 51
and *Led Zeppelin*, 55, 57, 69–70, 117, 124
as songwriter with band, 69–70, 185, 186, 238, 239–40, 241, 242–3, 323, 393–4
receives first big cheque, 83–4
and first American tour, 90, 91, 94, 95–6, 97, 98, 99, 100, 101, 102, 104, 107, 108, 109, 111, 122–3
at Farx Club, 124–5
and second American tour, 130–1, 135–6, 137, 141, 144–5
and *Led Zeppelin II*, 135, 145, 147–8, 150, 154
and girls, 137, 166–7
and UK tour, 159, 160
and third American tour, 161, 164, 166–7

Plant, Robert—*contd*
  and fourth American
    tour, 153–4
  and Albert Hall show,
    170
  and tour of continent,
    173–4
  and fifth American tour,
    176, 178
  time in Wales, 180–2,
    184–6
  and *Led Zeppelin III*, 185,
    186, 191, 192–3, 200
  and Headley Grange, 187
  show in Iceland, 187
  and Bath Festival, 188,
    190
  and sixth American tour,
    202
  and *Led Zeppelin IV*, 238,
    239–40, 240–1,
    242–3, 249, 253, 257,
    260–1, 262, 264, 266
  and seventh American
    tour, 253, 255
  in Japan, 254
  visits Thailand and India,
    254–5
  and Bombay Symphony
    Orchestra, 269
  on Grant's management
    style, 272
  buys sheep farm in Wales,
    275
  and *Houses of the Holy*,
    277, 278, 279
  and ninth American tour,
    280–1, 282, 283, 285,
    286, 294
  stage costume, 281
  on Bonham's behaviour,
    292
  difficulties in relationship
    with Bonham, 293
  considers solo career, 301
  and film of band, 307,
    309
  and Swan Song, 313, 314
  meeting with Presley,
    315–16

  and *Physical Graffiti*, 322,
    323
  and tenth American tour,
    330, 331, 333, 335
  and Earl's Court shows,
    340, 341
  travels with family, 342
  accident and injury,
    342–4
  and *Presence*, 345, 346,
    350, 351–2, 354–5
  falls from wheelchair, 351
  makes first stage
    appearances since
    accident, 352
  and punk, 364–5
  and eleventh American
    tour, 366–7, 368, 369,
    370, 372, 374–5,
    376–7, 379
  and death of son, 383–4,
    385
  difficulty in returning
    after son's death, 386
  attends meeting of band
    at Clearwell Castle, 388
  makes stage appearances,
    388–9
  and *In Through the
    Outdoor*, 390, 391,
    392, 393–4, 395
  and Knebworth shows,
    403, 404, 405
  attends *Melody Maker*
    awlards, 408
  and European tour, 409,
    410
  and death of Bonham,
    412, 414
  and end of Led Zeppelin,
    415, 316
  life and career after end
    of Led Zeppelin, 420,
    422–3, 424, 425, 426,
    430–2, 432–3, 433–5,
    436, 437, 439, 440,
    441, 442, 444, 445,
    446, 447–8, 448–9,
    450
  brief references,74, 89,

    100, 132, 149, 268,
    291, 297, 298, 325,
    396, 407, 411, 413
Plastercaster, Cynthia, 140
Plata, Manitas de, 11, 182
Playboy magazine, 22
Playhouse Theatre, London,
    128
Plaza Hotel, New York,
    144, 326, 334, 375
'Please Please Me', 253
Plumpton Place, 275, 309,
    408
Plymouth, 124
Polanski, Roman, 163
Polar Studios, 390–2
Police, The, 408, 440
Pontiac Silverdome,
    Michigan, 366, 372
Poole, Mac, 38, 39–40,
    84–5, 111, 124–5,
    133–4, 290, 291, 334,
    335
'Poor Tom', 185, 236
Pop Club, Bronby, 51
Pop Proms, 160
P-Orridge, Genesis, 213–14
Porter's Popular Preachers,
    121, 122
Portrait of Genius, 196
Pound, Ezra, 219
Pound Lane Primary
    School, Epsom, 59
Powell, Aubrey, 276–7, 352
Powell, Cozy, 291, 414,
    415
'Preacher's Blues', 150
'Preaching Blues', 71, 150
'Prelude', 421
Premier Talent, 89
Presence (seventh Led
    Zeppelin album),
    345–8, 350–5, 357,
    362, 367
Presidents, The, 183
Presley, Elvis, 21, 25, 30, 31,
    60, 61, 70, 106, 114,
    119, 138, 168, 182,
    209–10, 278, 279,
    315–16, 330, 384

Presley, Lisa Marie, 316,
    446
Presley, Priscilla, 446
Pretenders, the, 404
Pretty Things, the, 32, 299,
    313, 316, 342
Prince, 447
Principle of Moments, The,
    423
Private Eye, 50
Proby, P.J., 32, 52, 184,
    195
Procol Harum, 32
Psychic TV, 214
Puff Daddy, 437
Pye, 30, 41, 75, 115

Q magazine, 12, 266, 443
Quaglino's, 331
Quatro, Suzi, 331
Queen, 244, 435
'Quicksand', 213
Quinn, Anthony, 79

Rachman, Peter, 79
Radio Caroline, 380
Radio London, 310, 380
Radziwill, Princess Lee,
    270
Raft, George, 229
Raglan Castle, Great Tower
    of, 307
Railway Tavern,
    Birmingham, 27
Rainbow Suite,
    Birmingham, 311
Rainbow Bar & Grill, LA,
    284, 315, 334, 349
'Rain Song, The', 277, 307
Raising Sand, 442–3, 448
Raleigh, 175
Ralphs, Mick, 373
'Ramble On', 135, 145,
    147–8, 151, 277, 445
Ramones, the, 54
Rascals, the, 90, 111
Rashman, Elliot, 435
Rat Pack, the, 286
Rattles, The, 30
'Ravi', 196

Reading, 257
Reagan, Mary 'Ma', 171–2,
    247
'Rebel Rebel', 65
Record Mirror, 119, 200,
    240, 251
Redcats, the, 113–14
Redding, Noel, 139
Redding, Otis, 42, 176
Redditch, 85, 132–3, 413
Red Hot Chili Peppers,
    445
Reed, Lou, 335
Regal-Zonophone, 360
Reid, Terry, 12–13, 23, 24,
    25, 31, 90, 175, 311,
    361
Reinhardt, Django, 182,
    348–9
Reinhardt, Max, 302
Relf, Keith, 8, 25–6, 63, 65,
    72, 185
R.E.M., 423
Remastered, 55
Remasters, 432, 437
Renaissaince Pleasure Fair,
    Navato, 345
Renbourn, John, 160, 186,
    191, 195, 196, 346
Retaliation, 311
'Revolution', 48
'Revolution 9', 163
Revolver, 10, 127, 326
Rejkjavic, 187
Rhodes, 342–3
Rich, Buddy, 35, 132
Richard, Cliff, 18, 43, 47,
    61, 184
Richards, Keith, 10, 71,
    115, 144, 210, 268,
    303, 324, 325, 341,
    375, 389, 400
Richmond Athletics Club,
    74
Rimmer, William: *Evening
    (The Fall of Day)*, 314,
    315
Roaring Twenties, London,
    299
Robinson, Lisa, 122, 123

'Rock and Roll', 237–8,
    239, 250, 340, 367,
    376, 377, 445
Rock for Kampuchea
    charity show, 408
'Rock Island Line', 61
'Rock Me Baby', 66
'Rock My Plimsoul', 66
'Rocky Raccoon', 163
Rodgers, Jimmy, 55
Rodgers, Paul, 27, 313,
    316–17, 345, 421, 435
Rodney Bingenheimer's
    English Disco, LA,
    283–4, 285
'Rolling and Tumbling', 65
Rolling Stone, 124, 154, 199,
    119, 122, 144, 199,
    256–7, 280, 313, 326,
    354, 362, 378, 442
Rolling Stones, 10, 18, 30,
    69, 71, 74, 75, 82, 98,
    118, 123, 130, 157,
    186, 187, 216, 217,
    234, 237, 268, 269,
    275, 280, 281, 296,
    299, 300, 303, 321,
    324–5, 350, 370, 375,
    389, 392, 396, 397,
    439, 447
    albums, 43, 48, 51, 138,
        153, 211, 269, 303,
        324
    Altamont show, 164, 211,
        288
    and the occult, 210–11
    songs, 31, 65, 303
Rolling Stones Records, 82,
    300
Ronstadt, Linda, 362
Rooney, Mickey, 302
Rose, Tim, 26, 33, 37, 38,
    83, 359, 360
Rosen, Steve, 15
Rossetti, Dante Gabriel,
    325
Rotten, Johnny, 362, 365
Roundhouse, London, 74,
    84
'Route 66', 105

'Rover, The', 185, 236, 249, 321, 322
Roxy, the, LA, 331
Roxy, the, London, 365
Roxy Music, 283, 334, 399
'Royal Orleans', 347, 354
Royal Orleans Hotel, New Orleans, 287
Rundgren, Todd, 180, 317, 331, 399
Rush, Otis, 114
Rushock Parish Church, 414

Sabino, Karl, 423
Sacramento, 336
'Sad Eyed Lady of the Lowlands', 10
Saint, The, 79
St James Club, 341
St Paul, 372
Salewicz, Chris, 228, 370
Samwell-Smith, Paul, 6, 16, 43
Sander, Ellen, 141–2
Trips, 141–2
Sand Diego, 250, 282, 331
Sandra, Miss, 138
San Francisco, 89, 102, 109–10, 111–12, 120, 164, 168, 175, 287, 304, 342, 377–9
'San Francisco', 102
San Francisco Mime Troupe, 110
San Jose, 144
Santa Barbara, 167
Santa Clara Pop Festival, 144
Santa Monica, 302, 335–6
Civic, 345
Santana, 188
Saturday Book Show, 128
Satyricon, 138
Saucerful of Secrets, 48
Savages, 14
Savoy Brown, 148, 188
Savoy Hotel, London, 169, 415, 416
'Say Man', 30

Scabies, Rat, 365
'Scarborough Fair', 66
'Scarlet', 325
'Scarlet O'Hara', 41
Scene, the, London, 299
Schaefer Music Festival, 161
Schulps, Dave, 67, 199, 375
Science and Technology College, Manchester, 74
Scientology, 226
Scorpio Rising, 229–230, 302, 305
Scorsese, Martin, 302–3
Scotland, 398
Jimmy Page's house in see Boleskin House
Scream for Help, 423
Searchers, the, 90, 195
'Search For Nirvana, The', 196
Seattle, 103, 104, 136, 165–6, 331, 377, 384
Pop Festival, 165
Seatwave, 440
Secombe, Harry, 40, 43
Secret Adventures of Tom Thumb, The, 438
Secunda, Tony, 24, 25, 360
Segovia, 182
Selkirk, 360
Senators, The, 37, 133
'Session Man', 14
Seven Stars Blues Club, 105
Sex Pistols, 99, 362, 404, 426
Sgt Pepper, 10, 124, 210
Shade, Will, 65
Shadows, the, 42, 60, 61, 82, 93, 142
'Shake 'Em On Down', 191, 323
'Shake My Tree', 433
Shankar, Ravi, 196, 269, 320
'Shapes of Things', 6, 55
Shaw, Sandy, 32
Shea Stadium, 280

Sheehan, Dennis, 368, 383
Sheeley, Sharon, 195
Sheffield University, 74
'She Just Satisfies', 184, 195
'She Moved Through The Fair', 11, 55–6, 196, 246
Shepperton Studios, 312
Shepton Mallet, 187
Sheridan, Mike, 172
Sherman, Bobby, 282
'She Said Yeah', 25
'She's A Mod', 37
'She's A Rainbow', 43
'She's Fallen in Love with the Monster Man', 203
She Trinity, 338
She Waits For Night, 438
Shirley, Kevin, 441, 443, 448–9
'Shoom Lamma Boom Boom', 43
'Shop Around', 31
Showground Stadium, Sydney, 269
Sicily, 223, 302, 342
'Sick Again', 321, 322, 324, 330
Sidcup, 91
'Silhouettes', 298
Silhouettes, The, 156, 183
Silk Torpedo, 316
Simenon, Paul, 362
Simon, Paul, 191 see also Simon and Garfunkle
Simon and Garfunkle, 48, 153
Simply Red, 435
Simpson, Jim, 133, 291
Sinatra, Frank, 280, 286
'Since I've Been Loving You', 192–3, 324, 346, 445
Singapore, 269
Singer Bowl, Flushing Meadows, New York, 161, 168
'Sing Sing Sing', 87
SIR Studios, 347, 349

Sissy Stone, 38
Sisters of Mercy, 423
'666 The Number Of The Beast', 213
16 Hip Hits, 41
Sixty Six to Timbuktu, 437
Skinner, Stephen, 22, 259
Sky TV, 428
Slade, 72, 171
Slade, Chris, 421
'Slow Dancer', 422
Small Faces, 13, 15, 16, 48, 149, 320
'Smile of Your Shadow, The', 438
Smith, Chad, 445
Smith, Jimmy, 92
'Smoke Gets in Your Eyes', 253
'Smokestack Lightning', 30, 55
Snow, Mat, 12, 276
Snow Patrol, 441
Social Deviants, the, 360
Softley, Mick, 196
Solomon, King, 221, 222
Sol studio, 428
Solters Roskin & Sabinson (SR&S), 280
'So Many Roads', 114
'Somebody to Love', 24
'Something Else', 99
'Song of Mexico', 41
'Song Remains The Same, The', 277, 341, 367, 404, 445
Song Remains The Same, The (film of Led Zeppelin), 293–4, 306–9, 312, 355, 362–3, 364, 403, 414, 439, 440–1, 444
Sonny & Cher, 136
Sounds, 214, 256, 316, 340, 354, 363–4, 402
'South Bound Suarez', 392, 393
South Norwood, 77
South Side Johnny, 399
Sparky, Miss, 138–9
Spare, Austin Osman, 262

Speakeasy, the, London, 311, 324
Spector, Phil, 284
Speedway Fairgrounds, Montgomery, Alabama, 8
Spencer Davis Group/Rhythm and Blues Quartet, 14, 29, 171
Spiders, The, 37, 133
Spirit, 99, 100, 165, 245
Spokane, 103
Spooky Tooth, 311, 360
Sporting Life, The, 437
Springfield, Dusty, 32, 82
Staines, 129
'Stairway To Heaven', 100, 185, 242–6, 250, 251, 252, 253, 256, 259, 263–6, 279, 309, 322, 346, 354, 356, 374, 404, 421, 422, 430–1, 432, 434, 441, 445, 446
Stamp, Chris, 121
Staple Singers, the, 176
Star and Garter, Halesowen, 171, 172
Stargroves, 269
Starliners, the, 172
Starr, Ringo, 10, 32, 307
Starr, Sable, 285
Starship, 282, 292, 294, 330, 334, 335, 367
Status Quo, 296
Stax Records, 175–6
'Steal Away', 359
'Stealing, Stealing', 65
Steele, Tommy, 18
Stein, Mark, 166
Stephens, Geoff, 338–9
Steppenwolf, 188
Steve Gibbons Band, 422
Steve Miller Band, 111
Stewart, Ian, 237–8
Stewart, Rod, 7, 24, 29, 45, 57, 66, 130, 163, 283, 296, 298, 301, 331
Sticky Fingers, 269

Stigwood, Robert, 16
'Still of the Night', 433
Stills, Stephen, 13
Stjarscenen club, Gothenburg, 51
Stockhausen, Karl Heinz, 201
Stockholm, 50, 169, 390–2, 396
Stone the Crows, 256, 313, 373
Stormcock, 190
Stourbridge Art School, 71–2
'Street Fighting Man', 48
Stringbeats, the, 311, 361
Stripper, The, 161
Strummer, Joe, 363
Studio, 259
Sullivan, Big Jim, 7, 41, 44, 131, 183, 184, 196
Sullivan, Ed, 339
Sumlin, Hubert, 61, 114–15
Summers, Montague, 226–7
Summit Arena, Houston, 373
Sun, 444
Sunday Express, 224
Sunday Night at the London Palladium, 70
Sunday School studio, 437
Sunday Times,The, 442
Sunset Sound Studios, 250
'Sunshine Superman', 42, 44
Superhype, 82, 83
Superlungs, 13
Supershow, 129
Supersonic, 403
'Superstition', 376
Supremes, the, 96
Surrey, University of, 74
Sutch, Screaming Lord, 14, 36, 183, 203, 211
Sutcliffe, Phil, 337
Sutton Art College, 112–13
Swansea Top Rank, 373
Swanson, Gloria, 303

Swan Song, 312–15,
    316–17, 343, 345, 351,
    353–4, 389–90, 420,
    422, 426
Sweden, 124
Swedish TV, 129
'Sweet Baby', 241
Swingle's Celebrity Hotel,
    371–2
Switzerland, 271, 342
Sydney, 269
Sylmar earthquake, 250
'Sympathy for the Devil',
    211, 303
Szabo, Gabor, 196

Taj Mahal, 111
Taj Mahal Hotel, Bombay,
    255
Talmy, Shel, 7, 67
Tamla Motown, 42, 93
Tampa, 280, 281, 366,
    373–4
'Tangerine', 185, 246
Tapestry, 256
Tarantino, Quentin, 302–3
Tate, Sharon, 163
'Taurus', 100, 245
Taylor, Bobby, 113
Taylor, Dick, 115
Taylor, Elizabeth, 325
Taylor, James, 241
Taylor, Mick, 325
'Tea for One', 346
T-Bones, the, 55
Teen Club, Denmark, 47
Telegraph, 444
'Ten Little Indians', 15
Tennessee Teens, the,
    309
Ten Years After, 159, 161,
    188, 360, 380
'Ten Years Gone', 321, 322,
    324, 367, 370
Termen, Lev, 99
Terry, Sonny, 323
Texas, 333
Thailand, 254–5
'Thank You', 137, 148
Thatcher, Margaret, 398

'That's The Way', 185, 186,
    199, 255
Thee Charming Experience,
    LA, 140, 167, 203
Their Satanic Majesties
    Request, 43, 211, 303
Them, 7, 184
'There Are But Four Rolling
    Stones', 41
'Think About It', 63
Thinkfarm design company,
    445
Thin Lizzy, 148, 350
'This Is. . . .', 30
Thomas, Sir William ap, 307
Thompson, Bill, 188–9
Thompson, Tony, 424, 425
Thorgerson, Storm, 276,
    352, 353, 400–1
Thorup, Peter, 202
'Those Were the Days', 76
'Three Blind Mice', 66
Three Dog Night, 136
'365 Rolling Stones (One
    for Every Day of the
    Year)', 41
Three Week Hero, 52
Throbbing Gristle, 214
Thunderbirds, the, 113
Thunderchief, The, 438
Tibet, Dave, 214
'Ticket to Ride', 96
'Tidal', 437
Tidmarsh, Chris (Red E.
    Lewis; later known as
    Neil Christian),113–14
    see also Christian, Neil
Tight But Loose, 75
'Time Drags By', 184
Time Out, 154
'Tinker, Tailor, Soldier,
    Sailor', 68, 277
Toad the Wet Sprocket, 438
'Tobacco Road', 99, 184,
    338
Tokyo, 253–4
Tolkien, J.R.R
    The Hobbit, 241
    Lord of the Rings, 240, 241
'Tom Cat', 238

Tommy, 322
Tomorrow, 311
'Tomorrow's Clown', 395
Tonbridge, 219
Top Gear, 47, 128
Top of the Pops, 6, 129, 202,
    312, 403
Top Pops magazine, 158
Tornados, the, 352
Toronto, 389
Tory Party, 398–9
Tosh, Peter, 300
Tous En Scene, 145
Tower House, 10, 317–18,
    356, 357, 365, 414
'Tower of Strength', 423
Townshend, Pete, 6, 15, 69,
    144, 389
Tracey, Reg, 44
Traffic, 15, 48
'Train Kept A-Rolling', 46,
    51, 239, 395
Tramp, London, 324
'Trampled Underfoot',
    127, 321, 322, 324,
    330, 340, 341, 404,
    445
Transatlantic, 56
'Travelling Riverside Blues,
    101, 145, 150
Travers, P.L., 155
Trax disco, New York, 375
'Treat Her Right', 425
T.Rex, 148, 187, 271, 283,
    307
'Tribute to Bert Burns', 158
Trident Studios, 252
Troubadour, LA, 240, 331
Trouser Press, 117, 375
Truth, 45, 47, 48, 57, 62,
    66, 116, 117
Turd Burglars, 388
'Turn on Your Love Light',
    39
TV-Byen, 128–9
12 String Guitar, 191–2
21s Coffee Bar, London, 18
2001, 305

Uhelszki, Jaan, 371–2

UK Hall of Fame, 439
Ulster Hall, Belfast, 251–2
Uncle Earl, 438
UNICEF charity show, 408
United States *see* America
Unit 4 + 2, 90
Upchurch, Phil, 92
'Unplugged', 433
Uriah Heep, 288, 421
U.S.A Today, 442
US Rock and Roll Hall of
    Fame, 436
Utopia, 399
U2, 271

Vagabonds, the, 299
Valens, Richie, 238, 323
Valentine, Rudolph, 231
Vancouver, 145, 253, 331
Van Dike club, Plymouth,
    124
Vanilla Fudge, 80, 89, 90,
    95, 96 7, 98, 99, 100,
    101, 121, 125, 130,
    165, 166
Vanity Fair, 442
Van Ronk, Dave, 65–6
Variety, 144
Verrall, Ronnie, 131
Viagogo, 440
Victoria Hall, Selkirk, 360
Vietnam, 49, 120
Vigorelli football stadium,
    Milan, 252–3
Vikernes, Kristian (aka
    Count Grisnackh), 212
Vikings, the, 172, 291
*Village Green Preservation
    Society*, 48
Village Theater, New York,
    62
Villa Nellcote, 10
Vincent, Gene, 19, 60, 112,
    113, 114, 143–4, 271,
    392
Virgin Records, 256
Volumes, the, 30

'Waggoners Lad, The', 186
'Wait For Me', 195

Waiting For The Sun, 48
Wales, 180–1, 184–6, 275,
    341
Walker, Johnnie, 341
Walking into Clarksdale,
    436, 449
'Walk Tall', 184
Walk the Line, 442
Waller, Fats, 92
Waller, Micky, 184
'Walter's Walk', 102, 345
'Wanton Song, The', 321,
    330
Ward, Bill, 132, 291, 292,
    412
Warner Bros., 75
Washington, Dinah, 66
Waters, Muddy, 25, 30, 57,
    61, 65, 115, 149, 238
Waters, Roger, 342
Watts, Charlie, 115
Wayne, Carl, 172, 291
Way of Life, A, 37, 38, 39,
    74, 133, 240, 291
WBCN, 118, 120
'Wearing and Tearing',
    394–5, 396
Webb, Stan, 270
Webb, Terry, 37, 133, 134
Webster, Eileen, 188
Weedon, Bert: *Play in a
    Day*, 59
Weintraub, Jerry, 315
Weiss, Steve, 77, 97, 294
Welch, Chris, 19, 69, 73,
    83, 125, 154, 263, 270,
    293
'We'll Meet Again', 436
Wembley Arena, 256, 434
Wenner, Jaan, 119, 138
'We're Gonna Groove',
    145, 170
West, Keith, 311
West Hagley, 180
Western Spring Stadium,
    Auckland, 269
Westfallen Halle,
    Dortmund, 408
Wexler, Jerry, 80, 81–2,
    121, 146

'What Is and What Should
    Never Be', 135, 147,
    151
Wheatstraw, Peetie, 30
Wheels of Fire, 48
Wheldon, Huw, 113
'When the Levee Breaks',
    239, 246–7, 250, 278,
    279, 346, 448
'When You Walk In the
    Room', 195
Whisky A Go Go, LA, 89,
    103, 107, 109, 140,
    164
Whistler, James, 318
White, Bukka, 30, 61, 106,
    191, 323
White Album, The, 48, 163,
    353
'White Dog', 238
Whitehead, Peter, 170
'Whiter Shade of Pale, A',
    32
Whitesnake, 418, 433
'White Summer', 11, 55,
    246, 313, 367
Who, The, 10 11, 14, 15,
    16, 67, 69, 74, 90, 96,
    98, 118, 121, 130, 141,
    142, 170, 172, 194,
    275, 299, 321, 366,
    376, 389, 415, 440
'Whole Lotta Love', 61, 67,
    100, 125, 129, 135,
    147, 149–50, 151,
    157–8, 176, 179, 199,
    202, 245, 246, 270,
    278, 279, 322, 376,
    377, 409, 445
'Whole Lotta Shakin' Goin'
    On', 119
'Whole Of The Law, The',
    214
'Who's Gonna Buy Your
    Chickens When I'm
    Gone', 66
Whyton, Wally, 18
Wick, The, 324
Wilde, Marty, 395
Wilde, Oscar, 220, 318

Williams, Larry, 25
Williamson, Sonny Boy, 29, 30, 31, 71, 149, 150, 151, 184, 323
'Will the Circle Be Unbroken', 65
Wilson, Ann, 136
Wilson, B.J., 32
Wilson, Dennis, 163
Wilson, Nancy, 136
Wilton House school, 86, 87
Wimbledon Art College, 112, 201
'Winchester Cathedral', 338–9
Windsor, 411
Winner, Michael, 421, 423
Winter, Johnny, 188
Winterland Ballroom, San Francisco, 168
Winwood, Stevie, 14, 15, 24, 29, 76
Wish You Were Here, 191, 352
'With A Little Help From My Friends', 32, 76
Witherspoon, Jimmy, 30
Wolverhampton Gaumont, 30
Wolverhampton Wanderers, 366
Wonder, Little Stevie, 247, 376
Wonderwall, 189
Wood, Chrissie, 331
Wood, Ronnie, 7, 45, 324, 325, 331, 341, 375, 400

Wood, Roy, 414
Woodroffe, Jezz, 423
Woodstock, 120, 162–3, 181
Woodstock, 138
Wood Tavern, Hornsey, 124
Woodward, Joanne, 94
Worcestershire, 275, 412
Worth Farm, Little Horsted, 436
Wow, 192
Wyman, Bill, 315

XTC, 410

Yardbirds
and Beck, 5, 6, 7, 117
and Page, 5–6, 7, 8, 9, 11, 13, 16, 43, 50, 68, 102, 111, 117, 136, 149, 165, 196, 211, 349
last show, 9, 27, 47
and Jones, 14–15, 44
split up, 23, 77
and Plant, 25
material used by Led Zeppelin, 55, 57, 62, 63, 64, 185, 277, 367
in America, 62, 75, 89, 94
use of other artists' material, 62, 63, 64, 65
record labels, 76
brief references, 46, 51, 53, 56, 90, 99, 151, 175, 201, 215, 216, 299, 310, 320, 361, 380, 381, 386

Yeats, W.B., 213, 225
Yellow Submarine, 138
Yes, 322
Yorke, Gerald, 231, 232, 233, 302, 319
Yorke, Ritchie, 146
'You Better Run', 309, 310
'You Can't Sit Down', 92
'You Keep Me Hanging On', 96
'You'll Never Walk Alone', 404
'You Need Love', 57, 135, 149
Young, Neil, 185, 236, 241, 432
Younger Than Yesterday, 124
Young Rascals, the, 309
'Your Time Is Gonna Come', 54–5, 97
'You Shook Me', 25, 51, 56–7, 58, 67, 97

Zabriske Point, 138
Zacron, 201
Zanetta, Tony, 329
Stardust, 328
Zappa, Frank, 138, 139, 166, 188, 335
Zephyr, 97
Zeppelin, Countess Eva Von, 174
Zeppelin, Count Ferdinand Von, 174
ZigZag, 365
Zooma, 437
ZoSo symbol, 255, 261, 262–3, 450